LLEWELLYN'S

COMPLETE BOOK OF
CEREMONIAL MAGICK

LLEWELLYN'S

COMPLETE BOOK OF
CEREMONIAL
MAGICK

A Comprehensive Guide to the
Western Mystery Tradition

LLEWELLYN PUBLICATIONS
Woodbury, Minnesota

FIRST EDITION

First Printing, 2020

Cover design by Kevin R. Brown

Art credits for interior illustrations listed at the end of each individual book.

Llewellyn Publishing is a registered trademark of Llewellyn Worldwide Ltd.

Library of Congress Cataloging-in-Publication Data

Names: DuQuette, Lon Milo, editor. | Shoemaker, David G., editor.
Title: Llewellyn's complete book of ceremonial magick : a comprehensive
  guide to the western mystery tradition / edited by Lon Milo DuQuette &
  David Shoemaker.
Description: 1. | Woodbury, Minnesota : Llewellyn Worldwide. Ltd, 2020. |
  Series: Llewellyn's complete book series; 14 | Includes bibliographical
  references and index. | Summary: "Compiled by two of the leading figures
  in the magick community, this new title in Llewellyn's Complete Book
  series includes more than 650 pages of fascinating insights into the
  history and contemporary practice of ritual magick"—Provided by
  publisher.
Identifiers: LCCN 2019036892 (print) | LCCN 2019036893 (ebook) | ISBN
  9780738764726 (paperback) | ISBN 9780738761251 (ebook) 9780738760827 (hardcover)
Subjects: LCSH: Magic. | Ritual.
Classification: LCC BF1623.R6 L54 2020 (print) | LCC BF1623.R6 (ebook) |
  DDC 133.4/3—dc23
LC record available at https://lccn.loc.gov/2019036892
LC ebook record available at https://lccn.loc.gov/2019036893

Llewellyn Worldwide Ltd. does not participate in, endorse, or have any authority or responsibility concerning private business transactions between our authors and the public.

All mail addressed to the author is forwarded but the publisher cannot, unless specifically instructed by the author, give out an address or phone number.

Any internet references contained in this work are current at publication time, but the publisher cannot guarantee that a specific location will continue to be maintained. Please refer to the publisher's website for links to authors' websites and other sources.

Llewellyn Publications
A Division of Llewellyn Worldwide Ltd.
2143 Wooddale Drive
Woodbury, MN 55125-2989
www.llewellyn.com
Printed in the United States of America

Acknowledgments

The editors would like to express our deep gratitude to all the talented authors who contributed to this volume. Their wisdom and insights will serve seekers for many years to come. Special thanks to Elysia Gallo at Llewellyn, for her expert guidance and her unique ability to keep two crazy magicians on track and on task. And to our families, friends, and teachers, our deepest thanks for a lifetime of love, wisdom, and support.

Contents

Contents

· · · · · · · ·

Figures

• • • • • • •

Figures

Book Four

. . . .

. . . .

Figures

· · · · · · · ·

Tables

Tables

• • • • • • •

• • • • • • •

Editors' Introduction

Magick is not something you do. Magick is something you are!

~*Donald Michael Kraig*[1]

Magick is the science and art of causing change to occur in conformity with will.

~*Aleister Crowley*[2]

I was an eighteen-year-old atheist when my passion for all things magical and mystical was born out of a psychedelically triggered epiphany of self-realization. In a timeless slit of eternity I saw (in blinding Technicolor certainty) that all things in the cosmos—light, time, space, energy, matter, motion, and my *own self*—were merely cascading fractals of a supreme and awesome *singularity of consciousness*; furthermore, I giddily surrendered to the most "Self"-evident of self-evident Truths that this supreme *singularity of consciousness* was *God* and *myself*.

In the days and weeks that followed that curious awakening, I combed the stacks of my college library for books on Zen, yoga, and other varieties of Eastern mysticism, hoping to find in classical literature other examples and parallels to my chemically induced experience. I soon found the works of Alan Watts, Paramahansa Yogananda, and a wide selection of other material to capture my attention. My timing for such a quest could not have been more culturally synchronistic. The pop world of the mid-1960s viewed such esoteric studies and practices as being *where it's at*, hip, socially aware, and sexy. Oh, I was going to look so cool losing my ego!

For the next ten years or so, I made a real effort to become a good yogi (I truly don't regret a moment of mantra chanting, fasting, and pranayama), but eventually I came to the realization that I was fundamentally hardwired differently than the Eastern mystic I was trying to emulate.

1. Donald Michael Kraig, *Modern Magick: Twelve Lessons in the High Magickal Arts*, rev. and expanded ed. (St. Paul, MN: Llewellyn Publications, 2010), 88.
2. Aleister Crowley, *Magick in Theory and Practice*, 6th ed. (New York: Castle Books,1992), xii.

I was objective rather than subjective, active rather than passive. I began to seek out some sort of Western system of consciousness expansion and self-transformation. What I eventually found was Qabalah and six thousand years of philosophies, spiritual practices, arts, sciences, and mythologies that lie at the heart of Western philosophy and religion; indeed, it forms the foundation of Western civilization itself. I found "Magick."

Even under the best of circumstances ceremonial magick is an awkward and difficult study, especially at the beginning. There is no such thing as "Magick 101." It seems that wherever one chooses to begin, one should already be familiar *with* (or have mastery *of*) a half dozen obscure and esoteric subjects about which one is woefully undereducated. Fledgling magicians are forced to dive into the deep side of the pool and sink or swim. Looking back, I'm not sure why I didn't drown in the murky waters of the magical swimming pool. Perhaps I was too lazy to get out of the water.

One thing is for certain: at the beginning of my magical career, things would have gone dramatically smoother had I a textbook like *Llewellyn's Complete Book of Ceremonial Magick*—a single volume I could turn to to get a primary esoteric education in the most important subjects I needed to learn in order to properly prepare myself for postgraduate work. Such a tool would have shaved years off my magical learning curve.

I admit, I am the laziest man in the world, and even though I have written a number of books and songs and been involved in one way or another in numerous other publishing efforts, each time a project is presented to me I have to be dragged kicking and screaming into the process. When my friends at Llewellyn approached me about a massive project called the *Complete Book of Ceremonial Magick*, my initial response was, "It sounds like too much work!"

I think they thought I was joking. When pressed why I was reluctant to come on board, I responded by saying something like this:

> It would mean … first trying to contact a score of the most celebrated magical scholars and practitioners in the world and convince them to drop whatever it is they are doing and write the equivalent of a small masterpiece of a book that would encapsulate and illuminate the essence of an essential aspect of the science and art of ceremonial magick. Even if we could get these cloistered esoteric superstars to agree, they are all geniuses! Do you know how hard it can be to work with even one genius? Can you imagine trying to work with a couple dozen geniuses at once? This thing will probably drag on for years as we gather up and edit. No! It sounds like too much work!

Obviously, I changed my mind.

The project's profound and historical potential (and my own sense of responsibility to future generations) won out over my inherent slothful nature. Much to my surprise, I found it far easier than I expected to personally contact and secure the goodwill and participation of the brightest stars of the twenty-first century's magical firmament. Each was remarkably gracious and enthusiastic. Furthermore, the gods smiled and inspired each of our contributors to create for us real mini-masterpieces… some of the best work of their careers—true examples of magical genius. And *that* is the real magick of the *Complete Book of Ceremonial Magick*.

I would especially like to draw the reader's attention to the epilogue of this work, *The Future of Ceremonial Magick* by Brandy Williams. It will be apparent to the reader that the format Brandy is offering is different from that of the other sections. It is a true prophetic document and a breathtaking example of the visionary inner eye of a true magician. The reader is urged to read it in a meditative state.

A Special Thank You

As I've confessed, I am the laziest man in the world. The editorial labor necessary for a work of this scope is monumental and far beyond my skill or capacity to shoulder alone. This work would never have seen the light of day without the herculean efforts of my friend and co-editor, Dr. David Shoemaker (who is also the author of book 9 of this work). Thank you, Dr. Shoemaker, and let's hope our next project is a bit easier.

—Lon Milo DuQuette

Never let your love of Clarity overtake your lust for Mystery.
~Bill Nelson, musician/magician

As a young doctoral student in clinical psychology, I found myself frustrated by the status quo of the available training in clinical theory and practice. The emphasis in clinical psychology over the past several decades has been on empirically validated clinical approaches, favoring easily researchable modalities over the more traditional (but unfashionable) "depth" psychology of Freud, Jung, and others. This was a needed corrective to the occasionally slack critical thinking evident in the earlier approaches, but it limited the light of investigation to only one corner of the human experience. In this intellectual climate, I found myself seeking a psychological worldview that would satisfy my curiosity about the deeper mysteries of human consciousness. This quickly led me to the work of Carl Jung, and I soon realized that I was not only seeking a foundation of my psychological approach, I was seeking a renewal of my spiritual life. The mystery I was lusting after would not be discovered in any book or in any theory, but only in my own personal approach to the divine. I soon found the work of Israel Regardie in the form

· · · · · · · ·

of *The Middle Pillar*,[3] which introduced me to Qabalistic psychology and the writings of Aleister Crowley. When I finally delved into Crowley's writings, I knew I'd found my path.

In most of life, it is only occasionally that we meet an individual who truly shines with Self-hood, whose very presence is a lesson in a certain way of being and of living. When I began attending events presented by various magical orders, I found that these organizations were absolutely filled to the brim with such people!—and I am so very pleased and honored to say that the contributors to this volume are among the best and the brightest of these brilliant individuals. It has been a true delight to read and edit this collection and to hear the unique voices of the various authors discussing their respective areas of specialty with such clarity and passion.

In assembling this volume, we considered the diverse array of philosophies, spiritual traditions, and ritual styles that might reasonably fall within the conceptual net known as ceremonial magick. In each book of this volume, we will feature a different tradition, highlighting the key concepts, philosophical underpinnings, and ritual approaches that constitute its unique contribution to the field of magick. Text boxes in each book will give more detail about important historical figures or submovements relevant to the tradition. The sequence of books is roughly chronological, to aid the reader's ability to trace the evolution of magick across cultures and over the course of millennia. Furthermore, as many traditions built on the foundations of earlier doctrines and practices, approaching the work chronologically more clearly traces the influences each body of work exerted on the others. As one might expect, we were inevitably forced to explore some traditions in more detail and others only in passing. We encourage the reader not to assume that this represents doctrinal bias on the part of the editors but rather the limitations of the space and scope of this volume.

The very worthwhile price to pay when assembling a volume of this diversity and magnitude is that the unique viewpoints of the various authors may sometimes contradict each other. We made an editorial decision to embrace these differences as an inevitable, positive result of bringing together a group of such devoted and learned specialists rather than attempting to impose a uniformity of doctrine and interpretation that, in fact, is not actually there. Accordingly, we invite the reader to approach this volume with critical thinking skills fully engaged, and to let the interplay of views enrich your research as you come to your own conclusions. In a similar vein, we have made no attempt to standardize the spelling or usage of the technical terms and concepts that appear throughout this volume. As they say, reasonable people may disagree on such things, and the various traditions represented here often have their own unique usages as well.

To my good friend, co-editor, and brother in the Great Work, Lon Milo DuQuette (who, judging by his prolific career of writing, speaking, teaching, and making music, isn't as lazy as

---

3. Israel Regardie, *The Middle Pillar: The Balance Between Mind and Magic.*, ed. and annotated with new material by Chic Cicero and Sandra Tabatha Cicero (St. Paul: Llewellyn Publications, 2002).

· · · · · · · ·

he thinks): Thank you for sharing the very magical task of compiling and editing this work. It has been a challenging but extremely fulfilling journey, and I share your hope that generations to come may benefit from what we've assembled here.

And finally, to the reader: May you discover the eternal light of Magick within yourself, and bring that light to bear on your path, finding much joy and fulfillment in every step.

—David Shoemaker

BOOK ONE

———✦———

Foundations of Western Magic
by Sam Webster

In 1510 Heinrich Cornelius Agrippa gave us ceremonial magic as the topic of the third of his *Three Books of Occult Philosophy*. The practices and traditions discussed in the volume in your hand call themselves forms of ceremonial magick because of this. Agrippa created a critical compendium of magical lore that still enriches our practice to this day, but much of this lore was not considered magic by those who practiced it.

Scholars from Lynn Thorndike to Ronald Hutton have suggested there is a continuity in the development of Western ritual magic from ancient times to modern.[1] As a body, this stream of practice has been termed the *Western Mystery Tradition*, or more recently the *Western esoteric tradition*.[2] So much will have to be lightly touched upon here due to the limits of space, but those parts that become our magic will be the focus.

What Is Magic?

Before we can undertake a history of Western magic—particularly if the history is to be a short one—we need to have some idea about what we do and do not mean by the word.[3] Yet a precise definition is not easy to fashion.

---

1. For example, Lynn Thorndike, *A History of Magic and Experimental Science*; and Ronald Hutton, *The Triumph of the Moon: A History of Modern Pagan Witchcraft* and *Witches, Druids, and King Arthur*.

2. For a formulation of Western esotericism, see Antoine Faivre, *Access to Western Esotericism*. For a concise history, see Nicholas Goodrick-Clarke, *The Western Esoteric Traditions: A Historical Introduction*.

3. Herein and hereafter I will use the spelling *magic*, which is conventional in academic work. Aleister Crowley's custom of using the *k* will be better applied to work from within the contemporary magickal perspective.

· · · · · · · ·

Magic is thought of by many as being in opposition to *religion*. Magic is often defined as the manipulation of spiritual forces for specific, usually material ends, while religion is said to focus on worship and general supplication for help. This is a popular distinction, but counterexamples are not hard to find. We regard the animal sacrifices of the ancient Greeks to be religious, not magical—and yet the ancient Greeks always expected an answer. Even today, anyone attending a Catholic mass or Protestant service will note the specificity of petitional prayer.

Others define the difference between religion and magic as the difference between the legitimate and the illegitimate use of spiritual resources, with magic of course constituting the illegitimate. And indeed, every culture distinguishes between common acts of piety and esoteric or forbidden magic—but unfortunately for our purposes, these dividing lines are drawn very differently from one culture to another. The same magical square that a magician in London might formulate in private to attract celestial forces, a Hindu shopkeeper in New Delhi will hang openly behind the cash register to attract the blessing of the gods and good fortune.

Moreover, many practices have been thought of as magic at one time in history and yet not at another. For example, both Agrippa in 1500 and the Golden Dawn in 1900 used the term *magic* to describe their practices, while Iamblichus, who in 300 was at the root of these same practices, did not. Particularly for ancient peoples, these practices were not regarded as magic but simply as a part of their religion—the *operational* part.

Once we remove the cultural framework around the words *religion* and *magic*, no objective differences remain. This realization will guide our exploration of the ancient forms of magic, and we may see them as entirely a part of their religious framework while no less means of accomplishing ends.

And so, what is magic? In my view, magic is religious action or *operative religion*. It is any use of religious or spiritual resources to achieve a result, whether that result is spiritual or material. To put it flatly, magic is not *separate* from religion in any meaningful sense; rather, it is *part* of religion, specifically that part that seeks an outcome.

Equipped with this definition, we can now look at the ancient sources that are the foundations of Western ceremonial magic. The history that follows is a summary of a long journey, one whose beginnings are older than history itself, that takes us through the ancient cultures that contributed to our understanding of those practices we now call magic.

We'll look into the depth of time and consider the limited information our forebears had of the Bronze Age. The path becomes easier for us to follow as we enter the Iron Age, and from there we can trace the philosophical tradition through more than a thousand years of development, culminating in the practice of theurgy as developed and taught by Iamblichus of Chalcis around 300 BCE.

· · · · · · · ·

The tradition was interrupted by the rapid rise and domination of Christianity and the fall of the Roman Empire, but from about 500 on, we can again track the development of magical theory and practice through the Middle Ages and the early Renaissance. At last, this short history will bring us to the dawn of the modern era, when in 1510 Heinrich Cornelius Agrippa wrote his *Three Books of Occult Philosophy*, a scholarly compendium of magical lore that still influences and enriches our practice to this day.

Discussing aspects of this history in more depth and continuing the journey to the present day is the work of the rest of this volume. Later books cover planetary magick; the influence of the Kabbalah of the Jews, the Cabala of the Christians, and the Qabalah of the hermeticists; the grimoire traditions and the Enochian magick of John Dee; alchemy; the Abra-Melin system; and influential orders such as the Rosicrucians and Freemasons, and later the Golden Dawn, the Ordo Templi Orientis (O.T.O.), and the A∴A∴. In the final chapter, after this long journey, ceremonial magic is returned to its polytheistic roots.

Deep Time and the Bronze Age

Modern humans, of the species *Homo sapiens sapiens*, have been around for perhaps 300,000 years. The deep past, of course, always casts a subtle influence on the present, but only in the last few hundred years have we begun to possess real information about ancient cultures. Not until 1822, for example, was the ancient Egyptian language translated; the translation of Sumerian was only beginning in 1838.

When we look at the deep ancient world, then, we have to remember that until relatively recently we had only a dim and often erroneous idea about our inheritance. Our old ideas about the origins of the Western magical tradition were mostly projections based on whatever architecture, artifacts, and other fragments of the past had survived into the Iron Age. Even these scattered pieces had often themselves been changed along the way, transformed by ancient peoples before being written down and delivered to us in the form of myths, legends, and scriptures.

A variety of scientific developments, however, have increased our skill at reconstructing the past. We have better indications now of what humans were doing as deep as 33,000 BCE, when the Red Lady of Paviland was buried in what is now Britain. The body, which was covered in red ocher, was buried with seashell necklaces and rings and rods carved from the ivory of a mammoth's tusk. When the Red Lady was unearthed in 1823, scientists speculated that "she" was a prostitute from the time of the Roman Empire; only since the 1960s has analysis revealed that the skeleton is male and dates from tens of thousands of years earlier. The ocher and the adornments must have had some symbolic meaning and probably indicate some form of ritual activity. The Red Lady is now thought to be the oldest known ceremonial burial in Europe. These ancient cultures, however, are mostly cut off from us by the last ice age, which ended about 12,000 years ago.

· · · · · · ·

The stone circles of Europe were once thought to have been erected by the ancient Druids, who were contemporary with the ancient Romans. We now know that these were actually built by much older cultures beginning in about 3300 BCE. Even earlier are chamber tombs and cairns, which we can date to 4000 BCE at the latest, in the early Neolithic period. Long before these is the Göbekli Tepe in what is now Turkey, built in about 11,000 BCE by people who had not yet developed agriculture.

The historical record changes dramatically after a period of decline and destruction that began about 1200 BCE. Within about a half-century, most of the great cultures of the Western world at that time—including the Egyptian, Hittite, Minoan, Assyrian, Babylonian, and Mycenaean cultures—either collapsed or were significantly diminished. During this period, almost every important city on the eastern end of the Mediterranean Sea was destroyed; many of them were never occupied again. Historians still debate the causes—drought, warfare, widespread piracy, and the failure of rigid political systems to adapt to change are all possible contributors—but in any case, this collapse marked the end of the Bronze Age.

Here is where our story can really begin.

When the Lights Come on Again: The Iron Age and the Ancient World

We can trace the origins of our modern practices all the way back to about 900 BCE, to the culture that arose as humanity began to recover from the Bronze Age collapse. What survives from this prehistoric world is mostly Greek and Roman, along with some Hebrew elements. It was through the lenses of these great cultures that the still more ancient Egyptian and Mesopotamian cultures were understood.

This final period of prehistory, the Iron Age, was first named by the ancient Greek poet Hesiod in his poem *Theogony*. For Hesiod, the Iron Age was the third and most brutal of the mythic ages during which the gods had their origins. Together, the epic poems of Hesiod and Homer formed the cosmic narrative that became the basis for Mediterranean culture. Beginning with the conquests of Alexander the Great starting around 325 BCE, the swell of great empires spread these myths and legends broadly.

What comes forward from this ancient period are streams of knowledge and practice: philosophy, myth, spellcraft, fragments of worship practices, and bits of early science and math. Much of this lore would be hidden and inactive until the Renaissance, except for such pieces as were later absorbed and preserved—though in distorted forms—by the Church.

The line between the Iron Age and the beginnings of written history is not sharply defined. It was around this time that philosophy had its beginnings in attempts to find a rational basis for understanding and interpreting the ancient poetic myths. But it wasn't long before philosophers expanded their horizons and were trying to explain the whole world without reference to the literary traditions. We call these ancient philosophers the *pre-Socratics*, and the first—at least of

· · · · · · · · ·

those whose names and works have survived—was Thales (c. 624–546 BCE), who told us "all things are full of gods" and began organizing the discipline of geometry.

Pythagoras (c. 570–495 BCE), who is credited with coining the term *philosophy*, created a community of followers that long outlasted him. He taught using geometric proofs, and he required discipline and contemplation from his students. His contributions ranged from theories of musical harmonics to practices for the attainment of a good life. The doctrine of ethical reincarnation is attributed to him, as well as a number of mathematical theorems.

Our image of a holy man or sage comes, in part, from the mystic philosopher and healer Empedocles of Sicily (495–444 BCE). Empedocles was said to go about wearing elaborate purple robes, a crown, and golden sandals. This sartorial splendor was criticized by some in his own day as being eccentric and overdone, but it was the common garb of priestfolk during worship.

Empedocles claimed to remember other lives and to know that he was a divine being incarnate on earth. In his great cosmogonic poem *On Nature*, he wrote that the conflict between two divine forces, Strife and Love, was the dynamic that propels all action. In this poem, he also gave us the first Western presentation of the four elements, fire, air, water, and earth, which he called "roots." He took his leave of life (or at least of Sicily) by jumping into a volcano, leaving his sandals on the edge of the crater.

Socrates (470–399 BCE) was a stonecutter in Athens whose method of teaching was not to profess to know but only to ask. We have no writings of his, only what Plato, Xenophon, and a few other contemporaries wrote about him, and it may be that the Socrates we meet in Plato's dialogues is more of a literary construct than an accurate portrait. Socrates was noted for his unusual method of teaching, which consisted of asking a series of questions, and for his ethical virtues, which ultimately brought him into conflict with the leadership of Athens and led to his trial and his death by hemlock.

For magical practitioners, it is important to note that Socrates claimed to be guided by his personal *daemon*, mostly by being told what *not* to do. Scholars struggle with this, but the descriptions that we have make it clear he was dealing with the same phenomenon we know today as the *Holy Guardian Angel*.

Little is known about Diotima of Mantinea, but it is important that we acknowledge her as the one whom Socrates referred to as his teacher, according to Plato's *Symposium*. She introduced Socrates to the notion of divine ascent through beauty and love, starting with the particular love, as of an individual, and slowly learning to generalize and abstract that love until one can perceive and unite with the Good and Beautiful that are the Source of Being. Diotima's teachings illustrate why understanding ancient philosophy is vital to us. Philosophy was the theology of its time, and it provides the theoretical underpinnings for magical practice today.

· · · · · · · ·

Philosophical development in the West comes to a head with Plato (c. 428–347 BCE). Plato was the founder of the first institution of higher learning in the Western world, and while he was not the first to be called a philosopher, his formulation of the discipline is so influential that in the West he can be considered philosophy's inventor. Plato's dialogues summarize the thought of many thinkers before him, and in many cases it is only through Plato that we know of them at all. Importantly, Plato's work was preserved (though it was lost to the West from the fall of Rome to the Renaissance), and it came to form the basis for all philosophy and theory of magic thereafter.

Yet to Plato himself, the written word was not the most important part of his teachings. In the dialogue *Phaedrus*, he wrote that "he who has knowledge of the just and the good and beautiful ... will not, when in earnest, write them in ink, sowing them through a pen with words which cannot defend themselves by argument and cannot teach the truth effectually." The unwritten doctrines that expressed Plato's true understanding were to be conveyed by the spoken word.

Plato's philosophy developed in two major phases after his life. The first we call Middle Platonism, and it starts with Antiochus of Ascalon (c. 125–68 BCE), who rejected the hard skepticism of his teachers at the Third Academy, who denied humans the ability to know the absolute.

Plutarch (c. 45–120) is the preeminent writer of Middle Platonism. He also rejected the strict determinism of the Stoics and asserted the freedom of the will. He disagreed with the Epicureans and declared the soul immortal. For Plutarch, matter, although transformed by the Creator into the World Soul, was nonetheless the source of all evil. For him, the Supreme Being was transcendental to the world, yet worked within the world through the gods and daemons of popular religion.

In the Roman Empire at this time, participation in politics was limited by the imperial system to a small portion of elite society. For the leisured classes and anyone else who had an education, philosophy and religion had become venues for self-expression and advancement. This was an era that saw the writing of the *Corpus Hermeticum*, the *Sepher Yetzirah*, the *Chaldean Oracles*, the *Gnostica*, and the *Gospels*.

Neoplatonism, which emerged in the third century, is the name we give to the next phase of development in Platonic thought. Eventually, Neoplatonism split into two branches, one purely philosophical and the other theurgic and ritualizing. It is from this theurgic branch that the Western magical tradition springs, specifically "learned" magic.

When Plotinus (204–270) arrived in Alexandria to study philosophy, he despaired of finding what he sought until he was pointed to Ammonius Sakkas (dates unknown), who held the chair of philosophy at Alexandria. On returning to Rome, Plotinus taught his own vision of Platonic philosophy. The teachings of Plotinus bear some striking similarities to Vedantic thought, and recent scholarship suggests that his teacher's family may have come to Alexandria from northern

India. Plotinus's cosmology and ideas about the soul were the origin of the concepts that magic users today have about the world and ourselves.

Plotinus gave us a relatively simple fourfold cosmological model that was debated and elaborated upon by his successors but that would be familiar to any Qabalist. It consists of a hierarchy of four hypostases, or entitative stabilizations. The highest realm is that of the Creator and source of being, called *to hen,* the One. Next highest is the realm of *nous,* the intelligible mind, the domain of whatever can be apprehended only with the nondiscursive mind. Below that is the realm of *psyche,* the soul. The soul is perhaps most simply understood as that which leaves the body upon death, but here it constitutes an entire living cosmic domain and underpinning of the material world. This realm is the natural place of the gods of myth and culture in this system. The lowest realm is that of *hyle,* matter, which consists of the entire physical cosmos out to and including the eighth sphere of the fixed stars.

Plotinus's cosmology assumed that this fourfold cosmos is of similar character to the humans in it. The entitative unity of a human comes from the presence of the One in us. As Plotinus expressed it in his last words, "Strive to give back the One in yourself to the One in the All." The *nous* in humans, corresponding to the *nous* in the cosmos, is our intelligence. Yet in a real sense what are present in us are merely the participating images of the real One and the real *nous,* just enough to give us these qualities of unity and mind. Where we really begin is at the level of the *psyche,* or soul, which lives in the material world of *hyle,* in, on, or permeating the body.

We have Plotinus's thought because his lecture notes and essays were compiled and edited by one of his students, Porphyry of Tyre (c. 234–305). We are fortunate that Porphyry was an excellent writer, as is shown by his other works such as *On Abstinence from Animal Food, Aids to the Study of the Intelligibles,* and *Philosophy from Oracles,* which gives us parts of the Chaldean Oracles. The popularity of his *Against the Christians* can be inferred from the fact that the Roman emperor Theodosius II ordered the burning of every copy in 435—and then had to repeat the order in 448.

Porphyry's work was important to science, as his writing on the Aristotelian categories became the basis for biological taxonomies. But it is his *Letter to Anebo* that is important to Western magic. There are competing theories as to what this letter is really about, but in it Porphyry critiqued the modes of worship of the day and raised the idea—which Christians would later adopt—that the recipients of burnt and bloody sacrifice were demons and not gods.

Most scholars think that Porphyry's critique was literal and sincere. Many of his views in this letter, however, are contradicted by his later writings, which has led some to suggest that this text should be regarded as an example of "disputations and solutions," a common mode at the time for discussing philosophical topics, in which the author listed all the debates on a subject and then systematically answered each one.

· · · · · · · ·

We have the *Letter to Anebo* at all only because it is part of a work by Porphyry's own student, Iamblichus (c. 240–325).[4] Iamblichus was born in the town of Chalcis in northern Syria. He lived and taught in the Syrian city of Apamea, where the Chaldean Oracles are said to have been written and kept. Only a small portion of Iamblichus's books have survived. He is known today principally because later writers wrote about him, sometimes quoting passages from his works. In this way we have fragments from two commentaries on Platonic dialogues and from his work *On the Soul*. We also know about other works of his that are completely lost, including one on the Chaldean Oracles, with at least twenty-eight chapters.

One exception to this sad loss is the work generally referred to as *De mysteriis*, or *On the Mysteries*. This, Iamblichus's longest-surviving work, is properly titled *The Reply of the Master Abamon to the Letter of Porphyry to Anebo, and the Solutions to the Questions It Contains.* In this work, Iamblichus defends theurgy, which is advanced polytheistic practice, and he presents a rationale for cultic worship of heroes, spirits, archons, angels, and gods, leading eventually to union with the One that is All. It also explains the use of divination, divinization through divine possession, the art of sacrifice, and other allied practices generally termed magic today. Importantly, Iamblichus gives us the pedagogy that provides the skills needed to do all this and that underlie all magical practice. This work, like the rest of Iamblichus's writings and teachings, integrated worship and philosophy in a way that had not been seen before but which came to dominate Neoplatonic philosophy in the ancient world.

The last major philosopher of the ancient world whom we have space to cover is Proclus (412–485), who was the head of the later Athenian Platonic Academy. Many of the ideas that were first exposited by Iamblichus were developed—and sometimes criticized—a few generations later by this important thinker.[5] We have also been blessed by a collection of Proclus's hymns which show us an implementation of theurgic practice in verse.[6]

We are fortunate to have some of Proclus's longer works, such as *Platonic Theology* and *The Elements of Theology*, all of which had a profound influence during the Renaissance when they were translated and became available to Europe.

Most precious to us is Brian Copenhaver's 1988 translation of "On the Priestly Art According to the Greeks," as this is one of the very few explicit writings on the actual practice of theurgy.[7] Copenhaver speculates that this text is a précis, culled by a Byzantine philosopher, of a larger

---

4. The current best biography of Iamblichus is found in the introduction to *Iamblichus: De Mysteriis*, trans. Emma C. Clarke, John M. Dillon, and Jackson P. Hershbell, pp. xvii and following.

5. O'Meara, *Pythagoras Revived: Mathematics and Philosophy in Late Antiquity*.

6. See R. M. van den Berg, *Proclus' Hymns*.

7. Copenhaver, "Hermes Trismegistus, Proclus, and the Question of a Philosophy of Magic in the Renaissance," in *Hermeticism and the Renaissance*, 79–110.

· · · · · · · ·

work by Proclus. The text is especially important due to its influence on Ficino, and it figures prominently in his *Three Books on Life*. It explains the power and ubiquity of prayer and explains the use and theory behind what we call today *correspondences*.[8]

The excessive prevalence of men in this story is partly an artifact of the way history was written. Even if there is little information about them, we must remember Diotima of Mantinea, Socrates's teacher mentioned previously; Sosipatra of Ephesus (c. 325), mystic and teacher of philosophy; and Hypatia of Alexandra (c. 350–415), teacher, astronomer, and mathematician. Joan Breton Connelly's work shows the importance of women in the religious culture of the ancient world, mostly lost to us because the women did not write.[9]

Maximus the Thaumaturge

Maximus of Ephesus (c. 310–372) was a Neoplatonist philosopher, theurgist, and mage who studied at the school of Iamblichus's greatest pupil, Aedesius, alongside the famous sage Eusebius. Maximus became the most influential teacher of the future emperor Julian, who would attempt to reestablish classical paganism in the Roman Empire. Eusebius tried to warn Julian off becoming Maximus's pupil on account of his penchant for sorcery, relating an occasion when Maximus invited him and others to the temple of Hecate. There he saluted the statue of the goddess and told his audience that they would soon be witness to his lofty genius. He then burned a grain of incense while muttering an incantation, whereupon the statue of the goddess seemed to smile before bursting out laughing. Urging his audience not be afraid, he warned them that the stone torches in her hands would shortly burst into flame, which they immediately did. Eusebius advised Julian that such theatrical sorcery merely tricked the senses, insisting that the purification of the soul is of primary importance, and that was to be achieved by reason alone, which was the position of Plotinus rather than Iamblichus.

Julian nevertheless headed straight to Ephesus, where Maximus taught him Iamblichan theurgy, which was based primarily on the Chaldean Oracles and the magical religious rites that he had inherited as a son of the last solar priest-king of Emesa. Animal sacrifice and divination were central rituals. On assuming the throne, Julian attempted to establish a cult of Helios the Sun, as the supreme deity of Creation.

Eunapius, the Greek historian from whom we derive most of our knowledge of Maximus, met the great wizard in person, and gives us perhaps the best description of a pagan magus of late antiquity that has come down to us:

---

8. Eds. note: Magical correspondences are discussed throughout this volume, with extensive tables given in Book Eleven: Magician's Tables.

9. Connelly, *Portrait of a Priestess: Women and Ritual in Ancient Greece*.

• • • • • • • •

While still a youth [I] met him in his old age and heard his voice, which was such as one might have heard from Homer's Athene or Apollo. The very pupils of his eyes were, so to speak, winged; he had a long grey beard, and his glance revealed the agile impulses of his soul. There was a wonderful harmony in his person, both to the eye and ear, and all who conversed with him were amazed as to both these faculties, since one could hardly endure the swift movements of his eyes or his rapid flow of words. In discussion with him no one ventured to contradict him, not even the most experienced and most eloquent, but they yielded to him in silence and acquiesced in what he said as though it came from the tripod of an oracle; such a charm sat on his lips.[*]

Eunapius also recounts an episode in which the great philosopher and mystic Sosipatra was bewitched by a relative who had fallen in love with her. Maximus detected the spell and was able to counter it with a spell of his own. After the death of Julian just two years into his reign, Maximus was arrested and eventually executed.
—Guy Ogilvy

Guy Ogilvy has been a practising spagyrist and student of the Western esoteric tradition for many years. He has written several books on esoteric subjects under various names, including his latest, *The Great Wizards of Antiquity* (Llewellyn, 2019), the first of a trilogy on the history of magic and alchemy in the West. He has appeared on several television networks in Britain, Japan, and the US to share his expertise on magic and alchemy.

[*] Philostratus and Eunapius, *The Lives of the Sophists*, trans. Wilmer Cave Wright, (Cambridge, MA: Harvard University Press, 1921), 427.

Our Theurgic Foundation

The fall of the Western Roman Empire in the fifth century and the dominance of Christianity thereafter disrupted the development and continuity of this branch of philosophy and religious practice. Some religious and magical technologies were passed on in spite of the interruption, such as the collection of spells and recipes called the *Kyranides*. The Northern peoples and their practices would be absorbed into the hegemonic cultures of the Mediterranean during the earlier medieval period (500–1100), and fared about as well as the Southern peoples. Others survived because they had been translated into Arabic or Hebrew but were little known in Christendom for a thousand years until the recovery of magic in the Renaissance.

The Renaissance, however, would see the recovery of ancient magic in a new and vital way we will examine below, but what was central to that recovery was the last great fluorescence of

· · · · · · · ·

traditional pre-Christian religion, a profound synthesis of religious thought. This synthesis was developed by the ritualizing, theurgic branch of Neoplatonism, and it began with Iamblichus.

What is critical about this, and not always recognized, is that this synthesis provided a complete theory and justification for all traditional ancient worship. It provided for every level of development and education, from the holiday visits of common worshipers, to the temple to ask for boons, to the needs of cities and states for divine blessings, to the exalted practices of the philosophers and priestfolk, and even to the completely immaterial mind-only practices of the rare and few.

What we have of this is most thoroughly presented in Iamblichus's *De mysteriis*. Other philosophers such as Proclus and Damascius (c. 458 to after 538) would add to this understanding, but not in such a practical manner as in *De mysteriis*.

It is fair to argue that theurgy is the central pillar of all magical practice in that it is the basic technique for worshiping the gods, attracting their presence and power to enable those practices of wonders and transformations we call magic. Divination, spirit conjuration, and divine possession are all embraced by, and made actionable in, theurgic practice. In this way, *De mysteriis* is the cornerstone of the entire Western magical tradition. No other work provides as strong and thorough a theoretical basis for all the practices we call magic today as this one does.

Yet never does Iamblichus refer to *magaia* in *De mysteriis*. He appears to have thought of the practices not as magic but rather as a kind of advanced religiosity and deep spirituality.

In *De mysteriis*, Iamblichus, who was in fact a Syrian noble of a priestly family, wrote in the character of an Egyptian priest. With great vigor and eloquence, he answered each of Porphyry's challenges to worship and spiritual advancement, and in the process he delineated a justification for worship of the gods as well as for the advanced form of that worship, which is theurgy.

Prayer, sacrifice, and divination were the tools used by Iamblichus and the theurgists. *De mysteriis* gave a critical analysis of each. Not satisfied with merely being in the gods' good graces, the practitioner used sacrifice and prayer to come into a closer relationship with the deity, eventually to the level of union.[10] Divination was employed to refine theurgic practice by seeking the deity's instructions to improve it.

Where philosophy was used to speculate upon the nature of the gods and how to approach them, divination augmented that understanding with revelation. Then the practices of sacrifice and prayer actively applied and tested that knowledge, resulting in better communications with the gods.

---

10. Sandwell, 266; Lane Fox, 207–208; Scheid, 95.

The Iamblichan Paradigm of Theurgy

In Iamblichus's view, the theurgist lives in a world created by a divine hierarchy that is descended from the One, the supreme and ultimate grand unity of being. The world gets its structure according to the principles of mediation; as a mean is required between all extremes, the hierarchy has many layers, all in keeping with the cosmic strata.

These strata are derived from Plotinus: unity, mind, soul, and matter. The material realm, the cosmos, is organized by the classical Ptolemaic cosmology. The earth, along with the four elements, are at the center. This terrestrial realm is surrounded by the celestial realm, which includes the moon, the sun, and the rest of the planets, and ends with the sphere of the fixed stars. Outside the cosmos, the divine realm begins.

The power of creation and divine presence ever flows from the One. It flows down the hierarchy of divinities and daemons in emanation, *prohodos*, and it flows in return, *epistrophe*. It is this returning current that the theurgist exploits to ascend the hierarchy, eventually back to the One.

The deities of worship, myth, and legend are, in philosophical terms, the Platonic ideas or forms. The deities emanate their essences (their selves) into the cosmos, giving otherwise formless and insensible matter its distinct characteristics. When manifested in material form, these divine ideas are called words, or *logoi*, and so the texture, color, shape, and what we call today the chemical or medical properties of things, as well as all other characteristics, are to the theurgist the literal presence of the deity in the object. These anagogic *logoi* of the gods that can be found in matter are called *sunthemata*, or tokens, and by contemplating and sacrificing these "wondrous deposits," the theurgist becomes herself divinized.[11]

Moderns will recognize this as the ancient understanding of correspondences, although that term was not used until after the Renaissance. Proclus, in his *On the Hieratic Art*, explained that the "sympathy of lower things for those above" is the inherence of the *logoi* of the divine ideas present in objects, prayers, and thought. The *logoi* are not only the distinguishing characteristics in all things, they *are* themselves the divine presence. When Proclus wrote of their "use made in the priestly art," he explained how and when these things are applied and their *logoi* are activated.

Proclus wrote that the divine light comes "to what is capable of sharing it," using the analogy of a warm candlewick that, having been made fit (*epitedeiotes*) by being warmed, can be lit by a flame that is merely held nearby without touching. It is through the performance of the invocation that the theurgist is "warmed" and that the contact with the divine is made. In this analogy, the lighting of the wick represents the "divinization of mortal entities," and the illumination that

---

11. *Iamblichus: De Mysteriis*, 10.5, p. 349, and 1.12, p. 53.

· · · · · · · ·

results is the approaching of the divine. Proclus cites Chaldean Oracle, fr. 121: "For the mortal who has approached the fire will possess the light from God."[12]

The human theurgist is a microcosm of the larger world. Within her constitution is the One in the soul, the manifestation of the One in the individual that grants unity and individuality. She also possess *nous*, or nondiscursive mind, which resides above and complements her discursive mind, *dianoia*, for it is *nous* that is able to experience the *logoi* directly. Most properly, her rank is that of a soul, and from the mean between *nous* and *hyle* she takes her own proper place in the divine hierarchy, albeit as its least member.

The theurgist's soul, like those of all humans, is imbued with the divine *logoi*. The gods, who are the source of the *logoi*, are present to her and within her as part of her very constitution. She shares in the composite life of the body and is constrained by its lawful needs, and yet with the help of the gods she is able to free herself from the body, its limits, and its passions, and ultimately to attain the rank of the angels and coadminister the cosmos.

Bridging the gap between the material body and the incorporeal soul is the aetheric and/or pneumatic vehicle, called the *augoeides soma* or *ochema*, the egg-like body or vehicle.[13] Once purified, this vehicle becomes the tool for the ascent to the creative cause and the screen on which "blessed visions" arise as the gods communicate to the theurgist.

Theurgy is an advanced religious practice, and so the would-be theurgist must be prepared. At the beginning, she undergoes a time of study. She learns of the world from Aristotle, and she learns of higher things from the Platonic dialogues (including their copious commentaries), the *Corpus Hermeticum* (in whatever form it existed in Iamblichus's time), the Chaldean Oracles, Pythagorean mathematics, and other supportive works. Parallel to this was the cultivation of virtue, moderation, and piety in all actions. Supporting all this was her lifelong practice of ordinary, traditional worship and cult.

The theurgist is then to practice devotion, making sacrifice and spending long hours in invocation. First, she will be illuminated by the gods as she comes to know them firsthand, and she will be purified by their *sunthemata*, which are activated by their presence in offerings. Later, she will become united with their will, and she will join in their projects. Eventually, she will be joined to the gods in ineffable union, *theosis*.

As part of her approach to the divine, she invokes and makes offering to each and every daemon, angel, and archangel. First, she worships the terrestrial gods of her culture and of the places around her. This is the first step up the hierarchy of divine beings, which proceeds up

---

12. "Fr." means "fragment." Scholars have attempted to catalog the Chaldean Oracles in various ways over the years, since we literally only have "fragments" of the original work.

13. Shades of Carlos Castaneda here.

• • • • • • • •

through the celestial realm to the *noeric* (soul) gods, to the *noetic* (mind) gods, and finally to the henadic realm of the many gods that are one.

When she is able to stand on the firm foundation given by the terrestrial gods, she next worships the sun and practices *photogogia*, light-guiding, filling herself with divine fire. From the sun, she asks to know and converse with the personal daemon, called today the Holy Guardian Angel, who was given her by the demiurge at her creation and who will guide her on her theurgic path. One after another, she invokes the gods until she comes to know them all and awakens their *logoi* within her, uniting herself to the cosmos and eventually leading her up to union with the One, *henosis*.

As she advances along this path, her sacrifices become less material. She gradually dispenses with "bodies," or material offerings, as she moves to symbols, word images, and actions. Eventually, as her *epitedeiotes*, or "fitness," to receive the gods improves, she dispenses with symbols as well, making purely immaterial offerings.

As the divine union becomes more pure and stabilized, as her will becomes more united with the gods, the theurgist's actions become those of demiurgic mimesis, imitating the Creator as she fulfills her purpose, continuing creation so that the promise of the *Timaeus* (41b–c) is fulfilled, that the cosmos be complete or else be imperfect.

Notably, there are no *voces magicae*, what we call barbarous tongues, listed as part of this preparation. Nor are there any arcane practices, strange symbols, and the like. There are places for these things in theurgy, and if the theurgist is trained in the use of these tools, or if she is an initiate of such mysteries as provide them, they will provide divinely empowered access or activity. But, though they may be helpful, they are not necessary.

In essence, theurgy was for the most part performed simply by participating in ordinary cultic activities. These activities were performed, however, with the understanding and intention of being moved by the activated *sunthemata* along the path to greater intimacy with the gods. By taking what we might call the "theurgic view," the theurgist makes her participation in all religious activity—even that from outside her own culture—serve her theurgic advancement and attainment. This is key to understanding the practices of Agrippa's occult philosophy and, later, those of the Golden Dawn.[14]

The Medieval Age

With the fall of the Roman Empire in the West, reckoned from about 500 CE, a new era dawned. This age was profoundly dominated by the Church and Christianity. Never had the West seen a

---

14. Eds. note: See Book Eight: The Golden Dawn.

religion that was so militant and aggressive, so dedicated to removing all other spiritualities from its domain.

As the Church spread into the lands of the Franks, Germans, and Britons, it worked primarily to convert the local leadership. But there were also the traditional religious practices of those peoples to be dealt with. These practices were "pagan," which is to say non-Christian, so the Church could not allow them to continue; yet they were also vibrant and necessary to life, so they proved impossible to erase. In the interest of easing conversions, however, the Church made accommodations.

In spite of the Church's condemnation, magic was widespread and in use in every stratum of society.[15] This was a time of limited medical knowledge and few life-supporting technologies, and magic, in the sense of the use of spiritual resources for material ends, was one of the very few recourses available for the stricken. Every European culture had developed its own collection of spells and recipes designed to alleviate troubles. After the spread of Christianity, these collections were still made and used, but where once they had called on the deities and spirits of the local cultures, they now called more often on saints, angels, and the Holy Trinity, either in whole or in part.[16]

Incantations, amulets, and actions laden with meaning or power were still used to aid the needful and smite enemies.[17] Divination was still used to prognosticate or diagnose.[18] But more often than not, a Christian "coat of paint" was added so that the people would redirect their devotions to Christian deities and their loyalties to Church authorities. Within a few generations, the "pagan" origins of these practices were a faint memory, and everyone was a baptized Christian.

The text of the *Kyranides*, which contains elements from the Greek magical papyri, shows how these ancient spells endured well into the Christian period.[19] Formalized speech, physical objects having natural "occult" properties or consecrated with verbal formula, and images of the afflicted or cursed, usually empowered by invoking Christian spiritual entities, were common.[20] The Church alternately promoted and condemned these practices, for it presumed that

15. Bailey, *Magic and Superstition in Europe*, 80; Kieckhefer, *Magic in the Middle Ages*, 56–57; Flint, *The Rise of Magic in Early Medieval Europe*, 3–8; and Fanger, *Conjuring Spirits: Texts and Traditions of Medieval Ritual Magic*.

16. Bailey, *Magic and Superstition in Europe*, 83.

17. Bailey, *Magic and Superstition in Europe*, 80–83.

18. Bailey, *Magic and Superstition in Europe*, 82, 87–90.

19. Anonymous, *Kyranides: On the Occult Virtues of Plants, Animals & Stones*, 67. Compare with Betz, *The Greek Magical Papyri in Translation*, LXIII. 7–12, p. 295, and another version VII. 411–416, p. 129. See also Section 1.2, fn4.

20. Formalized speech: Bailey, *Magic and Superstition in Europe*, 83–84, and Kieckhefer, *Magic in the Middle Ages*, 69–70. Objects: Bailey, 84–87. Images: Bailey, 87.

the powers invoked were not those of the Christian Trinity or the saints but those of non-Christian demons.[21] Making the sign of the cross or saying the *Pater Noster* could be acceptable, but because they could be also deployed for dishonorable purposes such as cursing, they were not entirely encouraged. The blessing of Church-ordained priests, on the other hand, was considered helpful to all magics, and could be requested to empower spells and amulets. Consecrated eucharists were used by priests in a talismanic fashion to protect and to bless with fertility and good fortune cities, villages, fields, and flocks.[22]

Book-derived magic, including the conjuring of spirits and demons, was practiced among the educated and often mislabeled as necromancy.[23] Yet the usual hallmark of theurgy, the use of such practices for spiritual advancement, was absent here. Scholars have identified certain texts and practices that can be considered theurgy, and some of these were possibly influenced by Iamblichus. Claire Fanger, in the compilation *Invoking Angels*, outlines the major forms of theurgy that were emerging in the thirteenth to sixteenth centuries.[24] This collection of essays, edited by Fanger, presents a number of Christian texts that show some of the characteristics of theurgy we have seen in the Iamblichan paradigm. These texts clearly were used to invoke beings, namely angels, in order to receive knowledge and experience visions.[25] In the absence of polytheism, however, the practice was limited by having only one god to invoke.

By the High Middle Ages, 1000–1250, and the dawn of the Renaissance beginning according to various opinions as early as the fourteenth or fifteenth century, the religions that the Church worked so diligently to suppress were mostly gone. As for their magics, although the serial numbers were filed off and fresh coats of paint applied in new colors, much of the same underlying methods were there but now the new God and his angels and saints were the divine ones invoked.

Michael Scott: The Wizard of the North

Michael Scott (1175–c. 1232) was a multilingual, wandering Scotsman who studied astrology in Toledo, taught mathematics to Leonardo Fibonacci in Bologna,* and spent some years as court astrologer and scientific advisor to the great Holy Roman Emperor Frederick II, the King of Jerusalem, Germany, Italy, Sicily, and Burgundy. Frederick was a great zoologist, so it's likely that Scott's translation of Aristotle's nine-volume *History of Animals* caught his attention. As a member of the famous Toledo School of Translators, he

21. Bailey, *Magic and Superstition in Europe*, 4; Flint, *The Rise of Magic in Early Medieval Europe.*

22. Bailey, *Magic and Superstition in Europe*, 86.

23. Bailey, *Magic and Superstition in Europe*, 78, 101–106; Kieckhefer, *Magic in the Middle Ages*, 151–175.

24. Fanger, *Invoking Angels: Theurgic Ideas and Practices, Thirteenth to Sixteenth Centuries*, 15 and throughout.

25. Fanger, *Invoking Angels*, 8, 65–67, re: Iamblichus, 56; *Iamblichus: De Mysteriis*, 2.9, 105–107.

· · · · · · · ·

was a colleague of Yehuda ben Moshe, the translator of the infamous Arabic grimoire *Picatrix*, a compendious handbook of talismanic magic. Scott referred to a book he studied in Toledo that contained spirits that, when the book was opened, would cry out, "Say what you want and it shall be done forthwith."** Scott was long accredited, perhaps erroneously, with writing a book on demonic magic owned by Abbot Trithemius, the teacher of Cornelius Agrippa. He certainly wrote works on alchemy, astronomy, physiognomy, and chiromancy, many of which survive, but his success during his lifetime was largely based on his great learning, shrewd intelligence, and ability to perform apparent wonders. Our idea of the classic medieval wizard may be based chiefly on him. Scott had already earned a formidable reputation as a magus by the time he made an impressive entrance at Frederick's multicultural court in Sicily, dressed in a pointy hat and flowing robes cinched at the waist. Frederick is said to have done his best to expose the wizard's deception, but when the wily Scott defeated all his best efforts, he asked him to accept a position at court.

Scott gained a pernicious reputation as the most feared sorcerer and alchemist in Europe. Dante even found a place for him in his *Inferno*, specifically in the fourth bolgia of the Eighth Circle of Hell, reserved for sorcerers, astrologers, and false prophets.

Despite his reputation, he was a well-qualified clergyman and was offered an archbishopric in Ireland by Pope Honorius III, which he turned down because his knowledge of Irish Gaelic was limited.

Scott became known to history by many titles, including the Wizard of the North, the White Wizard, and the Lost Genius. He is now acknowledged by historians of science for his contributions to such subjects as medicine, anatomy, reproduction, and the rare phenomenon of supernumerary rainbows, which he appears to have observed in the Sahara in the company of Tuareg tribesmen.[26] He is celebrated by some stage magicians as a brilliant illusionist and hypnotist who used his understanding of physiognomy for "cold reading" his audience.

—Guy Ogilvy

* Fibonacci discovered the magical sequence of numbers named after him that illustrates the fractal nature of the universe. He dedicated his *Liber Abaci*, which included the sequence, to Scott.
** Lynn Thorndike, *Michael Scot* (London: Nelson, 1965).

These centuries were also a time of narrowing choices for the Jewish community.[27] In the 1400s, Jews were persecuted in Austria and expelled from Cologne, Augsburg, and many other

26. See Scott, "Michael Scot and the Four Rainbows."
27. Seltzer, *Jewish People, Jewish Thought*, 450; David B. Ruderman, *Kabbalah, Magic, and Science*, 8–9.

cities and districts of Germany.[28] Jews were expelled from Spain in 1492 and from Portugal in 1497. In 1536, the Inquisition was permanently established in Portugal for the purpose of exposing Jews. The Talmud was burned in Italy in 1553, Hebrew books were censored by the Church in 1554, and Pope Paul VI ordered the Jews of Rome into a ghetto in 1555.[29]

This same period saw the development of the Jewish mystical tradition called Kabbalah,[30] from the first appearances of foundational works such as the *Bahir* and the *Zohar* in the thirteenth century to the sixteenth-century reinterpretations by Isaac Luria and others in the Galilean community of Safed, which developed in reaction to the increasing persecution of the Jews.

Kabbalah drew on earlier mystical traditions, including the *Merkabah* (chariots) and *Hekhalot* (palaces) schools of mysticism, the mysticism of the *Sefer Yetzirah*, based on the letters of the Hebrew alphabet, and Neoplatonism with its hierarchy of cosmic realms.

Fanger cites both Moshe Idel and Gershom Scholem as presenting significant arguments as to how the various aspects of Jewish practice constitute a kind of theurgy, both through its attempts at *unio mystica*, divine vision, and through its pursuit of practical results.[31] Idel argues that the simple practice of the commandments, even in the absence of any ritual activity, were also an effective form of theurgy.[32]

The Renaissance

The medieval period is often called the Dark Ages for good reason. So much knowledge and so many writings had been forgotten or lost with the fall of the Roman Empire and the rise of the Church that little was known or understood about the ancient world except for what it suited the Church to preserve. Of the classical philosophers, only Aristotle was preserved in something approaching completeness, and that was largely because his work had been given life in the context of the Church by Thomas Aquinas.

Out of Plato's many writings, the West still possessed only one dialogue, the *Timaeus*, and some small fragments of other works. What little else was known of Plato came mostly from one book, *The Consolation of Philosophy*, that became popular during the late Middle Ages. This summary of philosophy was written by the Roman senator and philosopher Boethius in 534 as a way to pass the time while awaiting his execution for treason.

28. Seltzer, *Jewish People, Jewish Thought*, 321.

29. Seltzer, *Jewish People, Jewish Thought*, 451.

30. Eds. note: See Book Two: Qabalah.

31. Fanger, *Invoking Angels*, 23–26, re: Idel, *Kabbalah: New Perspectives*, 35–58, especially 40–41, and Scholem, *Major Trends in Jewish Mysticism*, 4.

32. Fanger, *Invoking Angels*, 23; Idel, *Kabbalah: New Perspectives*, 158.

· · · · · · · ·

The rest of Plato's works, along with the works of Plotinus, Iamblichus, and many others, had been preserved by the Arabs, who had translated them into Arabic, and by the Byzantine Greeks. But the Roman Catholic Church was at war with the Islamic World throughout much of the Middle Ages, and the Greek and Latin sides of the Church had been divided ever since the Great Schism of 1054.

If these works from the ancient world had remained lost to the West, the Western magical tradition might have ended during the Middle Ages. The rebirth of that tradition came about because these texts were rediscovered by the West. And that rediscovery can be traced back to a meeting in 1438 between Cosimo de' Medici and a Greek scholar. At least that's the popular version of the story. Historians disagree about whether there was ever an actual meeting between the two. But the Greek scholar's influence on Cosimo is certain.

This scholar, Georgius Gemistus, was the first person to call himself a *Hellene*—the Greek equivalent of a Pagan—in Christian times. Through his writing and teachings, Gemistus reintroduced Plato to the Western world. Because of his profound knowledge of Plato, he was known as Plethon, meaning "like-Plato."[33]

Many people know about the Medicis, and in particular Cosimo, who was a wealthy merchant and banker, a patron of art and scholarship, and the effective ruler of Florence, Italy. Far fewer have heard of Plethon, who came from the Peloponnese in Greece. In 1438 Plethon traveled to Italy, along with a delegation from the Eastern Orthodox Church, to attend the Council of Ferrara. The council was one of several attempts that were made to reconcile the Eastern Orthodox and Roman Catholic Churches. (The council, like all the other attempts, was ultimately unsuccessful; the Orthodox and Catholic Churches were unable to resolve their differences and remained divided.)

It was in Ferrara that Plethon may have met Cosimo.[34] Neither man was a delegate to the council, but both were among the many great men who attended and watched from the sidelines. Cosimo was also paying for the event.

We can't be sure that Cosimo and Plethon met in Ferrara, nor in Florence, where the council was moved after a year to avoid an outbreak of plague. But popular history holds that it was Plethon who inspired Cosimo to seek out and acquire critical Platonic and Neoplatonic texts, the *Corpus Hermeticum*, the Orphic Hymns, and other ancient Greek writings. It is also possible that Cosimo acquired from Plethon a short version of the Chaldean Oracles. Cosimo later funded the education of Marsilio Ficino, who translated these texts into Latin for the first time.

33. Woodhouse, *George Gemistos Plethon*, 186–188.
34. Woodhouse, *George Gemistos Plethon*: Ferrara, 136–153, Florence, 171–188, and humanism, 154–170.

Marsilio Ficino

Cosimo de' Medici began sending his agents to find and purchase works by Plato and other Greek philosophers. But as Greek was no longer widely spoken in the West, the texts would have to be translated into Latin.

Cosimo found the translator he needed in Marsilio Ficino, the young son of his personal physician. He arranged to have Ficino taught Greek by an exiled Orthodox priest. Between 1462 and 1484, Ficino translated all of Plato's dialogues into Latin. He also translated works of many of the Neoplatonists, including Plotinus, Porphyry, Iamblichus, and Proclus.

Cosimo lay on his deathbed when he acquired a manuscript of what we now call the *Hermetic Corpus*. Ficino stopped working on Plato in order to translate it as quickly as possible so he could read it to Cosimo in his final hours.

Ostensibly a commentary on Plotinus, Ficino's own *Three Books on Life* contains in its third book a functional presentation of theurgy that many later writers exploited and built upon.[35] Ficino's works, though, are heavy with theory; the practicalities of theurgy received only light treatment from him.

Even so, we have stories of him singing the Orphic Hymns accompanied by the lyre. These invocations, along with his instructions in the third book, made for a kind of celestial therapy that dared not call itself magic, or at least not yet. That would come with his students and, more powerfully, a generation later with Agrippa.

Renaissance Kabbalah

Kabbalah entered the world of the Renaissance though Ficino's student, the young Count Giovanni Pico della Mirandola. Kabbalah was thought by some to be the secret teachings of Moses, but for Pico it supported the divinity of Christ and other Christian theological positions, which meant that it could be used to provide a Christian justification for magic. The tale of Pico and the Kabbalah lies outside our scope, but it has been well covered by others.[36]

Through their own works, two of Pico's students added considerably to an understanding of these teachings. Johannes Reuchlin published *De Verbo Mirifico* in 1494 and *De arte Cabalistica* in 1517, and Franciscus Gregorius published *De harmonia mundi totius cantica tria* in 1525.

To understand Kabbalah itself, we can turn to the father of its modern study, Gershom Scholem, and his student Moshe Idel. According to Scholem, *Kabbalah* is the traditional and most commonly used term for the esoteric teachings of Judaism and for Jewish mysticism, "especially

---

35. Ficino, *Three Books on Life*, trans. Carol V. Kaske and John R. Clark.

36. Walker, *Spiritual and Demonic Magic from Ficino to Campanella*, 54–59; Yates, *Giordano Bruno and the Hermetic Tradition*, 84–116; Wirszubski, *Pico della Mirandola's Encounter with Jewish Mysticism*.

· · · · · · · ·

the forms which it assumed in the Middle Ages from the 12th century onward."[37] Scholem, Idel, and a host of scholars since then have explored the richness of this kind of Jewish mysticism, finding in it a beautiful and lively depth.

Neoplatonism is an essential dimension of Kabbalah. As Scholem has written, "Inasmuch as early Kabbalah needed a theoretical foundation it was largely influenced by neoplatonism."[38] Kabbalah can even be seen as a kind of theurgy. In *Kabbalah: New Perspectives*, Moshe Idel dedicates a chapter to exposition of *devekut*, the practice of cleaving to Yahweh (YHVH), the patron deity of the Jewish people.[39] Idel noted that source texts on the subject employ Aristotelian, Neoplatonic, and hermetic terminology as "a garb used by the mystics in order to articulate their experiences."[40] Idel also wrote that the Neoplatonic and hermetic influences have "strong magical interests, widely known as theurgy." This fusion of purpose and nomenclature between Neoplatonic theurgy and Kabbalah also extends to the idea of the transformation of the soul through the use of *devekut* through ordinary worship.

Agrippa and the Modern Era

At last we come to the modern era, which can be said to have begun in 1517 on October 31, the precise moment of its beginning marked by the blow of a hammer as Martin Luther nailed his *Ninety-Five Theses* on the door of the Cathedral of Wittenberg.

The dominant figure in Western magic in the early modern era was Heinrich Cornelius Agrippa von Nettesheim (1486–1535). Agrippa is considered a humanist and was contemporary with Erasmus (1466–1536), with whom he corresponded, and Martin Luther (1483–1546), whom he first supported and later denounced.[41] In intellectual history, he is known most positively for his *De vanitate*, considered an important work on early modern skepticism.

It was his writing on the occult, however, and especially his *Three Books of Occult Philosophy* (*TBOP*) that made him most famous. Perhaps *infamous* is the better word—his fame was so great that he is considered to have been a major influence on the popular legend of Faust selling his soul to the Devil, especially in the plays of Christopher Marlowe and Johann Wolfgang von Goethe.[42]

---

37. Scholem, *Kabbalah*, 3.

38. Scholem, *Kabbalah*, 96.

39. Idel, *Kabbalah: New Perspectives*, 35–58.

40. Idel, *Kabbalah: New Perspectives*, 39.

41. Nauert, *Agrippa and the Crisis of Renaissance Thought*, 109–110, 168. This is the main biography of Agrippa.

42. Lehrich, *The Language of Demons and Angels*, 1.

· · · · · · · ·

Agrippa considered himself to be a son of Cologne, Germany; however, little is known of him before 1507, the date of his earliest surviving letter.[43] He matriculated at the University of Cologne in 1499 and received a licentiate in art in 1502. He later claimed doctorates in canon and civil law and at times claimed to be a doctor of medicine.[44]

Besides his intellectual career, Agrippa was also a man of action, seeing military service in Spain and Italy. This is perhaps what led to his claim of knighthood on the title page of *TBOP*.[45] There is also evidence of his service to the Holy Roman Emperor and the Pope. This service brought Agrippa to stay in Italy between 1511 and 1518, where he was exposed to the Italian humanists and the work of Ficino, Pico, and Reuchlin. He married an Italian native of Pavia and attempted to settle, lecturing at the University of Pavia on the hermetic *Pimander*.[46]

Agrippa's knowledge of the occult was not solely theoretical. He claimed to be able to manufacture gold alchemically, but said that the process was too expensive to be profitable.[47] Perhaps more important, there is significant evidence in his letters that he formed occult groups, possibly oathbound to secrecy, wherever he traveled.[48] Of their influence we can only speculate.

Three Books of Occult Philosophy

Agrippa finished writing his first version of *Three Books of Occult Philosophy* in 1510. Twenty years passed before the publication of its first volume, which Agrippa spent serving first the city of Metz[49] and then the nobility of Europe.[50] At the same time, he was studying Kabbalah and hermeticism, and he added discussions of both subjects to *TBOP* before its first volume was published in 1530. This volume caused such an uproar among the censors that the publication of the remaining two volumes was delayed for three years.[51]

In *TBOP,* Agrippa drew on the works of Pico, Reuchlin, and Gregorius as well as on other sources of Kabbalistic knowledge.[52] The brothers Paolo and Agostino Ricci were major contrib-

---

43. Nauert, *Agrippa and the Crisis of Renaissance Thought*, 4.

44. Nauert, *Agrippa and the Crisis of Renaissance Thought*, 10.

45. Nauert, *Agrippa and the Crisis of Renaissance Thought*, 15–17, 37–39.

46. Nauert, *Agrippa and the Crisis of Renaissance Thought*, 37–40.

47. Nauert, *Agrippa and the Crisis of Renaissance Thought*, 24.

48. Nauert, *Agrippa and the Crisis of Renaissance Thought*, 17–24. Compagni, *Cornelius Agrippa: De occulta philosophia, libri tres*, 2.

49. Lehrich, *The Language of Demons and Angels*, 5.

50. Compagni, *Cornelius Agrippa: De occulta philosophia, libri tres*: Holy Roman Emperor Maximilian, William IX Palaeologus, 4, Margaret of Austria, 7.

51. Nauert, *Agrippa and the Crisis of Renaissance Thought*, 112–113.

52. Compagni, *Cornelius Agrippa: De occulta philosophia, libri tres*. Sources: Gregorius, 621, Pico, 624, Reuchlin, 626. For a list of the individual works by Gregorius, Pico, and Reuchlin cited here, see the index of Compagni's book.

• • • • • • • •

utors and possibly known by Agrippa personally.[53] Paolo Ricci is known for his translation of the *Sha'arei Orah* of Joseph ben Abraham Gikatilla, while Agostino Ricci was the author of a number of works and a likely source of Agrippa's knowledge of the important Kabbalistic text the *Zohar*.[54] Another source of information was Pietro Galatino's *Opus de arcanis Catholicae veritatis*, published in 1518. Agrippa possessed a copy of this Latin text on the Kabbalah by 1532 and cited it in *TBOP*.[55]

With its influences from Neoplatonism and theurgy, Kabbalah fit well into *TBOP*. Agrippa could not have known that Kabbalah had, as a matter of historical fact, been informed by Neoplatonism. But he certainly saw the parallels, and he realized that Kabbalah could serve as a vehicle for presenting Iamblichan theurgy in a suitably "de-paganized" form to be acceptable for use by Christians.

The final two volumes of *TBOP* were published in 1533, and Agrippa died just two years later. Over time, many editions of *TBOP* were produced, many of them unauthorized. At one point a spurious fourth book was published; this incorporated some of Agrippa's own work on geomancy but also contained rites intended to summon specific demons, which were outside the scope of Agrippa's original project.[56] *TBOP* was translated into English in 1651, and this edition was plagiarized to produce Francis Barrett's *The Magus* and the DeLaurence edition of Agrippa's *Philosophy of Natural Magic*.[57] In his study of the history of grimoires, Owen Davies notes the presence of Agrippa's *Three Books* (and often the spurious fourth) in all the time periods and most of the locales he explores.[58]

The influence of *TBOP* is hard to overstate.[59] *TBOP* informed the cunning-folk and underpinned many of the grimoires that came after it. Giordano Bruno (1548–1600), John Dee (1527–1608), the Rosicrucian documents (1614–1617), and the Freemasons (1717) were all influenced by it. By the 1850s Freemasonry metastasized into "Fringe Masonry," with orders and lodges that reasserted social hierarchy and explored more esoteric spirituality.[60] This kind of Freemasonry

53. Assumed to be brothers by the French Humanist Symphorien Champier and reported by Nauert, *Agrippa and the Crisis of Renaissance Thought*, 41, 131–132.

54. Nauert, *Agrippa and the Crisis of Renaissance Thought*, 131–132; Compagni, *Cornelius Agrippa: De occulta philosophia, libri tres*, 626.

55. Nauert, *Agrippa and the Crisis of Renaissance Thought*, 133; Compagni, *Cornelius Agrippa: De occulta philosophia, libri tres*, 621.

56. Nauert, *Agrippa and the Crisis of Renaissance Thought*, 228, 325n11.

57. Barrett, *The Magus, Celestial Intelligencer*; Agrippa, *The Philosophy of Natural Magic* and *Three Books of Occult Philosophy*, xl.

58. Davies, *Grimoires: A History of Magic Books*, 47, 52, 54, 141, and throughout.

59. Nauert, *Agrippa and the Crisis of Renaissance Thought*, 229, 322–334, especially 325–326.

60. Goodrick-Clarke, *The Western Esoteric Traditions*, 131–154; Howe, "Fringe Masonry in England, 1870–1885," *Ars Quatuor Coronatorum*, 242–280.

• • • • • • • •

became the container for the French occult revival, the medium of transmission of hermetic and other ancient thought systems, and the population with the appropriate skills to be able to produce several magic or theurgic societies such as the Élus Coëns, or *Martinists* (c. 1766), and the Hermetic Order of the Golden Dawn (1888).[61] The Golden Dawn extensively used the concepts and language of *TBOP* to structure its teachings, rituals, and other practices.[62]

This can be seen as the successful result of Agrippa's purpose for *TBOP*: the reformation and redemption of occult philosophy—magic—for contemporary use. Agrippa accomplished this task by reorganizing the grimoire magic of his day on the basis of Iamblichan theurgy. Theurgy gave Agrippa a coherent theory for explaining the nature of magical practice and its use for spiritual advancement. Then, by translating theurgical concepts—particularly the Neoplatonic cosmology and divine hierarchy and the theurgical notions of the soul, its parts, and its vehicle—into their Kabbalistic equivalents, Agrippa made this "pagan" spirituality sufficiently Christian to be acceptable for use in his time.

So now we have come to the end of our journey through the past. We have seen how the ancient world bequeathed to us—as filtered through the perceptions of the Greeks and Romans—their religious insights and a portion of their magical practices; how the Neoplatonists, especially Iamblichus, developed this inheritance into theurgy, which became the foundation for the Western magical tradition; how Christianity tried to end this tradition even while carrying pieces of it forward; how the recovery of ancient texts by way of Byzantium and the Islamic world led to its renewal; and how Agrippa gave us a masterful and influential *summa* of our great inheritance.

Throughout the rest of this book, dear reader, you will find the best and brightest of us explaining the depths of that inheritance and providing you with the tools and means to practice its many branches.

May you have success!

Bibliography

Agrippa von Nettesheim, Heinrich Cornelius. *The Philosophy of Natural Magic*. Chicago, IL: DeLaurence, Scott & Co., 1913.

———. *Three Books of Occult Philosophy*. Edited and annotated by Donald Tyson. Translated by James Freake. St. Paul, MN: Llewellyn Publications, 1993.

———. *Three Books of Occult Philosophy, Book One*. Translated by Eric Purdue. Introduction by Christopher Warnock. Renaissance Astrology, 2012.

---

61. Goodrick-Clarke, *The Western Esoteric Traditions*, 191, 138–145, 196–203.

62. Goodrick-Clarke, *The Western Esoteric Traditions*, 138–145, 196–203.

· · · · · · · ·

Anonymous. *Kyranides: On the Occult Virtues of Plants, Animals & Stones.* Renaissance Astrology Facsimile Editions, 2005.

Armstrong, A. H., ed. *Classical Mediterranean Spirituality: Egyptian, Greek, Roman.* London: Routledge & Kegan Paul, 1986.

Bailey, Michael D. *Magic and Superstition in Europe.* Lamham, MD: Rowman & Littlefield, 2007.

Barrett, Francis. *The Magus, Celestial Intelligencer: A Complete System of Occult Philosophy.* London Forgotten Books, 2008. First edition published in London in 1801.

Berg, R. M. van den. *Proclus' Hymns: Essays, Translations, Commentary.* Leiden, Netherlands: Brill, 2001.

Betz, Hans Dieter, ed. *The Greek Magical Papyri in Translation.* Chicago, IL: University of Chicago Press, 1986.

Burkert, Walter. *Homo Necans: The Anthropology of Ancient Greek Sacrificial Ritual and Myth.* Translated by Peter. Bing. Berkeley, CA: University of California Press, 1983. Originally published in German in 1972.

Compagni, V. Perrone, ed. *Cornelius Agrippa: De occulta philosophia, libri tres.* Leiden, Netherlands: E. J. Brill, 1992.

Connelly, Joan Breton. *Portrait of a Priestess: Women and Ritual in Ancient Greece.* Princeton, NJ: Princeton University Press, 2007.

Copenhaver, Brian P. "Hermes Trismegistus, Proclus and the Question of a Philosophy of Magic in the Renaissance." In *Hermeticism and the Renaissance*, edited by Ingrid Merkel and Allen G. Debus, 79–109. Washington, DC: Folger Shakespeare Library, 1988.

———. *Hermetica.* Cambridge, UK: Cambridge University Press, 1992.

Davies, Owen. *Grimoires: A History of Magic Books.* Oxford: Oxford University Press, 2009.

Dickie, Matthew. *Magic and Magicians in the Greco-Roman World.* London: Routledge, 2001.

Faivre, Antoine. *Access to Western Esotericism.* SUNY series in Western Esoteric Traditions. Albany, NY: State University of New York Press, 1994.

Fanger, Claire, ed. *Conjuring Spirits: Texts and Traditions of Medieval Ritual Magic.* University Park, PA: Pennsylvania State University Press, 1998.

———. *Invoking Angels: Theurgic Ideas and Practices, Thirteenth to Sixteenth Centuries.* University Park, PA: Pennsylvania State University Press, 2012.

Faraone, Christopher A., and Dirk Obbink, eds. *Magika Hiera: Ancient Greek Magic and Religion.* New York: Oxford University Press, 1991.

Ficino, Marsilio. *Three Books on Life.* Translated by Carol V. Kaske and John R. Clark. Tempe, AZ: Arizona Center for Medieval and Renaissance Studies, 2002.

· · · · · · ·

Finamore, John F. *Iamblichus and the Theory of the Vehicle of the Soul*. Chico, CA: Scholars Press, 1985.

Flint, Valerie I. J. *The Rise of Magic in Early Medieval Europe*. Oxford: Oxford University Press, 1991.

Goodrick-Clarke, Nicholas. *The Western Esoteric Traditions: A Historical Introduction*. New York: Oxford University Press, 2008.

Graf, Fritz. *Magic in the Ancient World*. Translated by Franklin Philip. Cambridge, MA: Harvard University Press, 1997.

Hornung, Erik. *Conceptions of God in Ancient Egypt: The One and the Many*. Translated by John Baines. Ithaca, NY: Cornell University Press, 1982.

Howe, Ellic. "Fringe Masonry in England, 1870–1885," *Ars Quatuor Coronatorum* 85 (1972).

Hutton, Ronald. *The Triumph of the Moon: A History of Modern Pagan Witchcraft*. New York: Oxford University Press, 2001.

———. *Witches, Druids, and King Arthur*. London: Hambledon and London, 2003.

Iamblichus. *Iamblichus: De Mysteriis*. Translated by Emma C. Clarke, John M. Dillon, and Jackson P. Hershbell. Boston, MA: Brill, 2004.

Idel, Moshe. *Kabbalah: New Perspectives*. New Haven, CT: Yale University Press, 1988.

Kieckhefer, Richard. *Magic in the Middle Ages*. Cambridge, UK: Cambridge University Press, 1989.

Kingsley, Peter. *Ancient Philosophy Mystery, and Magic: Empedocles and Pythagorean Tradition*. Oxford: Clarendon Press, 1995.

Lane Fox, Robin. *Pagans and Christians*. New York: Knopf, 1986.

Lehrich, Christopher I. *The Language of Demons and Angels: Cornelius Agrippa's Occult Philosophy*. Boston, MA: Brill, 2003.

Mylonas, George E. *Eleusis and the Eleusinian Mysteries*. Princeton, NJ: Princeton University Press, 1961.

Nauert, Charles G., Jr. *Agrippa and the Crisis of Renaissance Thought*. Urbana, IL: University of Illinois Press, 1965.

O'Meara, Dominic J. *Pythagoras Revived: Mathematics and Philosophy in Late Antiquity*. Oxford: Clarendon Press, 1990.

Petropoulou, Maria-Zoe. *Animal Sacrifice in Ancient Greek Religion, Judaism, and Christianity, 100 BC–AD 200*. New York: Oxford University Press, 2008.

Plotinus. *Enneads*. Translated by A. H. Armstrong. Cambridge, MA: Harvard University Press, 1966–1988. 7 volumes.

Remes, Pauliina. *Neoplatonism*. Berkeley, CA: University of California Press, 2008.

• • • • • • •

Ruderman, David B. *Kabbalah, Magic, and Science: The Cultural Universe of a Sixteenth-Century Jewish Physician.* Cambridge, MA,: Harvard University Press, 1988.

Sandwell, Isabella. *Religious Identity in Late Antiquity: Greeks, Jews and Christians in Antioch.* Cambridge, UK: Cambridge University Press, 2007.

Scheid, John. *An Introduction to Roman Religion.* Bloomington, IN: Indiana University Press, 2003.

Scholem, Gershom. *Kabbalah.* New York: Dorset Press, 1974.

———. *Major Trends in Jewish Mysticism.* New York: Schocken Books, 1988.

Scott, Tony. "Michael Scot and the Four Rainbows." *Transversal: International Journal for the Historiography of Science* 2 (June 2017): 204–225.

Seltzer, Robert M. *Jewish People, Jewish Thought: The Jewish Experience in History.* New York: Macmillan, 1980.

Shaw, Gregory. *Theurgy and the Soul: The Neoplatonism of Iamblichus.* University Park, PA: Pennsylvania State University Press 1995.

Thorndike, Lynn. *A History of Magic and Experimental Science.* London: Macmillan, 1923.

Walker, D. P. *Spiritual and Demonic Magic from Ficino to Campanella.* University Park, PA: Pennsylvania State University Press, 2000.

Wallis, R. T. *Neoplatonism.* London: Duckworth, 1972. 2nd edition. 1995.

Wirszubski, Chaim. *Pico della Mirandola's Encounter with Jewish Mysticism.* Cambridge, MA: Harvard University Press, 1989.

Woodhouse, C. M. *George Gemistos Plethon: The Last of the Hellenes.* Oxford: Clarendon Press, 1986.

Yates, Frances A. *Giordano Bruno and the Hermetic Tradition.* New York: Vintage Books, 1969.

About the Author

Sam Webster, PhD, MDiv, Mage, hails from the Bay Area and has taught magick publicly since 1984. He graduated from Starr King School for the Ministry at the Graduate Theological Union in Berkeley in 1993 and earned his doctorate at the University of Bristol, UK, studying Pagan history under Prof. Ronald Hutton. He is an Adept of the Golden Dawn, a cofounder of the Chthonic-Ouranian Templar order, and an initiate of Wiccan, Druidic, Buddhist, Hindu, and Masonic traditions. His work has been published in journals such as *Green Egg* and *Gnosis*, and 2010 saw the release of his first book, *Tantric Thelema*, establishing the publishing house Concrescent Press (Concrescent.net). He founded the Open Source Order of the Golden Dawn (OSOGD.org) in 2011 and the Pantheon Foundation (PantheonFoundation.org) in 2013. Sam serves the Pagan community as a priest of Hermes.

• • • • • • •

Book Two

Qabalah
by Anita Kraft & Randall Bowyer

Qabalah is ubiquitous in ceremonial magic. The history of Qabalah is long, and its literature is vast. Our brief survey can offer only a few glimpses of this astounding tradition. We hope these glimpses will inspire students to pursue deeper knowledge.

The Hebrew word *Qabalah* (קבלה) means "tradition."[1] In esoteric contexts, it means the tradition of Jewish mysticism.[2] *Tradition* implies continuity of ideas and practices, yet the greatest Qabalists have always been innovators. Each school of Qabalists has sought new mystical interpretations, while carefully preserving historical continuity. Scholars have described Jewish mysticism as "simultaneously conservative and radical."[3] Qabalah is a lively tradition of creativity, forever changing and growing.

This tradition of innovation led to surprising developments in the Renaissance. Christian magicians created a *Hermetic* Qabalah, reinterpreting fundamental qabalistic theories and practices in

---

1. Scholars of Judaism usually transliterate the word as *Kabbalah,* while scholars of the Renaissance often favor *Cabala*. Ceremonial magicians tend to prefer *Qabalah*. These are all valid ways of representing the word in our alphabet, although *Qabalah* better approximates the Hebrew orthography. We have generally transliterated Hebrew words as the Golden Dawn did: we assume most students of ceremonial magic will find *sephiroth* more recognizable than *sfirot*. Since our criterion was familiarity, our transliterations are not uniform and do not always reflect Hebrew spelling.

2. Jewish mystics began calling their work *Qabalah* in the twelfth century. Therefore, academic usage defines *Qabalah* exclusively as Jewish mysticism from the Middle Ages onward. Yet medieval mysticism developed from ancient tradition. So, in popular usage, *Qabalah* embraces the whole evolution of Jewish mysticism.

3. Fine, *Safed Spirituality,* 17. Gershom Scholem calls Qabalah "deeply conservative and intensely revolutionary," *Major Trends in Jewish Mysticism,* 120. Scholem discusses this central paradox of mysticism in *On the Kabbalah and Its Symbolism,* 7–11.

non-Jewish terms. Hermetic Qabalah evolved into the Golden Dawn magical system, the basis of ceremonial magic today.

Some Historical Notes
Prophecy and Apocalypticism (Sixth through Second Centuries BCE)

The Babylonian exile and the destruction of the Temple (sixth century BCE) threatened the Jewish faith.[4] The prophet Ezekiel offered hope of a return from exile. Ezekiel's vision of God enthroned upon a chariot has inspired mystical practices ever since (see inset). As Ezekiel foretold, the Jews returned home and rebuilt the Temple.

Ezekiel's Vision

The prophet Ezekiel's cautiously precise account of his experience has had immeasurable influence through the centuries. The chariot-throne inspired Jewish mysticism; the four living creatures inspired Christian iconography. Renaissance humanists mingled Ezekiel's powerful images with Greek philosophical themes in the tarot. The following quotations come from Ezekiel 1:4–6, 10, 14, 26, and 28.

And I looked, and, behold, a whirlwind came out of the north, a great cloud, and a fire infolding itself, and a brightness ...

Also out of the midst thereof came the likeness of four living creatures. And this was their appearance; they had the likeness of a man.

And every one had four faces, and every one had four wings. ...

As for the likeness of their faces, they four had the face of a man, and the face of a lion, on the right side: and they four had the face of an ox on the left side; they four also had the face of an eagle. ...

And the living creatures ran and returned as the appearance of a flash of lightning. ...

And above the firmament that was over their heads was the likeness of a throne, as the appearance of a sapphire stone: and upon the likeness of the throne was the likeness as the appearance of a man ...

As the appearance of the bow that is in the cloud in the day of rain, so was the appearance of the brightness round about. This was the appearance of the likeness of the glory of the Lord.

---

4. These brief sketches of qabalistic history summarize several historical surveys (which sometimes disagree on details). We make no claim to original scholarship. Also, we gratefully acknowledge a substantial debt to Hava Tirosh-Rothschild, whose lectures on the history of Jewish mysticism (Indiana University, autumn 1993) inspired us to learn a little more.

• • • • • • • •

During the Second Temple Period (516 BCE–70 CE), prophecy took the form of apocalyptic visions. Prophets described ascending to the heavens, where angels explained cosmological mysteries and revealed future events. Apocalyptic texts offered assurance that God was in control of an orderly cosmos. The book of Daniel (second century BCE) included visions of Ezekiel's chariot and Isaiah's messianic king. Expectations of a Messiah increasingly shaped Jewish beliefs.

Apocalyptic literature enriched Judaism with several other ideas. It featured a well-developed angelology. It taught that God created everything in heaven and on earth with sacred words. It hinted that exceptional people could learn those words and wield their power.

Rabbinic Judaism, Chariot and Palace Mysticism (First through Sixth Centuries CE)

The destruction of the Second Temple in 70 CE ended biblical Judaism. Sacrificial rites ceased, and the power of the priesthood faded away. A group of erudite sages stepped forward to transform the religion. Scripture replaced the Temple as the focus of Jewish spirituality. Prayer and pious behavior replaced sacrifice. These innovations enabled Judaism to survive the Greater Exile that began in 135 CE.

The new Jewish leaders inherited many duties expected of holy men in ancient times. Serving as judges, scholars, soothsayers, exorcists, and rainmakers, they preferred the simple title *rabbi,* "teacher."

Rabbinic Judaism recognized two sources of authority. The Bible declared the written law, available to all. But an oral law, reserved for the elite, expounded the Bible. This oral tradition was already well established when the rabbis came to power. Within it was an even more recondite tradition of mystical practice. Eventually the rabbis recorded portions of the oral law in the Mishnah and Talmud. Simultaneously they recorded portions of their mystical tradition in the Chariot and Palace texts.

The rabbinic sages aspired to experience what biblical figures had experienced. They wanted to see the divine chariot *(merkavah)* and prophesy like Ezekiel. They wanted to enter the seven heavenly palaces *(heikhaloth),* receiving revelations like Enoch.[5] They wanted to understand how God created the world with words, as Genesis told.

The Chariot and Palace texts were instruction manuals for attaining such experiences.[6] They gave advice on necessary preparations. They provided lengthy prayers and incantations (couched in abstruse language to veil their purpose). The prayers emphasized divine names, especially

---

5. The apocalyptic books of Enoch, no longer canonical, include revelations of astronomical and meteorological mysteries.

6. Several of these books survive. Some are mystical, others clearly magical. For example, the fourth-century *Sepher ha-Razim (The Book of the Mysteries)* resembles a grimoire: it lists the angels of the seven palaces and what powers each can confer.

· · · · · · · ·

God's holiest name, the *Tetragrammaton*.[7] Sacred names and amuletic seals were passwords for the angelic sentinels at the palace gates. Gradually ascending through all seven celestial spheres, worthy aspirants would finally behold the chariot.

Before daring these astral adventures, aspirants received formal initiation and instruction. They fasted and strictly maintained ritual purity. They armed themselves with virtue, plus an arsenal of sacred names and amulets. These spiritual practices were dangerous. Even the visions of the lower heavens could cause insanity or death.[8] In time, speculation on the mysteries of creation became the prevailing form of Jewish mysticism. The "work of Genesis" *(maaseh Bereshith)* was safer than the "work of the chariot" *(maaseh merkavah)*.

The fourth-century *Sepher Yetzirah (Book of Formation)* is the most important text from this period.[9] It declares that God created the world by means of "thirty-two mysterious paths of wisdom."[10] These paths are the twenty-two Hebrew letters plus ten *sephiroth*.[11] The word *sephiroth* is untranslatable: its meanings include "numerals," "spheres," "eons," and possibly "sapphires." The connections among these meanings are not obvious today. Ancient astronomy envisioned the heavens as a system of ten concentric crystalline *spheres*. The Bible compared the heavens to *sapphire* (as in Ezekiel 1:26). Qabalah describes the ten sephiroth as emanating from God, like the *eons* in Gnostic cosmology. Ten *numerals* represent all numbers, as the alphabet represents all words—and as the ten *spheres* represent all of creation. The book's unknown author, fond of playful ambiguity, surely intended multiple meanings. Qabalists today are still clarifying their understanding of the sephiroth. The short, cryptic *Sepher Yetzirah* laid the foundation of all later Jewish mysticism.[12]

The Early Qabalistic Period (Twelfth through Thirteenth Centuries)

After the sixth century CE, no new Chariot or Palace texts appeared. The current of Jewish mysticism flowed quietly underground. In the middle of the twelfth century, it burst forth with fresh vigor.[13]

---

7. God's true name consists of the Hebrew letters *yod heh vau heh*. Tradition forbids speaking it, or even writing it unnecessarily. *Tetragrammaton,* "four-letter name," is one of several substitutes for this sacrosanct and powerful word. The ineffable name is prominent throughout Jewish mysticism.

8. An often-repeated tale from the Babylonian Talmud (*Chagigah* 14b) names four mystical companions. Only one returned unscathed from his experience. See Ariel, *The Mystic Quest*, 20, and Scholem, *Major Trends in Jewish Mysticism*, 52–53.

9. The date of the *Yetzirah* is uncertain. Scholars place it anywhere from the first to the sixth century.

10. Friedman, *The Book of Creation*, 1.

11. The plural ending for feminine nouns in Hebrew is *-oth* (rhyming with English *both*). Hence, one *sephirah* (ספירה) but ten *sephiroth* (ספירות).

12. The numerous translations of the *Sepher Yetzirah* disagree on many points, large and small. We advise studying more than one translation.

13. Or perhaps mysticism died out in the West and Eastern masters reintroduced it. Lacking evidence, historians can only guess about Jewish mysticism in the Dark Ages.

Sepher ha-Bahir

The Book of the Brilliance is a key manuscript in the evolution of Qabalah. In fact, this twelfth-century text first used the word *Qabalah* to mean Jewish mysticism. The *Bahir* ascribes its opening words to the second-century adept Nehunia ben ha-Qanah. References to the Chariot also help set the book in the context of earlier mysticism.[*]

The *Bahir* appeared between 1150 and 1200 in Provence but incorporated older material. Its unknown author likely had some connection to Isaac the Blind. (Scholars disagree about the specifics of that connection.) In brief homilies interpreting biblical verses, the *Bahir* established much of the qabalistic symbolism used today.

The *Bahir* propounded a new conception of God by reimagining the sephiroth. The *Sepher Yetzirah* had introduced the sephiroth as tools that God used in creating the world. In the *Bahir,* the sephiroth became parts of God, dynamic emanations constantly interacting. The book envisioned one God with ten emanations—an eternal equilibrium produced by ceaseless motion.

The *Bahir* arranged the sephiroth in a particular sequence, "one above the other."[**] It gave each sephirah a name. It introduced organic symbolism, including the tree metaphor, to explain the sephiroth. The qabalistic Tree of Life originated here. The *Bahir* conceptualized the divine as a plurality of forces—both male and female.

Renaissance scholars Flavius Mithridates and Guillaume Postel translated the *Bahir.* Aryeh Kaplan published the first English translation in 1979.

The *Yetzirah* and the *Zohar* are more famous, but *Sepher ha-Bahir* made comparably vital contributions to the development of Qabalah.

[*] Kaplan, *The Bahir*, 1, 25, 32.
[**] Kaplan, *The Bahir*, 45. The text usually calls the emanations *attributes (middoth)* rather than *sephiroth.*

An entirely new set of works solidified themes from Chariot literature, adding new interpretations. Earlier mystics had believed their souls literally ascended to the planets. Qabalists believed the ascent happened within themselves. Chariot and Palace texts had symbolized divine energy as fire. Qabalistic texts preferred water: God's energy flows like a fountain through the sephiroth. Qabalists did not just behold divinity, but actively participated in the life of the divine. Different mystical schools emerged simultaneously in the twelfth century, each making unique contributions.

An unknown master from Provence composed *Sepher ha-Bahir (The Book of the Brilliance)* sometime after 1150 (see inset). Slightly later, Isaac the Blind (c. 1160–1235) became the first Qabalist definitively identified by historians. Dedicating his whole life to the study of Qabalah, Isaac led a Provençal qabalistic school. He wrote a commentary on the *Sepher Yetzirah* and developed new mystical doctrines. Isaac said God exists beyond the sephiroth, in a manner beyond human comprehension: intellect can only express it negatively, saying God is *not limited* or God is *not*. The subtle yet daring speculations of Isaac the Blind remain central to Qabalah today.

Different innovations came from a German school of "pious ones," or *Hasidim*.[14] They emphasized love of God and stern asceticism. The Hasidim combined Chariot mysticism with a magical system based on the Hebrew alphabet. Using *gematria* (calculating numerical values of words), they sought God's hidden will in the Bible. The German Hasidim also studied the lore of demons and ghosts.

Eleazar of Worms (c. 1176–1238) was a gifted, prolific writer from a leading Hasidic family. German Hasidism culminated in his books. His interests included ethics, Chariot mysticism, the *Sepher Yetzirah,* and numerical symbolism. Eleazar's ideas—especially his mystical technique of combining letters—inspired Abraham Abulafia a generation later (see inset).

Abraham Abulafia

Abraham Abulafia (1240–c. 1292) was absolutely not a typical Spanish Qabalist. He was not a rabbi, and he preferred philosophy to Talmudic studies. He rejected the sephiroth as idolatrous. Modern scholarship, however, considers Abulafia a pivotal figure in the history of Qabalah.

A wandering sage, Abulafia traveled throughout the Mediterranean region. He conferred with mystics of other faiths. Abulafia's unique system of mystical practices shows some curious similarities to Sufism and even Yoga.

Abulafia scorned speculative mysticism. His only interest was experiencing union with God, which would produce ecstasy and prophecy. (Hence scholars label his teachings the Prophetic school or the Ecstatic school.) Abulafia believed the names of God were secret keys to attainment. His mystical system incorporated breathing, singing, positioning the hands and head, and pronouncing divine names.

Insisting that meditation on earthly things cannot reach the divine plane, Abulafia meditated on the alphabet. Letters and words preceded creation, existing before God said "Let there be light." Words suggest the earthly things they signify, but letters are ideal for meditative purposes. Abulafia meditated on letters, individually and in combination *(tzeiruph)* with other letters. He also pondered their numerical values. Abulafia's work with the letters greatly influenced practical Qabalah.

Believing all languages derive from Hebrew, Abulafia considered any alphabet suitable for meditation. He applied his methods to the Greek and Latin alphabets, contemplating words in several languages. He taught his idiosyncratic mysticism to Jews and Christians alike.

---

14. The plural ending for masculine Hebrew nouns is *-im* (rhyming with English *team*). So, one *Hasid* (חסיד) but many *Hasidim* (חסידים).

Abulafia's mysticism was solitary, seeking an internal and entirely personal experience of God. He recommended isolation, considering separation and withdrawal necessary to reach religious perfection. Abulafia stated that human teachers are useful only until a spiritual teacher appears. Abulafia's teachings could have influenced the magical system of Abramelin. (See Book Six: The Magick of Abra-Melin.)

At age forty, Abulafia attained union with God. He emphasized the divine ecstasy of this union, describing it with erotic imagery. Abulafia's understanding of divine union as orgasmic bliss later inspired Hasidic theories of prayer.

After his experience of union, Abulafia began writing prophetic books. Like many Qabalists, he came to believe he was the Messiah. Abulafia had the wisdom to see his mission of redemption as primarily internal and personal. Nonetheless, he did attempt to convert the Pope.

Some of Abulafia's voluminous writings have survived. His ideas shaped Jewish qabalistic practice. Abulafia's universalism appealed to Renaissance humanists, deeply influencing Hermetic Qabalah. Scholar Moshe Idel has written extensively on Abulafia.

Abulafia's Prophetic school was one of several mystical schools in medieval Spain. Some mixed Neoplatonism with Qabalah, producing systematic metaphysical doctrines. Others explored Gnosticism, speculating on the nature of evil.

Joseph Gikatilla (1248–c. 1305), one of Abulafia's students, condensed qabalistic thought into well-organized treatises. His *Gates of Light* explained the sephiroth and theoretical Qabalah. His *Nut Garden* explained the letters and practical Qabalah. In later centuries his ideas influenced Hermetic Qabalah.

Isaac Kohen of Castile (late thirteenth century) mythologized evil, introducing "full-blown Gnostic dualism."[15] His *Treatise on the Left Emanation* postulated a demonic parallel universe called the Other Side. (Later Qabalists called it the *Sitra Ahra* and the *Qlippoth*.) Samael, Asmodeus, and Lilith rule there. As human virtue empowers the sephiroth, sin empowers the Other Side. Kohen believed good and evil will someday meet in battle. The Messiah will vanquish the demons and deliver the Jewish people. Kohen's ideas made a deep impression on Moses de León.

The Zoharic Period (Thirteenth Century to the Present)

Sepher ha-Zohar (The Book of Splendor) marked an epoch in the history of Qabalah. It appeared, piece by piece, during the last quarter of the thirteenth century. Moses de León (c. 1240–1305)

---

15. Dan and Kiener, *The Early Kabbalah*, 37.

wrote this massive qabalistic collection.[16] He combined themes from Palace mysticism, German Hasidism, and the Provençal and Spanish qabalistic schools. The result was a masterpiece of theoretical Qabalah unlike any previous qabalistic book.

The *Zohar* is not a textbook but a collection of tales, with characters and plot. The narrative follows several rabbis, sharing biblical insights as they experience progressively more miraculous events. The *Zohar* even offers a love story, the eternal romance of Tiphareth and Malkuth.[17] The demon Samael threatens their sexual union, so Qabalists must assist the sacred marriage theurgically. "Through an action below, an action above is aroused."[18] The highly symbolic language of the *Zohar* established a new mystical vocabulary.

For two centuries, *Sepher ha-Zohar* made little impact outside the Iberian Peninsula. But in 1492, Jewish refugees carried their manuscripts to new countries. As printed versions appeared, the *Zohar* rapidly became "the Bible of Kabbalah."[19]

The theme of exile recurs throughout Jewish history. In 1492 religious nationalism prompted the expulsion of all Jews from Spain. Tens of thousands fled to the more tolerant Ottoman Empire. Many Spanish Qabalists settled in the Galilean town of Safed. Their various traditions merged in a remarkably creative new school. Soon Qabalists from all over the Jewish world came to study at Safed.

Moses Cordovero (1522–1570) was the principal architect of the Safed school's qabalistic synthesis. His *Garden of Pomegranates* "systematized and integrated all the speculative elements of cabalism to his time."[20] Abulafia's practices also inspired him.

Isaac Luria (1534–1572) succeeded Cordovero as leader of the Safed school. Many consider him the greatest of all Qabalists. Luria's vivid imagination and intense mystical visions expanded the symbolism and theology of Qabalah. He built an extensive theology around the concept of exile. Luria believed sparks of divine fire are trapped—or exiled—in the demonic realm. Because human virtue can liberate the sparks, striving for spiritual perfection has cosmic significance. Qabalah has the power to hasten the Messiah's coming and end the Jews' exile.

Luria's thought centered on recurring cycles of birth and death, of cosmic expansion and contraction. He speculated on the world's creation and destruction. He believed even God dies and gives himself rebirth (as recounted in Genesis). Luria taught that human souls enter new bodies

---

16. It is more accurate to say Moses de León wrote *most* of the *Zohar*. Some sections (like *The Faithful Shepherd*) seem to be the work of disciples imitating the master's style.

17. These are the sixth and tenth sephiroth on the Tree of Life. In the *Zohar* they are individual personalities, the Blessed Holy One and the Shekhinah. The *Zohar* describes their love in vivid, even erotic, language.

18. *Zohar* 3:31b, quoted in Matt, *Zohar*, 24.

19. Matt, *Zohar*, 11. Christians first published the *Zohar* (beginning about 1558) because they believed it supported trinitarian doctrines.

20. Blau, *The Christian Interpretation of the Cabala in the Renaissance*, 10.

• • • • • • • •

after death. He believed he could read the history of a soul in a person's face. Having written the *Zohar* in a past life, Luria could read it with special insight. Luria's highly original mysticism added deeper mythical dimensions to the *Zohar*.

Modern Hasidism and Modern Judaism (Eighteenth Century to the Present)

Israel Baal Shem Tov (c. 1700–1760) started a new Hasidic movement in Poland. Rabbi, amulet maker, and healer, he energized Luria's abstruse metaphysics with emotional enthusiasm. His revived Hasidism considered emotion more important than erudition. During prayer, emotion can overwhelm rational consciousness, exalting the pious to communion with God. Because even familiar daily prayers can produce communion, the Hasidim consider prayer dangerously powerful: "It is only by God's grace that we remain alive after praying."[21] Hasidism itself remains alive and well today, representing "practical mysticism at its highest."[22]

Another influential eighteenth-century movement, the Jewish Enlightenment, differed from Hasidism in virtually every way. Advocating modernism and acculturation, Jewish Enlightenment rationalists condemned mysticism of any kind. They despised Qabalah as "a system of metaphysical delirium,"[23] and reviled the *Zohar* as "a book of lies."[24]

In the twentieth century, academic inquiry into Qabalah gradually displaced Jewish Enlightenment prejudices. Gershom Scholem (1897–1982) contended that Qabalah was in fact the heart and soul of Judaism. A large and valuable body of scholarship on Jewish mysticism exists today.

The academic study of Qabalah has also stimulated lively interest among contemporary Jews. Women and men, observant and secular, find the essence of their Jewish heritage in Qabalah.

Meanwhile, qabalistic initiation continues among the Orthodox. Most conspicuously, the twenty-first-century Hasidim cultivate lives of traditional Jewish piety, steeped in Qabalah. After two millennia of change, the ancient Jewish mystical tradition is thriving today.

Hermetic Qabalah in the Renaissance (Fifteenth through Seventeenth Centuries)

Throughout the Middle Ages, Christians knew virtually nothing of Qabalah, Judaism, or the Hebrew language. They generally regarded Jews not with curiosity but with fear of Jewish sorcery.

In the fifteenth century, humanist scholars rediscovered the ancient Hermetic tradition.[25] Seeking the unity of all knowledge, they blended Christian faith with pagan philosophy and

---

21. The pseudepigraphic *Testament of Rabbi Israel Baal Shem,* quoted in Dan, *The Teachings of Hasidism*, 107.

22. Scholem, *Major Trends in Jewish Mysticism*, 341.

23. Kalisch, *Sepher Yetzirah*, 9. An important American Reform rabbi, Isidor Kalisch (1816–1886) produced the first English translation of the *Sepher Yetzirah* in 1877. He believed the book contained philosophy, not mysticism.

24. Heinrich Graetz, quoted in Scholem, *Major Trends in Jewish Mysticism*, 191. A leading historian, Graetz (1817–1891) evinced a seething hatred of the *Zohar*.

25. For more on the Hermetic tradition, see Book One: Foundations of Western Magic.

• • • • • • • •

theurgy. Qabalah, reinterpreted in Hermetic and Christian terms, became the keystone of their universal synthesis. Inextricably linked with Qabalah, ceremonial magic emerged from this same Renaissance synthesis.

Giovanni Pico della Mirandola (1463–1494) was the first Christian Qabalist. Pico believed Qabalah unified all philosophies and religions while upholding Christianity. In 1486 he proclaimed, "No science offers greater assurance of Christ's divinity than magic and the cabala."[26]

For the next two centuries, Qabalah fascinated European intellectuals. Enthusiasm for Jewish mysticism elicited unheard-of empathy for Jews and interest in Jewish thought. Universities began teaching Hebrew. Latin translations of Jewish texts appeared, alongside the first books of Hermetic Qabalah. Persecutions continued, but the humanists fought for tolerance.

Johann Reuchlin (1455–1522) faced the Inquisition to halt the burning of Jewish books. Less successfully, he attempted to convert Jews with qabalistic arguments about the name Jesus. Adding the letter *shin* to the Tetragrammaton (God's true name), Reuchlin revealed "the name of YHSVH, the true Messiah."[27] Christian Qabalists, at least, welcomed this Pentagrammaton.

Two striking innovations—both anticipated by Abulafia—extracted Hermetic Qabalah from its Jewish matrix. Hermetic Qabalah asserted that qabalistic truth is not restricted to Judaism or the Hebrew language. This idea exalted Qabalah to universal importance but uprooted it from its native soil. Hermetic Qabalah also deemed initiation unnecessary, radically altering the nature of qabalistic learning. Instead of receiving formal initiation into a master's secret teachings, Hermetic Qabalists studied books.

Cornelius Agrippa (1486–1535) blended Christian, Jewish, and pagan traditions into a system he called *ceremonial magic*. At the center of his synthesis was Hermetic Qabalah. Agrippa's *Occult Philosophy,* the "magical encyclopedia of the Renaissance,"[28] revolutionized sixteenth-century magical practice. Five hundred years later, ceremonial magicians continue to build on Agrippa's qabalistic foundation.

By the seventeenth century, "some knowledge of cabala was part of the equipment of every scholar in every part of Europe."[29] Christian Knorr von Rosenroth (1636–1689) produced the crowning work of Renaissance scholarship on Qabalah. Knorr's *Kabbala Denudata* remained the standard reference for Hermetic Qabalists until the twentieth century.[30]

---

26. Pico, quoted in Shumaker, *The Occult Sciences in the Renaissance*, 16.

27. Reuchlin, *On the Art of the Kabbalah: De Arte Cabalistica*, 353.

28. Donald Tyson, "On the *Occult Philosophy*," in Agrippa, *Three Books of Occult Philosophy*, xlii.

29. Blau, *The Christian Interpretation*, 100. Blau may have overstated his point.

30. Paul Kléber Monod observes that *Kabbala Denudata* "is an immensely complex work, and any attempt to sum it up in a few words will be inadequate." See *Solomon's Secret Arts*, 108.

. . . .

Modern Hermetic Qabalah and the Golden Dawn School (Nineteenth Century to the Present)

Qabalah, like most spiritual interests, lost prestige during the Enlightenment. In the nineteenth century, Éliphas Lévi (1810–1875) revitalized Hermetic Qabalah. Lévi maintained that Hermetic, Jewish, and Christian dogmas "complete and explain one another and their synthesis will be the religion of the future."[31] Lévi's ideas influenced Freemasonry, Theosophy, and the Hermetic Order of the Golden Dawn.

The Golden Dawn was a formally organized school of Hermetic Qabalah.[32] Its founders lectured on Qabalah; they translated the *Yetzirah* and portions of the *Zohar*. They introduced English readers to these essential qabalistic texts, "the kernel of that oral tradition."[33] However, the Golden Dawn was not a literary association but a system of initiation.

Initiates learned the theory of Hermetic Qabalah and the practice of ceremonial magic. The Golden Dawn structured its initiatory, magical, qabalistic synthesis on the Tree of Life. The initiation rituals symbolized a gradual ascent through the sephiroth.

Anchoring Hermetic Qabalah in an initiatory tradition (like Jewish Qabalah) was an important development. The Golden Dawn school introduced several other significant innovations. It improved Agrippa's system with better knowledge of Qabalah. It forged Lévi's rhapsodic ideas into workable rituals. Its secret interpretation of the *Sepher Yetzirah* thoroughly integrated the tarot with the Tree of Life. The Golden Dawn school enriched qabalistic symbolism with new correspondences, including elaborate color symbolism.

After the schism of 1900, initiates published many of the order's secrets. Israel Regardie (1907–1985) produced the clearest and most influential revelation. Regardie's *Golden Dawn* revolutionized twentieth-century magical practice. Despite his Jewish heritage, Regardie was emphatically a Hermetic Qabalist. He maintained that Qabalah "could and should be employed without binding to it the partisan qualities of any one particular religious faith."[34]

---

31. Lévi, *The Book of Splendours*, 120. Themes of reconciliation and synthesis, typical of Renaissance humanism, dominated Lévi's thought.

32. We mention the Golden Dawn only as a school of Qabalah; for more on the order's history, teachings, and members, see Book Eight: The Golden Dawn. By speaking of the Golden Dawn in the past tense, we intend no disrespect to those who carry on its work today. We are simply considering the teachings of the original order (1888–1900), as distinct from later developments.

33. Westcott, *An Introduction to the Study of the Kabalah*, 12. William Wynn Westcott (1848–1925) published the second English translation of the *Sepher Yetzirah* (London, 1890). Samuel Liddell MacGregor Mathers (1854–1918) published the first English translation of *Zohar* extracts. His *Kabbalah Unveiled* (London, 1887) relied on Knorr's Latin text in *Kabbala Denudata,* not the original Aramaic.

34. Regardie, *A Garden of Pomegranates*, v.

· · · · · · · ·

Generations of students have preserved the order's qabalistic doctrines with surprisingly few alterations.[35] The Golden Dawn system has become the standard of modern ceremonial magic and Hermetic Qabalah.

The marvelously innovative Golden Dawn school deserves serious study. Students must understand, however, that Qabalah neither began nor ended with the Golden Dawn. The founders did extraordinary work with the qabalistic information available to them in 1888. Far more information is available today. Students will find popular introductions, translations of ancient texts, and scholarly monographs by the thousands. We hope these brief historical notes will motivate students to explore.

Some Basics of Theoretical Qabalah

Qabalists divide their tradition into theoretical and practical branches. Theoretical Qabalah, involving the ten sephiroth, is more contemplative, more mystical. Practical Qabalah, involving the twenty-two letters, is more active, more magical. Together, these complementary approaches embrace the thirty-two paths of wisdom enumerated in the *Sepher Yetzirah*.

Theoretical Qabalah provides the foundational theologies upon which practical Qabalah operates. It includes metaphysical and mystical speculation concerning deity, souls, angels, and demons. It contemplates creation, the evolution of the divine and the divine realm. Theoretical Qabalah expounds the sephiroth, the four worlds, and the veils of negative existence. It informs the ascent toward knowledge of (and perhaps union with) divinity.

Theoretical information has always dominated published writings on Qabalah. One reason for this is that the sephiroth are relatively stable and unchanging. The ten sephiroth resemble well-known destinations, while the letters resemble the journeys to those destinations. Each person's journey is unique.

Theoretical Qabalah often takes the form of stories and homilies. These seem intended to instruct initiates while hiding the true meaning from outsiders. Readers unfamiliar with the underlying symbols and definitions may find the *Bahir* and the *Zohar* frustrating.

It is important to remember that there is no single, unvarying qabalistic theology. Every period, every school, every individual Qabalist has a unique understanding of the tradition. This brief introduction mentions only a few widely accepted concepts. It emphasizes the teachings of the Golden Dawn school of Qabalah.

---

35. Many variations on Golden Dawn themes exist. Aleister Crowley (1875–1947) [Eds. note: See Book Nine: Thelema & Aleister Crowley] tinkered with tarot attributions. Charles Stansfeld Jones (1886–1950) reassigned letters to paths; his students have considerably developed English-language *gematria*. Kenneth Grant (1924–2011) reimagined the Other Side, which his students have extensively explored. Yet these and other variants remain solidly within the Golden Dawn school.

• • • • • • • •

The Tree of Life

A diagram called the Tree of Life is the most familiar symbol of Qabalah (figure 1). It is a visual summary of the *Sepher Yetzirah*. It shows the sephiroth as ten circles, and the letters as twenty-two lines connecting the circles.

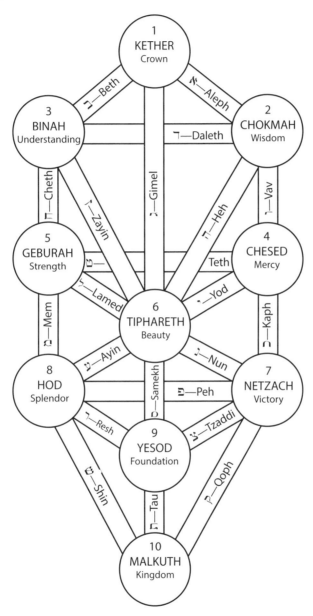

Figure 1. The Tree of Life of the Golden Dawn

Qabalists have imagined the Tree of Life differently over the centuries. The Tree of Life that the Golden Dawn adopted is one version among many.[36] Because of the Golden Dawn's influence, however, it is the most common Tree in ceremonial magic.

The Sephiroth

The *Sepher Yetzirah* introduced the ten sephiroth. It described them as instruments or tools that God used when creating the world. The ten sephiroth represent all of existence just as ten digits represent all numbers.

Sepher ha-Bahir described the sephiroth as parts of God, ten aspects of one divine consciousness. The *Bahir* spoke of the sephiroth as individuals with distinct personalities and gave them names.

The sephiroth are vessels of divine force. Each contains distinct powers, including a divine name, an archangel, a choir of angels, and an intelligence. These beings vary in their powers, functions, and missions. Their individual names allow Qabalists to work with specific aspects of the divine. Qabalists understand there is true power in knowing a name. To master the divine and angelic names is to possess a certain control of the sephiroth.

The correspondences of the sephiroth come mostly from Jewish Qabalah. Hermetic Qabalists added correspondences such as the tarot and non-Jewish deities.[37] The Golden Dawn used the qabalistic tarot correspondences extensively with both the sephiroth and the paths, which will be discussed later. This emphasis on the tarot attributions to the Tree of Life is a point of departure for some modern magicians with the Golden Dawn system. A thorough account of the tarot exceeds the scope of this chapter.

Kether (כתר), "Crown," is the first sephirah on the Tree of Life. Kether is the first emanation, the first manifestation of God's will. No thought or differentiation exists here. Kether is the sphere of the "first moved."[38] The divine name is *Eheieh* (אהיה), "I am." The archangel is *Metatron* (מטטרון), the Prince of Countenances, "who bringeth others before the face of God."[39]

---

36. The Golden Dawn borrowed its Tree of Life from the Jesuit polymath Athanasius Kircher (1602–1680). Kircher's Tree of Life diagram assigned Hebrew letters to the twenty-two connecting lines, going from top to bottom in alphabetical order. Kircher's Tree is the favorite of Hermetic Qabalists. Jewish Qabalists generally prefer Isaac Luria's arrangement of the letters. Strictly theoretical Qabalists prefer a Tree consisting of sephiroth only, omitting the letters.

37. For more correspondences, see Book Eleven: Magician's Tables. For many additional correspondences, see Aleister Crowley's "777" in *777 and Other Qabalistic Writings*.

38. The concept of the "first moved," or *primum mobile*, comes from ancient philosophy. God is the "first mover" or "first cause" who sets the cosmic system in motion. Qabalists identify this "unmoved mover" with Ain Soph. Some prefer to think of Kether as everything that exploded from the Big Bang and coalesced into the universe.

39. Regardie, *The Golden Dawn*, 96.

· · · · · · · · ·

Chokmah (חכמה), "Wisdom," is the second sephirah. Chokmah is the sphere of the stars (often represented by the twelve constellations of the zodiac). Masculine, vigorous, and active, Chokmah is the Father, eternally united with the Mother, Binah. It is the Word, or *logos,* the written law. Chokmah is the *yod* (י) of the Tetragrammaton. The divine name is *Yah* (יה), "God." The archangel is *Raziel* (רזיאל), "the Prince … of the knowledge of hidden and concealed things."[40]

Binah (בינה), "Understanding," is the third sephirah. Binah is the sphere of Saturn, the dark waters of creation. It is the flowing waters of divinity. Binah is the feminine potency who is co-equal with Chokmah. Binah is the supernal Mother, the Queen, "the great feminine form of God, the Elohim, in whose image man and woman are created."[41] Binah is the Qabalah, the oral law. Binah is the *heh* (ה) of the Tetragrammaton. The divine name is *Tetragrammaton Elohim* (יהוה אלהים), "Lord God." The archangel is *Tzaphqiel* (צפקיאל), "the Prince of the Spiritual Strife against Evil."[42]

These three sephiroth constitute the supernal triad. Below the supernal triad is the abyss and the "false sephirah" *Daath* (דעת), "Knowledge." Daath is not a sephirah and should not appear as such on the Tree. (If it did appear on the Tree of Life, Daath would occupy the empty space in the center of the first six sephiroth.) It is a barrier that aspirants must cross to reach the supernal triad.

Chesed (חסד), "Mercy" or "Loving-kindness," is the fourth sephirah. It is also called *Gedulah* (גדולה), "Greatness." The word *Chesed* has multiple meanings, including "love" and "charity" (like the Greek *agapē*). Chesed is the sphere of Jupiter. A masculine potency, it represents peace and benevolence. Moses at Sinai, begging God to have mercy on his people, illustrates Chesed. It is the mercy that a king acquires once he has received wisdom and understanding. The divine name is *El* (אל), "God." The archangel is *Tzadqiel* (צדקיאל), "the prince of Mercy and Beneficence."[43]

Geburah (גבורה), "Strength," is the fifth sephirah. It is also called *Din* (דין), "Judgment." Geburah is the sphere of Mars. A feminine potency, it represents war and violence. It is the violent rushing waters of a tsunami, water in its most destructive form. It is the flaming sword of God sitting in judgment. The Golden Dawn warned of the dangers of imbalance between Geburah and Chesed: "Remember that unbalanced force is evil, that unbalanced severity is but cruelty and oppression, but that also unbalanced Mercy is but weakness which would allow and abet evil."[44] When Geburah is out of balance with Chesed, its wrath can turn to evil. Geburah then becomes

---

40. Regardie, *Golden Dawn*, 96. The Golden Dawn documents seem to confuse the names *Raziel* (רזיאל) and *Ratziel* (רציאל); see Regardie, *The Golden Dawn*, 64 and 96. *Raz* (רז) means "mystery," while *ratz* (רץ) means "messenger." Ratziel is a perfectly respectable angel, but Raziel is the archangel of Chokmah.

41. Mathers, *The Kabbalah Unveiled*, 25.

42. Regardie, *The Golden Dawn*, 97.

43. Regardie, *The Golden Dawn*, 97.

44. "On the General Guidance and Purification of the Soul," in Regardie, *The Golden Dawn*, 75.

• • • • • • • •

the gateway to the demonic realm of the Other Side. The divine name is *Elohim Gibur* (אלהים גבור), "Mighty God." The archangel is *Kamael* (כמאל), "the Prince of Strength and Courage."[45]

Tiphareth (תפארת), "Beauty," is the sixth sephirah. Tiphareth is the sphere of the Sun. A masculine potency, it represents balance, spirituality, compassion, and harmony. Occupying the center of the Tree, Tiphareth has a direct connection to every sephirah except Malkuth. It is the manifested, reflected light of God. Tiphareth is the Blessed Holy One, the Son of Chokmah and Binah. He is the bridegroom to the bride Shekhinah (Malkuth). Tiphareth is the *vau* (ו) of the Tetragrammaton. The divine name is *Tetragrammaton Eloah va-Daath* (יהוה אלוה ודעת), "Lord God and Knowledge."[46] This twelve-letter name is unique to the Golden Dawn school. In Jewish Qabalah the divine name of Tiphareth is the Tetragrammaton. The archangel is *Raphael* (רפאל), "the Prince of Brightness, Beauty, and Light."[47]

Netzach (נצח), "Victory," is the seventh sephirah. Netzach is the sphere of Venus. A masculine potency, it represents eternal love and harmony. Netzach is the ability to persevere and to conquer using passions and emotions. Netzach displays the qualities of Binah (such as intuition and insight) and Chesed (mercy and love), but on a lower level. The divine name is *Tetragrammaton Tzabaoth* (יהוה צבאות), "Lord of Hosts." The archangel is *Haniel* (האניאל), "the Prince of Love and Harmony."[48]

Hod (הוד), "Splendor," is the eighth sephirah. Hod is the sphere of Mercury. A feminine potency, it represents the intellect. Hod shows the qualities of Chokmah (such as wisdom) on a lower level. This manifests in Hod as learning and ritual. Hod is the realm of the magician. The divine name is *Elohim Tzabaoth* (אלהים צבאות), "God of Hosts." The archangel is *Michael* (מיכאל), "the Prince of Splendour and of Wisdom."[49]

Yesod (יסוד), "Foundation," is the ninth sephirah. Yesod is the sphere of the Moon and reflects the Sun of Tiphareth. This interesting sephirah represents the genitals of God. It is the location of the union between Tiphareth above and Shekhinah (Malkuth) below. Yesod is the well of souls, where souls are deposited before birth. Yesod is the astral plane. The divine name is *Shaddai El Chai* (שדי אל חי), "Almighty Living God." The archangel is *Gabriel* (גבריאל), "the Prince of Change and Alteration."[50]

Malkuth (מלכות), "Kingdom," is the tenth sephirah. Malkuth is also called *Kavod* (כבוד), "Glory," and *Shekhinah* (שכינה), "Presence." Malkuth is the sphere of the elements. A feminine potency, it is the most complex of all the sephiroth (see inset). Malkuth represents the terrestrial world and the gateway to the world of the divine. It is the funnel for all the other sephiroth into the material

---

45. Regardie, *The Golden Dawn*, 97.

46. Regardie, *The Golden Dawn*, 64.

47. Regardie, *The Golden Dawn*, 97.

48. Regardie, *The Golden Dawn*, 97.

49. Regardie, *The Golden Dawn*, 98.

50. Regardie, *The Golden Dawn*, 98.

plane. Malkuth is the Daughter of Chokmah and Binah. She is the bride of Tiphareth. Malkuth is the final *heh* (ה) of the Tetragrammaton. The divine name is *Adonai ha-Aretz* (אדני הארץ), "Lord of the Earth." The archangel is *Sandalphon* (סנדלפון), "the Prince of Prayer." [51]

The Shekhinah

The *Bahir* postulated a feminine, visible, knowable aspect of God, the *Shekhinah*. The Shekhinah, or "Presence," is the channel through which the divine waters flow. Also called *Kavod*, or "Glory," she is the boundary between the divine world and creation. She receives the life force from the masculine Tiphareth and dispenses the force to creation. She is a passive force, with no identity of her own. Like a mirror, she is always full but only reflecting energy from above and below. The Shekhinah is the point of contact between God and creation.

The Shekhinah is the Daughter of Chokmah and Binah. Unlike Binah, who is a flowing fountain, the Shekhinah is a closed well. "A garden inclosed is my sister, my spouse; a spring shut up, a fountain sealed" (Song of Songs 4:12). The *Zohar* states, "When the need arises, She becomes a spring; when the need arises, She becomes a well." [*] The Shekhinah must be protected from the evil outside the garden, so when evil threatens she becomes a well. "If life on earth is corrupt, Shekhinah turns into a well, and the waters must be drawn by righteous heroes." [**]

The relationship between Tiphareth and Shekhinah is based on sexual intercourse. The Shekhinah is the Sabbath bride, ushered into the synagogue with the song "Lekha Dodi (Come, My Beloved)." The meaning of this qabalistic song from Safed is mostly lost to non-qabalistic Jews.

Hasidim understand communion *(devequth)* as a mystic sexual union with the divine feminine presence: "Moving your body in worship, thus reminding yourself that the Shekinah is standing before you, will rouse you to a state of intense excitement." [***] Hasidim engage in theurgic coitus, intending to assist Tiphareth and the Shekhinah in their union.

The Shekhinah has many correspondences. She is a rose, earth, fountain, garden. She is both pure and highly sexualized. She is the guardian on the Ark of the Covenant. She is the God that spoke to Moses on Sinai. She is the gateway to the divine.

[*] Matt, *Zohar*, 181.
[**] *Zohar* 1:60a-b, in Matt, *Zohar*, 292.
[***] *Testament of Rabbi Israel Baal Shem*, quoted in Dan, *The Teachings of Hasidism*, 110.

---

51. Regardie, *The Golden Dawn*, 98. There are two other archangels of Malkuth: Metatron, the Prince of Countenances, reflected from Kether, and *Nephesh ha-Messiah*, or "the Soul of the Messiah," as the emissary to Earth.

· · · · · · · ·

The Three Trinities and the Tetrad of Malkuth

The Tree of Life holds three triangles or trinities (figure 2). Each comprises a male, a female, and a union. The highest trinity is the supernal triad, also called the Crown, King, and Queen. Kether, Chokmah, and Binah are three combined into two, to make one. Chokmah and Binah are not a duality but a singularity: they are never separated. The supernal triad exists above the abyss of Knowledge and beyond Reason. In the Golden Dawn's color symbolism (Queen scale), these sephiroth are white, gray, and black, respectively.

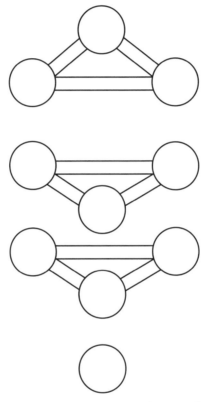

Figure 2. The Three Triads on the Tree of Life

The second trinity includes Chesed, Geburah, and Tiphareth. They form a downward-pointing triangle, as if reflecting the triangle above. This triad concerns leadership and governance, mercy and power. Reconciling these opposites is Tiphareth, the Sun, whose light brings forth beauty and peace. The primary colors blue, red, and yellow correspond to these sephiroth.

The third trinity consists of Netzach, Hod, and Yesod. They form another downward-pointing triangle, a second reflection. This triad governs the elements and natural forces. The secondary colors correspond to these sephiroth. The blue of Chesed and the yellow of Tiphareth make the emerald green of Netzach. The red of Geburah and the yellow of Tiphareth make the brilliant orange of Hod. The blue of Chesed and the red of Geburah produce the brilliant purple of Yesod.

Malkuth is unique in the Hermetic tradition. In Jewish Qabalah, Malkuth stands alone at the bottom of the Tree, connecting only to Yesod and not part of any triad. However, in Hermetic Qabalah, Malkuth connects to Hod and Netzach as well as Yesod, forming a tetrad. Malkuth is the final convergence of all things above. As the sphere of the four elements, Malkuth has four colors, three of which are duller versions of Netzach (olive), Hod (citrine), and Yesod (russet). The fourth color (black) demonstrates how far Malkuth is removed from the primal bright white light of Kether. At the same time, black suggests a return to the nothingness of *Ain* to be reborn in Kether. This mystery exemplifies the qabalistic formula "Kether is in Malkuth and Malkuth is in Kether."

The Three Pillars

The ten sephiroth form three columns or pillars (figure 3). As in the three trinities, there is a male, a female, and a union.

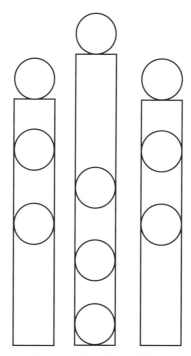

Figure 3. The Three Pillars

The Pillar of Mercy, on the right-hand side of the Tree, represents the element of fire. It includes the masculine sephiroth Chokmah, Chesed, and Netzach.

The Pillar of Severity, on the left-hand side of the Tree, represents the element of water. It includes the feminine sephiroth Binah, Geburah, and Hod. These two pillars balance each other.

The Pillar of Mildness, in the center, represents the element of air. It includes Kether, Tiphareth, Yesod, and Malkuth. This Middle Pillar reconciles the other two.

The Middle Pillar Exercise is a simple, purely qabalistic meditation taught by the Golden Dawn.[52] Through visualization and intonation, students establish the Middle Pillar within themselves. By internalizing the Tree of Life, students embody its symbolism of balance.

The Veils of Negative Existence

The Tree of Life is the central construct of Qabalah. Other systems, symbols, and mystical theories have developed from it. These additional theories expand the symbolism of the Tree. They explain various aspects of creation and the divine, starting with what existed before creation.

Figure 4. The Veils of Negative Existence

What existed before the universe is concealed and transcendent. No words can describe this pre-existence. It is possible to speak of it or imagine it only in negative terms. Qabalists call it negative existence, understanding God in this pre-existence as *Ain* (אין), "not" or "nothing" (figure 4). Out of pure negativity came *Ain Soph* (אין סוף), "without end" or "limitless." And finally came *Ain Soph Aur* (אין סוף אור), "no end of light" or "limitless light." "And God said, Let there be light: and there was light" (Genesis 1:3).

52. Golden Dawn initiates received the Middle Pillar Exercise between the Portal and Adeptus Minor grades. See Regardie, *The Golden Dawn*, 90. Regardie considers the Middle Pillar as a tool for healing and for working magic in *Foundations of Practical Magic*, 137–160. Basically, the student visualizes the four central sephiroth in turn, while intoning their divine names. Kether is a brilliant light just above the head. Tiphareth is sunlight shining from the heart. Yesod is a radiance from the genitals. Malkuth is a glow emanating from just below the feet. Imaginative students will find many ways to embellish the exercise.

· · · · · · · ·

Positive existence began when the limitless light focused itself into a single point, called the Crown. As the universe emanated from Kether, the Crown, God became manifested and (somewhat) knowable. God remains omnipresent and infinite, but it is possible to describe the manifested God in positive terms.

The Four Worlds

The four worlds represent the four stages of creation or four fundamental states of being.[53] Each world corresponds with a letter of the Tetragrammaton and an element. Hermetic Qabalah assigns each world a suit of tarot cards as well as a court card.

Qabalists conceptualize the four worlds in two ways. One way regards the worlds as four distinct Trees of Life. The Golden Dawn assigned a complete "scale" of color symbolism to each of these Trees.[54] The other way considers all four worlds as specific sephiroth on a single Tree.

Atziluth (אצילות), "Nearness," is the first world, closest to God. Atziluth is the world of archetypes, where an idea originates—the point of inspiration. Atziluth is the *yod* (י) of Tetragrammaton, the Father, corresponding to the element of fire. In the tarot it is the suit of wands and the four knights (or princes) among the court cards. On the Tree, Atziluth is associated with Chokmah and the divine names of God.

Beriah (בריאה), "Creation," is the second world. Beriah puts in motion the idea conceptualized in Chokmah. An emotional attachment gives the idea momentum. Beriah is the *heh* (ה) of Tetragrammaton, the Mother, the element of water. In the tarot it is the suit of cups and the four queens. On the Tree, Beriah is associated with Binah and the archangels.

Yetzirah (יצירה), "Formation," is the third world. Yetzirah is the world of formation, where an idea gradually becomes a reality. Yetzirah is the *vau* (ו) of the Tetragrammaton, the Son, and the element of air. In the tarot it is the suit of swords and the four kings. Yetzirah is the largest of the worlds, encompassing all the sephiroth from Chesed to Yesod. Tiphareth is its center. Yetzirah corresponds with the angels.

Assiah (עשיה), "Making" or "Action," is the final world, the physical world. In Assiah, the ideal becomes manifested existence: the Shekhinah gives birth to the original conception. Assiah is the final *heh* (ה) of the Tetragrammaton, the Daughter, and the element of earth. In the tarot Assiah is the suit of pentacles and the four knaves (or princesses). Assiah is associated with Malkuth and the intelligences.

---

53. An anonymous work called *Massekheth Atziluth (Tractate of Nearness)* first mentioned the four worlds. Current academic dating puts the work around 1000–1250 CE.
54. For the four scales of color symbolism, see Book Eleven: Magician's Tables. Artist and initiate Moïna Mathers (1865–1928) developed this intricate system of 140 symbolic colors.

A simple example may explain this fourfold process of creation. Atziluth is the moment of waking, when a single thought—*java*—enters your mind. In that second you have conceptualized what you need to manifest, a cup of coffee. The passion of Beriah overrides all desire to stay under the covers, propelling you out of bed. Nothing will keep you from manifesting that cup of java. Yetzirah is the brewing process: step by step, your java takes form, engaging all your senses. Your morning is happening, you are awake, and the day is taking shape. At last, the fully manifested java pours from Yesod into the vessel of Assiah. The fourfold act of creation is complete, and your inspiration is fulfilled. You have an actual cup of coffee.

The Parts of the Soul

The Hebrew Bible uses five different words for "soul." Qabalists believe each word signifies a distinct part of a human being. The *Bahir* discusses the five names of the soul: *nephesh, ruach, neshamah, chiah,* and *yechidah*. However, the *Zohar* mentions only three: the nephesh, ruach, and neshamah. Lurianic Qabalah restored the other two: chiah and yechidah.

In Hermetic Qabalah, four of these five parts of the soul correspond to the four worlds. Therefore, a human birth replicates the fourfold process by which God created the universe.

Yechidah (יחידה) means "individuality" or "oneness." This part of the soul is not associated with a part of the world, but rather the divine, the oneness of God and Man before man is created. It is also associated with Adam Qadmon (see below).

Chiah (חיה), "life," is associated with Atziluth, Chokmah, fire, and the *yod*. It is the life force, the spark of life. "It is the undiluted Life-Force itself, and it is our true identity."[55]

Neshamah (נשמה), "spirit," is associated with Beriah, Binah, water, and the *heh*. It is intuition, "that part of us that rises above the thinking process and vibrates in greater harmony with the ultimate reality."[56] It is the superior man of the *I Ching,* or Freud's superego.

Ruach (רוח), "breath" or "mind," equates to Yetzirah, the lower seven sephiroth from Chesed to Yesod, and is *vau*. This is where the soul manifests intelligence and reason. It is the ego and the inferior man of the *I Ching.*

Nephesh (נפש), "soul," equates to Assiah and Malkuth. This is the birth of the soul into the material body. It is the basic instincts, the animal part of the soul where survival and necessities drive actions. It is the id.

---

55. DuQuette, *The Chicken Qabalah of Rabbi Lamed Ben Clifford,* 101.
56. DuQuette, *The Chicken Qabalah of Rabbi Lamed Ben Clifford,* 100.

Adam Qadmon

Plato teaches that man is a little model of the universe, a microcosm. The Bible teaches that man is made in the image of God. The Tree of Life diagram interweaves biblical and platonic themes. It represents simultaneously the macrocosmic universe, the Creator of the universe, and the microcosmic man.

Adam Qadmon (אדם קדמון), "Primeval Man," is an anthropomorphized version of the Tree of Life and the sephiroth. It is the archetypal human, the perfected person. Adam Qadmon is Adam before the fall from the Garden of Eden. Some Qabalists regard Adam Qadmon as a fifth world, aligning with the *Yechidah* (the highest part of the soul).

Adam Qadmon embodies the Tree of Life. The supernal triad is the head of the body. Chesed and Geburah are the right and left arms. Tiphareth is the body or trunk. Netzach and Hod are the right and left legs. Yesod is the phallus, the genitals of Adam, and Malkuth is the feet.

The viewer sees the *backside* of Adam Qadmon, not the front. As God said to Moses, "thou shalt see my back parts: but my face shall not be seen" (Exodus 33:23).[57] The right hand is on the Pillar of Mercy and the left hand is on the Pillar of Severity. This point has caused considerable confusion in Hermetic Qabalah. The right hand of God is always the masculine side and the left hand is always the feminine side.

An easy way to learn the Tree of Life is to practice drawing it. The geometry is basic and requires only a compass and a ruler. One line plus three-and-a-half circles will pinpoint the locations of the sephiroth (see inset). Repeatedly drawing the Tree renders every detail familiar. Labeling the Tree with correspondences also helps make the system of qabalistic symbolism familiar.

Some Basics of Practical Qabalah

The two branches of Qabalah complement and balance each other. Theoretical Qabalah takes a more contemplative, armchair approach to the mysteries. Practical Qabalah takes a more active, hands-on approach. As theoretical Qabalah speculates on the ten sephiroth, practical Qabalah works with the twenty-two Hebrew letters.

The Alphabet

Of course, it is possible to study Qabalah without speaking Hebrew. There are enough books in English to occupy students of theoretical Qabalah for years. Practical Qabalah, however, demands at least a familiarity with the Hebrew alphabet.

---

57. Another possibility is that looking at Adam Qadmon is like looking into a mirror; cf. the Odes of Solomon 13:1.

How to Draw the Tree of Life

Step 1: Using a ruler, draw a long vertical line. This is the Middle Pillar (figure 5).

Step 2: Choose a point at the top of the line. This is Kether.

Step 3: Set a compass so that its radius is one-fourth the length of the line. Place the pivot of the compass on the Kether point. Draw a semicircle below Kether. The point where the semicircle intersects the line is Daath.

Figure 5. How to Draw the Tree of Life, Steps 1–3

Step 4: Place the pivot of the compass on the Daath point. Draw a circle around Daath. The points where the circle intersects the semicircle are Chokmah and Binah. The points where the circle intersects the line are Kether and Tiphareth (figure 6).

Figure 6. How to Draw the Tree of Life, Step 4

Step 5: Place the pivot of the compass on the Tiphareth point. Draw a circle around Tiphareth. The points where this circle intersects the previous circle are Chesed and Geburah. The points where the circle intersects the line are Daath and Yesod (figure 7).

Figure 7. How to Draw the Tree of Life, Step 5

Step 6: Place the pivot of the compass on the Yesod point. Draw a circle around Yesod. The points where this circle intersects the previous circle are Netzach and Hod. The points where the circle intersects the line are Tiphareth and Malkuth (figure 8).

• • • • • • • •

Figure 8. How to Draw the Tree of Life, Step 6

Step 7: Reset the compass so that its radius is one-fourth the distance between Tiphareth and Yesod. Draw ten smaller circles around the focal points of the sephiroth (figure 9).

Figure 9. How to Draw the Tree of Life, Step 7

Step 8: Using a ruler, connect the focal points of the sephiroth to delineate the remaining paths (figure 10).

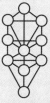

Figure 10. How to Draw the Tree of Life, Step 8

Step 9 (optional): Using a ruler, measure half the radius of a sephirotic circle. Widen the paths to this measurement (figure 11). (Technically the width of the paths should equal 30° of the sephirotic circles, or one-twelfth the circumference; however, if the circles are fairly small, the difference between $2\pi r \div 12$ and $r \div 2$ is imperceptible.)

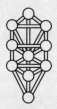

Figure 11. How to Draw the Tree of Life, Step 9

Step 10 (optional): Label the paths and sephiroth with helpful information or fill them in with appropriate colors.

At first sight, the Hebrew alphabet may seem outlandish (table 1). Written from right to left, it contains only consonants—some of them challenging to pronounce. A full account of the Hebrew alphabet exceeds the scope of this book. The first few pages of any introductory book on Hebrew will answer many questions.[58]

An easy way to learn the Hebrew alphabet is to practice writing it. Beginners should practice the simple block style until the letters become easily recognizable. The Ashuri script calls for a calligraphic pen or brush. Numerous books and websites offer detailed instruction on how to form the letters. Writing Hebrew qabalistic terms also helps make the technical vocabulary of Qabalah familiar. Some students may profit from toys and games designed to teach children the alphabet.

Qabalists consider the Hebrew language sacred. It is the language of the Bible, the language with which God created the universe. The letters of the Hebrew alphabet are tools of creation, repositories of divine power. Qabalists work with the letters to reveal mystical insights or even to produce magical effects.

Methods and Uses of Practical Qabalah

A fundamental premise of Qabalah is that every word of the Bible "holds supernal truths and sublime secrets."[59] Even when the literal sense appears unimportant or uninspiring, it is meaningful. So Qabalists seek deeper truths concealed below the surface meaning of the text. They approach the Bible as a divine code that the pious must decipher. Qabalists employ traditional methods or practices to reveal hidden biblical wisdom. The chief methods are *notariqon, gematria,* and *temurah.* The use of such practices constitutes "practical Qabalah."

Critics invariably object that anyone skilled in practical Qabalah can make a text say *anything.* It is true that Qabalists often use these methods quite playfully.[60] Nonetheless, Jewish Qabalists take their play seriously: discoveries must follow established rules of interpretation.[61] Since God's will is infinite, however, Qabalists affirm that the Bible conceals infinite treasures.

---

58. An introduction to Biblical Hebrew is ideal, but Modern Hebrew is generally similar. Pronunciation varies with dialect. We have mostly followed Golden Dawn custom, preferring the Sephardic pronunciation of Biblical Hebrew. Thus, we say *Kether,* but Ashkenazi Jews (including Regardie, in some of his books) say *Keser,* while Israelis say *Keter.* These are all acceptable pronunciations of כתר.

59. *Zohar* 3.152a, in Scholem, *Zohar,* 121.

60. DuQuette's *Chicken Qabalah* exemplifies this playfulness. See especially his chapter on practical methods, "Chapter 10: Last Lecture—Games Qabalists Play," 181–199.

61. Jewish liturgy enshrines the thirteen principles of Rabbi Ishmael (90–135 CE); see Adler, *Synagogue Service,* 34. Later authorities increased the number of rules for biblical exegesis to forty-nine.

Letter and Final Form (Script Style)	Name of Letter in English Transliteration	Numerical Value	Letter and Final Form (Block Style)	Simplified Pronunciation for Anglophones
א	*aleph*	1	א	silent glottal stop
ב	*beth*	2	ב	*b* or *v*
ג	*gimel*	3	ג	*g* (as in *go*) or *gh* (as in German *Tag*)
ד	*daleth*	4	ד	*d* or *dh* (as in *smooth*)
ה	*heh* or *hé*	5	ה	*h*
ו	*vau*	6	ו	*w* or *u* (as in *due*) or *o* (as in *doe*)
ז	*zayin*	7	ז	*z*
ח	*cheth*	8	ח	*ch* (as in German *Bach*, but whispered)
ט	*teth*	9	ט	*t* (as in *stake*)
י	*yod*	10	י	*y* or *i* (as in *Lisa*)
כ ך	*kaph*	20	ך כ	*k* (as in *cat*) or *kh* (as in German *Bach*)
ל	*lamed*	30	ל	*l*
מ ם	*mem*	40	ם מ	*m*
נ ן	*nun*	50	ן נ	*n*
ס	*samekh*	60	ס	*s*
ע	*ayin*	70	ע	glottal stop
פ ף	*peh* or *pé*	80	ף פ	*p* or *ph* (as in *graph*)
צ ץ	*tzaddi*	90	ץ צ	*tz* (as in *quartz*)
ק	*qoph*	100	ק	*q* (as in *kit*)
ר	*resh*	200	ר	*r*
ש	*shin*	300	ש	*sh* or *s*
ת	*tau*	400	ת	*t* (as in *take*) or *th* (as in *both*)

Table 1. The Hebrew Alphabet

At its heart, practical Qabalah is a way of meditating on sacred words. Its methods are the flint and steel that spark intuition. Qabalists also use practical methods to deepen their understanding of traditional prayers and customs. They may employ practical Qabalah to conceal secret knowledge, particularly when designing amulets. Qabalists sometimes use notariqon, gematria,

· · · · · · ·

and temurah to construct words of power or magical names. Hermetic Qabalists tend to dwell on the magical applications of these methods. Some writers shun *all* practical Qabalah as tainted by magical practices.[62]

For a more balanced view, we have selected various (mostly Jewish) examples of practical Qabalah. They illustrate how practical Qabalah enriches Jewish tradition, magically and otherwise. We have also drawn a few examples from ceremonial magic.

Notariqon

Notariqon (נוטריקון), "abbreviation," uses acronyms in various ways. Jews employ notariqon in everyday language, as shorthand for Hebrew names. For example, *Ari* (ארי), "Lion," stands for *Ashkenazi Rabbi Isaac,* the revered Qabalist Isaac Luria.

Qabalists seek deeper meaning in words by considering them as acronyms. For example, they consider *chen* (חן), "grace," an acronym of *chokmah nistarah,* or "hidden wisdom." Wherever "grace" occurs in scripture, Qabalists see it as hinting at some concealed wisdom. Conversely, they perceive the hidden wisdom of Qabalah as a pathway to divine grace.

Likewise, *amen* (אמן) traditionally stands for *El melekh neeman,* "God is a faithful king." It affirms one's trust in God at the end of every prayer.[63]

Qabalists also create acronyms to abbreviate words, sentences, or whole psalms. Traditional Jewish amulets often use this form of notariqon, simultaneously conserving space and concealing secrets. For example, the letter ש, commonly seen on a mezuzah, stands for *Shaddai* (שדי), "Almighty." Jewish folklore further interprets *Shaddai* (שדי) as "Guardian of the doors of Israel" (שומר דלתות ישראל).[64] The abbreviation ש also appears on protective amulets.[65]

---

62. Regrettably, one such writer was the pioneering scholar Gershom Scholem, who devoted only one page of his monumental survey to explaining practical methods. He protested that "what really deserves to be called Kabbalism has very little to do with these 'Kabbalistic' practices" (*Major Trends in Jewish Mysticism,* 100). Scholem's bias encouraged academics to ignore the practical side of Qabalah, skewing scholarship for generations.

63. Some say *Adonai* (אדני) instead of *El* (אל); see Regardie, *A Garden of Pomegranates,* 111. However, the synagogue liturgy and the *Sepher Yetzirah* both say *El* is a faithful king; see Adler, *Synagogue Service,* 130-B, and Kalisch, *Sepher Yetzirah,* 17 and 47.

64. Blu Greenberg repeats this bit of folklore (disapprovingly) in *How to Run a Traditional Jewish Household,* 211. The *mezuzah,* affixed to the doorpost of a Jewish home, contains a tiny scroll of biblical verses in accordance with Deuteronomy 6:9 and 11:20. Belief in the mezuzah's protective power, and the practice of carrying a mezuzah as an amulet, are both ancient.

65. Schrire, *Hebrew Magic Amulets,* 99. Lévi notes the frequent occurrence of ש on talismans in *Transcendental Magic,* 222 (associating the letter not with *Shaddai* but with the Pentagrammaton).

· · · · · · · ·

Another example of notariqon often found on Hebrew amulets is the word *argaman* (ארגמן), "purple." This seemingly random word invokes the archangels Auriel, Raphael, Gabriel, Michael, and Nuriel.[66]

Qabalists ordinarily form acronyms from the initial letters of words. Sometimes, however, they employ the final letters. For example, *Tzamarkhad* (צמרכד), another name for the archangel Metatron, appears on many amulets. It represents Genesis 1:1–5, being formed from the last letter of each verse.[67]

Basic rituals of ceremonial magic include some familiar examples of notariqon. The divine name *Agla* occurs in the Golden Dawn's Ritual of the Pentagram. *Agla* (אגלא) stands for *Atoh gibor le-olam Adonai*, or "Thou art mighty forever, my Lord." This sentence comes from the central prayer of Jewish liturgy, the *Amidah*.[68]

Another divine name, *Ararita*, occurs in the Golden Dawn's Ritual of the Hexagram. Ararita (אראריתא) conceals an affirmation of God's unity: "One, the Beginning of his Unity, the Beginning of his Oneness, his Exchange is One."[69] Notariqon condenses this mystical affirmation into *one* word.

Ceremonial magicians do not restrict their use of practical Qabalah to Hebrew. For example, Israel Regardie disliked the divine name associated with Tiphareth, *Tetragrammaton Eloah va-Daath*. He found it inconveniently long for purposes of intonation. Instead Regardie intoned *Iao*, the Greek name of a Gnostic deity with solar associations.[70] At first glance, this substitution looks absurdly out of place. Transliterated to Hebrew, however, the Greek letters IAΩ become יאו, an acronym of יהוה אלוה ודעת. Regardie cleverly solved his problem through bilingual notariqon.

Gematria

Gematria (גמטריא), "calculation," utilizes the fact that Hebrew letters also function as numerals. Each letter has an inherent, perfectly ordinary, numerical value: א is 1, ב is 2 (table 1). Qabalists consider words as the sums of their letters and seek meaning in those sums. For example, *raz* (רז) means "mystery," and its letters total 207. *Aur* (אור) means "light," and it also adds to 207. The identity of their numerical values suggests a connection between the words. Qabalists may consider "light" mystically synonymous with "mystery," or infer that mysteries can bring enlightenment.

---

66. Schrire, *Hebrew Magic Amulets*, 104.

67. Agrippa, *Three Books of Occult Philosophy*, 477.

68. See Adler, *Synagogue Service*, 15 and elsewhere. For the Ritual of the Pentagram, see Regardie, *The Golden Dawn*, 53, or Crowley, *Magick*, 618.

69. Reuchlin, *On the Art of the Kabbalah*, 351. See also Verman, *The Books of Contemplation*, 101–102, and Agrippa, *Three Books of Occult Philosophy*, 476–477. For the Ritual of the Hexagram, see Regardie, *The Golden Dawn*, 296–297, or Crowley, *Magick*, 621–622.

70. Regardie, *Foundations of Practical Magic*, 145.

· · · · · · · ·

Qabalistic texts call the unknowable creator *Ain Soph* (אין סוף), meaning "limitless" or "infinite." Again, the numerical value is 207. Qabalists may conclude that light—the first manifestation of Ain Soph (Genesis 1:3)—is an infinite mystery.

Qabalists sometimes conceal a word by substituting another with the same numerical value. For example, the angel Raziel revealed divine mysteries to Abraham Abulafia, who published them under the name *Raziel*.[71] The pseudonym hinted at Abulafia's identity because *Raziel* (רזיאל) equals *Abraham* (אברהם).

By making similar numerical substitutions, pious Jews avoid writing the Tetragrammaton unnecessarily. Some write יוי because those letters equal 26, the sum of the Tetragrammaton. Others prefer יה because the *names* of those letters, *yod* (יוד) and *hé* (הא), equal 26.[72] Another way of writing (or speaking) the Tetragrammaton is to spell out the name: *yod heh vau heh* (יוד הה וו הה) equals 52, or 2 × 26.[73] Some even write ד because the Tetragrammaton contains *four* letters.[74] Such numerical paraphrases of sacred names often appear on Jewish amulets.

Five Hebrew letters have "final forms," used only at the end of words. Occasionally Qabalists assign alternate numerical values to these final forms.[75] For example, *chen* (חן), "grace," usually equals 58, as *barukh* (ברוך), "blessed," usually equals 228. But the alternate values make each word equal 708.

Basic rituals of ceremonial magic offer examples of gematria. The Lesser Ritual of the Pentagram contains four sacred names: the Tetragrammaton, *Adonai* (אדני), *Eheieh* (אהיה), and *Agla* (אגלא). Notariqon turns these four divine names into יאאא, which equals 13; 13 equals *echad* (אחד), "one," so these names, through their diversity, assert God's unity.

The name *Ararita* (אראריתא) equals 813, the sum of all of the letters in Genesis 1:3. So *Ararita* mystically signifies "And God said, Let there be light: and there was light." Hence the Ritual of the Hexagram pairs *Ararita* with *lux*—Latin for "light."[76]

---

71. Scholem, *Major Trends in Jewish Mysticism*, 127.

72. Counting the *names* of letters, instead of the letters themselves, is a specific technique of gematria. Qabalists call it *mispar shemi*, or "name number." Our other examples of gematria are *mispar hekhrechi*, "essential number," the simplest and commonest form. Schochet lists a dozen different techniques of gematria in "The Principle of Numerical Interpretation," in Locks, *The Spice of Torah*, XXI–XXIV.

73. Note that this example and the previous example spell the name of the letter ה differently. Both הה and הא are accepted spellings. The Golden Dawn advised spelling out the Tetragrammaton rather than speaking some approximation like *Jehovah*: see Regardie, *The Golden Dawn*, 53. Lévi advised the same in *Transcendental Magic*, 379.

74. Schrire, *Hebrew Magic Amulets*, 95.

75. See figure 12. Using alternate values for final forms is another specific technique of gematria—*mispar gadol*, or "big number." Hermetic Qabalists seem to use it more than Jewish Qabalists, presumably because of Reuchlin's exposition of the alphabet: see *On the Art of the Kabbalah*, 317.

76. See Regardie, *The Golden Dawn*, 298, or Crowley, *Magick*, 621.

• • • • • • • •

Gematria is the most popular method of practical Qabalah. Many Qabalists (Jewish and Hermetic) spend years cataloguing words with the same numerical value.[77] Students interested in gematria should keep a notebook of their own findings.

Temurah

Temurah (תמורה), "exchange," comprises several techniques. The simplest of these utilizes anagrams. When the same letters spell different words, Qabalists use those words to explain each other. For example, "There is no good higher than joy (ענג), and there is no evil worse than affliction (נגע)."[78]

Similarly, bread (לחם) and salt (מלח) symbolize the polarity of Chesed and Geburah—mercy and judgment. Thus, the ancient Jewish custom of dipping bread into salt at meals acquires deeper meaning. Dipping the bread expresses a silent prayer that mercy may prevail over judgment.[79]

Sometimes anagrams highlight affinities between words, as in Genesis 6:8, where Noah (נח) found grace (חן). The word *temurah* itself (תמורה) is an anagram of *terumah* (תרומה), "offering." Qabalists may infer that temurah, rightly practiced, becomes a sort of mystical offering.

More complex techniques of temurah utilize substitution ciphers or codes. Qabalists use these ciphers to reveal the Bible's secrets and to conceal their own. Qabalists frequently use ciphers to write the Tetragrammaton without impiety. The numerous standard ciphers have names summarizing how they work. For example, *Athbash* (אתבש) is one of the most popular ciphers: א, the first letter of the alphabet, becomes ת, the last, and ב, the second letter, becomes ש, the penultimate—hence אתבש. Athbash encrypts the Tetragrammaton as מצפץ, often seen on Jewish amulets (table 2).

The *Athbash* (אתבש) Cipher	The *Avgad* (אבגד) Cipher
א becomes ת	א becomes ב
ב becomes ש	ב becomes ג
ג becomes ר	ג becomes ד
ד becomes ק	ד becomes ה
ה becomes צ	ה becomes ו

Table 2. Two Examples of Temurah Cipher (continued)

77. David Godwin offers his notes on gematria (and other useful information, with minimal use of the Hebrew alphabet) in *Godwin's Cabalistic Encyclopedia*. Notes on gematria constitute the "other writings" in Crowley's *777 and Other Qabalistic Writings*. Gutman Locks catalogues the numerical value of every word in the first five books of the Bible in his *Spice of Torah*. Several other collections are available.

78. *Sepher Yetzirah*, in Friedman, *The Book of Creation*, 5.

79. Isaac Luria recommended dipping the bread thrice. Bread (לחם) equals 78, and $78 \div 3 = 26$, so three dips betoken the Tetragrammaton. See Locks, *The Spice of Torah*, II. Yehuda Shurpin summarizes bread and salt symbolism in the article "Why Do We Dip the Challah Bread in Salt?" on Chabad.org. It may interest some readers that bread and salt combined would be $78 + 78$.

• • • • • • • •

The *Athbash* (אתבש) Cipher	The *Avgad* (אבגד) Cipher
ו becomes פ	ו becomes ז
ז becomes ע	ז becomes ח
ח becomes ס	ח becomes ט
ט becomes נ	ט becomes י
י becomes מ	י becomes כ
כ becomes ל	כ becomes ל
ל becomes כ	ל becomes מ
מ becomes י	מ becomes נ
נ becomes ט	נ becomes ס
ס becomes ח	ס becomes ע
ע becomes ז	ע becomes פ
פ becomes ו	פ becomes צ
צ becomes ה	צ becomes ק
ק becomes ד	ק becomes ר
ר becomes ג	ר becomes ש
ש becomes ב	ש becomes ת
ת becomes א	ת becomes א

Table 2. Two Examples of Temurah Cipher (continued)

In *Avgad* (אבגד), another popular cipher, each letter becomes the next letter in the alphabet: א becomes ב and ג becomes ד—hence the name אבגד. Avgad transforms the Tetragrammaton into כוזו, an encrypted name found on mezuzah scrolls.[80]

Aiq Bekar

Another technique of temurah, *aiq bekar* (איק בכר), warrants a separate explanation. Qabalists use this technique less for decoding the Bible than for encoding names. Aiq bekar takes encryption to another level. This type of temurah is also the key to understanding the planetary magic squares.[81] Aiq bekar sorts the twenty-two letters and the five final forms into nine triads or "chambers" (figure 12). As the name indicates, the letters איק—equivalent to 1, 10, 100—form the first triad. The letters בכר, or 2, 20, 200, form the second. Aiq bekar allows Qabalists to exchange

---

80. Schrire, *Hebrew Magic Amulets*, 96. Additional amuletic inscriptions were common on mezuzah scrolls before the rationalist philosopher Maimonides fulminated against them in the twelfth century. See also Silverberg, "Maimonides and the Protective Function of the *Mezuza*."

81. For these squares and their use, see Book Three: Planetary Magick.

any letter with others from its chamber. For example, "mystery" (רז) can become "son" (בן) or "truthful" (כן).

3	ג	2	ב	1	א
30	ל	20	כ	10	י
300	ש	200	ר	100	ק
6	ו	5	ה	4	ד
60	ס	50	נ	40	מ
600	ם	500	ך	400	ת
9	ט	8	ח	7	ז
90	צ	80	פ	70	ע
900	ץ	800	ף	700	ן

Figure 12. The Nine Chambers of Aiq Bekar

The nine chambers also function as a substitution cipher. Freemasons and magicians employ this code, which Agrippa's *Occult Philosophy* popularized. The cipher indicates letters by specifying their location in the nine-chamber grid using rectilinear figures. It indicates א through ט (the units, 1–9) by adding one dot (figure 13). The cipher indicates י through צ (tens, 10–90) with two dots. It indicates ק through ץ (hundreds, 100–900) with three dots.[82]

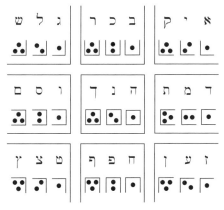

Figure 13. The Nine Chambers Exploded as a Code-Matrix,
Showing the Hebrew Alphabet Encrypted by the Aiq Bekar Cipher

82. Agrippa, *Three Books of Occult Philosophy*, 561. A Masonic variant indicates units by location alone, tens by adding *one* dot to the location, and hundreds by adding *two* dots. See Mackey, *An Encyclopaedia of Freemasonry and Its Kindred Sciences,* vol. 1, 151, but note that Mackey's explanation jumbles some Hebrew letters.

• • • • • • • •

Agrippa also taught how to form characters (sigils) from names encoded by *aiq bekar*.[83] The procedure is simply to combine the separate rectilinear figures into one. Only the magician who created it can reconstruct the name from the finished character (figure 14).

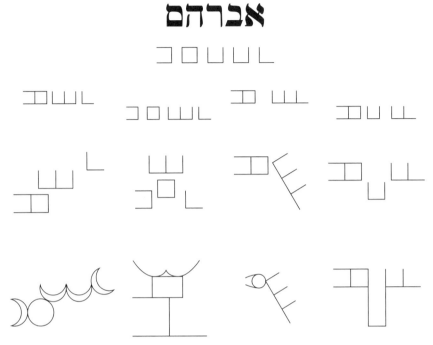

Figure 14. The Name Abraham *in the Aiq Bekar Cipher, and Some Sigils Formed from It*

The nine chambers facilitate a reductive technique of gematria, reducing hundreds or tens to units. Instead of 200, the numerical value of ר becomes 2. Instead of 20, כ also becomes 2.[84] For example, "mystery" (רז), normally 200 + 7, becomes 2 + 7 by this technique. The numerical value of *Ararita* changes from 813 to 12. This technique of gematria, in turn, facilitates another application of the nine chambers.

The use of "magic squares" for talismanic purposes is ancient. The simplest magic square is a grid of nine compartments. The grid arranges the numbers 1 through 9 so that each row adds to 15 (figure 15). Qabalists see this square as concealing the divine name יה through gematria. Qabalists also see this magic square as the aiq bekar chambers rearranged, so they use it for encryption,

---

83. Agrippa, *Three Books of Occult Philosophy*, 561.

84. This technique of gematria is *mispar qatan*, or "little number." See Schochet, "The Principle of Numerical Interpretation," in Locks, *The Spice of Torah*, XXI–XXII. Aiq bekar relies on the alternate numerical values of the final forms, explained previously. So in this context, *mispar qatan* works in conjunction with *mispar gadol*, or "big number."

· · · · · · · ·

alongside the reductive technique of gematria described above. They first reduce all letters in a word to units. Then they indicate the word, as a series of numbers, with lines on the grid.

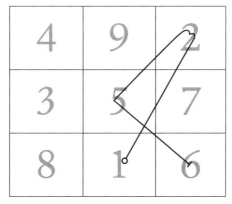

Figure. 15. The Nine Chambers of Aiq Bekar Rearranged as a Magic Square, with the Name Abraham *Indicated by Lines Drawn on the Square*

For example, *Abraham* (אברהם) is normally 1 + 2 + 200 + 5 + 40. The alternate value of final *mem* makes it 1 + 2 + 200 + 5 + 600. Reduction turns these numbers into 1 + 2 + 2 + 5 + 6. On the grid, *Abraham* begins with a mark in box 1 (for א). (See figure 15.) From that mark, a line extends to box 2 (for ב). The next letter (ר) is also a 2, indicated by "a crook or wave in the line."[85] The line continues to box 5 (for ה), then ends in box 6 (for ם). Removed from the grid, the lineal figure becomes a mystifying sigil.

The Golden Dawn taught the use of aiq bekar and the planetary magic squares. It also taught a simpler device for generating sigils, the rose of twenty-two petals (figure 16). These petals represent the letters of the Hebrew alphabet, arranged in three concentric circles. The inner circle contains the three mother letters. The middle circle contains the seven double letters. The outer circle contains the twelve single letters. Lines drawn from one petal to another form sigils on the rose. The process is identical to that used on the magic square.[86]

85. Regardie, *The Golden Dawn*, 483.

86. For fuller instructions, see Regardie, *The Golden Dawn*, 482–483. This "rose" appeared on the lamen of the Golden Dawn's secret Second Order. Depictions of the Rose-Cross Lamen sometimes scramble the correct arrangement of letters. The arrangement depends on the King Scale colors corresponding to the letters. The middle circle goes counterclockwise in standard rainbow sequence, from red to violet.

· · · · · · · ·

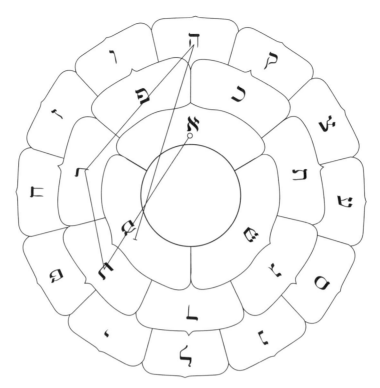

Figure 16. The Rose of Twenty-Two Petals, with the Name
Abraham *Indicated by Lines Drawn on the Rose*

To summarize these methods, notariqon changes words into other words using acronyms. Simple temurah does the same using anagrams, while complex temurah uses ciphers. Gematria turns words into numbers. Certain types of temurah—aiq bekar and related techniques—transform names into geometrical abstractions.

Some Notes on Qabalah in Ceremonial Magic

From a strictly qabalistic viewpoint, ceremonial magic comprises several advanced applications of temurah. Exchanging letters for symbols, ceremonial magicians can change names into sequences of colors or stones.[87] They can transform names into unique scents by compounding incenses.[88] Magicians can devise environments where every sight, sound, scent, taste, touch, and action invokes one name. The possibilities are numerous.

---

87. For example, the colors bright pale yellow, yellow, orange, scarlet, and deep blue spell *Abraham* (אברהם): blending them will produce a unique color representing the name. The stones topaz, agate, peridot, ruby, and beryl likewise spell *Abraham*. For these correspondences, see Book Eleven: Magician's Tables.

88. Again, *Abraham* could be a blend of galbanum, mastic, frankincense, dragon's blood, and myrrh.

• • • • • • • •

Magical Correspondences

Ceremonial magicians produce these transformations through correspondences (table 3). The system of magical correspondences stems from the *Sepher Yetzirah*, the foundation book of Qabalah. The *Yetzirah* sorts the Hebrew alphabet into three categories. It specifies some of the things God created using each letter.

Letter and Final Form (Block Style)	Name of Letter in Hebrew (Script Style)	Correspondence According to the *Sepher Yetzirah*	Tarot Correspondence According to the Golden Dawn
א	אלף	Air	The Fool
ב	בית	Mercury	The Magician
ג	גמל	Moon	The High Priestess
ד	דלת	Venus	The Empress
ה	הא or הה	Aries	The Emperor
ו	וו	Taurus	The Hierophant
ז	זין	Gemini	The Lovers
ח	חית	Cancer	The Chariot
ט	טית	Leo	Strength
י	יוד	Virgo	The Hermit
ך כ	כף	Jupiter	The Wheel of Fortune
ל	למד	Libra	Justice
ם מ	מם	Water	The Hanged Man
ן נ	נון	Scorpio	Death
ס	סמך	Sagittarius	Temperance
ע	עין	Capricorn	The Devil
ף פ	פא or פה	Mars	The Tower
ץ צ	צדי	Aquarius	The Star
ק	קוף	Pisces	The Moon
ר	ריש	Sun	The Sun
ש	שין	Fire	Judgment
ת	תו	Saturn	The World

Table 3. Essential Correspondences of the Hebrew Alphabet

Each of the three *mother* letters (אמש) is unlike any other.[89] These unique letters suggest the distinct elements. With each mother letter, God formed one of the three elements that compose all matter.[90]

Each of the seven *double* letters (בגדכפרת) represents two sounds. The letter's position within a word determines its sound.[91] These changeable letters suggest the mobility of the planets, or "wandering stars." With each double letter, God formed one of the seven planets of ancient astronomy.

Each of the twelve *single* letters (הוזחטילנסעצק) represents just one sound.[92] These unvarying letters suggest the stability of the fixed stars. With each single letter, God formed one of the twelve constellations in the zodiac.

Thus, the *Sepher Yetzirah* makes the rich symbolism of astrology and alchemy part of qabalistic symbolism. From a magical viewpoint, these yetziratic correspondences integrate Qabalah into the Western esoteric tradition.

The Golden Dawn adopted the letters' traditional correspondences to elements, planets, and zodiacal signs. It also correlated the twenty-two letters with the twenty-two major arcana of the tarot.[93] These essential correspondences are the basis of ceremonial magic.

For example, a magician desiring a more balanced life would employ the letter ל. *Lamed* corresponds to Libra in the zodiac and Justice in the tarot. An airy sign ruled by Venus, Libra signifies the due balance of intellect and emotion. Accordingly, ל governs "Works of Justice and Equilibrium."[94]

---

89. א represents a silent glottal stop (the little puff of air preceding the *a* in *apple*); it makes no sound although the mouth is open. מ represents *m*; it makes a sound although the mouth is closed. ש represents two sounds (*sh* and *s*), but the rules governing double letters do not apply. The letters א and מ form the Hebrew word for "mother" (אם).

90. Magical literature usually mentions four elements—earth, water, air, fire—and often adds spirit, the fifth element. But there are only three mother letters, so the *Sepher Yetzirah* mentions only three elements. The Golden Dawn circumvented this difficulty by assigning secondary correspondences to two letters. Thus, ת represents the element of earth as well as the planet Saturn, and ש represents spirit as well as fire.

91. Initial letters are always hard sounds: ב is a hard *b* in *binah* (בינה), "understanding." Final letters are always soft sounds: ב is a soft *v* in *kokav* (כוכב), "star." Either sound can occur in the middle of words. Thus, ב is a hard *b* in *qabalah* (קבלה), "tradition," but a soft *v* in *gevurah* (גבורה), "strength." Although the fourth-century *Yetzirah* designated ר a double letter, ר represents only one sound today. Aryeh Kaplan discusses this puzzle in his *Sefer Yetzirah*, 160–161.

92. In fact, the consonants ו and י sometimes represent vowel sounds.

93. Many manuscripts of the *Sepher Yetzirah* exist, with many variations. They commonly disagree about which planets correspond to which double letters. The Golden Dawn therefore created its own arrangement, assigning planets based on their astrological sympathy with the associated tarot cards. So Venus goes with the Empress (ד), while Mercury goes with the Magician (ב). Again, a full account of the tarot exceeds the scope of this chapter.

94. Crowley, "777," 12, column XLV, in *777 and Other Qabalistic Writings*.

· · · · · · · ·

Figure 17. A Talisman Incorporating Correspondences of the Letter Lamed,
Employing Notariqon, Gematria, and Temurah

A magician could invoke balance with a talisman incorporating symbols that correspond to ל. The following example is one of many possible designs (figure 17). The background is the emerald green of Libra.[95] The design features a pair of scales in equipoise atop the sword of Justice. The sword alludes to the tarot image and to Libra's ruling element, air. Above the scales is the name *Hagiel* (הגיאל), the intelligence of Libra's ruling planet, Venus. The name appears as an aiq bekar sigil, bilaterally symmetrical to represent balance. *Hagiel* equals 49 (7 × 7), and Libra is the seventh zodiacal sign. *Libra* is the Latin word for a pair of scales. The equivalent Hebrew word, *moznayim* (מאזנים), equals 148, and 148 also equals *Netzach* (נצח), the sephirah of Libra's ruling planet, Venus. Further, 148 is the sum of the divine names associated with the supernal triad: *Eheieh* (אהיה) is Kether, *Yah* (יה) is Chokmah, and *Tetragrammaton Elohim* (יהוה אלהים) is Binah. These three sephiroth exist in eternal equilibrium. Their positions on the Tree of Life vaguely suggest a pair of scales. So these divine names, abbreviated as אייא, empower the talisman. א appears on the right, balanced by יא on the left. The palindrome אייא equals 22. Of the traditional thirty-two paths of wisdom, the

95. For colors and other correspondences, see Book Eleven: Magician's Tables.

· · · · · · · ·

twenty-second path is ל. This example illustrates how easily the use of magical correspondences can mesh with practical Qabalah.

After *designing* this talisman, the magician would *construct* it under favorable astrological conditions.[96] The magician would also *consecrate* the talisman in a ceremony of carefully balanced actions. The altar cloth would be emerald green. The incense would be galbanum. The magician would recite inspiring words about balance and conjure Hagiel to indwell the talisman.[97]

Learning the Language of Magical Correspondences

Once the sephiroth and the letters are familiar, students should become conversant with the principal correspondences. The elaborate symbolism of Hermetic Qabalah resembles a second language. Students become fluent by using it frequently. Immersion accelerates the process. Learning this language—like learning other aspects of Qabalah—mostly requires patience and persistence.

An easy way to learn correspondences is to use them playfully in everyday life. The Tree of Life functions as a filing cabinet for the universe. With a little ingenuity, everything will fit somewhere. For example, students may classify cars astrologically or assign cats to the sephiroth.

This lighthearted way of assimilating qabalistic symbolism makes an entertaining game for groups of students. Qabalistic theme parties are helpful too. For example, everyone could bring food or music representing Chesed. Group activities are always instructive because no two people see symbols quite the same.

Tarot decks incorporating Golden Dawn symbolism can serve as helpful qabalistic flashcards.[98] Ordinary card games, slightly modified, become surprisingly effective tools for learning tarot correspondences.[99]

An excellent method of study is physically interacting with tangible qabalistic symbols. For example, memorizing that oak represents Geburah is good, but searching the woods for five perfect oak leaves makes an enduring memory. Contemplating symbolic objects by arranging them on altars is an absorbing, tactile sort of meditation.[100]

---

96. For astrological considerations in ceremonial magic, see Book Three: Planetary Magick.

97. The initial desire, design, construction, and consecration of the talisman follow the pattern of manifestation through the four worlds.

98. Of course, students can make their own flashcards of correspondences, qabalistic terminology, and so forth.

99. For example, the simple game of Crazy Eights works well with a 78-card deck. Cards can match by number or suit as usual, but also by element, planet, zodiacal sign, or any other correspondence that the players agree to accept. Wild cards are unnecessary.

100. Anita Kraft's *Qabalah Workbook for Magicians* gives detailed instructions for this method, designed especially for beginning students.

• • • • • • • •

Few people learn best from rote memorization. However, reviewing lists of correspondences at bedtime is often helpful. It is encouraging (and indicates real progress) when qabalistic symbolism begins to appear in dreams.

A System of Symbols

For ceremonial magicians, Qabalah is first and foremost an immense system of symbols. The *Sepher Yetzirah* established the system; medieval Qabalists expanded it. Agrippa tabulated their system of correspondences; the Golden Dawn school embellished Agrippa's work. Hermetic Qabalah encompasses the symbolism of astrology, tarot, and other esoteric traditions. The result is not just a hodgepodge of symbols but an orderly system. This systematic structure is what makes qabalistic symbolism so powerful.

The prosaic rational mind articulates systems; the poetic intuitive mind speaks in symbols. Only in conjunction can these opposite mentalities create—or understand—a *system of symbols*. The qabalistic symbol system unites opposites, resolves dichotomies, and bridges worlds. Qabalah provides a common language between waking life and dream, between mundane and magical realms. Qabalah is not the only such language, but it proffers the largest vocabulary of any.

In other words, qabalistic symbolism is excellent for interpreting dreams and oracles. Qabalistic symbolism is equally useful for devising sigils, talismans, magical formulas, and rituals. For knowing oneself or for communicating one's will to the universe, qabalistic symbolism is unsurpassed.

It is no coincidence that the Lesser Ritual of the Pentagram is purely qabalistic. Students of ceremonial magic begin their practice with this classic, paradigmatic ritual.[101] They visualize the sephiroth, intone divine names while visualizing Hebrew letters, and internalize elemental correspondences. This simple ritual demonstrates the essential unity of qabalistic symbolism and ceremonial magic.

Similarly, it is no coincidence that the discipline of astral travel relies on Qabalah. The Tree of Life serves as a map for the astral traveler. The methods of practical Qabalah function as a traveler's phrasebook for the astral realm. Qabalistic symbolism provides a systematic itinerary of astral exploration and a lexicon for interpreting experiences.

Magical Formulas

Qabalistically speaking, the construction of magical formulas combines correspondences with notariqon. Magicians transmute words (usually divine names) into symbolic structures or patterns of ritual action. This is less abstruse than it sounds.

---

101. The Lesser Ritual of the Pentagram was the first magical ceremony taught to Neophytes of the Golden Dawn. In fact it was the *only* magical ceremony entrusted to initiates of the Outer Order. For the text of the ritual, see Book Eight: The Golden Dawn.

• • • • • • • •

For example, the Tetragrammaton—the preeminent magical formula—is the true name of the Creator. The four letters *yod heh vau heh* therefore symbolize all of creation. Magicians identify the letters with the elements composing the material world—fire, water, air, earth. They assign the letters and elements to the four directions—south, west, east, north. The result is a sort of qabalistic mandala representing the totality of existence. This mandala could be a circle divided into quarters or an altar displaying four symbols.[102] This is the static aspect of a magical formula, functioning as a symbolic structure.

The Tetragrammaton can also function as a pattern of ritual action. In this dynamic aspect, the name of the Creator symbolizes the *process* of creation. The four letters traditionally correspond with the four worlds—Atziluth, Beriah, Yetzirah, Assiah. The letters *yod heh vau heh* likewise correspond with Father, Mother, Son, Daughter. (This universal formula embraces both macrocosmic creation and microcosmic procreation.) The result is a ceremony symbolizing the divine creative work. It could be a fourfold ritual summoning elemental forces or a four-stage invocation.

A previous example illustrates both aspects of the Tetragrammaton formula in use. The talisman for a more balanced life suggests the Tetragrammaton by its cruciform arrangement (figure 17). The four Hebrew letters on the talisman allude to the Tetragrammaton through practical Qabalah.[103] The consecration ritual would occur within a quartered circle, ideally in a square temple. On the altar would be the equal-armed Cross of Equilibrium. The consecration would culminate in a fourfold invocation of the powers of Netzach. The magician would invoke the *deity*, the *archangel*, the *angelic choir*, and finally the *intelligence*.[104] These four stages of invocation represent manifestation through the four worlds.

The formula of Tetragrammaton is by no means the only magical formula. Aleister Crowley devoted several chapters of *Magick in Theory and Practice* to magical formulas. He succinctly declared that "every true name of God gives the formula of the invocation of that God."[105]

Magicians sometimes abbreviate complex sequences of symbols, even entire series of rituals, into magical formulas. For example, the Golden Dawn conferred initiatory rituals corresponding to earth, air, water, fire, and spirit. The familiar archangels Auriel, Raphael, Gabriel, and Michael rule the four elements. Adding Nuriel (the ruler of the fifth element) produces the previously mentioned acronym *argaman* (ארגמן), "purple." This terse invocation of archangels is the for-

---

102. The chariot-throne of Ezekiel's vision could be a structural representation of the Tetragrammaton. The four ingredients of the Temple incense (frankincense, onycha, galbanum, storax) may also betoken the Tetragrammaton. See Exodus 30:34–37.

103. Temurah turns the acronym איא into יאי, a well-known abbreviation from the *Shema* (Deuteronomy 6:4): "The Lᴏʀᴅ our God is one Lᴏʀᴅ."

104. These would be *Tetragrammaton Tzabaoth, Haniel*, the *Elohim*, and finally *Hagiel*. Hagiel's sigil appears on the talisman because the intelligence represents the final materialization of force in Assiah.

105. Crowley, *Magick*, 169. For more on magical formulas, see *Magick*, 148–173.

mula of the Golden Dawn's elemental initiations. A single word encapsulates all five initiatory ceremonies and years of concomitant study.

Further Study

Qabalah does not appeal to everyone. Some readers may find it boring or befuddling. We assure them it is possible to practice ceremonial magic without *mastering* Qabalah. On the other hand, some readers may already feel the fascination of this ancient tradition. We assure them Qabalah can deepen their understanding, empower their magic, and enrich their lives.

Qabalah is a huge field of study, steadily expanding. Students at any level will find an overwhelming wealth of information.

Lon Milo DuQuette's *Chicken Qabalah* offers a painless, entertaining introduction to modern Hermetic Qabalah. Israel Regardie's *Garden of Pomegranates* is more serious in tone. Anita Kraft's *Qabalah Workbook for Magicians* offers a hands-on approach to learning about the sephiroth.

A useful survey of Jewish mysticism is David Ariel's *Kabbalah*. An updated edition of his *Mystic Quest,* it presents scholarly information for general readers.

We suggest that beginning students study several secondary sources before reading actual qabalistic texts. It helps to become familiar with the terminology and symbolism beforehand: medieval Qabalists generally wrote for initiates, not for curious outsiders.

The *Sepher Yetzirah* is available in many English translations, most of them annotated. Aryeh Kaplan's *Sefer Yetzirah* is thorough. Kaplan also translated and annotated *The Bahir*. The *Zohar* is a substantial work. A few excerpts appear in Gershom Scholem's *Zohar: The Book of Splendor*. More excerpts appear in Daniel Matt's *Zohar: The Book of Enlightenment*. Considerably more excerpts appear in Isaiah Tishby's three-volume *Wisdom of the Zohar*.

Students seeking a more nuanced understanding of Qabalah should acquaint themselves with Judaism in general. Helpful topics include the Bible and the Talmud, plus Jewish liturgy, customs, history, and folklore. Even the slightest acquaintance with Hebrew helps in studying Qabalah of any kind. A little Latin helps in studying Hermetic Qabalah.

Over time, the study of Qabalah instills mental habits, subtly shaping the way students think. Thus, Qabalah may have benefits extending beyond the esoteric realm into ordinary life. A few examples come readily to mind: not surprisingly, they fall into a familiar pattern. Students of Qabalah learn to believe in themselves and trust their inspirations (Kether). Thus, they think creatively, disregarding convention (Chokmah) while knowing their personal limitations (Binah). Students work with joy and a certain playfulness (Chesed), balanced by determination and discipline (Geburah), so they learn to see harmonious connections between apparent opposites (Tiphareth). Students of Qabalah cultivate the complementary powers of unrestrained imagination (Netzach) and organized memory (Hod). Combining these powers, they improve their skill in creative visualization (Yesod). Ultimately, they learn to integrate disparate information into a unified body of knowledge (Malkuth). Note that the mental habits on the right-hand pillar pertain to liberty, while those on the left pertain to discipline. The habits on the middle pillar complete the three triads, and Malkuth integrates everything.

A Note of Caution

Anything powerful is dangerous. Intensive study of Qabalah involves real psychological perils. For example, some students become obsessed with gematria, mistaking irrational notions for mathematical certainties. Students can reduce their risk of obsession by maintaining balance and not revering gematria unduly.

Furthermore, some students of Qabalah develop grandiose delusions, mistaking themselves for Chosen Ones. (Self-proclaimed Messiahs are rife throughout qabalistic history; sometimes their followers suffered greatly.) Students can reduce their risk of messianic ideation by staying humble and laughing at themselves.

A good defense against all such dangers is "hearty human companionship,"[106] ideally within an esoteric fraternity. "Initiation is a preservative against the false lights of mysticism."[107] The early Jewish mystics, understanding the dangers of their tradition, forbade solitary study.

Rightly practiced, Qabalah itself can help students avoid its dangers. Qabalah teaches balance, extolling equilibrium as divine perfection. Qabalah also teaches humility, perpetually reminding students of how little they know.

A Final Thought

No one can master all qabalistic lore in one lifetime. Ceremonial magicians cannot rival the *depth* of learning that initiates of Jewish Qabalah attain. Magicians can, however, cultivate a *breadth* of learning that the Orthodox disregard. Renaissance humanism still inspires Hermetic Qabalah; ceremonial magic still seeks harmony, synthesis, and universal truth.

So magicians can apply methods of practical Qabalah to sacred texts in Greek or English. They can use structures of theoretical Qabalah to understand the Sumerian pantheon or Ismaili cosmology. They can examine parallels between Palace texts and Masonic or Mithraic initiations. They can explore similarities between Hasidic prayer and Tantric or Thelemic ritual. They can employ qabalistic symbolism to interpret their dreams or their initiatory experiences. They can adapt Abulafia's teachings to invoke their Holy Guardian Angels or to seek divine union. Ceremonial magicians can do a lot with Qabalah.

---

106. Crowley, "The Dangers of Mysticism," *The Equinox* I:6 (September 1911): 157.
107. Lévi, *Transcendental Magic*, 93.

Bibliography of Works Consulted

Adler, Herbert M., and Arthur Davis, eds. *Synagogue Service: New Year: A New Edition of the Festival Prayers with an English Translation in Prose and Verse*. New York: Hebrew Publishing Company, n.d.

Afterman, Allen. *Kabbalah and Consciousness*. Riverdale-on-Hudson, NY: Sheep Meadow Press, 1992.

Agrippa von Nettesheim, Heinrich Cornelius. *Three Books of Occult Philosophy*. Edited and annotated by Donald Tyson. Translated by James Freake. St. Paul, MN: Llewellyn Publications, 1993.

Ariel, David S. *Kabbalah: The Mystic Quest in Judaism*. Lanham, MD: Rowman and Littlefield, 2006.

———. *The Mystic Quest: An Introduction to Jewish Mysticism*. New York: Schocken, 1992.

Birnbaum, Philip, trans. *Ethics of the Fathers*. New York: Hebrew Publishing Company, 1949.

Blau, Joseph Leon. *The Christian Interpretation of the Cabala in the Renaissance*. New York: Columbia University Press, 1944.

Blumenthal, David R., ed. *Understanding Jewish Mysticism: A Source Reader*. New York: Ktav, 1978.

Budge, E. A. Wallis. *Amulets and Superstitions*. 1930. Reprint, New York: Dover, 1978.

Case, Paul Foster. *The Tarot: A Key to the Wisdom of the Ages*. 1927. Reprint, Richmond, VA: Macoy, 1975.

Colquhoun, Ithell. *Sword of Wisdom: MacGregor Mathers and the Golden Dawn*. New York: G. P. Putnam's Sons, 1975.

Crowley, Aleister. *777 and Other Qabalistic Writings of Aleister Crowley*. Edited and introduced by Israel Regardie. 1973. Reprint, York Beach, ME: Samuel Weiser, 1983.

———. "Liber MCCLXIV: The Greek Qabalah." Edited by Bill Heidrick. *The O.T.O. Newsletter* 2, nos. 7 and 8 (May 1979): 9–43.

———, et al. *The Equinox: The Review of Scientific Illuminism*. Introduced by Israel Regardie, vol. I (1–10) and III (1). York Beach, ME: Samuel Weiser, 1993.

———, with Mary Desti and Leila Waddell. *Magick: Liber ABA, Book Four, Parts I–IV*. 2nd rev. ed. Edited, annotated, and introduced by Hymenaeus Beta. York Beach, ME: Samuel Weiser, 1997.

Dan, Joseph, ed. *The Teachings of Hasidism*. With the assistance of Robert J. Milch. West Orange, NJ: Behrman, 1983.

———, and Ronald C. Kiener, trans. *The Early Kabbalah*. New York: Paulist Press, 1986.

Dresden, Sem. *Humanism in the Renaissance*. Translated by Margaret King. New York: McGraw-Hill, 1968.

· · · · · · ·

DuQuette, Lon Milo. *The Chicken Qabalah of Rabbi Lamed Ben Clifford: A Dilettante's Guide to What You Do and Do Not Need to Know to Become a Qabalist.* York Beach, ME: Weiser Books, 2001.

Farr, Florence. *The Way of Wisdom: An Investigation of the Meanings of the Letters of the Hebrew Alphabet Considered as a Remnant of the Chaldean Wisdom.* Reprint, Edmonds, WA: Sure Fire Press, n.d.

Fine, Lawrence, trans. *Safed Spirituality: Rules of Mystical Piety, the Beginning of Wisdom.* New York: Paulist Press, 1984.

Friedman, Irving, trans. *The Book of Creation.* New York: Samuel Weiser, 1977.

Fuller, J. F. C. *The Secret Wisdom of the Qabalah: A Study in Jewish Mystical Thought.* London: Rider & Co., 1937.

Gaster, Moses, ed. and trans. *The Sword of Moses: An Ancient Book of Magic.* Edmonds, WA: Holmes Publishing Group, 2000.

Godwin, David. *Godwin's Cabalistic Encyclopedia: A Complete Guide to Cabalistic Magick.* 2nd ed. St. Paul, MN: Llewellyn, 1989.

Godwin, Joscelyn. *The Theosophical Enlightenment.* Albany, NY: State University of New York Press, 1994.

Greenberg, Blu. *How to Run a Traditional Jewish Household.* New York: Simon and Schuster, 1983.

Greenberg, Moshe. *Introduction to Hebrew.* Englewood Cliffs, NJ: Prentice-Hall, 1965.

Harrison, R. K. *Biblical Hebrew.* Chicago: NTC, 1993.

Hoffman, Edward, ed. *The Kabbalah Reader: A Sourcebook of Visionary Judaism.* Foreword by Arthur Kurzweil. Boston, MA: Trumpeter, 2010.

Idel, Moshe. *Hasidism: Between Ecstasy and Magic.* Albany, NY: State University of New York Press, 1995.

———. *Kabbalah: New Perspectives.* New Haven, CT: Yale University Press, 1988.

———. *Language, Torah, and Hermeneutics in Abraham Abulafia.* Translated by Menahem Kallus. Albany, NY: State University of New York Press, 1989.

———. *The Mystical Experience in Abraham Abulafia.* Translated by Jonathan Chipman. Albany, NY: State University of New York Press, 1988.

———. *Studies in Ecstatic Kabbalah.* Albany, NY: State University of New York Press, 1988.

Janowitz, Naomi. *The Poetics of Ascent: Theories of Language in a Rabbinic Ascent Text.* Albany, NY: State University of New York Press, 1989.

Kalisch, Isidor, ed. and trans. *Sepher Yezirah: A Book on Creation; Or, The Jewish Metaphysics of Remote Antiquity.* 1877. Reprint, San Jose, CA: Supreme Grand Lodge of AMORC, 1987.

Kaplan, Aryeh, trans. *The Bahir.* 1979. Reprint, York Beach, ME: Samuel Weiser, 1989.

———. *Meditation and Kabbalah.* York Beach, ME: Samuel Weiser, 1982.

———, trans. *Sefer Yetzirah: The Book of Creation.* Rev. ed. York Beach, ME: Weiser, 1997.

Klein, Mina C., and H. Arthur Klein. *Temple Beyond Time: The Story of the Site of Solomon's Temple at Jerusalem.* New York: Van Nostrand Reinhold, 1970.

Knight, Gareth. *Esoteric Training in Everyday Life.* Oceanside, CA: Sun Chalice, 2001.

Kraft, Anita. *The Qabalah Workbook for Magicians: A Guide to the Sephiroth.* Newburyport, MA: Weiser, 2013.

Lévi, Éliphas. *The Book of Splendours: The Inner Mysteries of Qabalism.* York Beach, ME: Samuel Weiser, 1984.

———. *Transcendental Magic: Its Doctrine and Ritual.* Translated by Arthur Edward Waite. 1896. Reprint, York Beach, ME: Samuel Weiser, 1990.

Locks, Gutman G. *The Spice of Torah: Gematria.* Introductory essay, "The Principle of Numerical Interpretation," by Rabbi J. Immanuel Schochet. New York: Judaica Press, 1985.

Mackey, Albert Gallatin. *An Encyclopaedia of Freemasonry and Its Kindred Sciences.* Two volumes. Rev. ed. New York: The Masonic History Company, 1919.

Marcus, Jacob Rader. *The Jew in the Medieval World: A Source Book, 315–1791.* 1938. Reprint, Cincinnati: Hebrew Union College Press, 1990.

Mathers, Samuel Liddell MacGregor, trans. *The Kabbalah Unveiled.* 1887. Reprint, York Beach, ME: Samuel Weiser, 1986.

Matt, Daniel Chanan, trans. *Zohar: The Book of Enlightenment.* Ramsey, NJ: Paulist Press, 1983.

Monod, Paul Kléber. *Solomon's Secret Arts: The Occult in the Age of Enlightenment.* New Haven, CT: Yale University Press, 2013.

Novick, Léah. *On the Wings of Shekhinah: Rediscovering Judaism's Divine Feminine.* Wheaton, IL: Quest Books, 2008.

Patai, Raphael. *The Hebrew Goddess.* 3rd ed. Detroit, MI: Wayne State University Press, 1990.

Pico della Mirandola, Giovanni. "Oration on the Dignity of Man." Translated by Elizabeth Livermore Forbes. In *The Renaissance Philosophy of Man*, edited by Ernst Cassirer, Paul Oskar Kristeller, and John Herman Randall, Jr. 1948. Reprint, Chicago, IL: University of Chicago Press, 1961.

Platt, Rutherford H., Jr., ed. *The Forgotten Books of Eden.* New York: Alpha House, 1927.

· · · · · · ·

Regardie, Israel. *Foundations of Practical Magic: An Introduction to Qabalistic, Magical, and Meditative Techniques.* 1979. Reprint, Wellingborough, UK: Aquarian, 1982.

———. *A Garden of Pomegranates: An Outline of the Qabalah.* 2nd rev. ed. Saint Paul, MN: Llewellyn, 1970.

———. *The Golden Dawn.* Four volumes, 1937–1940. 6th rev. ed. Saint Paul, MN: Llewellyn, 1989.

———. *The One Year Manual: Twelve Steps to Spiritual Enlightenment.* Rev. ed. York Beach, ME: Samuel Weiser, 1981.

———. *The Tree of Life: A Study in Magic.* 1932. Reprint, New York: Samuel Weiser, 1972.

Reuchlin, Johann. *On the Art of the Kabbalah: De Arte Cabalistica.* Translated by Martin and Sarah Goodman. 1983. Reprint, with introduction by Moshe Idel. Lincoln, NE: University of Nebraska Press, 1993.

Scholem, Gershom. *Major Trends in Jewish Mysticism.* 1941. Translated by George Lichtheim. 3rd rev. ed., 1961. Reprint, New York: Schocken, 1988.

———. *On the Kabbalah and Its Symbolism.* Translated by Ralph Manheim. 1960. Reprint, New York: Schocken, 1988.

———. *On the Mystical Shape of the Godhead: Basic Concepts in the Kabbalah.* Translated by Joachim Neugroschel. 1962. Reprint, New York: Schocken, 1991.

———. *Origins of the Kabbalah.* Edited by R. J. Zwi Werblowsky. Translated by Allan Arkush. 1962. Reprint, Princeton, NJ: Princeton University Press, 1990.

———, ed. *Zohar: The Book of Splendor.* Introduction translated by Ralph Marcus. 1949. Reprint, New York: Schocken Books, 1976.

Schrire, Theodore. *Hebrew Magic Amulets: Their Decipherment and Interpretation.* 1966. Reprint, New York: Behrman, 1982.

Sellers, Ovid R., and Edwin E. Voigt. *Biblical Hebrew for Beginners.* 1941. Reprint, Naperville, IL: Alec R. Allenson, 1974.

Seltzer, Robert M. *Jewish People, Jewish Thought: The Jewish Experience in History.* New York: Macmillan, 1980.

Shumaker, Wayne. *The Occult Sciences in the Renaissance: A Study in Intellectual Patterns.* 1972. Reprint, Berkeley, CA: University of California Press, 1979.

Shurpin, Yehuda. "Why Do We Dip the Challah Bread in Salt?" Chabad.org. https://www.chabad .org/library/article_cdo/aid/484194/jewish/Why-Do-We-Dip-the-Challah-Bread-in-Salt.htm. Accessed September 3, 2019.

Silverberg, David. "Maimonides and the Protective Function of the *Mezuza.*" The Maimonides Heritage Center. https://mhcny.org/parasha/1046.pdf. Accessed September 3, 2019.

• • • • • • •

Stirling, William. *The Canon: An Exposition of the Pagan Mystery Perpetuated in the Cabala as the Rule of All the Arts.* 1897. Reprint, London: Research Into Lost Knowledge Organisation, 1981.

Tishby, Isaiah, and Fischel Lachower, eds. and trans. *The Wisdom of the Zohar: An Anthology of Texts.* 1949. Translated by David Goldstein, 1989. Reprint, London: Littman Library of Jewish Civilization, 1994.

Verman, Mark. *The Books of Contemplation: Medieval Jewish Mystical Sources.* Albany, NY: State University of New York Press, 1992.

Waite, A. E. *The Holy Kabbalah: A Study of the Secret Tradition in Israel as Unfolded by Sons of the Doctrine for the Benefit and Consolation of the Elect Dispersed through the Lands and Ages of the Greater Exile.* 1929. Reprint, New Hyde Park, NY: University Books, 1969.

Walker, D. P. *Spiritual and Demonic Magic from Ficino to Campanella.* 1958. Reprint, University Park, PA: Pennsylvania State University Press, 2000.

Westcott, William Wynn. *An Introduction to the Study of the Kabalah.* Circa 1908. Reprint, Kila, MT: Kessinger, n.d.

———, trans. *Sepher Yetzirah, or Book of Formation.* Rev. ed. 1893. Reprint, San Diego, CA: Wizards Bookshelf, 1990.

——— [Gustav Mommsen, pseud.]. "A Society of Kabbalists." *Notes and Queries* 6 (December 8, 1888): 449.

———. "A Society of Kabbalists." *Notes and Queries* 7 (February 9, 1889): 116–117.

Zalewski, Pat. *Kabbalah of the Golden Dawn.* 1993. Reprint, Edison, NJ: Castle, 2000.

About the Authors

Anita Kraft is an accomplished Qabalist and has been a magician for over twenty-five years. She has traveled and lived all over, attending universities in Europe and the US. She has written and lectured on Qabalah and ceremonial magick and is the author of *The Qabalah Workbook for Magicians: A Guide to the Sephiroth.* She currently resides in the Midwest, where she is getting a postgraduate degree in mental health.

Randall Bowyer has been a student of the Western Esoteric Tradition since 1979. He lives in the United States and is moderately reclusive.

Art Credits

Figures 1–16 by the Llewellyn Art Department.

Figure 17 by James Clark.

BOOK THREE

Planetary Magic
by David Rankine

Since the astrologers of the first civilization in ancient Sumer identified the seven classical planets (Sun, Moon, Mercury, Venus, Mars, Jupiter, Saturn), the influence of the wandering stars, or deathless powers, as they were known, has permeated the Western Mystery Tradition for more than 5,000 years. The planets represent the higher powers of the universe, their orbits the cycles of energetic currents that surround us and can be felt at times subtly or more obviously in our lives. Humanity has looked to the heavens for guidance and meaning, interpreting the celestial as divine and recognizing the interplay of heaven and earth—As above, so below.

The presence of the planetary energies is always all around us though, found in the days of the week in various languages, the sevenfold symbolism appearing repeatedly from rainbow to heptatonic scales in music. Across ancient cultures, the deities of the planets shared qualities that emphasized the qualities of the planetary energies and have become the accepted perceptions across cultures, such as Venus with love, Mercury with communication, the Sun with wealth, etc. These qualities form the symbol sets of colours, scents, crystals, planets, animals, etc., for each planet.

The deities associated with the planets have been perceived in basically the same way for more than two millennia, resulting in a tremendous buildup of power in their images and symbols as connecting gateways to them. They take their names from the Roman gods: Sol, Mercury, Venus, Luna, Mars, Jupiter, and Saturn. Most of these planetary gods were part of an extended family within the Roman pantheon, which also includes the gods of the trans-Saturnian planets (named in recent centuries after those gods by astronomers for consistency).

The family tree shows:

• Uranus is the father of Saturn and Venus

• Saturn is the father of Jupiter, Neptune, and Pluto

• Jupiter is the father of Mercury and Mars

The two luminaries of the Sun and Moon, or Sol and Luna, were brother and sister, and come from an earlier line, derived from the Greek Titans Hyperion and Theia, as opposed to the Olympians attributed to the other planets. This separation of the seven into five "real" planets and two luminaries (Sun and Moon) occurs frequently in planetary attributions. The Romans equated their own deities to those of the earlier Greeks, and in so doing they absorbed many of the qualities and myths of the Greek deities into their own. As a result, it would be more accurate to say that the planetary gods in the Western Mystery Tradition are Romano-Greek in nature.

The attribution of deities to the seven classical planets began with the Sumerians (who, through cultural shifts and conflicts, became the Babylonians), which may have provided the inspiration for the Greeks. When the Greeks conquered the ancient Babylonians, they named the planets after the deities in their own pantheon with corresponding qualities. This sequence of attributions is shown in table 1.

Planet	Babylonian	Greek	Roman	Common Qualities
Sun	Shamash	Helios	Sol	Solar gods
Mercury	Nebu	Hermes	Mercury	Messengers of the gods
Venus	Ishtar	Aphrodite	Venus	Goddesses of love
Moon	Sin	Selene	Luna	Lunar deities
Mars	Nergal	Ares	Mars	War gods
Jupiter	Marduk	Zeus	Jupiter	Father gods, bringers of order
Saturn	Ninib	Kronos	Saturn	Planters of seeds

Table 1. The Pantheons and Their Planetary Attributions

"We are also to show forth, what Divine, gifts, powers & Virtues, man receiveth from the celestial bodies (that is) the seven planets; called by the Astrologers the seven erratic or wandering Stars." [1]

Working with planetary deities is beneficial through receiving energy from the deity to assist your work or striving toward a greater purity and power expressed by the deity (theurgy). Both these approaches, like the gods, are not new, and are seen in ancient Greek writings, with requests for divine aid permeating practical magical work such as the *Greek Magical Papyri* (fourth century

---

1. *Janua Magica Reserata*, 1641, reproduced in Skinner and Rankine, *The Keys to the Gateway of Magic*, 91.

BCE—fifth century CE). It is also seen in more devotional writings like the *Orphic Hymns* (third century CE), where offerings were made to the deity being praised with hymns to encourage a gift of divine energy.

Theurgic practice was the core of Neoplatonism and was written about at length by philosophers such as Plotinus (205–270 CE), Iamblichus (c. 245–325 CE), Proclus (412–485 CE), and pseudo-Dionysius the Areopagite (sixth century CE). Pseudo-Dionysius is of particular significance, as he marks a conflation of Neoplatonism with Christianity. This theme is also seen in the development of some grimoires where the influence of the planetary gods is visible, like the fifteenth-century Greek *Hygromanteia*, which is the precursor to the *Key of Solomon*. This theme of Christian Neoplatonic style was revived by Marsilio Ficino (1433–1499 CE) in the Renaissance, with his translation of the works of the aforementioned philosophers as well as the significant *Corpus Hermeticum*, which contributed to the development of the Hermetic tradition.

Planetary Symbols

The alchemical and hermetic writings of the Middle Ages and Renaissance contained numerous symbols for the classical planets, with the symbols that have become standardised first reproduced in 1482 CE in *Poeticon Astronomicon*, the Italian publication of Hyginus. The planetary symbols are all made from combinations of three constituent parts: the circle, the crescent, and the equal-armed cross.

Sun

The symbol of the Sun is a circle with a dot in the centre. The circle represents the life-giving energies of the infinite, the cycle of life, death, and rebirth. The central dot emphasises the primal nature of these energies, and the vital nature of the sun for life on Earth. The absence of anything connected to the circle indicates the way the solar energy emanates universally, sometimes shown by rays coming off the circle in all directions.

Mercury

The symbol of Mercury is a circle atop an equal-armed cross, with a crescent horns-up intersecting the top of the circle. Here the life essence of the circle is conjoined with the crescent of time, dominating the cross of matter. The union of time and life emphasises the quicksilver nature of Mercury, speeding over the elemental cross. As the crescent only slightly touches the circle, it can be seen that Mercury's influence is one of subtlety rather than direct action.

Venus

The symbol of Venus depicts a circle atop an equal-armed cross. The life-giving energies of the circle dominate the cross of matter. This form shows the power of Venus as the force of generation and attraction, with the essence of life dominating the physical world.

Moon

The symbol of the Moon is a crescent usually facing to the left, or occasionally to the right. The cyclic nature of the Moon is entirely indicated by its symbol of the crescent, which changes form through every part of the lunar cycle.

Mars

The symbol of Mars is a circle with an arrow (originally an equal-armed cross) connected to it at the northeast point of the circle. It emphasises the energy and vitality of Mars, with the life-giving circle expressing its energy through action, indicated by the arrow being at a diagonal and to the upper right (corresponding to the right arm and hand, the dominant active force in most people).

Jupiter

The symbol of Jupiter is an equal-armed cross with a left-facing crescent joined to the left-hand arm of the cross. The emphasis is on expansion rather than contraction, with the crescent facing outward, expressing the balance of form outward in time producing change, rather than limiting it inward to a static state.

Saturn

The symbol of Saturn is an equal-armed cross with a left-facing crescent attached to the bottom of the cross by its upper tip. This symbolically expresses the qualities of Saturn, with the equal-armed cross of matter and form dominating the crescent, which represents time in the context of the lunar cycle of ebb and flow. The Saturn symbol is thus one of solidity and its restriction.

In the ancient world, rulership of different parts of the body was attributed to the planets. This was known as *melothesic (zodiacal) man*, and it was believed that by working with the appropriate planets, healing could be performed on the body (table 2). These attributions developed into the astrological rulership of the body by the twelve astrological signs (which are of course ruled by the planets). The planets were also attributed to human life, being known as the Seven Ages of Man. Shakespeare referred to this in his famous quote in *As You Like It* (act 2, scene 7), which begins, "All the world's a stage, and all the men and women merely players."

Planet	Melothesic Man	Planetary Age	Virtue
Moon	Sense of taste, left-hand side, belly, stomach, womb	First Age of Man—birth to 4 years old	Growth
Mercury	Speech and thought, bile, buttocks, tongue	Second Age of Man—5 to 14 years	Education
Venus	Sense of smell, liver, flesh	Third Age of Man—15 to 22 years	Emotion
Sun	Sense of sight, right-hand side, brain, heart, sinews	Fourth Age of Man—23 to 41 years	Virility
Mars	Genitals, kidneys, left ear, veins	Fifth Age of Man—42 to 56 years	Ambition
Jupiter	Sense of touch, arteries, lungs, semen	Sixth Age of Man—57 to 68 years	Reflection
Saturn	Bladder, bones, phlegm, right ear, spleen	Seventh Age of Man—69 years to end of life	Resignation

Table 2. The Planets, the Human Body, and the Ages of Man

Planetary Magic and Kabbalah

The Hebrew attributions to the planets date back to the roots of the Jewish Kabbalah (first to second centuries CE). These were subsequently reinforced by the synthesis of kabbalistic material into the grimoires with their largely planetary focus during the Middle Ages and Renaissance, feeding heavily into the Western Mystery Tradition. At first glance the seven classical planets might not seem a good fit onto the ten sephiroth ("emanations") of the Tree of Life, but there is a long tradition and history of planetary associations with the Kabbalah (figure 1).[2]

The planetary influence in Kabbalah can be seen in the two mystical schools that combined in the later practices: *Maaseh Merkavah* (*Workings of the Chariot*), which primarily emphasised the first chapter of the book of Ezekiel, and *Maaseh Bereshith* (*Workings of the Beginning*), which focused around the first chapter of the book of Genesis. The word *merkavah* ("chariot") refers to the vision of Ezekiel's chariot found in the book of Ezekiel in the Bible. The Merkavah mystic, or rider, sought to gain entry to the presence of God on his throne through fasting and repetitious use of hymns and prayers. When the rider was in trance, he would send his spirit up through the Seven Palaces, using a combination of magical amulets and long, memorized incantations to ensure that he passed the guardian angels and demons of the palace gates.

The Merkavah cosmology is specifically planetary, focusing on the sephiroth that correspond to the seven classical planets, from Yesod, the sephira of the Moon, up to Binah, the sephira of Saturn, these being the seven planets he traversed leaving Malkuth (the earthly realm) to ascend

2. The other three sephiroth correspond to the four elements, the zodiac, and the first swirlings of creation.

· · · · · · · ·

to the divine presence. Echoes of the Merkavah tradition can be found in the grimoires, from the use of planetary amulets and long invocations to fasting and prayers for purification.

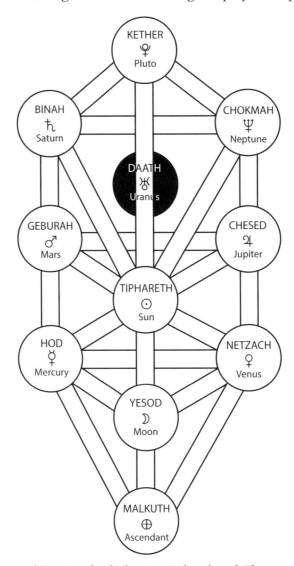

Figure 1. Image of the Tree of Life Showing Sephiroth with Planetary Attributions

In the Maaseh Bereshith school of Kabbalah, the planetary influence is again significant. The earliest and arguably most significant kabbalistic text, the *Sepher Yetzirah (Book of Formation)* was written in the first or second century CE. Chapter 4 of the six within it focuses on the sevenfold associations of the planets and their connections.

Seven doubles: ….

And with them He formed,

. . . .

Seven planets in the Universe,

Seven days in the Year,

Seven gates in the Soul, male and female.[3]

The "seven doubles" refers to the seven double letters of the Hebrew alphabet, so-called as there are two ways of pronouncing each letter depending on their position in a word. The seven double letters correspond to the planetary sephiroth on the Tree of Life, which directly relate to the days of the week, as described in creation (i.e., the book of Genesis). The six planetary sephiroth of Yesod, Hod, Netzach, Tiphareth, Geburah, and Chesed correspond to the days from Sunday to Friday and are known as *Sephiroth ha-Benyin* (the "Sephiroth of Construction"), with the sephira of Binah corresponding to the sabbath, which takes its name from the Hebrew word for Saturn, *Shabbathai*. From this sevenfold symbolism a whole range of other associated qualities are used in Kabbalah, including the concept of the *Cube of Space*, with the six directions and the centre corresponding to the seven planets.

Types of Planetary Magic and Spiritual Creatures

Planetary magic usually falls into three main areas of work: talismanic, theurgic, and spirit work. The creation of amulets (for protective qualities) and talismans (for attractive qualities) occurred with great frequency in the ancient world, and manifested strongly through the Renaissance grimoires, especially the planetary pentacles of the *Key of Solomon*. The planetary energies are seen as being stronger on their day of the week and during the hours of the day that they govern. For this reason, planetary magic is always done on the day of the planet where possible, and definitely during the hours of the planet.

Planetary Hours

Planetary hours can be traced back to ancient Egypt, where the priests attributed a different ruling god to each of the twenty-four hours of the day. The ancient Greeks adopted this idea and adapted it into the system that we are familiar with.

Planetary hours are not the sixty-minute hours that we are accustomed to using in normal timekeeping. The period of daylight that extends from sunrise to sunset is divided into the twelve "hours" of the day. The period of darkness extending from sunset to sunrise of the next day is divided into the twelve "hours" of night. As the duration of daylight and darkness varies, the planetary hours are sometimes called the "unequal hours."

Almanacs, ephemerides, and the internet are all sources you can use to discover the sunrise and sunset times, enabling you to calculate the planetary hours in advance and time your ceremonies appropriately.

---

3. *Sepher Yetzirah* 4:6.

Tables 3 and 4 give attributions for planetary hours of the day and night.

Hour	Sunday	Monday	Tuesday	Wednesday	Thursday	Friday	Saturday
1	Sun	Moon	Mars	Mercury	Jupiter	Venus	Saturn
2	Venus	Saturn	Sun	Moon	Mars	Mercury	Jupiter
3	Mercury	Jupiter	Venus	Saturn	Sun	Moon	Mars
4	Moon	Mars	Mercury	Jupiter	Venus	Saturn	Sun
5	Saturn	Sun	Moon	Mars	Mercury	Jupiter	Venus
6	Jupiter	Venus	Saturn	Sun	Moon	Mars	Mercury
7	Mars	Mercury	Jupiter	Venus	Saturn	Sun	Moon
8	Sun	Moon	Mars	Mercury	Jupiter	Venus	Saturn
9	Venus	Saturn	Sun	Moon	Mars	Mercury	Jupiter
10	Mercury	Jupiter	Venus	Saturn	Sun	Moon	Mars
11	Moon	Mars	Mercury	Jupiter	Venus	Saturn	Sun
12	Saturn	Sun	Moon	Mars	Mercury	Jupiter	Venus

Table 3. Attributions of Planetary Hours of the Day

Hour	Sunday	Monday	Tuesday	Wednesday	Thursday	Friday	Saturday
1	Jupiter	Venus	Saturn	Sun	Moon	Mars	Mercury
2	Mars	Mercury	Jupiter	Venus	Saturn	Sun	Moon
3	Sun	Moon	Mars	Mercury	Jupiter	Venus	Saturn
4	Venus	Saturn	Sun	Moon	Mars	Mercury	Jupiter
5	Mercury	Jupiter	Venus	Saturn	Sun	Moon	Mars
6	Moon	Mars	Mercury	Jupiter	Venus	Saturn	Sun
7	Saturn	Sun	Moon	Mars	Mercury	Jupiter	Venus
8	Jupiter	Venus	Saturn	Sun	Moon	Mars	Mercury
9	Mars	Mercury	Jupiter	Venus	Saturn	Sun	Moon
10	Sun	Moon	Mars	Mercury	Jupiter	Venus	Saturn
11	Venus	Saturn	Sun	Moon	Mars	Mercury	Jupiter
12	Mercury	Jupiter	Venus	Saturn	Sun	Moon	Mars

Table 4. Attributions of Planetary Hours of the Night

> ### *Example Calculation: Mercurial Hours*
> Wednesday is the day of Mercury. The process is then as follows.
>
> Consulting an almanac, you see the sun rises at 7:00 a.m. that day and sets at 8:48 p.m. So the hours of daylight are from 07:00 to 20:48, giving 13 hours and 48 minutes.
>
> 13 × 60 + 48 = 828 minutes of daylight
>
> 848 ÷ 12 = 69
>
> This means each of the 12 daylight "hours" will be 69 minutes long.
>
> Consulting table 3, you see that the first and eighth daylight hours of Wednesday are ruled by Mercury. So for the first hour of the day, the ritual should be performed between 7:00 a.m. and 8:09 a.m. (69 minutes).
>
> For the eighth hour, further calculation is needed:
>
> Add together the "hour" length for 7 "hours" (7 × 69 = 483 minutes, or 8 hours and 3 minutes). Then add this to the sunrise time (7:00 a.m. + 8 hours and 3 minutes = 3:03 p.m.).
>
> This means the eighth hour starts at 3:03 p.m. and finishes at 4:12 p.m. (3:03 + 69 minutes).

The Middle Ages and Renaissance also saw the clear codification of planetary spiritual creatures into hierarchies, with the archangels ruling, each with their order of angels beneath them. Each planet also has a planetary intelligence (or angel), which serves to control the planetary spirit (or demon). Distinct from this hierarchy are the seven Olympic spirits, which differ from most angels and demons in that they are said to be comprised of the four elements rather than the more common, purest form of air (or occasionally fire), which is said to form their bodies.

The planetary archangels can be seen as overseers, directing the energy of the planets. You should call to the archangels to direct a particular planetary energy into your ceremony. In contrast, the angels can be seen as the workforce under the archangels, who enact their will. The planetary intelligences embody the positive qualities of their planets and act as the overseeing focus for the planetary spirits, which are comprised of ungoverned, pure planetary energy without focus. The planetary spirit should always be directed by the appropriate planetary intelligence or archangel. The planetary intelligences and spirits are mainly worked with for making and empowering amulets and talismans.

This is the influence of the seven planets,
are principally drawn from the Superior Angelical powers,
& Celestial intelligent Angels, as aforesaid,
Disposing the soul of man, which is the seat of those Virtues. [4]

4. *Janua Magica Reserata*, 1641, reproduced in Skinner and Rankine, *The Keys to the Gateway of Magic*, 92.

This sequence of overseeing is best illustrated in the *Hygromanteia*, which contains a list of planetary demons for every hour of the day for the whole week, and their corresponding controlling angels. The process of conjuration begins by calling on the planetary god first, then the angel, then the demon, who all have specific functions they are called for.

The nine orders of angels were first listed by pseudo-Dionysus the Areopagite in *The Celestial Hierarchy* around 500 CE, and this has been the accepted hierarchy of the angelic orders ever since (table 5). The planetary intelligences (and spirits) first appear in Agrippa's *Three Books of Occult Philosophy*, published in 1531–1533 CE, though they were drafted around 1508–1509 CE. It is very unlikely that Agrippa would have made them up, and he probably learned about them from his teacher, the Abbot Trithemius. The source of their origin remains a mystery at this point.

Heaven	Divine Name	Planet	Number	Archangel	Order of Angels	Intelligences	Spirit
Superior Hierarchy							
			1	Metatron	Seraphim		
			2	Raziel	Cherubim		
7	Yahveh Elohim	Saturn	3	Tzaphkiel	Thrones	Agiel	Zazel
Middle Hierarchy							
6	El	Jupiter	4	Tzadkiel	Dominations	Jophiel	Hismael
5	Elohim Gibor	Mars	5	Khamael	Powers	Graphiel	Bartzabel
4	Eloa va-daath	Sun	6	Michael	Virtues	Nakhiel	Sorath
Inferior Hierarchy							
3	Jahveh Sabaoth	Venus	7	Uriel	Principalities	Hagiel	Kedemel
2	Elohim Sabaoth	Mercury	8	Raphael	Archangels	Tiriel	Taphthartharath
1	Shaddai El Chi	Moon	9	Gabriel	Angels	Malka[5]	Schad

Table 5. Planetary Hierarchy

In contrast to both talismanic and spirit work, which are external, the theurgic practice of planetary magic is more internal. Theurgy seeks to refine the spiritual nature of the magician in a quest for the qualities of perfection embodied by the planetary gods. As alchemy has the six inner white and six outer red steps (the zodiacal twelve, ruled by the planets), so too does planetary magic encourage inner transformation and outer manifestation through these areas of practice. Devotional practices, including meditation, contemplation, and the use of hymns (prose that praises the divine), are all theurgic practices.

---

5. *Malka* is commonly used as shorthand for Malkah be-Tharshisim ve-ad Be-Ruachoth Shechalim.

Use of the Kameas

The names of the planetary spiritual creatures are converted into sigils on planetary magic number squares known as *kameas*. Sigils may be a pictorial depiction of a name (as here) or of an intent (discussed below). The kameas have a number of rows and columns equal to the planetary number (so 3 × 3 for Saturn, 4 × 4 for Jupiter, etc.), and every row, column, and diagonal add up to the same number. As the names of all these spiritual creatures are Hebrew, and every letter of the Hebrew alphabet has a numerical value, the name of the spiritual creature can be converted to a series of numbers and mapped onto the appropriate kamea, creating its sigil. The possible problem of letters with numerical equivalents higher than the numerical range contained within the kamea is solved by a process of numerical reduction called *Aiq Beker*, or the Qabalah of Nine Chambers (table 6). The name *Aiq Beker* comes from the attribution of the letters to the first two chambers, hence AIQ (Aleph, Yod, Qoph) BKR (Beth, Kaph, Resh).

1	2	3
Aleph (A: 1)	Beth (B: 2)	Gimel (G: 3)
Yod (I, Y: 10)	Kaph (K: 20)	Lamed (L: 30)
Qoph (Q: 100)	Resh (R: 200)	Shin (Sh: 300)
4	5	6
Daleth (D: 4)	Heh (H, E: 5)	Vav (V, O, U: 6)
Mem (M: 40)	Nun (N: 50)	Samekh (S: 60)
Tav (Th: 400)	Final Kaph (K: 500)	Final Mem (M: 600)
7	8	9
Zain (Z: 7)	Cheth (Ch: 8)	Teth (T: 9)
Ayin (Aa, O, Ngh: 70)	Peh (P, Ph: 80)	Tzaddi (Tz: 90)
Final Nun (N: 700)	Final Peh (P, Ph: 800)	Final Tzaddi (Tz: 900)

Table 6. Aiq Beker

If the letter has a higher number than found in the kamea, the number is dropped to the highest number available in the appropriate square of the Aiq Beker table (e.g., 200 down to 20). The guidelines for drawing sigils in this manner are:

- Work out the numerical sequence for the Hebrew letters of the name.
- A circle is usually drawn in the square where the sigil begins and ends. A bar can also be drawn across the starting line in place of a circle to mark the beginning or end of the name.
- When a name starts and ends in the same square, the sigil can be "closed" by joining the end of the final line to the beginning of the first line.

• • • • • • • •

- If a name begins with two letters with the same numerical value, a bifurcation like a curvy *m* may be used, with the line to the next square drawn from the centre of the bifurcation.

- When two consecutive letters within a name have the same numerical value, a small loop is drawn resembling a curvy *u*, with additional *u*'s for each additional consecutive repetition of the same numerical value.

Example of Sigil Construction

Following the guidelines described, here is the process for the Saturnian planetary intelligence Agiel. The name *Agiel* is written in Hebrew as *AGIAL*, which converts to the numerical sequence of 1 (A), 3 (G), 10 (I), 1 (A), 30 (L). The Saturn kamea contains the numerical range 1–9, so by Aiq Beker the 10 is reduced to 1 and the 30 is reduced to 3. The sequence of numbers for drawing the sigil then becomes 1, 3, 1, 1, 3.

4	9	2
3	5	7
8	1	6

The first number is 1 (for A), so a circle is drawn in the centre of the square corresponding to 1 (figure 2). The second number is 3 (for G), so a line is drawn from the circle to the square corresponding to 3. The third number is a 1 (for I, reduced from 10), so a *u* is drawn and a line drawn to the square for the number 1. The next letter in the name is A, also with a numeration of 1, so a double *u* is drawn to show that there are two consecutive letters attributed to this number. Finally the line is drawn to the square with 3 again (for L, reduced from 30 to 3). As this is the last letter of the sigil, the end is marked with a small circle.

The sigils for the Olympic spirits are not drawn using this principle, as they are Greek in origin and their creation was not through this technique, which uses Hebrew.

The technique for creating sigils on kameas can also be used to create a sigil of your intent to use on an amulet or talisman. You can apply exactly the same techniques but use English (or another language that is your primary one) for the word or word sequence. It is best to keep the intent concise and precise or the sigil may become complicated. The benefits of using this English alphabet form of kamea sigilisation is its simplicity, with the numbers always in the 1–9 range (table 5).

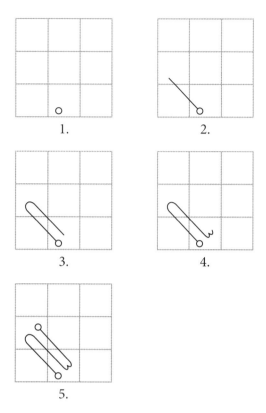

Figure 2. *Example of Sigil Construction*

1 A, J, S	2 B, K, T	3 C, L, U
4 D, M, V	5 E, N, W	6 F, O, X
7 G, P, Y	8 H, Q, Z	9 I, R

Table 7. *English-Language Table for Sigil Making*

So if you were to make a sigil for the intent "I will pass my exam," it would be formed using this sequence:

I	W	I	L	L	P	A	S	S	M	Y	E	X	A	M
1	5	1	3	3	7	1	1	1	4	7	5	6	1	4

Looking at the table of types of planetary magic (listed in the "Planetary Amulets and Talismans" section later in this book), you would choose the Mercurial kamea, which is 8 × 8. Note that with the two 3s and three 1s together, there will be a double and a triple loop in the sigil.

• • • • • • • •

The Planetary Kameas

Although the use of the kameas for creating sigils was first mentioned in Agrippa's work, the kameas themselves were used prior to this. A manuscript called *The Book of Angels, Rings, Characters, and Images of the Planets: Attributed to Osbern Bokenham* (1441–1445) on planetary magic makes specific reference to the use of the kameas inscribed on thin metal sheets in talismanic magic. So even when uninscribed, the basic kameas can be used to contribute to a planetary matrix as a base image added to the shrine or altar.

Kamea of Saturn

"From Saturn man receiveth a sublime contemplation, profound understanding, solidity of Judgement, firm speculation, stability and an immovable Resolution."[6]

4	9	2
3	5	7
8	1	6

Table 8. Kamea of Saturn:
Number of squares = 9; row/column total = 15; square total = 45

Kamea of Jupiter

"From Jupiter an unshaken prudence, temperance, benignity, piety, Modesty, justice, faith, Grace, Religion, Equity & Regality, &c."[7]

4	14	15	1
9	7	6	12
5	11	10	8
16	2	3	13

Table 9. Kamea of Jupiter:
Number of squares = 16; row/column total = 34; square total = 136

Kamea of Mars

"From Mars, constant Courage & fortitude, not to be terrified, truth, a fervent Desire of animosity, the power & practice of Acting, and an Inconvertible Vehemency of the mind."[8]

6. *Janua Magica Reserata*, 1641, reproduced in Skinner and Rankine, *The Keys to the Gateway of Magic*, 91.

7. *Janua Magica Reserata*, 1641, reproduced in Skinner and Rankine, *The Keys to the Gateway of Magic*, 91.

8. *Janua Magica Reserata*, 1641, reproduced in Skinner and Rankine, *The Keys to the Gateway of Magic*, 91.

· · · · · · · · ·

11	24	7	20	3
4	12	25	8	16
17	5	13	21	9
10	18	1	14	22
23	6	19	2	15

Table 10. Kamea of Mars:
Number of squares = 25; row/column total = 65; square total = 325

Kamea of the Sun

"From the Sun Nobleness of mind perspicuity of Judgement & Imagination, the nature of Knowledge & opinion, Maturity, Counsel, Zeal, Light of Justice, Reason & judgement to Distinguish Right from wrong purging Light from the Darkness of Ignorance, the Glory of truth found out, & Charity the mother & Queen of all Virtues."[9]

6	32	3	34	35	1
7	11	27	28	8	30
19	14	16	15	23	24
18	20	22	21	17	13
25	29	10	9	26	12
36	5	33	4	2	31

Table 11. Kamea of the Sun:
Number of squares = 36; row/column total = 111; square total = 666

Kamea of Venus

"From Venus a fervent Love, most sweet hope, the Motion of Desire, order, Concupiscence, Beauty, Sweetness, Desire of Increasing & propagation of itself."[10]

22	47	16	41	10	35	4
5	23	48	17	42	11	29
30	6	24	49	18	36	12
13	31	7	25	43	19	37
38	14	32	1	26	44	20
21	39	8	33	2	27	45
46	15	40	9	34	3	28

Table 12. Kamea of Venus:
Number of squares = 49; row/column total = 175; square total = 1,225

9. *Janua Magica Reserata*, 1641, reproduced in Skinner and Rankine, *The Keys to the Gateway of Magic*, 91.
10. *Janua Magica Reserata*, 1641, reproduced in Skinner and Rankine, *The Keys to the Gateway of Magic*, 91.

• • • • • • • •

Kamea of Mercury

"From Mercury A piercing faith & belief, Clear reasoning, the Vigour of Interpreting & pronouncing, Gravity of speech, Acuteness of will, Discourse of Reason, & the swift motion of the Senses."[11]

8	58	59	5	4	62	63	1
49	15	14	52	53	11	10	56
41	23	22	44	48	19	18	45
32	34	35	29	25	38	39	28
40	26	27	37	36	30	31	33
17	47	46	20	21	43	42	24
9	55	54	12	13	51	50	16
64	2	3	61	60	6	7	57

Table 13. Kamea of Mercury:
Number of squares = 64; row / column total = 260; square total = 2,080

Kamea of the Moon

"From the Moon, a peacemaking Consonancy, fecundity, the power of Generating & growing greater, of Increasing & Decreasing; A Moderate Temperance & faith, which being Conversant in Manifest & occult things, yieldeth Direction to all, also Motion to the tilling of the Earth, for the manner of Life, & giving growth to itself & others."[12]

37	78	29	70	21	62	13	54	5
6	38	79	30	71	22	63	14	46
47	7	39	80	31	72	23	55	15
16	48	8	40	81	32	64	24	56
57	17	49	9	41	73	33	65	25
26	58	18	50	1	42	74	34	66
67	27	59	10	51	2	43	75	35
36	68	19	60	11	52	3	44	76
77	28	69	20	61	12	53	4	45

Table 14. Kamea of the Moon:
Number of squares = 81; row / column total = 369; square total = 3,321

11. *Janua Magica Reserata*, 1641, reproduced in Skinner and Rankine, *The Keys to the Gateway of Magic*, 91.

12. *Janua Magica Reserata*, 1641, reproduced in Skinner and Rankine, *The Keys to the Gateway of Magic*, 92.

• • • • • • • •

Spiritual Creature Sigils

Note that these sigils are all shown constructed on their appropriate planetary kamea.

The Archangels		
Saturn	Tzaphkiel	 *Figure 3. Tzaphkiel Sigil*
Jupiter	Tzadkiel	 *Figure 4. Tzadkiel Sigil*
Mars	Khamael	 *Figure 5. Khamael Sigil*
Sun	Michael	 *Figure 6. Michael Sigil*

Table 15. The Planetary Archangels and Their Sigils (continued)

· · · · · · · ·

The Archangels		
Venus	Uriel	Figure 7. Uriel Sigil
Mercury	Raphael	Figure 8. Raphael Sigil
Moon	Gabriel	Figure 9. Gabriel Sigil

Table 15. The Planetary Archangels and Their Sigils (continued)

Planetary Archangels

The Saturnian archangel is Tzaphkiel ("Beholder of God"). He is known as the Angel of Paradise because of his role in the Garden of Eden, and in modern times is the patron of all those who fight pollution and love and protect nature. Tzaphkiel is also the patron of artists, bringing illumination and inspiration to those who seek to create beauty in the world.

Tzadkiel ("Righteousness of God") is the Jupiterian archangel of benevolence, memory, and mercy. He is often depicted with a dagger in his hand, representing the power of the intellect. Tzadkiel is a comforter, associated with invocation and prayer. He is the archangel to help overcome despondency and to forgive others for their negative deeds. Tzadkiel can also be appealed to for help with financial matters and for achieving justice in a situation.

Khamael ("He who sees God") is the Martial archangel, a warrior who represents divine justice, is said to grant invisibility, and rules over martial qualities like power and invincibility. Khamael is the ideal angel to call upon to help you take personal responsibility and to develop self-confidence. He will help you deal with the consequences of your actions and to find justice, but only if you stick to the truth.

Michael ("He who is like God") was the first angel created and is often seen as the leader of the angels, or the "first among equals." He is usually shown wielding a sword or lance, and sometimes the scales of justice. Michael is the Solar archangel and helps those who call upon him to achieve goals and destinies. Michael is particularly called on to achieve a legitimate goal or for protection,

Uriel ("Light of God), also known as Auriel or Oriel, is the archangel of Venus and of peace and salvation. He is often depicted with a flame or lamp in his hands. Uriel embodies the power of light as illumination and spiritual passion. Uriel is associated with magical power and the application of force, and can help cause a positive breaking of bonds when needed and overcome inertia. He is also the patron of astrology and has been linked strongly with electricity.

Raphael ("Healer of God") is the Mercurial archangel charged with healing humankind and the earth. Often depicted with a pilgrim's staff, he is the patron of travelers, and he protects those on journeys, especially those involving air travel. Raphael's special charges are the young and innocent. Raphael is the archangel of knowledge and communication and may be called upon to help with any related areas, such as improving your memory, learning languages, exams, dealing with bureaucracy, and business matters.

Gabriel ("The Strength of God") is the angel who usually delivers messages to humanity, embodying the link between humans and the universe and the divine as expressed by the Moon. As the Lunar archangel, Gabriel is the guide to the inner tides of our unconscious. Gabriel can help with developing the imagination and psychic abilities. He is also associated with domestic matters, especially the development of the home, or finding a new home.

The Intelligences		
Saturn	Agiel	*Figure 10. Agiel Sigil*
Jupiter	Jophiel	*Figure 11. Jophiel Sigil*
Mars	Graphiel	*Figure 12. Graphiel Sigil*
Sun	Nakhiel	*Figure 13. Nakhiel Sigil*
Venus	Hagiel	*Figure 14. Hagiel Sigil*
Mercury	Tiriel	*Figure 15. Tiriel Sigil*

Table 16. The Planetary Intelligences and Their Sigils (continued)

• • • • • • • •

The Intelligences		
Moon	Malka be-Tarshishim ve-ad be-Ruah Sheharim[13]	Figure 16. Malka Sigil

Table 16. The Planetary Intelligences and Their Sigils (continued)

The Spirits		
Saturn	Zazel	Figure 17. Zazel Sigil
Jupiter	Hismael	Figure 18. Hismael Sigil
Mars	Bartzabel	Figure 19. Bartzabel Sigil
Sun	Sorath	Figure 20. Sorath Sigil

Table 17. The Planetary Spirits and Their Sigils (continued)

13. Malka is named as the intelligence of intelligences—no standard intelligence is given by Agrippa.

· · · · · · · ·

The Spirits		
Venus	Kedemel	*Figure 21. Kedemel Sigil*
Mercury	Taphthartharath	*Figure 22. Taphthartharath Sigil*
Moon	Chasmodai	*Figure 23. Chasmodai Sigil*
Moon	Schad Barshrhmoth ha-Shartathan (spirit of spirits)	*Figure 24. Schad Sigil*

Table 17. The Planetary Spirits and Their Sigils (continued)

Planetary Amulets and Talismans

Practical work with the planets may positively increase something in your life associated with the planet, or alternatively remove or transform something negative. Whichever of these it may be, you are acting to improve yourself and your situation, to more effectively follow your path and achieve your goals. The process of attraction, repulsion, or transformation will determine the best way to achieve your goal, such as using an amulet or talisman.

An amulet is a protective charm and works through repulsion to protect the bearer from specific forces or events. A talisman is a charm of attraction used to attract specific energies to enhance a specific aspect of the bearer's situation. For example, you might make a lunar amulet for protection if you were going on a cruise, or a talisman if you were working on developing your psychic abilities.

Amulets and talismans may be carried on you to receive the benefits on an ongoing basis (particularly for amulets) or may be placed in a suitable safe place. So a Mercurial amulet to protect your car would stay in the car, whereas a Mercurial talisman for better communication might be located near your telephone or computer.

Planet	Type of Magick
Sun	Career success and progression, establishing harmony, healing and improving health, leadership skills, acquiring money and resources, promotion, strengthening willpower
Mercury	Business success, improving communication skills, developing knowledge and memory, diplomacy, exam success, divination, developing influence, protection when traveling by air and land, learning music
Venus	Increasing attractiveness and self-confidence, beauty and passion, enhancing creativity, improving fertility, developing friendships, obtaining love
Moon	Developing clairvoyance and other psychic skills, ensuring safe childbirth, divination, glamour and illusions, lucid dreaming, protection when traveling by sea
Mars	Controlling anger, increasing courage, enhancing energy and passion, increasing vigour and sex drive
Jupiter	Career success, developing ambition and enthusiasm, improving fortune and luck, general health, acquiring honour, improving sense of humour, legal matters and dealing with the establishment, developing leadership skills
Saturn	Performing duty, establishing balance and equilibrium, dispelling illusions, protecting the home, legal matters, developing patience and self-discipline

Table 18. The Planets and Their Associated Types of Magick

The process of talismanic magic may be summed up in four stages: preparation, creation, purification and consecration. This process is equally valid for both amulets and talismans.

Preparation involves determining the intent and the components to be used in the talisman, i.e., the material you will make the talisman out of and the words and sigils used. Once you have decided on your talisman base (card, metal disc, crystal), you need to acquire it. Preparation also involves calculating the appropriate planetary hours during which you will perform the creation, purification, and consecration. You may also choose to include meditation on the planet if you feel you need to develop your understanding of the energies of the planet.

Creation is the construction of the talisman. Draw, etch, or engrave the sigils onto your talisman, indicating your intent and the names of the spiritual creatures or forces you will draw upon to empower your talisman. Appropriately coloured card is easiest. Metal discs can be expensive and difficult to source, though they are more durable, as are crystal discs. (Those listed in table 19 are easier to obtain in a disc form.)

• • • • • • • •

Planet	No.	Metal	Colour	Crystal
Saturn	3	Lead	Black	Obsidian
Jupiter	4	Tin	Blue	Lapis lazuli
Mars	5	Brass[14]	Red	Bloodstone
Sun	6	Gold	Gold/yellow	Amber
Venus	7	Copper	Green	Malachite
Mercury	8	Aluminium[15]	Orange	Agate
Moon	9	Silver	Silver/purple	Selenite

Table 19. The Planets and Their Metals, Colours, and Crystals

"The Talismans, Pentacles, Mystical Images, Sigils, Characters and other suchlike Talismans, which are the main tools for working with Occult Science, can be created with different materials. You can make them on virgin parchment, on metal plates, on magnetic stones, on jasper, agate and on other precious stones." [16]

In the grimoires, the amulets and talismans were usually made on circular disks of metal. However, when using card, it works well to use a number of sides equal to the planetary number (e.g., triangle for Saturn, square for Jupiter, etc). If you choose to use white card, the ink colour for all the appropriate seals or sigils you decide on should be of the relevant planetary colour.

Hence a Jupiterian talisman would be on a square piece of blue card. Glyphs usually included on talismans are the astrological sigil of the planet, the divine name, the name and/or sigil of the archangel, the name and/or sigil of the planetary spirit and intelligence, and any other appropriate symbols desired.

Purification is the precursor to the final step of consecration. Purification makes sure there are no unwanted influences attached to your talisman, effectively making it completely neutral and ready to act as a receptacle and lens for the forces you attract through its action. Purification can also include ritual bathing in a bath fragranced with the appropriate planetary essential oil so that you too are pure.

Consecration is the activation of the talisman as a focus for the desired planetary energy. Hymns may be included in the consecration ceremony to request assistance, to enhance the effectiveness of both amulets and talismans.

---

14. Brass is used for the creation of charms instead of the planetary metal for Mars, which is iron due to the belief that spiritual beings dislike iron.

15. As mercury is a liquid at room temperature and is extremely toxic, it is for obvious reasons unsuitable for creating charms. Aluminium is a light metal used in the construction of aircraft, and hence movement between realms (air and earth) makes it a suitable metal for use.

16. *Key of Solomon*, 1796, reproduced in Skinner and Rankine, *The Veritable Key of Solomon*, 81.

• • • • • • • •

Ceremony for Talismanic Preparation

Place the following items on the altar:

- The talisman
- An appropriately coloured piece of natural material big enough to wrap the talisman in
- Bowl of spring water
- Bowl of sea salt
- Censer of incense
- Red candle

Place your talisman on the piece of coloured fabric on the altar.

Perform your preferred space clearing/banishing ritual.

Purify your talisman to remove all influences—pass it through the incense smoke, saying:

I purify you with the element of air.

Now pass the talisman (carefully and quickly) through the candle flame, saying:

I purify you with the element of fire.

Sprinkle the talisman with a drop of water from the bowl and say:

I purify you with the element of water.

Sprinkle a few grains of salt over the talisman and say:

I purify you with the element of earth.

The talisman is purified and ready to be consecrated.

State the intent of the talisman in a single concise sentence (prepared beforehand). As you do so, draw the sigil of the planet in the air over the talisman, visualising it in its planetary colour. See the sigil shining with an inner brilliance, then visualise a taut line of force in the planetary colour from your dominant hand to the sigil. Lower your hand so the sigil descends with it, into the talisman.

Intone in sequence the hierarchy of planetary spiritual creatures for the planet, a number of times equal to the planetary number. Start with the divine name, then the archangel, then the order of angels, the name of the heaven (i.e., the planet), the planetary intelligence, and finally the planetary spirit.

· · · · · · · ·

Now raise your arms upward so they make a *V*, and declare:

I will take of the divine spirit [divine name], *emanating from the heavens,*
Focused through the archangel [name], *who directs the* [order of angels],
Manifesting through the power of the heaven of [planet], *expressed through*
[planetary intelligence] *and* [planetary spirit].
I have created this talisman for my glory.
I have formed it and I have made it.

As you make this declaration, feel the planetary force descending from the heavens and collecting in your hands. See the energy there as a glow of the planetary colour surrounding your hands. Bring your hands down simultaneously and place them on the talisman, saying:

I join this talisman to my life, that the (repeat intent).
As above, so below.
This is my will, it is so.

Wrap the talisman in the fabric and put it in a safe place.

Here is an example sequence of the calling of the hierarchy of spiritual creatures for a talisman of Mars:

Elohim Gibor, Khamael, Seraphim, Mars, Graphiel, Bartzabel (× 5)

Now raise your arms upward so they make a *V*, and declare:

I will take of the divine spirit Elohim Gibor, emanating from the heavens,
Focused through the archangel Khamael, who directs the Seraphim,
Manifesting through the power of the heaven of Mars, expressed through
Graphiel and Bartzabel.
I have created this talisman for my glory.
I have formed it and I have made it.

Planetary Magic Circle

You may prefer to use a magic circle that is created specifically for the purpose when doing planetary workings. The one given here is for solitary work, and the size can be increased appropriately for group workings. First prepare the space by removing any distractions and cleaning it. The circle is a suitably planetary seven foot in diameter.

· · · · · · · ·

Requirements:
- Spirit light (may be a lamp with a wick or a candle)
- Incense (optional)
- Small bowl of sea salt
- Small bowl of spring water

For the creation of the circle, you may use a wand or dagger, or your preferred hand (i.e., right hand if right-handed, left if left-handed), whichever is your choice. If using your hand, the gesture of benediction works very well. This is made by extending the forefinger and middle finger, and curling the ring finger and little finger into the palm, with the thumb curled over so it rests on the ring and little fingers.

Light the spirit light and the incense (if you are using any). Declare:

Hekas o hekas este bibeloi. [17]

Add the salt to the bowl of water, proclaiming:

Be pure.

See the water glowing with a brilliant white glow. Pick up the bowl of consecrated water and walk from the east, in a clockwise circle, sprinkling the consecrated water. When you have returned to the east, go back to the altar, replace the bowl on the altar, and pick up your preferred tool, or make the gesture of benediction. Again go to the east and walk clockwise with your arm outstretched downward toward the floor, and see a circle of white flames being formed at the tip of the weapon or the fingers of your preferred hand, and say:

> *United the seven deathless powers form the greater unity.*
> *That unity is my circle, bound in time and space.*
> *Within is my universe illuminated by the magic of the wandering stars.*
> *As above, so below.*

When you have returned to the east, return to the centre and place your weapon on the altar, and continue with your ceremony.

At the end of the ceremony, pick up the weapon or make the gesture again, and walk counterclockwise from the north, again with arm pointed at the floor and seeing the white flames die away as you complete the circuit back to the north.

---

17. "Begone all unholiness!" (Greek).

Sympathetic Magic

When working planetary magic, one of the most powerful tools you have is the principle of contagion, also known as the law of attraction. Each planetary energy has a symbol set that has been powered by centuries or millennia of practice. By working with the symbol set, you draw the energies of the desired planet into your life, by creating a focus of harmonic influences that magnify your intent toward the desired result. As an example, if you were nervous about passing an exam, you would work with Mercury, and might wear some orange clothing and anoint yourself with lavender oil, carry a citrine quartz or agate, have orange candles in your study, burn a stimulating Mercurial oil such as lemon, etc. Of course any magic for results requires avenues to manifest through, and you would still need to study for the exam! Magic works to enhance, not to create out of nothing.

When considering additional symbolism for attraction, it is important to remember that the planets also represent the higher aspects of the four elements and rule the zodiacal signs, so their influence and symbols may be relevant to consider and include those listed in table 20.

Planet	Higher Aspect of	Rules
Sun	Fire	Leo
Moon	Water	Cancer
Mars	Fire	Aries, Scorpio
Mercury	Air	Gemini, Virgo
Jupiter	Water/air	Sagittarius, Pisces
Venus	Earth	Taurus, Libra
Saturn	Earth	Capricorn, Aquarius

Table 20. Planets, Elements, and Rulerships

Theurgic Work

Magic is not just about ritual practice, and it is important to remember the more "passive" side of magic—the being and becoming through inner work. For this, meditational and contemplative practices that help you focus on developing your positive qualities and transforming any negative ones are extremely important. Ultimately magic is the journey to achieving your own genius and radiating it, and theurgy is the heart of this.

In 1987 I coined the phrase "magic takes on the religion of the age,"[18] and now over thirty years later, I would add that "magic takes on the technology of the age." Magic has been called the technology of the sacred, and there is no reason why technology should not be used to enhance magical practice. A great example of this is the *Symphonies of the Planets*—recordings

---

18. *"A New Look at Some Old Gods."* Lecture by David Rankine at Leeds University Occult Society, 1987.

· · · · · · · ·

made by the Voyager space probe of the sounds emanating from the planets it passed. Whilst only Jupiter and Saturn are included from the classical planets, the recordings are amazing to use as background for planetary meditations and rituals.[19] Music that inspires, such as Holst's *The Planets*, may be used, though ambient instrumental music that is not intrusive works best as a background for meditation and contemplation.

Devotional practices are not simply a matter of worship; they are aspirational, seeking to develop the link between you and the divine to strengthen or refine qualities in yourself that they represent. This is the essence of devotion, which is a personal, private practice, best treated as such and not diluted through broadcasting it on social media for attention. A shrine to a deity acts as a gateway between you and that deity, and should be treated as a sacred space, not a photo opportunity. If you do feel a desire to engage in discussion or publication of current practices, remember the virtue of silence is not only to maintain the undiluted integrity of your work but also to encourage humility and keep the ego controlled.

It is better to concentrate on one planetary deity and the associated qualities at a time, so you can keep the focus pure. A shrine that you attend daily is strongly recommended for theurgic work. Shrines do not have to be complex or cluttered with statues and paraphernalia. The essentials for a shrine are a suitably coloured cloth as the base (usually on a small table or similar item), coloured candles (preferably of the planetary colour and number), a representation of the deity (statue or image) that you find pleasing to look at, and a censer or holder to burn incense or joss on. Beyond this, a few items that are particularly symbolic of the deity, such as a crystal, may be added, and fresh flowers are a nice touch. Of course a shrine should be kept clean and preferably be in a private space where it is not accessible to others. The following example of devotional practice may be adapted for any of the other planetary deities using their symbols, hymns, etc.

Example of Planetary Devotion for Mercury

The shrine is set with an orange cloth, with a statue of Mercury at the rear in the centre and eight orange candles, four on either side of the statue in a line along the back of the shrine. In front of the statue is a small censer with charcoal for burning galbanum or frankincense.[20] A piece of agate is placed in front of the censer, so a T-shape is formed by the items, with the image of a caduceus (symbol of Mercury and healing) placed on the left of the censer and agate, and a pen on the right (symbolic of writing, said to have been created by Mercury) and a bottle of lavender essential oil. On the wall behind the shrine, place a good-sized (say A4) picture of the Mercury sigil. You might also put the Orphic hymn in a large font on the wall next to the sigil

---

19. The recordings can be found on YouTube with a search for "Symphonies of the Planets."

20. Although frankincense is now usually seen as Solar, in the Orphic Hymn to Hermes it is specified as the offering. In such cases where the symbolism has changed or is shared, it is a matter of choice which you use.

· · · · · · · ·

for ease of reading, keeping your hands free. As this devotion is to Mercury, ideally perform it during a Mercurial planetary hour of the day.

First have a purification bath, allowing your body and mind to relax and let go of any stresses of the day. You can add appropriate essential oils or herbs to the bath. (If you place the herbs in a muslin bag, you will still get the benefits of their qualities without making a mess.) Dry yourself and put on a simple robe. (White or black are good neutral colours if you do not have a whole set of planetary colours!) Approach the shrine with a sense of joy and anticipation.

Light the candles and the charcoal (or joss), and recite the Orphic Hymn to Hermes[21] (Mercury) whilst offering frankincense, censing the statue and the rest of the shrine:

> Hermes, draw near, and to my pray'r incline, angel of Jove [Zeus], and Maia's son divine;
> Studious of contests, ruler of mankind, with heart almighty, and a prudent mind.
> Celestial messenger, of various skill, whose pow'rful arts could watchful Argus kill:
> With winged feet, 'tis thine thro' air to course, O friend of man, and prophet of discourse:
> Great life-supporter, to rejoice is thine, in arts gymnastic, and in fraud divine:
> With pow'r endu'd all language to explain, of care the loos'ner, and the source of gain.
> Whose hand contains of blameless peace the rod, Corucian, blessed, profitable God;
> Of various speech, whose aid in works we find, and in necessities to mortals kind:
> Dire weapon of the tongue, which men revere, be present, Hermes, and thy suppliant hear;
> Assist my works, conclude my life with peace, give graceful speech, and memory's increase.

Sit in front of the shrine, cross-legged or on a chair as works best for you. Take the agate off the altar and hold it between your hands in your lap, connecting you to the shrine energetically and also putting a Mercurial item in connection to your body.

Relax, close your eyes, and still your breathing, taking time to enter a meditative state. See the Mercury symbol in orange on a blue background. As you visualise the symbol, contemplate the qualities associated with Mercury, such as communication, deception, flexibility, healing, and memory. Consider how strong each of these forces is in your life, and which of them you are actively trying to cultivate or transform. Allow your inner vision to be inspired by your thoughts, and see what images and events it brings up.

After you have spent some time (5–15 minutes) contemplating the qualities of Mercury, decide which quality you feel you should focus on. Place some more frankincense on the charcoal, and as the lemony fragrance surrounds you, allow it to give you a singular clarity so you consider only the chosen quality. See the sigil of Mercury again flowing in front of you the same size as

---

21. Thomas Taylor's 1792 translation of the Orphic Hymns is still widely used due to his poetic turn of phrase, making the rhyme and flow of the hymns ideal for devotion.

you, glowing orange. Feel the power of that quality emanating from the orange Mercury, then see it moving forward to be absorbed into your body. As you absorb that quality, anoint yourself with lavender oil,[22] making the Mercury sigil on your heart, and state:

As above, so below.
This is my will, it is so.

Take time to write up your impressions and thoughts, then blow out the candles and move away from the shrine, walking backward so you continue to look at the shrine as you step away, showing your respect for the planetary deity.

Obviously change does not happen overnight, and such a practice should be performed daily for a period of time, such as a month. If you can perform it during the appropriate planetary hour every day, it quickly builds up power and helps accelerate the process of change as your self-discipline and determination drive your unconscious to manifest the changes in your conscious self. Daily practice greatly strengthens the willpower essential for successful magic and transformation.

Planetary Water

Planetary water may be easily made for use in planetary magic. To make it, place a planetary crystal (e.g., citrine quartz for Mercury) in a clean glass bottle or jar with spring water, and seal it. Place it in a dark, cool space for a period of days equal to the planetary number (so eight for this Mercurial example) to charge. If you are making solar water, it can be placed on a shelf where it receives direct sunlight during the day, and conversely moonlight for lunar water. The other planetary waters should all be left in a dark space (equating to the darkness of space) without the light of the sun or moon influencing the planetary energy.

Planetary water can be used for a variety of purposes, such as anointing, and is particularly useful when added to enhance the planetary influence. Examples of this are adding some to a ritual purification bath, adding a few drops to a coloured magical ink, and using some during the consecration of magical items (including statues on devotional shrines).[23]

---

22. Unlike lavender oil, most essential oils should not be anointed directly on the skin, so check beforehand and dilute the oil in a base oil such as sweet almond in a ratio no less than 1 part to 50 parts base oil.

23. Note that since many minerals contain poisonous substances, they should not be drunk or consumed internally.

Trans-Saturnian Planets

Although planetary magic traditionally focuses on the seven classical "planets," mention should be made of the more recently discovered Uranus (1789) and Neptune (1846). Following its discovery in 1930, Pluto was also incorporated into planetary magic, though with its reclassification in 2006 as a dwarf planet, some people have chosen to stop considering it a planet, whilst others include other dwarf planets such as Ceres and Eris.

Uranus ("sky" or "heaven") is the Roman god who fathered Saturn, who castrated Uranus with a diamond sickle and threw his genitals into the sea. Some versions of the myth state that Venus was born from his blood and the foam of the sea. Uranus was equated to the Greek Ouranos and his associated myth. Uranus is associated with the element of air and the day Wednesday, and rules the sign of Aquarius in the zodiac. The colour is purple, and associated materials are titanium, amethyst, labradorite, and tourmaline. Uranus is associated with change and technology, especially electricity, and the archangel Uriel has been associated with Uranus. In modern Qabalah, Uranus is often attributed to the non-sephira of Daath on the Tree of Life.

Neptune (the etymology of his name is uncertain) is the Roman god of the sea, horses, and earthquakes, who was son of Saturn and brother to Jupiter and Pluto. He was originally associated with springs and streams prior to his identification with the Greek sea god Poseidon, so all water can be associated with him. Neptune is associated with the element of water and the day Monday, and rules the sign of Pisces. The attributed colour is gray (or seagreen), and the associated materials are tungsten, pearl, rutile, rutile quartz, and shell. The magic of Neptune is that of the sea, tidal and subject to sudden changes. As the archangel of water, Gabriel can be worked with for Neptune. Neptune is often attributed to the supernal sephira of Chokmah in modern Qabalah, in which case the archangel Raziel is appropriate.

Pluto is the Roman god of the underworld and wealth. His name comes from the Latin *pluton*, which is derived from the Greek word *ploutos*, meaning "wealth." Pluto was another son of Saturn, and thus brother to Jupiter and Neptune. In later times he was equated with the Greek underworld god Hades and the whole "abduction of Persephone" myth associated with him, with Persephone becoming Proserpina. Pluto is associated with the element of earth and the day Saturday, and rules Scorpio. The attributed colour is white (which is the reflection of the entire spectrum, and hence the quality of invisibility), and associated materials are diamond, ebony, fluorite, platinum, and zircon. The magic of Pluto is that of invisibility, treasure, and the underworld. Some people attribute Pluto to the sephira of Kether on the Tree of Life in modern Qabalah, as marking an edge of our universe whilst also embodying the concept of the hidden (invisible). With this attribution, the archangel Metatron is considered a suitable archangel to work with for Pluto.

Planetary Fragrances

Fragrance plays an important role in magic. Not only does it stimulate memory, but it also enhances mood and has traditionally been used to attract the attention of spiritual creatures, through burning incense and wearing suitable oils. Fragmentary writings from Mesopotamia mention seven planetary fragrances associated with the classical planets and their gods (table 21). The fragrances are calamus, cedar, cypress, galbanum, labdanum, myrtle, and storax, but the only specific associations known for certain amongst these are cedar as being sacred to Marduk (Jupiter) and myrtle as being sacred to Shamash (the Sun). A reference in the *Greek Magical Papyri* gives us a complete set of planetary attributions, listing the seven Greek gods who were associated with the classical planets and their scents:

"The proper incense of Kronos is storax, for it is heavy and fragrant; of Zeus, malabathron; of Ares, kostos; of Helios, frankincense; of Aphrodite, Indian nard; of Hermes, cassia; of Selene, myrrh."[24]

Planet	Incense Plant	Latin Name
Sun	Frankincense	*Boswellia carterii*
Mercury	Cassia	*Cinnamomum cassia*
Venus	Spikenard	*Nardostachys jatamansi*
Moon	Myrrh	*Commiphora myrrha*
Mars	Kostos	*Sassurea lappa*
Jupiter	Malabathron (Indian bay leaf)	*Cinnamomum tamala*
Saturn	Storax	*Liquidambar styraciflua* L.

Table 21. Planets with Their Associated Incense Plants and Latin Names

Centuries later, the grimoires give different sets of fragrances and a whole range of incenses, based on availability and a very different cultural situation. Some of these ingredients include animal parts and toxic metals, and the use of these faded away as perceptions of magic and the world changed. The planets were no longer worshiped as gods, but were seen as part of the Christian Creation. Looking at Agrippa's *Three Books of Occult Philosophy* (1531–1533) and the *Heptameron* (1485) against modern attributions, we see the attributions given in table 22.

---

24. *PGM* XIII.17–20.

Planet	*Heptameron*	Agrippa	Modern
Sun	Red sandalwood	Mastic	Amber, cinnamon, frankincense, orange, sandalwood (red)
Mercury	Mastic	Cinnamon	Galbanum, lavender, lemon, mastic, rosemary, storax
Venus	Pepperwort	Saffron	Benzoin, lilac, lily, rose, sandalwood (white)
Moon	Aloes	Myrtle	Camphor, jasmine, vanilla, ylang-ylang
Mars	Pepper	Lignum aloes	Black pepper, dragon's blood, ginger, opoponax
Jupiter	Saffron	Nutmeg	Cedar, copal, hyssop, juniper, saffron
Saturn	Sulphur	Pepperwort	Myrrh, patchouli, pine, vetivert

Table 22. Attributions of Planetary Incenses across Time

For modern rites, unless you are using a blended incense, it is better to use a resin (at least one is given for each planet in table 20), as it will burn sweet the whole time. If you burn herbs, the smell quickly resembles a bonfire and is not conducive to concentration.[25] If you choose to make your own planetary incense using appropriate ingredients, remember it should always be at least two-thirds resin base for the same reason.

Building the Planetary Matrix

In addition to wearing an item of the appropriate planetary colour and a scent of the planet, carrying a consecrated crystal can also add strength to the planetary matrix you create about yourself when performing planetary magic. Using all of these symbols not only helps to send a continuous passive message to your unconscious but also actively forms a matrix of the desired planetary energy around you, to act as a magnet for drawing the appropriate energy to you and to your actions, both magical and mundane. For this reason, more examples of planetary crystals are given in table 23. Both loose crystals and crystals in jewelry are equally good to have on your person, as long as they have been consecrated. For jewelry, it should also be mentioned that certain parts of the body correspond more strongly to planetary influences, which is relevant for the wearing of items such as rings. On the hand there is Venus (thumb), Jupiter (index finger), Saturn (big finger), the Sun (ring finger), and Mercury (little finger). Other relevant areas for jewelry include the throat (Venus, e.g., strings of crystals), heart (Sun, pendant), and brow (Moon, circlet or crown).

---

25. When burning incense, always check if there is a smoke detector in the room, and if necessary disable it for the duration of the ritual, remembering to make sure it is working again once the smoke has cleared and before going to sleep.

· · · · · · · ·

Planet	Crystals
Sun	Amber, cat's-eye, diamond, sunstone, tiger's-eye, topaz, zircon
Mercury	Agate, aventurine, citrine quartz, labradorite, opal
Venus	Amazonite, emerald, jade, malachite, peridot, rose quartz, zoisite
Moon	Aquamarine, beryl, chalcedony, moonstone, pearl, quartz, selenite
Mars	Bloodstone, carnelian, garnet, hematite, magnetite, pyrite, ruby
Jupiter	Amethyst, ammonite, azurite, lapis lazuli, sapphire, sodalite, turquoise
Saturn	Jet, obsidian, onyx, serpentine, smoky quartz

Table 23. Planets and Their Crystal Attributions

The more you add to the planetary matrix, the stronger you can make it. So you might anoint yourself with a planetary number of drops of an oil for the planet, like eight drops of lavender, each day. One key to the planetary matrix is subtlety. You are working with unseen energies, and if you suddenly make yourself more noticeable, that is not unseen! Fortunately the items of the planetary matrix can all be discreet, such as planetary coloured underwear, the crystal in jewelry or in a pocket, the fragrance subtle and not overpowering, etc.

The planetary matrix can also be added to in non-ritual circumstances through the use of an oil burner, using candles, playing suitable music, or even eating foods associated with the planets. The more you put in, the stronger the critical mass of your planetary matrix will be to attract the divine force.

The energies of the planets were not all perceived as having positive relationships. A summary of the planetary relationships given by Agrippa is shown in table 24.

Relationship	Sun	Mercury	Venus	Moon	Mars	Jupiter	Saturn
Sun toward		Enemy	Love	Enemy	Enemy	Love	Friend
Mercury toward	Enemy		Friend	Enemy	Enemy	Friend	Friend
Venus toward	Love	Love		Love	Love	Love	Enemy
Moon toward	Enemy	Enemy	Friend		Enemy	Friend	Friend
Mars toward	Enemy	Enemy	Love	Enemy		Enemy	Enemy
Jupiter toward	Friend	Friend	Friend	Friend	Enemy		Friend
Saturn toward	Friend	Friend	Enemy	Friend	Enemy	Friend	

Table 24. Planetary Relationships According to Agrippa

· · · · · · · ·

These relationships should be considered when working out days and times of rituals. Although the planetary hour and day should always be used where possible, sometimes this is not practical for any number of reasons. Refer then to chart 24 and look at the days of planets that have a "friend" or "love'" relationship with the planet you are working with as alternative options.

Dreaming with the Planets

Using the dreaming mind to seek answers to questions is a practice that goes back to the dream incubation temples of the ancient world. In the grimoires there is a planetary version of this practice,[26] where a seal is created during the appropriate planetary hour and placed under the dreamer's pillow. After a purificatory bath and before going to sleep, a prayer is said and the angel of the day named, with the question being voiced out loud (e.g., "Gabriel, am I being deceived by my friend N?"). The angel may then appear or speak to you in your dream to offer guidance or an answer to your question.

There are different individual prayers for each of the seven named angels; however, the prayer given below in table 25 (Psalm 4:6–10) is for all of them and may be used accordingly on any day of the week. It may be spoken in Latin or English according to preference.

6	sacrificate sacrificium iustitiae et fidite in Domino multi dicunt quis ostendit nobis bonum	Offer up the sacrifice of justice, and trust in the Lord: many say, Who showeth us good things?
7	leva super nos lucem vultus tui Domine dedisti laetitiam in corde meo	The light of thy countenance, O Lord, is signed upon us: thou hast given gladness in my heart.
8	in tempore frumentum et vinum eorum multiplicata sunt	By the fruit of their corn, their wine, and oil, they rest:
9	in pace simul requiescam et dormiam	In peace in the self same I will sleep, and I will rest:
10	quia tu Domine specialiter securum habitare fecisti me	For thou, O Lord, singularly hast settled me in hope.

Table 25. Prayers from Psalm 4:6–10

26. Wellcome 4669, 1796, reproduced in Skinner and Rankine, *A Collection of Magical Secrets*, 123–133.

Some of the angels listed in table 26 are not the classical archangels. They are specifically angels of the night though, so it may be supposed they were considered appropriate emissaries for dream interpretation. Raphael is here given as Solar and Michael as Martial. For centuries both Michael and Raphael were attributed to the Sun at different times. Michael as Martial is less common in his warrior aspect. Uriel also is more commonly Venusian but has also been attributed to the other earthy planet of Saturn.

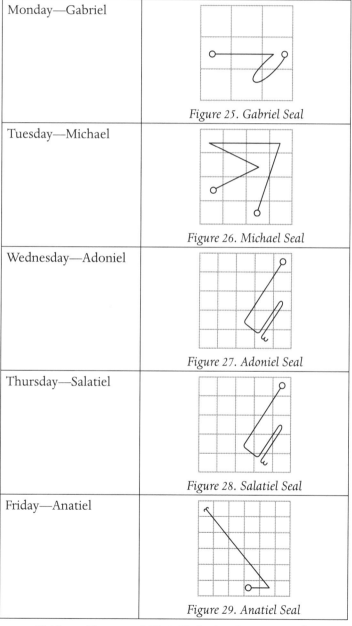

Monday—Gabriel	*Figure 25. Gabriel Seal*
Tuesday—Michael	*Figure 26. Michael Seal*
Wednesday—Adoniel	*Figure 27. Adoniel Seal*
Thursday—Salatiel	*Figure 28. Salatiel Seal*
Friday—Anatiel	*Figure 29. Anatiel Seal*

Table 26. Planets and Their Night Angels (continued)

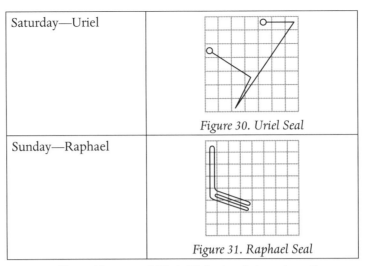

| Saturday—Uriel | *Figure 30. Uriel Seal* |
| Sunday—Raphael | *Figure 31. Raphael Seal* |

Table 26. Planets and Their Night Angels (continued)

Planetary Lamens

For conjuration the magician would normally wear a lamen pinned to their robe on their chest over their heart. A lamen can be a piece of cloth or paper and would include the seal of the creature being called. Bearing the mark of the spiritual creature can facilitate communication as well as provide protection. It could also be seen as a beacon on the physical plane, which combined with the conjuration to provide a clear location. If working with the planetary intelligences and spirits, the seal of the spirit would be on the outside and the intelligence would be on the inside, facing the heart, as an additional protection. The same principle is found when conjuring demons, with the seal of the controlling angel or archangel on the underside facing the heart.

For planetary work that is talismanic or theurgic, a general-purpose planetary lamen can be created with the seven-rayed planetary heptagram on it to add to the planetary matrix. The sigil of the planet can be added in the centre of the heptagram and, if desired, the seal of the archangel drawn on the underside facing the heart. Either type of heptagram is suitable, and you should choose the type which appeals to you more.

The Heptagram, or Seven-Rayed Star

The heptagram (or septagram) is the seven-pointed planetary star that is used by a number of magical traditions, including in the grimoires, the Golden Dawn, Thelema (the Astrum Argenteum and the Babalon star), and the Fairy tradition (the Faery or Elven star). It has two forms, known as the 7/2 heptagram (figure 32) and the 7/3 heptagram (figure 34), the latter numbers referring to the number of points you move around the star to draw the next line of the heptagram in the single continuous stroke that creates it.

· · · · · · · ·

Figure 32. The 7/3 Heptagram

Figure 33. Sigillum Dei Aemeth

The 7/2 heptagram is perhaps best known in the famous Sigillum Dei Aemeth ("Sigil of God's Truth") in the thirteenth-century grimoire *Liber Juratus* (figure 33). This image was adopted by Dr. John Dee in the sixteenth century and became a central part of Enochian magic. The seven points are also associated with the seven vowels of ancient Greek, which are attributed to the planets, and used in some ancient spells. The sequence of the seven vowels from alpha to omega was sometimes written as shorthand to represent all the planets, and it was seen as being a powerful spoken or sung charm in its own right (table 27). Use of the seven vowels as a repeated mantra is a good practice for developing the power of your tone for ritual use.

Vowel	Sound	Planet	Colour	Position
Alpha	A	Moon	Silver	Middle right
Epsilon	E	Mercury	Orange	Bottom left
Eta	Ē (EE)	Venus	Green	Upper left
Iota	I	Sun	Gold	Upper right
Omicron	O	Mars	Red	Bottom right
Upsilon	U	Jupiter	Blue	Middle left
Omega	(Ō) OO	Saturn	Black	Top

Table 27. The Seven Vowels of Ancient Greek

You can see it is easy to remember the positions of the planets on the points of the heptagram as the days of the week move around clockwise from the top (figure 34). The top point is Saturn (Saturday), to Sun (Sunday), Moon (Monday), Mars (Tuesday), Mercury (Wednesday), Jupiter (Thursday), and Venus (Friday).

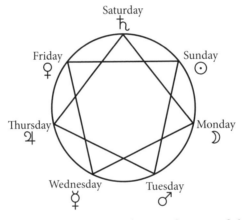

Figure 34. The 7/2 Heptagram Showing the Days of the Week

Conclusion

The power of the planets is immense, accessible, and all-permeating in our lives. Working planetary magic is arguably the most efficient way to optimize and harmonize the swirling of forces we are all surrounded by. Appreciating the nature of these energies and being able to direct their flows and ride their currents not only helps improve quality of life, but more importantly helps develop quality of soul. At its core, planetary magic is the union of a greater whole (our solar system), and by practicing it we embody the axiom of "As above, so below," becoming a harmonious microcosm that consummates the Great Work, i.e., the work of making humanity great.

Suggested Reading List

Agrippa von Nettesheim, Heinrich Cornelius. *Fourth Book of Occult Philosophy*. London: Askin Press, 1979.

———. *Three Books of Occult Philosophy*. Edited and annotated by Donald Tyson. Translated by James Freake. St. Paul, MN: Llewellyn Publications, 2005.

Barry, Kieren. *The Greek Qabalah: Alphabetic Mysticism and Numerology in the Ancient World*. York Beach, ME: Samuel Weiser, 1999.

Betz, Hans Dieter, ed. *The Greek Magical Papyri in Translation*. Chicago, IL: University of Chicago Press, 1992.

Denning, Melita, and Osborne Phillips. *Planetary Magick: Invoking and Directing the Powers of the Planets*. St. Paul, MN: Llewellyn Publications, 1992.

Digitalis, Raven. *Planetary Spells and Rituals*. St. Paul, MN: Llewellyn Publications, 2010.

Fischer-Rizzi, Susanne. *The Complete Incense Book*. New York: Sterling, 1998.

Gettings, Fred. *Dictionary of Occult, Hermetic, and Alchemical Sigils*. London: Routledge & Kegan Paul, 1981.

Kerényi, Karl. *The Gods of the Greeks*. Translated by Norman Cameron. London: Thames & Hudson, 1951.

Kupperman, Jeffrey S. *Living Theurgy*. Glastonbury, UK: Avalonia, 2014.

Marathakis, Ioannis. *The Magical Treatise of Solomon, or Hygromanteia*. Singapore: Golden Hoard Press, 2011.

McLean, Adam, trans. *The Magical Calendar*. Grand Rapids, MI: Phanes Press, 1994.

Moore, Thomas. *The Planets Within: Marsilio Ficino's Astrological Psychology*. London: Associated University Presses, 1982.

Rankine, David. *Climbing the Tree of Life*. Glastonbury, UK: Avalonia, 2005.

———. *Conjuring the Planetary Intelligences*. London: Hadean Press, 2019.

———, and Sorita d'Este. *Practical Planetary Magick*. Glastonbury, UK: Avalonia, 2007.

Skinner, Stephen, and David Rankine. *A Collection of Magical Secrets*. Glastonbury, UK: Avalonia, 2009.

———. *The Keys to the Gateway of Magic*. Singapore: Golden Hoard, 2005.

———. *The Veritable Key of Solomon*. Singapore: Golden Hoard, 2008.

Taylor, Thomas, trans. *The Hymns of Orpheus*. Philadelphia, PA: University of Pennsylvania Press, 1999.

. . . .

About the Author

David Rankine is an author, esoteric researcher, and magician who lives in Glastonbury, England, with his partner, occult artist and tattooist Rosa Laguna. David has been making major contributions to the modern occult revival since the early 1980s, through lectures, workshops, presentations, articles, and books. His esoteric expertise covers a wide range of topics, including the Grimoire tradition, Qabalah, planetary and elemental magic, Greco-Egyptian magic, and the Western esoteric traditions.

David has authored thirty books to date, as well as hundreds of articles for magazines and journals. He is known for his lively and informative style when lecturing and facilitating workshops. He is fascinated with planetary and elemental magic, which he sees as the foundations of the Western esoteric traditions, and he wrote on these topics in his books *Practical Planetary Magick* (2007) and *Practical Elemental Magick* (2009). Both these topics also feature in many of his other works, especially on the grimoires and Qabalah.

For more information on David and his work, visit davidrankine.com.

Art Credits

Figures 1–2 and 10–34 by the Llewellyn Art Department.

Figures 3–9 by James Clark.

BOOK FOUR

⊕

Alchemy
by Dennis William Hauck

The word *alchemy* comes from the Arabic phrase *al-khemia*, which means "from the land of Khem." Khem is the Egyptian hieroglyph for "black," which specifically refers to the rich, black soil found in the Nile River delta. Thus, alchemy became known as the "Black Art," which also evokes the dark, secretive practices of the alchemists.

Scholars consider the era of Egyptian alchemy to span the centuries from 5000 BCE to 350 BCE. That was followed by a period of Greek alchemy in Egypt from the arrival of Alexander the Great (332 BCE) to the Arabian invasion (642 CE). Arabian alchemy flourished for another five hundred years before the heyday of alchemy began in Europe around 1200 CE.

According to ancient Egyptian texts, the first alchemist was Thoth. He arrived during a period known as *Zep Tepi* (around 10,000 BCE), when godlike beings roamed the earth. The Egyptians considered Thoth the primordial source of all thought—the inventor of writing, philosophy, theology, law, literature, magic, alchemy, mathematics, and all the sciences.

Thoth represents the archetypal concept of mind, the wellspring for all human insight and inspiration. An Egyptian motto says, "May Thoth speak to you daily." According to the Ebers Papyrus (1550 BCE), a 68-foot-long scroll on medical alchemy that is the oldest book in the world, "Man's guide is Thoth, who bestows on him the gifts of his speech, who makes the books, and illumines those who are learned therein, and the physicians who follow him, that they may work their cures."[1]

---

1. Bryan, *Ancient Egyptian Medicine*, 21.

· · · · · · · ·

Thoth is the Greek word for the Egyptian *Djehuty*, which means "like an ibis." Djehuty was an ancient lunar god associated with the ibis because of the bird's unique crescent-shaped beak. He performed magical acts of manifestation and symbolized the transformative power of the eternally changing moon. His magic holds the universe together. Without his words, the gods themselves would not exist and nothing in the cosmos would ever change or evolve.

The Greek god Hermes and Egyptian god Thoth were worshiped as a single entity in the Hellenistic city of Hermopolis, and the Hermetic writings were associated with an ancient Egyptian priest known as Hermes Trismegistus ("Thrice Greatest Hermes"). The teachings attributed to him inspired an explosion of interpretive texts in philosophy, religion, alchemy, and magic that were housed in the Great Library of Alexandria (305 BCE).

Eventually, the library grew to over 400,000 scrolls and became a center of learning that attracted scholars from all over the world. In that fertile environment, alchemy evolved from a disorganized collection of smelting procedures and tincturing recipes into a Hermetic science focused on understanding the universal principles of transformation. From Alexandria, the teachings spread to the Arabian lands, Mesopotamia, India, and China.

In a tragic loss to humankind, the Great Library of Alexandria caught fire during a power struggle between Ptolemy XIII and his sister Cleopatra in 48 BCE. The library was engulfed in a firestorm that ignited from soldiers fighting on the city's docks. The surviving scrolls were moved to two nearby temples that served as a library for another three centuries.

Then, in 290 CE, Roman Emperor Diocletian decreed the destruction of all alchemy manuscripts in Egypt, which resulted in a significant loss of precious texts. In 391 CE, Christian zealots attacked one of the temples, destroyed all the scrolls, and turned the building into a Christian church. Finally, in 415 CE, Christian mobs destroyed the remaining temple library. They dragged Hypatia, the last librarian, into the street and accused her of teaching Greek philosophy. Using abalone shells, they scraped the flesh from her body while she was still alive.

The extinguishing of the light of Alexandria and the suppression of Greek philosophy were the results of the dogmatic control of knowledge and fear of new ideas that was gripping the world. Known as the Dark Ages, it was a period of stagnant intellectual growth and lack of innovation that lasted from the fall of the Roman Empire (476 CE) to the beginning of the second millennium (1000 CE).

Fortunately, alchemy and the Hermetic teachings survived in the Arabian lands and were rekindled in Europe with the infusion of copied Alexandrian manuscripts brought to Spain by Arabian invaders. The Arabs crossed over from Morocco in 711 CE and occupied Spain for more than seven centuries. The Islamic rulers proved very tolerant, and Spain soon became a haven for philosophers, alchemists, magicians, and freethinkers of all persuasions. By 1100, Latin translations of alchemy and Hermetic manuscripts were spreading throughout Europe. Alchemy would thrive in Europe for the next seven hundred years.

• • • • • • •

Hermetic Philosophy in Alchemy and Theurgy

One of the copied Alexandrian scrolls brought by the Arabs to Spain was the *Emerald Tablet*, a short but profound document in which Hermes summarized the esoteric principles of creation (figure 1). The Tablet became the core document in European alchemy, and nearly every alchemist had a copy of it hanging on the wall or tucked away in a revered spot in their library. They believed it contained a secret formula that showed how to transform anything.

Figure 1. Emerald Tablet

See if you can sense the universal formula hidden in the words of the Emerald Tablet as you read the following translation.[2] Note that when the tablet refers to the "Universe," it is talking about the material universe in which we live. When it speaks of the "Whole Universe," it is referencing both the material universe ("Below") and the spiritual universe ("Above").

2. Hauck, *The Emerald Tablet: Alchemy for Personal Transformation*, 45.

* * * * * * *

The Emerald Tablet

In truth, without deceit, certain, and most veritable.

That which is Below corresponds to that which is Above, and that which is Above corresponds to that which is Below, to accomplish the miracles of the One Thing. And just as all things have come from this One Thing, through the meditation of One Mind, so do all created things originate from this One Thing, through Transformation.

Its father is the Sun; its mother the Moon. The Wind carries it in its belly; its nurse is the Earth. It is the origin of All, the consecration of the Universe; its inherent Strength is perfected, if it is turned into Earth.

Separate the Earth from Fire, the Subtle from the Gross, gently and with great Ingenuity. It rises from Earth to Heaven and descends again to Earth, thereby combining within Itself the powers of both the Above and the Below.

Thus, will you obtain the Glory of the Whole Universe. All Obscurity will be clear to you. This is the greatest Force of all powers, because it overcomes every Subtle thing and penetrates every Solid thing.

In this way was the Universe created. From this comes many wondrous Applications, because this is the Pattern.

Therefore, am I called Thrice Greatest Hermes, having all three parts of the wisdom of the Whole Universe. Herein have I completely explained the Operation of the Sun.

The first principle presented in the Emerald Tablet is known as the *Doctrine of Correspondences*, which describes a vertical relationship between spirit or energy in the realm Above and matter or manifestation in the realm Below. A penetrating examination of this vertical axis of reality can be found in a work in the *Corpus Hermeticum* called the *Divine Pymander* (or "Divine Mind"). Attributed to Hermes Trismegistus, the text describes his meeting with the One Mind and what it revealed to him about the nature of reality.[3]

The Tablet goes on to elaborate on the nature of the One Thing, which alchemists interpret as the First Matter, or primordial stuff of creation. The first two sentences of this paragraph present the Four Elements in the order of Fire, Water, Air, and Earth. Associated with each of the elements are alchemical operations: Calcination (Fire), Dissolution (Water), Separation (Air), and Conjunction (Earth).

The fourth paragraph is the most mystical part of the Emerald Tablet and reveals how to enter the spiritual realm using the alchemical operations of Fermentation (spiritizing matter) and Distillation (a purifying circulation of rising vapors and falling condensate).

The fifth paragraph describes the powerful Quintessence (Fifth Element) that is created by following these instructions. In the next section, we learn this process is a universal Pattern that

3. Trismegistus, *The Divine Pymander,* trans. John Everard.

governs transformation on all levels. It is not only the secret pattern embedded in Nature but is also the formula that the alchemists follow in the Great Work.

The final paragraph identifies the author as Hermes Trismegistus, which is Latin for "Thrice Greatest Hermes." The oldest reference to his name is in a papyrus of notes from a meeting of the Ibis cult near Memphis in 172 BCE.[4] He is said to be thrice-great because he exists on all three levels of reality: the physical, the mental, and the spiritual. Free of the cycle of rebirth and existing outside of time, he has grasped the "Operation of the Sun," or the inner workings of the universe.

The unique spiritual technology developed in Alexandria was based on a deeply intuitive understanding of the intimate connection between mind and matter. Born of a union of laboratory observations with the spiritual practices of priests and magicians, the new Art of Transformation sought to understand how things can be perfected by working simultaneously with both physical and spiritual techniques.

The Birth of Cosmogonic Magic

In a parallel development in Alexandria, the ancient Egyptian cult of Heka evolved into an organized collection of beliefs and practices that became the basis for modern magic. Heka magic consisted of spells and rituals intended to communicate directly with the gods to ask for assistance and good fortune. While every god had their own heka spells, the central focus of the cult was the god Heka, who took on human form. Often depicted as a boy, he was considered a source of creativity and provided the energy for transformation. Written spells and amulets from the Heka cult dating back to 4500 BCE have been discovered, and it was actively practiced until around 500 CE.

In Alexandria, there was a merging of Heka practices and the Neoplatonist philosophy of Plotinus (204–270 CE) and Porphyry (234–305 CE) that gave birth to a spiritualized magic known as *theurgy*, or "divine working." The Neoplatonists described reality as a series of emanations from the One, an ineffable presence outside the universe that was sometimes referred to as "The Good." From the One (called *To Hen* by the Greeks) emanates the Divine Mind (*Nous*, or consciousness). From the Divine Mind proceeds Soul (*Psyche*), which includes both individual and world soul. Finally, Soul is the seed of Nature (*Physis*, or physical manifestation).

Theurgy is based on the idea that one can follow the divine emanations back to their source. In other words, a person can evoke and even direct the divine energies by a purifying initiation that includes active meditation, rigorous prayer, fasting, or devotional rituals. The beneficent energies (or spirits) released could then be influenced to disclose mysteries, accomplish tasks, animate objects, or even inhabit a human being as a medium.

---

4. Copenhaver, *Hermetica*, xiv.

· · · · · · · ·

Plotinus called the union of the inner divinity of the Soul with the Divine Source *henosis*, and he created a school where methods of meditation were taught to help his pupils achieve that state. Porphyry was a student at his school.

The Syrian philosopher Iamblichus (250–325 CE), who was a pupil of Porphyry, expanded the methods of theurgy to include the practice of invocations and rituals to evoke the presence or action of a deity.[5] He envisioned magic as a psychospiritual discipline whose goal was to bring divine energies into the everyday world through the purified consciousness of the magician. Ceremonial magic was the tool that connected the higher or astral identity of the magician with the divine presence.

Iamblichus further modified the Neoplatonic teachings by reaffirming the original Platonic idea of the soul's descent or embodiment in matter. To Iamblichus, all matter was as divine as any other part of the cosmos, for it was all within One Mind. In *Theurgia: De Mysteriis Aegyptiorum* (*Theurgy: On the Mysteries of Egypt*), Iamblichus wrote:

> After the theurgic discipline has conjoined the individual Soul with the several departments of the universe and all the divine powers that pervade it," he wrote, "it leads the Soul to the Creator of the world, places it in his charge, and frees it of everything pertaining to the realm of matter—uniting it with the Sole Eternal Reason (*Logos*). What I am saying is that it unites the Soul individually with the One—Father of himself, self-moving, who sustains the universe. Thus, it establishes the theurgic soul in the creative energies, in the conceptions and qualities of those powers. Finally, the Soul becomes part of the entire demiurgic mind. This, according to the Egyptian sages, is the final "Return" as taught in the Sacred Records.[6]

Iamblichus traced the origin of theurgy to ancient Egypt and said it was Hermes himself who revealed the divine plan in the minds of philosophers: "Hermes, the god who presides over learning from ancient times," he wrote, "is rightly considered the common patron of all priests and presides over true knowledge about the gods. Our ancestors dedicated the fruits of their wisdom to him by attributing all their own writings to Hermes."[7]

For Iamblichus, theurgy was a series of operations aimed at recovering the transcendent essence of reality by following divine signatures on both material and spiritual levels of being. The work was with the Soul and not the mind. Ultimate reality could not be grasped with the human mind, because the One Mind is supra-rational and outside of space and time. By working

---

5. Eds. note: See Book One: Foundations of Western Magic for more on Iamblichus.

6. Iamblichus, *Theurgia: On the Mysteries of Egypt*, 282.

7. Iamblichus, *Theurgia: On the Mysteries of Egypt*, 25.

· · · · · · ·

"like with like" between levels, powerful symbols and deep intimations develop that embody transcendent energy beyond the reach of words.

The Sacred Goal of the Great Work

Under the Neoplatonist influence in Alexandria, alchemy and theurgy evolved into spiritual disciplines that shared the same goals of the Great Work. Isolating and purifying the Soul, or spiritual essence of plants and minerals, was always part of practical laboratory work in alchemy. But now the emphasis was on the human soul and the evolution and perfection of the whole universe.

The powerful Science of Soul that developed in Alexandria was a unique blend of practical chemistry, psychology, spirituality, and magic. Both alchemists and theurgists believed all matter was alive with the divine signatures of its creator, which caused substances to slowly evolve into a perfect expression of divine intent. Their goal was to speed up this natural process of perfection—to resurrect the spiritual essences trapped in matter and cause that which already exists in a latent state to become active and grow.

"The Great Work is, above all things, the creation of man by himself," noted French magician Eliphas Levi. "That is to say, the full and entire conquest of his faculties and his future; it is especially the perfect emancipation of his will, assuring full power over the Universal Magical Agent. This Agent, disguised by the ancient philosophers under the name of the First Matter, determines the forms of modifiable substance, and we can really arrive by means of it at metallic transmutation and the Universal Medicine."[8]

The First Matter in Alchemy and Magic

The concept of the First Matter (*Materia Prima*) was central to both theurgy and alchemy and united their practitioners in the Great Work (figure 2). The First Matter is the primordial chaos that contains all possibilities. It is an unorganized state of energy or proto-matter that is the same for all substances and exists in an invisible state between energy and matter. According to the Hermetic viewpoint, the First Matter emerged from Chaos and is controlled by the light of consciousness from the One Mind.

Alchemists believed the First Matter was a real substance that could be extracted from matter and made visible and tangible, and they even listed it as an ingredient in their experiments. The primary tool for manipulating it was the spiritual connection they made with the First Matter, in which their consciousness identified with it and changed it. Meditation, prayer, and ritual were tools used by both alchemists and magicians in their pursuit of the First Matter.

---

8. Levi, *Transcendental Magic*, 58.

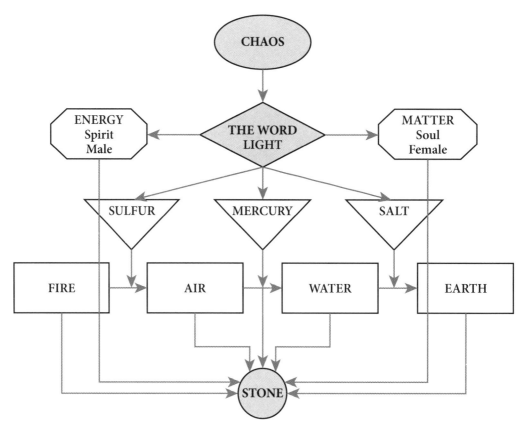

Figure 2. First Matter

The work with the First Matter is clearly demonstrated in the alchemists' work with the metals. It was thought the metals matured naturally underground, slowly changing from base metals like lead into noble metals like silver and gold. This process could be speeded up by accessing the First Matter responsible for it, which in the case of the metals was mercury.

Mercury was considered the First Matter of the metals because it has the power to dissolve and balance the other metals. To transform metals, it is necessary to melt them in fire, but mercury is naturally in a liquid state, able to take the shape of any container and reflect a clear image of anything near it. As quicksilver, it seemed alive and always changing. As a heavenly body, it was always closest to the sun and appeared to follow its own path in the heavens—sometimes even going backward.

Swiss Renaissance alchemist Paracelsus (1493–1541) elevated mercury to a universal power in a triad of primordial forces known as the *Tria Prima*, or "Three Essentials." Fiery Sulfur (brimstone) was equated with energy; Salt (cubic sodium compounds) represented matter; and shiny, reflective Mercury was associated with light. The *Tria Prima* became the prevalent working the-

· · · · · · · ·

ory of medieval alchemists and is still represented in modern scientific theory as energy, matter, and light ($E = mc^2$).

In magical work, Sulfur is the *anima*, or the transformative Soul that burns through time. Salt is the *corpus*, or physical effect to be manifested. Mercury is the *spiritus*, or transformative power of consciousness. In terms of application, Sulfur is the expansive force or binding agent between the spiritual realm above and the manifested world below. Salt is the contractive force or substantiating agent. Mercury is the force of conscious will or transforming agent (Levi's Universal Magical Agent).

Hermetic alchemy and the Three Essentials became part of the doctrine of many esoteric groups, including the Freemasons, Theosophists, Ordo Templi Orientis, Aurum Solis, Golden Dawn, and various Rosicrucian orders and Templar groups.[9] According to Eliphas Levi, the Hermetic doctrines are a perennial philosophy that keeps resurfacing in different forms, no matter how much it is suppressed.

Levi observed, "Behind the veil of all the hieratic and mystical allegories of ancient doctrines, behind the darkness and strange ordeals of all initiations, under the seal of all sacred writings, in the ruins of Thebes, on the crumbling stones of old temples and on the blackened visage of the Sphinx, in the marvelous paintings of the Vedas, in the cryptic emblems of old books on alchemy, in the ceremonies practiced by all secret societies, there are found indications of a Hermetic doctrine which is everywhere the same and everywhere carefully concealed."[10]

Practices and Techniques of Hermetic Alchemy

Concealment and secrecy are fundamental characteristics of Hermetic practice. The term "Hermetically sealed" means making a container perfectly sealed and airtight. That kind of closed-off, uncontaminated spiritual environment is where Hermetic meditation, rituals, and initiations take place.

In practice, the real path of Hermetic enlightenment is not theoretical verbiage but the cultivation of silence. In the *Discourse on the Eighth and Ninth,* Hermes tells his son Tat to become "a pure receptacle, a womb that understands in silence."[11] He instructs him to "sing while you are silent" and let the cosmic hymn flow through him by remaining quietly receptive. Disciples of Hermes, still known as "Sons of Hermes," reach the primal presence of the One only by passively receiving—and then actively uniting with—its creative energies. At that point their own consciousness becomes divinely inspired.

9. Eds. note: See Book Eight: The Golden Dawn for more on the Golden Dawn, and Book Nine: Thelema & Aleister Crowley for more on the Ordo Templi Orientis.

10. Levi, *Transcendental Magic*, 1.

11. Meyer, *The Nag Hammadi Scriptures*, Codex IX, Section 6.6.

• • • • • • • •

Rosicrucian Alchemy

Alchemy was an essential part of the teachings of the Rosicrucian Order from its inception. The mystical fellowship was allegedly founded in 1407 by Christian Rosenkreuz (literally, "Rosy Cross"). The original Order of the Rosy Cross consisted of eight bachelor doctors who dedicated themselves to the "higher good" and started healing the sick without payment. For them, the Rosy Cross was a symbol of higher love and understanding.

Over the years, the original group grew into a secret brotherhood of alchemists and sages whose goal was to transform the arts, sciences, religion, and politics of Europe into a more enlightened view of the world. In the early seventeenth century, the brotherhood went public with the release of three manifestos: the *Fama Fraternitatis* (*Fame of the Brotherhood of the Rosy Cross*, 1614), the *Confessio Fraternitatis* (*Confession of the Brotherhood of the Rosy Cross*, 1615), and, in 1617, an alchemical text called the *Chymical Wedding of Christian Rosicross*, which opened with Dee's Monad symbol.

Between 1614 and 1620, over four hundred books were published that discussed the Rosicrucian manuscripts. By 1700, the Rosicrucians had grown into an influential movement of alchemists, magicians, scientists, and philosophers, who sought to apply alchemical operations to perfect both individuals and society. Prominent alchemists who were adherents of the group included John Dee (1527–1608), Heinrich Khunrath (1560–1605), Francis Bacon (1561–1626), Robert Fludd (1574–1637), Elias Ashmole (1617–1692), Thomas Vaughan (1621–1666), Robert Boyle (1627–1691), Isaac Newton (1643–1727), Count St. Germain (1691–1784), and Count Cagliostro (1743–1795).

Rosicrucian alchemy is a melding of practical and spiritual techniques based on the universal principles of transformation. Thus, the operations of alchemy apply not only to lab work but also to the psychological and spiritual transformation. The path to initiation in the Rosicrucian system involves nine stages of inner and outer transmutation of the threefold human soul, the threefold human spirit, and the threefold human body.

Rosicrucian philosophy gave birth to nearly fifty new Rose Cross organizations. The influential Fraternity of the Gold and Rosy Cross was founded by alchemist Samuel Richter (1690–1760?) in Germany in 1740, and new Rose Cross degrees and rites were added to the Masonic orders in the 1770s. The *Societas Rosicruciana* (Rosicrucian Society) was formed in Scotland and limited its membership to Christian Master Masons. The Rosicrucians heavily influenced many other groups, including the Martinists, Knights Templar, Golden Dawn, Anthroposophical Society, and the Theosophical Society.

Modern Rosicrucian organizations include the Rosicrucian Fellowship, founded by Danish mystic Max Heindel (1865–1919) in California in 1909, and the Lectorium Rosicrucianum, founded in Holland by Jan van Rijckenborgh (1896–1968) in 1924. The largest organization, the Ancient Mystical Order Rosae Crucis (AMORC), was founded by Harvey Spencer Lewis (1883–1939) after he was initiated into the Rosicrucian mysteries in France. In 1915, he opened the headquarters in New York and then moved it to San Jose, California, in 1927.

The Sons of Hermes in Europe

The rising influence of Hermeticism in Europe spread into the Church and blossomed in several Christian mysticism movements. One of the most popular was the Quietist Movement, born in Spain in the writings of Catholic nun Teresa of Avila (1515–1582) and priest Miguel de Molinos (1640–1696).

Like the Sons of Hermes, the Quietists believed it possible to have an inner experience of the divine within the human soul, which can achieve divine union while still on earth. We know from their journals and diaries that many Renaissance alchemists practiced Quietist techniques in the privacy of their chambers. The four stages of this powerful method are given in the following section.

The Quietist Method[12]

Step 1—Quieting

To begin the Quieting process, sit comfortably with your spine upright and close your eyes. Do not perform Quieting while lying down. The best time to practice is early morning, after a nap, on a day off, or other time of solitude without interruptions.

This basic process of Quieting takes place on all levels of body, mind, and soul. Beginning on the level of your body, slowly withdraw your attention from physical sensations and sensory inputs. Start "softening" the body by relaxing the muscles and releasing tension.

On the level of mind, Quieting requires stilling the constant chatter of thoughts and the swirling chaos of emotional energy. During this initial stage, the mental faculties are not yet completely purified, and one tends to be distracted by lingering thoughts, emotions, memories, fantasies, planning, worrying, and other lingering impressions in the mind. Simply ignore these without deliberately trying to control them in any way. Try not to invest any energy pushing them away or attempting to bury them. Let them dissolve by not any paying attention to them.

Other distractions that arise during this kind of activity are insights, breakthroughs, and self-reflected comments such as "Am I doing this right?," "I feel so peaceful," etc. All these attachments—even the positive ones—will cause the mind to descend into worldly concerns.

---

12. Hauck, "Searching for the Cosmic Quintessence," *Rose+Croix Journal*, 9.

The mind should be clear, without any ideas or impressions. It may take some time to achieve this state, but it will manifest eventually if you maintain an attitude of dissolution and surrender and keep reducing everything to a state of simple awareness. When mental quieting has been attained, the attention should be rested behind the eyes or forehead.

On the level of soul, the Quieting process is one of release from earthly desires. It is a way of soothing our inner being by letting go of nagging feelings of guilt, greed, pride—intrusive desires of any kind. It is also necessary to overcome feelings of deficiency, sinfulness, or inferiority and to realize the Soul is infinite and not tied to this world or to the acts of any temporal ego that emerged from it. Successful quieting of the Soul results in a feeling of loving innocence and transcendent peacefulness.

Once body, mind, and soul are quieted, the work focuses on the Cultivation of Silence. The primary work here is on the individual will, which becomes lost or absorbed into the divine presence within the sacred Stillness. Remember, it is the Stillness itself that dissolves you.

Do not set a time limit or use an alarm to end the Quieting phase. Do it as long as you can, and when you feel it is time, gently withdraw from this Inner Laboratory and end the session. Clarity of intent is what makes this work. Once that is lost, it is time to stop.

Step 2—Reversion

Once Quieting is mastered, move directly from that phase to the second step, which is Reversion. During Reversion, the focus is on surrendering yourself completely to the divine will and seeking higher guidance to replace your own personal will. Ironically, this occurs most easily when a person is at the end of their rope—frustrated and disappointed in their efforts to change themselves. It can happen to anyone trying to do something extraordinary with their lives and being thwarted by peers, family, careers, social expectations, dogma, or other cultural restrictions.

To really understand Reversion, you need to understand the ways in which you have rejected the divine in your life. Some people throw themselves into daily chores, busy work, obligations, and jobs and never acknowledge the spiritual level of their lives. They do not believe in mystical experiences, or they think accepting such ideas would somehow interfere with their practical goals. Others are consumed by soul-robbing careers that demand all their time and energy, and they do not have the luxury of experimenting with spirituality. Still others are hardened into a materialistic approach to the world through greed, rejection, abuse or painful experiences, or just lack of love in their lives.

The practice during this stage is to reflect on your failures to accept spiritual realities. Reflect on how that has robbed your life of depth and meaning. Acknowledge the ways in which your soul has been damaged because of it. All that should remain is the sincere urge to be healed and made whole again.

· · · · · · · ·

Step 3—Recollection

The third step in the Quietist method is Recollection, which is a process of transcending duality and affirming the divine Source of all things. The work of Recollection begins with intense mental focus in which one concentrates on the withdrawal of the Soul from worldly temptations and enters devout contemplation on the power of spiritual passion. The two previous steps must be mastered before proceeding to the Recollection stage.

The primary tool of Recollection is deep contemplation, which must be practiced inside the heart and not intellectually. A deep piety will develop in your heart that is beyond any that can be achieved through religious dogma or ceremonial performances. This pureness in the heart becomes a steadfast guide, as the Soul desires to be led by the divine Will only.

From the Hermetic viewpoint, this emerging spirit is Thoth/Hermes, the inner guide that is born within the purified heart. In practice, one must agree to the necessity of divine assistance—something totally separate from one's being—that will provide the confidence and actualized faith to proceed to the final stage in this process.

It is very important to persevere in a state of deep contemplation and continue residing in the heart until your personal ego dissolves. In terms of spiritual chemistry, the vessel of the soul must be hermetically sealed so nothing from the mundane world contaminates it. Suddenly, you feel "refreshed and renewed" by the unmistakable presence of divine grace.

At that point, *contemplation must cease immediately without discursive thinking of any kind, and the methods by which you achieved this state must be abandoned.* Your soul must allow the divine to work within it—and through it. The Soul must bloom naturally without hindrance and allow the influx of grace to continue if possible.

Step 4—Infused Contemplation

The final step of the Quietist method may take some time to achieve, because the flowering of the Soul depends on maintaining an open gateway to divine grace. Proceeding directly from the previous step, one now enters a state of passive contemplation in which one witnesses the infusion of divine energy. It is experienced as an expansive fascination and profound humbling in the presence of something greater. One feels completely fulfilled and fully alive and requires nothing else. The frenzied search for truth ends and one exists in a state of gnostic bliss. It is a rare and wonderful state that human beings can—and have—achieved.

Each individual soul is also part of the greater Soul of the universe. Therefore, one's soul is also the center of the universe, because a person can become one with the divine Mind by cohabitating the same sacred space.

To stay in this holy place, continuous self-denial and mortification are required. Pride and self-love on any level must be banished, so that all that remains is the simple and pure desire to remain in the presence of the divine, which is the Soul's desire and true home.

• • • • • • • •

Grounding Divine Energy

The initiate's role during Infused Contemplation is to become the perfect vessel for divine energy. Thinking this or trying to visualize it is not enough. One must continue in this final phase in a wholly passive state. Physical sensations will eventually disappear. Memory and imagination will now be absorbed in the divine, and a feeling of ecstasy will permeate one's being as the energy condenses into a new incarnation.

Iamblichus named this new body the *Augoeides*, from the Greek term meaning "luminous body." It is also known as the "Cloak of Hermes," the tangible body of light or transformed spiritual body worn by the initiate who has overcome the limitations of physical consciousness. In the Golden Dawn tradition, Aleister Crowley taught that the Augoeides is born within the initiate as a separate identity—a higher spirit or guardian angel.

But the Augoeides is just one form that can be taken by the grounding of divine energy. Alchemists refer to the conscious projection or manifestation of desires in the physical world as *chemicalization*, although it has nothing to do with laboratory chemicals. The term refers to the use of certain methods to condense one's spiritual powers into etheric "chemicals" that can react and have an effect in the real world. The steps in this psychospiritual process are outlined below in the following section.

Chemicalization

Step 1—Sealing

The first step is to get a clear image of what it is you want to accomplish. Then try to isolate the relevant essences and primal forces associated with your goal. Next, seal these raw ideas and emotions in the Vessel of Transformation. The vessel could be a ritual space or your own mind, but it must be hermetically sealed and purified of outside influences. The work is in the Inner Laboratory, and it may take some effort to connect with the archetypal essences of the situation or desire. Each must be identified as separate "chemicals," with their own identities and properties.

Step 2—Agitation

This is a process of stirring up the energies or bringing them to life in the sealed vessel. It involves active imagination—visualizations and guided imagery designed to encourage the trapped essences to express and release their archetypal energies.

Step 3—Combustion

Having released the volatile "inner vapors," you now set them afire with forceful, focused intention. You need to turn up the fire to gain control and direct the energy toward completion of your goal. It begins with a period of purposeful chaos and inflammation. In this tumultuous state, you will find the truth you are looking for not in the mind but in the blood—in your feelings and desires.

· · · · · · · · ·

Next is a courageous and unrelenting intrusion of your intention into the inner cauldron. It is the aggressive application of your will over the seething powers trapped inside. Finally, as you gain control, the energy changes. It becomes more coalesced and starts flowing on its own—like lava.

Step 4—Withdrawal

The willful fires are abruptly withdrawn and the aggressive focusing of the flame of consciousness turned off. Total silence—without any thoughts or emotions—must prevail. The essences in the vessel are now cooking in their own heat, digesting in their own juices. There may be a black period of doubt or depression within you, but this is part of the process. To succeed, you must let go without losing interest.

Step 5—Manifestation

After the ritual ends, the original desire or goal gradually begins to reappear in your life. But you must not rush it or want it too badly. Never talk about it or share the experience with others at this point. Enthusiasm must be contained—let the desire gain power slowly. Allow the energy to congeal on its own and flow at its own pace toward the target. The pregnancy of your intention must have time to mature in the darkness. Soon, perhaps unexpectedly, your desire will manifest into reality.

The process of projection and manifestation requires a lot of inner work and discipline. You must learn to sacrifice yourself, for you are an ingredient in this process. The purification and concentration of your desire, willpower, and imagination reignite your Secret Fire on a higher level that fuels the continuing transformation as an independent force or servitor.

The Operations of Alchemy

The names of laboratory operations can vary in alchemical manuscripts, and even the number of operations can exceed seventy. For instance, in the astrological arrangement, there are twelve operations that work through the zodiac.[*] The Great Work in this system follows the houses of astrology: Aries (Calcination), Taurus (Congelation), Gemini (Fixation), Cancer (Dissolution), Leo (Digestion), Virgo (Distillation), Libra (Sublimation), Scorpio (Separation), Sagittarius (Ceration), Capricorn (Putrefaction/Fermentation), Aquarius (Multiplication), and Pisces (Projection).

Generally, most procedures in alchemy reduce to six or seven basic operations. This is because there are different names for the same processes. Calcination and incineration, coagulation and congelation, separation and purgation, cibation (adding water at the right time) and solution (or dissolution), are all names for similar operations. Sometimes the operations are part of each other. For example, putrefaction (or digestion) is part of the fermentation process, and sublimation is a form of distillation.

* * * * * * * *

In the planetary/metals sequence, which we will see at the end of this book in the Azoth drawing (figure 16), there are seven operations corresponding to the planets and their metals, beginning with Saturn/Lead and working up to the Sun/Gold. However, there are two arrangements of this drawing. In the Ptolemaic system (140–1600 CE), the Earth is at the center of the universe, and the Sun, Moon, and planets circle around it. In this scheme, the Sun is at ray four (conjunction) and the Moon at ray five (fermentation) in the Azoth drawing. The Copernican system (1543–present) reflects the true arrangement, with the Sun at the center of our solar system. This modern Ladder of the Planets pattern (figure 16), which is favored by psychologists and contemporary magicians, has the Moon at ray six (distillation) and the Sun at ray seven (coagulation).

To confuse matters more, the alchemists liked to scramble the order of the operations, and very few drawings depict the operations in their proper order. Yet one thing that does seem to stay the same are the four phases of transformation. The first is the Black phase, which involves the destruction of existing structures or habits. The second White Phase is a period of purification of the surviving essences. The third, very brief Yellow phase represents the hint of gold or dawning of inner light that is taking place. The final Red Phase of empowerment is the ultimate fusion of spirit and matter.

In the esoteric alchemy of the Golden Dawn and Rosicrucian orders, the White and Red are the dominant phases of the Great Work. In these traditions, the White Phase of inner purity and the Red Phase of outer projection each consists of three to six alchemical operations.

The White and Red phases come together in the adept (on earth) during the final operation of Conjunction. This is ancient Egyptian or Ptolemaic alchemy with the earth at the center, and it represents an important distinction from other spiritual or religious movements. It implies the final stage of perfection is not on high in some ethereal heaven but right here on earth in matter. In this view, the spiritization of matter (and the human body) is the true goal of the Great Work.

* Pernety, *Dictionnaire Mytho-Hermétique (Mytho-Hermetic Dictionary)*, 99.

Ritual and Prayer in the Laboratory

The alchemist's laboratory was a sacred space in which the spiritual powers above merged with the physical work below (figure 3). Alchemical experiments became rituals in which the alchemist identified with the substance at hand and suffered with it through its transformations. The practical work of chemistry was done simultaneously with prayer and meditation.

Figure 3. Laboratory

There was usually a special chamber or tabernacle in the lab called the *Oratorium* where the alchemist could find privacy to meditate or pray. *Ora et Labora* ("Pray and Work") was the guiding dictum of alchemists. In the following two experimental procedures—making tinctures and elixirs—we will see how the merging of physical and spiritual took place.

Making a Spiritized Tincture [13]

Step 1—Preparing the Menstruum

Menstruum is the alchemist's word for the alcohol, acid, glycerin, oil, or other solvent used to extract essences from a substance. For herbal tinctures or elixirs, the preferred menstruum is high-proof grape alcohol. However, it is difficult to make and expensive to procure. Most modern practitioners use taste-free Everclear (190 proof), Spirytus (192 proof), Balkan Vodka (179 proof), or popular vodkas (80 proof).

13. Hauck, *Spagyric Alchemy*, 23.

You will also need a clean jelly jar or small Mason jar with a volume of around 100–200 ml (3.4–6.8 ounces). If the jar has a metal lid, you will have to cover it in plastic wrap. Metal spoons or other utensils should also never come in contact with the menstruum or tincture. Metal grounds and changes the spiritual energy you are trying to capture and control. Remember, the vessels of the alchemists were treated like ritual items and not everyday bottles, flasks, and glasses.

Step 2—Signatures and Timing

Before you begin working with the herb, get to know its signatures by handling it and paying attention to its color, odor, and physical structure. Make an infusion (tea) from the herb and taste it. Research the folklore and properties of the herb. The more you know about it, the better. Apply your knowledge and familiarity with the herb to try to connect with the soul of the herb in meditation. This will release and capture the herb's archetypal power.

All major operations on the herb, such as picking, drying, crushing, mixing, and extraction, should ideally be begun during the correct planetary hour on the planetary day ruling the herb. (Planetary charts can be downloaded from Alchemystudy.com/download/Planetary_Charts.pdf.)

Wash and clean the herb whose tincture will be made. The favorite healing herb of the alchemists was the jupiterian plant *Melissa* (lemon balm), but any edible herb can be used. Start by drying the herb in an *open* oven at low heat (less than 180°F or 82°C) for 2–3 hours. Pre-dried herbs and bulk teas can also be used if you do not have access to fresh plants.

Step 3—Begin the Extraction

Begin the extraction process in the planetary hour of the ruling planet of the herb. Begin with meditation and prayer to create a sacred space within the vessel. Then take the dried herb and crush it by hand into small pieces. You can also use a mortar and pestle or a coffee grinder to grind it to a coarse powder. You can use metal utensils with the dried herb but not with the menstruum or tincture. Place about 40 ml (1.4 ounces) of the powder per 100 ml (3.4 ounces) of volume in your jar. With focused intent, pour the menstruum over the herb until it is saturated but not over two-thirds full. Hermetically seal the jar with a tight lid.

Step 4—Incubation

Start the incubation process by wrapping the jar in cloth or foil. It should not be exposed to light during the initial incubation period. Then place the jar in a warm location, near (not on) a radiator, furnace, or water heater. Shake the jar vigorously once or twice a day. While shaking it, visualize the herb willingly giving up its essences or soul.

Step 5—Distillation

The fluid inside will evaporate as it warms up and then condense again. As this natural inner distillation repeats, the soul of the herb is regenerated by minute degrees closer to perfection. This

. . . .

circulation and maceration ("chewing") is responsible for the tincturing process. The fluid will become darker with each passing day. Alchemically, the coloration (or tincturing) is the extraction of the Sulfur (soul essence) from the Salt (plant matter) by the Mercury (spirit of alcohol).

Continue this process for two to three weeks, until the color of the tincture is dark. This is your "Philosophical Child" and must be treated with a caring attitude. Let no one else handle the jar or even view its contents. Each time you handle it, visualize the sulfurous soul being born in the murky herbal mass in the darkness of the Hermetic womb of the jar.

Step 6—Animating the Mercury

After the color of the liquid is sufficiently darkened, let the jar cool to room temperature before opening. Opening the jar is considered the moment of birth for the resurrected soul of the herb. Like the birth of a child, the first moments of breath are crucial to survival.

In a process known as "Animating the Mercury," the alchemist brings the tincture to life outside the womb of the sealed jar. While carefully opening the jar, visualize the forces that animate the living world. As the Emerald Tablet tells us, "Its father is the Sun; Its mother the Moon. The Wind carries it in its belly; Its nurse is the Earth."[14] The enlivening solar spirit of Celestial Fire from above is carried by the air and enters the body through breathing. From below, the nurturing lunar spirit of Manifestation grounds the energy in a living soul.

Allow the tincture to breathe while warming the jar in your hands and meditating on this divine process. The soul of the herb is now resurrected and enlivened by the intervention of spirit.

Step 7—Retrieving the Living Tincture

Now the tincture is a living thing and can survive on its own. Press out any remaining liquid from the mass of plant matter. Then filter the solution (using medium filter paper or coffee filters) until it is clear of particles or debris. The resulting tinctured liquid contains the Sulfur or soul of the herb (its essential oils) united with its Mercury or spirit (the alcohol).

Making the Elixir[15]

Step 1—Incinerating the Dregs

If you wish to go on and make the Elixir, save all the dregs or waste products from the tincturing process. These consist of phlegm (liquid scum, foam, and goo) and feces (solid waste and residue) removed by filtering. The solids are the depleted salts or dead body of the herb—what the alchemists called the *caput mortum* ("dead head").

---

14. Hauck, *The Emerald Tablet*, 45.

15. Hauck, *Spagyric Alchemy*, 31.

The word *elixir* is from the Arabic *Al-iksir*, which literally means "from the ashes." The elixir process is all about purifying and resurrecting the immortal essences within the cremated remains of the herb.

Place the dregs in a heatproof bowl, pot, or frying pan and cover with a wire screen. Ignite the alcohol-soaked material and let it burn. The mass will begin to incinerate and roast. Let the dead plant matter burn itself out and cool.

Step 2—Purifying the Ashes

Take the ashes from the initial combustion and grind to a fine powder with a mortar and pestle. Then place the ashes in a covered crucible or heatproof dish. Heat in an oven, at the highest temperature possible, until the ashes have turned grayish white. Continued heating at higher temperatures will turn the ashes pure white. Heating for several days at 3000°F (1650°C) would turn them red. Store the purified ashes in a clean and clearly labeled flask. You may have to repeat this process many times to get enough ashes to work with. Alchemists sometimes refer to these ashes as the "new body," or resurrected Salt.

Step 3—Tincturing the Ashes

Mix the tincture from the previous work with the purified ashes at the correct planetary hour on the planetary day ruling the herb. Pour the entire tincture over the ashes in the flask. If the tincture is still living, there should be a slight fizzing sound. Shake vigorously, then hermetically seal the flask.

Step 4—Incubating the Tinctured Ashes

Put the flask in an incubator or by a heat source to digest. Shake three times daily. During this time, much of the purified ashes (or resurrected Salt) will be absorbed into the tincture. After three weeks, pour off any remaining liquid, leaving the new Salt residue in the flask. Now seal the flask and let it sit for another few weeks in an incubator or in a warm spot out of direct light.

Step 5—Animating the Elixir

Open the jar and let the material breathe for the first time in the birthing process described in step 6 of the tincturing operation (Animating the Mercury). Leave the flask open and let the material dry up and granulate. Scrape this regenerated Salt out of the jar after it has dried, then grind it to a fine powder in a *warm* mortar. Store the reanimated elixir in a clean dark-glass flask or jar.

The elixir powder at this stage, known as the Powder of Projection, represents the resurrection of the soul of the herb into a new higher or spiritized body. The combination of the alchemist's grounding spirit and the Celestial spirit from above makes the elixir magically healing. Depending on the characteristics (or "signatures") of the herb, the elixir can be used to cure a variety of specific conditions.

. . . .

In general, the process of projection is used to transmute a lesser substance or situation into a higher or more perfect form. Projection opens a channel between the alchemist below and the divine energies above. It requires intense focusing and deliberate direction of etheric energies on the part of the alchemist. This mysterious marriage of mind and matter is when the alchemist becomes the magician.

Alchemist-Magician John Dee

Dr. John Dee (1527–1608) was a true Renaissance man who achieved world renown as a mathematician, alchemist, magician, mapmaker, cryptographer, astrologer, and philosopher. His library was one of the largest in England, with nearly four thousand rare texts and manuscripts, and his alchemical laboratory rivaled any in the world at the time.

When he entered Cambridge College at the age of fifteen, Dee began a five-year regimen of sleeping only four hours a day, so he could devote more time to studying Hermetic philosophy and alchemy. "I was so vehemently bent to study," said Dee of his time at Cambridge, "that for those years I did inviolably keep this order: only to sleep four hours every night; to allow to meet, eat, and drink two hours every day; and of the other eighteen hours all were spent in my studies and learning."

Dee grew into an imposing figure with a commanding presence. Biographer John Aubrey described his physical appearance in his manuscript *Brief Lives* (1693): "He had a very fair, clear, rosy complexion and a long beard as white as milk. He was tall and slender—a very handsome man. He wore a gown like an artist's frock, with hanging sleeves, and a slit. A mighty good man was he."[*]

Dee was a close confidant of Queen Elizabeth I, who issued him a license to practice alchemy and make gold. As a favor to the Queen, it is said, he "controlled the Elements" and cast a spell on the Spanish Armada by causing bad weather to thwart the invasion of England. He is said to have been the inspiration for Prospero in Shakespeare's *The Tempest* (1610) and also the model for Goethe's *Faust* (1587).

While most alchemists of his time sought the Philosopher's Stone for its alleged ability to transmute base metals into gold, Dee viewed it as much as a philosophy as a physical object. He described it as a state of magical consciousness that could transmute the human soul into a more perfect state. "The Philosopher's Stone," he stated, "is the force behind the evolution of life and the universal binding power which unites minds and souls in a higher human oneness."[**]

[*] Clark, *Aubrey's Brief Lives*, 255.
[**] Halliwell, *The Private Diary of Dr. John Dee*, 87.

Dr. John Dee—Alchemist and Magician

Perhaps the greatest European master of projection and chemicalization was British alchemist-magician Dr. John Dee (1527–1608). He invented a system of ceremonial magic based on the evocation and commanding of heavenly spirits and revealed the Enochian language in which they communicated.[16] He was given a license to practice alchemy by Queen Elizabeth I and was considered a master occultist and astrologer.

In addition, Dee was one of the leading mathematicians in the world. Convinced that Euclidean geometry was sacred and originated from the One Mind, just as Pythagoras taught, he constructed a multilayered symbol that incorporated all the planetary energies and their angelic correspondences. He used the ancient ciphers of alchemy as geometric figures and applied Euclidean geometry to capture their deeper meaning and relationships.

Figure 4. Monad

He called his sigil the *Monad*, from the Greek word meaning the "ultimate One"—the singular entity from which all properties are derived (figure 4). Dee said his geometric proof would revolutionize all areas of knowledge and urged astronomers to stop peering through their telescopes trying to understand the heavens and instead spend their time meditating on his Monad. If one could drop the Monad cipher into a great sea of First Matter, he noted, then the universe as we know it would emerge.

The Monad ritual described below is a geometric meditation using a square and compass, the classic tools of sacred geometry used in Freemasonry. Take a moment between each step to reflect on the esoteric properties of the construction.

---

16. Eds. note: See Book Seven: Enochian Magick & Mysticism for a thorough overview of the Enochian tradition.

The Monad Ritual

1. At the center of a white piece of unlined paper, make a single dot. This is the Monad, the dimensionless One or Hermetic source outside creation that modern science views as the inexplicable singularity of the Big Bang.

2. Using the Monad point as center, draw a circle with a 1-inch (2.5 cm) radius (figure 5). The circle delineates the manifested universe. Now look at what you have drawn. It is the cipher for the Sun, and what is about to unfold is the Operation of the Sun. This is also the cipher for the perfected metal gold.

Figure 5. Sun

3. Now draw a semicircle of the same radius intersecting the top of the cipher for the Sun (figure 6). This crescent represents the Moon facing the Sun and reflecting its light. This union of Fire (Sun) and Water (Moon) is the Sacred Marriage of the King and Queen in alchemy. The overall figure you have created also represents the Horns of Taurus or the Cornucopia of creation.

Figure 6. Moon

4. At the very bottom of the circle, draw a vertical line downward for 3 inches (7.5 cm). This is the vertical axis of reality, or *Axis Mundi*, that connects the spiritual or energetic realm above with the material or manifested world below.

5. At 1 inch (2.5 cm) down the vertical axis, draw a horizontal line 2 inches (5 cm) wide centered at right angles to the vertical line (figure 7). This is the horizontal axis of reality, and it symbolizes the fundamental duality of creation. It represents the polarities of male-female, King-Queen, light-darkness, good-evil, right-left, and positive-negative that make the world go round.

Figure 7. Construction

6. The cross we constructed provides deep insight into reality. Known as the Cross of the Elements, it is where the Soul is crucified, torn between opposites. Dee calls the point where the lines meet the "Copulative Center," meaning a fertile inner point of balance and repose. It represents human consciousness, just as the center point above in the Sun represents the Divine Mind.

7. The two lines and their crossing point make up a *Tria Prima* of forces representing Body or Salt (the horizontal line), Soul or Sulfur (the vertical line), and Spirit or Mercury (the crossing point). The *Tria Prima* plus the Four Elements constitute the Septenary, or seven-fold pattern of creation.

8. A Quaternary, or Cubic Space, is created by the four intersecting lines, which stand for the Four Elements. The Quintessence, or Fifth Element, is indicated by their shared crossing point that represents mind or consciousness.

9. Here Dee reveals the Octad, which is concealed "in a most secret manner" in the geometric relationship of the four lines plus the four right angles. He advises the initiate to study this relationship "with great attention." The hidden Octad refers to an unseen or etheric reality all around us. In *Discourse on the Eighth and Ninth*, Hermes Trismegistus calls it "the realm beyond words" behind physical reality.[17]

10. At the bottom of the vertical line, draw two 1-inch-radius (2.5 cm) semicircles—one touching the bottom of the line on the left side and the other on the right side. The two semicircles form the astrological sign of Aries, which is the first sign of the zodiac and traditionally when the Great Work begins. It is also associated with the Fire Element and the burst of life in the spring. "To begin the work of this Monad," notes Dee, "the aid of Fire is required." The point at the bottom where the two semicircles meet represents another kind of consciousness—the instinctive life force or Mind of Nature.

17. Meyer, *The Nag Hammadi Scriptures*, section 6.6.

· · · · · · · ·

11. The construction is complete, but the ritual continues as its deeper meanings are revealed. Take a minute to study the entire Monad, paying attention to the overall relationship between the lines.

12. Within the body of the Monad, Dee has concealed all the glyphs of the seven planets and their associated metals. By tracing the connecting lines and arcs in different ways, one can locate all seven heavenly spheres and thereby reveal how the archetypal forces relate in Nature. See if you can find the corresponding alchemical ciphers in Dee's Monad symbol.

13. The merged planetary ciphers are arranged from left to right and top to bottom around the Cross of the Elements (figure 8). According to Dee, by placing the planetary ciphers in their proper relationship, the symbols come alive. In this arrangement, the Sun at the top of the Monad is the only symbol that is always the same and, in that sense, incorruptible like gold. No matter which way the Monad is turned—upside down, left to right, right to left, or its mirror image—the cipher of the Sun and gold is always the same. The shape or phase of the Moon, however, is tied to the position of the Sun.

Figure 8. Ciphers

14. The heart of the Monad and the one cipher that embodies all the others is Mercury (figure 9). Mercury is the key to transformation and is considered the First Matter of the metals. Just as is depicted in the Monad, Mercury is the source of all the metals and amalgamates them together as one.

Figure 9. Mercury

15. The planetary metals are arranged around the Cross of the Elements. The primal duality of Saturn/Lead is represented in the left-right mirror image of its cipher, each of which is composed of one of the Aries semicircles and the vertical axis (figures 10 and 11). The duality of Jupiter/Tin is revealed in the 90-degree mirror image of its ciphers along the horizontal axis (figures 12 and 13). Each cipher is composed of the lower quadrant of the Cross of Elements and its corresponding Aries semicircle.

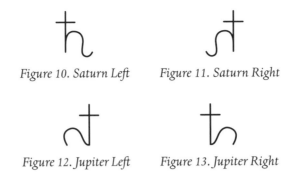

Figure 10. Saturn Left   *Figure 11. Saturn Right*

Figure 12. Jupiter Left   *Figure 13. Jupiter Right*

16. The ciphers for Mars/Iron and Venus/Copper form their own male-female duality on the vertical axis, where they lie in conjunction on top of each other (figures 14 and 15).

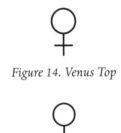

Figure 14. Venus Top

Figure 15. Mars Bottom

17. The ritual is now complete. For additional insights into the Monad, review the twenty-four theorems of John Dee's treatise *The Hieroglyphic Monad* published in 1564.[18]

Mystery of the Azoth

Another powerful drawing that incorporates the occult symbology of alchemy is a meditative mandala known as the *Azoth of the Philosophers* (figure 16), by German alchemist Basil Valentine (1394–1450). *Azoth* is from the Arabic word for mercury, in the sense of a Universal Solvent (also known as the *Alkahest*). The letters *A* and *Z* in the word convey the idea of unlimited application to everything from A to Z or from alpha to omega.

18. Dee, *The Hieroglyphic Monad*, 1975.

• • • • • • • •

Figure 16. Azoth

This drawing was considered blasphemous by the Church, and it was circulated secretly in several different forms during the late Middle Ages. The following ritual is a step-by-step working of the mandala, which reflects the corrected or Copernican order of the planets preferred by most modern alchemists and magicians.

The Azoth Ritual

Step 1—The Alchemist

The ritual begins in the circle at the very center of the mandala. Fix your attention on the face of the bearded alchemist for a few minutes and try to identify with him—like you are looking into a mirror. The downward-pointing triangle superimposed over his face is the cipher for the Water Element, and it suggests divine grace pouring down from above like rain. So within the triangle at the center of the drawing is the face of God, and the drawing clearly implies that the face of God and the face of the alchemist are the same.

Now broaden your attention to include the schematic body of the alchemist, which is shown in perfect balance with the Four Elements as depicted in his outstretched arms and legs. His right foot is firmly planted on Earth and his left is in Water. In his right hand is a torch of Fire and in his left hand an ostrich feather symbolizing Air.

• • • • • • • •

Step 2—Suspended in Duality

The alchemist stands balanced between the masculine and feminine powers. Try to understand the differences between these opposing forces as you explore the symbols that surround them. Sol, the archetypal Sun King, is seated on a lion to his right, and Luna, the archetypal Moon Queen, is seated on a great fish in the ocean to his left. Above the King is the torch of Fire; below him is Earth. Above the Queen is the feather of Air; below her is Water.

Sol holds a scepter and a shield indicating his strength and authority over the visible world, but the fiery dragon of his rejected unconscious waits patiently in a cave beneath him. Luna holds the reins to a great fish, symbolizing her gentle taming of nature, and behind her is a chaff of wheat, which stands for her connection to fertility and growth. The bow and arrow she cradles in her left arm symbolize the wounds of the heart and body she accepts as part of her existence.

Step 3—The Three Essentials

Move your attention to the large inverted triangle that stands behind the circular emblem of the alchemist. Again, this is the cipher for Water, but now it carries the *Tria Prima*, or three primordial forces, pouring down. Sulfur as energy is depicted in the left corner as the Sun. It is labeled *Anima*, or Soul. On top of it, a salamander plays in fire—the classic alchemical symbol for energy.

In the right corner, Mercury as light is depicted as the reflecting Moon. It is labeled *Spiritus*, or Spirit. On top perches the Bird of Spirit ready to take flight. Finally, Salt as matter is depicted at the bottom as the Cube of Elements. It is labeled *Corpus*, or body. The five stars hovering around it suggest it also contains a hidden Fifth Element, the invisible Quintessence, or life force.

Step 4—The Ray of Saturn

In a circular pattern around the body of the alchemist are seven rays or emanations indicating a progressive level of transformation. These operations are numbered from one to seven and contain the cipher of the corresponding planet and metal. Following each ray is a circle (called a *roundel*) containing a scene that elaborates on the work to be performed at that stage.

The first ray is the downward-pointing black ray labeled number one. It represents the beginning of the Ladder of the Planets and is marked by the cipher that stands for both the metal lead and the planet Saturn. The square symbol for Salt is also shown, which indicates our work begins in the unredeemed matter of the physical realm.

This heavy oppressive darkness—whether in the laboratory or in the mind—is where the Great Work begins. Symbols of the Black Phase of alchemy are the Crow, the Raven, the Toad, and the *Massa Confusa*, or First Matter.

The first roundel (between rays one and two) shows a black crow perching on top of a skull. Next to it on the outer ring is the Latin word *Visita*, which means "to visit or start a journey." This is the initial Black Phase of alchemy, during which the subject is purified by breaking it down during mortification and calcination. Calcination is the heating of a substance in a crucible or over an open flame until it is reduced to ashes. Psychologically, this is the destruction of ego and its attachments to possessions and material reality. Reflect on what this ray says about your own situation.

Step 5—The Ray of Jupiter

The second ray is marked with the cipher that stands for both the metal tin and the planet Jupiter. The corresponding second roundel depicts the black crow watching itself being dissolved. The word on the outer ring near this roundel is *Interiora*, which means "the interior or innermost parts."

This is the beginning of the White Phase of purification. Symbols include a white Skull or Skeleton, the White Swan, and Two Fish (Soul and Spirit) swimming in opposite directions. The operation at this stage is a further process of mortification known as *dissolution*. Dissolution is dissolving the ashes from calcination in water or acids. This represents a further breaking down of the artificial structures of the psyche. Again, reflect on how this operation would take place in your own personality.

Step 6—The Ray of Mars

The third ray is marked with the cipher signifying both the metal iron and the planet Mars. It is also marked with a smaller cipher for Sulfur, one of the *Tria Prima* forces. Iron and sulfur come together chemically in vitriol, or sulfuric acid, the aggressive liquid fire of the alchemists.

The third roundel depicts the alchemical operation of separation. The remains of the black, earthbound crow are being picked apart by two white soul-birds, who retrieve any viable parts. Separation is the isolation of the components of dissolution by filtration and discarding any unworthy material. What valuable essences would such an operation reveal in you?

This step is the first coming together of the birds of Soul and Spirit and represents the conclusion of the White Phase of purification. In the ring above this roundel is written *Terrae*, which means "from the earth." It refers to the genuine material being separated out from the dregs of matter at this stage. Continue this operation on the inner level by trying to recognize and preserve the genuine parts of your personality as you remember your origin state of innocence.

Step 7—The Ray of Venus

The fourth ray is marked with the cipher that stands for both copper and Venus. The fourth roundel depicts the birds of Soul and Spirit leaving the earth together, lifting a five-spiked crown representing the Fifth Element, or Quintessence, recovered from the preceding operations.

In the ring above the roundel is inscribed the word *Rectificando*, which means "by rectification" or "setting things right." This is the turning point in alchemy, when the matter undergoes spiritization. Known as the Green Phase, it is symbolized by the Green Lion, the Cockerel and Hen, the King and Queen holding hands, and scenes of marriage and copulation.

Here begins the sacred work of conjunction, which is the recombination of the saved essences from separation into a new incarnation. On the personal level, this is the Integration of the Personality—a return to wholeness and renewed confidence. Reflect on what the empowerment of your true self would look like.

Step 8—The Ray of Mercury

The fifth ray is marked with the cipher for the metal mercury (quicksilver) and the planet Mercury, as well as an identical smaller symbol indicating Mercury of the Three Essentials. The fifth roundel has the inscription *Invenies*, which means "you will discover." The scene in the roundel shows the birds of Soul and Spirit nesting in a tree, brooding over the alchemical egg.

The operation here is fermentation, in which the essences of Soul and Spirit give birth to a new life. It begins with the putrefaction or decay of the product from the earthly conjunction. In a sense, it dies and is resurrected on a higher level as a new embodiment known as the Child of the Philosophers. This marks the beginning of the Red Phase of empowerment.

Fermentation is a subtle process best understood as a rebirth on a new level of spiritual reality—like the crushing of grapes to make the spirit of wine. It is initiated by the crushing of the ego or the utter destruction of worldly connections, including physical death. Some of the tools of fermentation are deep reflection and meditation, spiritual fasting, and psychoactive drugs. This phase is often associated with the rainbow or Peacock's Tail, which depict a rapid cycling through brilliant colors. In shamanic initiations, fermentation is achieved by using "plant allies" containing psychedelic substances.

Step 9—The Ray of the Moon

The sixth ray contains the cipher that stands for both the metal silver and the Moon. Distillation is the operation at this stage, and it involves the boiling and condensing of vapors from the fermented solution. The circulatory process gradually increases the purity and potency of the product of fermentation. This is the second or higher working with the element Water in the Great Work. It results in the production of the extremely pure White Stone, which represents the resurrected Soul or living essence of a substance.

Distillation is represented in the fifth roundel by a unicorn lying on the ground in front of a rose bush. According to legend, the unicorn runs tirelessly from pursuers but lies down meekly when approached by a virgin. The virgin symbolizes the purified matter at this stage, which has returned to a state of innocence and potential. The five blooms on the rose bush symbolize the Quintessence, or life force, that has been elevated and purged of contaminating forces.

· · · · · · · ·

Above the roundel is the word *Occultum*, meaning "secret or hidden," since the essences at this stage are carried invisibly by vapors. This is the level of hidden spiritual manifestation in the Azoth. Often unnoticed by others, the sublimation of psychic forces within us creates a new spiritual level of being.

Step 10—The Ray of the Sun

The seventh ray displays the cipher that stands for both gold and the Sun, and the corresponding roundel shows an androgynous youth emerging from an open grave. It is marked with the Latin word *Lapidem*, meaning "the Stone."

This is the conclusion of the Red Phase and the final operation of the Azoth. Known as *coagulation*, it begins in the concentrated solution resulting from distillation. Often referred to as the "Mother of the Stone," this solution produces an extremely pure precipitate or solid body (the White Stone). This new body, which represents the resurrected essence or Soul, is then infused with Spirit, or energy from above.

Coagulation is seen as a sacrificial act. In other words, Soul surrenders to Spirit and is assimilated into it. The sacrifice is often depicted as a pelican feeding its young with its own blood. It is also shown by brief appearances of the White Lion (Soul) in sequences with the Red Lion (Spirit). We see it again in drawings showing the White Queen in marriage ceremonies giving up her name or identity to the Red King.

The purified essences of Soul and Spirit coagulate into a perfected body known as the *Philosopher's Stone*. Existing simultaneously on all levels of reality, it represents the ultimate perfection of matter and is said to be the same for all substances. The Philosopher's Stone is sometimes depicted as a shining red crystal or symbolized by the immortal Phoenix bird rising in fire from its own ashes.

Step 11—The Ascended Essence

If we take an overview of the entire drawing, we notice a mysterious winged caricature that resembles a winged disk or Egyptian *Aureus*. Located where the head of the alchemist should be, its wings are touched on the left by the fire of the salamander and on the right by the Bird of Spirit. These symbols point to the Hermetic concept of the Augoeides, or Ascended Essence. We see it here, poised to rise up out of this drawing into the new realm of being.

Step 12—The Hidden Key

There is one last message hidden in the Azoth drawing. All the Latin words contained in the outer ring compose a summary of what has taken place: *Visita Interiora Terrae Rectificando Invenies Occultum Lapidem*. It says, "Visit the innermost parts of the earth; and by setting things right (rectifying), you will find the hidden Stone."

· · · · · · · ·

Furthermore, the first letters of these seven Latin words spell out the word *VITRIOL*. Vitriol is sulfuric acid, the highly corrosive liquid fire that drives the whole wheel of transformation. It is both the fundamental acid behind chemical change in the alchemist's laboratory and the inner or Secret Fire that brings about the spiritual transformation of the alchemist.

Golden Dawn Alchemy

The Hermetic Order of the Golden Dawn was a magical order devoted to the study and practice of theurgy. Rooted in the Rosicrucian movement, the Golden Dawn was founded in 1888 by three Scottish Rite Freemasons: William Westcott, William Woodman, and Samuel Mathers. Golden Dawn teachings are at the heart of many contemporary movements, including Thelemic groups like Aleister Crowley's A∴A∴, Ordo Templi Orientis (O.T.O.), Aurum Solis, and the Ecclesia Gnostica Catholica, as well as independent magical orders such as Wicca, the Brotherhood of Light, Builders of the Adytum, and Fraternitas Saturni.

Alchemy was an advanced practice of the Golden Dawn that was viewed as a way of linking the powers of the divine above and the physical below. William Westcott wrote a "flying roll" on alchemy called *The Science of Alchymy: Spiritual and Material*. The group also had a practicing alchemist on staff by the name of William Alexander Ayton (1816–1909). An Anglican vicar, Ayton had a well-equipped laboratory where he produced magical elixirs and stones. He spent most of his time studying alchemy but lived in constant fear that his bishop would find out what he was doing. Ayton's translation of *The Life of John Dee* by Thomas Smith was essential reading for members.

A large library of other alchemical texts, which included all the classical works, was available to higher grade members. Alchemy was introduced at the second level and continued into advanced instruction at the third level. Both practical and spiritual alchemical operations and rituals were taught. In fact, member Israel Regardie (1907–1985) once noted that a secret alchemical process was at work behind all Golden Dawn rituals.

Conclusion: The Black Art

The practices and techniques of Hermetic alchemy we have discussed all share a common source of their power. As we noted at the beginning, the Black Art practiced by Egyptian priests originated from the land of Khem—from the miraculously fertile black dirt of the Nile Delta. That kind of inexplicable, chaotic, and infinitely powerful darkness is the source of all true magic. It can be found in the dark matter/energy at the ends of the universe and in the darkest recesses of the human mind. It is a source of unlimited power.

The alchemists called that secret blackness the *First Matter*, and they believed it was the ineffable source of both consciousness and physical reality. The hidden connection between mind

• • • • • • • •

and matter is what makes the Great Work of alchemy and theurgy possible. The roots of both alchemy and magic are planted in the same black soil of the First Matter.

Sources (Bibliography)

Ayton, W. A. *The Alchemist of the Golden Dawn: The Letters of the Revd W. A. Ayton to F. L. Gardner and Others, 1886–1905*. Edited by Ellic Howe. Paris: Aquarian Press, 1985.

Begich, Nick. *Towards a New Alchemy: The Millennium Science*. Anchorage, AK: Earthpulse Press, 1997.

Blavatsky, H. P. *The Theosophical Glossary*. Los Angeles, CA: Theosophy Company, 1952.

Bryan, Cyril, trans. *Ancient Egyptian Medicine: The Papyrus Ebers*. Chicago, IL: Ares Publishers, 1980.

Clark, Andrew. *Aubrey's Brief Lives*. Oxford: University of Oxford Clarenden Press, 1898.

Copenhaver, Brian P. *Hermetica: The Greek Corpus Hermeticum and the Latin Asclepius in a New English Translation*. Cambridge, UK: Cambridge University Press, 1992.

Dee, John. *The Hieroglyphic Monad*. Boston, MA: Red Wheel Weiser, 1975.

Fowden, Garth. *The Egyptian Hermes: A Historical Approach to the Late Pagan Mind*. Princeton, MA: Princeton University Press, 1986.

Halliwell, James Orchard. *The Private Diary of Dr. John Dee*. London: BOD Ltd., 2013.

Hauck, Dennis William. *Alchemical Guide to Herbs and Food*. San Francisco, CA: Amazon Publishing, 2016.

———. *The Emerald Tablet: Alchemy for Personal Transformation*. New York: Penguin Arkana, 1999.

———. "Searching for the Cosmic Quintessence: How Alchemists Meditated in the Middle Ages and Renaissance." *Rose+Croix Journal* 10 (2014).

———. *Spagyric Alchemy: Isolating the Life Force in Plants*. San Francisco, CA: Amazon Publishing, 2017.

Iamblichus. *Theurgia: On the Mysteries of Egypt*. Translated by Alexander Wilder. New York: Metaphysical Publishing Co., 1911.

Levi, Eliphas. *Transcendental Magic: Its Doctrine and Ritual*. Translated by A. E. Waite. London: Rider & Co., 1896.

———. *Transcendental Magic: Its Doctrine and Ritual*. Translated by A. E. Waite in 1896. Reprint, San Francisco, CA: Amazon Publishing, 2017.

Mathers, S. L. MacGregor. *Astral Projection, Ritual Magic, and Alchemy: Golden Dawn Material*. Edited by Francis King. Rochester, VT: Destiny Books, 1987.

Meyer, Marvin, ed. *The Nag Hammadi Scriptures*. San Francisco, CA: HarperOne, 2009.

· · · · · · · ·

Pernety, Antoine-Joseph. *Dictionnaire Mytho-Hermétique (Mytho-Hermetic Dictionary)*. Seattle, WA: 2011. First printing 1758.

Shaw, Gregory. *Theurgy and the Soul: The Neoplatonism of Iamblichus*. University Park, PA: Pennsylvania State University Press, 1995.

Trismegistus, Hermes. *The Divine Pymander*. Translated by John Everard. Seattle, WA: Kessinger Publishing, 2010.

Zalewski, Pat. *Alchemy and Golden Dawn Ritual*. London: Rosicrucian Order of the Golden Dawn, 2011.

Suggested Reading List

Abraham, Lyndy. *A Dictionary of Alchemical Imagery*. Cambridge, UK: Cambridge University Press, 1999.

Burckhardt, Titus. *Alchemy: Science of the Cosmos, Science of the Soul*. Louisville, KY: Fons Vitae Press, 2006.

Case, Paul Foster. *Hermetic Alchemy: Science and Practice*. Boston, MA: ROGD Press, 2009.

Churton, Tobias. *The Golden Builders: Alchemists, Rosicrucians, and the First Freemasons*. New York: Barnes and Noble, 2002.

Cunningham, Scott. *Earth, Air, Fire & Water: More Techniques of Natural Magic*. Woodbury, MN: Llewellyn Publications, 2002.

Garstin, E. J. Langford. *Theurgy, or The Hermetic Practice: A Treatise on Spiritual Alchemy*. Berwick, ME: Ibis Press, 2004.

Greer, John Michael. *The New Encyclopedia of the Occult*. Woodbury, MN: Llewellyn Publications, 2005.

Grillot de Givry, Emile. *Witchcraft, Magic & Alchemy*. Mineola, NY: Dover Occult, 2009.

Guiley, Rosemary Ellen. *The Encyclopedia of Magic and Alchemy*. New York: Facts On File, 2006.

Hanegraaff, Wouter J. *Western Esotericism: A Guide for the Perplexed*. New York: Bloomsbury Academic, 2013.

Harkness, Deborah E. *John Dee's Conversations with Angels: Cabala, Alchemy, and the End of Nature*. London: Cambridge University Press, 2006.

Harpur, Patrick. *The Secret Tradition of the Soul*. New York: Evolver Editions, 2011.

Hauck, Dennis William. *The Complete Idiot's Guide to Alchemy*. New York: Penguin Alpha, 2008.

Heldstab, Celeste Rayne. *Llewellyn's Complete Formulary of Magical Oils: Over 1200 Recipes, Potions & Tinctures for Everyday Use*. Woodbury, MN: Llewellyn Worldwide, 2012.

Helmond, Johannes. *Alchemy Unveiled*. Salt Lake City, UT: Merkur Publishing, 1997.

· · · · · · · ·

King, Francis, and Stephen Skinner. *Techniques of High Magic: A Handbook of Divination, Alchemy, and the Evocation of Spirits*. Rochester, VT: Destiny Books, 2000.

Levi, Eliphas. *Transcendental Magic: Its Doctrine and Ritual*. Translated by A. E. Waite in 1896. Reprint, San Francisco, CA: Amazon Publishing, 2017.

Linden, Stanton J., ed. *The Alchemy Reader: From Hermes Trismegistus to Isaac Newton*. New York: Cambridge University Press, 2003.

Roob, Alexander. *Alchemy & Mysticism: The Hermetic Museum*. Berlin: Taschen, 1997.

Sutin, Lawrence. *Do What Thou Wilt: A Life of Aleister Crowley*. New York: St. Martin's Griffin, 2000.

Tambiah, Stanley Jeyaraja. *Magic, Science, Religion, and the Scope of Rationality*. Cambridge, UK: Cambridge University Press, 1990.

U. D., Frater. *Practical Sigil Magic: Creating Personal Symbols for Success*. Woodbury, MN: Llewellyn Publications, 2012.

Wolf, Fred Alan. *Mind into Matter: A New Alchemy of Science and Spirit*. Needham, MA: Moment Point Press, 2000.

About the Author

Dennis William Hauck is an author and lecturer in consciousness studies. His primary focus is on levels of awareness and the mechanisms of transformation of consciousness. He works to merge various philosophical and scientific traditions into a coherent theory that can be applied to personal transformation. He has contributed to several related areas, including the history of science, psychology, and the serious study of paranormal and mystical experiences.

Hauck is a leading authority on Hermeticism and alchemy. He has translated several important alchemy manuscripts and published a dozen books on the subject, including *The Emerald Tablet: Alchemy for Personal Transformation* (Penguin, 1999), *Sorcerer's Stone: A Beginner's Guide to Alchemy* (Penguin Citadel, 2004), and *The Complete Idiot's Guide to Alchemy* (Penguin Alpha, 2008). His work has been featured in *USA Today, The Wall Street Journal, The New York Times, Chicago Tribune, The Boston Globe, Harper's,* and other periodicals, and he has been interviewed on nearly 300 radio and TV programs, including NPR's *Morning Edition, Sally Jessy Raphael, Geraldo, The O'Reilly Factor, Extra*, and *CNN Reports*.

Hauck is the current president of the International Alchemy Guild (www.AlchemyGuild.org) and serves as curator of the Alchemy Museum in San Jose, California (www.AlchemyMuseum .info). He is also founder of the International Alchemy Conference (www.AlchemyConference.net) and an instructor in alchemy (www.AlchemyStudy.com). His website is www.DWHauck.com, and his Alchemy Study Facebook group is at www.Facebook.com/groups/studyalchemy. Hauck lives in the Sierra Mountains east of Sacramento, California.

· · · · · · · ·

Art Credits

Figures 1 and 16 © Dennis William Hauck.

Figure 3 © University of Wisconsin Digital Collection: http://digital.library.wisc.edu/1711.dl /UWSpecColl.DuveenD0897.

Figures 2 and 4–15 by the Llewellyn Art Department.

BOOK FIVE

Demonology & Spirit Evocation
by Dr. Stephen Skinner

Demonology could be defined as the study of demons and their names, hierarchy, and abilities. As such, it is an integral part of the practice of magic. Whenever I am asked if I believe in demons or spirits, I usually reply no, because my knowledge of these entities does not spring from my belief in them but from my observation, evocation, and interaction with them over an extended period of time, in my case, more than fifty years.

Belief is secondhand knowledge, repeated from what you have heard or been told. *Knowledge* is the result of experience, of testing and repeating the same procedures, and getting the same results. Belief requires only faith, but knowledge requires method, observation, and repeated experiment—in short, the application of the scientific method. The usual dichotomy between religion and science would be much better expressed as the difference between belief and knowledge. When it comes to spirits, demons, and demonology, knowledge is a much firmer footing than belief.

The popular view of demons and demonology has changed a lot over the last three centuries. In the seventeenth century in the Western world, the belief in the existence of spirits and demons was as strong as (if not stronger than) it had been in the ancient world. But with the coming of the Enlightenment and the waning of strongly held Christian beliefs (especially Catholicism), a more materialistic view of the world took over. With the founding of the Royal Society in London in 1660, the emphasis fell on what was measurable and testable, rather than on Church dogma. Even though Isaac Newton was as interested in magic and alchemy as he was in mathematics and physics, the popular view ignored that and ceased to believe in spirits and demons.[1]

Running parallel to that in the eighteenth century was a strong undercurrent of practitioners who still used grimoires to call spirits. In fact, some of the most prominent people in England—such as Lord Somers, Solicitor General for England and Wales, and Sir Joseph Jekyll, the Master of the Rolls (the supreme legal functionary in England) and the Lord High Admiral—continued to collect grimoires, practice magic, and call both angels and demons.

In the nineteenth century, materialism probably reached its peak when man had spanned long distances with rail networks, built canals, and invented all sorts of machines. Strangely, at the end of the nineteenth century, in 1888, the Hermetic Order of the Golden Dawn was founded to teach magic, and members still understood what demons and spirits were. But in the early twentieth century, the new "science" of psychology began to beguile even the advocates of magic such as Aleister Crowley and Dion Fortune. Crowley even went as far as to say that "Ceremonial Magic fines down, then, to a series of minute, though of course empirical, physiological experiments," and that "the spirits of the Goetia are portions of the human brain."[2] Dion Fortune was not far behind in her psychologising of magic. Spirits and demons had been discarded as the active agents of magic and magicians, and "New Thought" and psychology reigned supreme.

The latter half of the twentieth century saw a lot of self-help gurus promising magical results from positive thinking, visualisation, and affirmations, the seedbed of the New Age movement.

These are all useful psychological techniques that can certainly help in one's day-to-day life, but they are not magic in the sense that would have been understood by John Dee, Eleazar, or King Solomon, or indeed by any of the hundreds of practitioners of magic since their time. Magic depends on the help of disembodied spirits or demons, without which no amount of visualisation or straining of the brain can effect the changes that spirits or demons can produce.

Increasingly, people looked to psychology to explain magic, or simply discarded it as an outmoded form of thinking. For a while the theories of anthropologists held sway as science looked to "primitive" societies to explain magic. However, with the hippie revolution of the 1960s, materialistic explanations began to fall away. During the late twentieth and early twenty-first centuries, the publication of many grimoires (magician's handbooks) brought back the so-called "spirit model" of magic, confirming that magicians dealt with spirits not with psychological complexes. With this greater availability of information, the world at large has begun again to understand what magic really is. The New Age visualising and manifesting model, and the

---

1. Newton's notebooks on mathematics and physics were "saved for the nation"' and now reside in major UK libraries; however, his even more extensive writings on alchemy, prophecy, and magic were bought by a private collector and finally ended up in the National Library in Jerusalem.
2. Crowley, *The Book of the Goetia of Solomon the King*, 4, 3.

• • • • • • • •

psychological model that says it's "all in the head," began to fade away. With the old verities coming back into focus, people are realising that magic cannot be done by just straining your own mental faculties, but needs the assistance of gods, angels, daemons, or spirits, or "spiritual creatures," as Dr. John Dee used to refer to them. Only cooperation with such spiritual creatures can produce results that can truly be described as magic or miracles.

The *Goetia*

The *Goetia* is the first part of the grimoire the *Lemegeton*. It is effectively a register of seventy-two spirits or demons, with their seals and qualities plus a method of evoking them. It dates back to the mid-seventeenth century or maybe a bit earlier. The title of this book was chosen with reference to the chapter "Of Goetia and Necromancy" in H. C. Agrippa's *Three Books of Occult Philosophy*, and simply meant that form of magic dealing with demons. However, Agrippa's view of *goetia* does not really map onto the ancient Greek meaning of *goetia*, or the concept of the *goes*, despite modern attempts to link the two. *Goetia* is often mistakenly explained as a derivation of the Greek for "howling." In the twentieth century, the *Goetia* was edited by S. L. MacGregor Mathers from manuscripts in what was then the British Museum but is now the British Library, and was later published without permission by Aleister Crowley in 1904.

Demons

It is well known that the word *demon* comes from the Greek *daemon*, but it is not so well known what other changes took place with the meaning of the word over time. Before the ascendancy of Christianity, around 400 CE, there was no doubt that a daemon occupied the middle ground between men (and women) and the gods. There were good daemons and evil daemons (*cacodaemones*), and they sometimes performed the function of spiritual intermediaries, carrying messages between gods and man, and vice versa.

The ancient hierarchy of "spiritual creatures,"[3] of spirits, angels, archangels, daemons, demigods, and gods, was extensive. But with the coming of Christianity, these were all (except for angels) swept into the dustpan of history and demoted to being demons and banished beneath the earth. There was no longer any room in the heavens or on Earth for them. According to Christian doctrine, their function as mediators between man and god was assumed by Jesus Christ, the Virgin Mary, and the Holy Ghost. Christianity also added in the doctrine of the "fallen angels," and these demoted angels also became demons. Demonology then became the study of these demons, just as angelology was the study of the remaining angels who did not "fall."

---

3. In the sense of "not physical," with no implication of holiness.

Egypt

In Egypt in the first centuries of the Christian era, Graeco-Egyptian magicians called upon the aid of all of these "spiritual creatures," because it was logically thought by them that man alone cannot produce magical results or "miracles," no matter how hard he wishes, meditates, or prays, as magic is not done by either meditation or prayer. But with the help of one or another of these entities, various types of miraculous outcomes could be arrived at. To evoke and coerce one of these spiritual creatures to carry out the magician's will, however, it was necessary to do certain very specific things. In broad outline, these were:

a. To provide a conducive atmosphere, by using the correct incense;

b. To perform the ritual on the correct day and in the correct hour;

c. To perform the ritual in a clean and pure place, away from "the haunts of men," where there was little chance of disturbance or interruption;

d. To use the correct conjurations, which had to be pronounced clearly and correctly, preferably from memory;

e. To establish the magician's credibility by him claiming to be a god, or a part of a magical lineage, or reciting the names of other magicians;

f. Pronouncing the words of power, which would typically be the names of the spirit's superiors, or a god, to compel the spirit to action (most words of power were in fact names);

g. To bind the spirit with an oath before requesting or demanding the desired boon;

h. To provide protection for the magician in the form of a protective floor circle and/or a consecrated lamen to wear on his chest. For the Graeco-Egyptian magicians, even the gods and demigods were dangerous and had to be handled carefully.

Belief was not required, and magic was seen as a technique. These techniques are recorded in detail in many pages of the *Papyri Graecae Magicae* (the *Greek Magical Papyri*), of which more than 13,600 lines have survived.[4]

The amazing thing about these techniques is that they are almost exactly the same procedure as was found a thousand years later in Mediaeval grimoires, or in nineteenth-century Solomonic magic texts. Of course, the language and some of the names have changed, but the *method* has remained the same. If magic was just some kind of made-up nonsense, as many twenty-first-century sceptics might believe, then the method would have been reinvented with each generation … but it hasn't.

4. See Skinner, *Techniques of Graeco-Egyptian Magic*.

• • • • • • • •

At about the same time, just north of Egypt in Palestine, Jesus Christ was regarded as a wonder-worker, if not actually a magician.[5] No particular censure was attached to this view of Jesus by his contemporaries, as he was obviously a wonder-worker, and therefore this was expected of him, even he was not immune from the suspicion that he might have used a spirit or demon to help him perform his miracles. In fact, for the early Christians, explaining the difference between his miracles and the magic performed by other contemporary magicians such as Eleazar was a real problem. At that time, and subsequently, daemons or spirits were considered a necessary part of magic without which it simply would not work.

In the Bible, the Pharisees accuse Jesus of driving out demons by the power of a very specific spirit: Beelzebub, a prince of demons.[6] In Matthew 12:24–25, 27, Jesus speaks of using this demon's name for that purpose, and asks the Pharisees, in a very matter-of-fact way, which name they use:

> But when the Pharisees heard it, they said, "This fellow doth not cast out devils, but [except] by Beelzebub the prince of devils."

> And Jesus knew their thoughts, and said unto them …

> "And if I by Beelzebub cast out devils, by whom [in what name] do your children cast them out?"

Of course, the heavy irony would not have been lost on the Pharisees. The key thing is that the technique of using a senior demon's name to control lesser ones was accepted as commonplace by both Jesus and the Pharisees. It does not matter who used the name of Beelzebub. The important point is that it was seen as an acceptable procedure, used by magicians, rabbis, and holy men. This procedure has definitely always been a part of Solomonic magic as it has been practiced over the last two millennia.

It was only with the advent of Christianity that magic began to be seen as something derived *from* the Devil rather than an art used to *control* demons for the benefit of the magician.

Demonology

Demonology may be defined as "the study of demons or beliefs about demons, their hierarchy and qualities, especially the methods used to summon and control them." The original Greek word *daimon* indicated an intermediary between man and the gods, carrying prayers from man to the gods, and their responses and help in the opposite direction, with no particular implication of evil. The sense of "demon," from the time of Homer onward, was a benevolent being,

---

5. Smith, *Jesus the Magician*.
6. See also Mark 3:22; Matthew 10:25, 12:24–28; and Luke 11:15, 18–19.

but with the coming of Christianity, all such pagan entities were "demonized," and so demons began to be looked upon as inherently evil. In English, the name now holds connotations of malevolence.

The problem is that the objects of its study (demons) cannot be seen and felt by the ordinary man. In fact, the problem is exactly the same as that faced by Edward Jenner in 1796 when he discovered how to protect against smallpox by inoculation with cowpox. How was he going to explain that taking the pus from a cow and inserting it into a cut made in a child's arm would protect them for life from the horrors of smallpox? Without an electron microscope he could not even show them a smallpox virus. His patients, who formed a long queue around his garden, had to take it on faith.

The situation is the same for demonology. Demons cannot be shown to the average man, and even the effects of their behaviour cannot be shown without sometimes attracting scorn and derision. At least Jenner had a "new" field, and his explanation of viruses and their behaviour was not clouded by more than 1,700 years of obfuscation and deliberate distortion. Up until 400 CE, most citizens of the Roman Empire would have known what a daemon was, and been wary of it. But with the coming of institutional Christianity, supported by the full force of Rome, all of the detailed knowledge of magic and the behaviour of daemons was swept into a dusty corner and given just one label: demon.

So there are many difficulties in the way of a complete description of demonology in a materialistic world where the existence of the subject under discussion is not even recognised. Demons cannot be shown in the normal course of things, but their presence can be detected by their effects, just as viruses cannot be shown under an optical microscope (as they are too small), yet their existence is accepted by everyone in the modern world. Viruses are taken as a matter of faith, as are radio waves, which cannot be seen except for the patterns they produce on an oscilloscope. In the ancient world, daemons were thought of in the same way.

Spirit Evocation

Demons can, however, be observed under very limited circumstances that require as much preparation as the most stringently prepared scientific experiment. This process is *spirit evocation*. Evocation is quite different from invocation. Evocation deals with spirits and demons, but invocation deals with the gods. Both processes come from the pre-Christian pagan world. Exorcism is nowadays used by Christian priests to drive demons out of possessed humans, but in past times it was used by magicians.[7] The modern trend is to paint possession as some kind of extreme mental disorder, but this is clearly not the case, as several examples of the reality of spirit possession will show.

---

7. The word *exorcism* is also used in grimoires in the same sense as *evocation*, which is slightly confusing.

• • • • • • • •

One clear example of exorcism from the ancient world was the driving out of demons by Jesus Christ from the possessed man he met in Gadara, on the banks of the Sea of Galilee. This unfortunate man had been bound in chains but had broken them by applying "superhuman" strength, the first hint of the objectivity of the demons possessing him. When Jesus drove out the demons, he knew that they had to go somewhere and would not just evaporate into thin air (as they might if they were just a symptom of mental disease). Jesus selected a herd of swine grazing on an adjoining hill in which to implant them. The enraged swine ran down the slope and drowned themselves in the adjoining sea.[8] This, in anyone's language, is proof of both the effectiveness of the exorcism and the reality of the demons. Otherwise, what might be the logical explanation for the simultaneous insane self-destructive actions of a nearby herd of pigs?

A more calculated description of exorcism by the magician Eleazar appears in the works of Josephus, and it took place in front of a large number of witnesses, including an emperor. Eleazar, having been asked to exorcise a possessed man, proceeded with the exorcism and the application of his consecrated ring to the man's nose. At the same time, he commanded the demon to prove it had exited by overturning a cup of water set at some distance from the exorcism. In due course, as the unfortunate victim collapsed, the water in the cup was spilled and the person recovered. Now it is easy to explain this might have happened by trickery, but what I am trying to show here is the physicality of phenomena produced by the fleeing demons. Josephus's account was written within living memory of the event.

So much for driving out demons. But what about calling up demons or spirits that are not lodged in an unfortunate human? This is done by the process of evocation.

The earliest accounts of evocation centre around King Solomon and are contained in the *Tanakh* (the Old Testament). Solomon is reputed to have called up demons (or *jinn*, if you prefer) to help him with the tasks of building his famous Temple around 950 BCE. Many stories of these events have become the stuff of legends, recorded both in the Jewish and Christian worlds and later in the Islamic world, for Solomon's actions were part of the background of all three monotheistic religions, Judaism, Christianity, and Islam. A more detailed and technical description of Solomon's interaction with demons and their building of the Temple appear in the second-century-CE book *The Testament of Solomon,* which also gives more information on the method used. Whatever the truth of these accounts, the style of ritual magic that involves calling up demons or spirits (using very specific techniques) has come to be called *Solomonic magic.*

Evocation from Constantinople to England

These methods were adopted by Greek-speaking magicians living in Egypt, and traveled with them to the then centre of the Greek-speaking world, Constantinople, in the fifth and sixth

8. Mark 5:1–20.

centuries, where they were refined. The *Hygromanteia* is one of the few surviving Greek texts of Solomonic magic from that time. When Constantinople was sacked in 1453 by Muslim invaders, the manuscripts containing these methods traveled with fleeing monks to Italy, where they were translated into Latin as the *Key of Solomon*. The *Key* was then translated into other European languages, including English, in the fifteenth and sixteenth centuries.

During the fifteenth and sixteenth centuries, a lot of experimentation in evocation took place in England. One of the best-known examples of this was the experimentation with invoking angels and spirits into a crystal done by Dr. John Dee in the late sixteenth century. Dee was well aware that his basic methods and equipment were drawn from the grimoires that he owned. (It is well known that his main Sigillum Dei Aemeth comes from the grimoire *Liber Juratus*, and his Table of Practice from the *Summa Sacre Magice*, and he undoubtedly knew this.) He was cautious and so did not refer to them as magic in a time when this might have led to his death. Magic was practiced by the upper levels of society, from manuals of magic called *grimoires*, by those who could read Latin and Greek, such as Dee, and who also had the space and time to carry out full ceremonial ritual. But it was also practiced in a rather abbreviated form by village cunning-men, who also provided medical and sometimes midwife services. These cunning-men, such as Old Cornelius or Moses Long in Oxford, also used grimoires, divination, astrology, and herbal medicine from Thomas Culpeper's *Complete Herbal* rather than full-scale ritual evocation.[9]

Although there were many magicians and demonologists before him, Reginald Scot, who published *The Discovery of Witchcraft* in 1584 and took a very rational approach to magic and witchcraft, has come to be called "England's first Demonologist."[10] Scot attempted to explain that many of the accusations brought against witches were just motivated by village spite directed against quarrelsome old women, but he did not condemn the more learned practitioners of evocation. History, however—or his printers—played a nasty trick on Scot, for when his book was reprinted long after his death in 1665, new sections were added that included practical grimoire and cunning-man material that directly contradicted his contentions. Instead of showing the supposed fatuousness of magic, it supplied a usable compendium of its methods.

That, in a nutshell, is how the Solomonic method of spirit/demon evocation reached England from its inception in Egypt two thousand years ago.

Soon after, the Bible was translated into English in 1611, at the command of King James I. Across both the Greek (New Testament) and the Latin (Old Testament),[11] there are no less than thirty-four different terms describing daemons, spirits, wood nymphs, and other "spiritual crea-

---

9. For a typical grimoire, see Skinner and Rankine, *The Cunning Man's Grimoire*.

10. Almond, *England's First Demonologist: Reginald Scot & 'The Discoverie of Witchcraft,'* 2011.

11. The original was in Hebrew and Aramaic, but King James's translators worked primarily from the Latin Vulgate.

tures." The translators of the King James version of the Bible reduced all of these to just one prejudicial term: demon.

Demons were assumed to reside in Hell, a convenient repository of all things evil, which barely existed before the coming of Christianity, unless you consider the Greek Hades or the Jewish Gehenna as its theological ancestor.

Just as Hell developed a hierarchical structure,[12] so did both demonolcy and angelology. In the case of angelology, the heavy lifting was done in the fifth to sixth centuries by pseudo-Dionysus the Areopagite. He started with the Jewish angel categories of Seraphim and Cherubim, but, running out of names, he picked all sorts of words out of the New Testament such as Thrones Principalities, and Powers and made them into the names of different categories of angels.

Demonologists took longer to arrange their hierarchy, but during and after the Middle Ages a structure was devised that paralleled human affairs, and this is the structure found in most grimoires.

Grimoires

Grimoires, or "grammars," of sorcery were the working manuals of magicians. In almost all cases these grimoires were for the personal use of the magician and not for publication. They were not designed, as a modern book might be, to explain or justify a particular practice, but were for the use of the magician who wrote them. Of course, one disadvantage of these manuscripts (as they usually are) is that the writer had no need to explain everything for the beginner, but simply wrote the important things he needed to remember or that he needed to pass on to his apprentice. Magic has seldom been taught in a classroom, but has always been part of a chain of master-apprentice transmission.

Magic, and specifically Solomonic magic, is a complex process and involves a very precise technology. How can it be referred to as a "'technology"? It is a technology because it uses clearly defined methods and equipment—methods that produce repeatable results.[13]

Strange as it may seem, purity is always an important part of Solomonic magic, and this first requirement is often overlooked by beginners who wish to rush into the more dramatic part. But magic requires a precise accumulation of equipment that is pure, preferably new, and free of the contamination of other influences or a previous owner. The grimoires always stress this, but it is often the first thing to be overlooked by the novice.

---

12. The doctrines and geography of Hell were elaborated upon in the *Divine Comedy,* a poem written by Dante in 1308–1320 that outlined it in graphic detail.

13. The results of evocation will produce repeatable results nine times out of ten, as long as the same correct method and equipment are used. Any chemist will tell you that the same degree of repeatable reliability is experienced with chemical reactions. There will always be a time when some impurity affects the work, hampering the reaction, or evocation.

· · · · · · · ·

Solomonic magic is not the easy route to anything, but once mastered, it provides repeatable operations. The objective of science is to document observations and then draw conclusions from them that will enable repeatable experiments to be made. In this sense magic is quite scientific. Aleister Crowley's slogan "The Method of Science, the Aim of Religion" is a reflection of this, as the Aim of Religion is to deal with spiritual creatures such as god(s) and angels, while the Method of Science is the derivation of rules that can be used to repeat the experiment successfully.

The Circle

The protective circle dates back at least 2,500 years. Classical Indian texts such as the *Ramayana* (dating from the fourth to the fifth century BCE) record Lakshman drawing such a circle on the ground to protect Sita, his wife, from a demon. Unfortunately, Sita stepped over this boundary and was captured by the demon Ravana, an indication of the fate of any magician who similarly stepped over the boundary of the magic circle.

Assyrian texts tell of protective circles called *uṣurtu,* drawn with a mixture of flour and water and then consecrated. Hebrew examples include Honi the Circle Drawer, who used such a circle to invoke rain. In Egypt, the boundary often took the form of the *ouroboros,* a circle designed as a snake swallowing its own tail. This could be drawn with chalk (as were Mediaeval magicians' circles) or even made of real snakeskin. On one papyrus we even have the exact words and symbols that need to be inscribed.* These are just some of the examples of the use of the magic circle in ancient times.

At least one modern edition of the *Goetia* replicated the ouroboros theme (see figure 2). More sophisticated versions of this form of protection, like a magnetised iron chain, were used in the Middle Ages.

There are many tales of the fate that befell the unwary who stepped out of the circle, such as a priest who was attacked so ferociously by the demons he had called that he later died of his wounds.**

The shape of the circle has an effect on the spirit, who will circle around a few times but not find an easy entrance. The effect is the same as if we were confronted by a razor-sharp wall in a completely alien environment. We might well refrain from trying to walk through it.

* *Papyri Graecae Magicae (PGM)* III. 291–306.
** Recorded by Caesarius of Heisterbach.

The practical manuals of magicians from the Middle Ages until the present are called grimoires, and these detail the times, tools, and talismans needed for such experiments. They are not history, theory, or theology, but a recording of the methods used. Every grimoire stresses the dangers of evocation. Solomonic grimoires explain that the magician needs to be surrounded by a properly consecrated circle and protected by a lamen worn on the breast.

Protection from spirits, demons, and even gods was necessary. Despite New Age practitioners visualising angels and gods as uniformly good and even treating them like helpers or pets, the ancients knew better and were never so complacent. There are a number of instances recorded in the Bible of the Ark of the Covenant (belonging to the Jewish god Yahweh) striking down dead even its own worshipers. This theme was even expanded upon in its later appearances in Indiana Jones films.

Method and Equipment for Dealing with Demons

Protection in Solomonic magic is quite detailed and specific but always contains three main ingredients: a protective floor circle to mark the limits beyond which the spirit/demon may not step, several pieces of magical equipment such as a sword, sceptre, or wand, and personal protection for the magician in the form of a properly constructed phylactery (this is not simply a talisman or common amulet).

The primary protection is the circle drawn on the ground before any operation of evocation. The rationale is that the practitioner needs to be protected from the spirit or demon by a line they cannot cross. The *Heptameron*, one of the most widely respected grimoires, says of these circles that "they are certain fortresses to defend the operators safe from the evil Spirits."[14] There have always been stories of spirits harming magicians who evoked them without taking this precaution. Even in the twenty-first century, I often hear accounts of people who have not bothered to draw and consecrate the circle but attempted an invocation sitting in an armchair in their front room. Fortunately, careless amateurs are usually protected from their folly by their inability to carry out the complex and demanding procedures of evocation. If they do the method correctly, they will get results, and they will need protection.

Circles vary, from the simplest, containing one or two godnames, to complex circles containing all ten godnames, archangelic names, and angel names of the Kabbalistic Tree of Life (figures 1 and 2).

---

14. Agrippa, *The Fourth Book of Occult Philosophy*, 59–60.

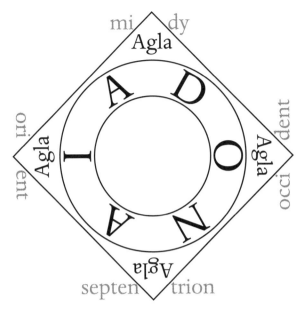

Figure 1. A Very Simple Protective Circle:
The circle's corners are marked with *AGLA*,
an acronym of אגלא, *Atah Gibor le-Olam Adonai*,
meaning "You, O Lord, are mighty forever."
This phrase forms part of a daily Jewish prayer.
Between the circles is the Hebrew word for Lord, *Adonai*.[15]

15. Wellcome MS 983.

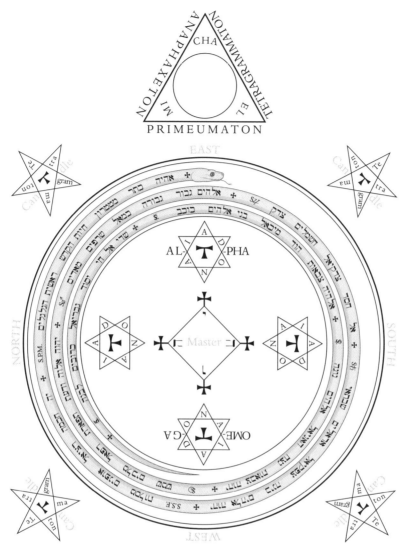

Figure 2. A Complex Circle:
Containing ten godnames, archangel names, and angel names.[16]

The boundary is always circular (or more correctly annular) but is sometimes set within a square. Between the circles are usually written protective names, ranging from godnames, through archangels and angels, to the names of demon princes or even the secret names of the seasons or of the sun, moon, and earth (figure 3). Those names (according to the *Heptameron* and those grimoires that follow its pattern) change every season.

16. From the frontispiece in Crowley's *The Book of the Goetia of Solomon the King*.

· · · · · · · ·

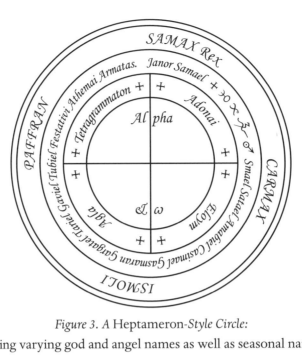

Figure 3. A Heptameron-Style Circle:
Showing varying god and angel names as well as seasonal names.[17]

There are many more complicated versions of the circle.[18] One of the common ingredients in constructing such a circle is that after painting or drawing the circle, the operator must go over it with a sharp, consecrated sword or knife. Spirits appear to be quite afraid of sharp iron instruments, and the circle-drawer uses that knowledge to make an effective barrier.

Greek magicians using the *Hygromanteia* were instructed to leave the dagger or black-handled knife on the floor at the circle entrance with its tip pointing outward. The magician was enjoined by the grimoire not to step out or even lean over the circle perimeter.

If the circle was outdoors, then it would be cut in the turf using the same knife. An example of this kind of woodland circle appears in the evocation of the spirit Oberion (figure 4).[19] Note that in this circle, the names are still Hebrew godnames, plus some Greek Christian names like Χρυς.

17. Skinner and Rankine, *The Veritable Key of Solomon*, 139.
18. Many other examples of circles can be found in Skinner, *Techniques of Solomonic Magic*, 152–180.
19. See Harms, Clark, and Peterson, *The Book of Oberon*, 467–473.

THE CIRCLE FOR RAISING Oberion.

Figure 4. Circle for Evoking the Spirit Oberion, Set Outside in the Woods[20]

Triangle of Art

As already described, the basic protection for the magician included a floor circle painted or inscribed with chalk that protects the magician from any attacking spirit. The magician aims to constrain the spirit, on the other hand, within a triangle outside of the circle. Drawn at floor level and called the Triangle of Art, its history is less clear, but it has been certainly used for more than three centuries. It is a locus for the spirit's manifestation, not so much as a portal but more as a temporary constraint that is also designed to force the spirit to tell the truth in response to the magician's questions. Theoretically the circle is used because it was considered a perfect geometric shape, but in practice it confuses the spirit, which will continue to circle around looking for an entrance until it is confined to the Triangle of Art.

---

20. From the magazine *The Straggling Astrologer,* 1824. Edited by Robert Cross Smith, aka Raphael.

• • • • • • • •

There are other forms of protection that complement the circle, such as the wearing of a phylactery, the splashing of holy water, and so on, but there is no space to consider these here.

Key of Solomon

Although there are many manuscript grimoires numbering in the many hundreds spread round the libraries and private collections of the world, only a dozen or so have been published. Of these perhaps the best known is the *Key of Solomon*, or *Clavicula Salomonis*. There are approximately 150 known manuscripts of this work, but only two volumes have ever been published.[21]

The *Key* outlines the preparation needed before an evocation and gives the invocations needed to call the spirits and the design of the circle to be used. It also contains a large number of planetary talismans, which, if consecrated at the right time with the right incense and right invocations, can be used for a wide range of purposes, including the acquisition of honour and riches, success in gambling and love, and so on. The *Key of Solomon*, despite its attribution to Solomon, actually comes from a Greek source called the *Hygromanteia*, or *Magical Treatise of Solomon*.[22]

A necessary part of any manual of demonic evocation is a Register of Spirits, which gives a list of the names and describes what each spirit is able to do. Each spirit is limited to a particular sphere of action, which is called its "Office," and cannot deal with anything outside that limit. So, for example, a spirit that will aid the magician in matters of the heart will be unable to bring money to the magician. Spirits are specialists, and so before calling a spirit, you have to ensure that the thing you want, the boon you want granted, falls into their area of expertise; otherwise any effort expended in calling it will be wasted. For this you need a Register of Spirits containing the names of spirits and their Offices. But this is not present in the *Key of Solomon*.

Office of Spirits

The first such Register of Spirits extant in a European language is to be found in the Greek *Hygromanteia*. In Latin one of the first was recorded in 1508 by the Abbott Trithemius. He called the text *De Officio Spirituum* (*On the Office of the Spirits*). There is no record of its current whereabouts, but there was a grimoire called *A Book of the Offices of Spirits* by John Porter (a contemporary with Dr. John Dee) dated 1583, which is probably an English translation of that text.[23] The word *Offices* here means the function of the spirit, the range of things the spirit is capable of doing, or allowed to do. In the *Offices of Spirits* the hierarchical structure is clear. This book gives the title and function of each of $4 + 3 + 75 + (4 \times 12) = 130$ spirits. These numbers show the

---

21. S. L. MacGregor Mathers, *The Key of Solomon*, 2000. Plus a further three manuscripts were published in Stephen Skinner and David Rankine, *The Veritable Key of Solomon*, 2008.

22. Marathakis, *The Magical Treatise of Solomon, or Hygromanteia*.

23. Porter, *A Book of the Offices of Spirits*, 2011.

. . . .

structure and hierarchical nature of this grimoire. It actually begins with its very first sentence by outlining the four "Kings of the Air" (or sublunary spirits):

Urience / Uriens / Uraeus, King of the East.[24]

Paymon, King of the West.

Amaymon, King of the South.

Egine / Egyn, King of the North.

These four are also called the four *Demon Kings,* and they are very important in the practice of magic. The *Office of Spirits* continues, by saying that above them are three supreme demons, "Lucipher [*sic*], Beelzebub and Satan." The origin of these names is fascinating, but suffice it to say that Lucifer was Greek for "the light bringer"; Beelzebub, בַּעַל זְבוּב, or in Greek, βααλζεβούβ, "Lord of the Flying Ones," was a Philistine / Palestinian god;[25] and Satan was simply the Opposer, or "Counsel for the Prosecution," in the biblical book of Job.

There are a number of other lists of the Princes of Hell. One such demon classification was based on a Christian list of the seven deadly sins—Lucifer: pride; Mammon: greed; Asmodeus: lust; Leviathan: envy; Beelzebub: gluttony; Satan: wrath; and Belphegor: sloth[26]—but this list is rather arbitrary. Another is the more standard Jewish list of Princes of the Qliphoth: Satan and Moloch, Beelzebub, Lucifuge ("flee from the light"), Ashtaroth, Asmodeus, Belphegor, Baal, Adrammelech, Lilith, and Nahemah.[27]

However, here we are more concerned with the ways that magicians perceived the hierarchy, rather than either Christian theologians or Jewish rabbis. After the 3 Supreme Rulers and 4 Demon Princes of the four quarters come a further 75 demons of various ranks. This is very numerically close to the 72 demons of the *Goetia.*[28] They are divided into ranks that reflected Mediaeval society. Their divisional distribution is a bit difficult to count, as many are given two

24. This King is often called *Oriens,* but this is a longstanding confusion with the Latin word for *east.* Oriens was on some grimoire diagram placed next to the actual name of the King, and at some point the name and direction were confused, and Oriens was mistaken for the name of the King in the East. From manuscripts such as the *Clavis Inferni* (Skinner and Rankine, *The Grimoire of St. Cyprian: Clavis Inferni*) it is clear that the name was originally *Urieus.* Not only does *Urieus* sound like *Uraeus,* the serpent headdress of ancient Egypt, but its symbol was the winged *Ouroboros,* one of the clearest indications of the origin of this King's name in ancient Egypt. Its orientation in the east, at the place of the rising sun, also accords well with an Egyptian origin.

25. The usual translation is the derogatory "Lord of the Flies" or "Lord of the Dungheap." Christian demonology lists Beelzebub as one of the seven Princes of Hell.

26. The Princes of Hell identified by the German bishop Peter Binsfeld in 1589.

27. Skinner, *Complete Magician's Tables,* table K93. Aleister Crowley later amended this list to include his favourites.

28. The spirits are not the same as those listed in the *Goetia,* but some have similar names, and others are common to both texts in their function.

· · · · · · · ·

ranks. For example, Darbas (number 15) is both a Prince and a King. However, if you take the highest rank each time (as in human terms Princes often became Kings), you get the following distribution—King: 11; Prince: 14; Duke: 11; Earl: 7; Marquise: 5; Viscount: 2; Lord and Governor: 6; Ruler: 6; Prelate: 1; Sundry:[29] 12—making a total of 75.[30]

Why was a hierarchy so important? It is because the magician needs to know at what level to ask for a boon, and what name of a more senior demon or god must be used in order to compel the lesser demon. For example, it was quite common to threaten a recalcitrant lesser spirit with the wrath of its King, despite that fact that the magician might not have been able to actually honour this threat.

The same sort of structure appears in the *Goetia* where the relevant figures are: Kings: 12;[31] Dukes: 23; Presidents: 12; Marquises: 12; Earls, Counts, Princes and Prelates: 12; Knights: 1, making a Total of 72.[32]

However in the *Goetia* the three supreme demons are omitted, and in other seventeenth-century grimoires they are sometimes just reduced to their initials, L:B:S, perhaps through fear of ecclesiastical persecution of anyone found in possession of a text featuring names as inflammatory as Lucifer, Beelzebub, and Satan.

The most extensive Register of Spirits extant is the *Lemegeton*, also known as *Clavicula Salomonis Regis* or the *Lesser Key of Solomon*. After the *Key of Solomon*, it is the next most well-known grimoire.

A Regal Spirit

Attested in a number of manuscripts, the spirit Birto was allegedly conjured up in front of King Edward IV of England and his wife, Elizabeth Woodville.* The method is unique and consists of two circles of the same size, one for the spirit (marked "Birto") and one for the magician (marked "Magister"). However, in between these two circles there must be a drawing or a model of a wyvern (a two-legged dragon with a very sharp tail). It is thought that the wyvern is reminiscent of Melusine, the ancestress of Elizabeth Woodville. In addition, the magician carries a sceptre proclaiming the name of the Demon King (in this case, Egyn, King of the North). Taken together, the sceptre and the wyvern give the magician the credibility he needs to call up Birto. This is probably the only spirit that needs the magician to create a viable wyvern in order to succeed with his evocation.

* Skinner and Clark, *The Clavis or Key to the Mysteries of Magic*, 398–399.

---

29. Magnus Petis, Horseman, Count, Knight, Captain, Giant, and Ox.

30. This is followed by a delineation of a further 12 demons who report to the 4 Kings of the four quarters.

31. Nine, but 12 after reconstruction. The lists in the *Goetia* are defective after repeated copying and show only 9 Kings, when in fact there was originally one King for each zodiacal sign.

32. Skinner and Rankine, *The Goetia of Dr. Rudd*, 103–174, 366–381.

The *Lemegeton*

The *Lemegeton* was the title given to a collection of five grimoires, four of which were designed as a Register of Spirits. These five constituent grimoires are:

I. *Goetia*, or *Liber Malorum Spirituum seu Goetia*, which deals with 72 evil spirits

II. *Theurgia-Goetia*, which deals with spirits of mixed nature

III. *Ars Paulina (parts I and II)*, which deals with good spirits

IV. *Ars Almadel*, which deals with angels

V. *The Notory Art* (or *Ars Notoria*), which also utilises angels

All five books were extant and well known to Trithemius in 1508, but some under different names. Four of these were mentioned separately by Agrippa in 1531 at the end of book 3 of his *Three Books of Occult Philosophy*[33] in the chapters "Of Goetia and Necromancy" and "Of Theurgia." In those chapters Agrippa speaks disapprovingly of the *Goetia* in order not to attract the attention of the Church or the Inquisition. This was a technique initially adopted by Trithemius, who heavily criticised every grimoire he ever mentioned but with his tongue firmly in his cheek. Further on, Agrippa lists "Apponius" (Peter de Abano) as the author of a book "on the Goetia," without specifically noting that de Abano's *Heptameron* was the actual source of the conjurations in the *Goetia*.

In the chapter "Of Theurgia," Agrippa quotes "the *Ars Almadel*, the *Notory Art*, the *Ars Paulina*, the *Art of Revelations*, and many suchlike." The first three are all constituent books of the *Lemegeton*. Hence, Agrippa mentions three of the five books of the *Lemegeton* by name and two by subject matter.

Taken together, these five books are surprisingly complementary and interrelated, each having a good claim to belong to the Solomonic cycle (except the last one) and each having contents that date back at least to 1500. Tools mentioned in one are often used in another.

---

33. On pages 695–699 of the Tyson edition of *Three Books of Occult Philosophy*.

There are two main published versions of the *Lemegeton,* one edited by Joseph Peterson[34] and one by myself and David Rankine.[35] The latter is taken from a manuscript copy of the papers of Dr. Thomas Rudd.[36]

Although Peterson's edition is the standard version of the *Lemegeton,* the edition produced by Rudd incorporates extra material, such as complementary thwarting angel sigils, circles from the *Heptameron,* and also a rather unique method of controlling the spirits using a model of the metal container that Solomon reputedly imprisoned the spirits in. Let us look at each of these books of the *Lemegeton* in turn.

The *Lemegeton* copied by Rudd can probably be dated to 1641, as one of the examples given in the *Ars Paulina* (book 2) is dated March 10, 1641.

Part I. Goetia, or Liber Malorum Spirituum seu Goetia [37]

As we have seen, the *Goetia* contains a list of 72 demons, with descriptions of their appearance and their Office, as well as the number of legions they commanded, and sometimes what King they reported to. The latter is incomplete, and it can be seen that although originally the names were grouped by their King, this has been somewhat lost during multiple redactions. Each of the demons has its sigil, and in the Rudd edition, each demon also has the name and seal of the angel who controls and thwarts it.

The *Goetia* has become rather infamous of late, having the sigils of its 72 spirits spread around the internet over the last few decades so that they even appear on a range of t-shirts, which is something I am sure the original author would be far from happy about. In addition to its functions as a Register of Spirits, the *Goetia* has a set of evocations of increasing intensity that have been drawn from the *Heptameron* of Peter de Abano.[38] They culminate with an invocation of the spirit's King designed to force his attendance.

---

34. Peterson, *The Lesser Key of Solomon: Lemegeton Clavicula Salomonis.*

35. Skinner and Rankine, *The Goetia of Dr. Rudd.*

36. Following an error first propagated by A. E. Waite in his book *Ceremonial Magic*, it is often said that Dr. Rudd was a fictional creation of Peter Smart, and not a real person. This is a mistake as there is ample evidence of Rudd's existence (see box on Dr. Rudd in Book Seven). Furthermore, Peter Smart very clearly marks the beginning of each sheet in Rudd's manuscript (just as we might mark folio numbers), a procedure which would be ridiculous if Smart was not copying an existing manuscript but just making it up. In addition, there are a number of references to "T.R." providing the source material for Weyer's *Pseudomonarchia Daemonorum.* It cannot be proved that this T.R was Thomas Rudd but it seems to be quite possible.

37. "The Book of Evil Spirits or Goetia."

38. This grimoire was one of the components of Agrippa's *Fourth Book of Occult Philosophy.* In fact, only two parts of that book were by Agrippa, with the other parts by de Abano, Villanganus, etc. Because of this, many writers have said the obvious: that the whole book is not by Agrippa; but then they have mistakenly taken to calling it a book by "pseudo-Agrippa." It would more correctly be referred to as a book "by Agrippa and others." See Abano, *Heptameron.*

· · · · · · · ·

The grimoire continues with tables of the planetary hours, and secret seasonal names; construction of the circle and details of incense and spirit/angel names for each day of the week; consecration of the tools of evocation; and instructions concerning timing and practice.

Part II. *Theurgia-Goetia*

The *Theurgia-Goetia* is concerned with spirits of a mixed nature, i.e., good and evil. Perhaps the most obvious feature of this grimoire is its insistence upon orientation. In fact, it embodies yet another rule of evocation, which is that the magician must know, and should face, the direction from which the spirit is due to come. To that end, the first illustration in the text is an elaborate compass rose, showing the direction in which all of its spirits are located. It is not polite, nor does it reflect well on the competency of the magician, if he is showing his back to the spirit when it arrives (see figure 5).

Originally these directions were (as with a mariner's compass) meant to be wind directions, but the confusion between "wind" and "spirit" in the Latin word *spiritum,* which means both "spirit" and "breath," made the transition in meaning easy.

The directional rules of the *Goetia* by comparison are simpler, but even it suggests that you must face the Triangle of Art, which should then be placed on the side of the circle from which the spirit is expected to arrive. Unfortunately, the *Goetia* is a bit vague about directions. In contrast, the *Theurgia-Goetia* gives very precise compass points for each spirit. For example, Rasiel should be expected from due North whereas Dorochiel will come from "West by North," but Usiel should come from exactly NW—a total of 32 different directions are delineated in detail.

The title *Theurgia-Goetia* is a bit strange, as Graeco-Egyptian magicians went to some lengths to separate these two types of procedures. Accordingly, I do not think that the magician who adopted the name for this grimoire really understood that *theurgia* was a practice reserved for the gods, and he used these two words to simply indicate mixed good and evil spirits.

This grimoire is effectively a ritual version of the first book of Trithemius's, *Steganographia,* which was compiled by 1500.[39] The *Steganographia* has always been a mysterious book: some critics have claimed it was a book of cryptography, some a book of magic. On the face of it, it claims to teach how to use angels to carry secret messages between two widely separated persons (a function that would have been most useful in a pre-email world). Dr. John Dee was very excited when he first saw it, for both these reasons. I suspect that the carriage of secret messages via angelic aid may have been the prime purpose, followed by the inevitable addition of cryptography to keep the messages secret even if accidentally revealed.

---

39. The order of the spirits in the *Theurgia-Goetia* differs from that in the *Steganographia.*

• • • • • • • •

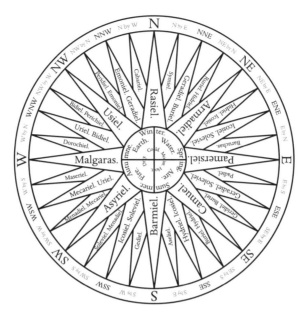

Figure 5. The Compass Rose in the Theurgia-Goetia:
Showing the exact direction from which each spirit can be expected to arrive.

At least one manuscript of the *Steganographia*,[40] which shows sixteen compass segments corresponding with the names of the sixteen Dukes, is more complete than the printed edition, which shows just three of the sixteen Dukes. Although Trithemius died in 1516, the *Steganographia* was not published until 1621 at Darmstadt and again in 1635, but only partially.

As in the *Goetia,* there is a strict hierarchy in the *Theurgia-Goetia* that is headed by four Emperors (Caspiel, Carnesial, Amenadiel, and Demoriel) corresponding with the four cardinal directions, while the sixteen Dukes are allocated the inter-cardinal points, plus other directions. The eleven so-called Wandering Princes fill in the remaining points of the compass.

The manuscript has obviously been redacted a number of times, with some scrambling and reordering of the folios, because the folios covering the actual method of invocation have moved away from the beginning of the manuscript and been placed just after the details relating to Pamersiel. The procedure to call forth any of the spirits of the *Theurgia-Goetia* (not just Parmersiel) is as follows:[41]

1. Choose a place in some island, wood, or grove that is well hidden,

40. National Library of Scotland Adv. MS 18.8.12.

41. Pamersiel is the fourth demon prince or king (according to which source you read) ruling in the east. His invocation is found in the *Theurgia-Goetia,* the second part of the *Lemegeton.* The general instructions for the evocation of *all* spirits in the *Theurgia-Goetia* were listed under his name, rather than just the specific instructions relevant to him.

• • • • • • • •

2. or in a private room in your house set aside for such operations, preferably an upper room (as the spirits of the *Theurgia-Goetia* are specifically airy spirits).

3. The magician should wear the seal of the Spirit on his breast and a girdle of lion skin about his waist, as mentioned in the *Goetia*.

4. Make a Circle in the form as shown in the previous book *Goetia*.

5. Call the spirits into a Crystal stone four Inches in diameter, set on a Table of Practice, "with the secret Table of Solomon" or the Seal of Solomon inscribed on it.[42]

6. Declaim the conjuration a number of times in order to give the spirit time to arrive.[43]

7. An unspoken instruction is to face the correct direction, as indicated by the spirit compass rose (see figure 5), and burn the correct incense, or frankincense.

Although this text suggests that this method is a sort of "spirit telegraph" to communicate with distant friends, it is in fact really a method of angel invocation. The magician faces the quarter of the angel, invokes the angel, and submits his request (what he wants the spirit to accomplish), cryptographically encoded on a piece of paper. The mental effort involved in encrypting it is part of the magical procedure, a little like Austin Osman Spare encoding his request in a sigil. There is thus no human recipient. This method is more sophisticated, as it addresses the direction to face and a particular named spirit rather than just "the Universe," as with Spare. Timing is, as always, also important.[44]

Part III. Ars Paulina

The *Ars Paulina* is divided into two parts that are sufficiently different for them to be thought of as distinct books.

Located at the beginning of the grimoire is the Table of Practice, which is similar to all such Tables of Practice, including Dr. Dee's *Tabula Sancta*. The Table of Practice is designed to support the skrying crystal or glass receptacle filled with water. Its design was typically a hexagram. On the Table (or etched into it) should be seven planetary seals, located at the vertices of the hexagram, with the Sun seal located in the centre.

---

42. In practice, the Seal of Solomon has another purpose (sealing the stopper of the spirit bottle), and you should instead use the Table of Practice as used in the *Ars Paulina* (see next section). See figure 6.

43. These primary conjurations are missing from some versions of the text but have been inserted in Skinner and Rankine, *The Goetia of Dr. Rudd*, 215–304.

44. There is a branch of Chinese metaphysics called *Chi Men Tun Chia* (or *Qi Men Dun Jia*) that retains the knowledge of the connections between spirits and the secret doors that open under certain conditions of timing and direction. The *Theurgia-Goetia* and *Ars Paulina* (part 1) retain hints of this art.

· · · · · · · ·

Ars Paulina (**Part 1**)

The *Theurgia-Goetia* is focussed on direction, but the *Ars Paulina* is focussed on time, and planetary rulership. Planetary hours are of prime importance in Western magic and are mentioned in almost every grimoire. The first book of the *Ars Paulina* is a Spirit Register, which lists spirits according to the specific planetary hours of the night and day. These are different from the planetary rulerships of the hours in that they are the same pattern of rulers for every day.

The *Ars Paulina* was reputedly delivered to the Apostle Paul at Corinth. In his *Epistles*, Paul speaks about himself in the third person[45] ascending to the Third Heaven, where he "heard unspeakable words, which it is not lawful for a man to utter." The *Apocalypse of Paul* goes on to speak about the Fourth Heaven, where he is said to have seen a soul being prepared for reincarnation, and then on to the other Heavens up to the Tenth.[46] These passages gave some credibility to the attribution of the *Ars Paulina* to that Apostle, but beyond that there is no significance in the title.

Each of the twelve hours of the day (which run from sunrise to sunset) and twelve hours of the night (which run from sunset to the next sunrise) has a name and is allocated a ruling angel. The angel in turn rules a varying number of Dukes, who have in their train an army of servants. Not all are listed, but just a selection are named. A very basic seal featuring planetary and zodiacal symbols is provided for each hour. Only one simple conjuration is provided for use with all hours, with the angel name changed.

Timing

Often, the correct time to call a spirit is limited to what planet the spirit is allied with. A solar spirit, for example, should be called only on a Sunday, whilst a spirit of Jupiter should be called only on a Thursday. In addition to this, a spirit is much easier to call within its own planetary hour. These hours are outlined in most grimoires, including the *Key of Solomon*. For example, the best time to call a Jupiterian spirit on a Thursday (the day of Jupiter) is in an hour of Jupiter, which is the first hour of Thursday (just after sunrise) or the eighth hour or the fifteenth hour after sunrise, etc. These hours are all measured from sunrise, but are not measured by the clock. Instead, the time between sunrise and sunset in minutes is taken and divided by twelve. This gives the length of one planetary hour (this may be longer than sixty minutes in summer, but shorter than sixty minutes in winter). Use this "planetary hour" count from sunrise, one hour at a time.*

* See the Planetary Hours box in Book Three: Planetary Magic.

---

45. In 2 Corinthians 12:2–4.

46. Robinson, "The Apocalypse of Paul," in *The Nag Hammadi Library in English*, 257–259.

Figure 6. Table of Practice for the Ars Paulina[47]

Ars Paulina (**Part 2**)

The second part of the *Ars Paulina* is derived from book 2 of Trithemius's *Steganographia*. This grimoire has a close connection with astrology and has a number of different uses. This part of the *Ars Paulina* gives the angels ruling each of the 360 degrees of the twelve signs of the zodiac, which combines both time and direction. It is interesting that Peter de Abano also gives magical images for each of these 360 degrees, which again connects the author of the *Heptameron* with the sources of the *Lemegeton*.

This is helpful if you know the exact sign and degree of your birth time. Then you can determine the angel ruling your birth, or the "Lord or Lady of your Geniture." This idea connects with the idea of a personal genius that conveys the influences of heaven (be they good or bad) to the person born under their rulership, or even with a guardian angel. For example, Latrael is attributed to the third degree of Libra, and Tzamiel is attributed to the tenth degree of Aquarius. For those who do not know the exact degree of their birth, an angel is also attributed to each whole sign.

These 360 angels (or spirits) are sometimes referred to as the *monomoiria*. At least two Gnostic sects revered the monomoirai: the Phibionites (a sect infamous for its use of sex and lewd practices in its rites) and the Marcosians. However, there is no certainty that the practices in the *Ars Paulina* had anything to do with either of these sects. Interestingly, these spirits are referred to here as *daemones*, which is suggestive of their Gnostic origins. Two seals are given for each sign,

---

47. Also usable for the *Theurgia-Goetia*.

and these are the same as those that appear in Paracelsus's *Of the Supreme Mysteries of Nature*, first published in 1656. Their inscriptions are mostly in Greek, but also in Latin.

A prayer is provided for these angels, but the magician is also encouraged to use "prayers to God, they being composed to your fancy but suitable to the matter in hand."[48] Further on, it is noted that "this prayer may be altered to the mind of the worker, for it is here set for an Example." Acceptable requests include to "illuminate your mind taking away all that is obscure and dark in thy memory, and make you knowing in all Sciences sacred and divine in an instant." This anticipates the purpose of the *Ars Notoria*, which is to enable you to comprehend all sciences in an instant. Again, the facing direction is stressed as being most important, and a "Crystal Stone" is to be used for the manifestation of the angel, in which you will "at last see strange sights and passages in the stone, and at last you will see your Genius." This method is suggestive of communication with your Holy Guardian Angel.

Part IV. Ars Almadel

The *Ars Almadel* deals solely with the conjuration of angels. These angels are divided into four *choras*, which are usually translated as "Altitudes" and are usually compared to the skrying practice in the 1580s of Dr. John Dee and Edward Kelley, who received the Calls of the 30 Ayres (or Aethyrs). But *chora* does not equate with *Ayre*. The original Greek word for *chora*, as it was used in Alexandria, referred to the suburbs surrounding that city and their directions, so *chora* is an indication of the cardinal directions, as is later confirmed in the text, where they are described as "the four Corners of the world East, West, North and South, the which are divided into twelve parts, that is every part [contains] three [zodiacal signs]." So in this book, direction and time (zodiacal signs) are again united.

The *Ars Almadel* dates back at least to the late fifteenth century, as it was mentioned by Agrippa. According to Turner,[49] a copy of it can also be found in a fifteenth-century manuscript in Florence.[50] Its techniques may derive from the techniques of Jewish angel magic as shown in manuscripts like the *Temunoth ha-Almadel*, תמונת האלמדל.[51]

A manuscript in the British Library credits Christofer Cattan, a Genovese, with being the inventor of the Almadel (the wax tablet used in conjuring the angels), or "l'inventore de detti Almadel Arabico."[52] Cattan was famous for his very influential geomancy published in French in 1558 and in English in 1591, but the mention of "Arabico" suggests that he may have translated it but did not invent it.

---

48. *Ars Paulina II*, in Skinner and Rankine, *The Goetia of Dr. Rudd*, 340–341.
49. Robert Turner, author of *Elizabethan Magic*.
50. Florence MS II-iii-24. See Turner, *Elizabethan Magic*, 140.
51. British Library Oriental MS 6360, f.13v.
52. British Library Additional MS 8790.

It is tempting to think that the name of this book came from the Arabic *al-Mandal*, meaning "magic circle," but strangely the particular procedure used in this grimoire is not one that utilises a circle. Of course the Circle of Art might simply have been taken for granted by the author, who here simply concentrates mainly on the equipment on the Table of Practice.

The method consists of assembling a six-inch-square wax tablet, which incorporates four candles at the corners, with strategically placed holes that allow the smoke from an incense burner placed below it to curl up and around the scrying crystal placed on the tablet, supported by a golden seal. The tablet has the usual godnames[53] engraved upon it within four squares, with a hexagram located at the centre, acting as a Table of Practice.

The colouring of the wax differs from one chora to another. Only one invocation is used, but with a change of angel names. Each chora has special qualities attributed to it. For example, the first chora improves fertility in women, animals, and crops. Specific angels, like Borachiel and Hellison, belong to this chora. There is just one invocation that is effective for all four choras. In recent times, magicians such as Frater Ashen Chassan have explored the choras in detail.[54]

Part V. The Notory Art (or Ars Notoria)

The last book is often missing from manuscripts of the *Lemegeton*. It is very interesting in its own right, but it is very different from the other four books. Because its method is so different, I suspect that it was not originally part of the *Lemegeton*.

What this grimoire promises is to teach the main subjects of the Mediaeval curriculum very rapidly, or at the least enable these subjects to be absorbed very rapidly. Although some subjects like logic, rhetoric, and grammar are mainly ignored today, being able to argue a topic logically and both speak about it persuasively and write about it are in fact very useful skills. Likewise, the *Ars Notoria* promised to teach languages such as Latin rapidly, as well as geometry and philosophy.

This book was definitely written before 1236, as it was mentioned by Michael Scot on that date. The earliest manuscript I am aware of is a parchment in the Mellon Collection, Yale University Library, MS 1, which is dated circa 1225.

The text of the English translation of *Ars Notoria* by Robert Turner was actually printed at around the same time as most of the manuscripts of the *Lemegeton* were written (1657). In fact, the manuscript versions of the *Ars Notoria* were usually copied directly from the printed translation of Robert Turner, rather than the other way around. But even the printed book is unworkably incomplete, as the method cannot be used without the elaborate illustrations, or *notae*, which are completely missing from the printed version and all seventeenth-century manuscripts.

---

53. Helion, Heloi, Heli, Iod, Hod, Agla, Tetragrammaton, Iah, Adonai, Helomi, Pine, Anabona, etc.
54. Garner [Frater Ashen Chassan], *Gateways Through Light and Shadow*.

The *Ars Notoria* is not, as many people think, the "notorious art," but is named after the magical diagrams, or *notae*, which are a key part of its method. The aim of the *Ars Notoria* was to use these *notae* both to prompt memory and to provide a scheme that would induce a rapid understanding in the operator of any particular art or science. It is easy to imagine eager students using this art as an aid to cramming or absorbing the essence of a subject. In a time of few books, the ability to understand the ground plan of a subject or memorise whole chunks of material was highly prized and indeed a necessary skill of the scholar. Knowledge was literally defined as how much you knew or could remember.

By about the seventeenth century, and certainly in the twentieth century, knowledge was redefined as the ability to find specific information from the huge range of available books. In the twenty-first century, knowledge may be redefined again as the art of using the internet most effectively to find that same information. But in the Middle Ages, the ability to memorise, absorb, and organise material was paramount. It is precisely for that purpose that the *Ars Notoria* was devised. Its methods promised the student that, with the memorisation of certain very elaborate diagrams accompanied by the correct prayers, whole subjects could be rapidly absorbed.

The method of this book, which was originally independent but after the seventeenth century was included amongst the magical procedures of the *Lemegeton*, relied upon the aid of spirits or angels in achieving these scholarly ends more rapidly. As Robert Turner so aptly explains:[55]

> The *Ars Notoria*, the magical art of memory, flourished during the Middle Ages, although its origins are attributed to Solomon and Apollonius of Tyana. It is a process by which the magician could instantly gain knowledge or memory of all the arts and sciences. … To set the process into operation, the appropriate *notae* were contemplated whilst reciting angelic names and magical orisons [prayers].[56]

The attribution of the *Ars Notoria* to Solomon gives it a reason for being included in the *Lemegeton*. There was some question about the morality of using angels rather than the labour of honest study, but in practice most students would use this art as an aid rather than an end in itself. If you like, it was the more technically advanced equivalent of a prayer to help you pass exams. Nowadays prayers are seen as free-form supplications and request lists, but the *Ars Notoria*, like the other grimoires in the *Lemegeton*, made a much more precise technology out of it. The *Ars Notoria* had such procedures taped almost eight hundred years ago, but only for worthy and studious objectives, not the cars, money, love, and career dreams of the present century.

55. The twentieth-century Robert Turner in his book *Elizabethan Magic,* not his namesake who originally translated this book into English in 1657.
56. British Library Sloane MS 3648, f.1.

• • • • • • • •

The beautiful *notae* were the key to the procedure. Sadly, all printed editions except the most recent, and many manuscript versions of the *Ars Notoria*, are missing these essential ingredients.[57] Some of the *notae* were abstract, but some were like summary sheets for the subject. For example, the *notae* for grammar show the nine parts of speech in circles, and the *notae* for geometry show the line, triangle, square, pentagram, six-pointed star, and circle in order. However, those *notae* that appear in some manuscripts [58] are much more like large disordered sigils than organised subject outlines.

Many copies are known to exist, and John Dee had at least two manuscript copies of the *Ars Notoria* in his library, as did Robert Fludd and Simon Forman, who made three copies. Ben Jonson, the Elizabethan playwright, also owned a copy of the *Ars Notoria*.

The *Ars Notoria* was also mentioned by Trithemius, who also makes a claim that "he had written a book giving an occult method by which a person totally ignorant of Latin could learn in an hour's time to write anything he wished in that language," a book with very similar objectives to the *Ars Notoria*.[59] Going back even further, the *Ars Notoria* was also mentioned by Peter de Abano,[60] whose contribution to the invocations of the *Goetia* has already been noted.

William Lilly (1602–1681), the astrologer, had two copies of the *Ars Notoria*:

> One whole year [1633–1634] and more I continued a widower, and followed my studies [in astrology and magic] very hard; during which time a scholar pawned unto me, for forty shillings, *Ars Notoria*, a large volume wrote in parchment [by Simon Forman], with the names of those angels, and their pictures, which are thought and believed by wise men, to teach and instruct in all the several liberal sciences, and is attained by observing elected times, and those prayers appropriated unto the several angels.[61]

It is interesting that Lilly mentions "their pictures," by which he probably meant the *notae*.

The rationale for the *Ars Notoria* being "Solomonic" comes from the introduction to the whole *Lemegeton*, which is found in several manuscripts, including Sloane MS 3648, in which it is said that Solomon learned all his knowledge using the *Ars Notoria*:

---

57. See Turin, Biblioteca Nazionale MS E. V.13, and Paris, Bibliothèque Nationale MS Lat. 9336. Some of these *notae* are reproduced in black-and-white versions in Fanger, *Conjuring Spirits*, on pages 114, 116, 120, 122, and 127–131, where they are discussed at some length. Five complete full-color sets of notae are included in Skinner and Clark, *Ars Notoria: The Grimoire of Rapid Learning by Magic*.

58. Such as Bibliothèque Nationale MS lat. 9336.

59. Thorndike, *A History of Magic and Experimental Science*, 439.

60. In his brilliant *Conciliator* and also in his *Lucidator*.

61. Lilly, *William Lilly's History of His Life and Times*, 45–46.

The fifth part is a Booke of orations and prayers that wise Solomon used upon the alter in the Temple [in Jerusalem] which is called *Artem Novam* [another name for the *Ars Notoria*]. The which was revealed to Salomon by the holy angel of God called Michael, and he also received many breef Notes [hence *Notae*] written by the finger of God which was declared to him by the said Angel, with Thunder claps, without which Notes [King] Salomon had never obtained to his great knowledge, for by them in [a] short time he knew all arts and sciences both good and bad which from these Notes [*Notae*] is called *Ars Notoria*.

In this Book is contained the whole art of Salomon although there be many other Books that is said to be his yet none is to be compared with this, for this containeth them all, although they be titled with several other names, [such] as the *Book Helisol* which is the very same as this last is, which [is] called *Artem Novam & Ars Notoria*, &c.

In the Middle Ages generally, but especially in the *Ars Notoria*, imagination and magic were made to serve memory and scholasticism. In the magical literature that circulated between the fifth and ninth centuries, there are many tales of ancient rabbis conjuring an angel called Sar-Torah, the "Prince of the *Torah*." This angel functioned like the angels of the *Ars Notoria*, and may have even been the model upon which it was based. Sar-Torah endowed the rabbis with the spectacular memory skills necessary for memorising vast swathes of the *Torah*. The angel then taught the rabbis a formula for giving others the same gift.[62]

This literature has been made available by Michael Swartz,[63] who gives us rare glimpses of how ancient and medieval Jews viewed this process of rapid learning aided by angelic conjuration. He examines many of the magical rituals for conjuring angels and ascending to heaven in the Merkabah chariot, a magical practice that is still very much a part of the practical Kabbalah today. So here you have the reason why the *Ars Notoria* became part of the *Lemegeton*, as it was yet another technique of Solomonic angel conjuration.

Part VI. The Picatrix

The *Picatrix* comes from a completely different magical lineage. Just as Solomonic magic comes from Greek sources (and possibly Hebrew sources before that), so the *Picatrix* is part of a magical lineage that came from Arabic sources, via the court of Alphonso X of Castile to Europe. This style of magic did not evoke spirits but utilised complex astrology to determine the precise time to create a talisman that would take its energy from the images inscribed upon it at the precise time that stellar influences were aligned and at their strongest.

Accordingly, the *Picatrix* is not associated with Solomonic magic nor even in a sense ritual magic. Originally written in Arabic, this book was first translated into Spanish and then into

62. British Library Sloane MS 3648, f.1. See Swartz, *Scholastic Magic*.
63. Complete translations of the principal Sar-Torah texts can be found in Swartz, *Scholastic Magic*.

· · · · · · · ·

Latin in 1256. It was not until the mid-twentieth century that it was translated into German. Two limited translations were made from the Arabic text after that. A translation of the full Arabic text of *The Goal of the Sage: An English Translation of Maslama al-Qurṭubī's Ġāyat al-Ḥakīm* (*Picatrix*) by Liana Saif is expected soon, and this will answer many questions about this text.

Suggested Reading List

Kiesel, William. *Magic Circles in the Grimoire Tradition.* Three Hands Press, 2012.

Leitch, Aaron. *Secrets of the Magickal Grimoires.* Woodbury, MN: Llewellyn Publications, 2005.

Scot, Reginald. *Discoverie of Witchcraft.* 1584, 1661, 1665. Reprint, London: Elliot Stock, 1886. Especially book xv, ch. i–iv, pp. 376 et seq.

Skinner, Stephen. *Techniques of Solomonic Magic.* Singapore: Golden Hoard, 2015.

Bibliography

Abano, Peter de. *Heptameron, or Magical Elements.* In Agrippa, *The Fourth Book of Occult Philosophy.* Revised edition. Edited by Stephen Skinner. Berwick, ME: Ibis Press, 2005.

Abraham of Worms. *The Book of Abramelin: A New Translation.* Edited by Georg Dehn. Translated by Steven Guth. Lake Worth, FL: Ibis Press, 2006.

Agrippa von Nettesheim, Heinrich Cornelius. *The Fourth Book of Occult Philosophy.* Edited with introduction and commentary by Stephen Skinner. Translated into English by Robert Turner. Berwick, ME: Ibis Press, 2005. Contains *Of Magical Ceremonies; Heptameron; On the Nature of Such Spirits; Arbatel of Magick; Of the Magick of the Ancients; Of Geomancy; Of Astronomical Geomancy.*

———. *Three Books of Occult Philosophy.* Translated by James Freake. Edited by Donald Tyson. St. Paul, MN: Llewellyn, 1993.

Almond, Philip. *England's First Demonologist: Reginald Scot & 'The Discoverie of Witchcraft.'* New York: Tauris, 2011.

Baker, Jim. *The Cunning Man's Handbook.* Glastonbury, UK: Avalonia, 2014.

Chassan, Frater Ashen [Bryan Garner]. *Gateways Through Stone and Circle.* Nephilim Press, 2013.

Crowley, Aleister. *The Book of the Goetia of Solomon the King.* Boleskine, Foyers, Inverness: Society for the Propagation of Religious Truth, 1904.

Davies, Owen. *Grimoires: A History of Magic Books.* Oxford: Oxford University Press, 2009.

Fanger, Claire, ed. *Conjuring Spirits: Texts and Traditions of Medieval Ritual Magic.* University Park, PA: Pennsylvania State University Press, 1998.

———. *Invoking Angels: Theurgic Ideas and Practices, Thirteenth to Sixteenth Centuries.* University Park, PA: Pennsylvania State University Press, 2012.

· · · · · · ·

Foreman, Paul. *The Cambridge Book of Magic: A Tudor Necromancer's Manual*. Edited and translated by Francis Young. Cambridge: Texts in Early Modern Magic, 2015.

Garner, Bryan [Frater Ashen Chassan]. *Gateways Through Light and Shadow*. Foreword by Stephen Skinner. Portland, OR: Azoth Press, 2016.

Harms, Daniel, James Clark, and Joseph Peterson. *The Book of Oberon: A Sourcebook of Elizabethan Magic*. Woodbury, MN: Llewellyn Publications, 2015.

Honorius of Thebes. *The Sworn Book of Honorius: Liber iuratus Honorii*. Text, translation, and commentary by Joseph Peterson. Lake Worth, FL: Ibis, 2016.

James, Geoffrey. *Angel Magic: The Ancient Art of Summoning and Communicating with Angelic Beings*. St. Paul, MN: Llewellyn Publications, 1997.

Karr, Don, and Stephen Skinner. *Sepher Raziel: Liber Salomonis*. Vol. 6, Sourceworks of Ceremonial Magic series. Singapore: Golden Hoard, 2010.

Kieckhefer, Richard. *Forbidden Rites: A Necromancer's Manual of the Fifteenth Century*. Stroud, Gloucestershire: Sutton, 1997. Reprint, University Park, PA: Pennsylvania State University Press, 1998.

King, Francis. *Magic: The Western Tradition*. London: Thames & Hudson, 1984.

King, Francis, and Stephen Skinner. *Techniques of High Magic*. Singapore: Golden Hoard, 2016.

Lilly, William. *William Lilly's History of His Life and Times*. London: 1724.

Marathakis, Ioannis, trans. and ed. *The Magical Treatise of Solomon, or Hygromanteia*. Introduction by Stephen Skinner. Vol. 8, Sourceworks of Ceremonial Magic series. Singapore: Golden Hoard, 2011.

Mathers, S. L. MacGregor, trans. *The Book of the Sacred Magic of Abramelin the Mage*. London: Watkins, 1900.

———. *The Key of Solomon the King (Clavicula Salomonis)*. London: Redway, 1889; London: Kegan Paul, 1909; reprint, York Beach, ME: Samuel Weiser, 2000.

McLean, Adam, ed. *A Treatise on Angel Magic*. Edinburgh: Magnum Opus Sourceworks, 1982.

———. *The Magical Calendar*. Edinburgh: Magnum Opus Sourceworks, 1979.

Peterson, Joseph, ed. and trans. *Grimorium Verum*. Scotts Valley, CA: CreateSpace, 2007.

———. *The Lesser Key of Solomon: Lemegeton Clavicula Salomonis*. York Beach, ME: Weiser, 2001.

Porter, John. *A Book of the Offices of Spirits*. Transcribed by Frederick Hockley. Edited and with an introduction by Colin D. Campbell. York Beach, ME: The Teitan Press, 2011.

Rankine, David. *The Grimoire of Arthur Gauntlet*. London: Avalonia, 2011.

Robinson, James, ed. *The Nag Hammadi Library in English*. San Francisco, CA: HarperCollins, 1990.

Rudy, Gretchen. *The Grand Grimoire*. Seattle, WA: Trident & Ars Obscura, 1996.

· · · · · · ·

Shah, Idries. *The Secret Lore of Magic: Books of the Sorcerers*. London: Muller, 1957.

Skinner, Stephen. *The Complete Magician's Tables*. 5th ed. Singapore: Golden Hoard, 2017.

———. *Techniques of Graeco-Egyptian Magic*. Singapore: Golden Hoard, 2014.

Skinner, Stephen, and Daniel Clark. *Ars Notoria: The Grimoire of Rapid Learning by Magic*. Woodbury, MN: Llewellyn Publications, 2019.

———. *The Clavis or Key to Unlock the Mysteries of Magic of Rabbi Solomon*. Translated by Ebenezer Sibley. Singapore: Golden Hoard, 2018.

Skinner, Stephen, and David Rankine. *A Collection of Magical Secrets*. Translated by Paul Harry Barron. London: Avalonia, 2009.

———. *The Cunning Man's Grimoire*. Vol. 9, Sourceworks of Ceremonial Magic series. Singapore: Golden Hoard, 2018.

———. *The Goetia of Dr. Rudd*. Vol. 3, Sourceworks of Ceremonial Magic series. London: Golden Hoard, 2007.

———. *The Grimoire of St. Cyprian: Clavis Inferni*. Vol. 5, Sourceworks of Ceremonial Magic series. Singapore: Golden Hoard, 2009.

———. *The Keys to the Gateway of Magic*. Vol. 2, Sourceworks of Ceremonial Magic series. London: Golden Hoard, 2005.

———. *The Practical Angel Magic of John Dee's Enochian Tables*. Vol. 1, Sourceworks of Ceremonial Magic series. London: Golden Hoard, 2004.

———. *The Veritable Key of Solomon*. Vol. 4, Sourceworks of Ceremonial Magic series. Singapore: Golden Hoard, 2008.

Smith, Morton. *Jesus the Magician*. Newburyport, MA: Hampton Roads, 2014.

Swartz, Michael D. *Scholastic Magic*. Princeton, NJ: Princeton University Press, 1996.

Thorndike, Lynn. *A History of Magic and Experimental Science*. Vols. I–VIII. New York: Columbia University Press, 1923–1958.

Turner, Robert. *Elizabethan Magic*. London: Element, 1990.

Waite, A. E. *The Book of Ceremonial Magic*. 1910. Reprint, New York: University Books, 1961.

About the Author

After graduating from Sydney University, Dr. Stephen Skinner began his career as a geography lecturer at what is now the University of Technology in Sydney. He authored *The Search for Abraxas* in 1972, and migrated to London the same year, where he wrote the *Techniques of High Magic* in 1976. Soon after, he produced *Terrestrial Astrology* (aka *Geomancy in Theory and Practice*), which is still the most complete work in English on Western divinatory geomancy. He collaborated with Dr. Donald Laycock on a dictionary of the angelic language discovered/used by Dr. John Dee, and edited Crowley's *Astrology* and the *Magical Diaries of Aleister Crowley: Tunisia 1923*.

Highly illustrated coffee-table books on *Nostradamus, Millennium Prophecies: Apocalypse 2000* followed. In 2003 he wrote *Sacred Geometry*, and soon after he edited Agrippa's *Fourth Book of Occult Philosophy*. From 2004 till 2010 he collaborated with David Rankine to produce the Sourceworks of Ceremonial Magic series, producing *The Veritable Key of Solomon, Lemegeton* (including the *Goetia*), *Janua Reserata, Sepher Raziel: Liber Salomonis,* and *Clavis Inferni*.

Skinner's *Complete Magician's Tables* is a tabular summary of the correspondences of the Kabbalah; angels and demons; the gods of many cultures; the constituents of magic in Latin, Greek, Babylonian, and Egyptian sources; and gemstones, plants, perfumes, and incenses—a total of over 840 comparative tables.

He was awarded a PhD in Classics by the University of Newcastle for his research into the Greek text of the magical papyri (*PGM*) and its connection with the Latin grimoires. The first part of this thesis has been published as *Techniques of Graeco-Egyptian Magic*, and the second part as *Techniques of Solomonic Magic*.

Skinner's most recent books are a full-colour version of Sibley's *Mysteries of Magic,* and the *Ars Notoria,* with full sets of *notae* never before published. He lives in Singapore. Visit his website at www.SSkinner.com.

Art Credits

Figures 1–3 and 5–6 by James Clark.
Figure 4 from *The Straggling Astrologer*, special thanks to Daniel Clark.

· · · · · · ·

Book Six

✦

The Magick of Abra-Melin
by Marcus Katz

The *Book of Abramelin,* a magical *grimoire* that gives the instructions to achieve the knowledge and conversation of one's personal Holy Guardian Angel, was written in German during the fourteenth and fifteenth centuries. The authorship is given as "Abraham of Worms," a possible—albeit, disputed—pseudonym of Rabbi Jacob ben Moses ha Levi Möllin (c. 1365–1427), also known as Maharil.[1]

I will review the Abramelin to provide a summary of the practice and revisit my own experience of completing the ritual during 177 days of work in 2004. Any writing on the Abramelin cannot help but be personal. All is purposed in this universe and seen as such, following the knowledge and conversation of the Holy Guardian Angel. I was given the circumstances to perform the Abramelin Operation exactly seven years following my initiation into the grade of Adeptus Minor. I found myself writing *After the Angel* (my journal of the experience) exactly seven years following the completion of the Abramelin. I was requested—out of the blue—to write this section in this present book exactly seven years since I published *After the Angel*. These cycles of seven years rippled out in time—into both the past and the future—from the moment of completion of the ritual.

The *Book of Abramelin* is similar in many senses to other occult grimoires, being a collection of autobiographical material, magic squares, folklore, and a series of instructions that present an extended ritual whose aim is to bring about the knowledge and conversation of one's personal

---

1. Abraham of Worms, *The Book of Abramelin,* xxiii.

Guardian Angel. However, it has been seen by many, including notorious occultist Aleister Crowley, as something of another order:

> The majority of old magical rituals are either purposely unintelligible or actually puerile nonsense. Those which are straightforward and workable are, as a rule, better adapted to the ambitions of love-sick agricultural labourers than educated people with a serious purpose. But there is one startling exception to this rule. It is *The Book of the Sacred Magic of Abra-Melin the Mage*.[2]

This ritual is presented as six or eighteen months in length and comprises an increasingly rigorous set of spiritual practices culminating in an invocation of the Angel and subsequent calling and controlling of the unredeemed spirits.

The book—hereafter referred to as *Abramelin*—exists in several translations, originally French, German, and Hebrew, and was introduced into the Western Esoteric Initiatory System in 1897 through the translation from the French into English by Samuel Liddell MacGregor Mathers (1854–1918). The French version has the Operation lasting six months and the German version gives eighteen months for the whole Operation.[3] It was then promulgated as an essential component of initiatory progress by Aleister Crowley (1875–1947) and assigned to the work of the *Adeptus Minor* grade in the initiatory system.[4]

The *Abramelin* stands in the medieval grimoire tradition in its format and content, with the notable exception of its ambition: a direct and ongoing relationship with the Guardian Angel, which is unique in this grimoire. However, the statement of authority through the autobiography, the anonymous teacher, the magic squares, and the rituals of purification, confession, and invocation are all firmly rooted in the Western occult tradition.[5]

These grimoires were a rich seam for Mathers and the founders of the Hermetic Order of the Golden Dawn. Mathers translated several such works, including the *Key of Solomon the King* and

---

2. Crowley, *The Confessions of Aleister Crowley*, 172–173.

3. I personally conducted the six-month version and feel that whilst the Operant should choose, there could be a danger of losing focus and intensity in the eighteen-month version. In this piece I have used the Mathers translation for reference and cited page numbers from a contemporary publication of the original Dover edition of his work, *The Book of the Sacred Magic of Abramelin the Mage*, first published in 1975. I have used this version as it was the guide to my own performance of the Abramelin. In the twenty-eight quotes herein, there are only minor differences among the presently available translations from the French or the German.

4. Eds. note: See Book Nine: Thelema & Aleister Crowley.

5. See "Jewish Elements in Magic," in Butler, *Ritual Magic*, 43, and on Abramelin, 296–297.

the *Grimoire of Armadel*.[6] The *Abramelin* can be treated as a classical work alongside these titles and the *Three Books of Occult Philosophy* by Henry Cornelius Agrippa.[7]

Whilst the other grimoires tend toward evocations of the spirits, talismans, and planetary magic, there are echoes of the aim of the *Abramelin*. As one example, we find the mention of the Holy "daimon" in Agrippa:

> Every man hath a three-fold good demon as a proper keeper or preserver, the one whereof is holy, another of the nativity and the other of profession. The holy demon is one, according to the doctrine of the Egyptians, assigned to the rational soul, not from the stars or planets, but from a supernatural cause from God himself, the president of demons, being universal and above nature.[8]

We will first look at the nature of the ritual as given in the most unique section of the *Abramelin* and without which the other sections of the book remain inert.

The Abramelin Operation

The ritual and contemplative practices described in the *Abramelin*, hereafter called the *Operation*, are divided into three periods of demanding preparation, each of two lunar months, which build in intensity—in daily practice and in cumulative effect. At the conclusion of these preparatory six months, there is an intense seven-day period of which the first three days consist of calling upon the good spirits and the grace of knowledge and conversation with the Holy Guardian Angel. If this is successful, the final three days involve the summoning of the evil spirits, under the instruction of the Angel, and obtaining their "oath" to obey the Operator and their Angel.

There is no banishing ritual necessary to conclude the Operation, as the Angel remains with the Operator and the evil spirits are only too glad to depart and get as far away from the Operator as possible. In this, the Operation is very different from other forms of magical ceremony, invocation and summoning.

The three preparatory two-month periods of the ritual might be summarised as:

• Removal—of the Psyche of the Operator through confession and constant prayer

• Relocation—of the Awareness of the Operator through ritualised activity

• Remembrance—of the Angel of the Operator through banishing and invocation

---

6. Mathers, *The Grimoire of Armadel* and *The Key of Solomon the King*.

7. See Leitch, *Secrets of the Magickal Grimoires*, 19–22, and Tyson, *Three Books of Occult Philosophy*.

8. Tyson, *Three Books of Occult Philosophy*, 527.

· · · · · · · · ·

Who Wrote the *Book of Abramelin*?

Abraham of Worms, "Son of Simon," given as the author of the *Abramelin*, states that he was born in 1362 C, and that he wrote the manuscript for his own son, Lamech, in 1458, when he would have been age 96.

In the autobiographical section of the work, he writes at length about his life and thoughts about both the occult practices and major events of the time. After a series of exhaustive travels, during which he met "Abra-melin" the Mage and learnt from him the method described in the book, he appears by his own description to have settled in Würzburg, Germany, where he married and raised a family. The true identity of the author remains in debate, with Georg Dehn proposing that the author was Rabbi Jacob ben Moses ha Levi Möllin (1375—1427), who was a noted student of the Talmud and survived the persecution described in the book.

Unfortunately, there are no references that confirm the details given in the autobiography section, such as court documents that would have named the figure if he had indeed been a court advisor, as claimed in the text. The reference to a son, Lamech, also cannot be verified to any possible author of the time.

Similarly, the identity of Abramelin himself remains a mystery, as the figure may have been a fictional character used as a literary device to provide the book a magical authority. A pseudonymous or blended author in a magical book is a common device in other esoteric literature, such as Hermes Trismegistus, the purported author of the Hermetic texts, or Christian Rosenkreutz, the eponymous hero of the Rosicrucian writings.

As is so often the case, it may be that the only true magical tradition is the invention of a magical tradition.

The first two-moon period is filled with prayer and study. Every day without fail, at fifteen minutes before sunrise, the practitioner must enter the Oratory, having bathed fully and properly, wearing fresh clothing. It was the fresh clothing that turned out to be one of the demanding parts of the ritual in actual practice rather than the early awakening each day. The practitioner then engages in fervent prayer and oration, kneeling before the window, which is open.

A lamp is lit whilst this practice is performed. Whilst the nature of this oration varies, it is at heart a constant prayer of thanks, confession, and supplication to divine will. The most important aspect of the practice here is that it seeks to earnestly connect to the divine will and opens the heart of the practitioner.

Later in the day, at least two hours must be set aside for study, usually after dining. The study is of holy books, religious texts, mystical treatises, and other inspirational works. As the practice intensifies, the amount of time naturally increases as the practitioner finds themselves refocusing their attention on spiritual matters.

· · · · · · · ·

The oration is repeated in the evening, and any ashes from the lamp or incense that is used are taken out and emptied. Whilst this appears a minor detail in the text, in practice the burning and emptying of the resultant ash has a profound spiritual significance once the Operation is being conducted—it symbolises the burning of the soul to meet the Angel.

This practice is repeated every day, taking up several hours. At least one contemporary book suggests that the process is reduced to just one time of prayer each day:

> But just once a day will probably be sufficient in the beginning. You could, of course, go for two times if you're a trooper, but this is hard to do immediately, and you don't want to fail right at the outset.[9]

However, it is my recommendation that the ritual is followed to the letter to build the intensity of the Work, rather than it be diluted to gain a sense of accomplishment. The feeling of failure to meet the standards of the ritual is an essential component of the first two months. It brings a sense of humility rather than achievement, which might aggrandize the ego of the practitioner.[10]

On the Saturday of the week, the sheets of the bedroom chamber are changed and the chamber perfumed. Again, whilst this seems an inconsequential instruction, in practice the weekly cleansing of the sleeping area is an essential response to much of the Operation continuing throughout the sleep of the practitioner. During the nights of the practice, there are intense dreams, visions, and other significant changes in the state of consciousness of the practitioner, particularly in the second period.

After two months of this daily practice, which would have to be totally abandoned should more than one performance be missed—for whatever reason—the second period of two moons commences.

In the second period, the prayers are increased in length, depth, and intensity, and one seeks as much retreat from the world as possible. The hands and face are now ritually bathed in fresh water before any oration, and every Saturday incense is burned whilst the orations are continued day and night.

In addition to this intensification and withdrawal, the practitioner now fasts every Saturday in preparation for the final ritual. As ever, making substantial changes to diet as well as the other factors at play during the Operation is not a matter to take lightly.

---

9. Newcomb, *21st Century Mage*, 152n2.

10. See Townsend, *The Gospel of Falling Down*, 62: "The greatest treasure we will ever discover is found not 'out there' but back at home, yet it is often only truly discovered after the failure of the original quest to find it."

During the third and final two months, the withdrawal continues, and a third set of prayers is added into the regime, at noon. In effect, the days now become a constant prayer only interrupted briefly by moments of everyday life.

Perfume and anointing are added into the ritual, preparing the practitioner and the tools for the final working. Incense is now almost continually burned. This continues for two months without ceasing and stretches the individual beyond anything they may have ever experienced.

The final days of the Operation concentrate on preparing the place of invocation, the use of specific psalms, a stripping of the last vestiges of individual self from the practitioner, and a complete day of absolute silence whilst the Oratory is left in its working state. Many hours of prayer then follow, and after further fasting, on the third day, with the grace of the divine, is attained the knowledge and conversation of the Holy Guardian Angel.

One is told to then leave the Oratory for an hour, then return and remain in the Oratory with the Angel for the rest of the day.

The next three days are concerned with calling and binding to obedience the chief evil spirits and the sub-princes of evil. These include Lucifer, Leviathan, Belial, and even Satan. Once these are bound, one can then command them to marshal their sub-princes, including Beelzebub and Asmodeus. Under the command of these eight sub-princes are entire ranks of Servitors, for example, Kemal, Sarisel, Roffles, and Rukum, in a vast array of names and roles.

One is also granted four personal servant spirits for the tides of the day—a lesser-noted aspect of the Operation, yet one that in practice is extremely profound and important to the magical work of the Adept after the Angel.

A final day is then taken up to call and bind to oath the lesser spirits and then, at last, a day of rest and celebration is allowed for the successful practitioner to conclude the entire working.

The book notes that perhaps only one person in one hundred will be able to successfully complete the working, and even that is given to grace as well as the correct performance of the ritual:

> I swear by the True God that out of an hundred persons who might undertake this operation, there would be only two or three who would actually attain to it.[11]

It is a demanding Operation unlike any other in the Western corpus, and focuses entirely on the individual's relationship with the divine, rather than gaining power to control spirits or some other ancillary purpose:

> It is absolutely necessary to perform this Operation unto the praise, honour, and glory of God; unto the use, health and well-being of your neighbour, whether friend or enemy; and generally for that of the whole earth.[12]

---

11. Mathers, *The Book of the Sacred Magic of Abramelin the Mage*, 156.

12. Mathers, *The Book of the Sacred Magic of Abramelin the Mage*, 53.

• • • • • • • •

Concerning the Selection of the Place

If one were to undertake this Operation, there are many practical considerations, most of which are dealt with very well and in detail throughout the *Abramelin*. Whilst Abramelin gives an account of the ideal place for the ritual, he also points out "in this point as in all the others, we should rule and govern ourselves according to the means at our disposal." [13]

The ideal situation is to have a lodge and terrace, with an uncovered balcony, and a window that looks out from the apartment to the terrace. There should also ideally be an oratory in which the main work of prayer is conducted. A sliding door allows one to open and close access to the divine realm.

In some cases the layout has been created within an otherwise unsuitable apartment, in other cases it has been built out from an existing home, and in my case it was simply provided to specification by the Angel, including two bags of river sand. [14]

It is also possible to prepare an outdoor space for the Operation, instructions about which are included in the book. However, there are many issues in maintaining an outdoor space unless it is within your own property, is nearby, and has ease of access.

The Ritual Implements

The oratory should have a lamp, a censer for incense, and an altar.

The Lamp

The lamp should ideally be an oil lamp, which can be lit and extinguished at ease throughout the periods of the Operation. At one point during the final seven days of the ritual, it must be left lit overnight with an open window in the room, so care must be taken to ensure this can be done in a safe manner.

The River Sand

The Operation requires sand in which the evil spirits may make their appearance known, in the same manner that the Angel signs the silver plate (see below). This river sand is used in the final stage of the Operation and can be poured onto a plate or bowl.

The Silver Plate

A silver plate is used in the final stage of the Operation in which the Angel makes itself known. This can be a small square of silver or a silver-covered plate. The Angel will make a visible mark upon the silver as the first indication of the successful conclusion of the Operation.

---

13. Mathers, *The Book of the Sacred Magic of Abramelin the Mage*, 76.
14. Marcus Katz, *After the Angel*, 123n106.

The Robe, Crown, Wand, and Incense

The practitioner requires a white linen robe and a girdle of silk, as well as a crown. The crown can be a simple gold circlet. Various oils, perfumes, and incense are required, plus a wand—ideally constructed of almond wood:

> You should also have a Wand of Almond-tree wood, smooth and straight, of the length of about from half an ell to six feet.[15]

The Oil of Abramelin

The anointing oil specified and used throughout the Operation is based on a biblical recipe comprising five ingredients: myrrh, cinnamon, cassia, olive oil, and "kaneh bosem," which is most often identified as calamus, or "cane balsam" (Exodus: 30:22–24). The Abramelin instructions follow the biblical quote in the phrasing that "thou shalt make it an oil of holy ointment, an ointment compound after the art of the apothecary" (Exodus: 30:25).

The ingredients and measures differ in translations, but those in the original biblical version are:

- Myrrh, 1 part
- Cinnamon, ½ part
- Cassia, same as myrrh in weight
- Olive oil, ¼ of the combined weight of the other ingredients
- Calamus, same amount as cinnamon

In the Mathers translation, he used galangal instead of calamus, and did not include cassia. Another alternative version was created by Aleister Crowley, using oils:

- 8 parts cinnamon
- 4 parts myrrh
- 2 parts galangal
- 7 parts olive oil

However, the increased amount of cinnamon, particularly as an essential oil, leads to a more caustic liquid that can burn the skin.

---

15. Mathers, *The Book of the Sacred Magic of Abramelin the Mage*, 77. He notes that the measurement given in French may also refer to "an arm's length" rather than specifically six feet.

· · · · · · · ·

The Requirement of Vegetarianism

The instructions of the Abramelin are explicit regarding the adoption of a vegetarian diet. During the ritual you are advised, "You shall eat during this whole period neither the flesh nor the blood of any dead animal." [16] Further, for the ritual and the following year, "You shall touch no dead body of any description soever." [17]

There is a further specific in this regard, during the Operation, with relation to one's own body: Take well heed during the Six Moons or Months to lose no blood from your body, except that which the expulsive Virtue in you may expel naturally of its own accord. [18]

At specific points, the dietary regime is tighter. During the three days of working with the unredeemed spirits at the conclusion of the ritual, "You shall fast, for this is essential, so that when you are working you may find yourself freer and more tranquil both in body and mind." [19] There are several further specifics, and the general instruction that "your only object during your whole life should be to shun as far as possible an ill-regulated life, and especially the vices of debauchery, gluttony, and drunkenness." [20]

One hundred and forty days into the ritual, I noted in my journal that I had realised something about blood and the ritual, although it was not clearly stated in the whole. [21] There was a similar insight later about "all that lives, lives."

The realisation was that the ritual is not only a spiritual event but also a *physical* event—every component of the body is aligned to the Angel through the kneeling, breathing, and repetition of the sensory anchors. This is coupled with dietary and sleeping regimes, all of which place the body in a peculiar and specific state.

As a result, any wound to the body would trigger an automatic survival mechanism, which in turn would draw away from the intent of the ritual. This could happen even with the smallest loss of blood or injury, such is the intense but delicate state into which the physical body has been placed. There are many such requirements in the Operation that further unpack their meaning only during the performance and over time.

Seclusion

Whilst the book recommends seclusion, this is a purely practical consideration, for it reduces the responsibilities on the practitioner during the Operation. It is advised that for "servants," the

---

16. Mathers, *The Book of the Sacred Magic of Abramelin the Mage*, 130.

17. Mathers, *The Book of the Sacred Magic of Abramelin the Mage*, 130.

18. Mathers, *The Book of the Sacred Magic of Abramelin the Mage*, 130.

19. Mathers, *The Book of the Sacred Magic of Abramelin the Mage*, 129.

20. Mathers, *The Book of the Sacred Magic of Abramelin the Mage*, 128.

21. Katz, *After the Angel*, 160.

· · · · · · · ·

problem will be balancing your work and the duties of the Operation, whereas for those who are "indentured," it would be impossible because one could be called for work in the middle of a waiting phase in the Operation. In contemporary terms, a job with regular hours might work with the Operation, but as with all things, once the working is commenced, all life becomes subservient to the demands of the ritual. A job with irregular hours or call-outs would not be practical to even commence the Operation. The important factor is that even if one should conduct business, it should be "modest and patient" and not the cause of anger or anxiety.[22]

In the present author's case, I had been given what appeared to be a once-in-a-lifetime opportunity of a six-month period during which I would not have to work and would receive income to support myself and family. I took this as a definite sign to commence the work. I did not expect that within a few weeks of commencing the Operation, my situation would radically change, and I would find myself having to again find employment whilst not giving up the Operation. This utterly unexpected twist was almost certainly part of the ritual, as the employment turned out to be abusive and contributed to the "winnowing of the soul" during the first two phases of the Abramelin.[23]

Age, Gender, and Marital Status

The specifications for the age and qualities needed for the Operation are obviously dated to the time of writing, when the average age expectancy, state of health, etc., would have been very different from today, as would be the social and religious views. Abramelin states that the age needed for the Operation is between twenty-five to fifty, and this seems to be given in context of health; it is also stated that one should be free of "inherited diseases" such as "virulent leprosy."[24] I would consider that a minimum age of twenty-five is about right, possibly older, and so long as one's health is reasonable and sufficient to conduct the Operation as given, there is no maximum age. I can only postulate that conducting the Operation toward the latter part of life may have a different focus for the Operator and a different communication from the Angel.

Whilst the *Abramelin* states that "whether he be free or married importeth little," it is recommended that you are single or commence in the first year of marriage.[25] If one were to conduct the Operation in the first year of marriage, or at any time in a marriage, this would need to be discussed between both partners. There will be an immediate and long-term impact of the working in any relationship.

22. Mathers, *The Book of the Sacred Magic of Abramelin the Mage*, 67.

23. I detail this strange turn of events in Katz, *After the Angel*.

24. Mathers, *The Book of the Sacred Magic of Abramelin the Mage*, 55.

25. Mathers, *The Book of the Sacred Magic of Abramelin the Mage*, 55.

• • • • • • • •

In terms of gender, it is clearly stated that whilst "there be only Virgins who are suitable" (amongst women), the advice is "that so important a matter should not be communicated to them, because of the accidents that they may cause by their curiosity and love of talk."[26] It should be highlighted that Mathers states in a footnote to this portion, "Here comes another touch of prejudice. In the present day many of the profoundest students of the Qabalah are women, both married and single."[27] Again, my counsel would be that the gender of the Operator is certainly something to be taken into account, but the Operation is available for all. There was nothing in my own experience that seemed as if it would be gender-specific.

I believe that the "qualities" given in chapter 3 of book 3 of the *Abramelin* are of far more import than specific age or gender, these being tranquillity, temperance, and not given to "avarice or usury."[28]

Varying the Instructions

As one practitioner of the Abramelin, "Ishariyah," writes: "Practice is what counts in this matter. This Operation is not a theory. It is the real thing. You have to do it. If you merely contemplate it, or change it, you will never really know it."[29]

However, there are several cases where a practitioner has written about the Holy Guardian Angel, or other mystical experience, and then revealed that they did not perform the Abramelin but rather devised a four-week version of the ritual, underwent a single significant experience they took as the Angel, or indeed crossed the Abyss in a vision.

These are not in any way comparable to the performance and result of the Abramelin any more than spending a year travelling abroad compares with watching an episode of a travel show.

One is advised only to follow the instructions of the book, with the assistance of the Angel, whether the practitioner is aware of it or not. If the practitioner is not sure whether they have achieved the knowledge and conversation, then it is not the Angel. One must have faith and stick to the instructions:

Ye have here to do with the Lord, Who not only beholdeth the outer man, but Who also penetrateth the inmost recesses of the heart. But having taken a true, firm, and determined resolution, relying upon the Will of the Lord, ye shall arrive at your desired end, and encounter no difficulty.[30]

---

26. Mathers, *The Book of the Sacred Magic of Abramelin the Mage*, 55–56.

27. Mathers, *The Book of the Sacred Magic of Abramelin the Mage*, 55, fn.

28. Mathers, *The Book of the Sacred Magic of Abramelin the Mage*, 55.

29. Ishariyah, *The Abra-Melin Experience*, 3.

30. Mathers, *The Book of the Sacred Magic of Abramelin the Mage*, 54.

· · · · · · ·

Superstitions about the Book

The most common superstition about the *Abramelin* is that the magic squares can somehow come to life and cause evil effects merely by their presence. This derives in part from Mathers, who originally lost his manuscripts for the publication of the *Abramelin* in Paris and had to delay his publishers whilst putting up posters for the return of his briefcase. He went on to write in his introduction:

> If left carelessly about, they [the squares] are very liable to obsess sensitive persons, children, or even animals.[31]

There is indeed a potential for obsession with magical work, which could be projected onto ritual or symbolic items such as the squares. However, there are "occult guards" that protect both the Operant and the squares—and their spirits—from misuse.[32]

The Requirements to Begin the Operation

I believe that the profound impact of the Abramelin is enough to overcome the usual notion of linear time and space. In ritual work, we often find that our sense of time is challenged, and ultimately we come to see it as "the moving likeness of eternity."[33] The principle and only requirement to perform the Abramelin is that *you have already done so in the future*. As such, a ripple has promulgated—apparently backward in time from our perspective—to the present moment when you commence the Operation. If you do not feel this, it is unlikely that you have succeeded in the Operation, nor will you succeed if you attempt it.

There also may be a particularly significant event that offers an invitation to attempt the ritual. In my case it was a six-month payment package that came at a time when I had exhausted all other distractions. It seemed unlikely that such an opportunity would ever again present itself.

Useful Preparation for the Operation

The structure of the Western Esoteric Initiatory System holds the Abramelin Operation as a fundamental transition point between the status of student and adept. It is a test of all prior work, a self-evident award, and a graduation ceremony rolled into one. The manifestation of the results may vary, but I hold that there is essential preparation for the Operation that corresponds to the likelihood of success.

One of the most significant preparations is one of philosophy rather than practicality. I suggest that the practitioner apply radical analysis of their belief structure and the notion of duality. This

---

31. Mathers, *The Book of the Sacred Magic of Abramelin the Mage*, xviii.

32. Mathers, *The Book of the Sacred Magic of Abramelin the Mage*, xvii.

33. Plato, *Timaeus*, E8.

· · · · · · · ·

might be accomplished through a combination of psychotherapeutic work, NLP (neuro-linguistic programming), and the Western Esoteric Initiatory System.[34]

I observe that some who have completed the Abramelin remain locked in a simplistic framework of "inner and outer," or "good and evil," which becomes further locked by their practice of the Operation. I do not believe that the Angel is truly apparent when viewing the world in these limited models.

An overhaul—through magical work or spiritual contemplation—of one's ideas of time and space is also essential to avoid the Abramelin consolidating an imbalanced view.

Prepare to Die

The Abramelin is a ritual of exhaustion, and as such the practitioner should be prepared to lose everything rather than gain anything in particular—even their Angel. Preliminary practice for this aspect of the Operation can include initiatory rituals, death and rebirth practices, and contemporary works such as *A Year to Live* by Stephen Levine.

Practice Constant Confession

The practice of unceasing prayer, also known as the Prayer of the Heart or the Jesus Prayer, is found in several branches of Christianity. It is a useful exercise prior to the Abramelin in that it foreshadows the constant attention placed on the contemplations during the Operation. The classic manual for this practice is *On the Prayer of Jesus* by Ignatius Brianchaninov.

Practice Devotion

It is uncommon to find the practice of devotion in magical work, yet this is a principle feature of the Abramelin. We may find it in *Liber Astarte* by Aleister Crowley, a six-month practice in which the practitioner devotes themselves to a chosen deity, practised at a lower grade than the Abramelin.[35] An alternative approach, within the Christian tradition, is *The Imitation of Christ* by Thomas A. Kempis, which can be used as a contemplative manual, taking each of the 118 contemplations as a daily prompt over three to four months.

Practice Divine Reading

To encourage a deeper and engaged reading of the spiritual material chosen throughout the Operation, the practice of Divine Reading is paramount. This Benedictine tradition works with scriptural reading in four phases: reading, meditating, praying, and contemplating. It is similar in essence to the four levels of Kabbalistic analysis: literal, symbolic, extended, and secret. A familiarity with active reading of spiritual texts will allow the practitioner an accelerated entry into

---

34. See "The Crucible Club" at www.marcuskatz.com.

35. Crowley, *Magick*, 460–471. Note that Crowley writes, "Do thou in no wise confuse this invocation with that [of the Holy Guardian Angel]."

this aspect of the Abramelin. However, there is something to be said for floundering with the spiritual reading in the beginning, which brings home a certain humility.

Practice Ritual

The Abramelin Operation is comprised of a series of interlocked ritual activities that in themselves are simple in practice, although the final phase is at the higher end of complexity in terms of ceremony and skill. A modicum of experience in Western ceremonial magic would likely benefit the practitioner.

However, there have been workings performed by those not approaching it from a background in ceremonial magic. The practitioner Ishariyah had "actively followed a spiritual path for 30 years" but "had never been particularly interested in the common perception of magical working, as I considered much of it to be lower astral work."[36] Similarly, the author William Bloom, who conducted the Operation in 1973 and published his diary under the pseudonym Georges Chevalier, had no deep practice in ceremonial ritual.[37]

Practice Mystical Contemplation

Those who discuss their experience of the Abramelin appear to fall into three distinct groups, based on their stated concerns, ongoing questions, and focus that follows the ritual. I believe that as the ritual fundamentally shifts the relationship between the practitioner and the universe, the manner in which that relationship is manifest is entirely dependent on the preexisting relationship.

One group attains some type of mystical or spiritual experience, where the outcome is described as a form of union with the universe; another group describes it as a connection to a new type of higher self; and a third group describes it as not an outcome but a command over the spirits.

These might be characterised as a mystical outcome, a psychological one, and a magical one. There is a fourth group, who successfully complete the ritual as given and gain the knowledge and conversation of their Holy Guardian Angel.

Choosing the Prayers and Reading Material

The *Abramelin* counsels that much time be spent in reading—and contemplating—spiritual works: "You shall set apart two hours each day after having dined, during the which you shall read with care the Holy Scripture and other Holy Books, because they will teach you to be good at praying, and how to fear the Lord."[38]

---

36. Ishariyah, *The Abra-Melin Experience*, 7–8.

37. Chevalier [Bloom], *The Sacred Magician*, 1976, and Bloom [Chevalier], *The Sacred Magician*, 1992.

38. Mathers, *The Book of the Sacred Magic of Abramelin the Mage*, 67–68.

The recommended literature would include Christian mystical works or other works found to be inspiring to the practitioner within their own tradition. The ultimate aim of this reading, in retrospect, is to "better know your Creator" and become increasingly open to one's own position relative to a vast and mysterious universe, in addition to learning new skills for prayer.[39]

The Abandoning of the Operation

If performed correctly, the Abramelin is a demanding work of magic that at the very least has a significant impact on the psychological state of the Operant. The repetitive ritual activity, adherence to a tight time schedule, and self-examination, coupled with the self-involved nature of the work, all contribute to a rapid and intense erosion of the psyche.

As the Operation progresses, further repetitions, intensification, and additional practises lead to an uncoupling of the usual sense of reality. The Operant may find themselves needing some form of escape, but this must be carefully considered—simple games might be one solution. Mathers notes that he translated the rule against *jeu* in the *Abramelin* as *gambling* rather than general *games* because he felt that recreation would be "almost a necessity during this period, to prevent the brain giving way from the intense nervous strain."[40]

The *Abramelin* does factor in ill health as a reason to adapt or abandon the Operation:

> And in the case that during this period you should be attacked with some illness, which would not permit you to go unto the Oratory, this need not oblige you to abandon your enterprise at once; but you should govern yourself to the best of your ability.[41]

The book suggests praying in bed, studying as you can, but should the sickness continue for the second period (or third six-month period in the eighteen-month version), then you should take this as a sign that you must await a more "fitting time."[42]

Crowley himself abandoned his first attempt at the Operation, for the performance of which he had moved to Scotland in 1899, in favour of visiting S. L. MacGregor Mathers in Paris during the midst of a crisis in the Hermetic Order of the Golden Dawn.[43] He wrote that as Mathers was a link to "Secret Chiefs," "if that meant giving up the Abra-Melin Operation for the present, all

---

39. Mathers, *The Book of the Sacred Magic of Abramelin the Mage*, 68.

40. Mathers, *The Book of the Sacred Magic of Abramelin the Mage*, 131.

41. Mathers, *The Book of the Sacred Magic of Abramelin the Mage*, 69.

42. Mathers, *The Book of the Sacred Magic of Abramelin the Mage*, 155. The paragraph in this section sets out the difference between "giving in for a while" and "conforming to His Holy Will."

43. Boleskine House, upon the shores of Loch Ness, where Crowley started the working, and which at one time was owned by Led Zeppelin guitarist Jimmy Page, suffered a major fire in 2015 and is now an empty shell.

· · · · · · · ·

right." [44] He then remained ambivalent about the Operation, returning to England "with a sort of feeling at the back of my mind that I might as well resume the Abra-Melin operation." [45]

It was not until he was travelling across China that he again resumed the Operation, writing, "I could construct my own temple about me and perform the Operation in my physical body," rather than astrally travelling to Boleskine House in Scotland, where he had set up for the Operation. [46]

However, following his eventual return to England, a bereavement, and an illness, he began to consider that he might be failing at the Operation. [47] In July 1906 he conferred with Cecil Jones, a magical colleague, and resumed regular invocations, culminating a few months later in a spiritual experience at Ashdown Park Hotel, Coulsdon, Surrey:

> On the ninth [October], having prepared a full invocation and ritual, I performed it. I had no expectation, I think, of attaining any special success; but it came. I had performed the Operation of the Sacred magick of Abra-Melin the Mage. [48]

The nature of the result, which Crowley tested further, and its relationship to the *Augoeides*, which we will discuss in the next section, is given more detail by a brief diary entry for the same date:

> Oct 9. I *did* get rid of everything but the Holy Exalted One, and must have held Him for a minute or two. I did. I am sure I did. [49]

Crowley took seven years to complete the Operation, attacking it with intensity and full focus on each attempt, through his own methodology. In the end, it is your Angel who will stand before you in accomplishment of this Operation. The question is simple: can you withstand the work? [50]

The Angel, Higher Self, and the Augoeides

There is often a conflation of terms when we read about the Holy Guardian Angel and Abramelin work, commencing with Crowley, who changed his view on the subject several times

---

44. Crowley, *The Confessions of Aleister Crowley*, 195.

45. Crowley, *The Confessions of Aleister Crowley*, 337.

46. Crowley, *The Confessions of Aleister Crowley*, 517.

47. A summary of this experience is provided in Churton, *Aleister Crowley: The Biography*, 122–125.

48. Crowley, *The Confessions of Aleister Crowley*, 532.

49. Crowley, *The Confessions of Aleister Crowley*, 532.

50. Mathers, *The Book of the Sacred Magic of Abramelin the Mage*, 54. Abramelin states, "Ponder the matter then well before commencing, and only begin the Operation with the firm intention of carrying it on unto the end, for no man can make a mock of the Lord with impunity."

· · · · · · · ·

during his life. This may be a matter of terminology, in an attempt to avoid the purely Christian notion of an Angel, but it can confuse students of the Work.

The Angel is not a form of self any more than a relationship with another person is a form of self. It is neither an unconscious self nor a higher self.

The Neoplatonic term *Augoeides* was featured and introduced into the Western esoteric tradition through the 1842 novel *Zanoni* by Edward Bulwer-Lytton (1803–1873). In the novel, which was influential for both Aleister Crowley and A. E. Waite, the mysterious Adept Zanoni speaks of the Augoeides as the "luminous soul."[51]

> There is a principle of the soul, superior to all nature, through which we are capable of surpassing the order and systems of the world. When the soul is elevated to natures better than itself, THEN it is entirely separated from subordinate natures, exchanges this for another life, and, deserting the order of things with which it was connected, links and mingles itself with another.
> —Iamblichus.[52]

The Augoeides was also referenced by Helena Petrovna Blavatsky (1831–1891) within theosophical teachings as "the luminous body of the spiritual soul, once rid of its (physical and psychical) vestures, or bodies."[53]

The Augoeides is seen as the "subtle vehicle" of the soul, and a "divine body."[54] This body can also be purged and energised by living according to the virtues. It can also be summoned. In *Zanoni*, the titular Adept calls upon "Adon-Ai," the "Son of Eternal Light," in a cave, which first appears as "a luminous and gigantic column, glittering and shifting."[55] Then out of that column emerges an angelic figure:

> A shape of unimaginable glory. Its face was that of a man in its first youth, but solemn, as with the consciousness of eternity and the tranquillity of wisdom; light, like starbeams, flowed through its transparent veins; light made its limbs themselves, and undulated, in restless sparkles, through the waves of its dazzling hair.[56]

---

51. Bulwer-Lytton, *Zanoni*, 2.IV.
52. Bulwer-Lytton, *Zanoni*, 4.IX.
53. Blavatsky, *Isis Unveiled*, 303fn80.
54. Mead, *Orpheus: The Theosophy of the Greeks*, IX, 281–291.
55. Bulwer-Lytton, *Zanoni*, 4.IX.
56. Bulwer-Lytton, *Zanoni*, 4.IX.

In this description, there is similarity to the Guardian Angel, and it is likely the seed of the concept that grew in Crowley's vision. As such, it is a reflection of the soul lit from its own light, finding a response in the universe—and not merely another version of self-identity.

The Cult of the Guardian Angel

The Church still maintains several movements dedicated to the angels, in much the same way as the cult of Mary or the cult of saints. One such movement is the "Opus Sanctorum Angelorum," sanctioned by Pope Paul VI in 1968.[57]

There are three stages in conjoining with the angels within this movement. There is a spiritual "promise" first made to the guardian angels, followed by a consecration ritual to the Guardian Angel, certifying oneself as a "spiritual warrior." [58] This is eventually followed by a third stage in which the candidate is consecrated to all angels.

Abramelin Diaries

There are few published full accounts of the Operation itself—the first being *The Sacred Magician* by William Bloom, which was originally published under a pseudonym, Georges Chevalier.[59] Bloom was twenty-five when in 1973 he set off to Morocco with his wife to practice the ritual in rural isolation. There is also a lesser-known account by Ishariyah (I. Golden), who was fifty-four when he undertook the ritual in 2003 in Australia. I discovered and purchased that book, *The Abra-Melin Experience*, during my own practice in 2004, when I was thirty-nine.

Author and researcher Aaron Leitch has also written on the Abramelin from his experience of the working in 1997,[60] and the Thelemic magician Bill Heidrick provides a lengthy "Abramelin Ramble" written between 1994–1995.[61] Athena W. completed the working in 2003–2004, and her notes are available online.[62] At the time of this writing, *The Abramelin Diaries* by Ramsey Dukes (Lionel Snell) is the most recently published account, following YouTube videos where he discusses his experience of the ritual in 1977.[63]

57. Grosso, 'The Cult of the Guardian Angel," in Parisen, *Angels & Mortals*, 128.

58. Grosso, "The Cult of the Guardian Angel," in Parisen, *Angels & Mortals*, 128–129.

59. Chevalier [Bloom], *The Sacred Magician*, 1976.

60. Aaron Leitch, "The Holy Guardian Angel," accessed September 24, 2019, http://kheph777.tripod.com/art_HGA.html.

61. Bill Heidrick, "An Abramelin Ramble," accessed September 24, 2019, http://www.digital-brilliance.com/kab/abramel.htm.

62. Athena W., "Abramelin Experiences," Enochian.org, accessed September 24, 2019, http://enochian.org/abramelin.shtml.

63. Ramsey Dukes, "Thoughts on Abramelin." YouTube video, accessed September 24, 2019, https://www.youtube.com/watch?v=IrtYoahG5Ww; and Dukes, *The Abramelin Diaries*.

· · · · · · · ·

The Appearance of the Holy Guardian Angel

The question most asked by those who have not attempted the Abramelin is about the appearance of the Angel, namely, whether it is a physical appearance. In the present author's case, it was a physical appearance, and I would propose that a successful Operation would likely involve such a manifestation. This is because the world is literally turned inside out during the culmination of the ritual, and as such, a physical presence is well within the parameters of this profound event.

To the practitioner who has been successful in the Operation, there is no astonishment at the physical manifestation, due to the other revelations that overwhelm the awareness at that time.

The Angel will always be unique to the individual. The fourth-century bishop Gregory Thaumaturgus suggested that angels are assigned by a "momentous decision." [64] The theologian Origen of Alexandria (c. 184–c. 253) speculated that angels are given their position through their own unique qualities, leading to contemporary authors suggesting that "we are paired with an angel individually suited to our personal pursuit of salvation." [65]

Israel Regardie (1907–1985) suggests, following Iamblichus, that "the outcome of the invocation of the Holy Guardian Angel does not result identically with various people" and "to whatsoever conception of his Angel he aspired, so will the outcome of the mystical marriage be." [66]

The Four Servant Spirits

On the calls for the second and third days of the final phase of the Operation, the practitioner calls upon the Dukes and Kings of the infernal hierarchies to provide four servant spirits unique to the practitioner. These may come from the lists provided in the *Abramelin* but may also be given individually, according to the whims of the Kings. The servant spirits are allotted times of the day when they are attendant and may also be "loaned" to other people for magical work. [67]

The Use of the Magic Squares

In the tradition of the grimoires, the *Abramelin* contains a significant section that provides a range of magic squares. These are grids of various sizes containing letters or numbers that create acrostic patterns of apparently nonsensical words such as *SEGOR*. In some cases, the letters and words may be translated from Hebrew, such as *MAIAM*, the Hebrew word for "water" in the magic square "to walk upon, and operate under, Water." [68]

---

64. Thaumaturgus, *Oration and Panegyric Addressed to Origen*, Oration 4.

65. Miller, *Lifted by Angels*, 109.

66. Regardie, "The Magician and the Holy Guardian Angel," in Parisen, *Angels & Mortals*, 92–93.

67. Katz, *After the Angel*, 189.

68. Mathers, *The Book of the Sacred Magic of Abramelin the Mage*, 231.

· · · · · · · ·

A Diary Entry

The Operation is not without significant impact on those around the Operator, which is difficult to communicate. Some forty days into the Operation, I recorded the first signs of influence on my wife and son, who managed to bear with me throughout the whole ritual. I provide these diary entries (published in *After the Angel*) as brief example of the importance of full consideration prior to attempting the working.

Day 39: 1st May 2004 (Saturday)

My oratories were performed this night with incense, after which I felt that the top of my head had been lifted off, and a wide empty plane had opened all around me, in which "presences" gathered—neither good nor bad, merely of a different order. It was very strange—I recall blinking, staring, and my stomach turning over. It was very visceral.

B [my wife] reported a nightmare where she was surrounded by threatening masked figures, and in the nightmare, I appeared and told her, "Everything changes into everything else."

Day 40: 2nd May 2004 (Sunday)

Orations performed.

My personality is beginning to revolt against the strain. I can feel every part of me screaming for either attention or to be withdrawn from the process. It is like a dark therapy.

Day 41: 3rd May 2004 (Monday)

Orations performed. R [my son] is reporting strong and meaningful dreams—this morning about an evil pure-white cat that he wanted to get rid of from the house, but B [my wife] and I wouldn't let him.

The wide open "headless" plane is still open. And I am starting to receive instruction. Really. And it is not at all like anything I imagined. But all too brief, I am too full for much to take within.

A plant pot crashed to the floor tonight in the hallway, making us all jump. It really could not have simply lifted itself off the stand and launched itself onto the floor. It feels as if everything is alive around us, and there are presences in the day, in the night, and in our dreams.

These squares are to provide magical results of varying plausibility if taken literally: "to prevent Caves from falling in" or "to cause a body to revive." [69] Others are to heal or cause sickness, find lost items, and other relatively common concerns such as to have as much money as one might need in times of trouble.

In the French version and Mathers's subsequent translation, the squares are incomplete—in one German version they are presented in full. There are specific instructions regarding the use of these squares, the main of which is "you will never demand of your Guardian Angel any Symbol wherewith to operate for an Evil end, seeing that you would grieve him." [70]

It is further indicated that "it is not necessary (in all cases) to use written symbols [the squares]" in favour of merely speaking or concentrating upon the square. [71] However, the book does present instructions for using the squares in ritual, and even encourages the operator that "the Evil spirits be exceedingly prompt and exceedingly obedient in the working of Evil." [72]

A general practice is also given for accessing the squares and spirits should an aim not be covered by the list of squares included in the book.

Preparation

1. Fast on the preceding day.

2. On the day, wash, enter the oratory dressed in white, and light the lamp and incense.

3. Place a drop of the anointing oil on a seven-sided tablet of gold, silver, or wax and place it upon the altar in front of the incense.

4. Kneel and call to Adonai for assistance.

5. Call upon the Guardian Angel for advice and to bless you with his appearance.

6. Await the presence of the Angel.

7. Once the Angel has appeared, concentrate your attention on your Angel.

8. You will then find that the name and square of the spirit required for the task—and his Duke—has appeared "written as it were in drops of dew, like a sweat exuding therefrom" upon the silver tablet. [73]

9. Copy the sign, leaving the tablet upon the altar, and return in the evening, when the name and square will have disappeared from the silver tablet.

10. Perform your regular prayer regime and wrap the tablet in a silk cloth.

69. Mathers, *The Book of the Sacred Magic of Abramelin the Mage*, 182, 196.

70. Mathers, *The Book of the Sacred Magic of Abramelin the Mage*, 125.

71. Mathers, *The Book of the Sacred Magic of Abramelin the Mage*, 131.

72. Mathers, *The Book of the Sacred Magic of Abramelin the Mage*, 135.

73. Mathers, *The Book of the Sacred Magic of Abramelin the Mage*, 133.

• • • • • • • •

It is suggested that if the Angel does not appear, then the aim of the ritual is not to be allowed by the divine, and that it is best to prepare the ritual on the eve of the Sabbath (Sunday) so as to conduct it on the Sabbath without making it unholy.

Use of the Given Square

Prepare the oratory with incense and the tools of the Abramelin ritual, including the bowl or plate of sand.

1. Light the incense and pray to the Angel with humility.
2. Stand fully robed with the girdle and headband, holding the wand and facing the arbor/door.
3. Call the Twelve Dukes as was done in the Operation. They will appear in sight.
4. Command the Dukes that they may not leave until the relevant Duke make appear in the sand the square and the name of the spirit that was received on the previous day upon the silver tablet.
5. At this point it will be evident that the spirit is present but invisible to sight.
6. Make the Duke and the spirit take the oath as was done in the Operation.
7. Dismiss the Dukes and spirit, first making a note of the square, because it will vanish as soon as the spirits are dismissed.
8. Close the ritual with the incense.

Success of the Magic Squares

There have been several occasions when the present author has successfully used the squares, subject to either necessity or experiment—and the grace of the Angel. The first was the 15th square, "That the Spirits bring all sorts of things to eat and drink."[74]

Our family was going through a time of hardship that had been made worse by myself falling foul of a short-term debilitating illness. I was unable to go into work and our money had completely run out, with no income for a further week. We worked with the spirits as a family with no clear hope of success.

The following day, there was a knock on the door. Even though I was very sick, I was able to get downstairs and open the door. I was surprised to see the human resources manager of my place of work. She told me that the company had been worried about my situation and knew that I had been unable to leave the house. As a gesture, they had asked the catering staff to put

---

74. Mathers, *The Book of the Sacred Magic of Abramelin the Mage*, 201.

together a meal. In fact, as it was a place with many catering students, they had all worked on the task and provided enough meals and food for a week.

I still have a photograph of our kitchen that day, full of trays and platters, bottles and dishes, brimming with food and drink—"all sorts of things to eat and drink."

The second notable occasion was more of an experiment than a necessity, with a magic square from another grimoire. I had been discussing with a friend the ridiculous aims of some of the squares. I chose a random square and performed a simple rite to activate it. I then forgot about it. Within a week, I found myself at a theatre in another city, reclining on floor cushions, listening to Arabic music and watching a *raqs sharqi* dance performance—all unexpectedly and without any intent on my part.

The oddest and most difficult aspect to explain was that I had totally forgotten the ridiculous aim of the magic square: "to summon thirteen dancing girls on a Wednesday." It was indeed a Wednesday.

The third example was in the searching of the magic squares to derive a name for a divination-related project. I had intended to search the squares for a combination of letters that would not be in general use. I also felt that there would be a trick in using a magical name for a whole project. As I vainly searched the squares for a workable combination of letters, I suddenly had the word *Tarosophy* spring into my mind, which became the guiding name and trademark of an entire lifetime project. It was only after I wrote it down and returned to close the *Book of Abra-melin* that I saw fully the square that I had last been viewing: "To Know the Secrets of Words."[75]

A final example was created for this current writing, to demonstrate the use of the squares. I selected the 16.10 square, *ORION*, "To find and take possession of all kinds of Treasures," namely "Coins."[76] This is also a square to recover lost money. I chose this square as it has such a definite purpose and outcome.

I created the square and activated it at 2:00 p.m. that afternoon. At 5:00 the following morning, I found myself suddenly awake and unable to sleep. I glanced at the emails on my phone and saw a notification that I had won a prize in the UK lottery.

I checked on the computer and the site was down for overnight repair. I made a cup of tea and refreshed the screen, only to discover, at 5:20 a.m., that I had indeed won 4.81 pounds on the lottery. I can only imagine that this precise amount is likely the total of coins lost from my pockets, fallen out at the cinema, and other losses of coins over the last few years.

---

75. Mathers, *The Book of the Sacred Magic of Abramelin the Mage*, 194. This is chapter 12, the 2nd square, *SIMBASI*.
76. Mathers, *The Book of the Sacred Magic of Abramelin the Mage*, 203–204.

· · · · · · ·

Aleister Crowley and the Abramelin

We have seen that Crowley held the knowledge and conversation of the Holy Guardian Angel as a central stage in the Great Work and his attempts at performing the Abramelin Operation.

We have also noted how Crowley compared the term *Holy Guardian Angel* to that of the *higher self*, *Khu*, *Augoeides*, etc., in his later writings only in the sense of deriding them as versions of *Higher Self* or *God within us*, which he deemed meaningless. He implored his student to abhor and abominate these terms—and much more—and instead "get on with your *practice.*" [77]

> We may readily concur that the Augoeides, the "Genius" of Socrates, and the "Holy Guardian Angel" of Abramelin the Mage, are identical. But we cannot include this "Higher Self"; for the Angel is an actual Individual with his own Universe, exactly as man is; or, for the matter of that, a bluebottle. He is not a mere abstraction, a selection from, and exaltation of, one's own favourite qualities, as the "Higher Self" seems to be. [78]

Crowley repeats several times that the Holy Guardian Angel is not an abstraction or a higher self—otherwise, "there would be no point" in the Abramelin. [79]

> He is not to be found by any exploration of oneself. It is true that the process of analysis leads finally to the realization of oneself as no more than a point of view indistinguishable *in itself* from any other point of view; but the Holy Guardian Angel is in precisely the same position. [80]

Contemporary practitioners have, in general, concentrated on the process of evocation and the commanding of the spirits in the *Abramelin*, after Crowley:

> Therefore we can infer that every ritual we perform to attain this Knowledge and Conversation not only brings us closer to the Holy Guardian Angel, but also increases our power over external circumstances and, why not, over the Spirits. [81]

The rejection of the Operation as a mystical experience—sometimes instead conflated with a "new age" gloss of self-development—in favour of seeing it as a gaining of implicit power and influence is also a common trend:

77. Aleister Crowley, *Magick Without Tears*, 208.

78. Aleister Crowley, *Magick Without Tears*, 276.

79. Aleister Crowley, *Magick Without Tears*, 282.

80. Aleister Crowley, *Magick Without Tears*, 282.

81. Massimo Mantovani, "Holy Guardian Angel for Fun and Prophet," in Morgan, *Thelemic Magick II*, 90.

• • • • • • • •

The real goal of the Abramelin Rite is to attain a Supernatural Assistant who will grant you the power to bind the spirits who would cause you harm and set them to working for you instead.[82]

The notion of power—an implicit statement of duality—is anathema to the spiritual experience of unification that attends the knowledge and conversation of the Holy Guardian Angel.

A Dark Song

A contemporary direct reference to the *Abramelin* is found in the 2016 film *A Dark Song*. The director, Liam Gavin, stated in an interview that the book appealed to him as it meant both the simplicity and the challenge of a single location shooting with a small cast. However, the film also captures the intensity, magical discipline, and spiritual development that are bound to the Operation.

There is one understated yet extremely relevant moment where the two characters (the woman performing it and the man assisting her) are sat quietly talking in the kitchen of the isolated house that has been hired for the duration of the ritual. They are talking about the weather, and in passing one mentions the month, to which the other quietly muses that they thought it was another month. In this reflective moment, we see that they have been entirely "de-coupled" from reality, which occurs in the actual Operation.

The ritual performed in the film bears little similarity to the Abramelin other than the relative isolation of the working and the length of it. However, some constraints such as sexual relations and diet are mentioned. There are also components that are subtly utilised, such as the increasing study of holy writings and the facing of demons prior to the climatic Operation. A particular point when the dynamic shifts between the characters is marked by a wound and blood, which is repeated as a motif at the conclusion of the film, and this is true to one of the instructions in the book with regard to blood.

The final sacrifice is also true to the Operation, as it involves a complete negation of the most important attachment of the main character—and a redemption (of sorts) for the other character. Despite the director having no significant involvement in esotericism, the theme of the work has been powerfully portrayed in the film.

It could be said that whilst the film is not about the Operation in function, it is about the Operation in purpose: the knowledge and conversation of the Holy Guardian Angel as an act of forgiveness, sacrifice, and grace.

---

82. Frater Rufus Opus, "Never Again Alone," in Cecchetelli, *The Holy Guardian Angel*, 53.

· · · · · · · ·

A. E. Waite and the *Abramelin*

A. E. Waite references the *Abramelin* in a short chapter within *The Book of Ceremonial Magic*, writing:

> The amateurs of occult science in the more dubious of its practical branches became possessed of this pearl of tradition in 1898, and I suppose that it is familiar enough in certain circles.[83]

Waite points out that the text differs in several ways from the usual run of grimoires, notably when it derides "all observations of times and seasons along the usual and accepted lines."[84]

He holds some contempt for the author:

> An exponent of Art Magic in the utmost simplification thereof, but that which he saves in ritual he expends in the dramatic elaboration of general *mise en scène*.[85]

Waite concludes by dismissing Mathers's statement of the importance and benefit of the book.

The Drop

A common experience following the conclusion of the Operation is the drop or comedown that attends the cessation of daily practice. One practitioner wrote that it is "like I have lost a friend."[86] After I completed the Abramelin, I was unable to write in my journal for thirty days. I then wrote a single page, of which the content still remains mysterious to me, mentioning specific terms such as "Black Tuesday" and "Interstate 5," which have no conscious meaning to me even now.[87] There is then no entry in my journal for another three months. During that time, I had an overwhelming feeling that I had fractured into two states, one where I had actually concluded the Operation with success and another where I had failed and was either trapped in an endless loop of performance or trapped in a fictional world created by the demonic entities.

Ishariyah notes the requirement to "re-integrate" himself with his family, "without losing the changes that have occurred in me."[88]

---

83. Waite, *The Book of Ceremonial Magic*, 93.
84. Waite, *The Book of Ceremonial Magic*, 94.
85. Waite, *The Book of Ceremonial Magic*, 95.
86. Ishariyah, *The Abra-Melin Experience*, 131.
87. Katz, *After the Angel*, 192–193.
88. Ishariyah, *The Abra-Melin Experience*, 130.

· · · · · · ·

After the Angel

The Abramelin Operation is both the culmination of the life of the Adept and the commencement of a new life. Ishariyah writes of the "great blessing" of the work, but also of the "next phase," which begins several months following the Abramelin.[89]

A successful conclusion of the Operation brings about several common and related experiences:

- A change of personality
- A change of life
- A change of priorities

The personality becomes more withdrawn from personal engagement, calmer and less attached to daily concerns. However, this is not a passive change—it can bring about a great release of energy and purpose, particularly should the Angel direct the person to a particular task. A single-mindedness is evident in the person, which can cause issues with the more mundane roles and responsibilities of life.

As such, life itself will change for the person as they adjust to the changes. In several cases, including my own, life will take itself along the line of least resistance, for better or worse. The person may remove themselves from the business of life, particularly to make themselves their own master. The practitioner may find themselves gravitating toward a more rural lifestyle: "For humans, for angels, for all planetary life, wilderness areas are necessary." [90]

This is a prime characteristic of the successful knowledge and conversation of the Holy Guardian Angel. As the *Abramelin* puts it:

> Now, at this point I commence to restrict myself in my writing, seeing that by the Grace of the Lord I have submitted and consigned you unto a MASTER so great that he will never let you err.[91]

There is no doubt—when in contact with the Angel—as to one's purpose, errors, and path following the conclusion of this Operation. There is no place left for fear, insecurity, or anxiety. There is no distraction nor doubt, for there is no one left to experience such things. The Angel is a coherent light of the soul in contact with itself, radiating outward. The trick is to maintain the knowledge and the conversation after the Operation.

---

89. Ishariyah, *The Abra-Melin Experience*, 134.
90. Dorothy Maclean, "Humans and Angels Now," in Parisen, *Angels & Mortals*, 260.
91. Mathers, *The Book of the Sacred Magic of Abramelin the Mage*, 85.

• • • • • • • •

Thomas Aquinas writes, "The Guardian Angels … teach us by lighting up our sense-images, and strengthen the light of our intelligence. Leading us to see everything more clearly, and like a skilled teacher, an Angel strives to compose and arrange sense-images in such a way as to give the mind better information to work on."[92]

In layman's terms, the world is turned inside out by this experience. We realise in every part of our awareness that the external world is actually our internal one, projected onto a vastly complex interactive screen. There are no people, places, time, or space—just the screen. And then something punches through the screen that is so real, so present, that either it is an experience of the self so insanely projected it appears as totally *other*, or it is indeed *other*, and we are relegated to the realisation of ourself as part of the screen. It is *we* who become the fiction, the *other*, and the Angel is held as the reality.

The priorities of life will be shifted to an increasingly spiritual or educational and developmental focus. The immediate concerns are lessened, and personal life comes to be experienced as a brief yet critical part of the species as a whole. It may not be possible to act upon the totality of these new priorities, but the Angel guides one to opportunities where they may be at least partly realised.

In making these adjustments, the overarching factor becomes the knowledge and conversation of the Angel. The task is then to forget everything other than this experience, a practice that recapitulates the work of earlier grades in the initiatory system. The zeal and recall exercises of the Zelator and Theoricus are essential foundational work for what follows after the Angel.

Aaron Leitch suggests that whilst it is unlikely that the practitioner will be able to maintain their oratory following the Operation, a "next best-case scenario is to maintain *some form* of oratory somewhere in your home."[93]

Crowley notes that the "discarded elements of the Adept" are neither wasted nor left "to become vehicles for obsession."[94] As they have built up into an adequate albeit artificial personality through the *Adeptus Exemptus* work, having been previously "sanctified and glorified" by the knowledge and conversation of the Holy Guardian Angel, they are put to work for their appointed purpose, now no longer impeded by the false personality—the attachment.

Every Guardian Angel comes with not only a message but a mission. It then remains to the practitioner whether they take on that mission or not.

92. Huber, *My Angel Will Go Before You*, 61.

93. Aaron Leitch, "Working with Your Holy Guardian Angel," in Cecchetelli, *The Holy Guardian Angel*, 75.

94. Crowley, *Magick Without Tears*, 318.

• • • • • • • •

The Abramelin in the Initiatory System

The knowledge and conversation of the Holy Guardian Angel is assigned to the sephirah of Malkuth, the "Kingdom," on the Tree of Life. Initially, this may seem odd, as this is the location of a relative beginner grade in the initiatory system—the Zelator. However, it conceals a deeper truth. The awareness of the Angel is an experiential shift in the relationship between the practitioner and the universe; it is a fundamental shift in identity and apprehension of reality. It is the third of such shifts in the initiatory system and precedes the fourth shift across the Abyss:

> It should never be forgotten for a single moment that the central and essential work of the Magicians is the attainment of the Knowledge and Conversation of the Holy Guardian Angel. Once he has achieved this he must of course be left entirely in the hands of that Angel, who can be invariably and inevitably relied upon to lead him to the further great step—crossing of the abyss and the attainment of the grade of Master of the Temple.[95]

As such, it is a perfect correspondence to Malkuth—the Kingdom. The corresponding tarot card of the Universe is assigned to the path between Malkuth and Yesod, representing not only our inner model of the world but also our experience of that model. Yesod appropriately means "foundation," the very foundation of our identity—our "self." We commence our Great Work in Malkuth because it is literally and simply exactly where we are.

The encounter with the Angel in Tiphareth is not experienced "in" Tiphareth—our "awareness" or consciousness—because we no longer possess an individual self-awareness. There is no real "Tree" after the Adept grade; it becomes merely a language spoken in a boundless place. So the vision of the Angel is experienced as the relationship between identity and the unknowable universe—it is this relationship that requires the language of mysticism rather than science, psychology, or magic.

Crowley himself refers to this experience and difficulty of expression in his final writings to a student, published as *Magick Without Tears*. He suggests that there are levels beyond the experience of the Holy Guardian Angel, further consolidating this mystical progression:

> Beyond that yet loftier vision which corresponds to our "Knowledge and Conversation of the Holy Guardian Angel", is that called Atmadarshana, the vision (or *apprehension*, a much better word) of the Universe as a single phenomenon, outside all limitations, whether of time, space, causality or what not.[96]

95. Crowley, "Epistola Ultima," in *Magick Without Tears*, 502.
96. Crowley, *Magick Without Tears*, 56.

Abramelin and Psychology

Whilst esoteric matters may be esoteric, they have fundamental effects on everyday life. As perspective is shifted through practice, crisis points are reached between one state of identity and another:

> The "dimension change" is inevitably a traumatic experience involving a psychological upheaval of some description.[97]

The Abramelin process also releases a significant amount of psychological material, namely that which belongs to projection and the shadow of the psyche. In this it is important to adhere to the instructions of the book, read spiritual material in a focused manner, and develop a clarity in confessions. As Robert Bly points out, "I'll mention the use of careful language, by which I mean language that is accurate and has a physical base. Using language consciously seems to be the most fruitful method of retrieving shadow substance scattered out on the world." [98]

We can also consider the parapsychology of the Angel in that, for example, "it lets us drop the controls of the ego and this surrender to the dynamics of higher consciousness." [99]

Contemporary Cultural References

The latest use of the *Abramelin* in popular culture is in the 2016 horror film *A Dark Song*, directed by Liam Gavin (see previous box). The film references the Abramelin by name at least twice and takes its theme as the invocation of the Holy Guardian Angel—in this case, to grant one specific favour. It has led to several social media site discussions as to the Abramelin and in particular Aleister Crowley's attempts at the ritual.[100] Whilst the ritual presented in the film is a mixed compendium of several other practices, grimoires, and traditions, it is ultimately true to the spirit of the Abramelin in terms of the redemptive nature of the Operation and the mental duress of its practice.

Several other films recall the relationship of the Adept and the Holy Guardian Angel, particularly in terms of the ascent narrative, without making direct reference to the ritual:

1. *Kontroll* (dir. Nimród Antal, 2003)

2. *Jacob's Ladder* (dir. Adrian Lyne, 1990)

---

97. Templar, *The Path of the Magus*, 87.

98. Bly, *A Little Book on the Human Shadow*, 42.

99. Michael Grosso, "The Cult of the Guardian Angel," in Parisen, *Angels & Mortals*, 128.

100. Reddit thread: "Curious about some things in A Dark Song (Spoilers, for sure)," accessed September 24, 2019, https://www.reddit.com/r/horror/comments/6g2p2j/curious_about_some_things_in_a_dark _song_spoilers/.

3. *Last Year in Marienbad* (dir. Alain Resnais, 1961)

4. *Inception* (dir. Christopher Nolan, 2010)

Conclusion

The *Book of Abramelin* provides a comprehensive ritual for practitioners to radically engineer their experience of the universe. It provides a unique bridge between the methodology of medieval magic and contemporary self-development work. The experience at the very least tests the faith of the practitioner, develops their spiritual practice, and forces a radical reevaluation of their belief system. Should it prove successful—for it is the most real of experiences, not merely a study—then it commences an utterly new life based on an entirely different experience of reality:

> When the entire system of the Universe is conterminous with your comprehension, "inward" and "outward" become identical.[101]

Suggested Reading List

In addition to those books listed in the bibliography and main text, I suggest the following titles as supplemental to the Abramelin Operation.

Auster, Paul. *In the Country of Last Things.* London: Faber & Faber, 1988.

An account of one who refuses to speak the "language of ghosts" and goes in search of her lost brother in the unnamed City. It is as harrowing an account of the futile nature of hope in the material world as some parts of the Abramelin experience.

Henderson, Joseph L. *Thresholds of Initiation.* Wilmette, IL: Chiron, 1995.

Henderson takes the account of growing into manhood in tribal societies and applies it to self-development. Of particular interest is the seven-stage grading system in which the experience of the personal Guardian Spirit is placed.

Katz, Marcus. *The Magister, Vol. 0: The Order of Revelation.* Keswick, Cumbria: Forge Press, 2016.

A further and comprehensive guide to essential reading on the Western Esoteric Initiatory System and the place of the Abramelin in the initiatory system may be found in this book.

Parisen, Maria, ed. *Angels & Mortals: Their Co-Creative Power.* Wheaton, IL: Philosophical Publishing House, 1990.

---

101. Crowley, *Magick Without Tears*, 204.

· · · · · · ·

An indispensable collection of essays ranging from Israel Regardie's "The Magician and the Holy Guardian Angel" to Matthew Fox's "Illuminations of Hildegard." It also contains papers from Marie-Louise von Franz, Geoffrey Hodson, and work on Rudolph Steiner.

Peake, Anthony. *The Daemon: A Guide to Your Extraordinary Secret Self.* London: Arcturus, 2008.

Peake presents a fascinating model of the human being having two distinct components, the *Eidolon* and the *Daemon*. We generally identify ourselves with the Eidolon, yet the Daemon exists in real time, slightly ahead of our lagging perception of ourself and the universe. Peake details numerous cases that he sees as the Daemon breaking through our usual sense of reality. Toward the end of the book he has a fascinating comparison of his work to that of Philip K. Dick and "Gnostic" theology.

Reed, Bika. *Rebel in the Soul.* London: Wildwood House, 1978.

A poetic presentation of Berlin Papyrus 3024, which provides a dialogue between a man and his soul as they despair of the world. It is estimated to be at least 4,000 years old, and the book provides several rituals or text that can inspire ritual. In a general sense, it provides a precursor for the *Abramelin*, separated from it by some several thousand years.

Underhill, Evelyn. *Mysticism.* London: Methuen & Co., Ltd., 1942.

Originally published in 1911, this book provides a comprehensive overview of the spiritual quest expressed in Christian mysticism and is an invaluable treasure trove to those undertaking the Abramelin experience. It covers areas such as visions, introversion, ecstasy and rapture, the unitive life, and the dark night of the soul.

Wolff-Salin, Mary. *Journey into Depth.* Collegeville, MN: Liturgical Press, 1999.

This book covers the experience of initiation within the Monastic tradition and compared to the training of a Jungian psychoanalyst. A timely work on the loss of the initiatory journey in contemporary society outside of these two specific areas and, of course, the whole of the Western esoteric corpus.

Bibliography

Abraham of Worms. *The Book of Abramelin: A New Translation.* Edited by Georg Dehn. Translated by Steven Guth. Lake Worth, FL: Ibis, 2006.

Auster, Paul. *In the Country of Last Things.* London: Faber & Faber, 1988.

Barrett, Francis. *The Magus.* Introduction by Timothy d'Arch Smith. Secaucus, NJ: Citadel Press, 1980.

Blavatsky, H. P. *Isis Unveiled.* Pasadena, CA: Theosophical University Press, 1972.

Bloom, William [Georges Chevalier]. *The Sacred Magician: A Ceremonial Diary*. Glastonbury, UK: Gothic Image, 1992.

Bly, Robert. *A Little Book on the Human Shadow*. New York: Harper Collins, 1988.

Brianchaninov, Ignatius. *On the Prayer of Jesus*. Boston, MA: New Seeds, 2006.

Bulwer-Lytton, Edward. *Zanoni*. London: Saunders and Otley, 1842.

Butler, Elizabeth M. *Ritual Magic*. Magic in History series. Stroud, UK: Sutton Publishing, 1998.

Cecchetelli, Michael, ed. *The Holy Guardian Angel*. Nephilim Press, 2013.

Chevalier, Georges [William Bloom]. *The Sacred Magician: A Ceremonial Diary*. St. Albans: Paladin, 1976.

Churton, Tobias. *Aleister Crowley: The Biography*. London: Watkins Publishing, 2011.

Crowley, Aleister. *The Confessions of Aleister Crowley*. London: Routledge & Kegan Paul, 1986.

———. *Magick*. London: Routledge & Kegan Paul, 1985.

———. *Magick Without Tears*. Phoenix, AZ: Falcon Press, 1982.

Dukes, Ramsey. *The Abramelin Diaries*. London: Aeon Books, 2019.

Henderson, Joseph L. *Thresholds of Initiation*. Wilmette, IL: Chiron, 1995.

Huber, Georges. *My Angel Will Go Before You*. Dublin: Four Courts Press, 1995.

Ishariyah. *The Abra-Melin Experience*. Daylesford, Victoria: Aurum Pty. Ltd., 2003.

Katz, Marcus. *After the Angel*. Keswick, Cumbria: Forge Press, 2011.

Leitch, Aaron. *Secrets of the Magickal Grimoires*. Woodbury, MN: Llewellyn Publications, 2005.

Levine, Stephen. *A Year to Live*. London: Thorsons, 1997.

Mathers, S. L. MacGregor, trans. *The Book of the Sacred Magic of Abramelin the Mage*. New York: Dover, 1975.

———. *The Grimoire of Armadel*. York Beach, ME: Red Wheel/Weiser, 2001.

———. *The Key of Solomon the King*. London: Routledge & Kegan Paul, 1981.

Mead, G. R. S. *Orpheus: The Theosophy of the Greeks*. London: Theosophical Publishing Society, 1896.

Miller, Joel J. *Lifted by Angels*. Nashville, TN: Thomas Nelson, 2012.

Morgan, Mogg, ed. *Thelemic Magick II: Being the Proceedings of the Tenth International Symposium of Thelemic Magick*. Oxford: Golden Dawn Publications, 1995.

Newcomb, Jason A. *The New Hermetics*. York Beach, ME: Red Wheel/Weiser, 2004.

———. *21st Century Mage*. York Beach, ME: Red Wheel/Weiser, 2002.

Parisen, Maria, ed. *Angels & Mortals: Their Co-Creative Power*. Wheaton, IL: Quest Books, 1990.

• • • • • • •

Peake, Anthony. *The Daemon: A Guide to Your Extraordinary Secret Self*. London: Arcturus, 2008.

Plato. *Timaeus*. London: Dent, 1965.

Reed, Bika, trans. *Rebel in the Soul*. London: Wildwood House, 1978.

Templar, Eldon. *The Path of the Magus*. Irchester, UK: Mark Saunders Books, 1986.

Thaumaturgus, Gregory. *Oration and Panegyric Addressed to Origen*. In *Ante-Nicene Fathers*, vol. 6. Translated and edited by Alexander Roberts and James Donaldson. Buffalo, NY: The Christian Literature Co., 1886.

Townsend, Mark. *The Gospel of Falling Down*. Winchester, UK: O Books, 2007.

Tyson, Donald, ed. *Three Books of Occult Philosophy*. St. Paul, MN: Llewellyn Publications, 1998.

Underhill, Evelyn. *Mysticism*. London: Methuen & Co., Ltd., 1942.

Waite, A. E. *The Book of Ceremonial Magic*. 1910. Reprint, New York: University Books, 1961.

Wolff-Salin, Mary. *Journey into Depth*. Collegeville, MN: Liturgical Press, 1999.

About the Author

Marcus Katz has studied and taught the Western Esoteric Initiatory System for over thirty-five years and was the first person to be conferred an MA in Western Esotericism in 2008 from the University of Exeter, UK.

He has authored and co-authored over forty books on tarot and esotericism, including the award-winning *Around the Tarot in 78 Days* (2012) with Tali Goodwin, and the groundbreaking *Tarosophy* (2011).

He teaches students through the online Crucible Club, which provides entry into the Order of Everlasting Day, established with the aim of preparing individuals to conduct the Abramelin Operation.

Marcus is co-director and course teacher of Magicka School, offering courses in Wicca, tarot, Kabbalah, alchemy, spellcrafting, and Egyptian magick. He was initiated into Gardnerian Witchcraft when he was eighteen through the direct lineage of Gerald Gardner and Patricia Crowther.

His research gives him access to rare and unique materials, including many unpublished works on tarot and Kabbalah. He has presented at the Golden Dawn Conference in London and the PCA/ACA conference in New Orleans, and has taught large groups in Australia, Singapore, and Hong Kong, and across Europe and the US. He co-organised the Tarosophy TarotCon events worldwide for seven years and taught at the prestigious Omega Institute in New York in spring 2011. He has traveled across Japan and Egypt—the latter in the footsteps of Aleister Crowley.

Marcus lives in the heart of the Lake District in England, where he is presently writing, with co-author Charlotte Louise, the second volume of the ten-volume *Magister*, a complete account of the Western Esoteric Initiatory System.

www.marcuskatz.net

www.magickaschool.com

www.tarotassociation.net

BOOK SEVEN

———✦———

Enochian Magick & Mysticism
by Aaron Leitch

Enochian magick is a system of angelic skrying (or crystal gazing) that arose in England during the early modern era (the time of Shakespeare and King James), between 1581 and about 1583. As a skrying system, it draws much from the larger *almadel* (or *armandel*) tradition, as found in texts such as the *Lemegeton* (especially the *Almadel of Solomon* and *Pauline Arts*), the *Grimoire of Armadel*, the *Book of Abramelin*, the *Art of Drawing Spirits into Crystals*, and many others. Meanwhile, it takes much of its form and procedure from earlier systems of Renaissance angel magick, as found in texts such as Agrippa's *Three Books of Occult Philosophy*, Trithemius's *De Septum Secundeis* and *Steganographia*, the *Book of Soyga*, the *Arbatel of Magic*, the *Sworn Book of Honorius*, the *Key of Solomon*, the *Heptameron*, and many related texts of Western magick and mysticism.

Enochian magick focuses upon some of the most exalted angels in the universe—those called the *Holy Hayyot*, who attend directly upon the Throne of God. It promises access to the very angels who participated in the creation of the universe, including the royal angels of the planets, the zodiac, the alchemical elements, and even the four corners of the earth itself. Perhaps most famously, it utilizes a specialized sacred language that the angels proclaimed is their very own native tongue, often erroneously termed *Enochian* today but originally called *Angelical*. (It was also referred to as the *first language of God-Christ* and even *Adamical* because it was supposed to be the language Adam used to speak with the angels in Eden.) Because of this, the system has developed a reputation for being extremely powerful—and dangerous.

Since the late 1500s, Enochian magick has been shrouded in deep mystery (and not a little misunderstanding!), yet it has simultaneously had a massive impact on the entire Western Mystery

• • • • • • • •

Tradition. The complex magic squares (wherein are encrypted the names of most of the angels and spirits of the system) have fascinated scholars and intimidated students for centuries. The history of English and European political intrigue and cloak-and-daggery associated with its reception and development has attracted many historians. And adept magicians have long attempted to make sense of the material, incorporating aspects of the magick into their own systems.

Foremost among these adepts were the founders of the Hermetic Order of the Golden Dawn (1888–1903), especially William Westcott and Samuel Mathers, who adapted several aspects of Enochian magick into their advanced curriculum—reserved strictly for "inner order" students. It was then adopted from the Golden Dawn by Aleister Crowley during his brief time in the Order, and subsequently became part of his Thelemic system. From these sources, portions of it made their way into Neopaganism as well as most modern systems of Western occultism. (If you have ever called the "guardians of the Watchtowers" to open a sacred circle, you have experienced the influence of Enochian magick.)

———

The Enochian system was first recorded in the journals of Dr. John Dee, adviser and unofficial court-philosopher to Queen Elizabeth I. An accomplished scholar and extremely influential in his political sphere, Dee was consulted by traders, navigators, military leaders, scientists, scholars, spies, and royalty from within England and across Europe. Dee helped form the future British Empire (even coining that term), helping to establish new trade routes and treaties, urging the Queen to capitalize upon the New World and to build her navy, furthering the advancement of science and education in his country, and even sometimes acting secretly on behalf of the Queen while traveling abroad. Later in his life, he felt he had exhausted all avenues of human knowledge, and decided to follow in the footsteps of the biblical prophets by seeking celestial wisdom directly from angelic beings.

Dee pursued this objective with the help of skryers, as he did not feel he had a natural ability for mediumship. The most successful of them was Edward Kelley, a man of some mystery who had an incredible skrying talent, an excitable temper, and a mysterious past. Kelley would work with Dee for several years, he the skryer and Dee the conjurer, and it was through his crystal gazing that the bulk of what we call Enochian magick and mysticism was transmitted.

Dee recorded the sessions in a series of journals that have come to us under several titles: *A True & Faithful Relation of What Passed for Many Years Between Dr. John Dee … and Some Spirits* (published with a preface by Meric Casaubon in 1659), *The Five Books of the Mysteries* (found today as *John Dee's Five Books of Mystery*, edited by Joseph Peterson), and Dee's personal grimoire including the *Heptarchia Mystica* and the *48 Claves Angelicae* (found today as *The Enochian Magick of Dr. John Dee* by Geoffrey James). More recently, the entirety of these journals has been published in two separate updated editions: *Dr. John Dee's Spiritual Diaries* by Stephen Skinner and the comprehensive *The Mystical Records of Dr. John Dee* by Kevin Klein.

Queen Elizabeth I

Queen Elizabeth I (September 7, 1553–March 24, 1603) was the daughter of King Henry VIII, the monarch who separated from the Catholic Church and founded his own Protestant Church in England. After his passing, and the closely-followed passing of his son (Edward VI), then-Princess Elizabeth's sister Mary came into possession of the throne. She remained a staunch Catholic, and her reign was marked by political and religious turmoil as she attempted to convert the nation back to papal authority. This earned her the title "Bloody Mary," a name still feared today by young people who dread to say her name in dark rooms, lest it evoke her vengeful spirit.

During Mary's reign, John Dee found himself in prison for his offense of casting a horoscope that indicated Elizabeth would make a more fitting queen than Mary. Elizabeth was also imprisoned by her sister, and for much the same reason. In time, of course, Mary would pass away and Elizabeth would ascend to the throne. She desired to preserve her father's church, and it was she (more than either Henry or Edward) who founded the Church of England as we know it today.

Elizabeth was a progressive queen who sought to establish her (then rather backwater) kingdom as a true world power, and she enlisted Dr. John Dee—England's most renowned astrologer, navigator, scientist, cryptographer, and scholar—as an advisor to this end. Together, Elizabeth and Dee created the "Elizabethan Era" of English history, known for its major cultural and technological strides and the colonialist English Empire that would develop to global prominence in the generations to come. In countless ways, the modern world we know today can be traced directly back to the court of Queen Elizabeth I and the calculated choices she made.

These journals were so complex and densely written (not to mention the fact they were written in "Shakespearean" English) that, they would remain largely unexplored for almost four hundred years. What material was adopted from them often came either from incomplete readings of the journals or from secondary sources entirely. (For example, the Golden Dawn were unaware of much of the *Heptarchia Mystica* when they formed their version of the Enochian system.) It would not be until the turn of the millennium (aided greatly by the advent of the internet) that Enochian students would come together and decipher the entirety of Dee's original system. I have presented my own efforts in this regard in my books *The Angelical Language, Volumes I and II*, and *The Essential Enochian Grimoire*.

• • • • • • •

Enochian Magick, from Dee to the Golden Dawn

There are two primary areas of study in modern Enochiana, which have been termed *Dee purist* and *neo-Enochian*. *Dee purism* is defined by the study of Dee's original skrying records, along with the Renaissance source material from which the man himself drew information (such as the Solomonic grimoires).

When the Golden Dawn formulated their recension of the system in the late nineteenth century, they had access to very limited resources. Either they had to work from secondhand sources, such as the sensationalized *A True & Faithful Relation* and a later document called *Book H* (which we will discuss later), or they had to sit alone in a British Library reading room and pore over Dee's handwritten journals with no help from other scholars. This would have been overwhelming for any researcher.

The result of these limitations meant that Mathers and Westcott did not transcribe the Enochian material exactly as Dee had recorded it. Instead, they merely drew the elements from Dee's material that most appealed to them, and applied those elements to the systems of magick they were already developing. What they created bears little relationship to Dee's magick—it has a different intent and exists within an entirely different (i.e., Victorian) context. Students of the modern Hermetic traditions have assumed Dee left behind little more than the skeletal framework of a system, which the Golden Dawn "fleshed out" into a comprehensive magical practice. However, the truth is that Dee did indeed record a *complete* system of Renaissance-style angel magick in his journals.

Meanwhile, the Golden Dawn adaptation of Enochiana is just as valid as what we find in Dee's original journals. Even if Mathers and Westcott adopted some incorrect information into the Order's system, that information has now had the better part of 150 years of practical application to become legitimate in its own right.

In this chapter we will discuss the evolution of Enochian magick from Dee's journals to the early Golden Dawn. We will see how the G. D. system was founded upon a mysterious Enochian document that predates the Order. And, with any luck, you will come away from this with a firm grasp of the differences between Dee purism and neo-Enochiana.

The Enochian Tradition

Before we can understand Dee's system of angel magick, it is first necessary to place it in its proper context. And to do that, I will need to demystify two points in particular: (1) the proper meaning of the term *Enochian* itself, and (2) the true identity of the so-called "Enochian" angels.

First, the term *Enochian* is not the proper name of Dee's magical system. It is not "Enochian magick," nor does it incorporate an "Enochian language." Nowhere in Dee's journals does he ever use these terms for the system he was recording. In fact, the term *Enochian* is properly defined as "of or pertaining to the biblical prophet Enoch."

The true Enochian tradition dates back to at least 600 BCE, during the Hebrew Captivity in Babylon. Scholars consider this the likely time and place where the oldest apocryphal text was written: the *"Ethiopic" Book of Enoch* (aka *1 Enoch*). In Dee's lifetime, this was known as a long-lost biblical text, but it was rediscovered in an Ethiopic Orthodox Christian Bible in the early seventeenth century. This is the book that contains the famous myth of the Watchers and their fall from God's grace, and the rise of the Nephilim (against whom the Great Deluge of the Old Testament was sent), and also records the spiritual journeys of the prophet Enoch himself through the seven Heavens.

As part of his celestial tour, Enoch was shown the famous *Tablets of Heaven*: celestial records of all things in the universe. Hebrew tradition has often called these tablets the *Sepher Raziel* (*Book of the Secrets of God*—not to be confused with the Jewish grimoires that borrow its name), and Christian tradition has called them the *Book of Life* or *Book of the Lamb*, wherein are recorded the names of all the saved. (We encounter this book in the Revelation of St. John, chapter 5, where it is sealed with seven seals that cannot be broken by anyone but Christ.)

Enoch himself was allowed to transcribe 366 books worth of the information contained in the Celestial Tablets. These Enochian books were then passed down through his family until they reached Noah. Noah supposedly found the instructions for the Ark within them, but then the books were lost during the Deluge.

In the earliest days of Christianity, the *Book of Enoch* (that is, *1 Enoch*) was extremely influential. The text seems to have had a direct impact on several books of the New Testament itself, not to mention the writings of many of the Church Fathers. (For a wonderful discussion of this subject, see the introduction to *The Book of Enoch the Prophet*, translated by Richard Laurence.) In fact, before Christianity became the official Roman religion, the *Book of Enoch* was included in the canon of many local churches' Bibles. And to this day it remains part of the canon of the Ethiopian and Eritrean Orthodox Tewahedo Churches.

Unfortunately, in the rest of the Western world, *1 Enoch* was driven literally underground by Church authorities who classified it as apocryphal at best and heretical at worst, and thus it was excluded from the Bible. It effectively vanished from the world for several hundred years. However, the story contained in the book was much harder to destroy, and the Enochian legend continued to spread throughout the world, capturing the interest of both Jewish and Christian scholars and mystics for centuries. There were even two attempts to write new versions of the text, called the *Hebrew Book of Enoch* (or *2 Enoch*) and the *Slavonic Book of Enoch* (or *3 Enoch*). Yet it is the story first told in *1 Enoch* that has always defined the Enochian tradition.

· · · · · · · ·

During the lifetimes of Dee and Kelley, the *Book of Enoch* was still lost, and its legend was still popular among European mystics. According to his journals, Dee asked an angel if he could be allowed to read the famous scripture. The angels eventually obliged him in this regard, but not as he likely expected. What the angels brought to Dee was not *1 Enoch* or one of the other apocrypha—instead they brought the Celestial Tablets that Enoch had transcribed, the *Book of the Lamb* itself, which Dee's angels referred to as the *Book of the Speech from God*. It was the arrival of these tablets, and everything that followed after them, that make Dee's journals part of the true—ancient—Enochian tradition.

The Enochian Angels

So who were these entities Dee and Kelley were speaking with? If you have done any research into the subject, you have undoubtedly encountered the assertion that Dee had discovered an entirely unique host of entities. And while there is a small kernel of truth to this, the statement is vastly misleading. Some have even gone so far as to insist they were not angels at all, but beings of a different sort who simply lied to Dee and Kelley about their true nature. Not a few students have begun to refer to them as "the Enochians," dropping the term *angels* entirely. And just a few, thankfully small in number, have gone so far as to suggest Dee was in contact with aliens from another planet or dimension!

Dee's angelic journals begin on December 22, 1581, somewhat before he met Edward Kelley and while he still employed a medium by the name of Barnabas Saul. Saul sat before a shewstone (aka a crystal ball) and gazed into its depths while Dee recited prayers in a nearby prayer room. After a while, an angelic entity appeared in the stone and began to speak with the men. When asked to identify itself, the angel gave its name as Annael.

Annael (sometimes spelled with a single *n*) is an archangel well known in grimoiric literature as the angel of Venus. She appears as such in the *Heptameron* with her fellow planetary archangels (figure 1).

Cassiel (Saturn)

Sachiel (Jupiter)

Samael (Mars)

Michael (Sol)

An(n)ael (Venus)

Raphael (Mercury)

Gabriel (Luna)

Figure 1. Archangels of the Seven Planets

• • • • • • •

These seven archangels are the chief governors of the entire universe, and they have appeared under different names and in different forms throughout biblical and biblio-mystical literature. In nearly all cases they are considered the archangels of the seven ancient planets, the seven days of the week, and the seven circles of Heaven.

The next question we must ask is why this particular angel chose to appear in the shewstone. Annael was not merely a random member of the seven highest archangels but is described by Dee as the "Chief Governor General of this great period." The meaning behind this obscure phrase is not found in the *Heptameron* but within another popular mystical text of the time,: the *Arbatel of Magic*.

The *Arbatel* is a very simple and eloquent grimoire from the late 1500s, outlining an occult philosophy based upon the sacred number seven. The Seven Spirits of God appear here as well, after a fashion—called in this case the seven "Olympian Spirits." Just like the archangels of the *Heptameron*, the Olympian Spirits are planetary in nature, so that each holds power over a specific astrological category of life.

Most importantly, these "spirits" are described as successive governors of the world. All of them hold the same authority, but each of them assumes the role of chief of the group for an "age" of 490 years (or 7 times 70). According to the text, the spirit of Saturn began his rule in 60 BCE, giving way to the spirits of Jupiter, Mars, and Sol in their turn. Beginning in 1411 CE, the spirit of Venus (named Hagith) took control and would rule until 1900 CE. Therefore, Hagith was in charge when the *Arbatel* was written, as well as when Dee performed his séances.

Thus, it is hardly surprising that Dee's very first angelic contact was not only one of the seven archangels but specifically the "Chief Governor General of this great period" as set forth in the *Arbatel*—the angel of Venus. Dee had merely applied the philosophy of the *Arbatel* to the seven archangels of the *Heptameron*, preferring beings more familiar to a devout Christian. Not only were the Olympian Spirits more obscure and lacking in biblical justification, but the very term *Olympian* lent them a dangerously Pagan connotation. Thus, Dee encountered Annael rather than Hagith. (Today, since 1900, the ruling archangel should be that of Mercury: Raphael.)

At this point, we are still discussing the first entry of Dee's *Five Books*, on December 22, 1581. Annael tells Dee and Saul how to proceed in further séances, and describes herself as the current governor set over the four principal archangels Michael, Gabriel, Raphael, and Uriel. These four are considered equal (or even greater) in power to the seven planetary archangels, being set over the four classical elements, the four zodiacal triplicities, and the four quarters of the world. Three of the four (Michael, Gabriel, and Raphael) are justified by direct mention in the canonical Bible, and legend holds that Michael and Gabriel actually sit at the right and left hands of God. Annael promises that Dee will receive audience with these angels, particularly Michael, and then swears never to appear again.

· · · · · · ·

The journals do not pick up again until the following March (1582), when a Sir Edward Talbot (aka Kelley) first appears as Dee's medium. As a test of Kelley's abilities, Dee set out to have him skry the angel Anchor—one of a group of three angels (Anchor, Anachor, and Anilos) mentioned in some obscure occult literature of the time. Dee used the same methods of invocation he had employed with Saul, which soon resulted in the appearance of an angel. However, this angel was not Anchor. When asked to identify itself, the being in the shewstone claimed to be none other than the archangel Uriel.

Sir Edward Kelley

Sir Edward Kelley (or Kelly, August 1, 1555–1598) is a mysterious figure in the diaries of Dr. John Dee. While legend has often held him to be a con artist or criminal, the historical record is not so clear. He was first introduced to John Dee as "Edward Talbot," and much speculation on his origins or true identity has been explored. (It has even been suggested, not unconvincingly, that he may have been a spy sent into Dee's household by the Catholic Church.)

Most of what we actually know of Kelley comes from Dee's journals, but recent years have seen the translation of several documents, originally in the Czech language, that not only continue Kelley's story where Dee left off but also contradict the more popular legends. We know for certain that Kelley was introduced to Dee as a professional skryer, an occupation more common then than it is today. Indeed, the journals prove Kelley was an excellent skryer, perhaps one of the best in history. He skryed the angels for Dee (who did not himself possess the Sight) for several hours a day, every single day, for several years. During this time, he traveled across Europe with Dee, stopping in several countries along the way to engage in prophecy via the angels as well as alchemical experiments.

Kelley claimed to possess the secret of transmuting lead into gold, and during their time in Prague, he left Dee's employ to take the position of Court Alchemist to the Holy Roman Emperor Rudolph II. Years later, Dee would report Kelley had died from a broken leg after an attempt to escape imprisonment by Rudolph. However, the recently translated Czech documents have presented a different story: wherein Kelley—having obtained a baronship (from which English authors have not quite accurately entitled him "Sir") and several mines from the emperor—actually lived a respectable life, had children, and passed away in dignity.

In classical magical literature, Uriel often plays the role of intermediary spirit—evoked not only for divination purposes but also to bring other spirits to the circle for questioning. This is exactly the role he takes in Dee's journals: introducing the men to the other three principal archangels, each of whom would be in charge of transmitting some specific aspect of the magical system. Over the hundreds of pages that follow, it is Uriel who appears to be master of the séances. He would open and close the sessions and bring other beings into the stone, and, if the men failed in some way, upsetting the angels, it was most often Uriel who halted the sessions to chastise them.

The first archangel Uriel brought to the stone was Michael (as promised by Annael), whose primary job seems to have been to reveal the magical furniture and equipment needed for the remainder of the work. Later came Raphael, who transmitted the entire text of the *Book of the Speech from God* in the form of forty-nine tables, and was therefore the first to reveal some form of the famous Angelical language. After him came Gabriel, who was in charge of the transmission of the forty-eight Angelical Keys that promised to unlock the mysteries of Raphael's holy book.

So now that we have established that Dee and Kelley were indeed talking to traditional Western angels, and that they were in fact receiving a system of angel magick, let's take a look at the system itself.

Dee's Enochian System—An Overview

Dee and Kelley's angelic magick came in three interrelated phases:

1. The first phase was concerned primarily with the magical furniture and tools that should be used when summoning angels, as well as methods for summoning a host of angels (called the *Heptarchia*—rulership of seven) under the charge of the seven planetary archangels.

2. The second phase centered on the *Book of the Speech from God* and the magick that could be worked through it.

3. The third and final phase centered on the Great Table of the Earth and its hierarchy of angels that could be contacted to influence the physical world.

Unfortunately, many Enochian scholars have presented these three phases as completely unrelated. However, Dee's journals do not present the material in that fashion. Each phase was given by the angels as the primer for the next phase, and the older information was always the basis for what would come later. Thus, what we find in the records is a single comprehensive system of angel magick. And even though Dee certainly had a penchant for cryptography and complex magic squares, the system he recorded is not so far removed from other examples of Medieval and Renaissance angel magick.

· · · · · · · ·

Phase One: The Heptarchia

After Annael gave Dee and Kelley over to the four archangels, Michael assumed the role of primary instructor. He delivered the designs for the Holy Table (figure 2), the Seal of the True God (often shortened to Seal of Truth—figure 3), the seven Ensigns of Creation (figures 10–16), the Holy Lamen (figure 4), and the Ring of Solomon (figure 5).

Figure 2. The Holy Table:
The top of the Holy Table of Practice. Made of
sweetwood, three-feet square, painted with consecrated gold
or yellow paint. It has to be elevated off the floor by
four wax tablets bearing the Seal of the True God upon them.

Figure 3. The Seal of the True God:

The Seal of the True God (aka the Seal of Truth).
Made of pure beeswax. A larger one was placed upon
the Holy Table, and four smaller versions were placed
beneath the table's legs.

• • • • • • • •

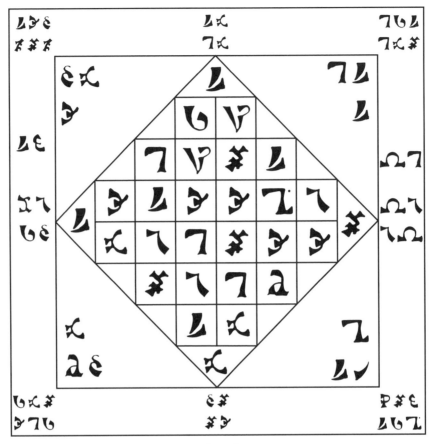

Figure 4. The Holy Lamen:
The Holy Lamen is made on plain paper
and carried hidden away in a cloth.

Figure 5. The Ring of Solomon:
The Ring of Solomon, delivered by the Archangel Michael.
It must be made of pure gold.

Figure 6. The Holy Table Set Up:
The Holy Table set up, with the Seal of the True God
and Ensigns of Creation. This table would have stood upon
a red silk cloth, with four smaller Seals of the True God
beneath its legs, and the whole covered with multicolored silk.

In recent years, it has been established that several of these tools are adaptations of tools already found in older grimoires. For example, the design of the Seal of the True God can be found in several sources, the primary one being *Liber Juratus* (figure 7).

Figure 7. Liber Juratus Seal:
An early form of the Seal of the True God, appearing in *Liber Juratus*.

• • • • • • • •

Even the construction of the seal appears to be derived from older sources. It is fashioned from beeswax and is the central focal-point where the angels will appear. (If you happen to use a crystal or other object for skrying, it would be placed upon the seal.) Compare this to descriptions in the *Book of Abramelin* of a "seven-sided tablet of wax," and of the Almadel of Solomon (found in the *Lemegeton*), which is also a beeswax tablet carved with magical names—both of which are used to skry angelic entities (figure 8).

Plus, as you can see, the design found on the top of Dee's Holy Table is also heavily influenced by the Almadel. One might go so far as to suggest the Seal of the True God and Holy Table, together, form an Enochian version of the Almadel itself.

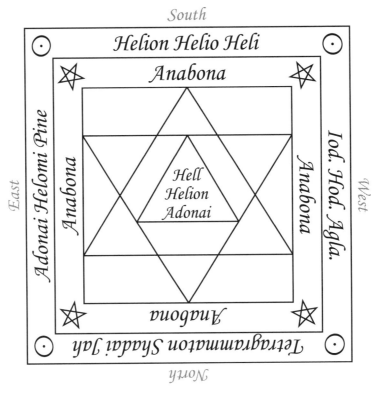

Figure 8. Almadel of Solomon:
The Almadel of Solomon, found in the *Lemegeton*.
Its design is similar to the Holy Table,
and it is made of beeswax, like the Seal of Truth.

At the same time, we can also see similarities between the Holy Table and the Table of Practice from the *Lemegeton's Pauline Arts* (figure 9).

Figure 9. The Pauline Arts *Table of Practice:*
Note its similarity to the Holy Table design.

Of course, some of the Enochian tools are unique to Dee's system. The designs of the Ring of Solomon and the Holy Lamen have no obvious precursors, though both of them (with very different designs) have their origins in Solomonic magick. The Seven Ensigns of Creation (figures 10–16), associated directly with the planetary archangels listed in the *Heptameron*, are also original to the Enochian system:

2⎮b / b⎮3	G b b	g.	**B** 22	2.4.6 / b b b / 2 4 6	b b / L / b	B r o g	Ⓑ
8 b / b / b 2	b̶b̶ 8	G b	GG b	152 b	152 b	52 BBB	B / ┼ / B
☽ q ⊠ B q	b o / o o	B / V / 7 9	b b b / b b b / b b b	11 / B / 5	b b / b / b b	b b / b	b / 8♭3 / b
b b / b b / b b	b₁₅ b / b b / b ₚb	b M / 166	7 △ bb	ⓑ 5	ᴳM✛	B	b A 1556
1 2 3 **B** 123 (⊠)		b	T b	ⱴBB 9	BBB 6 b	b b 72 F	♭

Figure 10: The Ensign of Venus and Annael

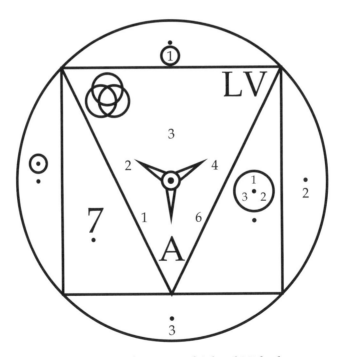

Figure 11. The Ensign of Sol and Michael

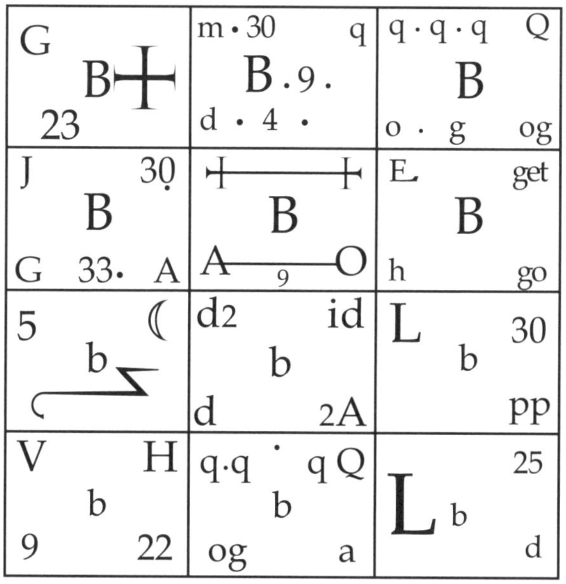
G B 23
m · 30 q B . 9 . d · 4 ·
q · q · q Q B o · g og
J 30 B G 33· A
B A 9 O
E get B h go
5 b
d2 id b d 2A
L 30 b pp
V H b 9 22
q·q · q Q b og a
25 L b d

Figure 12. The Ensign of Mars and Samael

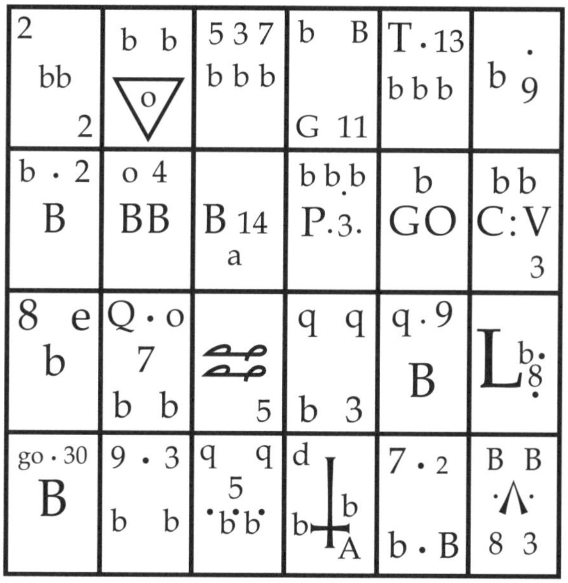
2 bb 2
b b o
5 3 7 b b b
b B G 11
T · 13 b b b
b 9
b · 2 B
o 4 BB
B 14 a
b b b P·3.
b GO
b b C:V 3
8 e b
Q · o 7 b b
5
q q b 3
q · 9 B
L b 8
go · 30 B
9 · 3 b b
q q 5 b b
d b b A
7 · 2 b · B
B B 8 3

Figure 13. The Ensign of Jupiter and Sachiel

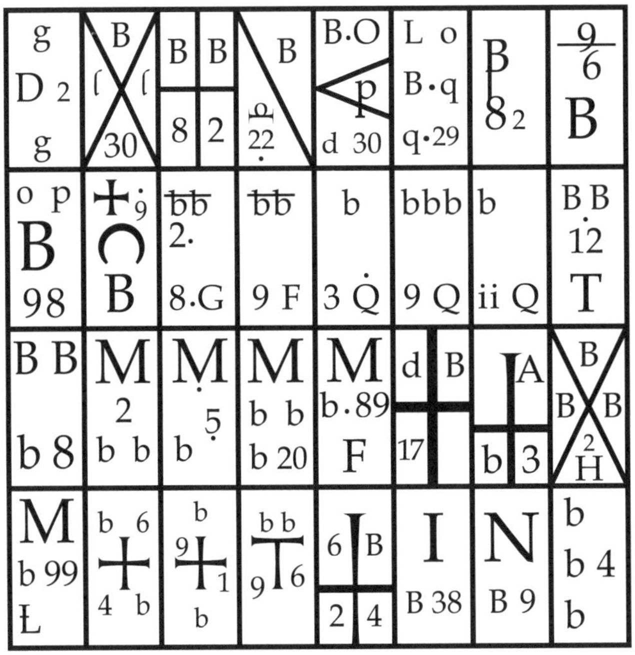

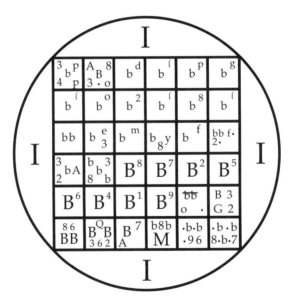

Figure 14. The Ensign of Mercury and Raphael

Figure 15. The Ensign of Saturn and Cassiel

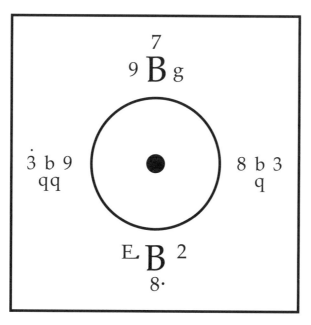

Figure 16. The Ensign of Luna and Gabriel

Dee's records contain no indication the Enochian tools and furniture are restricted for use with the angels described in his journals. In fact, they are intended for use in the summoning of absolutely any angelic entity. However, the tools draw their symbolism primarily from the Heptarchic angels. They embody all mystical considerations of the holy number seven, including the seven planets, the seven days of the week, and—most importantly—the seven biblical days of Creation.

There are forty-nine principal angels in this hierarchy, divided into seven groups of seven—a King, Prince, and five Governors for each planet / day of the week. All of the Angelical letters inscribed on the Enochian tools are from the names of these Heptarchic angels, with the exception of the Seal of the True God, which uses two sets of Qabalistic names that are related to the Heptarchia, but does not utilize Angelical characters. We will discuss these other names shortly.

The Heptarchic angels are unique to Dee's system. Their names are decrypted from a set of seven 7 × 7 tables revealed by Michael, called the *Tabula Collecta* (figure 17).

· · · · · · · ·

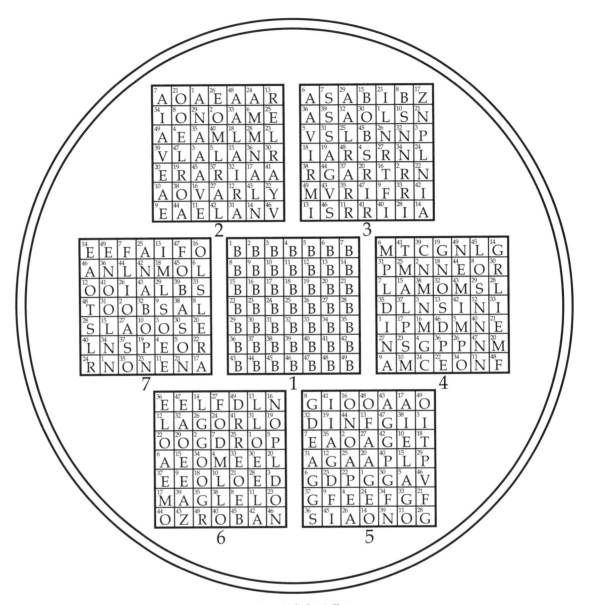

Figure 17. Tabula Collecta:
The seven tables of the bonorum (good) angels.

Though it is never elaborated on in the journals, these seven tables were assigned certain virtues:

Table 1: Wit and Wisdom

Table 2: Exaltation and Government of Princes

Table 3: Prevailing in Council and over Nobility

• • • • • • • •

Table 4: Trade and Merchandise, and Water

Table 5: Qualities of Earth

Table 6: Knowledge of Air and all who move in it

Table 7: Governance of Fire

Presumably, any one of these tables can be used as a talisman to learn about or invoke the virtues embodied in the table. There are also angels named in each one, such as Murifri (see Table 3 in the Tabula Collecta, sixth line down), who appeared to counsel Dee and Kelley during their own skrying sessions.

Dee was next instructed to decrypt these seven tables into the round *Tabula Bonorum*, which illustrates the names of forty-nine Heptarchic angels divided by their planetary attributions (figure 18).

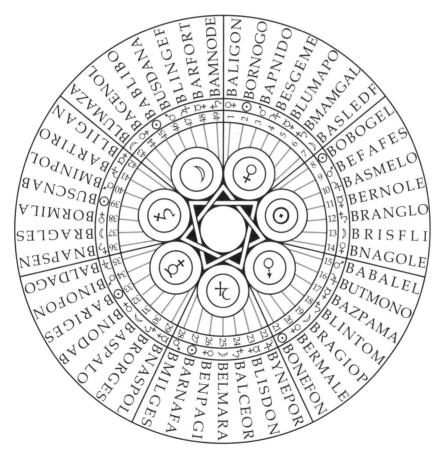

Figure 18. Tabula Bonorum:
The round table of the Heptarchia.

Each planet is subdivided into seven sub-planets, so that (for example) the King of Friday (Baligon) is the angel of Venus of Venus. His Prince (Bagenol) is the angel of Luna of Venus. The five Governors, then, are the angels of Saturn, Mercury, Jupiter, Mars, and Sol *of Venus*, respectively.

Beyond this, Dee and Kelley were also taught how to decrypt from the Tabula Bonorum the names of forty-two Ministers for each planet. They are divided into six groups of seven Ministers, and each group is active for four hours of the day ruled by their planet. In a series of visions, Dee and Kelley were given the various functions of these Ministers, most of them having power of various forces of nature, such as weather, metals, and the elements, as well as command over evil spirits, the rise and fall of kings, etc. Their names are also important in the creation of the talismans used to summon the King or Prince (or presumably one of the five Governors) of a given planet.

The entire Heptarchy, at least in Dee's time, was governed by the King and Prince of Venus (Baligon and Bagenol). When acting in this capacity, the King takes the name/title of King Carmara, and the Prince that of Hagonel. Though it is never mentioned in the journals, I suspect the ruling King and Prince should change when the ruling archangel changes over. In Dee's time the ruling archangel was Annael. If we follow the 490-year rule from the *Arbatel*, then Raphael should be in charge now, making the King and Prince of Mercury (Bnaspol and Blisdon) the rulers of the Heptarchia. Unfortunately, we are not told if they should take on the same titles as the previous rulers or if they have their own unique titles.

Finally, we must return to the Seal of the True God once more, in order to discuss the hierarchy of angels found upon it. The seal (pictured in figure 3) is covered in names that appear to be from the Angelical language, but they are, in fact, encrypted versions of Hebrew Qabalistic names.

Seven Secret Names of God

First, consider the seven Names of God written upon the outermost heptagon of the Seal of the True God. The names were given to Dee via the table shown in figure 19.

While these Names of God appear quite alien, they are not from the Angelical. They are actually compiled from the Hebrew names of the seven archangels of the Tree of Life from Binah to Yesod—traditionally known as the "seven spirits who stand before God" (Revelation 4:5). Starting in the upper-left corner of the table and reading downward, we find: **Zaphkiel**, **Zedekiel**, **Cumael** (a form of Kamael), **Raphael**, **Haniel**, **Michael**, and **Gabriel**. The final cell is occupied by an equal-armed cross, representing the earth. (The same cross appears in the very center of the seal.)

· · · · · · ·

Seven Unpronounceable Names of God

Just within the outer heptagon of the Seal of the True God are seven further Names of God, which the angels said were "unpronounceable." They were also given to Dee via a table, as seen in figure 20.

We can clearly see why these names are unpronounceable, because several of the characters are actually numbers with dots beneath them. However, these odd characters do in fact represent letters taken from the outer circumference of the seal: 21/8 = El; 8, 26, and 30 = L—which is a Name of God both in Hebrew (El) and Angelical (L).

Z	l	l	R	H	i	a
a	Z	C	a	a	c	b
p	a	u	p	n	h	r
h	d	m	h	i	a	i
k	k	a	a	e	e	e
i	i	e	e	l	l	l
e	e	l	l	M	G	✠

Figure 19. Table of the Seven Sephirothic Archangels:
These names appear in the outermost heptagon
of the Seal of the True God.

Meanwhile, *pronounceable* Hebrew angel names can be decrypted from this table. These are simply the Hebrew names of the seven planets with "-el" appended. Beginning again at the upper left corner of the table, but this time reading the letters in downward-left diagonal lines, we find the names of the seven planetary angels: **Sabathiel**, **Zedekieil** (a corruption of Zedekiel), **Madimiel**, **Semeliel** (a corruption of Semeshiel), **Nogahel**, **Corabiel** (a corruption of Kokabiel), and **Levanael**. These angels directly govern the planetary spheres in the realm of *Assiah* (the physical world). Their names appear decrypted at the very center of the Seal of the True God, surrounding the cross of the Earth.

S	A	A	I $\frac{21}{8}$	E	M	E 8
B	T	Z	K	A	S	E 30
H	E	I	D	E	N	E
D	E	I	M	O	30	A
I 26	M	E	G	C	B	E
I	L	A	O	I $\frac{21}{8}$	V	N
I	H	R	L	A	A	$\frac{21}{8}$

Figure 20. Table of the Seven Planetary Archangels:
These names appear just inside the outermost heptagon
of the Seal of the True God.

The rest of the angelic names that fill the seal are derived from the same table of planetary ruling angels, each name found by reading the table diagonally in a different direction. These angels are known today as the *Family of Light*—the Sons, Daughters, Sons of Sons, and Daughters of Daughters of Light. The exact place of these angels in the Heptarchic hierarchy is not entirely clear, except they are mentioned once in Dee's journals as ministering directly to the Heptarchic royalty. It also happens that some of the most famous of Dee's angels—who were of primary importance in the transmission of later phases of the magick—are found here, such as Ave, Madimi, and Illemese.

The Heptarchic system is not overly complex. If it has a reputation for being difficult to understand, it is only due to the magic squares and the methods used to decipher the angel's names from them. However, those decryption methods are not necessary in the practice of the magick—since all the names are already decrypted for us.

The actual practice of the system is also very straightforward, and not at all unlike other systems of Renaissance angel magick. It has a relationship to the *Heptameron* via the seven archangels, and the entire system has a strong relationship to the *Arbatel of Magic*. Not only do the archangels successively govern the cosmos as the *Arbatel* describes for the Olympian Spirits, but the occult philosophy described in the *Arbatel*'s "49 Aphorisms" can be considered a necessary primer for Dee's Heptarchic magick.

To summon a Heptarchic angel, you need the tools and furniture already described. The Holy Table and five copies of the Seal of Truth must be created—four small seals beneath the legs of the table, and a larger seal on its top, all covered with a multicolored silk cloth. (The multicolor represents Mercury, the planet associated with evocation and communication.) The Seven Ensigns of Creation can be fashioned of purified tin and arrayed upon the Holy Table, or painted upon it with consecrated gold or yellow oil paint.

You must also make talismans for the King and Prince you wish to contact, as well as one displaying the names of the forty-two Ministers who serve under them. As you sit at the Holy Table, the talisman of the royal angel is held in your hand and the talisman of the Ministers is placed beneath your feet. Invocations for the Kings and Princes are provided in Dee's journals, and as you recite them, the requested angel should appear over the Seal of Truth.

Missing Pieces?

It has been stated in many Enochian studies that information vital to Dee's system is missing from the records (often blamed on a maid who found Dee's journals many years after his passing and, ignorant of their importance, used several pages to drain pies). However, much less information is missing that you might assume, and while there are some bits missing or simply passed over without comment in Dee's journals, none of it strikes me as vital to working the magick.

If there is a major piece of the system missing, it would be a peculiar "globe" that is mentioned once or twice by Dee but is never illustrated in the surviving journals. (The references suggest it was originally in the record.) According to Dee, the globe is a diagram from which letters can be drawn for Heptarchic talismans. Atop the globe was the figure of King Carmara. Within the globe were the names of the seven Heptarchic Kings, along with certain characters that were likely the sigils of the Family of Light angels. (Thankfully, these sigils are not missing, as Dee preserved them elsewhere in his journals.) There were also further letters and numbers attached in some way to the names of the Kings—some of them written forward and some backward. Those letters, sadly, have indeed been lost.

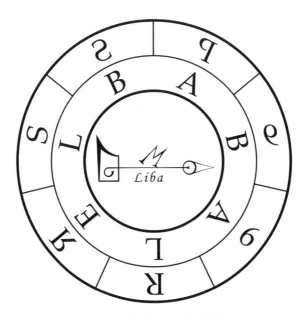

Figure 21. Dee's Heptarchia Talisman

Figure 21 is an example of a Heptarchic talisman as drawn by Dee for one of the Kings. In the center is the sigil of the Family of Light angel that directly serves the King. The name of the King is written around the sigil, and further letters (some forward, some backward) are written in the outermost circumference.

Personally, I would *love* to have that globe diagram so that the talismans for the remaining Kings and Princes could be properly fashioned. However, I also firmly believe that if that information was vital to the system, the angels would have made sure it survived for us. At the very least, Dee would have provided it in his personal grimoire (which still survives), but there is no mention of it there. As it stands, we have the necessary sigils for the Family of Light angels associated with the Kings. All we are truly missing are the peculiar letters that should go into the outer circumferences of their talismans. However, I see no reason why the talismans should not work without them.

Phase Two: The *Book of the Speech from God* and Gebofal

Once Dee had received the *Heptarchia Mystica*, the archangel Michael gave way to Raphael, who revealed the true heart and soul of the system: the holy *Book of the Speech from God*. In Angelical, its title is *Loagaeth* (pronounced "logah").

Emperor Rudolph

Rudolph II (July 18, 1552–January 20, 1612) was the king of Croatia, Hungary, and Bohemia and the archduke of Austria who ascended to the position of Holy Roman Emperor in 1576. However, he was unique among emperors for his general lack of interest in politics or asserting the power of his position. He is often regarded as being disinterested in his imperial role and duties. Instead, he chose to keep largely to himself, and turned most of his attention to art, mysticism, alchemy, and occultism.

As Dee and Kelley received the angelic communications during their travels across Europe, including a prolonged stay in Krakow with would-be benefactor Lord or Prince Albert Lasky, the angels urged them to go to Rudolph's court in Prague in order to present their work to him. Lasky, however, never funded their travel, so the two men journeyed to Prague on their own. Sadly, when Dee finally received an audience with the illusive emperor, the monarch seemed to be unimpressed with Dee's journals— and even less impressed with Dee's prophetic "messages from God." He seems to have mostly ignored the two men during their stay in Prague, that is, until Kelley reportedly had some success with his alchemical formulas for transmuting base metals into gold.

Dee returned to England, but Kelley remained and became an alchemist in Rudolph's court. Whether or not Kelley was very successful in this role is unknown, though we do know that Rudolph appointed him a baronship and gave him several silver mines, and Kelley lived out the rest of his life in Prague as a respected member of society. While Rudolph's disinterest in politics led many to see him as an ineffectual ruler, today we know his chosen focus on the arts and humanities not only led to a mini-Renaissance in his own kingdom, but in fact sparked the Scientific Revolution that would spread across the globe in the centuries after his passing.

Now, you already know what the *Book of Loagaeth* was supposed to be—the Celestial Tablets of Enoch, the seven-sealed Book of Life, the true *Sepher Raziel*. It consists of forty-nine individual tables (that is, 7 × 7), most of which have a 49 × 49 grid on the front and back. The grids are filled with letters that purport to be a new biblical doctrine: just as the New Testament was to the Old Testament, and the Quran was to the New Testament, so was the *Book of Loagaeth* a brand new Testament, which the angels promised would rectify all current faiths and reconcile them with one another. The angels promised that the redelivery of this new doctrine into the world (remember, it was once given to Enoch, but then revoked at the time of the Deluge) signaled the initiation of the End Times described in the Revelation of St. John. The new doctrine was supposed to spread around the earth for a time, and then the final Armageddon would take place.

· · · · · · ·

The only problem was the book was written entirely in the Angelical tongue, and the angels provided no translation for the text. This new doctrine was never intended to be preached from pulpits to the ignorant masses—instead, it was only to be understood by those mystics who learned how to unlock the mysteries of the book and receive the teachings directly from the angels.

To this end, forty-eight of the tables (numbers 2–49) were given keys with which to open them. Dee was told the first table belonged to the Christos (that is, the Logos) and could not be opened by human or angel. (Again, reference the Revelation of St. John, chapter 5, and the opening of the Seals of the Book.)

As for the keys that open the remaining forty-eight tables of *Loagaeth*, they are called the forty-eight Angelical Callings. These are a series of poetic invocations written entirely in Angelical, which serve to summon the angels associated with their assigned tables.

The system given by the angels for the proper use of both *Loagaeth* and its Keys was called *Gebofal* (a word that was never translated), as revealed by angels directly subservient to the archangel Gabriel. Gebofal appears to be a Christianized version of a Jewish practice called "counting the Omer," which involves the Qabalistic fifty Gates of *Binah* (Understanding). Therefore, I will take just a moment to explain the Jewish tradition first.

An *Omer* is a measurement of wheat. Counting the Omer is a fifty-day mystical observance prescribed in the Torah, in both Leviticus and Deuteronomy, and is associated with the festival of Passover. It gets its name from a passage in Leviticus 23:15–16:

> You shall count for yourselves—from the day after the Sabbath, from the day
> when you bring the Omer of the waving—seven Sabbaths, they shall be
> complete. Until the day after the seventh Sabbath you shall count, fifty day.

We find the instruction again in Deuteronomy 16:9–10:

> You shall count for yourselves seven weeks, from when the sickle is first put to
> the standing crop shall you begin counting seven weeks. Then you will observe
> the Festival of Shavu'ot for the Lord, your God.

The meaning behind this seven-week observance is found in the story of the Exodus. After the Passover event in Egypt, the Hebrew people began their journey into the wilderness. The next fifty days were not easy for them—they were pursued by the Pharaoh's army, nearly trapped on the shores of the Red Sea, and still had to endure weeks of travel through the hostile desert with little clue where they were supposed to go or how they were expected to survive. On the fiftieth day they arrived at Mount Sinai, where Moses received the Ten Commandments and formalized their Covenant with God.

Counting the Omer is both a religious observance of the Exodus and a mystical practice that recreates the event on a spiritual level. On the day after Passover, the mystic must remove himself from the world of man (symbolized by Egypt). As you may know, when you attempt to do this, the "Egyptians" tend to pursue you and attempt to drag you back. You also face inner obstacles to your progress—you must pass through the sea of your own subconscious habits and endure a frightening spiritual wilderness of the unknown.

Over the fifty-day process, the mystic must perform meditations aimed at removing himself from the earthly fifty Gates of Impurity, thereby entering the corresponding celestial Gates of Understanding. These celestial Gates are defined by the Tree of Life (figure 22): each of the lower seven sephiroth are divided into seven Gates—so we have (for example) the Gate of *Chesed* of Chesed, *Gevurah* of Chesed, *Tiphareth* of Chesed, *Netzach* of Chesed, *Yesod* of Chesed, and *Malkuth* of Chesed. Each Gate represents one aspect of God, specifically as illustrated in the Old Testament by some event involving one of the biblical prophets. To continue with Chesed as an example, its seven Gates correspond to Abraham, who was shown Mercy when the angel stopped him from sacrificing his son Isaac. Each of the seven Gates within Chesed is entered by meditating on the lessons taught by one biblical story or another involving Abraham.

The Jewish mystic begins the counting of the Omer by meditating on Chesed of Chesed and moving downward through the Gates, one per day, until reaching Malkuth of Malkuth on the forty-ninth day. By opening the forty-nine Gates of the lower seven sephiroth, the mystic has opened all of the Gates that lead directly to Binah. However, he is not permitted to open the final Gate because it lies within the pure divinity of the Supernals. That Gate can only be opened from the other side—it was opened once to let Moses pass through, and it will not open again until the Messiah does so during the End Times. (Later Christian variations on this system insist that the Gate also opened once to let Jesus ascend into Heaven.) Therefore, counting the Omer is not about entering the sphere of Binah. It is about opening all the Gates between us and the Supernals so that divine revelations and insight can filter down to us—symbolized in Exodus by reaching Mount Sinai and receiving the Ten Commandments.

Now, in this light, let us consider the practice of Gebofal. The *Book of Loagaeth* begins with the table of the Christos/Logos, which embodies the initial creative impulse of the universe. As we read in the first chapter of the Book of John:

> In the Beginning was the Logos, and the Logos was with God, and the Logos was
> God. [...] All things were made by him.

· · · · · · ·

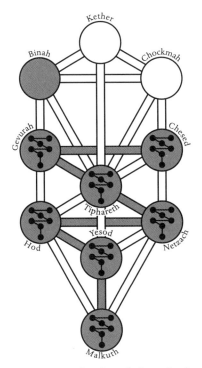

Figure 22. Tree of Life with the Fifty Gates

The next eighteen tables (that is, tables 2–19) embody the first six days of Creation, as evidenced by the poetry of the Angelical Callings used to open them. Each Call describes the creation of some aspect of the universe and God's establishment of angels to govern each one. There is also much apocalyptic imagery in the poetry, which seems to highlight the part that all of these ruling angels will play in the End Times.

Finally, the remaining thirty tables, which are all opened by the same Call used over and over, appear to represent the Seventh Day of Creation—meaning they embody the completed universe in the here and now. The angels explained that these represent thirty heavenly spheres—called *Aethyrs* (or *Ethers*)—that reach from God to Earth. The angels that reside within each Aethyr are the spiritual governors of specific geographical regions, called "Parts of the Earth," which we will return to shortly.

Taken as a set, the forty-nine tables of *Loagaeth* appear to represent the various astrological and elemental forces of the cosmos, beginning with the highest divine principal in the first table, and progressing downward until the physical Earth is reached in the forty-ninth table. Dee's angels often referred to the tables as the *Gates of Understanding*, or the *Gates of Wisdom*—both of which are references to the Supernal Realm where we find Binah (Understanding) and Chokmah (Wisdom).

Gebofal is a forty-nine-day process by which the aspirant moves downward from the highest point attainable by humans (table 2) until reaching the physical world once again (table 49). All of the Enochian skrying tools and furniture from the Heptarchia must be used, because the recitation of the Angelical Callings should result in the appearance of spiritual teachers who will expound upon the mysteries within the untranslated text of each table. The angels also suggested to Dee that he might enter the Gates of Understanding to make astral visits to the angelic cities within them, much as Enoch himself had done.

On each day, three times a day, the aspirant must open the Holy Book to the proper table, recite the Prayer of Enoch (as provided in Dee's records), and follow that with the Angelical Call associated with the table. What happens from that point would be strictly between the aspirant and the angels who arrive at the Call. The final table will be opened on the forty-eighth day, and upon the forty-ninth day the aspirant should receive direct revelations from God.

The Parts of the Earth are not addressed in the Gebofal practice, but instead appear to represent the kind of occult wisdom that can be obtained *through* the practice. And so, for that matter, is the Great Table of the Earth that Dee would receive in the next phase of the angels' teachings. In fact, the Parts of the Earth and the Great Table are directly connected.

Phase Three: The Great Table of the Earth or Watchtowers

When the Parts of the Earth system was revealed, it also began to reveal Dee's true motivation for wanting the magick in the first place. Everything up to that point had been very lofty and spiritual. However, Dee was absolutely dedicated to the notion that England was God's Kingdom here on Earth and that an English Empire should rightfully arise and rule the world. Remember that Dee is famous as England's first spy—because he regularly operated covertly on behalf of the Queen while visiting other countries. His reputation as a doddering old wizard, traveling around with a shady alchemist, was the perfect cover.

The Parts of the Earth system promised to give Dee direct influence over the tutelary zodiacal angels who governed every country in the known world. It also promised to allow his skryer to remotely view what was going on in those countries, and any secrets they were hiding. All he had to do was recite the Key of the Aethyrs, inserting the name of the particular Aethyr he wished to invoke, and the corresponding Gate would be open to him.

Each Aethyr encompasses three Parts of the Earth—except for the lowest one, which encompasses four, plus there is an extra "hidden" Part—making for a total of ninety-two Parts of the Earth. Each of these were given a name exactly seven letters long (figure 23).

Figure 23. The Great Table of the Earth Showing the Ninety-Two Parts:
The names of the ninety-two Parts of the Earth are arranged
according to this diagram, to create a massive table
twenty-five cells across and twenty-seven cells downward.

And this is the origin of the famous Great Table of the Earth (figure 24). The names of the ninety-two Parts are all arranged into a magical table in the peculiar fashion you see here. The resulting Great Table is, itself, divided into four quarters called the *Watchtowers*.

```
r Z i l a f A u t l p a  e  b O a Z a R o p h a R a
a r d Z a i d p a L a m     u N n a x o p S o n d n
c z o n s a r o Y a u b  x  a i g r a n o o m a g g
T o i T t x o P a c o C  a  o r p m n i n g b e a l
S i g a s o m r b z n h  r  r s o n i z i r l e m u
f m o n d a T d i a r i  p  i z i n r C z i a M h l
o r o i b A h a o z p i     M o r d i a l h C t G a
c N a b r V i x g a z d  h  Я O c a n c h i a s o m
O i i i t T p a l o a i     A r b i z m i i l p i z
A b a m o o o a C u c a  C  O p a n a B a m S m a l
N a o c o T t n p r a T  o  d O l o p i n i a n b a
o c a n m a g o t r o i  m  r x p a o c s i z i x p
s h i a l r a p m z o x  a  a x t i r V a s t r i m
m o t i b   a T n a n       n a n T a   b i t o m
d o n p a T d a n V a a  a  T a O A d u p t D n i m
o l o a G e o o b a u a     o a l c o o r o m e b b
O P a m n o O G m d n m  m  T a g c o n x m a l G m
a p l s T e d e c a o p  o  n h o d D i a l e a o c
s c m i o o n A m l o x  C  p a t A x i o V s P s И
V a r s G d L b r i a p  h  S a a i z a a r V r o i
o i P t e a a p D o c e     m p h a r s l g a i o l
p s u a c n r Z i r Z a  p  M a m g l o i n L i r x
S i o d a o i n r z f m     o l a a D a g a T a p a
d a l t T d n a d i r e  r  p a l c o i d x P a c n
d i x o m o n s i o s p  a  n d a z N z i V a a s a
O o D p z i A p a n l i  x  i i d P o n s d A s p i
r g o a n n Ч A C r a r  e  x r i n h t a r n d i ⌐
```

Figure 24. The Great Table of the Earth

This is the Great Table of the Earth as Dee received it. The angels explained this diagram to Dee and Kelley as follows: where the Parts of the Earth, taken individually, will grant you influence over specific areas of the world—namely, over nations—the Great Table gives you influence over entire quarters of the planet.

From the descriptions in the journals, it would appear that these "quarters" are more geopolitical than directional. From Dee's time to this very day, the division of the world into eastern, western, northern, and southern civilizations has been figured with Europe as the centerpoint. Thus, the Western Watchtower governs Western nations such as Britain, Greece, Rome, Spain, France, etc. (Today we would include North America as well.) The Eastern Watchtower governs the East Asian nations like China, Japan, Tibet, Mongolia, India, and the so-called Middle East. The Northern Watchtower governs northern nations such as Denmark, Finland, Iceland, Norway, and

Sweden. Finally, the Southern Watchtower governs southern nations like Australia, New Zealand, Fiji, Ethiopia, and most of Africa. (And, of course, South America would be included in that today.)

When the Parts of the Earth are arranged into the Great Table as we see here, their letters make up various names of God and an entire host of angels associated (not with the four elements!, but) with the four directions and the geopolitical regions encompassed by them (figure 25).

The angels in each Watchtower are given exactly the same powers as those in the other three. Thus, for example, if you need to call upon the angels of medicine, you would call upon those who reside in the area of the world where your patient lives. If they happen to live in China, you would call the angels of the Eastern Watchtower. To heal someone here in the US, you would call the angels of medicine from the Western Watchtower. In Africa you would call them from the Southern Watchtower, and in Norway you would call the angels from the Northern Watchtower.

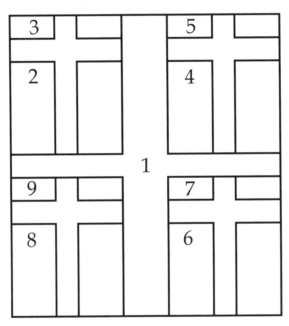

Figure 25. Powers of the Angels in the Great Table

1. Human Knowledge and Counsel
2. Medicine
3. Mixture of Substances
4. Metals and Stones
5. Transportation
6. The Four Elements
7. Discovery of Secrets
8. Transformation
9. Mechanical Crafts

This blank Watchtower could be any of the four. We can see here that each Watchtower is itself divided into four subquadrants. Further, this diagram illustrates the Divine Names and angelic powers found in each section. First and foremost are three Names of God found upon the horizontal arm of the Great Cross in the center. These three Names govern the hierarchy of the entire Watchtower. All together there are twelve such names in the Great Table (possibly corresponding to the zodiac).

Also arrayed upon the Great Cross we find the names of six of the twenty-four Elders of the Apocalypse, representing the twelve Tribes of Israel in pairs. They impart knowledge and judgment in human affairs (as tribal Elders are supposed to do). To summon them, you must use a Name of God found in the very center of the Great Cross in a swirl pattern. In Dee's time, the twenty-four Elders of the Apocalypse were associated with the zodiac—two Elders for each constellation. It is most likely Dee would have viewed them in this way, though he appears to have left it as a "given" in his records.

Within the four subquadrants of the Watchtower we have four Calvary Crosses. These Crosses each bear two Names of God that are used to summon the four angels found beneath the Cross's arms.

In the upper-left quadrant we find the angels of medicine, along with the names of several demons who can cause sickness.

In the upper-right quadrant we have the angels of precious stones, who actually have knowledge of the finding, collection, uses, and virtues of both metals and jewels. The powers attributed to the demons here are not recorded.

In the lower-left quadrant are the angels (and demons) of transformation. Dee does not tell us exactly what is meant by "transformation." However, most of the Watchtower angels seem to have powers related in some way to the practice of alchemy (metals, stones, medicines, etc.), and thus we might assume the powers of these entities concern alchemical transmutations.

In the lower-right quadrant are the angels (and demons) of the four elements. Note that the *only* angels in the Great Table who are, in fact, elemental in nature are the four listed in the lower-right subquadrant of each Watchtower. In Dee's lifetime, the four elements were mainly alchemical considerations—thanks in part to the famous doctor and occultist Paracelsus—and were secondarily astrological attributes for the four triplicities. It is from alchemy that we derive the four mixed virtues that form the elements: heat, coldness, moisture, and dryness. This would have likely been Dee's understanding of the elements as well.

Above the arms of the Cavalry Crosses we find the names of four further angels in each subquadrant. Of course, there is only one row of letters here, but each angel is found by anagramming the name of the angel before him. In the upper-left quadrant we have four angels who are skilled in the mixing of natural substances. In the upper-right quadrant are four angels who can transport things (or perhaps people) from place to place. In the lower left are four angels of the mechanical arts (indicating any work done with the hands, from painting and sculpture to carpentry and masonry, and even the building/repair of machines). Finally, in the lower-right quadrant are four angels who can reveal the secrets of all men. There are no demonic names associated with these angels at all.

To summon these four groups of angels, you must use a Name of God derived by taking the four letters above the arms of the Cross and prefixing it with a letter from the large Cross that binds all four Watchtowers together. Dee called this the *Black Cross*, very likely because it represents the alchemical Black Dragon, or decaying matter. Most of the letters from the Black Cross are used in the formation of demonic names found below the arms of the Calvary Crosses. Only a few letters are borrowed to make the Divine Names that govern the angels above the arms.

It may seem contradictory that both demonic and Divine Names should be drawn from something called the Black Cross. However, I feel this is also part of the alchemical symbolism of the Great Table. The Divine Names represent the immortal spirit (or Mercury) that can be extracted from decaying matter. The demons, of course, represent the decay.

Figure 26. The Tablet of Union

Students of the Golden Dawn will recognize the Black Cross under a different guise: the Tablet of Union (figure 26). There is no "Tablet of Union" in Dee's system; however, this diagram does appear in his journals. It was only used by the angels to show Dee how to divide the letters of three of the Parts of the Earth—Lexarph, Comanan, and Tabitom—onto the Black Cross. Therefore, Dee-purism ignores the Tablet of Union entirely. Personally, I find it valid in its own way, because where the Black Cross represents the inherent spirit within material dross, so does the Tablet of Union represent the inherent spirit within the four elements. (Just keep in mind that the Golden Dawn's method of using the Tablet of Union has no parallel in Dee's system whatsoever.)

Now using the Great Table is not just a matter of setting up the furniture and summoning the angels. Instead, a nineteen-day initiation process was outlined by which the aspirant establishes permanent contact with the entire hierarchy of Great Table angels at once. After that, the angels can be summoned and worked with at his leisure.

No invocations were provided for these angels, because Dee was instructed to write his own. As an angel famously told Dee, "Invocation proceedeth of the good will of man." Therefore, Dee was to create a *Book of Supplication* wherein he recorded invocations to each and every group of angels found in the Great Table. There were four invocations for each group—directed toward each of the four Watchtowers—for a total of thirty-six individual prayers, plus one prayer directed toward the God of Hosts (YHVH Zabaoth) and the twelve principal Divine Names of the Great Table. Dee did indeed write his own *Book of Supplication*, and it has been preserved in Geoffrey James's *Enochian Magick of Dr. John Dee*.

As for the nineteen-day initiation that Dee was to follow, I will outline it here as briefly as possible:

1) On the first four days, three times a day, Dee was to recite only the prayer to the God of Hosts through the twelve Divine Names of the Great Table. He was to ask God, in those Names, to send the angels of the Watchtowers to him and grant him their patronage.

2) Over the next fourteen days, the same prayer was to be recited three times a day, and the supplications of the Watchtower angels were added to it. Enochian scholars have debated for years how to divide thirty-six invocations between fourteen days. However, there is simply no way to evenly divide them in that fashion, and Dee's angels never suggested they should be divided at all. I believe all thirty-six invocations were to be recited each and every time—three times a day for fourteen straight days.

3) On the nineteenth day, the invocations will have taken effect. Dee was to clothe himself in a white linen robe and enter his oratory once more, to enjoy open conversation with the angels of the Great Table. Those angels, then, would have instructed him from there, and he should have had ready access to them from that time forward. He was told never to use the *Book of Supplication* nor the white robe again.

And that is John Dee's Watchtower system in a nutshell. It is a direct extension of the Parts of the Earth system, which is itself a direct extension of the *Loagaeth* system. At this point we have only one more brief point from Dee's records to cover: the so-called Reformed Table of Raphael, which bears directly upon the Golden Dawn's version of Enochian.

· · · · · · · ·

The Reformed Table of Raphael

Dee and Kelley stuck together for a few years after receiving the Enochian material, continuing to consult the angels on a regular basis about politics and other events in their lives. The two men would eventually drift apart, but not before—in April of 1587—it appears a last-ditch effort was made by the angels to keep the two men together.

First, we learn that the Family of Light angel Madimi had visited Kelley during the night and told him to share wives in common with Dee. Kelley appeared to be upset by this request, as were Dee and the two women.

```
r Z i l a f A y t l p a e   T a O A d u p   t D n i m
a r d Z a i d p a L a m     a a b c o o r   o m e b b
c z o n s a r o Y a u b x   T o g c o n x   m a l G m
T o i T t z o P a c o C a   n h o d D i a   l e a o c
S i g a s o m r b z n h r   p a t A x i o   V s P s N
f m o n d a T d i a r i p   S a a i x a a   r V r o i
o r o i b A h a o z p i     m p h a r s l   g a i o l
t N a b r V i x g a s d h   M a m g l o i   n L i r x
O i i i t T p a l O a i     o l a a D n g   a T a p a
A b a m o o o a C u c a C   p a l c o i d   x P a c n
N a o c o T t n p r n T o   n d a z N z i   V a a s a
o c a n m a g o t r o i m   i i d P o n s   d A s p i
s h i a l r a p m z o x a   x r i n h t a   r n d i L
m o t i b     a T n a n     n a n T a     b i t o m
b o a Z a R o p h a R a     a d o n p a T   d a n V a a
u N n a x o P S o n d n     o l o a G e o   o b a u a
a i g r a n o o m a g g m   O P a m n o V   G m d n m
o r p m n i n g b e a l o   a p l s T e d   e c a o p
r s o n i Z i r l e m u C   s c m i o o n   A m l o x
i z i n r C z i a M h l h   V a r s G d L   b r i a p
M o r d i a l h C t G a     o i P t e a a p D o c e
o c a n c h i a s o m t p   p s u a c N r   Z i r Z a
A r b i z m i i l p i z     S i o d a o i   n r z f m
O p a n a l a m S m a P     r d a l t T d   n a d i r e
d O l o P i n i a n b a a   d i x o m o n   s i o s p
r x p a o c s i z i x p x   O o D p z i A   p a n l i
a x t i r V a s t r i m e   r g o a n n P   A C r a r
```

Figure 27. The Reformed Great Table of Raphael

It was during this episode that Kelley reported having received instructions on his own concerning the Great Table of the Earth. He was told by a voice to "join Enoch his Tables" (meaning the Watchtowers, not the tables of *Loagaeth*). In other words, he was told to consider the entire Great Table rather than just one Watchtower. Then he was to number every square, starting in

• • • • • • • •

the upper left-hand corner and running rightward (for a total of 624). This came along with a message written in a number code that could be decrypted by replacing the message's numbers with letters from the numbered Great Table.

This, however, presented some problems, as translating the numbers of the message into letters from the Great Table produced no readable text. Then Kelley was visited in the night again, whereupon he was shown the *Reformed Great Table*.

This was simply a rearrangement of the Watchtowers within the Great Table. Arranging it in this way, and numbering the squares, finally revealed a message in Latin from the coded text. (Even still, it wasn't perfect. See Laycock's *Complete Enochian Dictionary*, 49–50.) Decoded, the message was from God himself, granting special permission for the wife-sharing to take place. Because of this, Dee "rejoices greatly" and consents to the sharing.

Next in the journals we see the message given to Kelley as he received the "Reformed" Great Table alone in his bedroom—and the messenger reveals himself to be the angel Raphael—hence the name of this version of the Great Table as used by the Golden Dawn: the Reformed Great Table *of Raphael* (figure 27). Over the next pages, the wife-sharing takes place, and Dee and Kelley have their last angelic sessions together. Nothing of further interest to us takes place, and the journals eventually come to an end.

Enochian Magick and the Early Golden Dawn

After Dee's passing, his system of Enochian magick fell mostly into obscurity. Many of his manuscripts and belongings were destroyed or stolen from his home while he was away in Europe. (Thankfully he had his angelic journals with him at the time.) And later, most of his Enochian material was hidden away in the false bottom of a chest, where it lay hidden for many years. (Once found, several pages of this material were lost when the previously mentioned maid used them to drain pies.)

In 1659, many of Dee's recovered angelic journals were published with a preface by Meric Casaubon under the title *A True & Faithful Relation of What Passed for Many Years Between Dr. John Dee ... and Some Spirits*. Casaubon's motives were political—hoping to prove that Dee, a famous and well-respected Anglican, had in fact been in contact with devils who wished to replace the New Testament with the *Book of Loagaeth*.

A True & Faithful Relation would go on to be the primary source for most Enochian researchers and practitioners who followed. One of these was Dr. Thomas Rudd, who has become famous for adding astrological and geomantic correspondences to Dee's system. (He also, inexplicably, added material from the *Goetia* to the seven Ensigns of Creation, for which there is no support in Dee's records.) See *A Treatise of Angel Magic* by Adam McClean for Rudd's Enochian-influenced system of angel magick.

· · · · · · · ·

Dr. Thomas Rudd

Dr. Thomas Rudd (c. 1583–1656) was a military engineer and mathematician working in the Low Countries (aka the Netherlands). King Charles I of England appointed him in 1627 to the position of chief engineer of all castles and fortifications within Wales, and later granted him the rank of the king's principal engineer. Historical records confirm that Rudd's advice was in demand across the United Kingdom in the building, refurbishing, and removal of several military complexes. His expertise in mathematics led him to publish two mathematical texts: *Practical Geometry, in Two Parts* and an edition of Euclid's *Elements of Geometry*. The latter had an attached introduction by Dr. John Dee, and Rudd was known to have taken an interest in Dee's writings, particularly his text on sacred geometry entitled *The Hieroglyphic Monad*.

It is perhaps because of this that Rudd gained a reputation as an occultist in his own right who was well versed in Hermeticism. Legend has placed him as the leader of a group of English magicians, though this is unverified. In time, a manuscript on angel magick would be attributed to him (published today as *A Treatise on Angel Magic*, edited by Adam McClean), though there is no way to verify if Rudd himself actually wrote it. Similarly, a version of the grimoire entitled *Goetia* was also attributed to him and is published today as *The Goetia of Dr. Rudd* (edited by Dr. Stephen Skinner and David Rankine). Whether these works were truly written by Rudd or simply attributed to him, they would go on to influence the development of Western occultism for generations to come, giving us the first steps into what is called *Neo-Enochiana* and providing a major influence on the early Golden Dawn.

Eventually the rest of Dee's journals were also published—this time without political motivation—and they have been available for the world to study ever since. I listed the best and easiest-to-obtain sources at the beginning of this chapter.

———

I have already described the activities of the founders of the Golden Dawn during the earliest days of the Order. They had to study Dee's journals at the British Library a little at a time. However, Dee's records are so prolific that they would not be fully vetted until the 1990s, when the internet allowed Dee enthusiasts and occultists from around the world to access his journals at will and to share and debate their findings with one another.

Meanwhile, members of the early Golden Dawn did not rely entirely upon Dee's journals for their information. They also drew material from the very obscure Enochian tradition that had evolved since the time of Dee, such as the writings of Dr. Rudd, and (most importantly) from a document of unknown origin called *Book H* (cataloged in the British Library as Sloane MS 307).

r	Z	i	l	a	f	A	u	t	l	p	a			T	a	O	A	d	v	p	t	D	n	i	m	24
a	r	d	Z	a	i	d	p	a	L	a	m			a	a	b	c	o	o	r	o	m	e	b	b	48
c	z	o	n	s	a	r	o	Y	a	u	b			T	o	g	c	o	n	x	m	a	l	G	m	72
T	o	i	T	t	x	o	P	a	c	o	C			n	h	o	d	D	i	a	l	e	a	o	c	96
S	i	g	a	s	o	m	r	b	z	n	h			p	a	t	A	x	i	o	V	s	P	s	i	120
f	m	o	n	d	a	T	d	i	a	r	i			S	a	a	i	x	a	a	r	V	r	o	i	144
o	r	o	i	b	A	h	a	o	z	p	i			m	p	h	a	r	s	l	g	a	i	o	l	168
c	n	a	b	r	V	i	x	g	a	z	d			m	a	m	g	l	o	i	n	L	i	r	x	192
O	i	i	i	t	T	p	a	l	o	a	i			o	l	a	a	D	a	g	a	T	a	p	a	216
A	b	a	m	o	o	o	a	C	v	c	a			p	a	L	c	o	i	d	x	P	a	c	n	240
N	a	o	c	o	T	t	n	p	r	a	T			n	d	a	z	n	x	i	V	a	a	s	a	264
o	c	a	n	m	a	g	o	t	r	o	i			l	i	d	P	o	n	s	d	a	s	p	i	288
s	h	i	a	l	r	a	p	m	z	o	x			x	r	i	i	h	t	a	r	n	d	i	J	312

e	x	a	r	p
h	c	o	m	a
n	a	n	t	a
b	i	t	o	m

b	O	a	Z	a	R	o	p	h	a	R	a			d	o	n	p	a	T	d	a	n	V	a	a	336
v	N	n	a	x	o	p	S	o	n	d	n			o	l	o	a	G	e	o	o	b	a	v	i	360
a	i	g	r	a	n	o	o	m	a	g	g			O	P	a	m	n	o	O	G	m	d	n	m	384
o	r	p	m	n	i	n	g	b	e	a	l			a	p	l	s	T	e	d	e	c	a	o	p	408
r	s	o	n	i	z	i	r	l	e	m	u			s	c	m	i	o	o	n	A	m	l	o	x	432
i	z	i	n	r	C	z	i	a	M	h	l			V	a	r	s	G	d	L	b	r	i	a	p	456
m	o	r	d	i	a	l	h	C	t	G	a			o	i	P	t	e	a	a	p	d	o	c	e	480
Æ	O	c	a	n	c	h	i	a	s	o	m			p	s	v	a	c	n	r	Z	i	r	Z	a	504
A	r	b	i	z	m	i	i	l	p	i	z			S	i	o	d	a	o	i	n	r	z	f	m	528
O	p	a	n	a	l	a	m	S	m	a	L			d	a	l	t	T	d	n	a	d	i	r	e	552
d	O	l	o	p	i	n	i	a	n	b	a			d	i	x	o	m	o	n	s	i	o	s	p	576
r	x	p	a	o	c	s	i	z	i	x	p			O	o	D	p	z	i	a	p	a	n	l	i	600
a	x	t	i	r	V	a	s	t	r	i	m			r	g	o	a	n	n	¶	A	C	r	a	r	624

Figure 28. The Frontispiece of Book H:
Displaying the Reformed Table of Raphael,
with the Tablet of Union in the center, written in black and red inks.

The best source I have found for *Book H* and its history is a book called *The Practical Angel Magic of Dr. John Dee's Enochian Tables* by Stephen Skinner and David Rankine. While the authors present some theories that are not generally supported today (such as the idea that Dee himself might have written *Book H*, which is *very* unlikely), it is not their speculative theories that make their book important. Instead, it is the history of *Book H* and its influence on the Golden Dawn that makes the book required reading for any student of the neo-Enochian system.

Book H consists of a series of lengthy invocations for all the angels of the Great Table. It assigns the same powers to the angels as we find in Dee's journals but uses an entirely different method of generating the angels' names from the Watchtowers, and a different method of summoning them. The prayers are similar, in essence, to those in Dee's *Book of Supplication*, though there is no evidence (based on the content of the prayers) that they were adapted from Dee's. In fact, the invocations in *Book H* are nearly *ten times* the length of those written by Dee! (And there is no mention of a nineteen-day ritual being necessary to use them.)

The unknown author also added a frontispiece to it, as pictured in figure 28. What you see here is a slightly modified version of Kelley's Reformed Table of Raphael. The original appears near the end of *A True & Faithful Relation*. It is only different from what you see here in that red ink has been used to denote the names of the angels, while black ink denotes the names on the Great and Calvary Crosses. Otherwise, it is the same as the Reformed Table that appears in Dee's journals: the ordering has been changed from the original Great Table, and the numbers you see running down the right-hand side are those added by Dee, as he numbered all the squares from 1 to 624 in order to decipher the message from God.

It would appear that the author of *Book H* studied *A True & Faithful Relation* and discovered the Reformed Table near the end—along with Dee's notation that he was "rejoicing" because this arrangement of the Great Table had "solved a significant problem." Naturally, our unknown author assumed the Reformed Table was a corrected version of the Great Table, and thus adopted it for *Book H*.

What he failed to do was carefully read the entries made by Dee over the days leading up to the Reformed Table, or else he would have known that it was specifically linked to the wife-swapping episode, and the "significant problem" that the Reformed Table solved was merely the decryption of the message from God giving Dee, Kelley, and their wives permission to co-mingle. Sadly, the moment the author made the choice to use the Reformed Table, he created a permanent schism between the two camps of Enochian study that would come to exist nearly two hundred years later.

The reason for this schism is that *Book H* was the primary authoritative text on Enochian magick used by the early Golden Dawn. What you see here is exactly how the Great Table looked to the first Adepts of the Order, including the black and red colors, as well as the Tablet of Union in the center. A more elaborate color scheme was applied to the Watchtowers in the Inner Order, but was never shown to members of the Outer. Meanwhile, *Book H* was used in the Inner Order as a grimoire for summoning the angels from this Reformed Great Table.

Unfortunately, *Book H* did not provide much context for itself. The only information it gave about the angels was found in the invocations, which mentioned their powers (basically the same as Dee had recorded them) and in which compass direction they governed. It did not explain anything that I have explained to you about the Great Table here, nor did it associate the angels within it with any specific choirs or give them any occult correspondences.

Thus, as far as we know, it was Mathers and/or Westcott who first applied the four classical elements to the individual Watchtowers, and the sub-elements (fire of water, air of earth, water of air, etc.) to each of the sixteen subquadrants. They were also the first to assign the Elders (or, as they called them, *Seniors*) to the planets rather than the older zodiacal attributions, and adapt the Divine Name in the center as the name of a solar angel who governs the Seniors. Each group of Seniors and their "King" were considered to embody the planetary forces when operating within a specific element—such as when Jupiter resides in a sign of the water triplicity (Cancer, Scorpio, or Pisces).

The Golden Dawn were also the first to attribute the Tetragrammaton (or four-lettered Name of God: YHVH) to the Tablet of Union and the squares of the subquadrants, as well as all of the geomantic, tarot, elemental, and other occult correspondences they apply to the individual squares. (I should also mention that the versions of the Watchtowers with multiple letters in many of the squares was also the invention of the Golden Dawn. They were the result of students being unsure about which letter should go in a square, such as a *u* versus a *v*, or an *e* versus an *a*. We have Chic and Sandra Tabatha Cicero to thank for laying those monsters to rest forever in the modern Golden Dawn.)

Book H also makes no mention of the forty-eight Angelical Keys. Therefore we might assume that Mathers or Westcott were the first to apply them to the Great Table instead. Their likely source for the Keys was Dee's personal grimoire, which survives in the Sloane collection at the British Library (and has been published in our time as *The Enochian Magick of Dr. John Dee*). In that grimoire, the forty-eight Keys are given with absolutely no explanation or instruction on how to use them, and no mention of the *Book of Loagaeth* is made. Dee had merely written them out so he could use them, and nothing more. Therefore, it is not hard to imagine why the early Golden Dawn adepts would have naturally applied those angelic Callings to the angels described in *Book H*.

As for how the words of the forty-eight Keys were to be pronounced, Dee's grimoire did in fact give pronunciation cues for the words. However, the earliest Adepts developed their own system of pronunciation, which has been affectionately called "Golden Dawn Liturgical Enochian" by

• • • • • • • •

some modern practitioners. The basic rule was to pronounce every letter in the name and to apply vowels where they were missing according to the rules of Hebrew. In practice, they would often allow letters to combine their sounds when they seemed to do so naturally (that is, to an English speaker), but there were no hard-and-fast rules on when to do so.

Over the years since, these rules have been greatly relaxed, and now each Adept seems to have their own pronunciations for the words. However, you can still hear echoes of Golden Dawn Liturgical Enochian in most of the Angelical used in modern Hermetic systems that have descended from the Golden Dawn or its influence.

Meanwhile, a vast amount of work has been done to decipher Dee's own pronunciation notes in both his journals and his personal grimoire, and we have a fairly good idea how the language might have sounded to him and Kelley. My own work on that particular subject can be found in the two volumes of *The Angelical Language*.

In Conclusion

This brief chapter has barely scratched the surface of the mysteries and practice of Enochian magick, both Dee-purist and neo-Enochian. I have also only hinted at the massive impact Dee and Kelley's contributions have had on our modern systems of magick. It would go on to influence Rosicrucianism, Thelema, Neopaganism, and Wicca, and a host of other traditions that have come down to us today. However, until relatively recently, most of the Enochian source material was left obscure and unexamined, wrapping what little was known in a shroud of mystery and misunderstanding. Since the dawn of the Information Age, much more has come to light, giving us a much better view into Dee's life, the time and place in which he lived, and what the motivations behind his Enochian magick may have been. I hope I have given you a solid glimpse into the origins of the tradition and its structure and intent, as well as how it survived to become a shining jewel of the Western Mystery Tradition.

Zorge,
Aaron Leitch, 2019

Sources

Agrippa, Henry Cornelius. *Three Books of Occult Philosophy*. Woodbury, MN: Llewellyn Publications, 2018.

Crowley, Aleister. "Liber LXXXIV Vel Chanokh: A Brief Abstract of the Symbolic Representation of the Universe Derived by Doctor John Dee Through the Skrying of Sir Edward Kelly." *Hermetic Library*. Accessed September 26, 2019. https://hermetic.com/crowley/libers/lib84.

Crowley, Aleister, Lon Milo DuQuette, and Christopher Hyatt. *Enochian World of Aleister Crowley: Enochian Sex Magick*. Tempe, AZ: Falcon Press, 2017.

· · · · · · · ·

Crowley, Aleister, Victor B. Neuberg, and Mary Desti. *The Vision & the Voice: With Commentary and Other Papers: The Collected Diaries of Aleister Crowley, 1909–1914 E.V.* York Beach, ME: Weiser Books, 1999.

De Abano, Peter. *Heptameron: Or Magical Elements.* CreateSpace Independent Publishing Platform, 2015.

Dee, John. *The Heptarchia Mystica of John Dee.* Edited by Robert Turner. Wellingborough, UK: Aquarian Press, 1986.

———. *A True & Faithful Relation of What Passed for Many Years Between Dr. John Dee and Some Spirits.* Preface by Meric Casaubon. London : Printed by D. Maxwell for T. Garthwait, 1659.

DuQuette, Lon Milo. *Enochian Vision Magick: An Introduction and Practical Guide to the Magick of Dr. John Dee and Edward Kelley.* York Beach, ME: Weiser Books, 2008.

Fell-Smith, Charlotte. *John Dee (1527–1608).* Berwick, ME: Ibis Press, 2004.

French, Peter J. *John Dee: The World of the Elizabethan Magus.* New York: Hippocrene Books, 1989.

Honorius of Thebes. *The Sworn Book of Honorius: Liber Iuratus Honorii.* Lake Worth, FL: Ibis Press, 2016.

James, Geoffrey, ed. and trans. *The Enochian Magick of Dr. John Dee.* St. Paul, MN: Llewellyn Publications, 1998.

Klein, Kevin, ed. *The Complete Mystical Records of Dr. John Dee: Transcribed from the 16th-Century Manuscripts Documenting Dee's Conversations with Angels.* Woodbury, MN: Llewellyn Publications, 2017.

Laycock, Donald C. *The Complete Enochian Dictionary.* Boston, MA: Weiser, 2001.

Leitch, Aaron. *The Angelical Language, Volume I: The Complete History and Mythos of the Tongue of Angels.* Woodbury, MN: Llewellyn Publications, 2010.

———. *The Angelical Language, Volume II: An Encyclopedic Lexicon of the Tongue of Angels.* Woodbury, MN: Llewellyn Publications, 2010.

———. *The Essential Enochian Grimoire.* Woodbury, MN: Llewellyn Publications, 2014.

Lumpkin, Joseph B. *The Books of Enoch: A Complete Volume Containing 1 Enoch (The Ethiopic Book of Enoch), 2 Enoch (The Slavonic Secrets of Enoch), 3 Enoch (The Hebrew Book of Enoch).* Fifth Estate, Incorporated, 2011.

McLean, Adam, ed. *A Treatise on Angel Magic: Being a Complete Transcription of Ms. Harley 6482 in the British Library.* Grand Rapids, MI: Phanes Press, 1990.

Peterson, Joseph, ed. and trans. *Arbatel: Concerning the Magic of the Ancients.* Lake Worth, FL: Ibis Press, 2009.

———. *John Dee's Five Books of Mystery.* York Beach, ME: Weiser Books, 2002.

• • • • • • •

———. *Lemegeton Clavicula Salomonis: The Lesser Key of Solomon*. York Beach, ME: Weiser Books, 2001.

Regardie, Israel. *The Complete Golden Dawn System of Magic*. New Falcon Publications, 2015.

———. *The Golden Dawn*. St. Paul, MN: Llewellyn Publications, 1982.

Scholem, Gershom. *Major Trends in Jewish Mysticism*. New York: Schocken, 1995.

Skinner, Stephen, ed. *Dr. John Dee's Spiritual Diaries (1583–1608)*. Woodbury, MN: Llewellyn Publications, 2012.

Skinner, Stephen, and David Rankine. *The Practical Angel Magic of Dr. John Dee's Enochian Tables: Tabularum Bonorum Angelorum Invocationes*. Woodbury, MN: Llewellyn Publications, 2010.

Trithemius, Johannes. *De Septem Secundeis (Seven Secondary Causes)*. Edited by Joseph H. Peterson. *Esoteric Archives*. Accessed September 26, 2019. http://www.esotericarchives.com/tritheim/tritem.htm.

———. *Steganographia*. Accessed September 26, 2019. http://trithemius.com/steganographia-english/.

Tyson, Donald. *Enochian Magick for Beginners: The Original System of Angel Magick*. St. Paul, MN: Llewellyn Publications, 1997.

Woolley, Benjamin. *The Queen's Conjurer: The Science and Magic of Dr. John Dee, Adviser to Queen Elizabeth I*. London: Flamingo, 2002.

About the Author

Aaron Leitch is a senior member of the Hermetic Order of the Golden Dawn and the academic Societas Magica. A scholar, practitioner, and teacher of Western Hermeticism, the Solomonic grimoire tradition, and Enochian magick, he has authored such titles as *Secrets of the Magickal Grimoires*, *The Angelical Language: Vols. I and II*, and *The Essential Enochian Grimoire*. Aaron and his wife, Carrie Mikell-Leitch, co-founded Doc Solomon's Occult Curios, where they handcraft traditional occult tools and supplies and offer classes on such subjects as grimoire magick and Abramelin. More recently, they established Solomon Springs, a forty-acre venue in the Florida wilderness for Pagan and esoteric festivals and gatherings.

Art Credits

All art in book 7 by James Clark.

BOOK EIGHT

⌲ ✦ ⌳

The Golden Dawn
by *Chic Cicero & Sandra Tabatha Cicero*

A single often-quoted sentence from the Neophyte Ritual of the Golden Dawn sums up the primary aspiration of the student of the Mysteries: "Long hast thou dwelt in darkness, Quit the Night and Seek the Day!" The very name of the Order, the Golden Dawn, alludes to the shining brilliance of the Divine Light of the Eternal breaking through the confines of darkness to herald the birth of a new day in the spiritual evolution of humankind. Beyond gaining skill in the art of magic, and the increase in psychic faculties that such performance brings with it, the aim of all rituals and practical magical work of the Golden Dawn is to create a spiritual bond between the magician and the Eternal, Immortal Self.

The Golden Dawn's impact on contemporary ceremonial magic cannot be overstated. While we as Golden Dawn magicians are naturally predisposed to favor our own tradition, we are certainly not the only authors to make this claim. The Golden Dawn has often been called "the most famous and influential occult order of modern times."[1] In his excellent book on *The Rosicrucians,* author Christopher McIntosh describes the Order as "the most impressive fruit to grow from the Rosicrucian tree."[2] And in his foreword to Ellic Howe's important text on the Order's history, Gerald Yorke writes: "The Hermetic Order of the Golden Dawn (G.D.) with its Inner Order of the Rose of Ruby and the Cross of Gold (R.R. et A.C.) was the crowning glory of the occult revival in the nineteenth century. It synthesized into a coherent whole a vast body of disconnected and widely scattered material and welded it into a practical and effective system,

---

1. Greer, *The New Encyclopedia of the Occult*, 202.
2. McIntosh, *The Rosicrucians*, 97.

· · · · · · · ·

which cannot be said of any other occult Order of which we know at that time or since."[3] It is a simple fact that without the Golden Dawn the esoteric and magical world of the twenty-first century would be very different from what it is today.

> There are many schools of magic in existence today, but many of them ultimately derive from the same source (...) The Hermetic Order of the Golden Dawn was the most important single source of the modern magical tradition.[4]

What is it about the Golden Dawn that makes it so significant? And what is it about the system that continues to attract aspiring magicians today, long after the passing of the Victorian age into which it was born?

It is easy to see how the Order was miles ahead of any esoteric fraternity of its era. It opened its doors to women as well as men, on a completely equal footing. And at a time when similar organizations were content with the mere theoretical *study* of magic and various occult topics, the Golden Dawn was created to be a society whose members learned and *practiced* magic.

Much of the magic contained within the teachings of the Order was not original. Its many component parts were drawn from several sources that would have been familiar to Hermeticists, alchemists, astrologers, natural philosophers, mages, and occultists from previous ages, comprising the various threads of what is known as the *Western Esoteric Tradition*. The range of studies undertaken by Golden Dawn magicians was impressive: ancient Egyptian religion and magic, classical Greek philosophy, the Greco-Egyptian Mystery religions, Hellenistic philosophy, Gnosticism, Neo-Platonism, Hermetism and Hermeticism, Jewish Kabbalah and Christian Hermetic Qabalah, Rosicrucian philosophy and Christian mysticism, astrology and planetary magic, tarot and other forms of divination, the principles of alchemy, evocation and spirit vision work, the creation of magical implements and sacred space, healing, aura control, godform assumption, the projection and movement of energy, dramatic invocation, consecration of talismans, and Enochian magic.

But what made the Golden Dawn truly unique was the genius of its founders to craft a single, organized framework from these diverse teachings, creating a comprehensive course for magical study, training, and practice. The design of the Golden Dawn system was balanced, logical, and practicable. Its structure includes several levels of initiation ceremonies accompanied by instruction and gradework, rituals, meditations, exercises, and examinations. The Order was created to be a school and a repository of esoteric knowledge, which was given to members in a gradual, step-by-step manner. Beginning students learned the principles of occult science and committed the

3. Howe, *The Magicians of the Golden Dawn*, ix.
4. King and Skinner, *Techniques of High Magic*, 9–10.

rudiments of magical knowledge to memory, while more advanced initiates explored these various esoteric avenues in greater depth and combined them with ritual techniques of practical magic.

Structural Roots and Direct Influences

By the nineteenth century, there was huge interest in Western esotericism in France and England. This movement, dubbed the Occult Revival, was led by individuals such as former Catholic clergyman Alphonse Louis Constant, better known as Eliphas Levi (1810–1875), an astute Qabalist and prolific author. His book on *The Dogma and Ritual of High Magic* (1854) would become a cornerstone of Western magic. Levi advanced the theory that the twenty-two Major Arcana cards of the tarot corresponded to the twenty-two letters of the Hebrew alphabet—a view that would later become an important part of the Golden Dawn's teachings. In addition, his writings on the Qabalah, the creation of talismans, and the idea of the Astral Light were largely embraced by the founders of the Golden Dawn. Another significant contributor to the Occult Revival was Frederick Hockley (1809–1885), a Spiritualist, Freemason, Rosicrucian, and profuse transcriber of unpublished works on Qabalah, alchemy, and magic. Hockley's experiments with spirit communications and clairvoyance using magic mirrors and crystals were carried out and meticulously recorded over a sixty-year span.

As England continued to explore the farthest reaches of the world, there was a great deal of interest in the ethnic and religious traditions of cultures both past and contemporary. The archaic Celtic civilization and the mysticism of the Far East attracted much attention. There was also considerable enthusiasm for anything having to do with ancient Egypt and Mesopotamia, fueled in no small part by Sir E. A. Wallis Budge, curator for the British Museum's Department of Egyptian and Assyrian Antiquities. In 1883 Budge began work for the museum, and through the 1880s he was able to secure numerous valuable manuscripts, cuneiform tablets, and Egyptian papyri for the British Museum, including a remarkably well-preserved version of the *Book of the Dead*. Such resources were rocket fuel for Victorian-era students of the occult.

The mid-1880s also witnessed a sizable growth in Masonry and quasi-Masonic organizations of all kinds. Freemasonry was a worldwide fraternity of men who, according to legend, traced their origins to the building of King Solomon's Temple and even earlier. However, the real roots of Freemasonry are to be found in the late medieval stonemasons' guilds of England and Scotland. Freemasons were taught basic morality and principled development of the human condition through symbols. Admission into Freemasonry required a belief in God as the Divine Architect of the Universe.

Although Freemasonry was not an occult society in and of itself, it nonetheless had considerable historical ties to occultism. Freemasonry was, and still is, the West's most influential fraternal order. Because of this, a huge percentage of Masonic ideas concerning the organization and

· · · · · · · ·

arrangement of lodges was adopted by occult societies and magical lodges. Initiation into the various degrees of Masonry involved an elaborate system of symbolic ritual. Masonic rites included secret passwords, signs, cryptic diagrams, knocks, oaths, blindfolds, and grips or handshakes. All of these features would directly influence the structure of the Golden Dawn's initiation ceremonies. Even the phrase "So mote it be" entered the vernacular of the Golden Dawn from Freemasonry.

The final and perhaps most important influence on the Golden Dawn was Rosicrucianism, a mystical and philosophical movement that first emerged in seventeenth-century Germany. The legendary Rosicrucians were said to be a secret order of Christian mystics who worked for the good of mankind and studied the art of alchemy and Hermetic philosophy. The Rosicrucians were first described in a series of cryptic manuscripts that started showing up in 1614, beginning with the *Fama Fraternitatis*, or "Announcement of the Fraternity." Not long after, two more manuscripts appeared: *Confessio Fraternitatis*, or "Confession of the Fraternity," and the *Chemical Wedding of Christian Rosenkreutz*. The *Fama* proclaimed the existence of a shadowy society of skilled mystics united under the symbol of the Rose Cross. It went on to describe the life of the fraternity's founder, Christian Rosenkreutz (or C.R.C.), and the discovery of the hidden vault wherein the founder and all the secrets of the Order were buried. The manuscript suggested that like-minded seekers contact the fraternity to share in its esoteric knowledge—a task made impossible by the lack of any instruction on how to contact the Fratres, combined with the admonition that anyone who *called* himself a Rosicrucian was an imposter! Whether real or imagined, no one actually found them. And in his later years, Lutheran clergyman Johann Valentin Andreae admitted to writing the *Chemical Wedding* as a joke and probably had a hand in writing the other manifestos as well.

Anna Kingsford

Anna Bonus Kingsford (1846–1888) is known today as a leading English anti-vivisectionist, proponent of vegetarianism, campaigner for women's rights, and one of the first English women to have earned a degree in medicine. She was also a profound mystic and an important influence on the founders of the Golden Dawn.

Much of what we know about Kingsford's life comes from the work of her friend and biographer, Edward Maitland. Their relationship was a very deep yet platonic friendship. When Kingsford began to receive a series of prophetic dream-visions—her "illuminations"—it was Maitland who made sure they were written down and preserved. These became the basis for *The Perfect Way, or the Finding of Christ* and *Clothed with the Sun*.

The two preached what they called the *New Gospel of Interpretation*, intended to restore lost esoteric truths of Christianity, especially truths that include the divine feminine. Kingsford's most potent formulation of this is the "Day of the Woman" prophecy: "And now I show you a mystery and a new thing [...] The word which shall come to save the world, shall be uttered by a woman. A woman shall conceive, and shall bring forth the tidings of salvation."*

In the early 1880s, Kingsford and Maitland became involved with the London Theosophical Society (TS). Eventually, they would split with the TS to go their own way, forming the Hermetic Society. It was at this time that Wynn Westcott and S. L. MacGregor Mathers, two of the soon-to-be founders of the Hermetic Order of the Golden Dawn, met Kingsford. Both would go on to lecture at Kingsford's Hermetic Society.

Kingsford was now at the height of her career. Highly charismatic, an entrancing speaker, beautiful, and ethereal, Anna riveted the attention of everyone near her. Mathers dedicated his important translation of *The Kabbalah Unveiled* (1887) to her and Maitland. His preface called Kingsford and Maitland's *The Perfect Way* the most occult book written in centuries. Kingsford's influence convinced Mathers that the magical order he and Westcott were forming should include women. Maitland later wrote that "in the course of the summer of this year, 1886, a proposal to study occultism was made to her by a notable expert."** The "notable expert" could be no one but Mathers.

In addition to adopting Kingsford's feminism, Mathers assisted in her anti-vivisection campaign and became a vegetarian. The official GD History Lecture praised Kingsford as one of the great Hermetists of the day. With its blending of Christianity and polytheism, its use of the term *Genius* for the Higher Self, and its valorization of the divine feminine, *The Perfect Way* clearly had a substantial influence on the GD curriculum. So much so that perhaps we can consider Anna Kingsford, as does Mary Greer in *Women of the Golden Dawn*, the "magical mother" of the Hermetic Order of the Golden Dawn.

—by M. Isidora Forrest

M. Isidora Forrest is the author of a number of books and articles on the Egyptian goddess Isis, including *Isis Magic* and *Offering to Isis*, as well as articles on selected deities in modern Neopagan practice and modern spiritual magic. She is a Prophetess in the House of Isis, a priestess of the international Fellowship of Isis, a Hermetic adept, a maenad for Dionysos, and a founder of the Hermetic Fellowship in Oregon.

* Edward Maitland, *Anna Kingsford: Her Life, Letters, Diary, and Work*, vol. 1, 344–345.
** Edward Maitland, *Anna Kingsford: Her Life, Letters, Diary, and Work*, vol. 2, 268.

Regardless of its origins, the idea of Rosicrucianism was very appealing. As Freemasonry spread across Europe in the eighteenth century and expanded again in the nineteenth century, all manner of arcane motifs, scriptural themes, ancient mystery religions, and secret societies such as the mysterious Rosicrucian Brotherhood were harvested for nuggets of inspiration. Consequently,

· · · · · · ·

several Masonic Rosicrucian fraternities were founded. The Rosicrucian movement spawned several groups concerned with the study of religious mysticism, philosophical and religious doctrines, alchemy, Qabalah, spiritual transformation, and general esotericism.

A Brief History of the Golden Dawn

The Hermetic Order of the Golden Dawn was the brainchild of Dr. William Wynn Westcott (1848–1925), a London coroner who was interested in all aspects of occultism. Westcott was a Master Mason and Secretary General of the *Societas Rosicruciana in Anglia*, or Rosicrucian Society in England (S.R.I.A.), a Masonic Rosicrucian research order. Westcott was interested in the many varieties of Masonry that thrived outside the conventional craft. He was actively involved in most of the esoteric orders that abounded in Britain at the time and was widely esteemed for his expertise on the Qabalah, alchemy, and Hermetic philosophy. He published an impressive volume of work in both the Hermetic and medical fields, including a translation of the famous Qabalistic text *Sepher Yetzirah* as well as Eliphas Levi's treatise on the tarot, *The Magical Ritual of the Sanctum Regnum*. He also edited a series of Hermetic and Gnostic texts and published them as individual volumes of his *Collectanea Hermetica* series.

The origin story of how the Golden Dawn came into being has more often than not been a source of confusion and deliberate mystification. According to Westcott's original version of events, he received some sixty pages of a manuscript written in cipher from an elderly Mason, the Reverend A. F. A. Woodford, in 1887. It was claimed that Woodford had received the manuscript from "a dealer in curios." The manuscript, which seemed to be old, was quickly deciphered by Westcott using the cipher found in Abbot Johann Trithemius's book *Polygraphiae*. It proved to be a series of ritual outlines for the initiation ceremonies of a quasi-Masonic occult order. An additional paper, also written in cipher, was inserted into the manuscript: a letter purporting to contain the credentials and address of a German Adept named Fraulein Sprengel. As the story goes, Westcott exchanged a series of letters with Sprengel, who authorized him to establish a new temple in England. Westcott fleshed out the outlines into full working rituals.

While the *Cipher Manuscript* is a genuine outline for an effective esoteric group, it is now considered highly likely that Westcott concocted the story about Fraulein Sprengel and her letters. During the Victorian era, esoteric groups needed an ancient "pedigree" in order to attract prominent Freemasons, Rosicrucians, and serious occultists into their ranks. After all, the Freemasons had the story of Hiram Abiff, the Rosicrucians had the legend of Christian Rosenkreutz, and the Theosophists had Blavatsky's occult "Masters." Surely Westcott must have felt the need to provide evidence that the Golden Dawn was not something merely created out of thin air, that it had a similar, noble history to back it up.

* * * * * * *

The pages of the Cipher Manuscript were probably ritual outlines for a prototype alchemical group known as the Society of Eight, which was founded in 1883 by Frederick Holland but never fully manifested. The papers were copied down by Kenneth Mackenzie, author of *The Royal Masonic Cyclopaedia,* a leading member of the S.R.I.A. and Grand Secretary of the Swedenborgian Rite of Freemasonry. After Mackenzie's death in 1886, Westcott became Grand Secretary of the S.R. and acquired all of Mackenzie's papers, including the folios of the Cipher Manuscript that were among the assorted documents of the Swedenborgian Rite. In any event, once Westcott had deciphered the ritual outlines, he began to implement his vision of a new occult society that was hands-on and practical, and not just another theoretical study group.

In February of 1888, the Isis-Urania Temple was inaugurated in London and the Order of the Golden Dawn was born. Westcott had already recruited two fellow Masonic Rosicrucians to be co-equal officers in the governing triumvirate for his new order: Dr. William Robert Woodman and Samuel Liddell "MacGregor" Mathers.

Of the three founding members of the Golden Dawn, Samuel Mathers was a most talented ritualist. He was also known for his translations of a series of grimoires, including *The Sacred Magic of Abra-Melin the Mage, The Key of Solomon the King,* and *The Grimoire of Armadel.* As a practical magician, Mathers had few equals. And of the three founding Chiefs, it was Mathers, the primary Chief of the Inner Order, who made the Golden Dawn into a truly magical initiatory order.

By the end of 1888, the Isis-Urania Temple in London had thirty-two members, nine women and twenty-three men. That same year, two more temples were established. A year after its founding, the Order had grown to around sixty members, about a third of whom were women. More temples were founded in the years that followed.

Members of the Order included quite a few doctors and writers. Many belonged to other esoteric groups such as the Freemasons and the Theosophical Society. In general, they were intelligent, creative people who sought out spiritual knowledge. Some of the more notable members of the original Order included William Butler Yeats, one of the greatest poets of the twentieth century; William Horton, a prominent graphic artist in the Art Nouveau movement; Reverend William Alexander Ayton, a clergyman and practicing alchemist; William Peck, city astronomer of Edinburgh; authors Arthur Machen and Algernon Blackwood; Arthur Edward Waite, a Christian mystic, occultist, and prolific author of several books on Freemasonry, Qabalah, and other esoteric subjects, as well as the creator of the most popular Golden Dawn–based tarot deck in the world (the Rider-Waite Tarot); Constance Wilde, the wife of playwright Oscar Wilde; and famed occultist Aleister Crowley.[5]

---

5. Eds. note: See Book Nine: Thelema & Aleister Crowley.

Women of the Golden Dawn

The Golden Dawn honored gender equality by admitting women to the highest ranks of membership and office. Some were suffragettes and New Women—part of the first wave of modern feminism. A number of extraordinary women became prominent teachers of the Order.

Moina Mathers (1865–1928, born in Switzerland as Mina Bergson) studied at the Slade School of Art in London. Her brother Henri Bergson was a Nobel Prize–winning French philosopher. She married Samuel Mathers in 1890 and changed her name to the more Celtic-sounding *Moina*. A pioneer in the art form of collage and a gifted clairvoyant, Moina was the first person to be initiated into the Order of the Golden Dawn. Her magical motto in the Order embodied her mission to always look forward: *Vestigia Nulla Retrorsum*, meaning "I never retrace my steps." Moina's paintings of Egyptian deities, wall decorations, and other artwork served to adorn the Isis-Urania Temple and illustrate the Order's teachings. Throughout her life, she remained dedicated to her husband and to the goddesses and gods of the pagan world. Moina led the Paris branch of the Golden Dawn for several years after her husband's death in 1918.

Annie Horniman (1860–1937) was a wealthy heiress who built two world-renowned theaters, including Ireland's famous Abbey Theater. Considered a driving force behind the Irish Literary Revival, Horniman was a staunch feminist, fiercely independent and outspoken. Although considered by some of her acquaintances to be overly zealous, fussy, and somewhat undiplomatic, she was by all accounts an excellent administrator and businesswoman. In the occult world, Annie was a skilled astrologer, tarot reader, and ceremonial magician. Her experience in the theatre undoubtedly benefited the staging of Golden Dawn rituals. Annie's Golden Dawn motto was *Fortiter et Recte* ("bravely and justly"), which fittingly expressed the way in which she faced the world around her.

Florence Farr (1860–1917) was a famous actress on the British stage who played leading roles in theatrical works by George Bernard Shaw and William Butler Yeats. Intelligent, self-educated, and doggedly independent, Florence joined the Isis-Urania Temple in 1890 under the motto *Sapientia Sapienti Dona Data* ("Wisdom is a gift given to the wise"). She taught weekly classes in tarot and Enochian magic and wrote a number of esoteric books. Her specialty was spirit vision work, and her experience in the theatre made her a gifted ritualist. In 1894 Florence became head of the London branch of the Order, until she resigned in 1900 to pursue a more Eastern focus.

Maud Gonne (1866–1953) was a gifted actress on the Irish stage, an activist whose fiery speeches incited riots, and one of the founders of Sinn Féin. Her Golden Dawn motto was fittingly *Per Ignem ad Lucem* ("Through fire to the light"). Maud's dislike of the

Masonic structure of the initiation rituals led to her resigning from the Order after a short period of time, although she continued to work with Yeats, Horniman, Farr, and Moina Mathers on ideas for rituals exploring the Celtic Mysteries.

The "golden age" of the original Order lasted only fifteen years. As with any organization involving human beings and their egos, problems eventually developed. Quarrels and power struggles ensued, and by 1903 the original Order of the Golden Dawn had ceased to exist and split into different factions. The work of the Golden Dawn continued in the form of offshoot orders that were established by former members of the original. The two primary offshoots were the *Order of the Alpha et Omega* (A.O.) and the *Order of the Stella Matutina* (S.M.). The A.O. survived until the outbreak of WWII, and the S.M. survived until 1978, when it was officially closed down.

The Ethos of the Tradition

The Golden Dawn was not created to be a religion or to replace one's religion, although religious imagery and spiritual principles play an important role in its activity. Nevertheless, the work of the system can certainly supplement and enhance one's religious experience regardless of the faith the magician practices. Tolerance for all true life-affirming spiritual paths was expected. As the Neophyte is told, "Hold all religions in reverence, for there is none but contains a ray from the ineffable Light you seek."[6] The Golden Dawn was intended to be a Hermetic Society of men and women, a fellowship of like-minded individuals: magicians and occultists, priests and priestesses, who were dedicated to the philosophical, spiritual, and psychic evolution of humanity through the preservation of the ancient, sacred wisdom of the West. The Order was meant to serve as the guardian of this Western spiritual wisdom, keeping its knowledge intact while at the same time preparing and training those aspirants called to the initiatory path of the mysteries.

The symbol of the Golden Dawn is a red cross above a white triangle (figure 1). Regardie explains its implication with eloquence: "Even upon the altar of the Temple are symbols indicating the rise of Light. A red Calvary cross of six squares as symbolic of harmony and equilibrium is placed above a white triangle—the emblem of the Golden Dawn. They form the symbol of the Supernal Sephiroth which are the dynamic life and root of all things, while in man they constitute that triad of spiritual faculties which is the intrinsically pure essence of mind. Hence is the triangle a fitting emblem of the Light. And the place of the Cross above the Triangle suggests not the domination of the sacred spirit, but its equilibration and harmony in the heart of man."[7]

6. Regardie, *The Golden Dawn*, 159.

7. Regardie, *The Golden Dawn*, 19–20.

Figure 1. Cross and Triangle

The Order System

The Golden Dawn order system is based entirely upon a hierarchical structure in which certain knowledge is retained for students who have reached specific grades or levels of achievement in their esoteric training. This is in keeping with the paradigm of a *school,* and the Golden Dawn is a school of the Mysteries that was designed in such a way as to correlate the various grade levels to specific esoteric ideas and cosmic principles. The primary philosophy behind the grade system is the *Qabalah,* a Hebrew mystical system that encompasses knowledge of the divine universe: its fundamental spiritual essence, composition, and evolution. The Qabalah teaches that the universe manifested from deity in ten stages, or emanations, known as the *sephiroth,* considered different aspects of divinity, divine powers, and expressions of God consciousness. The ten sephiroth that form the Qabalistic Tree of Life are listed in table 1.

No.	Name	Translation	Attribute
1.	Kether	The Crown	Oneness, unity
2.	Chokmah	Wisdom	Force, expansion
3.	Binah	Understanding	Form, contraction
4.	Chesed	Mercy	Construction
5.	Geburah	Power	Might, severity
6.	Tiphareth	Beauty	Balance, awareness
7.	Netzach	Victory	Emotion, desire
8.	Hod	Splendor	Intellect, reason
9.	Yesod	Foundation	Astral blueprint, matrix
10.	Malkuth	The Kingdom	Physical manifestation

Table 1. The Sephiroth, with English Translations and Attributes

The grades of the Golden Dawn correspond to the ten sephiroth, but they also have elemental and planetary associations. The titles and basic framework of these grades are taken from those of the Societas Rosicruciana in Anglia, which borrowed them in turn from the degree structure of an eighteenth-century German Rosicrucian group the *Orden des Gold- und Rosenkreuz*, or the Order of the Golden and Rosy Cross.

These ten grades are further divided into separate but interconnected orders. The First (or Outer) Order is the *Hermetic Order of the Golden Dawn*. The Second (or Inner) Order is the *Ordo Rosae Rubeae et Aurea Crucis*, usually referred to as the *R.R. et A.C.* These two Orders function as outer and inner courts of the mysteries. The Third (or Invisible) Order consists of grades that are not attained nor worked by living initiates, although some Golden Dawn groups give out these high titles honorarily. A list of the grades from lowest to highest is given in table 2.

FIRST ORDER: The Order of the Golden Dawn (First Degree of the System)				
Grade	**Symbol**	**Sephirah**	**Element**	**Planet**
Neophyte	⓪=◻0	—	—	—
Zelator	①=◻10	Malkuth	Earth	Earth
Theoricus	②=◻9	Yesod	Air	Luna
Practicus	③=◻8	Hod	Water	Mercury
Philosophus	④=◻7	Netzach	Fire	Venus
The Portal Grade (Second Degree of the System)				
Portal	—		Spirit	—
SECOND ORDER: The R.R. et A.C. (Third Degree of the System)				
Adeptus Minor	⑤=◻6	Tiphareth	—	Sol
Adeptus Major	⑥=◻5	Geburah	—	Mars
Adeptus Exemptus	⑦=◻4	Chesed	—	Jupiter
THIRD ORDER				
Magister Templi	⑧=◻3	Binah	—	Saturn
Magus	⑨=◻2	Chokmah	—	—
Ipsissimus	⑩=◻1	Kether	—	—

Table 2. The Grade Structure of the Hermetic Order of the Golden Dawn

Of all the initiation ceremonies, the Neophyte Ritual stands apart from the rest. Although it is considered a preliminary or probationary rite, hidden within its framework are all the fundamental magical formulae and techniques of the Order. The focus of the Neophyte Ceremony is the attraction of the Divine Light into the Temple by the presiding officers, to be implanted in the aspirant's auric sphere of sensation.

First Order Officers who actively perform the Neophyte Ceremony are *Hierophant* ("initiating priest"), *Hiereus* ("priest"), *Hegemon* ("guide"), *Keryx* ("herald"), *Stolistes* ("preparer"), *Dadouchos* ("torch-bearer"), and *Phylax* ("sentinel"). These Greek titles were derived from those of officiating priests of the ancient Greek mystery religions, such as the Eleusinian mysteries. These seven officers answered to a governing triumvirate known as the Greatly Honoured Chiefs, whose titles are *Praemonstrator* (the "prophesier," or teacher), the *Imperator* (or "commander"), and *Cancellarius* (or "chancellor," recorder).

The mythological narrative that serves as the magical backdrop and astral matrix for the Neophyte Ceremony is the Egyptian legend of the Hall of Judgment as described in the 125th chapter of the Egyptian *Book of the Dead*. This depicts the "Weighing of the Soul," in which the deceased (represented by the candidate) is brought into the Hall of Truth and judged as to his or her worthiness to receive the infinite Light. In this setting, the ritual enactment of the Weighing of the Soul represents the purification of the candidate before his or her reception into the Order.

This initiation is a process of spiritual alchemy wherein the Neophyte is the base material (the lead) that is to be transmuted into gold by the Work of transmutation hinted at by the Hierophant's speech to the candidate:

> The Voice of my undying and Secret Soul said unto me—"Let me enter the Path of Darkness and, peradventure, there shall I find the Light. I am the only Being in an Abyss of Darkness; from an Abyss of Darkness came I forth ere my birth, from the silence of a Primal Sleep."
>
> And the Voice of Ages answered unto my Soul—"I am He who formulates in Darkness—the Light that shineth in Darkness, yet the Darkness comprehendeth it not." [8]

Further initiations into the elemental grades are analogous to the alchemical processes of separation and purification.

The First Order consists of the grades from Neophyte through Philosophus. The grades from Zelator through Philosophus are known as the *elemental* grades and are each attributed to one of the four elements of fire, water, air, and earth. Each is also expressed through a different mythological narrative drawn from the Western Esoteric Tradition. Advancement through these levels is designed to expose the initiate to the elemental principles of nature as they exist out in the greater universe of the Divine and within the psychological makeup of the magician. These four principles are characterized as distinct sections of the subconscious mind and the auric sphere, and the Golden Dawn tradition symbolizes them collectively by the Egyptian god Osiris who was killed, dismembered, reassembled, and resurrected into a pure, spiritual form.

8. Regardie, *The Golden Dawn*, 151–152.

· · · · · · · ·

It is within the grades of the First Order where the students learn the language, symbols, and principles of magic; the Qabalistic Tree of Life; the letters of the Hebrew alphabet; the attributes of the elements, planets, and zodiacal signs; geomancy; gematria, or Hebrew numerology; divine Hebrew godnames, angelic hierarchies, and words of power; principles of alchemy; the Qabalistic parts of the Soul; the cards of the tarot; and so forth. Students must commit the rudiments of occult knowledge to memory before advancing to the performance of practical ritual magic. *That* is the domain of the Second Order.

Between the First and Second Orders is an additional grade of the *Portal*, which is a probationary period between the Inner and Outer Courts of the mysteries. This grade is attributed to the fifth element of spirit, which crowns and completes the other four elements. Here the initiate's assignment is to unify and assimilate the elements of the psyche that had been individually examined and cleansed during the work of the First Order.

Admission to the Second Order is by invitation only. The Inner Order consists of grades from Adeptus Minor to Adeptus Exemptus, and it is here that the initiate begins the practice of ceremonial magic, both in groups of one's peers as well as in solo work. The grade of Adeptus Minor (the "Lesser Adept") is where the majority of the published magical work of the Golden Dawn system takes place. The higher grades are divided into various subgrades that mirror the grades of the Outer Order: Neophyte Adeptus Minor (NAM), Zelator Adeptus Minor (ZAM), Theoricus Adeptus Minor (ThAM), and so on.

While the First Order can be seen as Osirian in emphasis, the Second Order is Rosicrucian. And while other Rosicrucian groups are oriented solely toward research or mysticism, the Golden Dawn's Inner Order is the preeminent *magical* manifestation of the Rosicrucian impulse. In 1892 Samuel Mathers finished the elaborate initiation ceremony into the ⑤=[6] grade of Adeptus Minor. Based on the legend of Christian Rosencreutz as presented in the *Fama Fraternitatis*, the Adeptus Minor Ceremony involves the discovery of C.R.C.'s tomb, known as the Vault of the Adepti (figure 2). Aided no doubt by the artistry of his wife, Moina, Mathers designed a highly elaborate version of the mystic Rosicrucian vault to serve as the primary temple and ritual chamber of the Second Order. All grade initiations pertaining to the R.R. et A.C. require this seven-sided chamber. This sacred space is reconsecrated once every year on or around the day of Corpus Christi, a Catholic feast day held in honor of the Eucharist. This tradition, adopted by the Second Order, was started by earlier Rosicrucians who referred to Corpus Christi secretively as "Day C."

Figure 2. A Modern-Day Vault of the Adepti

The Adeptus Minor Ceremony is impressive and eloquent. The mythological setting for the ritual is the reenactment of the death of Christian Rosencreutz and the resurrection of the Sacred Rosicrucian knowledge. The temple is opened by the officiating Adepti. The aspirant enters, announces his desire to be admitted into the Vault, and is rebuffed. Then the aspirant is sent to the anti-chamber, where he or she is divested of all insignia before returning to undertake an arduous period of trial and tribulation, including a symbolic crucifixion accompanied by the recitation of a potent and binding obligation. After this, the legend of Christian Rosencreutz is recounted to the aspirant. In due course, the door to the Vault is opened and the aspirant is admitted into the mystical seven-sided tomb, where the body of C.R.C., represented by the Chief Adept, is discovered. The secrets of the Vault, including its elaborate symbolism, are finally explained. Some of the prayers and speeches of this ceremony are hauntingly expressive of the aspirant's spiritual quest:

> Buried with that Light in a mystical death, rising again in a mystical resurrection,
> cleansed and purified through Him our Master, O Brother of the Cross and the Rose.
> Like Him, O Adepts of all ages have ye toiled. Like Him have ye suffered tribulation.
> Poverty, torture and death have ye passed through. They have been but the purification

of the Gold. In the alembic of thine heart, through the athanor of affliction, seek thou the true stone of the Wise.[9]

The $\textcircled{5} = \boxed{6}$ ceremony often has a powerful effect on those who experience it. According to Arthur Edward Waite, the ritual was quite inspiring: "It could not be denied that the culminating Grade, as the system was then developed, had the root matter of a greater scheme than had ever dawned in the consciousness of any maker of Masonic degrees under any Grand Lodge or Chapter, Conclave or Preceptory, in the whole wide world."[10]

Such sentiments explain why the Golden Dawn system has continued to grow and expand its influence far beyond the life span of the original Order and its immediate offshoots.

Dion Fortune

One of the best-known members to have emerged from the Alpha et Omega, Dion Fortune (born Violet Mary Firth, 1890–1946), was a trained psychotherapist and a Co-Mason. She joined the London Temple of the A.O. in 1919 under the motto *Deo Non Fortuna* ("By God, not by chance"). Beginning in 1921, she experimented with trance mediumship that culminated in the town of Glastonbury with archaeologist and psychical researcher Frederick Bligh Bond. While working in Glastonbury, Fortune met Christian occultist Charles Loveday. After a series of inner plane workings, Fortune, Loveday, and their coworkers had gathered enough material to found their own magical order, the *Fraternity of the Inner Light*, in 1924. This group would remain Fortune's esoteric focal point for the rest of her days. In 1925 she and Loveday were also involved in the Christian Mystical Lodge of the Theosophical Society, from which she resigned in 1927. This was also the year when she married Thomas Penry Evans and was expelled from the A.O. by Moina Mathers for publishing a series of articles that concerned the A.O. leadership. The fraternity she founded later changed its name to the *Society of the Inner Light* and is still active today.

Under her pen name, which was adapted from her magical motto in the A.O., Dion Fortune wrote several works of occult fiction, including *The Demon Lover, Moon Magic,* and *The Sea Priestess*. She also wrote a series of important texts on magic, including *The Cosmic Doctrine, Esoteric Orders and Their Work, Sane Occultism, Applied Magic,* and *The Mystical Qabalah*.

---

9. Regardie, *The Golden Dawn*, 309.
10. Waite, *Shadows of Life and Thought*, 161.

Essential Concepts

The range of studies undertaken by members of the various grades was quite broad. However, a number of themes and basic principles can be derived from the Order's teachings:

- *Macrocosm and Microcosm.* There is a connection between a higher divine reality called the *Macrocosm*, or the "Greater Universe," and the earthly realm of the Microcosm, the "Small Universe" of human beings. As above, so below.

- *Ultimate Divinity.* The Golden Dawn is ultimately monotheistic, although it conceives of the Ultimate Divinity as emanating itself through a multitude of forms, aspects, characteristics, and manifestations. Although the system may appear to be outwardly polytheistic, all deities are thought to be the various faces and rich expressions of the ultimate Divine Unity.

- *Immanence and Transcendence.* Ultimate Divinity is both immanent (within everything) and transcendent (beyond everything). The universe is completely divine, living, and animated.

- *The Universal Order.* The nature of the universe is ultimately good and constructive and leans toward balance. Evil is created from a state of imbalance.

- *The Way of Return.* Humanity has become separated from the Divine through *involution*, the process by which the spirit manifests into matter. Humans seek "the Way of Return" back to unity with the Divine through *evolution*, the process by which spirit reconnects with Divinity. Involution and evolution are both natural and necessary polar opposites in the process of creation. Although spiritual teachers can provide guidance, each individual aspirant must ultimately tread the way back to the Divine alone.

- *Hierarchies and Intermediaries.* Divine beings, deities, archangels, angels, and spirits act as links in a chain, the rungs on a ladder that aid the magician in climbing and descending the planes into higher realms of Being. Golden Dawn magicians are taught to always invoke the Highest first.

- *The Celestial Pattern.* Because the Macrocosm and Microcosm are linked, the individual human soul and aura contain a reflection of the celestial powers. These can be used to cause magical change through the manipulations of the aura and the Astral Light.

- *The Work.* As part of the discipline needed to return to the Divine, human beings must learn to understand the invisible realms that lie hidden behind the manifest universe. To that end, the Work embraces the passive practices of mysticism and active processes of magic. Armed with knowledge gained from esoteric practices, the fundamental objective of the magician is to achieve union with the Divine, a goal often called the *Great Work*.

Paul Foster Case

Paul Foster Case (1885–1954) was the best-known American member of the Alpha et Omega. In his early years, Case worked as a musician and a musical director in theatrical productions, which led to an interest in stage magic. A keen interest in the tarot resulted in his publication in 1916 of an excellent series of articles on *The Secret Doctrine of the Tarot* in the occult magazine *The Word*. In 1918 Case met Michael James Whitty, the editor of *Azoth Magazine* and Cancellarius of the Thoth-Hermes Temple in Chicago. Case joined the Chicago group and quickly advanced through the grades, becoming the Sub-Prae-monstrator of the Temple. His magical motto was *Perseverantia* ("perseverance").

Shortly thereafter, Case and Whitty worked on a text that formed the core of Case's excellent little book of tarot card meditations, *The Book of Tokens*. Whitty died in 1920 and Case succeeded him as editor of *Azoth*. It was during the same year that Case was initiated into the Second Order. Personal problems within the temple, combined with differences of opinion with Moina Mathers, resulted in Case resigning from the Order in 1921. In 1923 he created a correspondence course for his *School of Ageless Wisdom* in Boston. A few years later he moved to Los Angeles and founded a new esoteric school for practical occultism called the *Builder of the Adytum* (B.O.T.A.), which is active to this day. Case wrote a number of important books on tarot, Qabalah, Freemasonry, Rosicrucian-ism, alchemy, and magic.

Practical Magic in the Outer Order

Traditionally only one magical rite was ever given to Outer Order students for their own personal use—the *Lesser Ritual of the Pentagram*. The figure of the pentagram is undoubtedly the most important symbol in modern ceremonial magic. While this figure has been used in the Western occult tradition since the time of the Greek philosopher Pythagoras, the modern attribution of the elements to the five points of the pentagram in the manner most commonly used by magicians today was introduced by the Golden Dawn. The elements are assigned to the directions in accordance with the "four winds" attributions of the ancients: air–east, fire–south, water–west, and earth–north (figure 3).

The ritual opens with the Qabalistic Cross, vibrating four Divine Hebrew names and establishing a cross of Divine Light within the aura of the practitioner. The gestures given are similar to the Christian Cross, and the words are taken from the last few phrases of the Lord's Prayer, which is in turn based upon a Qabalistic Hebrew prayer. This Cross is Qabalistic because it is associated with the sephiroth of Kether, Malkuth, Geburah, Chesed, and Tiphareth. These sephirotic energy centers are activated within the magician's auric sphere by physical gestures, visualizations, and vibration of names and words of power. These spheres also represent a balancing of the four elements

• • • • • • • •

within the magician's aura: Kether—air, Malkuth—earth, Geburah—fire, and Chesed—water. And although the name of Tiphareth is not vibrated, the balancing element of spirit is indicated by the placing of the hands over the heart.

Figure 3. Elemental Attributions of the Pentagram

After establishing the Qabalistic Cross within the aura, the figure of the pentagram is then traced and visualized at the four cardinal directions, combined with the intonation or vibration of specific Divine Hebrew names. Following this, the magician calls upon four mighty archangels associated with the elements while imaging their majestic forms on the astral. The magician ends the ritual by repeating the Qabalistic Cross.

More than any other ritual, the Golden Dawn's Lesser Ritual of the Pentagram has been adopted and employed by magicians and occult groups from all across the spectrum of contemporary magical practice. By far the best known of the Golden Dawn's techniques, this little ritual is actually quite powerful and contains most of the techniques used in more complicated magical work. Simply put, it is one of the staples of Golden Dawn practice. "Those who regard this ritual as a mere device to invoke or banish spirits are unworthy to possess it. Properly understood, it is Medicine of Metals and the Stone of the Wise."[11]

There are two forms of this ritual, one for invoking magical energies into sacred space and the other for banishing the same. Respectively, they are the *Lesser Invoking Ritual of the Pentagram* (LIRP) and the *Lesser Banishing Ritual of the Pentagram* (LBRP). A banishing ritual is often performed as a preliminary cleansing rite or a prelude to more complex rituals, to clear the area of astral cobwebs beforehand. An invoking ritual has the opposite effect—it is designed to summon forces into the temple space. Traditionally, students were taught to perform the invoking version in the morning and the banishing in the evening. However, many students employ the LIRP to open a magical working and the LBRP to close the working down.

---

11. Crowley, *Collected Works of Aleister Crowley*, 204.

The LIRP uses the invoking form of the Lesser Pentagram, while the LBRP uses the banishing form (figure 4).

Figure 4. Lesser Invoking and Banishing Pentagrams

The Lesser Banishing Ritual of the Pentagram

Use your index figure, a black-handled dagger, or the Outer Wand of Double Power to trace the figures.

1. *The Qabalistic Cross.* Go to the eastern side (or the center) of the temple and perform the Qabalistic Cross:
   - Stand and face east. Imagine a brilliant white light touching the top of your head. Reach up with the index finger or the white end of the Outer Wand of Double Power to connect with this light and bring it to the forehead.
   - Touch the forehead and vibrate **"ATAH"** (*Ah-tah*, meaning "Thou art").
   - Touch the breast and bring the white end of the wand or index finger down until it touches the heart or abdominal area, pointing down slightly toward the ground. Imagine the light descending from the forehead to the feet. Vibrate **"MALKUTH"** (*Mal-kooth*, meaning "the Kingdom").
   - Touch the right shoulder and visualize a point of light there. Vibrate **"VE-GEBURAH"** (*veh-Ge-boor-ah*, meaning "the Power").
   - Touch the left shoulder and visualize a point of light there. See the horizontal shaft of light extending from the opposite shoulder to join this point of light. Vibrate **"VE-GEDULAH"** (*veh-Ge-doo-lah*, meaning "the Glory").
   - Imagine a completed cross of light running from head to feet and shoulder to shoulder. Bring the hands outward, away from the body, and finally bring them together again, clasped on the breast as if praying. See a point of light shining at the center of the brilliant cross. Vibrate **"LE-OLAHM"** (bow your head) **"AMEN"** (*Lay-oh-lahm, Ah-men*, meaning "Forever, unto the Ages").

2. *The Pentagrams.* Trace a large Lesser Banishing Pentagram. Thrust the implement through the center of the pentagram and vibrate **"YHVH"** (*Yod-hey-vav-hey*.) Keep your arm extended throughout; never let it drop. The pentagrams should be visualized in white light.

3. Turn and walk clockwise to the south and trace the same pentagram there. Charge the figure as before, intoning **"ADONAI"** (*Ah-doh-nye*).

4. Go to the west and trace the same pentagram. Charge it with **"EHEIEH"** (*Eh-hey-yay*).

5. Go to the north and draw the same pentagram, this time intoning the word **"AGLA"** (*Ah-gah-lah*).

6. *Invocation of the Archangels.* Keep the arm extended. Turn to face the east. Extend both arms out in the form of a Tau cross (a T-shape) and say, **"Before me, RAPHAEL."** Visualize before you the great archangel of elemental air rising out of the clouds, dressed in flowing yellow and violet robes and carrying a caduceus wand

7. Behind you, visualize another figure and say, **"Behind me, GABRIEL."** See the winged archangel of elemental water stepping out of the sea like the goddess Venus, dressed in robes of blue and orange, with cup in hand.

8. To your right, see another winged figure, the archangel of elemental fire, dressed in flaming red and green robes and carrying a mighty sword. Say, **"On my right hand, MICHAEL."**

9. See the great winged archangel of elemental earth at your left, rising up from the vegetation of the ground in earth-toned robes of citrine, olive, russet, and black, holding stems of ripened wheat. Say, **"On my left hand, URIEL."**

10. Then say, **"For about me flames the pentagram, and in the column shines the Six-Rayed Star."**

11. Close by repeating the Qabalistic Cross as in the beginning.

Practical Magic in the Inner Order

It is within the Second Order, the R.R. et A.C., where the real work of ceremonial magic begins on a personal, experiential level. Whereas the First Order is a school that teaches students the fundamentals of esoteric knowledge and prepares them for magical work, the Inner Order is where the student puts what he or she has learned to practical use. Adepts build and consecrate their own magical tools (figure 5), write and perform their own rituals based on traditional Golden Dawn formulae, create and consecrate talismans, practice techniques of skrying and spirit vision work, build and assume the images of godforms, and perform a wide range of advanced theurgical techniques.

Fueling the magic of the Order are practical, active methods for creating magical change in the Astral Light, the divine matrix that lies behind the mundane veneer of our physical world. Practitioners are taught procedures of meditation, visualization, vibration of godnames and words of power, dramatic invocation, focused intention and willpower, aura control, and the projection of energy. All of these techniques are used to hone the magician's skills and psychic faculties; they are powerful modes for unlocking latent spiritual powers that most humans can access only through practice and perseverance.

• • • • • • • •

Figure 5. The Elemental Tools of an Adept

Color is extremely important in the higher grades of the Golden Dawn system, because it is through the proper application of color, as well as through sounds and symbols ("names and images"), that the magician is able to forge a magical link with the divine intelligences.

In addition to creating an elaborate system of color scales, the GD utilized what it called *flashing colors*. These are essentially the same as complementary colors used by artists.

Complementary colors are two colors that lie directly opposite each other on a standard artist's color wheel. Flashing colors placed next to each other produce an optical "pulsing" effect that is helpful to the magician's practice.

The Exercise of the Middle Pillar is one of the better-known methods for establishing the central sephiroth of the Qabalistic Tree of Life within the magician's aura, or "sphere of sensation." By invoking the powers of the holy sephiroth with the auric sphere, the magician is able

• • • • • • • •

to utilize them for increased balance, vitality, and awareness. It also strengthens the aura against outside influences. Variants of this rite are used for a number of different purposes, including healing, the consecration of talismans, and preparation for godform assumption and communication with the Higher Self. Like the Pentagram Ritual, the Middle Pillar Exercise has often been co-opted by a wide range of modern spiritual traditions without any reference to its Golden Dawn roots.

In the basic exercise, the magician visualizes the Middle Pillar superimposed over his or her body, specifically the four sephiroth—Kether, Tiphareth, Yesod, and Malkuth—along with the so-called "invisible sephirah" of Daath, which is used here as a conjunction of the powers of Chokmah and Binah (figure 6). The godnames of these five energy centers are vibrated a number of times in conjunction with the visualizations.

Israel Regardie held that this simple exercise can increase one's field of attention, aid in the achievement of balance and equilibrium, and provide the student with a remarkable wellspring of power and spiritual perception. Practice of the Middle Pillar Exercise is concurrently stimulating and relaxing—it releases points of tension in both mind and body, often leaving one feeling joyful, rested, energized, and aligned with the divine forces inherent to the Qabalistic Tree of Life.

The Exercise of the Middle Pillar

This exercise can be performed either standing, sitting, or lying down. Begin with closed eyes and rhythmic breathing.

1. Imagine a sphere of white light just above your head. Vibrate the name **"EHEIEH"** (*Eh-hey-yay*) three times or more until it is the only thought in your conscious mind.

2. Imagine a shaft of light descending from your Kether (crown) center to your Daath center at the nape of the neck. Form a sphere of light at the Daath center. Vibrate the name **"YHVH ELOHIM"** (*Yode-heh-vav-heh El-oh-heem*). Intone the name the exact number of times that you vibrated the previous name.

3. Bring a shaft of light down from the Daath center to the Tiphareth center around your heart. Form a sphere of light there. Vibrate the name **"YHVH ELOAH VE-DAATH"** (*Yode-heh-vav-heh El-oh-ah v'-Dah-ath*) the same number of times as before.

4. See the shaft of light descending from the Tiphareth (heart) center into the Yesod center in the groin region. Imagine a sphere of light formed there. Intone the name **"SHADDAI EL CHAI"** (*Shah-dye El-Ch-eye*) the same number of times as before.

5. Visualize the shaft of light descending from the Yesod (groin) center into your Malkuth center at the feet and ankles. Vibrate the name **"ADONAI HA-ARETZ"** (*Ah-doe-nye ha-Ah-retz*) the same number of times as before.

· · · · · · · ·

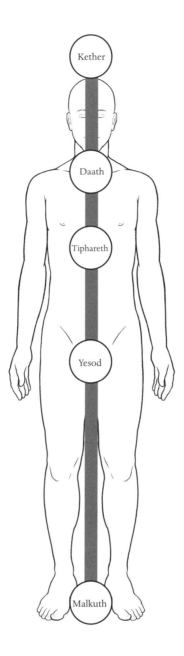

Figure 6. The Exercise of the Middle Pillar

6. Imagine the Middle Pillar complete. Then circulate the light you have brought down through the Middle Pillar around the outside of your body to strengthen your aura. (Perform each circulation a number of times.)

7. Using the cycles of rhythmic breathing, bring the light down one side of the body and up the other, from Kether to Malkuth and back to Kether. Exhale and visualize the light

· · · · · · · ·

descending the left side of the body. Inhale and imagine the light ascending the right side of the body back to Kether.

8. After performing this for a short space of time, imagine the ribbon of light descending from Kether down the front of your body to Malkuth and rising up your back, returning again to Kether. Inhale for rising, exhale for descending.

9. Still employing rhythmic breathing, visualize the sphere of Malkuth, then see the light rise again in a ribbon that spirals around the shaft of the Middle Pillar in the center of your body from Malkuth to Kether. When it reaches Kether, imagine a shower of light cascading down the outside of your body as it descends to Malkuth again. Circulate the light in this manner for some time.

10. Finally, focus some of the energy in Tiphareth, the heart center, before ending the exercise.

———

The practice of magic involves the invocation of the various forces and energies that comprise the building blocks of the manifest universe. Within the Western Esoteric Tradition, these forces are categorized as the elements, the Qabalistic sephiroth, the planets, and the zodiacal signs. The Golden Dawn developed a unique system for summoning and releasing these energies using the lineal figures of the pentagram and hexagram. The Pentagram Ritual of the First Order was expanded to include a series of separate pentagrams for invoking and banishing the five elements of fire, water, air, earth, and spirit, in addition to the twelve signs of the zodiac. Various forms of the hexagram are used to attract and dismiss the seven planets of the ancients and the ten sephiroth of the Tree of Life. Employing these lineal figures resulted in a framework for working Qabalistic and planetary magic that is systematic, logical, precise, and adaptable to the magician's specific objectives.

Figure 7. Planetary Attributions of the Hexagram

The hexagram is the symbol of the *Ruach Elohim*, or "Spirit of God." This Spirit has two essential principles—masculine and feminine—represented by the triangles of fire and water in perfect equilibrium. The usual form of the hexagram is the well-known "Star of David" formation, showing the sephirotic ordering of the planets. The six points of the figure are attributed

· · · · · · · ·

to the sephiroth on the Tree of Life and their planetary correspondences (figure 7). The two triangles of the hexagram are traced in a clockwise motion to invoke and anticlockwise to banish.

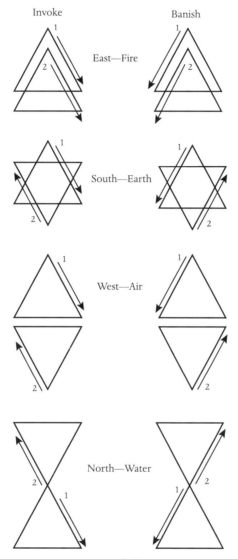

Figure 8. Four Forms of the Lesser Hexagram

Another standard ritual, the *Lesser Ritual of the Hexagram*, is used to establish a protective magic circle of planetary or sephirotic energies in the temple. This ritual is unique in its makeup because it employs four different variations on the basic form of the hexagram (figure 8). These four forms are based on the symbolic images of the elements: the Hexagram of Fire resembles flames, that of earth looks like the pentacle, that of air bears a likeness to a diamond or spear-head, and that of water resembles a cup. Although they are referred to as the Hexagrams of Fire, Water, Air, and

• • • • • • • •

Earth, they are not used to invoke these elements. Instead, the four hexagram forms reflect the presence of the planetary forces in the realm of the elements on the astral plane. Pentagram rituals are terrestrial and elemental; hexagram rituals are celestial and sephirotic.

There are three parts to the Lesser Ritual of the Hexagram. It opens with the Qabalistic Cross, then proceeds to the tracing of the four hexagrams, and ends with the Analysis of the Keyword, which refers to the letters *I.N.R.I.*, an important acronym of the cycle of life, death, and resurrection or rebirth connected to a host of religious and magical concepts. One of the power words emphasized in this ritual is *ARARITA*, a notariqon or acronym constructed from the Hebrew sentence *Achad Rosh Achdotho Rosh Ichudo Temurahzo Achad*, meaning "One is his beginning, One is his individuality, his permutation is One."

The Lesser Invoking Ritual of the Hexagram

This is the general-purpose Lesser Invoking Ritual of the Hexagram. It is not differentiated for any single planet or force. This is an appropriate ritual for creating a magic circle wherein a balance of all planetary or sephirotic forces is desired.

1. *Opening.* Face east and perform the Qabalistic Cross.

2. *The Hexagrams.* Go to the east. Trace the Lesser Invoking Hexagram of Fire toward the east. Thrust through the center of the figure and vibrate the word **"ARARITA."**

3. Go to the south and trace the Lesser Invoking Hexagram of Earth toward the south. Charge the center of the figure as before and vibrate **"ARARITA."**

4. Go to the west and trace the Lesser Invoking Hexagram of Air toward the west. Energize it by thrusting through the center of the figure and vibrate as before, **"ARARITA."**

5. Go to the north and trace the Lesser Invoking Hexagram of Water toward the north. Thrust and intone as before, **"ARARITA."**

6. *The Analysis of the Keyword.* Return to the east and perform the Analysis of the Keyword:
   - Extend your arms out in the shape of the Tau Cross (a T-shape), palms facing forward. Say with feeling, **"I.N.R.I."** (Pronounce each letter.) **"Yod Nun Resh Yod"** (*Yode-noon-raysh-yode*). As you pronounce the names of the Hebrew letters, trace them in the air before you, from right to left.
   - Return to the Tau Cross position and say, **"Virgo, Isis, Mighty Mother! Scorpio, Apophis, Destroyer! Sol, Osiris, Slain and Risen! Isis, Apophis, Osiris!"**
   - Through the previous oration, gradually raise the arms and lift the head upward. Vibrate strongly and slowly, **"IAO."**
   - Return to the stance of the Tau Cross, saying, **"The Sign of Osiris Slain."**
   - Put your right arm straight up in the air from the shoulder. The left arm should be straight out from the left shoulder so that the position of the two arms together resemble

the letter *L*. Hands are to be open flat, with palms forward. Turn your head so that you are looking over your left arm. Say, **"L, the Sign of the Mourning of Isis."**

- Raise the arms overhead to an angle of sixty degrees so that they form the letter *V*. Keep the arms straight and the palms facing forward. Throw the head back and say, **"V, the Sign of Typhon and Apophis."**
- Cross the arms on the chest to form the letter *X*. Bow your head and say, **"X, the Sign of Osiris Risen."**
- Say slowly and powerfully, **"L.V.X."** (Pronounce each letter separately and give the sign of each as you do so.) Say, **"LUX"** (*lukes*).
- Remain in the Sign of Osiris Slain and say, **"The Light …** (hold arms out in the Tau Cross position for a moment, then re-cross them again on the chest) **… of the Cross."**

———

One of the standard symbols worn by a Golden Dawn Adept is the Rose Cross Lamen, an emblem of the many occult forces utilized in the Order's work (figure 9). Within the magician's personal practice, the *Ritual of the Rose Cross* epitomized the Rosicrucian nature of the Golden Dawn's Inner Order. This rite utilizes the *Pentagrammaton*, or divine "five-lettered name," refer- ring to the Hebrew name of Jesus, *Yeheshuah* (YHShVH), as rendered by Christian Qabalists of the Renaissance. It is specifically the ineffable name of the Tetragrammaton (YHVH) with the letter Shin placed in the center of the name to represent the descent of the quintessential spirit into the realm of the four elements. Along with *Eth* (essence), *Ruach* (breath), and *Eheieh* (I am), the Pentagrammaton is one of the Hebrew names closely connected with the element of spirit.

Figure 9. The Rose Cross Lamen of the Adept

In this ritual, the figure of the Rose Cross is traced at six points: in the cross-quarters as well as zenith and nadir, above and below (figure 10). A seventh, central point is formed by the magician, standing in the center of the crosses at the end of the rite. The Ritual of the Rose Cross is a straightforward rite for soothing disruptive forces, both external and internal. The cross-quarters—southeast, southwest, northeast, and northwest—are areas where the elemental forces meet, blend, and sometimes clash with each other. Tracing the crosses in conjunction with the vibration of the Pentagrammaton at these points helps to calm and settle these energies, invoking balance and equilibrium wherever and whenever it is needed.

Together, the symbols of the rose joined to the cross present a multitude of ideas: the union of the divine masculine and divine feminine, regeneration and redemption, the blessings of the Christ impulse and consciousness, and strength through sacrifice. Additionally, it depicts the four points in space, with a fifth at the center. Like the pentagram, the Rose Cross is indicative of spirit ruling over matter, but while the pentagram depicts spirit as the head ruling over matter, the Rose Cross portrays spirit permeating the very *heart* of matter. The pentagram and the Rose Cross are both symbols of protection, but while the pentagram is more appropriate for summoning and dismissing specific energies, the Rose Cross is particularly suited for meditation, protection, balancing, blessing, and healing.

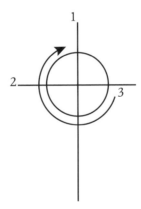

Figure 10. Tracing the Rose Cross

The Ritual of the Rose Cross

The room should be clear of any obstructions and the altar should be moved aside. The only implement needed will be a stick of incense. A number of other options are also available, including the Outer Wand of Double Power, the Lotus Wand, the Rainbow Wand, or a Rose Cross Wand.

1. *Opening.* Face east and perform the Qabalistic Cross.

2. *Rose Crosses.* Go to the southeast (SE) corner of the room and face outward. Trace a large cross and circle there with the incense or wand (figure 11). As you draw the cross, visualize

it in a golden light. The circle should be imagined as flaming red. While tracing this symbol, vibrate the name **"YEHESHUAH."** On the last syllable, thrust through the center of the circled cross, charging it.

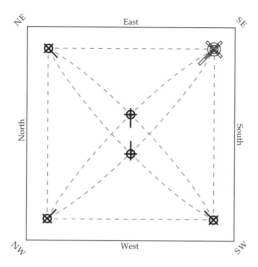

Figure 11. Movements in the Rose Cross Ritual

3. Keep the tip of the implement at the level of the center of the cross and walk to the southwest (SW) corner of the room. Draw the cross and circle (rose) as before and thrust the implement through the center of the figure, intoning, **"YEHESHUAH."**

4. Move to the northwest (NW). Trace the figure and intone, **"YEHESHUAH."**

5. Move to the northeast (NE). Trace the figure and intone, **"YEHESHUAH."**

6. Return to the SE and complete the circle. Touch the head of the implement to the cross already drawn there, but do not retrace or intone the name.

7. Now move diagonally across the room toward the NW, holding the implement high, but stop in the center of the temple and make the Rose Cross directly above your head. Vibrate the name **"YEHESHUAH"** as before.

8. With the implement held straight up in the air, walk to the NW corner of the room. Touch the tip of the implement to the center of the cross already formulated there. Do not retrace the cross or intone the name.

9. Move diagonally across the room again toward the SE, but lower your implement and stop in the center of the temple. Trace the Rose Cross below you and vibrate the name **"YEHESHUAH."**

10. Bring the tip of the implement up and continue to walk to the SE corner. Touch the tip of the implement to the center of the Rose Cross already traced there. Do not retrace or intone.

11. Move clockwise to the SW and touch the head of the implement to the cross already traced there.

12. Walk diagonally toward the NE, but stop in the middle of the room to touch the center of the cross above your head. Intone the name **"YEHESHUAH."**

13. Continue on to the NE and simply touch the implement to the center of the cross already formulated there.

14. Move diagonally across the room toward the SW, but stop in the middle of the temple to touch the cross below you. Vibrate the name **"YEHESHUAH."**

15. Continue on to the SW corner and simply touch the center of the cross already formulated there.

16. Move clockwise and link up with all the crosses by simply touching their centers with the wand (NW, NE, and SE). No need to intone as you do so.

17. Upon returning to the SE, the site of the first cross, touch the center and pause. Then retrace the golden cross over the original, only much larger. Trace a large circle and vibrate **"YEHESHUAH"** while tracing the lower half of the red circle (figure 12). Vibrate **"YEHOVASHAH"** while tracing the upper half of the red circle.

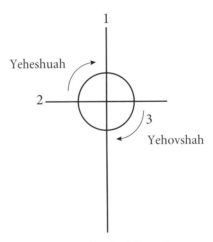

Figure 12. The Final Rose Cross

18. Walk clockwise to the center of the room. Observe all six Rose Crosses surrounding you, all connected by ribbons of light.

Spirit Vision

One important area of magical work in the Second Order is skrying, a method of clairvoyance also known as *spirit vision*. Within the Golden Dawn tradition, skrying and astral projection can be described as forms of self-hypnosis that use symbols as portals into the astral realm in order to effect changes in consciousness. From these higher levels of awareness, the magician often tries to see the underlying causes of things—to work at a problem from a higher angle or perspective—to get inside the machinery of the universe and see just what makes it tick.

The Second Order describes three such methods of clairvoyance, although they are not easily distinguished from one another. These include *skrying in the spirit vision* (or simply *skrying*), *traveling in the spirit vision* (astral traveling or astral projection), and *rising on the planes*. These three techniques can be described as *seeing, traveling,* and *rising*, although they can all be described generally as spirit vision workings. These are controlled astral visions: meaningful and intense experiences that are completely understandable. In these visions, the seer maintains complete control over his or her powers of choice, willpower, and judgment. Through these experiences, the magician is able to reach the deepest levels of what Carl Jung called the *collective unconscious* or what Hermetic philosophers called the *Anima Mundi*, the Soul of the World.

The Qabalah teaches that everything in the universe is created or prefabricated in the astral world of Yetzirah before it manifests in the physical world of Assiah. The astral plane is a level of reality that is higher than the physical world but lower than the divine world. It is a place that is in between: a domain of reflections, images, dreams, and visions. It is sometimes called the Treasure-house of Images and is said to contain the Akashic Records or the Akashic Library. This is a realm comprised of all the memories and experiences of humanity over the course of history, embedded within the substance of the ether.

Through spirit vision work, the magician views or enters the astral world and interacts with angels, spirits, and other entities—working with those archetypes that exist as a part of his own psychic makeup. But he is also working with the elementals and spirits as they exist out in the greater universe. To interact with one is to interact with the other. With skill and practice, the seer undergoes an intense daydream-like experience during which visions are seen and information obtained.

Golden Dawn spirit vision work is usually done by using a skrying symbol. This can be virtually anything: elemental or alchemical triangles, tarot cards, astrological symbols, geomantic tetragrams, sigils, Enochian pyramids, etc. All of these symbols may be used as astral doorways for visionary work, as well as tools for training clairvoyance and other psychic faculties. Traditionally the Golden Dawn employed a series of *tattva* cards borrowed from Eastern Theosophy and Hindu sources for this purpose. These are a series of emblems that conform to the five basic elements correlated to specific colors and shapes (table 3).

· · · · · · · ·

Tattva Name	Shape	Color	Element
Akasa	Oval/egg	Black	Spirit
Tejas	Triangle	Red	Fire
Apas	Crescent	Silver	Water
Vayu	Circle	Blue	Air
Prithivi	Square	Yellow	Earth

Table 3. The Tattvas and Their Correspondences

The five basic tattvas are used to create twenty compound or elementally mixed tattvas, which are symbolized by placing a small image of one of the tattvas inside that of a larger one. The three compound tattvas shown in figure 13 are taken from a set of tattva cards created by Israel Regardie and show the mixed emblems for Earth of Air, Spirit of Fire, and Fire of Earth.

The Order devised a method for using skrying symbols in conjunction with a common optical effect known as *negative after-images*, a phenomenon that dovetails perfectly with the Order's teachings on flashing colors. Negative after-images are the patches of complementary color formed in the retina of the eye by prolonged exposure of the eye to colors of high saturation. The after-image continues to appear in one's vision after exposure to the color ceases. In Golden Dawn spirit vision work, the transition between the symbol and its after-image is used as a trigger for the opening of a portal into the astral world.

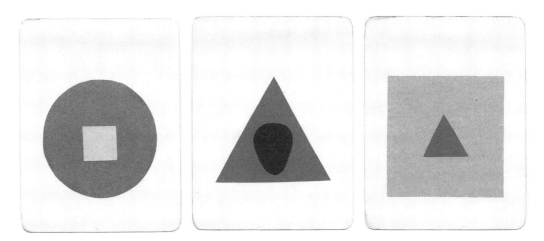

Figure 13. Israel Regardie's Tattva Cards

Florence Farr and Elaine Simpson briefly described their method and personal experience of a skrying vision in a side lecture labeled "Flying Roll No. IV," entitled "An Example of Mode of Attaining to Spirit Vision and What was seen by Two Adepti":

Rise, and perform the Qabalistic Cross and prayer. Then proceed to contemplation of some object, say a Tarot Trump. […] In this case you should have given previous study to the card, as to its symbolism, coloring, analogies, etc. […] Deeply sink into the abstract ideal of the card. […] Consider all the symbolism of the Tarot Card, then all that is implied by its letters, number, and situation, and the paths connected therewith. The vision may begin by the concentration passing into a state of reverie; or with a distinct sense of change. […] If you are highly inspired, fear not, do not resist, let yourself go; and then the vision may pass over you.[12]

Farr and Simpson go on to describe what they perceived in a skrying into the tarot card of the Empress.

Israel Regardie

"Francis" Israel Regardie (1907–1985) was the author of several notable books on ceremonial magic (figure 14). Born in England, Regardie's family moved to Washington D.C. and Regardie spent most of his life in the United States. He was an enthusiastic student of all things esoteric. In 1926, the young Regardie joined the Washington College of the *Societas Rosicruciana in America*, a non-Masonic Rosicrucian Order that used the initiation rituals of the Golden Dawn and had some correspondence with Wynn Westcott. In 1928, Regardie relocated to Europe to become secretary to Aleister Crowley.

By 1932, Regardie was a published author in his own right, with two of his most important books in print that year: *A Garden of Pomegranates*, which describes the mystical system known as the Qabalah, and *The Tree of Life*, a comprehensive textbook covering virtually every aspect of magic from the perspective of a practicing magician. Publication of *The Tree of Life* combined with a favorable book review by Dion Fortune brought Regardie an invitation into the Bristol Temple of the Order of the Stella Matutina, one of the primary offshoots of the Golden Dawn. He was initiated into the Order in January of 1933 and made rapid progress through the grades. He left the Stella Matutina at the end of 1934, having concluded that much of the Order's teachings would soon be lost. Three years later he published the bulk of the Order's teachings in four volumes titled *The Golden Dawn*.

In 1937, Regardie returned to the US, where he trained as a chiropractor and therapist. He continued to publish a number of books on magical topics until the end of his life, including *The Middle Pillar*, *The Philosopher's Stone*, *The Foundations of Practical Magic*, and *Ceremonial Magic*. In 1982, he initiated a small number of Golden Dawn students into the Adeptus Minor grade at a temple in Georgia.

---

12. King, *Astral Projection, Ritual Magic, and Alchemy*, 71.

Israel Regardie is often credited as the person most responsible for removing the veil of secrecy surrounding Western occultism. According to Francis King and Isabel Sutherland, "That the rebirth of occult magic has taken place in the way it has can be very largely attributed to the writings of one man, Dr. Francis Israel Regardie."*

* King and Sutherland, *The Rebirth of Magic*, 185.

Figure 14. Israel Regardie

Enochian Magic

The Enochian system of magic originated from the ceremonial skryings of Englishmen Dr. John Dee and Edward Kelly toward the end of the sixteenth century. Enochian magic has been a part of the Golden Dawn curriculum since the bare-bones outlines of the initiation rituals were first set down in the folios of the Cipher Manuscript. Divine Enochian names, as well as the Elemental Watchtower Tablets from which they were taken, are introduced to the student in the grades from Zelator through Portal. However, the Enochian system is not studied in depth by the student until he or she enters the Second Order.

Within the R.R. et A.C., Enochian magic is employed for invoking powerful elemental, planetary, and spiritual forces, as well as for spirit vision work in the various angelic realms represented by the squares on the Elemental Tablets, invocations using the Enochian Calls, and other aspects of the system including the *Heptarchia Mystica, Tabula Sancta, Sigillum de Emeth,* etc.

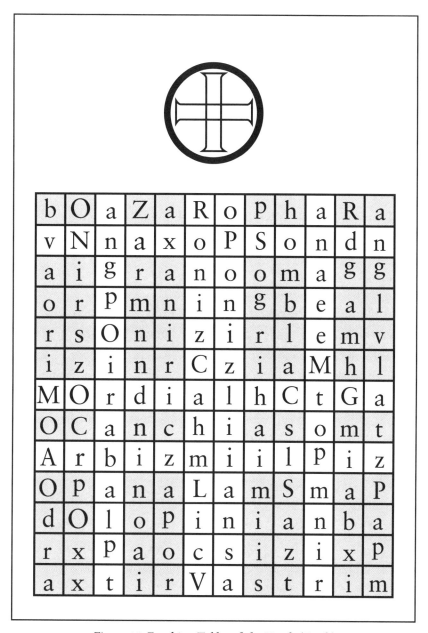

Figure 15. Enochian Tablet of the North (Earth)

A good example of Enochian as used in the practical workings of the Order can be found in the consecration ritual of the Four Elemental Weapons. The following excerpt from the Consecration of the Earth Pentacle calls upon the forces of the Enochian Tablet of Earth (figure 15), including the King and Seniors of the North. The magician is instructed to take up the Magic Sword, read an Invocation to the King of the element of earth, and trace an invoking pentagram of earth. Following this, the magician traces a Saturn hexagram and reads an invocation to six Enochian Seniors associated with earth:

"In the Three Great Secret Holy Names of God borne upon the Banners of the North, EMOR DIAL HECTEGA, I summon Thee, Thou Great King of the North, IC ZOD HEH CHAL, to attend upon this ceremony and by Thy presence increase its effect, whereby I do now consecrate this Magical Pentacle. Confer upon it the Utmost Occult Might and Virtue of which Thou mayest judge it to be capable in all works of the nature of Earth so that in it I may find a strong defense and a powerful weapon wherewith to rule and direct the Spirits of the Elements." [...] "Ye Mighty Princes of the Great Northern Quadrangle, I invoke you who art known to me by the honorable title, and position of rank, of Seniors. Hear my petition, oh ye mighty Princes, the Six Seniors of the Northern quarter of the Earth who bear the names of: LAIDROM. ALHCTGA. ACZINOR. AHMLICV. LZINOPO. LIIANSA."[13]

The Order took the Enochian skryings of Dee and Kelly in new directions, crafting it into a fully integrated system of Western magic and spiritual knowledge. "The thing that distinguishes Enochian Magic as taught by the Golden Dawn is that it makes possible an astonishingly effective and powerful synthesis of both theoretical and practical occult philosophy....In the hands of MacGregor Mathers and his colleagues the Enochian system stood revealed as a true concourse of all the forces in the microcosm Sephirotic, elemental, planetary and astral. It fused Kabbalah, tarot, astrology, and geomancy into a unified psychological field."[14]

It is undeniable that the Golden Dawn's inclusion of Enochian into its curriculum helped bring attention to Dee and Kelly's angelic workings and drive the current renaissance of interest in their work. Perhaps one of the greatest tributes to the Enochian system is the position of high respect afforded to it by the Golden Dawn; it is considered to be the apex and crowning jewel of the entire system. This is precisely why Enochian is not taught until all other aspects of the Golden Dawn curriculum have been thoroughly assimilated by the student.

At the outset, let it be said that a good deal of systematic study will be required to appreciate the value and subtle significance of this system. It is one of the most amazing magical schemes that I have ever encountered, since it provides a thorough-going and comprehensive synthesis of the entire magical system of the Golden Dawn. [...] Therefore, because it is a synthetic amalgamation of all the Order, the student will find it necessary and imperative to have made himself thoroughly familiar with all the other

13. Regardie, *The Golden Dawn*, 408–409.
14. Head, "An Introduction to the Enochian Teaching and Praxis," 6.

items of knowledge taught by the Golden Dawn. He must know his Tarot and Geomantic attributions so well that the names, symbols and ideas are all at his fingertips—this, naturally, in addition to the basic knowledge items of the Hebrew alphabet, Tree of Life, and the Qabalah generally. The formulae of practical Magic derived from the Z-documents, dealing with the symbolism of the Candidate, the Temple, and the Ceremony of the Neophyte Grade will require to be not only memorized and known, but understood. The student will need to be perfectly acquainted with the Pentagram and Hexagram Rituals, the formulae of the Consecration Ceremonies, the general art of invocation, and formulating Telesmatic images, and drawing Sigils.[15]

Several Second Order rituals contain Enochian material in varying degrees. Different aspects of the Enochian system are studied in every grade and sub-grade of the Inner Order.

The Magic of Light

There is a particular set of Second Order teachings collectively known as the *Z Documents*, the *Z Docs*, or simply the *Zeds*, which can be found in Israel Regardie's *The Golden Dawn*.

These manuscripts explain how various aspects of the Order's Neophyte Ceremony can be used as ritual formulae for endless varieties of practical magic procedures. One of these documents is known as *Z.2: The Formulae of the Magic of Light*.

The *Magic of Light* refers to the Golden Dawn's formula of practical magic, the various forms of which are hidden under many layers of symbolism within the Neophyte Ceremony.

There are five divisions of the Magic of Light, representing five different areas of occult work. These are classified under the five letters of *Yesheshuah*, the Pentagrammaton.

All works of ceremonial magic, including evocations and invocations, fall under the letter *Yod* and the element of fire. The consecration of talismans and the production of natural phenomena (rains, storms, earthquakes) fall under the letter *Heh* and the element of water. All works of spiritual development and transformation fall under the letter *Shin* and the element of spirit. This category is further divided into three types of magic that correspond to the three Yods or flames of the letter Shin. (These three flames are further assigned to the three Mother Letters: *Aleph*—Invisibility, *Mem*—Transformations, and *Shin*—Spiritual Development.) All forms of divination and astrology fall under the letter *Vav* and the element of air. Lastly, all works of alchemy fall under the letter *Heh Final* and the element of earth.

It is within these five divisions of practical magic that the magician begins to bring all aspects of the Golden Dawn system together. Everything that the student has learned up to this point is utilized: the study and memorization of the Hebrew alphabet, Qabalistic principles, astrological

---

15. Regardie, *The Golden Dawn*, 624–625.

· · · · · · · ·

correspondences, meditation, visualization, dramatic invocation, vibration, flashing colors, projection of energized willpower, assumption of godforms, various rituals of the pentagram and hexagram, and Enochian magic. All of this knowledge becomes part and parcel of the ritual tool kit of the practicing Golden Dawn magician.

Adepts study the outlines of magical rites provided in the Z.2 document to create their own unique versions of the same in fully expanded rituals. Israel Regardie supplied readers with rituals that he had created based on the Z.2 outlines as examples, but he also admonished students not to slavishly copy or simply cut and paste his versions. Skilled students are fully expected to fashion their own personal rituals using their own ingenuity and inspiration. Having the ability to create one's own effective rituals in this manner is one of the hallmarks of the advanced magician.

Advice for the Modern Practitioner

Today's Golden Dawn magicians have many options that were unavailable to their Victorian age counterparts. Several Golden Dawn temples and orders exist today. Some are traditional, others not so much. Some groups mix other elements or spiritual traditions with Golden Dawn teachings. There is nothing inherently wrong with this, so long as these groups make these distinctions clear to prospective members.

But you would be well advised to do your homework before joining any group. Ask questions in the magical community. Read books. Don't believe every claim you read on the internet. Better to work on your own than get involved with a sketchy teacher or a scam operation.

Self-initiation is also an option. Most of the original Golden Dawn's side lectures, supplementary Flying Rolls, and curriculum from Neophyte through Zelator Adeptus Minor have been published and are readily available for any interested student who is dedicated enough to pursue the studies on their own. One does not need to be a member of any acknowledged organization or temple to do the Work. There are probably many more people practicing solo or in small groups than is generally realized. The Golden Dawn current is very much alive and relevant in a world that could use a little more balance and sacredness of the kind stated in the Tiphareth clause of Adeptus Minor obligation:

> "I further promise and swear that, with the divine permission, I will from this day forward apply myself to the Great Work—which is to so purify and exalt my spiritual nature that with the Divine aid I may at length attain to be more than human and thus gradually raise and unite myself to my higher and divine genius, and that in this event, I will not abuse the great power entrusted to me." [16]

16. Regardie, *The Golden Dawn*, 301.

Sources

Crowley, Aleister. "The Holy of Holies." In *Collected Works of Aleister Crowley*, vol. 1. Des Plaines, IL: Society for the Propagation of Religious Truth, 1905.

Greer, John Michael. *The New Encyclopedia of the Occult*. St. Paul, MN: Llewellyn Publications, 2003.

Head, Thomas. "An Introduction to the Enochian Teaching and Praxis." In *The Complete Golden Dawn System of Magic*, vol. 10, by Israel Regardie. Phoenix, AZ: Falcon Press, 1984.

Howe, Ellic. *The Magicians of the Golden Dawn: A Documentary History of a Magical Order, 1887–1923*. New York: Samuel Weiser, 1997.

King, Francis, ed. *Astral Projection, Ritual Magic, and Alchemy: Golden Dawn Material by S. L. Mac-Gregor Mathers and Others*. Rochester, VT: Destiny Books, 1987.

King, Francis, and Stephen Skinner. *Techniques of High Magic: A Guide to Self-Empowerment*. Rochester, VT: Destiny Books, 1976.

King, Francis, and Isabel Sutherland. *The Rebirth of Magic*. London: Corgi Books, 1982.

Maitland, Edward. *Anna Kingsford: Her Life, Letters, Diary, and Work*. 2 volumes. London: George Redway, 1896.

McIntosh, Christopher. *The Rosicrucians: The History, Mythology, and Rituals of an Esoteric Order*. York Beach, ME: Samuel Weiser, 1997.

Regardie, Israel. *The Golden Dawn: An Account of the Teachings, Rites, and Ceremonies of the Order of the Golden Dawn*. 7th edition. Woodbury, MN: Llewellyn Publications, 2003.

Waite, Arthur Edward. *Shadows of Life and Thought*. Facsimile edition of original 1938 publication. Kila, MT: Kessinger Publishing Co., 1997.

Suggested Reading List

Cicero, Chic, and Sandra Tabatha Cicero. *The Essential Golden Dawn: An Introduction to High Magic*. St. Paul, MN: Llewellyn Publications, 2003. An introductory-level text that examines the history of the Golden Dawn and its principles and areas of study and practice.

———. *Golden Dawn Magic*. Woodbury, MN: Llewellyn Publications, 2019. Provides clear, step-by-step instruction in the main areas of practical Golden Dawn magic and how these procedures benefit the magician.

———. *Golden Dawn Magical Tarot*. St. Paul, MN: Llewellyn Publications, 1991. Tarot deck and accompanying book based on the teachings of the Order.

———. *Self-Initiation into the Golden Dawn Tradition*. St. Paul, MN: Llewellyn Publications, 1998. A rigorous text with knowledge lectures, meditations, pathworkings, rituals, exercises, and initiation rites for the solo practitioner and the working magical group.

· · · · · · · ·

Gilbert, R. A. *Revelations of the Golden Dawn*. London: Quantum, 1997. An exposé of the Order written by today's foremost Golden Dawn historian.

Golden Dawn Community. *Commentaries on the Golden Dawn Flying Rolls*. Dublin: Kerubim, 2013. Contains all the "Flying Roll" essays written by original Golden Dawn members and provides commentaries on each one by contemporary magicians.

Greer, Mary K. *Women of the Golden Dawn: Rebels and Priestesses*. Rochester, VT: Park Street Press, 1994. Describes the lives and magic of four remarkable women of the original Order of the Golden Dawn.

Howe, Ellic. *The Magicians of the Golden Dawn: A Documentary History of a Magical Order, 1887–1923*. New York: Samuel Weiser, 1972. Although written from a non-magical perspective, Howe's work remains an important text on the Order's history.

Küntz, Darcy, ed. *The Complete Golden Dawn Cipher Manuscript*. Edmonds, WA: Holmes Publishing Group, 1996. Provides a complete facsimile and translation of the foundational document that outlined the initiation rituals of the Order.

———. *The Golden Dawn Source Book*. Edmonds, WA: Holmes Publishing Group, 1996. A reference guide to the historical study of the origins, creation, and founding of the Order.

Regardie, Israel. *The Golden Dawn: An Account of the Teachings, Rites, and Ceremonies of the Order of the Golden Dawn*. 7th edition. St. Paul, MN: Llewellyn Publications, 2003. The twentieth-century's most influential magical text. The book that unveiled the teachings and rituals of the Golden Dawn to the world.

Wildoak, Peregrin. *By Names and Images: Bringing the Golden Dawn to Life*. Cheltenham, UK: Skylight, 2012. A valuable introduction to Golden Dawn magic and the mechanics behind the system.

Zalewski, Pat, and Chris Zalewski. *The Magical Tarot of the Golden Dawn*. London: Aeon Books, 2008. A detailed description of the tarot cards of the Golden Dawn and the methods used to work with them.

About the Authors

Charles "Chic" Cicero was born in Buffalo, New York. An early love of music, particularly of the saxophone, resulted in Chic's many years of experience as a lead musician in several jazz, blues, and rock ensembles, working with many famous performers in the music industry. His interest in Freemasonry and the Western Esoteric Tradition resulted in research articles on Rosicrucianism and the Knights Templar, printed in such publications as *Ars Quatuor Coronatorum* and the *1996–2000 Transactions of the Metropolitan College of the SRIA*. Chic is a member of several Masonic, Martinist, and Rosicrucian organizations. He is a past Grand Commander of the *Grand*

Commandery of Knights Templar in Florida (2010–2011) and is the current Chief Adept of the Florida College of the *Societas Rosicruciana in Civitatibus Foederatis*. A close personal friend and confidant of Dr. Israel Regardie, Chic established a Golden Dawn temple in 1977 and was one of the key people who helped Regardie to resurrect a legitimate branch of the Hermetic Order of the Golden Dawn in the United States in the early 1980s, with an initiatory lineage that dates back to the original Order of 1888. He met his wife and co-author, Sandra Tabatha Cicero, shortly thereafter. Chic served as the G.H. Cancellarius of the Hermetic Order of the Golden Dawn from 1985 to 1994, and as G.H. Imperator of the Order from 1994 to the present day.

Sandra "Tabatha" Cicero was born in rural Wisconsin. A lifelong fascination with the creative arts has served to inspire her work in the magical world. After graduating from the University of Wisconsin–Milwaukee with a bachelor's degree in fine arts in 1982, Tabatha worked as an entertainer, typesetter, editor, commercial artist, and computer graphics illustrator. In 2009 she obtained a degree in paralegal studies. She met Chic Cicero in 1983, and the Golden Dawn system of magic has been her primary spiritual focus ever since. Tabatha spent five years working on the paintings for *The Golden Dawn Magical Tarot*, which she began at the encouragement of Israel Regardie. Tabatha is a member of several Martinist and Rosicrucian organizations and is the current Imperatrix of the *Societas Rosicruciana in America* (www.sria.org). She has served as the G.H. Cancellaria of the Hermetic Order of the Golden Dawn from 1994 to the present day.

Both Chic and Tabatha are Chief Adepts of the Hermetic Order of the Golden Dawn as reestablished by Israel Regardie (www.hermeticgoldendawn.org), the oldest continuously operating Golden Dawn Order in the United States, as well as an international order with temples in several other countries.

Art Credits

Figures 1, 3–4, 8–10, 12, and 15 by the Llewellyn Art Department.

Figures 2 and 13 are photographs © Chic and Sandra Tabatha Cicero.

Figures 5, 7, and 11 by James Clark.

Figure 6 by Mary Ann Zapalac.

Figure 14 is a scan of Regardie's Tattva Cards © Chic and Sandra Tabatha Cicero.

BOOK NINE

Thelema & Aleister Crowley
by David Shoemaker

Each preceding book in this volume has explored a unique philosophy, ritual approach, or magical cosmology, and in each case it is clear that the hands of many thinkers and practitioners have shaped the tradition over time. In the present book, however, we find a unique example of a major magical tradition with a single founding luminary who is inextricable from the philosophies and practices of the tradition itself: Aleister Crowley. One of the most important and influential occultists of all time, Crowley was the founder and "prophet" of the system of attainment known as *Thelema*. A brilliant and controversial genius, Crowley has had a singular influence over the entire field of magick (always spelled with a *k* in Crowley's nomenclature) since he burst on the scene at the turn of the twentieth century.

Biographical Sketch

Edward Alexander ("Aleister") Crowley was born on October 12, 1875, in Royal Leamington Spa, England, to a prosperous brewing family. Raised in the strict Protestant sect known as the Plymouth Brethren, Crowley was steeped in the Bible from early childhood, and deeply internalized its symbol sets and poetic language. While he soon began to question fundamental Christian doctrines, the biblical mythology and morality he was exposed to in his formative years influenced his thinking and his personal spiritual development for the rest of his life. While attending Cambridge University, Crowley was introduced to occultism via Karl von Eckartshausen's *The Cloud upon the Sanctuary*, and he soon found himself drawn to the initiatory, magical organization known as the

Hermetic Order of the Golden Dawn.[1] Crowley had found the training ground he had been seeking, and here his magical adventure began in earnest.

Crowley rose quickly through the ranks of the Golden Dawn, and for a time he was taken under the wing of its cofounder S. L. Mathers. Eventually, a schism with many of the British members of the order led them to travel together to Paris. Their mutual affection was short-lived, however, and Crowley soon found himself disenchanted with Mathers and with the order itself. As he noted some years later in *Liber Causae*:

> The rituals were elaborated, though scholarly enough, into verbose and pretentious nonsense: the knowledge proved worthless, even where it was correct: for it is in vain that pearls, be they never so clear and precious, are given to the swine.
>
> The ordeals were turned into contempt, it being impossible for any one to fail therein. Unsuitable candidates were admitted for no better reason than that of their worldly prosperity.
>
> In short, the Order failed to initiate.[2]

Disillusioned with this experience, Crowley spent the next several years of his life immersed in various adventures, both exotic and domestic. He traveled to the Far East to study Buddhism and meditation with his former Golden Dawn colleague Allan Bennett, continued his hobby of mountaineering, and explored as many of the world's religious traditions as he could find, both in theory and in practice. He married his first wife, Rose Kelly, and settled into a brief period of domestic life at his newly purchased home on the shores of Loch Ness in Scotland, Boleskine House.

While on his honeymoon with Rose in Egypt, he experienced the pivotal moment of his magical career: the reception of *Liber AL vel Legis*,[3] also known as *The Book of the Law*. In an experience that by today's nomenclature would be considered a "channeled" writing, Crowley claimed to have had the Book dictated to him by Aiwass, an entity representing the forces of a New Aeon embodied by the Egyptian hawk-headed god Horus, or Ra-Hoor-Khuit. In the years following the reception of the Book, Crowley gradually came to feel that the purpose of his life was to serve as the prophet of this New Aeon, in the name of its central Law of Thelema (Θελημα), expressed in the now infamous maxim *Do what thou wilt shall be the whole of the Law*. We will discuss the implications of this Law, and the doctrine of True Will, in the paragraphs that follow. Crowley eventually took the magical motto *To Mega Therion* (The Great Beast), which was simultaneously a reference to a figure described in the Apocalypse of John, but also an inversion and

1. See Book Eight: The Golden Dawn.
2. Crowley, *The Holy Books of Thelema*, 1989, xlii.
3. Crowley, *The Holy Books of Thelema*, 1989.

• • • • • • • •

extension of that archetype as a positive and regenerative force of freedom, bringing the Law of Thelema to humanity.

Crowley dedicated the rest of his life to extending the Law of Thelema into the world through his teaching and writings, and through his administration of the magical orders he led until his death, the A∴A∴ and the Ordo Templi Orientis (O.T.O.). Aleister Crowley died on December 1, 1947, at his boarding house in Hastings, England.

Scientific Illuminism, Syncretism, and the A∴A∴

After his disheartening experiences with the Golden Dawn, Crowley worked with his then-mentor George Cecil Jones in 1907 to found the A∴A∴, his new take on a Qabalistically-based initiatory system, which stripped away much of the verbosity and excessive focus on doctrine found in the G.D. The core approach was termed *scientific illuminism*, or skeptical theurgy, and was centered on the idea that each aspirant must come to their own conclusions about beliefs, practices, and their results, based on their experience in the system. In essays such as "The Soldier and the Hunchback" and elsewhere, Crowley encouraged aspirants to adopt a distinctly skeptical and investigative approach to their work, and to avoid assuming any doctrine to be true until verified by inner experience. In *Liber Causae*, he noted:

> Should therefore the candidate hear the name of any God, let him not rashly assume that it refers to any known God, save only the God known to himself. Or should the ritual speak in terms (however vague) which seem to imply Egyptian, Taoist, Buddhist, Indian, Persian, Greek, Judaic, Christian, or Moslem philosophy, let him reflect that this is a defect of language; the literary limitation and not the spiritual prejudice of the man P.[4]

Crowley adopted a syncretic approach to the construction of his new system, bringing in elements of both Eastern and Western traditions. Again, in *Liber Causae* he wrote that he had constructed the system by "choosing only those symbols which were common to all systems, and rigorously rejecting all names and words which might be supposed to imply any religious or metaphysical theory."[5] More than any initiatory system that had come before, Crowley's A∴A∴ synthesized a great number of practices drawn from Hindu yoga, Buddhist, and Taoist traditions, alongside such traditional Western elements as Qabalah, astrology, tarot, Enochian studies, and ceremonial magick. His system included many of the philosophical traditions with which he had become acquainted during his tenure in the Golden Dawn, such as Neo-Platonism, Hermeticism, Rosicrucianism, and the Egyptian pantheon. It also carried forward many of the magical techniques he had learned in the G.D., such as astral travel, the vibration of God-Names,

---

4. Crowley, *The Holy Books of Thelema*, 1989, xliv. (Note: "P" is *Perdurabo*—one of Crowley's magical mottos.)
5. Crowley, *The Holy Books of Thelema*, 1989, xliii–xliv.

• • • • • • •

and the use of a vast system of Qabalistic correspondences of various words, phrases, colors, gods, spirits, incenses, and much more, as codified in his reference text *777*.[6]

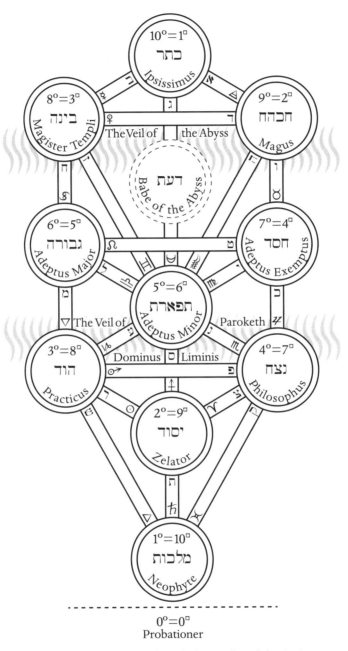

Figure 1. The Tree of Life with the Grades of the A∴A∴

6. Crowley, *777 and Other Qabalistic Writings*. Also, see Book Eleven: Magician's Tables.

• • • • • • • •

In addition to the integration of these diverse traditions and practices, Crowley's aim with the system of the A∴A∴ was to improve the efficiency of training. He stripped away the preliminary Knowledge Lectures of the Golden Dawn's system, generally expecting that those attracted to his system would be able to "bootstrap'" themselves through these materials largely through self-study in the early grades of A∴A∴. He also condensed the system of the grades themselves. For example, the array of traditional invocation and evocation rituals, construction of talismans and magical implements, Enochian work, and scrying techniques, which would have only been encountered in the Second Order of the original Golden Dawn, were now presented openly in the earliest stages of A∴A∴ (figure 1). Almost nothing in the curriculum of A∴A∴ was held back from public view, save for the initiation rituals themselves and a few key words and ritual procedures. In all of this, Crowley's guiding maxim was "Mystery is the Enemy of Truth."

Perhaps the most dramatic change in Crowley's revised system was the near-complete removal of any social context for training. Aside from the early-grade initiations, there are no group rituals in A∴A∴, and the order incorporates none of the social or fraternal aspects of groups like the Golden Dawn and many others. There are no "lodges" or "temples" in the conventional sense, and instruction is accomplished entirely through an aspirant's personal contact with a single assigned "Superior." Crowley's aim was to remove the interpersonal dramas, social status-seeking, and similar drawbacks that in his view had compromised the initiatory integrity of the Golden Dawn.

The Holy Guardian Angel

The *Holy Guardian Angel* (or *HGA*) is Crowley's term for that force, aspect of consciousness, or external entity that many other traditions have spoken of as the Higher Self, the Augoeides, the Higher Genius, and innumerable other names. Crowley discussed the Holy Guardian Angel in different ways at various stages of his life, and with considerable variation depending on his audience and his intention. At some points, he described the Holy Guardian Angel as if it were synonymous with the Higher Self—an aspect of our own conscious or unconscious existence. At other times, he quite definitively characterized the Holy Guardian Angel as an external entity of some sort. For example, his experience with his own Holy Guardian Angel, Aiwass, was of such a quality during the dictation of *The Book of the Law* that he perceived it as an external voice dictating to him.

In the system of the A∴A∴, from the very beginning, the path toward the "Knowledge and Conversation" (K & C) of the HGA is of singular importance. All of the tasks in the A∴A∴ curriculum up to the Adeptus Minor (Tiphareth) grade are designed to be stepping stones toward the K & C. These tools come in several varieties: magical rituals, meditation, the gradual raising of the kundalini through various practices, devotional practices, and much more; but all of these are simply tools to be used to attain Knowledge and Conversation. After the K & C, when the knowledge of the True Will is consciously and deeply ingrained in everyday living, one can choose to do a magical ritual and be assured that it is in line with the True Will. This is rarely the case before K & C.

There is communication with the HGA well before Adeptus Minor, to be sure, but it tends to be experienced through the vehicle of the unconscious mind, and veiled in the language of symbol. The experience of this is such that one may not sense a conscious communication at all for quite some time, but one gradually improves the ability to speak in this language of symbol; hence the requirement in A∴A∴ and other orders to memorize various magical "correspondences," for such symbols are in one sense the "native tongue" of the Angel.

Eventually, the aspirant begins to perceive these communications in a much more direct and conscious manner. In the system of A∴A∴, the so-called Vision of the Holy Guardian Angel is attributed to Malkuth, which is the sephira of the Neophyte ($1°=10^\square$) grade. It is often in the Neophyte grade that aspirants begin to have more of these conscious communications. It is a courtship—a gradually increasing and intensifying intimacy, a gradual improving of our ability to perceive the language of the HGA in our lives. Finally, at the Adeptus Minor ($5°=6^\square$) grade, the breakthrough of Briatic consciousness into our previously Yetzirah-bound mind forges a conscious link to the HGA. Thus, the defining characteristic of the true Adept of A∴A∴ is that he or she can communicate with the Angel consciously and at will.

The True Will

The core of the philosophy and religion of Thelema is to be found in the word itself: *thelema* is the Greek word for *will*. This "True" Will is understood to be much deeper than the simple will of the ego or the whims of the personality. It is one's life purpose, or basic nature, and the living out of that nature across the individual lifetime and even multiple incarnations.

The True Will is the will of the deepest inmost Self—the core of who one truly is as a spiritual being. Also, and importantly, it is an expression of the universal will, as particularized and expressed in the individual life. All too often, the True Will is erroneously conceptualized as a singular choice of a career or a single task to be accomplished in life. This is far too narrow a definition, as the True Will is the essence of one's real Self. It encompasses actions, thoughts, feelings, and behaviors, and it pertains to the way one lives, moment to moment, as well as the entire arc of one's lifetime. Clearly, the True Will is much, much more than a choice of career or a single life task to complete. There is often, however, a great deal of overlap between the True Will and what one chooses to spend one's time doing in life—one's occupation or favorite hobbies, for example. The True Will is very likely to overlap with one's passions, interests, and preferences. On the other hand, we've established that this is not the simple will of the ego-personality (or, in the terms of

Qabalistic psychology, the *ruach*). Sometimes aspirants find that their True Will—which ideally the ego facilitates—is not necessarily comfortable nor particularly harmonious with the ego's conceptions of itself. Often, the discovery of the True Will forces one to make painful choices about lifestyle, priorities, career, relationships, and many other things. Such growth processes are painful precisely because they make one stretch outside the comfort zone; but in this case, the aim is to harmonize these egoic choices in the day-to-day life with the deeper needs of the soul and the commandments of the HGA.

The True Will should equally explain one's choices in any given moment, and in any given situation, just as well as it explains the overall path of one's life. When contemplating one's True Will, one should try to take a step back from the everyday circumstances, career and life choices. The True Will explains the way one affects the universe, the choices one makes, and the paths one tends to take, whether one happens to be a stockbroker in New York City, a fisherman in Malaysia, or anything else. In other words, this central truth of Self will express itself in a certain way regardless of the mundane situations in which an individual finds themselves.

The process is incredibly individualized, and no two seekers will experience its peaks and valleys in the same way. It may be said without exaggeration that the aspirant must think of themselves as the prophet of their own Angel—as the high priest or priestess of a religion that is theirs alone. The aim of that religion is to deepen, intensify, and delineate with ever-increasing clarity the mystical and magical procedures that effectively invoke the Holy Guardian Angel. The development of this religion is essentially the work of the aspirant in the early stages of their journey. The body and mind are the vessel in which the Angel abides. The purpose of this vessel is to live out the True Will, which is the voice of the Angel in one's everyday life.

As mentioned earlier, the understanding of the True Will takes a quantum leap forward with the Knowledge and Conversation of the Holy Guardian Angel. This attainment typically climaxes as a result of intensive and focused ritual (such as the classic Abramelin approach) at the Adeptus Minor grade of A∴A∴, corresponding to the sphere of Tiphereth on the Qabalistic Tree of Life. With this attainment, the supernal realm of the neshamah—the spiritual intuition and the voice of the Angel itself—becomes apprehensible to the conscious mind for the first time.

The spiritual and mystical import of the True Will concept is self-evident from the discussion above; however, it carries implications for magical practice worthy of deep consideration. Most importantly, Crowley believes that when a magician is fully aware of their True Will, they are able to make more efficient choices about which magical aims to pursue, and when and how. Since the True Will of the individual magician is by definition the Will of the Universe and aligned with natural law, the magician's choices will therefore be aided by the momentum of the universe itself, much like a boat sailing with the current rather than against it. Indeed, Crowley's basic

• • • • • • • •

definition of magick itself is "the Science and Art of causing Change to occur in conformity with Will."[7] This applies equally to mundane, everyday actions as to traditional forms of ritual magick.

The doctrine of True Will has important interpersonal and societal implications as well. In his essay "Duty," Crowley writes:

> Abstain from all interferences with other wills. [...] To seek to dominate or influence another is to seek to deform or destroy him; and he is a necessary part of one's own Universe, that is, of one's self. [...] The essence of crime is that it restricts the freedom of the individual outraged. [...] Crime being a direct spiritual violation of the Law of Thelema, it should not be tolerated in the community. Those who possess the instinct should be segregated in a settlement to build up a state of their own, so to learn the necessity of themselves imposing and maintaining rules of justice. [...] The ultimate aim is thus to reintegrate conscience, on true scientific principles, as the warden of conduct, the monitor of the people, and the guarantee of the governors.[8]

An Overview of the Methods and Tools of A∴A∴[9]

There is no shortage of published material concerning the system of the A∴A∴, in terms of its overall approach and its training methods. This is certainly by design, as Crowley intended the methods and materials of A∴A∴ to be widely accessible and, in time, widely replicated. There is plenty of available material concerning what the system *is,* yet it is rare to find cogent and practical discussion of why and how the system *works.* In this section, we will explore the reasons why the methods and tools of A∴A∴ are arranged the way they are, why they unfold in a certain manner across the grades of A∴A∴, and how they lead the aspirant toward the K & C of the HGA and beyond.

There is a specific technology here, to be sure, but it tends to be discussed in terms of a grade-by-grade analysis, such as the way the tasks and the nature of each grade are attributed to the four elements or the corresponding sephiroth. We will consider it from this perspective as well, but also go beyond that approach and shift the focus to the *type* of training that occurs along the way. Our exploration here is not drawn directly from the writings of Aleister Crowley. Rather, it is an attempt by the present author to convey the essence of the system as a practical methodology.

The system of A∴A∴ below Tiphereth can be arranged into five training "tracks"—essentially, five different types of tools that work together to bring the aspirant to Knowledge and Conver-

---

7. Crowley, *Magick: Book 4: Parts I–IV,* 126.

8. Crowley, "Duty," in *The Revival of Magick and Other Essays (Oriflamme 2).*

9. Adapted from the chapter "The Methods and Tools of A∴A∴," in Shoemaker, *Living Thelema.*

. . . .

sation. These five training tracks unfold concurrently across the first order grades (Probationer through Dominus Liminis). We will briefly outline the five tracks and then cycle through and discuss each of them in more detail. Obviously, it is not possible to discuss every task assigned in A∴A∴ in this place.[10] Rather, we will emphasize the key practices that exemplify the five training tracks, and show how they complement each other in the unfolding path of the aspirant.

Track One: The development of magical skills and techniques

Track Two: The training of the mind—to focus, to empty, to become, and to remain receptive

Track Three: The stimulation and activation of the chakras and the raising of kundalini

Track Four: Devotional practices

Track Five: Balancing the psycho-magical constitution

Before we look at these in detail, it should be emphasized that everything in the A∴A∴ system below Tiphereth—everything leading up to the $5°=6^\square$ grade of Adeptus Minor—is devoted solely to the accomplishment of the K & C of the HGA. It is easy to lose sight of this, due to the diverse nature of the tasks assigned and the many traditions that are woven together in the system. Furthermore, every aspirant has their own prejudices and predispositions that may lead to magical myopia. In any case, the whole point of the system is not to accumulate a grab bag of unrelated magical techniques, but to become fully oneself. The aspirant must attain the K & C of the HGA, and discover with certainty the True Will. Then they must carry out that will with force and precision.

Track One

Track one is the development of magical skills and techniques. This track is actively worked from the very earliest stages of the A∴A∴—as early as Probationer.

Probationer

The Probationer is likely to be experimenting with a full spectrum of magical techniques, but by the time of the passage to Neophyte (assuming the Probationary year is successful), there will be even more specific emphasis on the traditional magical tools. Somewhat like learning an alphabet, one simply has to master the basics, and let them form a foundation for all that comes after. The focus here is on pentagram and hexagram ritual forms (Lesser, Greater, Supreme, etc.) as well as on developing competence with the corresponding elemental, planetary, and zodiacal invoking and banishing rituals.

---

10. For a grade-by-grade discussion of the tasks of A∴A∴, see Eshelman, *The Mystical and Magical System of A∴A∴*.

Karl Germer

Though Karl Johannes Germer is best known as the successor of Aleister Crowley, his true legacy is the corpus of Thelemic literature he saw published during his lifetime. Recognized as a Master of the Temple and chosen by Crowley to succeed him as head of the A∴A∴ and O.T.O., Germer made it his life's work to spread the Law of Thelema by preserving and publishing Crowley's writings.

Karl Germer and Aleister Crowley met in Germany in 1925 after being introduced by Hans Traenker. Germer was starstruck and became Crowley's devoted student and colleague. Establishing the Thelema Publishing Company with Crowley in 1929, Germer initiated the publishing program that he would carry on until his death. He eventually became Crowley's right hand and managed the affairs of the O.T.O. as Grand Secretary General while acting as Crowley's representative in the United States.

Maintaining the well-being of Crowley was Germer's first priority for as long as the two men knew each other. Even Germer's choice of wives was influenced by this devotion to Crowley, as their personal wealth and ability to support Crowley and his activities were primary considerations before a marriage proposal. As Crowley's health declined in post-war England, Germer ensured that he received frequent shipments of luxuries and basic goods from the US. This expense was largely shouldered by the members of Agape Lodge in Los Angeles, whose dues and donations were primarily earmarked to support publishing and Crowley's care packages.

As Crowley's viceroy in the US and chosen successor, Germer found himself frequently at odds with the local leadership of Agape Lodge and quickly became frustrated when their priorities appeared to diverge from his own. He saw the Southern California group as mostly a social venue where little serious work was being done to advance the Law of Thelema. The mystic in him felt that the A∴A∴ was a better vehicle of the Thelemic Current than the O.T.O. and that neither would survive if there was no foundation of published literature to support them. After Crowley's death, Germer devoted most of his time, energy, and the finances of the O.T.O. to bringing Crowley's remaining unpublished work to print. Such titles as *Magick Without Tears*, *The Book of Thoth*, and *Liber Aleph* would not be available today without his efforts.

Agape Lodge closed in 1949 and no further O.T.O. initiations were conducted during Germer's lifetime. He turned his attention to his A∴A∴ students and finding sources of funding for the publishing program. Upon his death in 1962, he left no successors or plans for the continuity of either order. The O.T.O. eventually reconstituted itself, but the A∴A∴ splintered into multiple claimant groups headed by Germer's remaining students. Though this failure to appoint suitable heirs would seem to leave a shadow over Germer's

legacy, his diligence in preserving Crowley's body of work is what enables these organizations to continue to exist and the Law of Thelema to have the reach it does today.
—Andrew Ferrell

Andrew Ferrell currently serves as the Vice-Chancellor and Grand Praemonstrator of the Temple of the Silver Star. As TOTSS Librarian and Archivist, Andrew is dedicated to preserving and sharing the printed legacy of Aleister Crowley, Karl Germer, Jane Wolfe, and Phyllis Seckler. He is an initiate of the O.T.O., an aspirant to the A∴A∴, and a lifelong student of the Mysteries. In the remaining hours of the day, he is an IT professional and enjoys talking and playing with his three dogs, "The Secret Chiefs."

Neophyte

The Neophyte is essentially formulating their own "astral atlas." There may also be experimentation with the Enochian system (although this is not specifically assigned until the Practicus grade) as well as various Solomonic and Goetic techniques.

What is essentially happening here, by design, is that much of the traditional instruction that would have occurred in the old Golden Dawn's Second Order is being handed to the Neophyte right at the outset, with only the preparation of Probationer as a preliminary. These skills are drilled in from the very beginning of the system—but why? It may not be immediately obvious why the ability to correctly perform a pentagram or hexagram ritual, or any of these other techniques, is necessarily related to the path toward Knowledge and Conversation. But consider: if one cannot design a ritual to effectively invoke a fundamental aspect of nature, such as a particular element or planetary influence, and make oneself an adequate vessel for the invocation and utilization of that specific force, how can one design the ultimate ritual of invocation—that of the HGA? The basics simply must be mastered. To be sure, learning any specific ritual form, such as a hexagram ritual, is in itself of little consequence; but as a tool for developing the capacity to invoke, safely contain, and direct magical force, it is invaluable.

The Neophyte is also trained and tested in the control of the Body of Light, and in the related techniques of scrying and so-called astral projection. The Neophyte is tested by his or her Superior in these procedures, to ensure the Neophyte has developed adequate facility with the Body of Light in order to competently explore the astral realms. This skill is important because the ability to speak the language of symbol, which is the natural language of the astral world—and of the subconscious mind—is directly related to the aspirant's growing capacity to receive consciously the various communications from the HGA. While initially, in the path of the aspirant, these impulses will likely be more or less subconscious—speaking through dreams and intuitive flashes of various kinds—the more consciously one can speak and understand this language, the closer one is to conscious communication with the Angel.

· · · · · · ·

Practicus

The Practicus moves on to work with divination. Why is this necessary? Keep in mind that divination is yet another method of using the conscious mind to receive subtle impressions from a set of symbols, and if one cannot sit down with a set of universal symbols like the Tarot or the I Ching and get something apprehensible and useful out of them, how can one possibly begin to tune into the subtle impressions that will be coming from the HGA? How can one build the right sort of spiritual 'radar,' with the necessary level of sensitivity to perceive the message of the HGA, if one cannot execute something as basic as a Tarot reading?

Philosophus

The Philosophus is tasked with mastering evocation and working with talismans. How do these practices lead the aspirant toward K & C? Consider the basic nature of evocation: it is the ability to externalize magical force, particularized to a specific form and type of energy of the magician's choosing. For example, the evocation of a particular spirit into a triangle requires the ability to tap into a specific energy source, and to effectively utilize the correct magical "muscles" to bring it down into manifestation. Whether one sees such an act as purely psychological or as an interaction with an actual external entity, one still has to have manifested *something* concrete; and by doing so, the aspirant strengthens the skills to interact compellingly, vibrantly, and effectively with the HGA when the time comes. We do not mean to imply that the nature of K & C will be exactly the same as that of conversing with a Goetic spirit; however, the skills strengthened by perfecting evocation will be directly applicable to the eventual K & C working.

Similarly, the ability to create and consecrate powerful talismans is an important preparation for K & C. What is the nature of a talisman? It is a physical object imbued with a specific force as chosen by the magician. And what is the aspirant, if not a talisman of the force of the HGA? If one cannot imbue a physical talisman with a specific force as simple as Mercury, for example, how can one possibly make the *entire being* a conscious talisman of the influence of the HGA?

Track Two

Track two is the training of the mind to focus, to empty, and to become and remain receptive. Here we have another set of tasks that is very likely to be approached from Probationer onward. While one can choose whatever practices one likes as a Probationer, it is very important to have some exposure to the basics of *asana* (postures) and *dharana* (concentration practices). Through these *raja yoga* practices, the aspirant is beginning to develop skill in stilling and focusing the mind, and training it to become receptive to subtle impressions. In addition, through the use of reflective meditations and study of the Holy Books, the aspirant will strengthen his or her ability to gain deeper understanding of important arcana of all sorts. Why is this important? Perhaps it is rather self-evident that if one cannot get the mind to be quiet—if one cannot still the flurry of everyday thought and allow the mind to become receptive to subtle impulses for something as simple as meditating on a line of text or a red triangle—how can one possibly achieve sufficient stillness of mind for the ultimate "meditation" of the final K & C working?

These raja yoga practices continue across the First Order grades, climaxing with Dominus Liminis. For example, *Liber Turris*[11] is assigned in the Practicus and Philosophus grades to strengthen the ability to destroy thoughts at their source in the brain. *Liber Yod*,[12] for the Dominus Liminis, serves as training in bringing the entirety of the mind to a single point of focused intensity. All of these practices, placed here just as the aspirant is on the final approach to Tiphereth, are entirely consistent with the aim of the Dominus Liminis to harmonize all the work done in the Order so far, and to aim with one-pointedness to the K & C of the HGA.

Finally, we have the practices of *Liber Jugorum*,[13] which develop the aspirant's control of thought, word, and deed. The Practicus attempts to control speech, the Philosophus action, and the Dominus Liminis thought. Why? If one cannot control one's speech in everyday life, how can one compose and deliver the most perfect invocation of the HGA? If one cannot control everyday actions, how can one create the perfect ritual to invoke the HGA? If one cannot control everyday thoughts, how can one, at that supreme moment of focus, direct all one's attention to the HGA? The control practices of *Liber Jugorum* strengthen many magical muscles necessary for ultimate success in the Great Work.

Track Three

Track three involves the stimulation and activation of the chakras and the raising of kundalini—the divine, life-giving, regenerative force resident in every human. Through various practices, this life force can be intensified and applied in specific, targeted ways to transformational processes in the body, in the mind, and in the subtle energy centers with which the magician works.

Many Probationers will be working with asana, and this practice is preliminary to more advanced kundalini work. Formal testing on asana is not required until the Zelator grade, where one must sit perfectly still in front of one's Superior for a full hour before being passed. When there is sufficient facility with asana, it is appropriate to begin working with *pranayama*—the control of breath. This also may start as early as Probationer, but formal testing does not occur until Zelator. One of the important things to note about this testing of pranayama is that the desired results (often described as "fine perspiration" and "automatic rigidity") are in fact early signs of kundalini activity. These are just the beginning stages, but it is evident that even at the level of Zelator, work is being done to initiate the flow of kundalini, and concrete results are beginning to manifest. In

11. Crowley, *Magick: Book 4: Parts I–IV*.
12. Crowley, *Magick: Book 4: Parts I–IV*.
13. Crowley, *Magick: Book 4: Parts I–IV*.

practice, these early results assist with the growing awareness of ecstatic energy states in the mind-body apparatus, and with the conscious direction of this energy to desired ends.

This process is greatly amplified through the practices given in Section SSS of *Liber HHH*,[14] which is assigned to the Practicus of A∴A∴. This beautiful and powerful practice—an instruction in Thelemic tantra—involves the conscious movement of energy between the base of the spine and the brain. The aspirant conceives of these opposite poles as being Hadit and Nuit, (essentially, the divine masculine and feminine archetypes in the Thelemic pantheon) and builds up a sort of courtship between them. After much extended practice, typically over the course of many days or longer, the aspirant brings the work to a climax as these poles are at last allowed to unite in ecstasy. What is the utility of this practice in terms of our training? In addition to the considerable mystical benefits, any such practice where the aspirant becomes a conscious vessel of magical force, and learns to direct it in a targeted fashion, is a means of developing important magical skills.

As with the other training tracks, the process of raising the kundalini is of fundamental importance in the A∴A∴ system. In a very real sense, the kundalini is the fuel that potentiates all the transformations we undertake in this system. All of the willed transformations of self are given more potency by virtue of this energy being raised and applied in the intended manner. Additionally, and very importantly, the spiritual ecstasy that occurs when these kundalini-related practices are brought to their conclusion is in itself transformative, healing, and evolutionary; its nature is to potentiate the transformation of the human into the more-than-human. The experience of this "divinized" ecstasy is so important in the path toward K & C that it can't be overstated. By the time the aspirant has completed the work of the first few grades of A∴A∴, the consciousness of the divine nature of this ecstasy should be so acute and so vivid that the very idea of God—the idea of our HGA—is the "sexiest" thing imaginable. Likewise, sex itself comes to be perceived as inseparable from holiness—it is, in fact, true worship of Nuit when practiced mindfully.

Track Four

Track four consists of devotional practices—the *bhakti yoga* of the A∴A∴ system. While this work is especially assigned to the Philosophus grade, corresponding to Netzach, the aspiration, the devotion, the fire, the passion for the path itself, and the progress toward union with the Angel are not new to the aspirant. Indeed, it is highly unlikely that an aspirant would even progress to the Philosophus grade at all without having been fueled by intense devotion and aspiration all along the way. All the truth and beauty that enraptures the aspirant, that unfolding mystery for which they continually reach, that siren song that calls them onward—all of these are simply one or another aspect of the Holy Guardian Angel active in their life and consciousness.

---

14. Crowley, *Magick: Book 4: Parts I–IV*.

• • • • • • • •

As noted earlier, these muscles of devotion and aspiration are cultivated most pointedly in the grade of Philosophus, corresponding to the sephirah Netzach; for it is just at this moment on the path, when one is nearly ready to begin the formal K & C working, that one must fully light the fires of aspiration. The key devotional instruction formally assigned to the Philosophus is *Liber Astarte vel Berylli*.[15] This is a beautifully constructed work in which one essentially creates one's own religious system devoted to a chosen deity. It is clear from the instructions in the book that the point here is to gain practice in the art of worship—to exercise and strengthen the muscles of devotion, so that in the very near future, as one undertakes the K & C working, one can direct this newly strengthened ability toward one's own HGA. This makes a good deal of sense, since it is unlikely that the Philosophus has full conscious contact with the HGA, and will therefore need other gods, symbols, and images as "stand-ins." In practice, this need tends to diminish quickly as the aspirant nears the climactic experiences of the Dominus Liminis and Adeptus Minor grades, and the HGA increasingly instructs them in all the essentials of their true religion, and they take their rightful place as the "prophet" of their own Angel.

Track Five

Track five is the balancing of the psycho-magical constitution. The aspirant must prepare themselves as a grail or other vessel for the indwelling of the light of the Angel. If the aspirant's development is unbalanced, the grail will topple. If they have failed to build themselves into a seamless and solid vessel, the grail will leak. They must fashion themselves into the perfect *form* that, by its design, invokes the desired *force*—the light of the HGA.

One way to conceptualize the process of attaining this balanced form is embedded in the passage through the elemental grades of the First Order of A∴A∴. At each grade, the aspirant builds a symbolic weapon to symbolize and concretize the inner changes occurring in that grade. These elemental weapons correspond, of course, to the four elements of earth, air, water, and fire, but we can also understand them in the context of Carl Jung's four functions of the psyche: sensation, intuition, thinking, and feeling, respectively. The pantacle (disk) is the weapon of earth, Malkuth, and sensation; the dagger is the weapon of air, Yesod, and intuition (spiritual intuition often first manifests through the subconscious, which is attributed to Yesod); the cup is the weapon of water, Hod, and thinking; and the wand is the weapon of fire, Netzach, and feeling, aspiration, and desire. Additionally, at the Dominus Liminis grade, the magick lamp is constructed as a symbol of the crowning of spirit over the other four elements. All of these things—the four elements, the four functions of the psyche, the four weapons—are representative of the balanced development of the psycho-magical constitution. By traversing these grades

---

15. Crowley, *Magick: Book 4: Parts I–IV.*

• • • • • • •

in a stepwise and balanced manner, one can indeed fashion oneself into a perfect grail for the light of the HGA, for it is said that a god will not indwell a temple improperly prepared.

Jane Wolfe

Jane Wolfe (1875–1958), Soror Estai, was an American silent film character actress, magician, and Thelemite. Chiefly, she is remembered as a skilled, graceful and persistent administrator. She helped found the Ordo Templi Orientis Agape Lodge in Pasadena, California, and for some time was the Lodge Master. It is no exaggeration to say that she was one of the people who kept the O.T.O. alive in the difficult years following Crowley's death. She was also a skilled magician.

Her early years were focused on practical things. Wolfe studied stenography, and worked in this field for ten years in New York. An attack of neuritis put an end to that pursuit, and she moved into acting, first in the theatre and then in the fledgling motion picture industry. She relocated to Los Angeles with Kalem Studios, and became a leading character actor. Her best-known film effort was a secondary role in *Rebecca of Sunnybrook Farm*, a Mary Pickford movie, made in 1917.

During her first years in California, Wolfe discovered spiritualistic practices. In the fall of 1913, she was given a copy of the book *Magic, White and Black* by Franz Hartmann. This book, subtitled *The Science of Finite and Infinite Life, Containing Practical Hints for Students of Occultism*, could be said to have influenced much of her later life in the way it tied personal discipline, in particular the control of the mind, to spiritual attainment.

This book whetted her interest in esotericism, and her biographer, Phyllis Seckler, documents that in August 1917 Wolfe used a Ouija board to contact several spirits. In 1918 she began to experiment with automatic writing, with the help of L. V. Jefferson. She connected with a spirit named "Fee Wah," who appeared periodically throughout the rest of her life, according to her biographical record.

In 1918 Wolfe began corresponding with Aleister Crowley, and two years later she renounced her career in Hollywood to join Crowley at his Abbey of Thelema at Cefalù, Sicily. The Abbey was a magical retreat/school modeled on the principles of Thelema and the training system of the A∴A∴. She lived there from 1920 until its closure in 1923.

Enough of Wolfe's diary entries have been conserved that we know how she progressed during her time at Cefalù. The students did daily magical developmental studies of beginning A∴A∴ degrees. Daily work included pentagram and hexagram rituals and Thelemic solar adorations. Wolfe also became adept at pranayama, asana, and dharana. These magical practices were taught to her directly by Crowley, and are carefully documented in her diaries. Her work there resulted in her admission as a Probationer in 1921.

· · · · · · · ·

Wolfe is most inspirational for her early mystic tendencies, gradually brought under her own control through her studies, and the management of both her mind and body. She seemed naturally at ease with astral workings, and at the same time, she skillfully used her own body to enhance and enable spiritual states. It is clear from her history that the discipline she developed using the practices learned at Cefalù greatly enhanced her ability to reach and control mystical states.

—Harper Feist

Harper Feist is a member of the O.T.O. and Local Body Master at Leaping Laughter Oasis (Minneapolis), and is also a member of A∴A∴. Outside, but related to, her spiritual pursuits, Harper holds a PhD in physical chemistry and is a martial artist, practicing the Japanese art of iaido. Her primary historical interests surround the intersection of magic and science in the Medieval and Renaissance periods, but she is also fascinated with the more personal history of her nineteenth- and twentieth-century magical grandmothers.

Ritual Construction Techniques

Crowley was a master at extracting doctrines and practices of true value from the verbose (and often corrupted, incomplete, or mistranslated) source materials of Western magical traditions. One of his greatest gifts to modern magical practice is his analysis of the components of effective ritual, outlined most succinctly in various chapters of *Magick in Theory and Practice*.[16] These include banishing, purification, consecration, general invocations, the oath or proclamation, specific invocations, bringing down the magical force, the completion of the work, and the License to Depart. While these basic components do not vary significantly from prior approaches, Crowley showed great ingenuity in his work with them over his lifetime, employing ecstatic states, sexual acts, psychoactive substances, dramatic action, and finely crafted poetic invocations rather than the often turgid and verbose tools of past traditions.

Banishing is a traditional term used for the clearing of the physical, mental, and spiritual space in which the magician is working. Crowley typically employed traditional rituals such as the Banishing Rituals of the Pentagram and Hexagram, which cleanse the microcosmic and macrocosmic realms, respectively.

Purification is a further cleansing of the magician and the space, typically symbolized as a washing with elemental water. The aim is to remove any unwanted or superfluous energies that might sully the purity of the magician's mental and physical space. *Consecration*, often seen as an action of the element of fire and carried out through the use of incense, elevates the purified magician/space by linking and dedicating it to the sacred aim of the rite.

---

16. Part III of Crowley, *Magick: Book 4: Parts I–IV*.

The *general invocation* is, as the term implies, a general raising of divine force. Any invocation that achieves this aim for the magician is a candidate for use, but common examples from the Western Hermetic and Thelemic traditions include the Preliminary Invocation of the Goetia, the First Call of the Enochian system, and the Priest's portion of the Anthem from Crowley's *Liber XV: The Gnostic Mass*:

> Thou who art I, beyond all I am,
> Who hast no nature and no name,
> Who art, when all but Thou are gone,
> Thou, centre and secret of the Sun,
> Thou, hidden spring of all things known
> And unknown, Thou aloof, alone,
> Thou, the true fire within the reed
> Brooding and breeding, source and seed
> Of life, love, liberty, and light,
> Thou beyond speech and beyond sight,
> Thee I invoke, my faint fresh fire
> Kindling as mine intents aspire.
> Thee I invoke, abiding one,
> Thee, centre and secret of the Sun,
> And that most holy mystery
> Of which the vehicle am I.
> Appear, most awful and most mild,
> As it is lawful, in thy child! [17]

The *oath* or *proclamation* is the magician's statement of purpose for the rite and/or an actual taking of an oath to execute the rite. With this act, the mental conception of the ritual's aim (thought) is translated into a concise verbal summary (word), and is then accomplished by the completion of the ritual itself (deed).

The *specific invocation* harnesses the generic force brought forth by the general invocation, and particularizes it to the specific energies necessary for completion of the ritual. Specific invocations may be ritualized, as in the case of the various Invoking Rituals of the Pentagram (for the four elements) or the Hexagram (for planetary and zodiacal forces). Specific invocations may also be poetic in nature, such as a set of stanzas dedicated to calling forth a particular deity, spirit, or other entity, as in this excerpt from Crowley's evocation of Bartzabel, the Spirit of Mars:

---

17. Crowley, *Magick: Book 4: Parts I–IV*, 594–595.

Hail! Hail! Hail! Hail! Hail!

Send forth a spark of thine illimitable light and force, we beseech Thee, that it may appear in the Heaven of Mars as the God Elohim Gibor.

O winged glory of gold! O plumes of justice and stern brows of majesty! O warrior armed with spear and shield! O virgin strength and splendour as of spring! That ridest in thy Chariot of Iron above the Storm upon the Sea! Who shootest forth the Arrows of the Moon! Who wieldest the Four Magick Weapons! Who art the Master of the Pentagram and of the blazing fury of the Sun![18]

Once the specific, desired magical force is present, it must be brought down from the highest, ineffable spiritual realms through increasingly dense astral planes, and finally into the physical world, so that the force may be used to consecrate the talisman, magical weapon, eucharist, or other "magical link" to complete the rite. This may be accomplished through the poetic invocation itself, as in the excerpt above, where we see the divine force, embodied by Elohim Gibor, brought down to the archangelic realm as manifested in Kamael, and the angelic "choir" the Seraphim. Subsequent stanzas of this invocation particularize the force further to the intelligence Graphiel and then finally to the spirit Bartzabel itself.

Once the talisman or weapon is consecrated or the eucharist consumed, the rite is concluded by the License to Depart—a dismissal of the spirits called forth, returning them to their proper abodes.

The Ordo Templi Orientis and the Integration of Sex Magick

Around 1912, Crowley came into contact with Theodor Reuss, who was the leader of the Ordo Templi Orientis (O.T.O.). The O.T.O. claimed to be an *Academia Masonica*, or a repository of esoteric rituals and practices of the Freemasonic tradition. They also claimed to possess a "supreme secret" supposedly drawn from tantric sexual practices that had been learned by adepts traveling in the East. According to Crowley, Reuss contacted him because Crowley had unknowingly published this supreme secret in *The Book of Lies*,[19] and he wanted Crowley to keep secret the full details. Crowley was admitted to the O.T.O. and eventually entrusted with the leadership of the order in the United Kingdom.

The introduction of sex magick and mysticism into Crowley's magical toolkit was nothing short of revolutionary. Sex magick rites gradually began to replace many of the more elaborate ritual techniques of traditional Western magick that Crowley had learned in the Golden Dawn. Crowley's work with sex magick techniques would dominate his personal magical practice for

---

18. Crowley, *The Vision & the Voice: With Commentary and Other Papers*, 275.
19. Crowley, *The Book of Lies.*

decades to come, documented in his *Rex de Arte Regia* diaries and elsewhere. In parallel with these developments, Crowley was simultaneously coming to terms with his own role as the Prophet of Thelema and the New Aeon. Remarkably, the central cosmology and pantheon of the New Aeon was inherently tantric, in the broad sense, and perfectly suited for implementation in a sex magick context: Nuit, the sky goddess and the embodiment of infinite possibilities, resembles the traditional Shakti, while her consort, Hadit, is the force of aspiration itself, not unlike Shiva. The product of their ecstatic union, the god Ra-Hoor-Khuit, or Horus, can be understood as an emblem of that spiritually awakened consciousness characteristic of the New Aeon: free, forceful, unashamed, and in harmony with universal Will.

Jack Parsons

John Whiteside "Jack" Parsons (1914–1952) was a pioneer in the field of rocket science, a writer, and an occultist. He experimented with early rocket engines, developed solid rocket fuel, and co-founded Jet Propulsion Laboratory. His contributions to science led NASA to name a crater on the moon in his honor. He also figures prominently in the history of Thelema in the early twentieth century because of his involvement with the Ordo Templi Orientis and A∴A∴, his own magical work, and the small body of writing he left behind.

Jack Parsons was initiated into the O.T.O. in 1941 at Agape Lodge in Southern California, the only functioning O.T.O. body at the time. He later entered the A∴A∴ as a student under W. T. Smith. Parsons advanced quickly in those systems and demonstrated a great deal of personal charm and leadership. Aleister Crowley eventually named him Master of Agape Lodge when he wanted to replace W. T. Smith. Parsons's tenure at the helm of Agape was not without controversy. At times, word of his ritual magick would alarm even Crowley.

One of his Parsons's documented rituals, known as the *Babalon Working*, was conducted with the assistance of a young pre-Scientology L. Ron Hubbard. From that operation came a document called *Liber 49*, which purports to be the fourth chapter of *The Book of the Law*. The Babalon Working was intended to invoke the goddess Babalon into manifestation on the physical plane. Parsons believed that the ritual brought his second wife, Marjorie Cameron, into his life, and he suspected her to be an incarnation of Babalon. The Babalon Working was a pivotal moment for Jack Parsons, and the visions he received during that time greatly influenced his later work and writings.

After taking the Oath of the Magister Templi in 1948, Parsons called himself *Belarion Antichrist* and positioned himself against what he viewed as the tyranny of Christianity.

He authored a document called *The Book of the Antichrist*, which contained a manifesto calling for freedom against religious and social oppression.

The most well-known of his written works is an essay titled *Freedom Is a Two-Edged Sword*, in which Parsons expounds eloquently on freedom, sexual liberation, government control, the power of women, Babalon, and other aspects of liberty as held by the Law of Thelema, "Do what thou wilt." Symbolically, Parsons describes the sword of freedom as having a two-edged blade, where one edge is the exercise of liberty and the other, the responsibility of the free individual to ensure the liberty of others.

Parsons's occult activities attracted the attention of the F.B.I., and at one point his security clearance was temporarily revoked, preventing him from working on government contracts. He left the O.T.O. in 1945 and continued his work with the occult and with dangerous chemicals until his death in 1952, when an accidental explosion in his garage took his life at the age of thirty-seven.

Regardless of the sensational aspects of his life, Jack Parsons can be viewed as a champion of the Thelemic principle of liberty. His life of science was dedicated to freeing humanity from the bonds of gravity. His occult life was dedicated to freeing the soul from the veils of the material world. But it is through his few written works that we get a picture of what drove him. His passionate writing is infused with energy and consistently articulates a theme of attaining personal freedom. Jack Parsons bore the torch of Thelema in its early days, and he can be remembered for his vision of what an advanced society, free from the bonds of repression, might look like.

—Rex Parsons

Rex Parsons has been pursuing his True Will as a star in the body of Nuit since 2010 e.v., if not well before that. He is an initiated member of the Ordo Templi Orientis and a former officer of 418 Lodge, O.T.O., and serves as a Temple Chief in the Temple of the Silver Star. In 2016 e.v., he was ordained a Priest of Ecclesia Gnostica Catholica. He regularly officiates celebrations of *Liber XV*, the Gnostic Mass, and performs other functions of the clergy. He is a contributor to the first two volumes of *Daughters of Babalon*, available from Lulu.com. He currently lives in the valley of Sacramento, CA.

In published writings such as *Liber Nu*,[20] *Liber Had*,[21] and *Liber H.H.H.*, Crowley wrote powerful and beautiful instructions on the mystical application of these forces, while his writings on their use in sex magick were largely reserved for the private papers of the highest degrees of the

20. Crowley, *Gems from the Equinox.*
21. Crowley, *Gems from the Equinox.*

• • • • • • •

O.T.O. However, some hints about these magical applications of sexual energy can be found in writings such as *Amrita*,[22] *Magick in Theory and Practice*, and elsewhere. The basic concept is that the generative force, which naturally resides in all humans as a function of procreation, can be harnessed and directed to specific magical aims in service of the will of the magician. Before this can be safely and effectively done, however, the magician must undergo rigorous training: a purification of the sex force, stripping away any accretions of societally based shame or negativity, followed by the consecration of the force to divine aims, all fueled and supported by the magician's training in yogic concentration techniques.

Aside from his compelling interest in the O.T.O.'s sex magick secrets, Crowley came to view the order as a primary vehicle of promulgating the Law of Thelema in the world at large, as well as a custodian of his own literary legacy. He restructured the order as a model of an ideal society that would allow individuals to exercise their True Will without undue restriction, while also optimizing the order's self-regulatory, creative, and governmental functions. In *Liber 194: An Intimation with Reference to the Constitution of the Order*, Crowley (writing as Frater Baphomet, his motto as the head of the O.T.O.) notes:

> By the study of [the Order's] Balance you may yourself come to apprehension of how to rule your own life. For, in True Things, all are but images one of another; man is but a map of the universe, and Society is but the same on a larger scale. [...] [The order] combines monarchy with democracy; it includes aristocracy, and conceals even the seeds of revolution, by which alone progress can be effected.[23]

While the membership of the O.T.O. was relatively miniscule in Crowley's lifetime, the order today has thousands of members worldwide. In accordance with Crowley's wishes, the O.T.O. functions as the custodian of his literary estate and maintains an impressive archive of Crowley's personal writings, magical implements, and other artifacts.

Key Rituals and Practices

Crowley was an incredibly prolific writer, and his output included countless books, essays, poems, plays, and even book reviews—but for magical practitioners, his creative and in some cases revolutionary rituals are the core of his legacy. It is beyond the scope of this book to examine all of these in detail, but it may be useful to explore several key ritual writings in outline.

22. Crowley, *Amrita: Essays in Magical Rejuvenation*.
23. In Crowley et al., *The Equinox*, vol. III, no. 10, 173–178.

· · · · · · · ·

Rituals of the Pentagram and Hexagram

Crowley adopted the traditional forms of these fundamental rituals when he learned them during his tenure with the Golden Dawn. He somewhat controversially made them publicly available in *The Equinox*,[24] along with many of the G.D.'s initiation rituals, and he later presented radically revised adaptations of these rituals in *The Book of Lies*, in the form of the *Star Ruby* (pentagram) and the *Star Sapphire* (hexagram). While these revised versions do not serve precisely the same purposes as the traditional forms, they do represent some of Crowley's earliest efforts to integrate his new Thelemic cosmology and philosophy into basic ritual practices. Also, contrary to the statements of some commentators, Crowley continued to teach the traditional forms of these rituals to the end of his life.

Liber Resh vel Helios [25]

Partially inspired by the Islamic custom of multiple prayer sessions spread throughout the day, Crowley developed the solar adorations contained in *Liber Resh* and assigned them to students as a basic daily practice. The aim is to align the magician's consciousness with the stations of the sun—dawn, noon, dusk, and midnight—through symbolic identification with the Thelemicized Egyptian deities Ra, Ahathoor, Tum, and Khephra, respectively.

The Mass of the Phoenix [26]

First published in *The Book of Lies*, the *Mass of the Phoenix* is another ritual recommended for daily use, and like *Liber Resh* involves the magician identifying him- or herself with the sun at dusk. It is a eucharistic ritual that climaxes with the consumption of a "Cake of Light" (essentially a small cookie scented with cinnamony Oil of Abramelin) that has been dabbed with a small amount of the magician's own blood.

Liber V vel Reguli [27]

Described by Crowley as the "Ritual of the Mark of the Beast: an incantation proper to invoke the Energies of the Aeon of Horus, adapted for the daily use of the Magician of whatever grade,"[28] *Liber Reguli* is essentially a special application of a pentagram ritual involving a simultaneous invocation of the four elements as well as spirit itself. As the quote above suggests, this is an explicitly Thelemic ritual, calling upon Therion, Babalon, Nuit, and Hadit, and employing averse (i.e., rotated so as to appear upside down) pentagrams.

24. Crowley, *The Equinox*, originally serialized 1909–1919.
25. Crowley, *Magick: Book 4: Parts I–IV*.
26. Crowley, *Magick: Book 4: Parts I–IV*.
27. Crowley, *Magick: Book 4: Parts I–IV*.
28. Crowley, *Magick: Book 4: Parts I–IV*, 561.

· · · · · · ·

Liber Samekh [29]

While living at his Abbey of Thelema in Cefalu, Sicily, in the early 1920s, Crowley wrote *Liber Samekh* for his student Frank Bennett. It was designed to be used as a months-long ceremonial working for Bennett to invoke his Holy Guardian Angel, and is a masterpiece of ritual construction and (especially) ritual commentary. In the "Scholion" that follows *Liber Samekh*'s ritual text, we find some of Crowley's most profound and direct writings on the nature of spiritual illumination, and some of his most detailed descriptions of the visualizations and other inner work to be used by the magician during the performance of the ritual.

Liber Pyramidos [30]

Originally written as a self-initiation ritual, *Liber Pyramidos* employs a unique "pyramidal" temple layout, and was designed to be a distillation of (and undoubtedly, in Crowley's mind, an improvement upon) the Neophyte initiation of the Golden Dawn. Its ritual formulae are distinct and powerful and can be used quite effectively as temple opening and closing ceremonies.

Liber XV: The Gnostic Mass [31]

Conceived as the central public and private ritual of the Ordo Templi Orientis and its Ecclesia Gnostica Catholica (Gnostic Catholic Church), the Gnostic Mass is one of the crowning examples of Crowley's ritual writing genius. The Mass unfolds as an interplay between the Priest, Priestess, and Deacon, who can be seen as representing the Sulphur, Salt, and Mercury of alchemy and the three *gunas* of Hindu philosophy. It incorporates ritual themes and structures from the Russian Orthodox and Roman Catholic Masses, as well as magical formulae drawn from Egyptian and Greek traditions. In many ways, it is a veiled ritual enactment of the technical secret at the center of the O.T.O.'s teachings, and it can be profitably studied in this light.

The Priestess is seated upon the altar and is (at her option) nude. Clothed or not, the Priestess can be seen as a representation of Nuit and the embodiment of divinity itself. The Priest, meanwhile, functions as a symbol of the aspiration to the divine—the Hadit force within each of us that yearns for ecstatic union with Nuit. The fruit of that union is seen as Ra-Hoor-Khuit, formulated as a Eucharist of wine and a Cake of Light that is consumed by the Priest. Each member of the assembled congregation also partakes of the Eucharist, as an affirmation of their participation in the mystery of the Mass that has just been enacted.

During the Mass, the Deacon and the congregation recite the *Creed*, which is worthy of study as a concise statement of core Thelemic assumptions about the laws of the universe that underlie the magick of the Mass.

---

29. Crowley, *Magick: Book 4: Parts I–IV*.
30. Crowley et al., *Commentaries on the Holy Books and Other Papers*.
31. Crowley, *Magick: Book 4: Parts I–IV*.

· · · · · · · ·

The Creed

I believe in one secret and ineffable LORD; and in one Star in the Company of Stars of whose fire we are created, and to which we shall return; and in one Father of Life, Mystery of Mystery, in His name CHAOS, the sole viceregent of the Sun upon the Earth; and in one Air the nourisher of all that breathes.

And I believe in one Earth, the Mother of us all, and in one Womb wherein all men are begotten, and wherein they shall rest, Mystery of Mystery, in Her name BABALON.

And I believe in the Serpent and the Lion, Mystery of Mystery, in His name BAPHOMET.

And I believe in one Gnostic and Catholic Church **of Light, Life, Love and Liberty, the Word of whose Law is THELEMA.**

And I believe in the communion of Saints.

And, forasmuch as meat and drink are transmuted in us daily into spiritual substance, I believe in the Miracle of the Mass.

And I confess one Baptism of Wisdom **whereby we accomplish the Miracle of Incarnation.**

And I confess my life one, individual, and eternal that was, and is, and is to come.

AUMGN. AUMGN. AUMGN.[32]

As the central public ritual of the O.T.O./E.G.C., the Gnostic Mass is presented regularly at many locations around the world and is one of the best ways to witness Thelemic ritual presented within the living culture of Thelemic communities. Any reader with even a passing interest in the magick of Aleister Crowley is strongly encouraged to attend a Gnostic Mass.

Post-Crowley Magick in the Twentieth and Twenty-First Centuries: Chaos Magick and Beyond

As a man bridging the Edwardian and early modern eras, Aleister Crowley was a magician of *our* time. This made him uniquely positioned to be seized upon as a hero by the counterculture of the 1960s, and to become the leading figure of the occult revival that followed, decades after his death. Crowley was hugely influential on figures such as the Beatles, Led Zeppelin's Jimmy Page, the Church of Satan's Anton LaVey, and experimental filmmaker Kenneth Anger. Crowley's collaboration with Gerald Gardner in the early twentieth century laid the groundwork for the emergence of the modern witchcraft/Wicca tradition and the broader neo-pagan movement. Likewise, several of Crowley's students went on to be important thinkers and writers in their own right, including Israel Regardie, Austin Osman Spare, and Kenneth Grant. These initiates contributed to the post-Crowley world of magick well into the late twentieth century, and their successors have continued their work to the present day.

---

32. Crowley, *Magick: Book 4: Parts I–IV*, 585.

Phyllis Seckler

Phyllis Seckler (Soror Meral) was one of the leading individuals responsible for establishing Thelema and the modern Ordo Templi Orientis (O.T.O.) in California. She was a IX° of the O.T.O. and an adept of the A∴A∴, and founded the College of Thelema. Her dedication to Thelema lives on in a number of organizations, as well as personally within her students.

Born in Canada in 1917 as Phyllis Evelina Pratt, Seckler later moved to California and worked as an art teacher, raising her young children after the end of her first marriage. She started taking acting lessons, and through her drama teacher at the time, Regina Kahl, she was introduced to Agape Lodge members, and even lived in the Lodge for a period of her life. (Aleister Crowley himself would later express delight at her sketches illustrating the interactions among the various individuals at Agape Lodge!)

Seckler was received into the A∴A∴ by Jane Wolfe in 1940, and after Wolfe's death in 1958, she received personal instruction from Karl Germer, head of both the O.T.O. and the A∴A∴, who recognized her as having achieved Knowledge and Conversation of the Holy Guardian Angel and the grade of Adeptus Minor $5° = 6^\square$. During this time, Seckler typed out copies of central Thelemic writings such as *The Vision and the Voice*, *Liber Aleph*, and other key texts so that they would not be lost. Many of these texts would later be published and achieve a wide circulation. Additionally, she spent a segment of her life married to Grady McMurtry, another key figure in the early history of the modern O.T.O. Together they initiated many of the earliest members of the modern O.T.O. in the United States. In 1979, she became the founding Master of 418 Lodge, a position she would continue to hold until her death a quarter century later.

Throughout her life, Seckler worked tirelessly to establish and grow a number of key Thelemic organizations in California, including the Ordo Templi Orientis, College of Thelema, Temple of Thelema, Temple of the Silver Star, and A∴A∴. Her writings included many essays in her journal *In the Continuum*, which contained a selection of key writings by Aleister Crowley not easily available in print, as well as her own writings on Thelema, magick, tarot, Qabalah, and other topics. (See the "Additional Suggested Readings" section.)

Seckler died peacefully among loved ones in 2004. Today, many of her personal students are among the most prominent and well-known writers and speakers in contemporary Thelema.

—Lauren Gardner

Lauren Gardner, PhD, is a counselor, educator, and psychotherapist in private practice in Chapel Hill, NC. Her esoteric background includes significant training in Golden Dawn, A∴A∴, Raja Yoga, and several related systems and traditions. Her doctoral dissertation examined the experiences of Pagans in psychotherapy.

Crowley's experimental and often transgressive approach to magick helped shape the so-called "chaos magick" movement. The work of magicians such as Peter Carroll and Phil Hine can easily be traced to the rule-breaking aesthetic of Crowley's corpus. Likewise, figures such as Genesis P-Orridge, Robert Anton Wilson, and Timothy Leary picked up Crowley's tools of mind- and culture-change and transmuted them into their own symbol sets and modes of work. P-Orridge channeled his efforts into the musical groups Throbbing Gristle and Psychic TV, and even founded a magical order of sorts, Thee Temple ov Psychick Youth (TOPY). Author Robert Anton Wilson explicitly discussed Crowley's philosophies in his writings, both fiction and nonfiction, and has been an initial source of inspiration for many aspirants who have gone on to work with Crowley's systems. Psychologist, LSD advocate, and counterculture icon Timothy Leary needs no introduction. While his broader work is well known, under the surface was a deep affinity for the mind-expanding and libertarian focus of Crowley's writings. Leary was even known to quote Crowley's "Do what thou wilt shall be the whole of the Law" maxim when appearing on television shows.

Crowley was the first prominent modern magician to live in the era of Freud, Jung, and other proponents of the depth psychology field. While his explicit exploration of this movement appears to have been rather fleeting, there is no doubt that he was undertaking work of a parallel nature. With Freud, he shared an appreciation of the importance of the sex force, and Jung's work with comparative religion and philosophy from the *psychological* point of view mirrored Crowley's attempts to translate his own similar research into *magical* practice. Crowley's essay "An Improvement on Psychoanalysis," published in *Vanity Fair* in 1916, is his most complete analysis of depth psychology as he knew it. It should be noted that this was written well before Jung's most important writings on alchemy and other esoteric traditions, and one wonders what Crowley would have thought had he ever reviewed Jung's mature work, or the transcendent *Red Book*,[33] which was not published until many decades after Crowley's death.

Crowley's efforts to integrate Eastern meditative techniques into the canon of Western magick prefigured the rise of a culture-wide fascination with yoga, tantra, and all things Eastern. His passionate support for the sexual liberation of humanity found itself powerfully expressed in the "free love" movements of the late 1960s, and the greater awareness and celebration of the diversity of sexuality and gender fluidity that is currently visible in our culture. To be sure, much work remains to be done to secure humanity's ultimate freedom, and the forces of superstition, intolerance, bigotry, and oppression are never far from our doorstep; but Aleister Crowley's magick—and indeed the whole of his life's work—is a potent example of one seeker's path to find the liberation inherent in living his own True Will.

---

33. Jung, *The Red Book.*

· · · · · · · ·

Organizational Contacts

Unlike many of the traditions described in this volume, Thelema exists in today's world as a living, growing community, embodied in the work of many organizations, large and small, and an even greater number of unaffiliated individual practitioners. Among these are two of the organizations formerly led by Crowley himself, the Ordo Templi Orientis (O.T.O.) and the A∴A∴, as well as more recently developed training options such as the Temple of the Silver Star (**totss.org**). More information about these organizations is easily found online, but a few additional words are warranted regarding the A∴A∴ (figure 2).

A∴A∴

Since the death of Karl Germer (Crowley's successor as the Head of the Order) in 1962, there has been no *universally acknowledged* governance of A∴A∴. After Germer's death, multiple claimants arose, each with its own leaders and its own (sometimes rather tangled) history. The only manifestation of A∴A∴ the present author and editors can *personally* vouch for in terms of its historical legitimacy, the competence of its leaders, and the linkage of its administrative Triad to the spiritual roots of the Order is the one that may be contacted via **onestarinsight.org**. This is not to denigrate the work of other A∴A∴ claimants—we know with certainty that much important work is being done by initiates of these organizations.

Figure 2. The Sigil of the A∴A∴

If you are called to the work of the A∴A∴, you are encouraged to do your own research and come to your own conclusions about which particular path is best for you. Ultimately, your own personal spiritual attainment will be the best indicator of the wisdom of your choice.

Grady McMurtry

Major Grady Louis McMurtry (1918–1985) is best known for reviving the Ordo Templi Orientis as Hymenaeus Alpha X°, after the death of Karl Germer, Frater Saturnus X°.

McMurtry joined the Order in June of 1941, taking both Minerval and I° on the same day. Then World War II intervened and McMurtry joined the cause in February of 1942, taking him away from Agape Lodge but resulting in his meeting Aleister Crowley that October. By November of that year, Crowley elevated McMurtry to the IX° with the motto *Hymenaeus Alpha* (777). In several letters (1942–1947) Crowley declared McMurtry to be his *Caliph*, or spiritual heir, and gave him authority "to take charge of the whole work of the Order in California. … This authorization is to be used only in emergency."

The death of Karl Germer in 1962, without designating an heir, created such an emergency. Phyllis Seckler, Soror Meral IX°, began contacting Order members and informing them of Germer's demise. When she contacted McMurtry about it, they began plans to rebuild the Order based on McMurtry's authorization from Crowley. She helped him move back to California, and they began meeting with surviving members of the Order. Only a few were still interested, most having lost connection during the years in which Germer refused to let the Order initiate or do any organizing or activities.

During McMurtry's leadership, the Order legally defended its right to Crowley's literary heritage and began publishing and initiating again, including incorporating the Order to give it firm legal standing in 1971. By October of 1977 McMurtry created Thelema Lodge in Berkeley, California, as the Grand Lodge, or center of operations. He was quite charismatic and encouraging to the young people of the '70s, and the membership quickly expanded. From less than a dozen members, the Order grew to having several local bodies across the US, with membership in the hundreds. It also began forming and implementing many of the committees and ruling bodies needed to fulfill Crowley's design for the Order. Today the Order's membership is counted in the thousands, with local bodies in over twenty-five countries and five Grand Lodges around the world.

—Marlene Cornelius

Marlene Cornelius was born a Thelemite. To her delight, she discovered Crowley through *The Book of the Law* and has been a member of the O.T.O. for thirty-four years and an aspirant to the A∴A∴ for almost thirty years. She also publishes hard-to-find Crowley and Thelemic history books through Red Flame (in the '90s) and Conjoined Creation (currently).

· · · · · · ·

Sources

Crowley, Aleister. *Amrita: Essays in Magical Rejuvenation.* Edited by Martin P. Starr. Kings Beach, CA: Thelema Publications, 1990.

———. *The Book of Lies.* York Beach, ME: Weiser, 1993.

———. "Duty." In *The Revival of Magick and Other Essays (Oriflamme 2).* Tempe, AZ: New Falcon/ Ordo Templi Orientis, 1998.

———. *The Equinox.* Facs. ed. Originally serialized 1909–1919. York Beach, ME: Weiser, 1992.

——— et al. *The Equinox.* Vol. III, no. 10. Edited by Hymenaeus Beta. New York: Thelema Publications, 1986.

———. *Gems from the Equinox.* Edited by Israel Regardie. York Beach, ME: Weiser, 2007.

———. *The Holy Books of Thelema.* York Beach, ME: Weiser, 1989.

———. *The Holy Books of Thelema.* Berkeley, CA: Conjoined Creation, 2015.

———. *Magick: Book 4: Parts I–IV.* Revised edition. Edited by Hymenaeus Beta. York Beach, ME: Weiser, 1994.

———. *777 and Other Qabalistic Writings of Aleister Crowley.* Edited by Israel Regardie. York Beach, ME: Weiser, 1993.

———. *The Vision & the Voice: With Commentary and Other Papers.* York Beach, ME: Weiser, 1998.

Crowley, Aleister, with H. P. Blavatsky, J. F. C. Fuller, and Charles Stansfeld Jones. *Commentaries on the Holy Books and Other Papers.* York Beach, ME: Samuel Weiser, 1996.

Eshelman, James. *The Mystical and Magical System of the A∴A∴.* Los Angeles, CA: College of Thelema, 2008.

Jung, Carl. *The Red Book.* Edited and translated by Sonu Shamdasani. New York: W. W. Norton & Co., 2009.

Shoemaker, David. *Living Thelema: A Practical Guide to Attainment in Aleister Crowley's System of Magick.* Sacramento, CA: Anima Solis Books, 2013.

Von Eckartshausen, Karl. *The Cloud upon the Sanctuary.* Originally published in 1793. Whitefish, MT: Kessinger, 2010.

Additional Suggested Reading

By Aleister Crowley

The Book of Thoth: A Short Essay on the Tarot of the Egyptians. The Master Therion [pseud.]. *The Equinox III* (5). York Beach, ME: Weiser, 1993.

• • • • • • • •

The Confessions of Aleister Crowley. Abridged one-volume edition. Edited by John Symonds and Kenneth Grant. New York: Arkana, 1989.

Eight Lectures on Yoga. Mahatma Guru Sri Paramahansa Sivaji [pseud.]. *The Equinox III* (4). New York: 93 Publishing, 1992.

The Law Is for All. Revised edition. Edited by Louis Wilkinson and Hymenaeus Beta. Scottsdale, AZ: New Falcon, 1996.

Liber Aleph vel CXI: The Book of Wisdom or Folly. Revised 2nd edition. Edited by Hymenaeus Beta. York Beach, ME: Weiser, 1991.

Little Essays Toward Truth. Revised 2nd edition. Edited by Hymenaeus Beta. Scottsdale, AZ: New Falcon, 1996.

Magick Without Tears. Abridged edition. Edited by Israel Regardie. Scottsdale, AZ: New Falcon, 1991.

"One Star in Sight." In *Magick: Liber ABA, Book 4*. Revised edition. Edited by Hymenaeus Beta. York Beach, ME: Weiser, 1994.

By Others

Campbell, Colin. *Thelema: An Introduction to the Life, Work & Philosophy of Aleister Crowley*. Woodbury, MN: Llewellyn Publications, 2018.

DuQuette, Lon Milo. *The Magick of Aleister Crowley: A Handbook of the Rituals of Thelema*. York Beach, ME: Weiser, 2003.

Grant, Kenneth. *The Magical Revival*. London: Starfire, 2015.

Hine, Phil. *Condensed Chaos: An Introduction to Chaos Magic*. Tempe, AZ: Original Falcon Press, 2010.

Hyatt, Christopher, ed. *Rebels & Devils: The Psychology of Liberation*. 3rd revised edition. Tempe, AZ: Original Falcon Press, 2013.

Kaczynski, Richard. *Perdurabo*. Berkeley, CA: North Atlantic, 2010.

Pendle, George. *Strange Angel: The Otherworldly Life of Rocket Scientist John Whiteside Parsons*. Orlando, FL: Harcourt, 2005.

Regardie, Israel. *The Eye in the Triangle*. Tempe, AZ: Original Falcon Press, 2017.

———. *Gems from the Equinox*. York Beach: Weiser, 2007.

Seckler, Phyllis (Soror Meral). *Kabbalah, Magick & Thelema: Selected Writings, Volume II*. Edited by David Shoemaker, Gregory Peters, and Rorac Johnson. York Beach, ME: The Teitan Press, 2012.

———. *The Thoth Tarot, Astrology & Other Selected Writings*. Edited by David Shoemaker, Gregory Peters, and Rorac Johnson. Sacramento, CA: Temple of the Silver Star, 2017.

· · · · · · · ·

Shoemaker, David. *Living Thelema: A Practical Guide to Attainment in Aleister Crowley's System of Magick*. 2013. Reprint, Sacramento, CA: Anima Solis Books, 2017.

Tau Apiryon and Soror Helena. *Mystery of Mystery: A Primer of Thelemic Ecclesiastical Gnosticism*. 2nd edition. Berkeley, CA: Conjoined Creation, 2014.

About the Author

Dr. David Shoemaker is a clinical psychologist in private practice, specializing in Jungian and cognitive-behavioral psychotherapy. David is the Chancellor and Prolocutor of the Temple of the Silver Star (totss.org), which offers a complete system of training in Thelemic magick and mysticism. He is also a senior initiate of the Ordo Templi Orientis and A∴A∴ (onestarinsight.org) and has many years of experience training initiates in these traditions.

Davide is a Past Master of 418 Lodge, O.T.O., in Sacramento, having succeeded Soror Meral (Phyllis Seckler), his friend and teacher. He also serves as a Sovereign Grand Inspector General of the order. He was the founding President of the O.T.O. Psychology Guild, and is a frequent speaker at national and regional events. His instructional podcast *Living Thelema* has been presented since 2010, and the popular book of the same name appeared in 2013. He is also the author or editor of numerous other publications focusing on Thelema, psychology, and magick.

In addition to his work in magick and psychology, David is a composer and musician. He can be contacted through his website at livingthelema.com.

Art Credits

All art in book 9 by James Clark.

BOOK TEN

—⊗—

Polytheistic Ceremonial Magic
by John Michael Greer

Ceremonial magic began as a polytheist tradition. The temples of Egypt where the Western magical tradition has its roots were built to honor many gods and goddesses. The Neo-platonist thinkers who fused magic with Greek philosophy to create the first fully developed Western occult traditions were Pagans who made offerings to the gods and goddesses of ancient Greece. It was only after the Christian minority seized political power in the classical world and made Pagan worship a crime punished by death that magic had to be adapted to the new regime, and very often the adaptations in question were fairly transparent: thus gods and goddesses were redefined as planets in astrological magic, as sephiroth in Cabalistic magic, and as saints and angels in Christian folk magic.

The occultists who revived ceremonial magic in the nineteenth century made use of these various redefinitions but rarely noticed the Pagan subtext hardwired into them. A millennium and a half of enforced Christianity had reshaped most Western magical traditions from top to bottom. Furthermore, many of the people who helped relaunch Western occultism in those years were themselves Christians to one degree or another, and most others were unwilling to face the social backlash that anyone who renounced Christianity could expect to suffer. Many years passed before such projects as Dion Fortune's public rites of Isis and Pan[1] resulted in the rebirth of full-blown polytheist religions in the Western world.

Even when that happened, polytheist approaches to ceremonial magic remained few and far between for too long. While such pioneering Neopagan movements as Gardnerian and

1. Gareth Knight's *Dion Fortune's Rites of Isis and of Pan* gives the text of these rites.

· · · · · · · ·

353

Alexandrian Wicca borrowed certain elements from ceremonial magic, those borrowings were used to flesh out traditions of religious ritual and folk magic; the broader possibilities open to the ceremonial magician were too rarely explored from that perspective. Remarkably often, too, the ceremonial elements brought into these Neopagan religions still had their full quota of Judeo-Christian symbolism. It was thus quite common in the late twentieth century, for example, for Wiccans who claimed to reject the Judeo-Christian God and all his works to invoke that god by his Hebrew names in the Lesser Ritual of the Pentagram, and call on four staunchly Judeo-Christian archangels to boot.

Gerald Gardner

Gerald Gardner is rightly known as the father of the modern witchcraft movement, but his work is a synergy of many magical streams that came before him, most notably Freemasonry, nineteenth-century Romantic paganism, and early twentieth-century ceremonial magick.

Gardner himself was a Royal Arch Mason, and seems to have borrowed several basic concepts from that august organisation, most notably the three degree initiatory system that is at its foundation. Masons have also traditionally referred to their system as the *Craft*, a term that is now also commonly used by modern witches.

Gardner's Masonic affiliations were noted by Aleister Crowley in his diary when Gardner came to Crowley's residence for tea on May Day in 1937, a meeting that would lead to Gardner becoming initiated into the magical order run by Crowley, the Ordo Templi Orientis.[2] Crowley also sold several books to Gardner, including a copy of *The Blue Equinox*, which would have a significant impact on Gardner's own work.

A study of Gardner's early notes for his *Book of Shadows* (or *Ye Bok of Ye Art Magical*, as it was originally called) shows that he cribbed a great deal from Crowley, as well as from the rituals of the Hermetic Order of the Golden Dawn and grimoires such as the *Key of Solomon* (itself translated by Golden Dawn leader S. L. MacGregor Mathers).[3]

For example, Gardner's witchcraft rituals often begin with the "casting of the circle," wherein the witch calls upon the Four Watchtowers. This is a concept originally dating from the Enochian magick of Dr. John Dee, court magician of Queen Elizabeth I, later used by the Golden Dawn, and which Gardner probably learned from reading Israel Regardie's publications of Golden Dawn material. Gardner's *Book of Shadows* also con-

2. Eds. note: See Book Nine: Thelema & Aleister Crowley for a fuller exploration of Aleister Crowley and the O.T.O.

3. Eds. note: See Book Five: Demonology & Spirit Evocation for more detail on the *Key of Solomon*.

• • • • • • • •

tains a version of the Golden Dawn *Lesser Banishing Ritual of the Pentagram* that appears to have been taken from Regardie's work.

The text of Aleister Crowley's famous public ritual *The Gnostic Mass* was a huge inspiration for Gardner, and he used several passages from it to form the basis for some of the witchcraft rituals he wrote, specifically the *Drawing Down the Moon* rite, the *February Eve Sabbat*, and the *Charge of the Goddess*. Gardner also seems to have used some aspects of the O.T.O.'s secret initiation rituals when formulating his witchcraft initiation ceremonies.

Gardner's work, although undoubtedly highly influential, is far from being an "authentic" tradition passed down by word of mouth from the pre-Christian era. Instead, Gardner's witchcraft is an amalgamation of many different threads of ceremonial magick practice, skillfully woven into a tapestry that evokes those ancient ways in the spirit of the practitioner.

—Rodney Orpheus

Rodney Orpheus is an Irish musician, writer, and technology designer. He has published two books, *Abrahadabra: Understanding Aleister Crowley's Thelemic Magick* and *Grimoire of Aleister Crowley*, and produced a couple of dozen records. He currently resides in London with his wife, Sulinna, and their cats.

A reaction against this sort of awkward pastiche was inevitable. During the last few decades of the twentieth century, as a result, the occult community in much of the Western world was riven by the unhelpful notion that Paganism and ceremonial magic were incompatible. To the very limited extent that this was true, it was purely a function of the fact that nearly all the living traditions of ceremonial magic active at that time invoked the Christian God through a hybrid Jewish-Christian Cabala and treated Pagan gods and goddesses as purely symbolic images. All that was necessary to break down the imaginary barrier between Pagans and ceremonial mages was the development of systems of ceremonial magic that, like the equivalent systems of the ancient world, invoked the deities and symbolism of polytheist faiths instead of the Christian God and Jewish and Christian symbolism.

With this in mind, beginning in 2008, I developed a system of ceremonial magic that used the technical methods of the Hermetic Order of the Golden Dawn, the most richly elaborated of modern magical systems, but took its symbolism from the traditions of modern Druidry. The basic teachings and practices of that system saw print in 2013 in my book *The Celtic Golden Dawn* and found an enthusiastic audience. One of my central projects since then has focused on working out ways to develop a more broadly based approach to polytheist ceremonial magic, since Druidry makes up a modest fraction of the modern movement of nature-centered spiritualities. The result is the system presented in the pages that follow.

. . . .

Like the one I presented in *The Celtic Golden Dawn*, this system derives from the rituals and practices of the Golden Dawn tradition. Is that the only kind of magic that can be adapted to the needs of the polytheist mage? Of course not. The Golden Dawn tradition is the system of ceremonial magic I've practiced most intensively over the years, however. If you happen to be an initiate of a different system of ceremonial magic and want to adapt that to polytheist use, the rituals given here may provide some inspiration in that project.

Requirements of Polytheist Ceremonial Magic

The rituals and practices that follow require little in the way of hardware and props, but they have two important requirements. The first requirement is that you have some relationship with a traditional pantheon of gods and goddesses. How you choose to relate to the pantheon in question is purely up to you. The relationship may be anything from a sympathetic appreciation of symbols and myths to daily worship at the altars of your gods, but you'll need some such connection in order to use what follows. What's more, whatever your religious and spiritual opinions happen to be more generally, the more you treat the gods and goddesses as real beings in your magical workings, the better the results will be.

Two cautions are worth mentioning here. First, don't mix pantheons in your magical work. If your broader spiritual life includes personal relationships with deities of two or more traditional pantheons, that's fine, but choose one pantheon to work with in your ceremonial magic, and stick with that. A pantheon, in one of its many senses, is an alphabet of forces, and jumbling together two or more pantheons in magical work is like jumbling together two or more alphabets in writing a letter—you're likely to produce pretty fair нῶởсεɔớь.[4]

The second caution has to do with using invented pantheons from fantasy novels, movies, video games, and the like. It's true that novels, movies, and games fill some of the same roles today that mythology filled in ancient times, but there's an important difference. The tellers of the old myths weren't simply making up stories for entertainment; the gods and goddesses whose traditional narratives they repeated were beings that some of their listeners had encountered personally in religious experiences, and from whom many people in their societies had received spiritual guidance and an assortment of blessings. Ask yourself this: if you were to find yourself right now in a situation where your life was on the line, would you consider praying for help to one of the deities in the pantheon you're considering? If not, it may not do you much good to invoke those deities for help in magic either. If you invoke fictional gods to empower your workings, you're likely to work fictional magic, rather than magic that will do things for you in the world of everyday fact.

---

4. This is the word *nonsense* written in letters from the Cyrillic, Greek, Hebrew, and Arabic alphabets. Point taken?

· · · · · · · ·

All these considerations relate to the first requirement of polytheist ceremonial magic. The second, which is closely related, is that you will need to have a patron deity—a god or goddess with whom you have a particularly close personal bond. Most of today's polytheist traditions encourage participants to seek out a patron deity, and a great many books on contemporary polytheist practice offer various methods for establishing a relationship with a god or goddess. How you go about doing this is therefore entirely up to you, but you'll need to have done this before you begin work on the rituals that follow.

What if you have more than one patron deity? In that case, pray to your patrons for guidance to find out which one of them you should invoke in magical ceremonies. Focus is one of the keys to magical success, and working in partnership with a single patron deity in your magical work will produce quicker and more powerful results than jumping from patron to patron. You can certainly continue to invoke your other patron or patrons in other contexts. It's just in magical practice that it's important to work with one patron at a time.

Polytheist Magic, Polytheist Religion

More generally, it's important to realize that ceremonial magic is not the same thing as religion. If you belong to an established polytheist tradition of one kind or another, you may have learned and adopted various rules regarding spiritual practices. The rituals in the pages below probably don't follow those rules, nor do the rites and practices you may have learned from other sources follow the same rules as the rituals that will be covered here. That is as it should be. Your kitchen stove and the water heater that provides you with hot showers both work with heat, but I don't recommend using the user's manual for one to make sense of the other!

Magic is not religion. Religion is the body of traditions, teachings, and practices by which we establish mutually beneficial relationships with the divine powers that shape the universe of our experience. Polytheist ceremonial magic builds on that foundation, providing operative mages—that is, people who practice magic—with tools to transform themselves and their lives using power that comes out of the relationship between the individual human and one or more gods or goddesses. You can participate in a religion without practicing magic, just as you can practice some kinds of magic and not participate in a religion.

Some corners of the polytheist community these days place a great deal of value on historical authenticity. Others place an equally great value on practicing only those traditions with which they have personal ethnic or cultural connections. They certainly have the right to make that choice for themselves, but magic has its own longstanding customs in such matters. The oldest surviving body of ritual texts in the Western occult tradition, the Graeco-Egyptian magical papyri, are a lavish gallimaufry of magical symbols and techniques derived from more than a dozen cultural and ethnic traditions of various eras, all of them efficiently reworked to fit the needs of operative mages in the third century CE. The same spirit has guided the entire history of magic, and there are good reasons for that.

Magic exists to accomplish things. If you go shopping for a hammer, let's say, you're not going to choose it based on whether the label claims it's an authentic hammer just like the ones used centuries ago, nor will you limit yourself to the kinds of hammers that happened to be used in the past by your ethnic or cultural ancestors. Instead, you'll choose the hammer that's best suited for the job—and yes, if that means that you pick up a hammer of English design made of German steel to help you build a shrine to an Egyptian god, that's what it means.

The same principle applies to magic. Operative mages set out to make things happen, and assemble the tools and techniques that are best suited to do that. Authenticity is important for museum pieces, but for a working system of magic meant to transform yourself, your life, and your world, it's irrelevant.

With these points in mind, we can proceed to the practices of polytheist ceremonial magic.

Polytheism and Neopaganism

Polytheism is a category of world religions that includes various ancient, indigenous, modern, and reconstructed or revived devotions, defined by their affirmation with religious regard of many gods. In some areas of the modern world, this category of religion shares demographical intersection with traditions and trends of Neopaganism, but is nevertheless globally distinct from these.

Polytheism today, as throughout history, represents a vibrant, international, cross-cultural array of religious traditions, pantheons, and pathways to devotion, worship, and practice, rather than a single thing, and includes many traditional and culturally specific expressions. When Neopaganism and polytheism intersect, it may be easy to mistake one for the other, or assume them to be expressions of the same thing; but as with all the myriad expressions of identity, distinction is vitally important in order to maintain clear lines of both the respect and the insights that serve as inroads to wisdom and growth. An individual may be Neopagan and polytheist without either being erased or replaced by the other.

Polytheisms from around the globe today face unprecedented hardships and violent oppression from a world rapidly secularizing to accommodate the pressures of Western expansion and economic sustainability, as governments and majority religious movements seek to deplatform, disempower, and erase their chances for representation and voice in the emerging twenty-first century. While Neopaganism is a distinctly modern concept born of intersecting spiritual practices of the twentieth-century West, polytheism includes non-Western cultures and identities that are put at risk not only by oppres-

---

sive evangelized and secularizing dominance but also by the casual erasure or disregard within adjacent (but distinct) Western movements such as Neopaganism.

Many polytheisms also have a place for intersecting or devotional practices of magic, mysticism, or esoteric mystery, but at their core they represent diverse religious traditions of devotion to many gods, who are affirmed and held as holding genuine existence independent of human consciousness and life. While there are many philosophical and occult roots that derive from ancient polytheistic peoples and cultures, these must be understood to be reflective of a system-wide polytheistic society rather than of polytheism itself; correlation and equation, like magic and religion, are distinct concepts.

When adapting contemporary magickal and esoteric practices to a framework of polytheistic religious identity, it is important to embrace a worldview that places humble devotion to the gods before magick or craft, for these are traditions of relation and of devotion before all else.

—Theanos Thrax

Theanos Thrax is a temple priest and polytheist consultant, educator, and author who writes on religion, identity, theistic orientation, and human rights topics. Residing in the woods of New England with four dogs, two cats, and an African raven, they serve as head caretaker of an Ophidiarium of sacred serpents.

The Circle of Presence

Magical practice in the standard Golden Dawn tradition begins and ends with a simple ritual called the *Cabalistic Cross*. This is a straightforward adaptation of the Christian practice of making the sign of the cross, and it's entirely appropriate if you happen to be a Christian. The cross is a Christian symbol, and the act of making the cross on your body is a Christian ritual; decking it out with divine names drawn from other traditions won't change that.

In place of the Cabalistic Cross, the system of polytheist ceremonial magic outlined here has a different ritual called the *Circle of Presence*. This is the basic opening and closing gesture you'll be using whenever you begin and end a magical working. The one thing you'll need in order to adapt it to your own spiritual needs is the name of your patron god or goddess, the deity with whom you have a personal relationship, as discussed previously. If your patron deity has more than one name, choose the one you prefer. In the rituals that follow, (PATRON) indicates where to speak the name of your patron deity.

Here and in other places, you'll be using a special mode of speech called *vibration*. To learn how to do this, chant a simple vowel tone, such as *ah*, and change the way you hold your mouth and produce the sound until it produces a buzzing or tingling sensation somewhere in your body. That's vibration. With practice, you'll find that you can fill your entire body with the sensation,

· · · · · · · ·

and even direct it outside your body. In the rituals that follow, every word printed IN CAPITAL LETTERS is to be vibrated.

Once you've settled on the name of your patron deity you'll be using, and practiced vibration enough to get some effect, you can proceed to the ritual. It is done as follows.

———

First, stand facing east. Raise your hands from your sides in an arc until your palms join above your head, fingers pointing up. Draw your joined hands down to your forehead, visualizing light descending from infinite space to a point above your head, and say, "In the name of …"

Second, draw your joined hands down to your heart. Visualize a ray of light descending from above your head to the center of the earth, and vibrate the name of your patron deity, (PATRON).

Third, separate your hands, and touch your right shoulder with the fingertips of your left hand and your left shoulder with the fingertips of your right hand, the hands crossing at the wrists. Say, "… my patron god(dess) …"

Fourth, raise the elbows straight up and bring your hands up, out, and down in a circular motion, bringing them back together, palm to palm, in front of your lower abdomen or groin (depending on your body's proportions). Visualize your fingertips tracing a circle of light. As you do this, say, "… I place myself within the circle of her (or his) presence …"

Fifth, bring the joined hands up to your heart again, fingertips pointing upward. Visualize the shaft of light descending from infinite space to the center of the earth, the circle of light you drew with your hands, and your heart shining like a sun. Say, "… and protection." This completes the ritual.

———

The Circle of Presence is a useful ritual in its own right and can be performed anytime you feel a need to call on the presence and protection of your patron god or goddess. As already noted, though, it also serves as the opening and closing gesture of the Lesser Ritual of the Pentagram. Once you've practiced it often enough that you can do it by memory, learning and practicing the Lesser Ritual of the Pentagram is the next step in your magical training.

The Lesser Ritual of the Pentagram

This is the workhorse ritual of Golden Dawn magic, the ritual you'll be doing more often than any other as you proceed to the summits of magical practice. In its original form, it's also one of the most thoroughly Judeo-Christian rituals in the entire system. Several significant changes thus need to be made to rework it for polytheist use.

First, as we've already seen, the Cabalistic Cross is replaced by the Circle of Presence, so that the ritual is oriented toward your own patron deity rather than the Jewish or Christian one.

Second, the pentagrams are drawn in a different way. In the version of the pentagram rituals used in standard Golden Dawn magic, the basic all-purpose banishing uses a pentagram traced from the point of earth to the point of spirit, the same gesture used to banish the element of earth. Why? Because an enduring theme of Christian teaching is the rejection of everything earthy as evil. The words of the Hegemon in the Theoricus grade of the Hermetic Golden Dawn—"Quit the material and seek the spiritual"[5]—sum up two thousand years of Christian moral and mystical teaching, and also express the basic intention of the version of the Lesser Ritual of the Pentagram taught by the Hermetic Golden Dawn.

That's an attitude that finds no justification in polytheist spirituality. From a polytheist perspective, the material world is not opposed to the spiritual world—quite the contrary, spirit finds its natural expression in matter, and matter finds its natural fulfillment in spirit. The way of tracing the pentagrams used in polytheist ceremonial magic needs to reflect that radical difference. We therefore trace the summoning[6] pentagram clockwise from the uppermost point, representing the descent of spiritual realities into manifestation through the elements of fire, air, water, and earth. The banishing pentagram is traced counterclockwise from the top point, representing the withdrawal of manifested realities into spirit through the same sequence of elements in reverse.

Third, the Hebrew divine names and archangels used in the Hermetic Golden Dawn's version of the ritual are relevant only to Christians, Jews, and those who are comfortable working with Judeo-Christian religious symbolism. Polytheist ceremonial magicians need to be able to replace them with names suited to their own religious needs.

For the Lesser Ritual of the Pentagram, then, you will need four divine names from your pantheon—if at all possible, two gods and two goddesses—and these four names need to have four and only four letters each (think ZEUS, ISIS, and so on). Why? Because the entire ritual is structured by a pattern of relationships between the numbers 1 and 4. There is one center and four quarters, one spirit and four elements, one practitioner relating to the four directions, and so on. In the ritual below, the deity names will be indicated by (DEITY 1), (DEITY 2), (DEITY 3), and (DEITY 4).

Experiments with names that have more or fewer letters show that rituals calling on these deities simply don't work as well. If your tradition has an alphabet of its own, such as the runes, the Ogham fews, or the Greek alphabet, you can use a deity whose name has four letters in

---

5. Regardie, *The Golden Dawn*, 190.

6. There has been a fair amount of confusion in occult circles from time to time about the relative meanings of the words *invoking* and *evoking*. I prefer the term *summoning* for both, to decrease the likelihood of mis-understanding.

that alphabet whether or not it has four letters in ours. Thus the Greek goddess Tyche, Τυχε in Greek, would be entirely appropriate to invoke in this ritual.

Modern Pagans very often assume as a matter of course that deities can only be assigned to directions on the basis of elemental symbolism. In this ritual, that is not required—you don't need an air deity in the east, a fire deity in the south, and so on—and in fact, it's not usually appropriate. (The Lesser Pentagram Ritual used in standard Golden Dawn practice, for example, assigns its four-lettered divine names to the four quarters without any regard for elemental symbolism.) Instead, the best rule is to have two gods facing each other and two goddesses facing each other—gods in the east and west and goddesses in the north and south, or vice versa. The most powerful deity should go in the east, and the rest may be arranged however the symbolism of your tradition and your own sense of appropriateness may guide you.

Once you've chosen your deities, you can proceed to the ritual, which is done as follows.

———

First, perform the complete Circle of Presence ritual, calling on your patron deity.

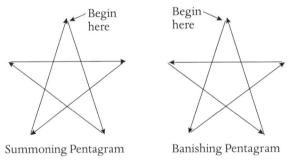

Figure 1. Spirit Pentagrams

Second, go to the eastern quarter of the space and trace a pentagram with the first two fingers of your right hand, beginning with the top point, as shown in figure 1. You draw clockwise to summon and counterclockwise to banish. Visualize the pentagram drawn in a line of pure white light. Point to the center of the pentagram and vibrate the name (DEITY 1).

Third, trace a line in the air around to the southern quarter, imagining it drawn in light. Draw the pentagram in the same way, point to the center, and vibrate the name (DEITY 2).

Fourth, repeat to the west, trace the pentagram, and vibrate the name (DEITY 3).

Fifth, repeat to the north, trace the pentagram, and vibrate the name (DEITY 4). Then trace the line back around to the east, completing the circle, and return to the center.

Sixth, stand at the center, facing the east, and say, "Before me the powers of air, behind me the powers of water, to my right hand the powers of fire, to my left hand the powers of earth.

For about me stand the pentagrams, and upon me shines the blessing of (PATRON)." Visualize the elements in the four directions when you say these words.

Seventh, repeat the Circle of Presence. This completes the ritual.

———

An example may be useful at this point. Here is one way that a worshiper of the gods and goddesses of ancient Egypt might perform the Lesser Ritual of the Pentagram.

———

First, perform the Circle of Presence ritual with these words: "In the name of THOTH, my patron god, I place myself in the circle of his presence and protection." The god's name is vibrated.

Second, trace the pentagrams in the four quarters and the circle that unites them, vibrating a divine name in each pentagram. In the east, the name is AMUN; in the south, ISIS; in the west, PTAH; and in the north, BAST.

Third, return to the center, visualize the elements, and say, "Before me the powers of air, behind me the powers of water, to my right hand the powers of fire, to my left hand the powers of earth. For about me stand the pentagrams, and upon me shines the blessing of THOTH."

Fourth, perform the Circle of Presence ritual again with the same words. This completes the ritual.

———

It's entirely possible to add additional symbolism from your tradition to this ritual. If you have traditional symbols, emblems, or beings that represent the four elements or the four directions, for example, you can call on these in the third step of the ritual in place of the references to the powers of the elements. For example, a Druid working with the symbolism of the Druid Revival traditions could choose to say, "Before me the Hawk of May, behind me the Salmon of Wisdom, to my right hand the White Stag, to my left hand the Great Bear."

The Middle Pillar Exercise

The next practice to learn, once you've memorized the Lesser Ritual of the Pentagram and gotten comfortable with it, is the Middle Pillar exercise. This is the basic internal energy practice of Golden Dawn magic. It's meant to waken and energize five energy centers in the subtle body, and then circulate energy through the subtle body as a whole.

The energy centers of the Middle Pillar are located above the crown of the head, at the throat, at the heart, at the genitals, and between the soles of the feet, extending a short distance into the ground. These are not the same as the chakras used in many Asian schools of mysticism. They are centers of resonance in what many systems of Western occultism call the *aura* and the Golden Dawn tradition calls the *Sphere of Sensation*—the roughly egg-shaped body of subtle energy that surrounds and interpenetrates the physical body. The centers of the Middle Pillar are located along the midline of the physical body, but are not physical organs.

This exercise can be adapted to fit whatever pantheon you prefer to work with. You'll need five deities, whose names can have any number of letters—the four-letter restriction applies only to the Lesser Ritual of the Pentagram. The standard approach, which follows the logic in Israel Regardie's fine little manual *The Art of True Healing*, is to use deities corresponding to the five elements—spirit, air, fire, water, and earth, in that order. One further complexity is that whichever option you choose, the deity of the fourth energy center, which is located at the genitals, should be the same gender you are.[7]

Along with your five deities, you'll also need five colors and five symbols. The default option if you're using the elemental scheme is white, yellow, red, blue, and brown, in that order, and the symbols are the sun, a cloud, a flame, a drop of water, and a stone. You don't have to use the default option. If your tradition has other symbols for the five elements, you can use them; if it associates the elements with other colors, you can use those.

However you do it, work out a suitable arrangement of correspondences, as shown in table 1.

Crown Center	DEITY 1	COLOR 1	SYMBOL 1
Throat Center	DEITY 2	COLOR 2	SYMBOL 2
Heart Center	DEITY 3	COLOR 3	SYMBOL 3
Genital Center	DEITY 4	COLOR 4	SYMBOL 4
Foot Center	DEITY 5	COLOR 5	SYMBOL 5
Thus a male Heathen who worships the Anglo-Saxon deities might choose this:			
Crown Center	Tiw	White	Sun
Throat Center	Woden	Blue	Raven
Heart Center	Hretha	Red	Flame
Genital Center	Ing	Green	Sheaf of barley
Foot Center	Eostre	Brown	Flowers
A female Heathen might instead choose this:			
Crown Center	Tiw	White	Sun
Throat Center	Woden	Blue	Raven
Heart Center	Thunor	Red	Hammer
Genital Center	Frig	Gold	Spindle
Foot Center	Eostre	Brown	Flowers

Table 1. Correspondences for the Middle Pillar Exercise

7. If you happen to be intersex or transgender, you may need to experiment to determine which gender the deity at the genital center should be. The wrong choice will produce a sense of energy blockage or "stuckness." Fortunately this will go away promptly when you repeat the exercise with the correct gender of deity.

· · · · · · · ·

Other correspondences could be chosen easily enough; these are just samples. Make your decision and give it a try. Once you've chosen your symbolism, the exercise is done as follows.

———

First, perform the complete Lesser Banishing Ritual of the Pentagram as given in the previous section. The banishing version of the ritual is always used in this exercise, to clear unwanted energies and influences from your sphere of sensation. Regular practice of a banishing ritual does for your energy body what regular bathing does for your physical body, and should be a daily exercise on the part of every ceremonial magician.

Second, imagine a ray of light descending from infinite space to form a sphere of light just above your head, about eight inches in diameter. This sphere is COLOR 1 and contains SYMBOL 1. When you have formulated it clearly in your imagination, vibrate NAME 1 three times.

Third, bring the ray of light to your throat, and form another sphere. This one is COLOR 2 and contains SYMBOL 2. When you have formulated it, vibrate NAME 2 three times.

Fourth, bring the ray of light to your heart, and form a third sphere, which is COLOR 3 and contains SYMBOL 3. NAME 3 is vibrated here three times.

Fifth, bring the ray of light to your genital center, and form a fourth sphere. This one is COLOR 4 and contains SYMBOL 4. NAME 4 is vibrated here three times.

Sixth, bring the ray of light to your feet, and form a fifth center. This one is COLOR 5 and contains SYMBOL 5. The name vibrated here, three times, is NAME 5.

Seventh, return your attention to the center at the top of the head. Bring a current of white light a few inches wide down the left side of the head and neck, the left shoulder and arm, and the left hip and leg, down to the center at the feet, then back up the right leg and hip, the right arm and shoulder, and the right side of the neck and head, back to the center at the head. Repeat this a total of three times; if possible, synchronize with the breath, so that the energy flows down with the outbreath and up with the inbreath, but it is more important to visualize the whole course than to make it happen within a single breath.

Eighth, in the same way, bring a current of white light from the center above the head, down the midline of the front of the body to the center at the feet, then back up the midline of the back of the body to the center above the head. Repeat a total of three times.

Ninth, breathing out, draw a current of white light straight down the midline of your body from the center above the head to the center at the feet, along the Middle Pillar. Breathing in, draw a current of energy back up the Middle Pillar of the body to the center above the head; breathing out, allow it to spray like a fountain out and over the whole body, cleansing the entire aura, pooling at the feet and being drawn back up the Middle Pillar with the next inbreath. You only need to do the current down the Middle Pillar from above once; do the rest of the cycle, up the Middle Pillar and down through the aura, a total of three times.

Tenth, perform the Circle of Presence. This completes the exercise.

· · · · · · · ·

Opening and Closing a Temple

The Lesser Ritual of the Pentagram and the Middle Pillar exercise are the daily practices of Golden Dawn magic, the disciplines that develop magical power and strengthen the energy body of the operative mage. Most people who are interested in magic, though, also have practical ends in mind—they want to wield magical energies to improve their own lives and the lives of others. The Golden Dawn tradition has plenty of methods for doing this too, and with a little alteration to refit them for polytheist use, they can be put to work to make changes in the world.

Practical magic in the Golden Dawn tradition is done in an open temple. A temple in this context doesn't mean a building set apart for the purpose of your magical work—though if you happen to have one of these, you can certainly use it! Any space can become a temple of magic for the duration of a magical working, and a special ritual is used to open a temple at the beginning of a working and close it at the end. In this polytheist version of Golden Dawn magic, you will open and close your temple in the name of your patron deity; you will vibrate his or her name where indicated by the word (PATRON).

You will need a few physical props for your magical temple. The first of these is an altar. Any item of furniture with a flat top around waist height, large enough to hold a few ritual items and small enough that you can move around it easily, can serve as an altar so long as you can set it in the middle of your working space. The altar is traditionally covered with an altar cloth, which can be as simple as an unhemmed length of fabric or as ornate as your budget or sewing skills will allow. The Hermetic Golden Dawn used a black altar cloth; you may do the same if you like, or choose a color or pattern more relevant to the spiritual tradition you practice. For example, as a Druid, I use a white altar cloth.

For the ritual of opening and closing, you'll also need a cup, bowl, or other container of water, and an incense burner. Choose these to match your tradition and your taste. You can use any incense appropriate to the magical working you have in mind. For general purposes, a good purifying incense such as frankincense is fine.[8] Stick, cone, or loose incense on charcoal are equally appropriate depending on your preferences.

To set up the temple before you begin the opening ritual, you need to know which way east is. An ordinary hiker's compass will tell you this if you're not sure. Set the altar in the middle of the space, with the water on the north side and the incense burner on the south side. Anything else you need for the ritual that you plan on performing once you have opened a temple also goes on the altar. Once the temple is set up, put on a robe if you prefer to wear one while working magic, light the incense, and proceed to open the temple as follows.

---

8. My book *The Encyclopedia of Natural Magic* (Llewellyn, 2000) is a good place to look up which incense to use for different kinds of magical workings.

· · · · · · · ·

First, stand at the west side of the altar, facing east. Raise your right hand, palm forward, to salute the divine powers you will summon during the ritual, and say, "In the name of (PATRON), and in the presence of all the gods and goddesses, I prepare to open this temple."

Second, perform the complete Lesser Invoking Ritual of the Pentagram to call magical energies into the space.

Third, standing at the west of the altar, facing east, pick up the vessel of water in both hands and raise it up. Say, "Let this temple and all within it be purified with water." Go to the east, dip the fingers of one hand into the water, and flick droplets of water three times to the east. Go around to the south, and do the same thing; repeat the same action in the west and the north. Return to the east, face east, lift up the vessel of water in both hands, and say, "The temple is purified." Then go back to the west of the altar and return the vessel of water to its place.

Fourth, standing at the west of the altar, facing east, pick up the incense. If you are burning stick incense, just the stick is fine; if you are using cone or loose incense, lift up the burner in both hands. Then say, "Let this temple and all within it be consecrated by fire." Go to the east, and with one hand, wave smoke from the incense three times to the east. Go around to the south and do the same thing; repeat the same action in the west and the north. Return to the east, face east, lift up the incense in both hands, and say, "The temple is consecrated." Then go back to the west of the altar and return the incense to its place.

Fifth, starting from the west of the altar, walk clockwise in a circle around the altar, passing the east four times. Each time you pass the east, bow your head in respect. This is the ancient and very widespread rite of *circumambulation*, still practiced in many polytheist societies around the world. As you walk, imagine your movements creating a whirlpool of energy that draws in magical power from the far reaches of the universe to your magical temple. When you have passed the east four times, circle back to the west of the altar and face east.

Sixth, spread your arms wide and say, "(PATRON), my patron god(dess), I ask you to bless and consecrate this temple of high magic, and aid me with your power in all the work I perform herein." Pause for a time and concentrate on sensing your patron deity's presence and power surrounding you.

Seventh, still standing at the west of the altar, facing east, raise your right hand again, palm forward, and say, "In the name of (PATRON), and in the presence of all the gods and goddesses, I proclaim this temple duly open." This completes the ritual.

———

Once you have opened the temple, you can do any magical working you wish inside the sacred space you've established. A little later on, we'll discuss some of the possibilities. Whenever you open a temple using the ritual just given, however, it's important to close the temple once you're finished with whatever you intend to do. The closing ritual is done as follows.

———

First, standing at the west of the altar, facing east, pick up the vessel of water in both hands and raise it up. Say, "Let this temple and all within it be purified with water." Repeat the process of purifying the temple with water exactly as you did in the third step of the opening ritual. Then go back to the west of the altar and return the vessel of water to its place.

Second, standing at the west of the altar, facing east, pick up the incense and say, "Let this temple and all within it be consecrated by fire." Repeat the process of consecrating the temple with fire exactly as you did in the fourth step of the opening ritual. Then go back to the west of the altar and return the incense to its place.

Third, starting from the west of the altar, walk counterclockwise in a circle around the altar, passing the east four times. Each time you pass the east, bow your head in respect. As you walk, imagine your movements dispersing the whirlpool of energy you created earlier and sending the intention of your working out into the universe to accomplish your will. When you have passed the east four times, circle back to the west of the altar and face east.

Fourth, spread your arms wide and say, " In the name of (PATRON), I set free any spirits who may have been imprisoned by this ceremony. Depart unto your rightful habitations in peace, and peace be between us." Pause for a moment, then perform the complete Lesser Banishing Ritual of the Pentagram.

Fifth, standing at the west of the altar, facing east, raise your right hand again, palm forward, and say, "In the name of (PATRON), and in the presence of all the gods and goddesses, I proclaim this temple duly closed." This completes the ritual.

———

Modern Witchcraft

The Witchcrafts of Gerald Gardner and Alex and Maxine Sanders were based around covens and initiatory practices. But today, there are far more solitary practitioners of Witchcraft than individuals who have gone through initiations or work in groups. This is due largely to the "rise of the book" in Witchcraft circles. During the 1950s and 1960s, obtaining Witch rituals required either an initiation or a willingness to create one's own. By the end of the 1970s, entrance into the world of Witchcraft could be obtained for the price of a mass-market paperback.

Gerald Gardner's *Book of Shadows* (a name for a collection of Witch rituals and magickal advice) was first reproduced in the 1964 pamphlet *Witch*, published by a critic of Gardner's soon after the old man's passing. However, *Witch* was not easily obtainable and had a short print run. That would change in the 1970s when both occult and mainstream publishers began printing how-to Witchcraft books complete with rituals. This gave Witchcraft to the masses, making the need for an initiator less urgent.

One of the most influential of those books from the 1970s was *The Spiral Dance*, written by California Bay Area resident Starhawk (born Miriam Simos in 1951) and published in 1979. *The Spiral Dance* articulated a different kind of Witchcraft from that of Gardner and Sanders, one infused with second-wave feminism and 1960s-era politics. It also included ideas from what's come to be known as the *Feri Tradition*, founded by Victor (1917–2001) and Cora Anderson (1915–2007) during the 1960s. The Witchcraft of the Andersons added new elements to the Craft and became one of America's first and largest homegrown traditions.

New Witchcraft traditions weren't just reserved for North America. The Witchcraft of Robert Cochrane (birth name Roy Bowers, 1931–1966) first went public in England in 1960. Though slow to gain traction, it would inspire several different traditions on both sides of the pond during the 1970s due to a series of letters written by Cochrane before his death. Today Cochrane is often hailed as the architect of "Traditional Witchcraft," a strain of the Craft inspired by English cunning-craft and other forms of folk magic.

Witchcraft continued to grow in popularity during the 1980s and '90s, with the Craft first written about by Gardner being hailed primarily as "Wicca." Today, Wicca is recognized as a religion by a variety of Western governments, and its primary symbol, the pentacle, can be seen on grave markers at national veterans cemeteries in the United States. Witchcraft has continued its pattern of growth in the new millennium, trending often on social media sites.

—Jason Mankey

Jason Mankey has been a practicing Witch for the last twenty-five years and is the author of *Transformative Witchcraft: The Greater Mysteries* and *Witch's Wheel of the Year: Rituals for Sabbats, Circles & Solitaries*, both published by Llewellyn. He lives with his wife, Ari, and two cats in California, where they lead two local covens.

The differences between the form of the Lesser Ritual of the Pentagram used in standard Golden Dawn practice and the form used in this Pagan version of the Golden Dawn are important to keep in mind. In the Hermetic Golden Dawn, the Lesser Banishing Ritual of the Pentagram is done at the beginning as well as the end of each working; in polytheist ceremonial magic, we do the Summoning Ritual at the beginning and the Banishing Ritual at the end. Since the Summoning Ritual in the form given here is meant to call magical energies into manifestation, and the

Banishing Ritual withdraws them from manifestation, using these two rituals to bracket the opening and closing ritual makes good sense and strong magic.

As with the other rituals we've covered, you can insert additional symbolism into the opening and closing rituals if you wish. If your tradition has a sacred well and a sacred fire, for example, or any other suitable symbolism relating to water and fire, you could insert those into the purification with water and the consecration with fire: thus, for example, an Irish Pagan might say, "Let this temple and all within it be purified by the waters of the Well of Segais," and "Let this temple and all within it be consecrated by the smoke of the fire of Bilé."

Elemental Pentagram Rituals

Many relatively simple magical workings can be done in an open temple with no further preparation, and a ritual for making and consecrating an herbal amulet is included at the end of this book. For more potent workings, though, it's often better to summon the magical energies of one of the four elements into the temple once it's open, and a specific set of rituals—the elemental pentagram rituals—are used for this purpose.

To use these rituals, you'll need to choose four deities from your pantheon who rule over the four traditional elements. These names can be as many letters as they happen to be—again, the four-letter rule applies *only* to the Lesser Ritual of the Pentagram, not to the elemental rituals or any other ritual in this system. You need a deity of air or the sky, a deity of fire or the sun, a deity of water or the sea, and a deity of earth or of fertility. Fortunately, these aren't hard to find in most traditional pantheons. You can invoke the same deities for the elements that you invoked in the Middle Pillar exercise, or different ones if you prefer. All that matters is that you settle on a set of names and use them consistently. In the rituals that follow, the names will be indicated by (EARTH DEITY), (WATER DEITY), (AIR DEITY), and (FIRE DEITY); as usual, every name in capital letters is to be vibrated.

The elemental pentagram rituals use the same basic structure as the Lesser Ritual of the Pentagram, and they begin and end with the Circle of Presence. You'll be tracing a different set of pentagrams for each ritual, starting from the point corresponding to the element, as shown in figure 2.

Figure 2. Elements and the Pentagram

These are not the versions of the elemental pentagrams used in the Hermetic Order of the Golden Dawn. As with the Lesser Ritual of the Pentagram, this is deliberate. The Golden Dawn versions are traced according to a complex theory that derives from the symbolism of the *Tetragrammaton*, the holy four-lettered name used for the Jewish and Christian God, and the results have practical difficulties—for example, using the Golden Dawn version, you can't invoke air without simultaneously banishing water, and vice versa! Tracing the pentagrams from the point assigned to each element, going clockwise to invoke and counterclockwise to banish, works equally well in practice and avoids these difficulties.

The rituals themselves are done as follows.

Pentagram Ritual of Earth

First, perform the Circle of Presence to invoke your patron deity.

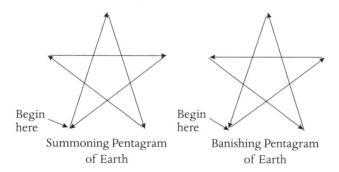

Figure 3. Earth Pentagrams

Second, go to the east and trace a pentagram of earth with the index and middle fingers of your right hand, clockwise to summon or counterclockwise to banish (figure 3). Imagine it drawn in emerald light. Point at the center of the pentagram and vibrate the name (EARTH DEITY). Trace a line of emerald light around to the south, then trace the same pentagram and vibrate the same name. Do the same to the west and north, and finally trace a line back around to the east to complete the circle.

Third, return to the west of the altar, face east, and say, "Before me the fertile plains, behind me the rolling hills, to my right hand the tall mountains, to my left hand the deep caverns, for about me stand the pentagrams, and upon me shines the blessing of (PATRON)."

Fourth, repeat the Circle of Presence. This completes the ritual.

Pentagram Ritual of Water

First, perform the Circle of Presence to invoke your patron deity.

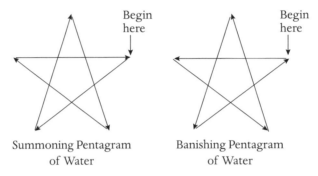

Figure 4. Water Pentagrams

Second, go to the east and trace a pentagram of water with the index and middle fingers of your right hand, clockwise to summon or counterclockwise to banish (figure 4). Imagine it drawn in blue light. Point at the center of the pentagram and vibrate the name (WATER DEITY). Trace a line of blue light around to the south, then trace the same pentagram and vibrate the same name. Do the same to the west and north, and finally trace a line back around to the east to complete the circle.

Third, return to the west of the altar, face east, and say, "Before me the dancing streams, behind me the great ocean, to my right hand the strong rivers, to my left hand the quiet lakes, for about me stand the pentagrams, and upon me shines the blessing of (PATRON)."

Fourth, repeat the Circle of Presence. This completes the ritual.

Pentagram Ritual of Air

First, perform the Circle of Presence to invoke your patron deity.

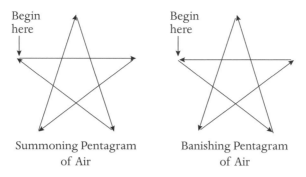

Figure 5. Air Pentagrams

Second, go to the east and trace a pentagram of air with the index and middle fingers of your right hand, clockwise to summon or counterclockwise to banish (figure 5). Imagine it drawn in golden light. Point at the center of the pentagram and vibrate the name (AIR DEITY). Trace a line of golden light around to the south, then trace the same pentagram and vibrate the same name. Do the same to the west and north, and finally trace a line back around to the east to complete the circle.

Third, return to the west of the altar, face east, and say, "Before me the rushing wind, behind me the silver mist, to my right hand the shining sky, to my left hand the billowing cloud, for about me stand the pentagrams, and upon me shines the blessing of (PATRON)."

Fourth, repeat the Circle of Presence. This completes the ritual.

Pentagram Ritual of Fire

First, perform the Circle of Presence to invoke your patron deity.

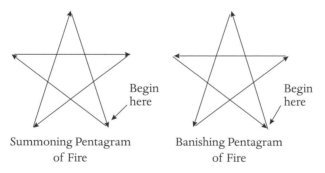

Figure 6. Fire Pentagrams

Second, go to the east and trace a pentagram of fire with the index and middle fingers of your right hand, clockwise to summon or counterclockwise to banish (figure 6). Imagine it drawn in crimson light. Point at the center of the pentagram and vibrate the name (FIRE DEITY). Trace a line of crimson light around to the south, then trace the same pentagram and vibrate the same name. Do the same to the west and north, and finally trace a line back around to the east to complete the circle.

Third, return to the west of the altar, face east, and say, "Before me the lightning flash, behind me the fire of growth, to my right hand the blazing sun, to my left hand the flame upon the hearth, for about me stand the pentagrams, and upon me shines the blessing of (PATRON)."

Fourth, repeat the Circle of Presence. This completes the ritual.

––––––

In magical workings, the elemental pentagram rituals are done after you open the temple and before you close it. Only one element is summoned in any ritual working, and once summoned, it must be banished again before closing the temple, to avoid leaving unbalanced energies behind in the place where you practice magic. The closing ritual and the final Lesser Banishing Ritual of the Pentagram finish the process of clearing away the energies, so the space you use for your temple can be used for other purposes.

The Supreme Ritual of the Pentagram

For most kinds of practical magic, it's appropriate to summon whichever elemental force is best suited to the work you have in mind. Not all magic aims at purely practical ends, though. Magical workings for spiritual development are also an important part of the operative mage's toolkit. It's through rituals of spiritual development that you build on the foundations laid down by daily practice of the Lesser Ritual of the Pentagram and the Middle Pillar exercise, to strengthen your connection with the gods and goddesses, with your patron deity, and with the currents of magical power that surge constantly through the universe.

For rituals of spiritual development, it's best to summon all four elements at the same time, since a state of balance among the elemental powers in the universe and in yourself is a key part of spiritual development through magic. The ritual used for this purpose is the Supreme Ritual of the Pentagram, which synthesizes the four elemental pentagram rituals into a single ceremonial form. The Supreme Invoking Ritual of the Pentagram is done as follows.

––––––

First, perform the complete Circle of Presence ritual, calling on your patron deity.

Second, go to the eastern quarter of the space, and trace the pentagram of air there, drawing it clockwise from the air point. Visualize the pentagram drawn in a line of pure yellow light. Point to the center of the pentagram and vibrate the name (AIR DEITY), the same name you use in the Pentagram Ritual of Air.

· · · · · · · ·

Third, trace a line in the air around to the southern quarter, imagining it drawn in white light. Draw a pentagram of fire in the south, tracing it clockwise from the fire point, visualizing it in red light. Point to the center, and vibrate the name (FIRE DEITY), the same name you use in the Pentagram Ritual of Fire.

Fourth, trace the line of white light around to the west. Trace a water pentagram there in blue light, clockwise from the water point, and vibrate the name (WATER DEITY), the same name you use in the Pentagram Ritual of Water.

Fifth, trace the line of white light around to the west. Trace an earth pentagram there in green light, clockwise from the earth point, and vibrate the name (EARTH DEITY), the same name you use in the Pentagram Ritual of Earth. Then trace the line of white light back around to the east, completing the circle, and return to the center.

Sixth, stand at the center, facing the east, and say, "Before me the powers of air, behind me the powers of water, to my right hand the powers of fire, to my left hand the powers of earth. For about me stand the pentagrams, and upon me shines the blessing of (PATRON)." Visualize the elements in the four directions when you say these words.

Seventh, repeat the Circle of Presence. This completes the ritual.

———

The Supreme Banishing Ritual of the Pentagram is done in exactly the same way, except that the pentagrams are all drawn counterclockwise from the relevant elemental point. Both versions should be practiced until you can do them from memory before you use them in a magical working. One convenient way to do this is to use both forms in a more potent version of the Middle Pillar exercise.

The Greater Middle Pillar Exercise

This working can be done once a week in place of your ordinary Lesser Ritual of the Pentagram and Middle Pillar exercise. The version presented here as an example uses the Irish pantheon, and the mage's patron is the Dagda. If you wish to use this exercise, of course, you should replace these with the appropriate names of your own patron deity and pantheon. You should also replace the Song of Amergin, the incantation that forms the center of the rite, with some similar incantation from your own tradition. For example, Heathen mages might choose to use the tremendous passage from the Old Norse Havamál in which Odin describes his self-sacrifice on the World Tree Yggdrasil. The incantation used should express some of the core spiritual truths of your tradition. In its Irish form, the exercise is done as follows.

———

• • • • • • • •

First, perform the complete Lesser Invoking Ritual of the Pentagram, calling on AN DAGDA in the Circle of Presence. The names for the four quarters are DANU in the east, LUGH in the south, BADB in the west, and BILÉ in the north.

Second, perform the complete Supreme Invoking Ritual of the Pentagram, using the same name in the Circle of Presence. Invoke air in the east in the name of NUADA, fire in the south in the name of BRIGHID, water in the west in the name of MANNANAN, and earth in the north in the name of ERIU. While invoking the elements, concentrate on feeling their presence and power flowing in through the pentagrams you have traced.

Third, standing in the center of the space, facing east, recite the Song of Amergin:

I am the wind on the sea;

I am the wave of the sea;

I am the bull of seven battles;

I am the eagle on the rock

I am a flash from the sun;

I am the most beautiful of plants;

I am a strong wild boar;

I am a salmon in the water;

I am a lake in the plain;

I am the word of knowledge;

I am the head of the spear in battle;

I am the god that puts fire in the head;

Who spreads light in the gathering on the hills?

Who can tell the ages of the moon?

Who can tell the place where the sun rests?[9]

While you recite each line of the Song of Amergin, imagine that you are what you describe: a wind of the sea, a hawk upon a cliff, a wise Druid, and the rest of it. Perceive yourself as a reality that goes beyond the body you presently inhabit. Believe that, like the Welsh wizard-bard Taliesin, you have been all things previously.[10]

Fourth, perform the complete Middle Pillar exercise in the usual way, except vibrate the name corresponding to each energy center nine times rather than three, and perform each of

---

9. Gregory, *Gods and Fighting Men*, part I, Book III: The Landing, www.sacred-texts.com/neu/celt/gafm/gafm09.htm.

10. Obviously, if you are working with a different pantheon and thus a different incantation, you will need to focus your contemplation in the ritual on the themes of the incantation you are using.

• • • • • • • •

the circulations of energy nine times instead of three. Done in the wake of the recitation of the Song of Amergin, this can be an extraordinarily potent experience.

Fifth, perform the complete Supreme Banishing Ritual of the Pentagram with the names already given to release the elemental energies you have summoned.

Sixth, perform the complete Lesser Banishing Ritual of the Pentagram with the names already given to clear away leftover energies and finish the exercise.

Consecration Ritual for an Amulet

This sample ritual is a basic ritual for making and consecrating an amulet to protect and bless a garden, using the traditions of natural magic. The amulet itself is a small bag of waterproof green cloth, into which will be put a moss agate and the dried leaves of comfrey (*Symphytum officinale*) and lovage (*Levisticum officinale*), two commonly available herbs. Do not make the amulet in advance. Instead, simply put the raw materials (the bag, the moss agate, and two little bowls—each containing half a teaspoon or so of one of the herbs) on the altar as shown in figure 7. You will also need a piece of silk or linen in which to wrap the amulet after it's made and consecrated.

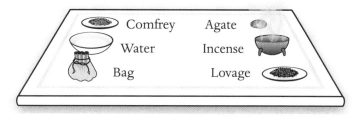

Figure 7. Altar for Sample Ritual

The pantheon for the following ritual is Roman, and the mage's patron is Vesta. If you wish to use this ritual, of course, it should be adapted to fit your own patron and pantheon.

———

First, stand at the west side of the altar, facing east. Raise your right hand, palm forward, to salute the divine powers you will summon during the ritual, and say, "In the name of VESTA, and in the presence of all the gods and goddesses, I prepare to open this temple."

Second, perform the Circle of Presence ritual with these words: "In the name of VESTA, my patron goddess, I place myself in the circle of her presence and protection."

Third, trace the pentagrams in the four quarters and the circle that unites them, vibrating a divine name in each pentagram. In the east, the name is JOVE; in the south, JUNO; in the west, MARS; and in the north, MAIA.

Fourth, return to the west of the altar, face east, visualize the elements, and say, "Before me the powers of air, behind me the powers of water, to my right hand the powers of fire, to my left hand the powers of earth. For about me stand the pentagrams, and upon me shines the blessing of VESTA."

Fifth, perform the Circle of Presence ritual again with the same words as before.

Sixth, standing at the west of the altar, facing east, pick up the vessel of water in both hands and raise it up. Say, "Let this temple and all within it be purified with water." Purify the temple with water in the usual way, then go back to the west of the altar and return the vessel of water to its place.

Seventh, standing at the west of the altar, facing east, pick up the incense and say, "Let this temple and all within it be consecrated by fire." Consecrate the temple with fire in the usual way, then go back to the west of the altar and return the incense to its place.

Eighth, walk clockwise in a circle around the altar, passing the east four times. Each time you pass the east, bow your head in respect, and imagine your movements creating a whirlpool of energy that draws in magical power from the far reaches of the universe to your magical temple. When you have passed the east four times, circle back to the west of the altar and face east.

Ninth, spread your arms wide and say, "VESTA, my patron goddess, I ask you to bless and consecrate this temple of high magic, and aid me with your power in all the work I perform herein." Pause for a time, and sense Vesta's presence and power surrounding you.

Tenth, still standing at the west of the altar, facing east, raise your right hand, palm forward, and say, "In the name of VESTA, and in the presence of all the gods and goddesses, I proclaim this temple duly open." Then perform the complete Invoking Pentagram Ritual of Earth, vibrating the name of CERES, the goddess of earth, in the four quarters.

Eleventh, say aloud, "I now create an amulet for the purpose of blessing and protecting my garden." Then put the herbs and the moss agate into the bag, and tie it shut. While you do this, imagine your garden thriving, a place of abundance and perfect safety. Make the image in your mind as clear and vivid as you possibly can. When you have finished making the amulet, place it in the center of the altar.

Twelfth, raise your arms in invocation and say, "Ceres, great goddess, protectress of all green and growing things, I ask you to strengthen this amulet with your power and wisdom so that it will bless and protect my garden." Then recite the following verses:

> Bounteous Ceres, thee I sing,
> Source of Jove the mighty king,
> Ancient goddess, Saturn's wife,
> Middle center of all life,

• • • • • • • •

Which forever streams from thee,

All-prolific deity.[11]

Repeat these verses three times. While you do so, concentrate on the presence of the goddess Ceres in and around your temple, and sense a stream of divine power descending from her into the amulet. Hold that image as long and as intensely as you can. When your concentration falters, say, "Ceres, great goddess, I thank you for your blessing and your help." Then wrap the amulet in the piece of silk or linen. This will keep the magical charge intact while you banish the energies you have invoked.

Thirteenth, perform the complete Banishing Elemental Pentagram Ritual of Earth, again vibrating the name CERES in each quarter, to release the energies you have invoked.

Fourteenth, pick up the vessel of water and purify the temple with water in exactly the same way you did in the opening. Return the vessel to its place.

Fifteenth, pick up the incense and consecrate the temple with fire in exactly the same way you did in the opening. Return the incense to its place.

Sixteenth, starting from the west of the altar, walk counterclockwise in a circle around the altar, passing the east four times. Each time you pass the east, bow your head in respect. As you walk, imagine your movements dispersing the whirlpool of energy you created earlier. When you have passed the east four times, circle back to the west of the altar and face east.

Seventeenth, spread your arms wide and say, " In the name of VESTA, I set free any spirits who may have been imprisoned by this ceremony. Depart unto your rightful habitations in peace, and peace be between us." Pause for a moment, then perform the complete Lesser Banishing Ritual of the Pentagram, using the same names as in the opening.

Eighteenth, standing at the west of the altar, facing east, raise your right hand again, palm forward, and say, "In the name of VESTA, and in the presence of all the gods and goddesses, I proclaim this temple duly closed." This completes the ritual.

A Final Note

The rituals and exercises given in this book are merely examples of what can be done with Pagan ceremonial magic. Every working performed by Golden Dawn mages, even the most complex, can be reworked in this same way to suit the needs of Pagan operative mages, and the same is true of other systems of ceremonial magic. Take the time to practice, master, and learn from the examples given here, and you'll find that it's easy to adapt other rituals the same way.

11. These lines are from the *Hymn to Ceres* by the great English Pagan Thomas Taylor (1758–1835). Always a careful scholar, Taylor based these lines on Roman myths that make Ceres rather than Rhea the wife of Saturn and the mother of Jupiter. See Sallustius, *Sallust, On the Gods and the World*, 153–155.

· · · · · · · ·

Bibliography

Greer, John Michael. *The Celtic Golden Dawn.* Woodbury, MN: Llewellyn Publications, 2013.

———. *The Encyclopedia of Natural Magic.* St. Paul, MN: Llewellyn Publications, 2000.

Gregory, Lady. *Gods and Fighting Men.* London: J. Murray, 1904. https://www.sacred-texts.com/neu/celt/gafm/index.htm. Accessed September 23, 2019.

Knight, Gareth, ed. *Dion Fortune's Rites of Isis and of Pan.* Cheltenham, UK: Skylight, 2013.

Regardie, Israel. *The Golden Dawn.* Edited by John Michael Greer. Woodbury, MN: Llewellyn, 2015.

Sallustius. *Sallust, On the Gods and the World.* Translated by Thomas Taylor. 1795. Reprint, Los Angeles, CA: Philosophical Research Society, 1976.

About the Author

John Michael Greer is the author of more than fifty books, including *The Celtic Golden Dawn* and the award-winning *New Encyclopedia of the Occult*, and a widely read weekly blog at www.ecosophia.net. A longtime student of Western esoteric traditions, he holds initiations in a range of Masonic, Rosicrucian, and Druid lineages, and served for twelve years as Grand Archdruid of the Ancient Order of Druids in America (AODA). He lives in Rhode Island with his wife, Sara.

Art Credits

Figures 1–6 by the Llewellyn Art Department.

Figure 7 by James Clark.

BOOK ELEVEN

———⊛———

Magician's Tables
by David Allen Hulse

The proper use of magical correspondences in the ritual work of a Magician is an essential part of any magical ceremony. The methodology behind any system of magical correspondences is derived from the renaissance *doctrine of signatures*. The philosophy of the doctrine of signatures looks to nature to find sympathetic correspondences. Thus, the walnut and the human brain are linked by this method of symbology, since the walnut is a hard shell enveloping a segmented nut that resembles the human skull surrounding a brain.

A complex system of symbolic correspondences has been developed by many different magicians and magical traditions by associating things of this world with the vast stretches of the cosmos, including the visible planets and the band of the zodiac. The core key symbols always involve the letters of the alphabet, the range of numbers, and the spectrum of the rainbow, all aligned to the elements, the planets, and the zodiac. Numbers are inevitably linked to words by associating a number value to each letter of a magical alphabet. It is the specific alignments between various symbol sets made by the magician that work with the logic of this doctrine of signatures.

For the practicing magician of the seventeenth century, the classical textbook to be consulted for such magical correspondences was *Three Books of Occult Philosophy* by Henry Cornelius Agrippa. For the practitioner of the magical arts in the nineteenth century, the classical textbook was *The Magus* by Francis Barrett (which was derived from Agrippa). For the twentieth century, the single most influential work concerning the doctrine of magical correspondences was Aleister Crowley's *777*.

· · · · · · · ·

My own publications concerning the magical tradition have focused on the categorization of the magical systems of the world, both East and West. This modest chapter cannot capture all the nuances found in my *Eastern Mysteries* and *Western Mysteries*. But given the limitation of space, I have crafted a lucid overview of the Qabalistic key to the Tarot found in the teachings of the Hermetic Order of the Golden Dawn as the true foundation of all magical endeavors. Magical correspondences will be provided for the elements, the planets, and the zodiac. The Western mandala known as the Tree of Life will be referenced throughout the following tables.

Those wanting a deeper grasp of the complexities of the symbolism for the Tree of Life should refer to the second key in *The Eastern Mysteries* concerning the Hebrew alphabet and the twelfth key in *The Western Mysteries* concerning the Tarot.

There is one common source from the nineteenth century for our modern magical tradition of symbolic correspondences. It is the magical fraternity of the Hermetic Order of the Golden Dawn, founded in England in 1887 by three Freemasons. These three founders (sometimes referred to as the three Secret Chiefs of the Order) were Dr. William Robert Woodman, Dr. William Wynn Westcott, and Samuel Liddell (MacGregor) Mathers. Two notable occultists from this order's members were Arthur Edward Waite and Aleister Edward Crowley, whose work in both magic and the Tarot continues to affect our modern magical community.

If we look at the work of Agrippa or Barrett, we will find no mention of the Tarot in their own doctrine of correspondences. But when we look to the esoteric teachings of the Hermetic Order of the Golden Dawn, we find that the key to their doctrine of signatures was a rectified order for the Tarot.

Eliphas Levi and the French occult movement of the nineteenth century aligned the esoteric symbolism of the Hebrew alphabet found in the tradition known as the *Qabalah* with the 78 cards composing the Tarot. The specific Hebrew text used as the lynchpin in this system of correspondences was the *Sepher Yetzirah* (*Book of Formation*), a short treatise giving the cosmological attributes of the 22 letters of the Hebrew alphabet. Wynn Westcott issued an English translation of this esoteric text, an indication that both Westcott and Mathers had access to this treatise as a means of solving the conundrum of how to allocate the Hebrew alphabet to the Tarot itself.

Eliphas Levi used the Marseille Tarot deck from France as the basis for attributing each letter of the alphabet to a specific Tarot card (table 1). Since the deck of 78 cards leads with 22 trump cards of an archetypal nature in their pictorial symbolism, known as the *Major Arcana*, Levi was able to pair one of 22 Hebrew alphabet letters to each of these cards. He used the actual images of the cards to make this alignment. Thus, he ascribed the first Hebrew letter of Aleph to key I, the *Magician*, since the arms, body, and legs of the Magician suggest in their shape the letter Aleph (א). Other symbolic images that identified in their shape the Hebrew alphabet included the lion's mouth in key XI, *Strength*, as the Hebrew letter Kaph (כ); the crossed legs, arms, and body in key XII, the *Hanged Man*, as the Hebrew letter Lamed (ל); and the falling mason's inverted body, legs, and arms in key XVI, the *Tower*, as the Hebrew letter Ayin (ע). This tradition was incorporated into both Papus's *The Tarot of the Bohemians* and Oswald Wirth's *The Tarot of the Magician*.

Heb	Tarot	Heb	Tarot	Heb	Tarot
א	The Magician	ח	Justice	ס	The Devil
ב	The High Priestess	ט	The Hermit	ע	The Tower Of God
ג	The Empress	י	The Wheel Of Fortune	פ	The Star
ד	The Emperor	כ	Force (Strength)	צ	The Moon
ה	The Pope	ל	The Hanged Man	ק	The Sun
ו	The Lover	מ	Death	ר	Judgment
ז	The Chariot	נ	Temperance	ש	The Fool
				ת	The World

Table 1. Eliphas Levi's Hebrew Key to the Tarot

However, with the advent of the Golden Dawn system of magic, both Westcott and Mathers, using Westcott's translation of the *Sepher Yetzirah* (published in 1887), unpublished materials at their access inherited from other occultists and magical orders, as well as the extensive library at the British Museum, discovered a different system of correspondences between the Hebrew alphabet and the Tarot. They forged a founding document known as the *Cipher Manuscript* to support this radical departure of symbolic correspondences from the system popularized by Eliphas Levi, acting as if their own esoteric teachings came from an existing Rosicrucian lodge in Germany. But the system they came up with for the Tarot was of their own invention and has shaped the contents of almost every modern published Tarot deck, including the decks of Arthur Edward Waite, Paul Foster Case, and Aleister Crowley.

When candidates came into the Golden Dawn for initiation into the mysteries, their first year of study focused on being able to write the Hebrew alphabet. Many would-be initiates were confused that this was the secret housed in the teachings of the Golden Dawn. But it truly was the crux of the matter, for the unique correspondences elucidated between the Hebrew alphabet and the Major Arcana of the Tarot were truly the treasure and greatest secret of the teachings of the Golden Dawn. Every ritual aspect of their ceremonies depended on this unique allocation for the Tarot, including the elaborate system of Enochian magic derived from John Dee's scrying work with Edward Kelley.

I have found in my own work with both the Tarot and magic in general that the system of magical correspondences devised by the Golden Dawn is the most workable and useful of any published esoteric system of allocations. This system can classify the contents of dreams and

· · · · · · · ·

waking visions. It can serve as a key to all esoteric texts and magical artwork. It greatly expands with years of practice. It can imbue the deepest symbolic meaning to any mundane occurrence in one's life. It grows internally with one's insight into the connections latent between the symbol sets. It becomes such a fabric of one's own mental processes that it is constantly running at a subconscious level. It needs to be at the foundation of the work of any practicing magician.

For the beginning student as well as the advanced practitioner, there will always be the tendency to modify this system of correspondences or completely replace it whole cloth with another. Aleister Crowley certainly did this by deviating from four of the Golden Dawn Major Arcana Tarot cards, and his student Frater Achad went even further by juggling the 22 paths of the Tree of Life that house the 22 cards of the Major Arcana in order to have greater astrological alignment between the sephiroth and adjoining paths. But I want to stress again the value of this system that Westcott and Mathers envisioned, for it is far richer than any other system or any other variation on a theme. Both Arthur Edward Waite and Paul Foster Case have preserved the integrity of this system in their own work with the esoteric nature of the Tarot, as well as Aleister Crowley (with the exception of four cards: the Emperor, Strength, Justice, and the Star).

As such, the next table to be shown in this chapter is this very recondite alignment of the Hebrew alphabet to the Tarot (table 2). Every practicing magician needs to deeply ingrain in his or her memory these extremely rich correspondences connecting the Hebrew alphabet with its cosmological attributes found in the *Sepher Yetzirah* to the 22 cards of the Major Arcana. Even if you have already been exposed to this system of correspondences, you need to make sure that it has been memorized to the point that every detail can be recalled on demand.

You will find in modern occult literature many a variation to the attributes listed in table 2. Thelemites swap the Emperor with the Star in accordance with the 57th verse of the first chapter of *The Book of the Law*: "All these old letters of my Book are aright; but צ is not the Star." [1]

Thelemites also keep the old tradition of positioning Justice at 8 and Strength at 11, but retain the Golden Dawn zodiacal attributes of Libra for Justice and Leo for Strength. Such symbolism should be viewed as secondary rather than primary.

The column labeled "Value" in table 2 displays the numerical value assigned to the Hebrew alphabet, which is different from the numeral associated to each Tarot card. In Eliphas Levi's system, the numerical sequence for the first ten Major Arcana cards was the same value as the numerical value of the Hebrew alphabet. But in the Golden Dawn system, the lead card of the Fool has the sequence number of 0 but the numerical value of 1 for Aleph. Thus, the Fool, which is Aleph and one, is also none. This is the great secret for the Tarot that the Golden Dawn system was able to decipher.

---

1. Crowley, *Liber L. vel Legis*, 7.

• • • • • • • •

Tarot	Hebrew	Value	Hieroglyph	Cosmos	Color
0. The Fool	Aleph (א)	1	Ox	△ / ⊛	Pale yellow
1. The Magician	Beth (ב)	2	House	☿	Yellow
2. The High Priestess	Gimel (ג)	3	Camel	☽	Blue
3. The Empress	Daleth (ד)	4	Door	♀	Green
4. The Emperor	Heh (ה)	5	Window	♈	Red
5. The Hierophant	Vav (ו)	6	Nail	♉	Red orange
6. The Lovers	Zain (ז)	7	Sword	♊	Orange
7. The Chariot	Cheth (ח)	8	Fence	♋	Yellow orange
8. Strength	Teth (ט)	9	Serpent	♌	Yellow
9. The Hermit	Yod (י)	10	Fist	♍	Yellow green
10. Wheel of Fortune	Kaph (כ)	20	Palm of hand	♃	Violet
11. Justice	Lamed (ל)	30	Ox goad	♎	Green
12. The Hanged Man	Mem (מ)	40	Water	▽	Blue
13. Death	Nun (נ)	50	Fish	♏	Blue green
14. Temperance	Samekh (ס)	60	Foundation	♐	Blue
15. The Devil	Ayin (ע)	70	Eye	♑	Blue violet
16. The Tower	Peh (פ)	80	Mouth	♂	Red
17. The Star	Tzaddi (צ)	90	Fish hook	♒	Violet
18. The Moon	Qoph (ק)	100	Back of head	♓	Red violet
19. The Sun	Resh (ר)	200	Face	☉	Orange
20. Judgment	Shin (ש)	300	Tooth	△	Red
21. The World	Tav (ת)	400	Mark/cross	♄ / ⊽	Blue violet

Table 2. The Golden Dawn Hebrew Alphabet Key to the Tarot

· · · · · · · ·

Arthur Edward Waite, in his introduction to Knut Stenring's translation of the *Sepher Yetzirah* (1923), makes this wry observation on the secret order for the Tarot:

> The proper placing of the Tarot Fool is the great crux of every attempt—and there are several—to create a correspondence between the Trumps Major and the Hebrew letters. If it be worthwhile to say so, the correct sequence, which emerges from unexpected considerations, has never appeared in print, and it is not to be confused with a Victorian allocation now well known, but which used to be regarded as important: it referred the cipher-card to Aleph, and therefore to the number one, so that we are confronted by the strange analogy of $0 = 1$, the alternative being—as we have seen—that $0 = 300$, otherwise 21 in the alphabetical order. [2]

In his usual pompous style, Waite reveals the real secret of $0 = 1$ as the true key to the Tarot, even though he states the opposite. His own Tarot design betrays this unique symbolism devised by the Golden Dawn (of which he was a member).

My twelfth key to book 2 of *The Western Mysteries* devotes a whole chapter to showing how Waite incorporated the symbolism of the Golden Dawn into each of his own 78 unique designs for the Tarot, which still serves as the basic blueprint for almost every modern Tarot deck.

This secret of allocating the Fool to both the number zero and the Hebrew letter Aleph is also hinted at in the 48th verse of the first chapter of Aleister Crowley's *The Book of the Law*: "My prophet is a fool with his one, one, one; are not they the Ox, and none by the book." [3]

The letters of the Hebrew alphabet each have a letter name, and for Aleph it is written as ALP (אלף), which is valued at 111. Each letter of the alphabet is in its shape a hieroglyph that is a translation of this letter name. For Aleph it is the Ox, as shown in the column labeled "Hieroglyph" in table 2. Thus, in the above verse by Crowley, the fool, the number 111, the Ox, and the value of none are all connected to Aleph as the Fool in the Tarot.

The color scale allocated to both the Hebrew alphabet and the Tarot cards of the Major Arcana shown in table 2 is derived from the Golden Dawn tradition that allocated four different color scales for the 22 Major Arcana cards. This scale is the most representative of the hues of the rainbow and is labeled the *King scale*, which corresponds to the highest of the four worlds in the Hebrew Qabalah. It is incorporated into the design for the Rose Cross used in the Golden Dawn system of magic.

---

2. Stenring, *The Book of Formation*, 11. Note that Waite may have been referring to his unpublished Tarot deck drawn between 1917–1923 by J. B. Trinick for Waite's own Rosicrucian order, since this book was originally published in 1923. The Waite-Trinick Tarot deck has only recently seen print in Goodman and Katz's *Abiding in the Sanctuary* as of 2011.

3. Crowley, *Liber L. vel Legis*, 6.

The Tarot cards in table 2 are ordered in a different way than in any previously published Tarot. Strength (Fortitude in some decks) and Justice are swapped, so that Strength is numbered 8 and Justice 11. This swap occurred when Mathers and Westcott were applying the attributes of the *Sepher Yetzirah* to the designs of the cards themselves. Waite himself swapped these two cards without giving a proper explanation for the exchange.

The Hebrew letters Teth and Lamed are both *simple* letters (the other two divisions being *double* and *mother* letters). The twelve simple letters are allocated to the twelve signs of the zodiac, and Teth is Leo, while Lamed is Libra. By establishing the Fool as Aleph and the lead card, Justice showing a woman holding a scale in one hand and a sword in the other would naturally fall to Teth and the sign Leo, while Strength showing a woman opening the mouth of a lion would fall to Lamed and Libra. By swapping these two cards, Strength becomes Leo (clearly showing the lion of Leo in its design), while Justice becomes Libra (clearly showing the scales of Libra in its design), which brings both cards into astrological harmony.

The most radical move by Westcott and Mathers was to displace Eliphas Levi's attribution of the Magician to Aleph and align Aleph to the Fool. The position of the Fool card eluded all previous commentators on the Tarot. This card was either put between key 20, Judgment, and key 21, the World, or it was allocated to last place and followed key 21. By placing the Fool to lead the deck and numbering it zero, the cosmological symbolism of the Hebrew alphabet matches perfectly the images of the cards themselves once Strength and Justice are exchanged.

Mathers and Westcott placed the 22 Major Arcana cards on a design of the Tree of Life derived from Athanasius Kircher. They revised the paths connecting the ten stations on the Tree of Life (known as *sephiroth*) to reflect their own unique connection of the Hebrew alphabet to the Tarot. This revised Tree of Life modified the existing paths of the traditional Jewish Qabalistic Tree of Life, which had a different scheme for the 22 paths connecting the ten sephiroth. In the original Tree of Life, the three horizontal paths were assigned to the three mother letters, the seven vertical paths were assigned to the seven planets, and the twelve slanting paths were assigned to the twelve signs of the zodiac.[4]

The Tree of Life is a map of the universe, a Western equivalent to the Eastern mandala. The diagram shows a series of ten circles symbolizing ten ever-expanding limits of the universe. The tenth station at the bottom is earth, the ninth station through the third stations are the seven planets (☽ ☿ ♀ ☉ ♂ ♃ ♄), the second station is the fixed stars composing the zodiac, and the first station is the white light of God, known as the *primum mobile*, or first swirling of creation. These ten stations should be seen as ten concentric circles, where the center is Earth and the tenth station and the outermost circle is the white light of the first station, the cause of all creation.

---

4. For a diagram of this proto–Tree of Life, see page 112 of my *Eastern Mysteries*.

• • • • • • • •

These ten stations, known in Hebrew as *sephirah* (singular) and *sephiroth* (plural), form in their symbolism developed by the Golden Dawn the most comprehensive exposition of the symbolic nature of the first ten numbers. These ten stations or numbers classify the astrological nature of our own cosmos and are given a complex coloring scheme in the Golden Dawn based on the rainbow of colors.

The 22 letters of the Hebrew alphabet serve as channels connecting these ten stations forming the Tree of Life. The combination of 10 stations and 22 paths form the 32 Paths of Wisdom described in the *Sepher Yetzirah*, illustrated in figure 1 and table 3.

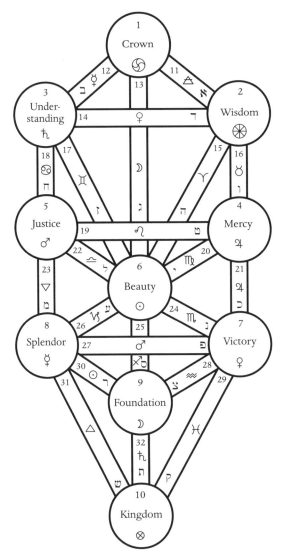

Figure 1. The Tree of Life as 32 Paths

Path	Cosmic Attribute	Path	Cosmic Attribute
1	Kether—Crown (Primum mobile)	17	ז Zain—The Lovers (♊)
2	Chockmah—Wisdom (Zodiac)	18	ח Cheth—The Chariot (♋)
3	Binah—Understanding (♄)	19	ט Teth—Strength (♌)
4	Chesed—Mercy (♃)	20	י Yod—The Hermit (♍)
5	Geburah—Severity (♂)	21	כ Kaph—Wheel of Fortune (♃)
6	Tiphereth—Beauty (☉)	22	ל Lamed—Justice (♎)
7	Netzach—Victory (♀)	23	מ Mem—The Hanged Man (▽)
8	Hod—Splendour (☿)	24	נ Nun—Death (♏)
9	Yesod—Foundation (☽)	25	ס Samekh—Temperance (♐)
10	Malkuth—Kingdom (⊗)	26	ע Ayin—The Devil (♑)
11	א Aleph—The Fool (🜁 / ⊛)	27	פ Peh—The Tower (♂)
12	ב Beth—The Magician (☿)	28	צ Tzaddi—The Star (♒)
13	ג Gimel—The High Priestess (☽)	29	ק Qoph—The Moon (♓)
14	ד Daleth—The Empress (♀)	30	ר Resh—The Sun (☉)
15	ה Heh—The Emperor (♈)	31	ש Shin—Judgment (△)
16	ו Vav—The Hierophant (♉)	32	ת Tav—The World (♄ / 🜃)

Table 3. The 32 Paths of Wisdom on the Tree of Life

It should be noted that in the Golden Dawn system of magic, the first ten stations on the Tree of Life, known as the ten sephiroth, are allocated to the 40 pip cards in the Minor Arcana of the Tarot. The four Aces fall to station 1, while the pip cards—numbered 2 through 10 in the suits of Wands, Cups, Swords, and Pentacles—are allocated to stations 2 through 10.

The Hebrew Qabalah has four levels to the cosmos and each level has its own Tree of Life. The highest world is named *Atziloth*, which is the Archetypal world. This world is the idea of creation itself, the impulse behind creation, and corresponds to the suit of Wands and the element of fire. The second world is named *Briah*, which is the Creative world. This world is the act of creating and corresponds to the suit of Cups and the element of water. The third world is named *Yetzirah*, which is the Formative world. This world is the pattern or blueprint behind creation and corresponds to the suit of Swords and the element of air. The fourth and final world is named *Assiah*, the world of Action. This world is the created world, which is the material world, and corresponds to the suit of Pentacles and the element of earth.

In light of the four worlds for the Tree of Life, the Golden Dawn worked out a complex system of color coding for the ten sephiroth and 22 paths of each of these four worlds. The four major color schemes of 32 colors for each of these four worlds are labeled the *King scale* for the world of Atziloth, the *Queen scale* for the world of Briah, the *Prince scale* for the world of Yetzirah, and the *Princess scale* for the world of Assiah. These four names are derived from the rectified order of the court cards in the Golden Dawn system for the Tarot, where the old Knight becomes the new King and the old King becomes the new Prince. This has eluded many a modern commentator and will be discussed in great detail in a later section dealing with the four elements.

Tables 4 and 5 show the four color scales for the ten sephiroth and the 22 paths in the four worlds. This scheme was first devised in the teachings of the Golden Dawn as envisioned by Moina Mathers, and was later popularized in the magical writings of Aleister Crowley. In his *Book of Thoth*, Crowley labeled the King scale as the Knight scale in order to help the reader understand that the old Knight is now the new King in the Golden Dawn allocations for color to the Tree of Life.

Sephirah (Path)	King Scale (Atziloth)	Queen Scale (Briah)	Prince Scale (Yetzirah)	Princess Scale (Assiah)
1—Kether	Brilliance	White brilliance	White brilliance	White flecked gold
2—Chockmah	Soft sky blue	Gray	Bluish-gray mother of pearl	White flecked red, blue, yellow
3—Binah	Crimson	Black	Dark brown	Gray flecked pink
4—Chesed	Deep violet	Blue	Deep purple	Deep azure flecked yellow
5—Geburah	Orange	Scarlet red	Bright scarlet	Red flecked black
6—Tiphereth	Clear pink rose	Yellow (gold)	Rich salmon	Gold amber
7—Netzach	Amber	Emerald	Bright yellow green	Olive flecked gold
8—Hod	Violet	Orange	Red russet	Yellow brown flecked white
9—Yesod	Indigo	Violet	Very dark purple	Citrine flecked azure
10—Malkuth	Yellow	Citrine, russet, olive, black	Citrine, russet, olive, black flecked gold	Black rayed yellow

Table 4. The Four Color Scales of the Four Worlds for the Ten Sephiroth

• • • • • • • •

Path	Tarot	King Scale (Atziloth)	Queen Scale (Briah)	Prince Scale (Yetzirah)	Princess Scale Assiah)
11—א	Fool	Pale yellow	Sky blue	Blue green	Emerald flecked gold
12—ב	Magician	Yellow	Purple	Gray	Indigo rayed violet
13—ג	High Priestess	Blue	Silver	Cold pale blue	Silver rayed sky blue
14—ד	Empress	Emerald green	Sky blue	Spring green	Bright rose rayed pale yellow
15—ה	Emperor	Scarlet	Red	Brilliant flame	Glowing red
16—ו	Hierophant	Red orange	Deep indigo	Deep olive	Rich brown
17—ז	Lovers	Orange	Pale mauve	New yellow	Reddish gray inclined to mauve
18—ח	Chariot	Amber	Maroon	Bright russet	Dark greenish brown
19—ט	Strength	Yellow	Deep purple	Gray	Reddish amber
20—י	Hermit	Yellow green	Slate gray	Green gray	Plum
21—כ	Wheel of Fortune	Violet	Blue	Rich purple	Bright blue rayed yellow
22—ל	Justice	Emerald green	Blue	Deep blue green	Pale green
23—מ	Hanged Man	Deep blue	Sea green	Deep olive green	White flecked purple
24—נ	Death	Blue green	Dull brown	Very dark brown	Vivid indigo brown
25—ס	Temperance	Blue	Yellow	Green	Dark vivid blue
26—ע	Devil	Blue violet	Black	Blue black	Cold dark gray near black
27—פ	Tower	Scarlet	Red	Venetian red	Bright red rayed emerald
28—צ	Star	Violet	Sky blue	Bluish mauve	White tinged purple
29—ק	Moon	Red violet	Buff flecked silver white	Translucent pink brown	Stone gray

Table 5. The Four Color Scales for the 22 Paths in the Four Worlds (continued)

• • • • • • • •

Path	Tarot	King Scale (Atziloth)	Queen Scale (Briah)	Prince Scale (Yetzirah)	Princess Scale Assiah)
30—ר	Sun	Orange	Gold yellow	Rich amber	Amber rayed red
31—ש	Judgment	Scarlet orange	Vermillion	Scarlet flecked gold	Vermillion flecked crimson and emerald
32—ת	Universe	Blue violet	Black	Blue black	Black rayed blue

Table 5. The Four Color Scales for the 22 Paths in the Four Worlds (continued)

The Golden Dawn system for assigning color correspondences to the Tree of Life gives four separate color schemes, one for each of the four worlds. The ten sephiroth are given four unique color schemes corresponding to the four worlds. The 22 paths are also given four unique color patterns. There are 16 possible combinations (4 × 4) of ten sephiroth with 22 paths by pairing four different color values of the sephiroth with four unique color values for the paths. Thus, the color scheme for the ten sephiroth in the Atziloth world can be connected by 22 paths in four different color values (one for each world). This is true for the other three worlds as well, each having four possible color schemes for the connecting paths.

The classic combination of 16 seen in most modern colored versions of the Tree of Life utilizes the Queen scale for the ten sephiroth and the King scale for the 22 paths. This is the fifth of 16 combinations and corresponds to △ of ▽ in the world of Briah. Both of these color schemes follow most closely the twelve gradations of the rainbow ranging from red to red violet and appear in almost every color illustration of the Tree of Life in modern magical literature.

Though the various shades of color seem arbitrary for each of the 128 color attributes shown in the color scales for the 32 emanations in four worlds, there exists a pattern to the King, Queen, and Prince color scales. The King scale corresponds to the father, the Queen scale to the mother, and the Prince scale to the son (based on the family division found in the Tetragrammaton). The union of the father with the mother results in the son. The combination of the King scale with the Queen scale results in the color attribute for the Prince scale. Look at the color scale for Chockmah: soft sky blue (King-Father) combines with gray (Queen-Mother) to form bluish-gray mother of pearl (Prince-Son). This logic holds true for all 32 emanations on the Tree of Life.

The Princess color scale does not follow this logic. It is its own scale and represents an earthy amalgam of colors. This scale can be interpreted by using the matching colors found in the other three scales. Thus, the Princess scale for Chockmah is white flecked red, blue, and yellow.

This can be seen on the Tree of Life using the Queen scale as Kether, Chesed, Geburah, and Tiphereth, which is white light speckled with ♃ (blue), ♂ (red), and ☉ (yellow).

Now that we have established the basic core correspondences in the Golden Dawn for the Tarot and the Tree of Life, we should study in detail the magical symbolism for the elements, the planets, and the zodiac, the magical building blocks of the cosmos. We will start with the elements, which in the Western tradition can be grouped as three alchemical elements, four elements at the four directions, five elements around the five points of a pentagram, and 16 counterchanges of four elements (each of the elements paired with itself and the other three), the last grouping of 16 (as 4 × 4) being extremely complex in its set of correspondences.

The Three Alchemical Elements

In the lore of alchemy there exist three basic elements that compose the entire universe. These three elements are Mercury (☿), Sulfur (🜍), and Salt (🜔). As color they are yellow for Mercury, red for Sulfur, and blue for Salt. These three symbols appear in Arthur Edward Waite's Wheel of Fortune card on the rim of the wheel.

This trinity of Salt, Sulfur, and Mercury symbolize female, male, and combined energies. Salt is the feminine, receptive force of water and the Moon. Sulfur is the masculine, active force of fire and the Sun. Mercury is the joining of male and female to form both the child and the hermaphrodite as air and the Stars.

These three elements also correspond to the three qualities of human life as portrayed in the Hindu theory of the three *Gunas* (or types of human behavior). These three aspects are labeled weighty inertia (Tamas), fiery activity (Rajas), and poise in quietude (Sattva) and are symbolized as tattvas by the yellow square (Tamas), the red upright triangle (Rajas), and the blue circle (Sattva). Salt is equivalent to Tamas, Sulfur to Rajas, and Mercury to Sattva.

Arthur Edward Waite utilized this variation of the three tattva colors of yellow, red, and blue as the three alchemical elements in designing his Wheel of Fortune card. The yellow serpent descending the wheel is 🜔, the rising red Hermanubis is 🜍, and the blue sphinx at rest on top is ☿.

This basic triple division for classifying our world is also found in the esoteric attributes of the *Sepher Yetzirah*, for the Hebrew alphabet is divided into three parts: three mother letters, which are the source of all sounds; seven double letters, which have two distinct pronunciations each; and twelve simple letters, which have only one pronunciation. The twelve simple letters are the zodiac, the seven double letters are the seven planets, and the three mother letters are the three elements.

These three mother letters are Aleph as the element of air, Mem as the element of water, and Shin as the element of fire. Their pronunciations hold the key to this elemental symbolism, for Aleph is the *ah* of a breath, Mem is the murmuring of running water, and Shin is the hiss of a

• • • • • • • •

fire. The three correspond to the alchemical trinity as Aleph for Mercury, Mem for Salt, and Shin for Sulfur. Table 6 delineates the elements as three.

Symbol	☿	☿	☿
Alchemy	Salt	Mercury	Sulfur
Color (Alchemy)	Blue	Yellow	Red
Cosmos	Moon	Star	Sun
Family	Mother	Child	Father
Yahweh	Heh (ה)	Vav (ו)	Yod (י)
IAO	A (Moon)	Ω (Stars)	I (Sun)
Gunas	Tamas	Sattva	Rajas
Quality	Inertia	Equilibrium	Activity
Motion	Downward	Centered	Upward
Tattva	Square	Circle	Triangle
Color (Tattva)	Yellow	Blue	Red
Hebrew	Mem (מ)	Aleph (א)	Shin (ש)
Sound	Murmuring	Exhaling	Hissing
Body	Belly, genitals	Heart, lungs	Brain
Element	Water	Air	Fire
Tarot	XII. The Hanged Man	0. The Fool	XX. Judgment
Cube	East to west	Above to below	North to south
Tree of Life	Binah	Kether	Chockmah
Number	3	1	2
Name	Understanding	Crown	Wisdom
Cosmos	Saturn	First cause	Fixed stars
Color (Tree of Life)	Black	White	Gray
Archangel	Gabriel	Raphael	Michael

Table 6. Alchemical Trinity of Elements

This division of the elements into three forms the basis for the most common division of the elements in the Western magical tradition. That division is the grouping of the elements into four (by adding earth to the three elements of air, water, and fire) to correspond to the four basic directions of the compass as north, south, east, and west.

• • • • • • • •

The Fourfold Division of the Elements

There is a beautiful portrayal of the symbolic components for the division of the elements into four in Arthur Edward Waite's portrayal of the Wheel of Fortune (figure 2), which he derived from Eliphas Levi's illustration of the Wheel of Ezekiel in *The Magical Ritual of the Sanctum Regnum Interpreted by the Tarot Trumps*. As the three alchemical elements divide the world into air, fire, and water, the division into four adds the additional element of earth to the mix.

These four elements within the alchemical tradition are derived from various parts of a hexagram, formed by the interlacing of two triangles (✡). Fire is the upright triangle (△), water is the downward triangle (▽), air is the upright triangle with the upper crossbar from the hexagram (⟁), while earth is the downward triangle with the lower crossbar from the hexagram (⍒). This interlinking of two triangles is also the basis in the East for the most supreme mandala of all, the *Sri Yantra*, composed of nine interlocking triangles.

Together these four elements can be aligned to the four directions. The Golden Dawn Lesser Pentagram Ritual assigns an element and a color to each of the four directions: the element of air and the color yellow are in the east, the element of fire and the color red are in the south, the element of water and the color blue are in the west, and the element of earth and the color green (or black) are in the north.

Figure 2. Waite's Wheel of Fortune Card

· · · · · · ·

The four elements are also the basis in the Tarot for the division of the Minor Arcana into four suits: the suit of Wands corresponds to the element of fire and the color red, the suit of Cups corresponds to the element of water and the color blue, the suit of Swords corresponds to the element of air and the color yellow, and the suit of Pentacles corresponds to the element of earth and the color green.

The binding element to this fourfold division used in the Golden Dawn is the four-lettered name of God in Hebrew known as the *Tetragrammaton* (יהוה) and variously translated as Yahweh, Iehovah, or Jehovah. In Hebrew it is written as Yod (י) valued at 10, Heh (ה) valued at 5, Vav (ו) valued at 6, and Heh (ה) valued at 5. Together they equal the mystic number of 26.

Each of these four letters of God reflects the division of the family into father, mother, son, and daughter. Yod (י) is the father, Heh (ה) is the mother, Vav (ו) is the son, and the final Heh (ה) is the daughter. The father is the element of fire, the mother is the element of water, the son is the element of air, and the daughter is the element of earth. Now this elemental division of the family unit into four is the basis of the Golden Dawn's revision in the Tarot to the order of the four court cards.

In the Tarot, the four Minor Arcana suits of Wands, Cups, Swords, and Pentacles each contain four figures derived from the court of a king: the King and his Queen and the Knight and his Page. Before the advent of the Golden Dawn, these four court cards (or coate cards, since they are all dressed in Medieval garb) fell to the family division of King as father, Queen as mother, Knight as son, and Page as daughter. But within the symbolism of the Golden Dawn for the Tarot, these four court cards assumed a different family order. The Knight became the father and the new King, the Queen remained the mother, the old King became the new Prince as the son, and the Page became his consort of Princess as the daughter. In this new order for the court cards, the Knight as the King remained mounted on his steed, the Queen remained seated on her throne, the new Prince commanded a chariot (which combined the mobility of the Knight with the throne of the Queen), and the Princess was stripped of her clothes and wrapped in her element.

Crowley, in devising his *Book of Thoth*, saw the possibility of the reader missing this subtle change in the court cards. He retained the old name of Knight rather than renaming him King, kept the Queen, and added the Prince and Princess.

In Crowley's magical record from May 3, 1920, he attempted to elucidate this misunderstood bit of symbolism unique to the Golden Dawn: "Why do the Tarot Cards give the Knight as the father, the King as the son? It is an echo of the legend of the Wandering Knight who wins the Queen, and whose son becomes the King. This, in turn, relates to the customs of matriarchy." [5]

---

5. Crowley, *The Magical Record of the Beast 666*, 116.

Further Clarification on the Court Cards

Eliphas Levi described the traditional order for the court cards of the Tarot as follows: "KING, QUEEN, KNIGHT, ESQUIRE. The married pair, the youth, the child…" (from *Doctrine and Ritual of Transcendental Magic*, p. 103, 1896). This traditional symbolism for the court cards depicting a King and a Queen as a married pair, a Knight as a youth, and a Page as a child was revised in the Golden Dawn teachings found in their *Book T*. In this esoteric Golden Dawn system, the traditional Knight was elevated to the status of the King astride his horse, while the traditional King became the Prince riding a chariot. The Page was transformed to a consort for this Prince as a Princess, while only the Queen remained as herself and became a consort for the Knight as the new King.

There are two main Tarot decks designed in the twentieth century that define almost all the symbolism found in every modern deck. These two decks are from A. E. Waite (illustrated by Pamela Colman Smith) and Aleister Crowley (illustrated by Lady Frieda Harris). When Waite designed his deck, he kept the traditional titles for the court cards as King, Queen, Knight, and Page. But when Crowley designed his deck, he incorporated the proper designs for the court cards as envisioned by the Golden Dawn. He correctly showed the Prince in his chariot and the King mounted on his horse. His one variation was retitling the new King as the Knight, so that it would be easier to identify the new King as the traditional Knight.

In looking at any modern variation on the Tarot, we can immediately identify it as coming from either Crowley or Waite. If the court cards show a Prince driving a chariot and a King on his steed, then they stem from the Golden Dawn system as illustrated by Crowley's Tarot. But if they have as court cards the traditional designs of King, Queen, Knight, and Page, then they are derived from the Waite Tarot deck.

It should be noted that the majority of Tarot decks published since 1970 have been influenced by Waite rather than Crowley. However, the Crowley/Harris *Book of Thoth* was the first Tarot design to show not only the correct court cards but also the proper titles and astrological correspondences for the Minor Arcana, as well as the correct Hebrew alphabet and astrological attributes for the Major Arcana according to *Book T* of the Golden Dawn.

This subtle point of symbolism has been missed by Arthur Edward Waite, Paul Foster Case, Israel Regardie, Robert Wang, and Christopher Hyatt, to name just a few contemporary commentators on the Tarot. If this fine point of symbolism is missed, then the two elements of fire and air are inadvertently swapped. If the Magician can comprehend this secret concerning the

• • • • • • •

court cards, then all the elemental secrets found in the esoteric teachings of the Golden Dawn can be fully comprehended. The correspondences for the four court cards are listed in table 7.

Traditional Title	Knight	Queen	King	Page
Revised G.D. Title	King	Queen	Prince	Princess
Crowley's Variation	Knight	Queen	Prince	Princess
Image	Knight on horseback	Queen on throne	Prince in Chariot	Princess naked in her element
Family	Father	Mother	Son	Daughter
Element	△	▽	⩘	⩔
Suit	Wands	Cups	Swords	Pentacles

Table 7. The Secret Order of the Court Cards

Each of the four letters of the Tetragrammaton correspond as well to the four Kerubic Angels of Lion, Eagle, Man, and Bull that drove the wheeled chariot of Ezekiel. (They also drive the chariots of the Princes in the court cards.) The Lion is Yod and fire, the Eagle is Heh and water, the Man is Vav and air, and the Bull is the final Heh and earth. The astrological symbols corresponding to these four angels can be numbered as 26, the same value as the Tetragrammaton written on the Wheel of Fortune. For the Lion is Leo, the 5th sign; the Eagle is Scorpio, the 8th sign; the Man is Aquarius, the 11th sign; and the Bull is Taurus, the 2nd sign: $5 + 8 + 11 + 2 = 26 = $ יהוה.

If we use the Latin Cabala Simplex values of Selenus (1624) to decode the word *ROTA* (an anagram for *TAROT*) written on the rim of the wheel, the number 48 is generated, as R = 16 + O = 15 + T = 18 + A = 1 (table 8).

If the value for the Tetragrammaton is subtracted from the value of ROTA, the number 22 is produced, symbolizing the 22 Tarot keys of the Major Arcana lining the rim of the Wheel of Fortune ($48 - 26 = 22$). If we add these two numbers instead, the number 74 is generated (as 26 + 48), which is the value of the letter name Lamed in full (למד = 30 + 40 + 4 = 74) that governs the next Tarot key, Justice.

· · · · · · · ·

A	B	C, K	D	E	F	G	H	I, J	L	M
1	2	3	4	5	6	7	8	9	10	11
N	O	P	Q	R	S	T	U, V	X	Y	Z
12	13	14	15	16	17	18	19	20	21	22

Table 8. Latin Cabala Simplex

Note that the Tetragrammaton as the Tarot also numbers to 22, as 9 + 4 + 5 + 4 = 22, for Yod = IX. The Hermit, Heh = IV. The Emperor, Vav = V. The Hierophant, and the final Heh = IV. The Emperor. The full set of correspondences for the four elements is shown in table 9.

Element	Alchemy	Zodiac	Hebrew	Latin	Quadrant
△	🜍	♌	י	A	Lower right
▽	🜔	♏	ה	O	Upper right
⏶	☿	♒	ו	T	Upper left
⏷	≈	♉	ה	R	Lower left

Table 9. The Four Elements in the Wheel of Fortune Card

In the "Alchemy" column in table 9, earth is symbolized as the sign for Aquarius (≈), representing the alchemical operation of dissolution. It is the dissolving of the three alchemical elements into one divine elixir. The Latin letters correspond in shape to the alchemical elements, while the quadrant ruled by each element (and each fixed sign) also governs one of the four quadrants of each directional Enochian Watchtower.

The four elements flow down the Tree of Life and touch all ten sephiroth. Air flows from Kether to Tiphereth to Yesod, forming the middle pillar. Fire zigzags from Chockmah to Geburah to Netzach. Water zigzags from Binah to Chesed to Hod. Earth is the joining of air, fire, and water at Malkuth.

Table 10 contains four unique color schemes for the four elements. The first color code is based on the four elements in Western magic. The second color code is based on the four humours of the body derived from the Greek physician Hippocrates. The third code is based on the Chinese elements, while the fourth code is based on the Hindu tattva system.

Each is a unique take on the four elements, but the primary scale to use is the first one, based on the three primary colors of red, blue, and yellow for fire, water, and air, and the fourth color of green (or black) for earth.

Symbol	△	▽	△̶	▽̶
Element	Fire	Water	Air	Earth
Color (Element)	Red	Blue	Yellow	Green/black
Yahweh	Yod	Heh	Vav	Heh
Hebrew	Shin	Mem	Aleph	Tav
Tarot	Judgment	Hanged Man	Fool	World
Family	Father	Mother	Son	Daughter
Suit	Wand	Cup	Sword	Pentacle
Court	Knight	Queen	King	Page
Direction	South	West	East	North
Season	Summer	Fall	Spring	Winter
Archangel	Michael	Gabriel	Raphael	Aurial
Sephiroth	2, 5, 7	3, 4, 8	1, 6, 9	10
Planets (Sephiroth)	♂ ♀	♄ ♃ ☿	☉ ☽	⊗
Humour	Yellow bile	Phlegm	Blood	Black bile
Temperment	Choleric	Phlegmatic	Sanguine	Melancholic
Body	Spleen	Brain/lungs	Liver	Gall bladder
Quality	Hot/dry	Wet/cold	Hot/wet	Dry/cold
Color (Humour)	Yellow	Blue	Red	Black
Trigram	Chen ☳	Tui ☱	Sun ☴	Ken ☶
Nature	Fire	Lake	Wind/wood	Mountain
Color (Trigram)	Red	Black	Green	White
Tattva	Agni	Apas	Vayu	Prithivi
Shape	△	☽	○	□
Color (Tattva)	Red	White (silver)	Blue	Yellow

Table 10. Additional Symbols for the Four Elements

The Pentagram of Five Elements

A further mystery to the division of the elements into four is the addition of a fifth element of spirit, which rules and animates the other four (figure 3). This division into five elements is placed upon the five points of the upright pentagram so that the lower right point is fire, the upper right point is water, the upper left point is air, the lower left point is earth, and the crowning apex point is spirit. The position of the four lesser elements on the pentagram is the same position as the four Kerubic angels in the Wheel of Fortune card, as well as the four quadrants of

· · · · · · · ·

the four Enochian Watchtowers. If the pentagram is traced beginning with the apex point and moving next to the lower right leg, the elements of spirit, fire, air, water, and earth are traced in order, reflecting the older Renaissance model of fire and air above water and earth.

Figure 3. Pentagram of Five Elements

This five-pointed star expands the sacred name of God known as the Tetragrammaton to the Holy name of Jesus as Yehoshuah, which places the letter Shin (ש) as a symbol of the fiery spirit in the center of the four elements. Yahweh (יהוה) becomes Yehoshuah (יהשוה), which was the great secret of the Renaissance Christian Qabalists. As *Yahweh* is labeled the *Tetragrammaton* (or word of four letters), *Yehoshuah* is labeled the *Pentagrammaton* (or word of five letters).

The pentagram is the primary symbol of both magic and the magician. It is referred to as the *Pentalpha*, since it is made up of the Greek letter Alpha (A) entwined five times. In the tradition of the Golden Dawn, this symbol is traced in the four directions to protect the magician during the ceremony of the Lesser Pentagram Ritual.

In Renaissance art, the upright pentagram was traced on the human body so that the apex point was at the head, the upright points at the arms, and the downward points at the legs.

Inverted, this pentagram has been associated with black magic or the darker arts in modern times. But the ancient symbol of a pentagram with its apex point pointing downward initially symbolized the light of the star descending on Earth as a blessing to humanity. This can be seen as a symbol for the Star of Bethlehem, which is a downward-pointing star shedding its light on Earth to mark the birth of the Messiah. This inverted pentagram symbolism is also used by the Masonic order of the Eastern Star to denote the guiding star for the Magi that leads to the birth of the Messiah.

This fivefold symbolism of the elements is an expansion of the table for four elements. The addition of a fifth element in alchemy is the operation of distilling the quintessence from the primal four elements. Table 11 illustrates the quintessential division of the elements.

Symbol	△	▽	☸	🜁	🜃
Element	Fire	Water	Spirit (Space)	Air	Earth
Pentagram	Lower right	Upper right	Apex	Upper left	Lower left
Yehoshuah	Yod (י)	Heh (ה)	Shin (ש)	Vav (ו)	Heh (ה)
Color (Elements)	Red	Blue	White	Yellow	Green (Black)
Platonic Solid	Pyramid	Icosahedron	Dodecahedron	Octahedron	Cube
Sides	4	20	12	8	6
Tarot	Wands	Cups	Major Arcana	Swords	Pentacles
Finger	Middle	Index	Thumb	Ring	Little
Sense	Sight	Taste	Hearing	Smell	Touch
Major Arcana	Emperor	Strength	Hierophant	Lovers	Hermit
Tree of Life	5 and 7	4 and 8	1 and 2	6 and 9	3 and 10
Direction	South	West	Center	East	North
Tattva	Agni	Apas	Akasa	Vayu	Prithivi
Shape	Triangle	Crescent	Oval	Circle	Square
Color (Tattva)	Red	White (Silver)	Black (Blue violet)	Blue	Yellow
Chinese Element	Fire	Water	Metal	Wood	Earth
Star	♂	☿	♀	♃	♄
Color (Star)	Red	Black	White	Green	Yellow

Table 11. Pentagram of Five Elements

In table 11, spirit can refer to space, as opposed to the four terrestrial elements. This is especially true in terms of the tattva Akasa. The five Major Arcana cards listed represent the five senses by way of their corresponding Hebrew alphabet letters. They are all taken from the twelve simple letters that represent the zodiac. The connections between the five senses and five select Hebrew alphabet letters are derived from the symbolism found in the *Book of Formation* (*Sepher Yetzirah*). The ten sephiroth on the Tree of Life refer to the five fingers of the right and left hands. For the right hand, the thumb is 1, the index finger is 4, the middle finger is 5, the ring finger is 6, and the little finger is 3. For the left hand, the thumb is 2, the index finger is 8, the middle finger is 7, the ring finger is 9, and the little finger is 10.

For the Chinese elements, earth and spirit are interchangeable, so that in one scheme metal is spirit while in an alternate scheme earth is spirit. The Chinese Taoist system of magic employs the pentagram as a symbol of creation and destruction. The five points of the pentagram correspond to the five Chinese elements as follows: apex point = metal, lower right = wood, upper right = water, upper left = earth, and lower left = fire.

The path of creation is the clockwise motion starting with the lower left leg of the pentagram and following the other four points in a clockwise motion, leading from fire to earth, metal, water, and wood, then returning to fire again. The path of destruction traces the actual shape of the pentagram and begins with the lower left leg of fire and then traces upward, following the path of the star to metal first, then wood, earth, and water, leading back to fire again.

One final system of dividing the elements will be detailed next, and that is the sixteen subdivisions of the four major elements of fire, water, air, and earth. It is at the heart of the system of magical correspondences found in the Golden Dawn system of magic.

Sixteen Combinations of the Four Elements

The four elements have sixteen possible pairings, and these sixteen form the most detailed descriptions for the elements. These sixteen subdivisions are illustrated by the sixteen divinatory shapes of geomancy, sixteen tattva counterchanges (as well as sixteen select *I Ching* hexagrams), sixteen letters of the Enochian alphabet, sixteen court cards of the Minor Arcana, and the sixteen secret channels normally not drawn on the Tree of Life that form the 33rd through 48th invisible paths. There are also sixteen color combinations for the four color schemes in the Golden Dawn for the Tree of Life in the four worlds, as well as sixteen quadrants of the Enochian Watchtowers.

The Golden Dawn teachings concerning these sixteen counterchanges for the four elements depend on a correct understanding of the four court cards, and most commentators on this subject confuse two cards, the Knight and the King. The older titles of Knight, Queen, King, and Page were transformed into King, Queen, Prince, and Princess by the Golden Dawn, and clarified by Crowley as Knight, Queen, Prince, and Princess.

The tables in this section will use the traditional titles for the court cards as Knight, Queen, King, and Page to make a clear distinction between the title of Knight and King, since the old Knight is the revised title of King while the old King is the revised title of Prince within the Golden Dawn tradition.

The correct allocation of the sixteen elements to the sixteen court cards is shown in table 12.

Court Card	Wands	Cups	Swords	Pentacles
Knight	Fire of fire	Fire of water	Fire of air	Fire of earth
Queen	Water of fire	Water of water	Water of air	Water of earth
King	Air of fire	Air of water	Air of air	Air of earth
Page	Earth of fire	Earth of water	Earth of air	Earth of earth

Table 12. Elemental Counterchanges for the Court Cards

Each of the four elements of fire, water, air, and earth are paired to all of the four elements. Thus, fire is subdivided into fire of fire, water of fire, air of fire, and earth of fire. Each of these four pairings is predominately fire, but each is in some way altered by its pair. Fire of fire intensifies the element of fire itself, while water of fire cools the fire by the influence of water. As symbols, fire of fire could be a fire consuming itself, while water of fire could be a flow of lava.

The tattva itself when paired to a tattva counterchange can serve as a portal to the astral landscape described by any specific elemental counterchange. The hexagrams of the *I Ching* corresponding to the sixteen elemental counterchanges can also serve as a means of imagining an astral elemental landscape.

Geomancy is an ancient form of divination that utilizes the earth as the divining table. Sixteen geomantic shapes are generated by four rows of either one or two points. These sixteen figures are given titles that indicate their divinatory meaning. The Golden Dawn attributes for geomancy are derived from Latin titles for these sixteen figures, but this divinatory system has its origins in Africa and the Middle East. The Enochian alphabet attributes can be correctly deciphered by linking these sixteen geomantic shapes to the sixteen elemental counterchanges. Table 13 lists the sixteen geomantic figures and their associated elemental counterchanges.

Within the Golden Dawn tradition these sixteen geomantic shapes are tied to sixteen select Enochian alphabet letters. The connection between the two is established through the astrological nature of these sixteen geomantic shapes. It is this connection that gives sixteen select Enochian letters their specific number values.

The zodiac signs associated with the court cards are each composed of the last 10 degrees of the preceding sign followed by the first 20 degrees of the predominate sign. The corresponding geomantic shape has both a planet and a sign associated with it, including the lunar nodes, known as the head and the tail of the dragon. The planets associated with the zodiac signs are their planetary rulers.

Figure	Title	Figure	Title	Figure	Title	Figure	Title
○ ○ ○ ○ ○ ○	Acquisitio △△	○ ○ ○ ○ ○	Puer ▽△	○ ○ ○ ○ ○ ○	Fortuna Major △△	○ ○ ○ ○ ○	Cauda Draconis ▽△
○ ○ ○ ○ ○ ○ ○	Laetitia △▽	○ ○ ○ ○ ○ ○ ○ ○	Populus ▽▽	○ ○ ○ ○ ○ ○ ○	Rubeus △▽	○ ○ ○ ○	Via ▽▽
○ ○ ○ ○ ○ ○ ○	Albus △△	○ ○ ○ ○ ○	Puella ▽△	○ ○ ○ ○ ○ ○ ○	Tristia △△	○ ○ ○ ○ ○ ○	Fortuna Minor ▽△
○ ○ ○ ○ ○ ○	Conjunctio △▽	○ ○ ○ ○ ○ ○	Carcer ▽▽	○ ○ ○ ○ ○ ○	Amissio △▽	○ ○ ○ ○ ○	Caput Draconis ▽▽

Table 13. Sixteen Geomantic Figures

Table 14 details the symbol sets for the sixteen counterchanged elements as court cards, astrology, geomancy, planet, and zodiac.

Element	Court Card	Astrology	Geomancy	Meaning	Planet	Zodiac
△ of △	Knight of Wands	20° ♏ – 20° ♐	Acquisitio	Gain, acquisition	♃	♐
▽ of △	Queen of Wands	20° ♓ – 20° ♈	Puer	Youth, rashness	♂	♈
🜁 of △	King of Wands	20° ♋ – 20° ♌	Fortuna Major	Wealth, fame	☉	♌
🜃 of △	Page of Wands	Elemental fire	Cauda Draconis	Exit, below	♄ + ♂	☋
△ of ▽	Knight of Cups	20° ♒ – 20° ♓	Laetitia	Joy, delight	♃	♓
▽ of ▽	Queen of Cups	20° ♊ – 20° ♋	Populus	People, crowd	☽	♋

Table 14. Sixteen Sub-elements as Court Cards, Geomancy, and Astrology (continued)

· · · · · · · ·

Element	Court Card	Astrology	Geomancy	Meaning	Planet	Zodiac
△ of ▽	King of Cups	20° ♎ – 20° ♏	Rubeus	Passion, temper	♂	♏
▽ of ▽	Page of Cups	Elemental water	Via	Path, journey	☽	♋
△ of △	Knight of Swords	20° ♉ – 20° ♊	Albus	Bright, wisdom	☿	♊
▽ of △	Queen of Swords	20° ♍ – 20° ♎	Puella	Beauty, innocence	♀	♎
△ of △	King of Swords	20° ♑ – 20° ♒	Tristia	Sadness, illness	♄	♒
▽ of △	Page of Swords	Elemental air	Fortuna Minor	Aid, small fortune	☉	♌
△ of ▽	Knight of Pentacles	20° ♌ – 20° ♍	Conjunctio	Union, meeting	☿	♍
▽ of ▽	Queen of Pentacles	20° ♐ – 20° ♑	Carcer	Delay, prison	♄	♑
△ of ▽	King of Pentacles	20° ♈ – 20° ♉	Amissio	Loss, give away	♀	♉
▽ of ▽	Page of Pentacles	Elemental earth	Caput Draconis	Enter, upper	♃ + ♂	♎

Table 14. Sixteen Sub-elements as Court Cards, Geomancy, and Astrology (continued)

There is a direct link between the sixteen court cards and the sixteen counterchanges of elements, and this link in turn determines the numbering of the Enochian alphabet by way of the sixteen geomantic figures. The path to solving the correct attributes for the sixteen elements is as follows: 16 elements → 16 court cards → 16 Major Arcana → 16 geomantic figures → select 16 Enochian letters. From these associations, the Hebrew letter for the corresponding Major Arcana is linked, and the number value of that Hebrew letter is then paired with sixteen select Enochian alphabet letters, all linked by the sixteen geomantic shapes.

The Numerology of Enochian Letters

How did the Golden Dawn derive numerical values for the Enochian alphabet? A table showing sixteen select Enochian letters as the sixteen geomantic figures is found on page 77 of volume IV of Israel Regardie's The Golden Dawn. There is no source for this table, but it clearly connects the Enochian alphabet with the divinatory shapes for geomancy. The Enochian table "Notes to the Book of the Concourse of the Forces" is found on page

298. This second table offers a correlation between the sixteen geomantic figures and sixteen select Hebrew alphabet letters based on the astrological attributes of the geomantic figures. Mathers was able to discover the correct astrological attributes for the Hebrew alphabet from the Qabalistic text the Sepher Yetzirah and connected them to the traditional astrological attributes of geomancy. If we combine these two tables, the numerical values for sixteen select Enochian letters can be obtained by paralleling Enochian to geomancy to astrology to Hebrew.

But where did the Golden Dawn derive geomantic attributes for sixteen select Enochian alphabet letters? The source Mathers used in numbering Enochian is found in *A Treatise of Angel Magic* by Dr. Rudd (being Ms. Harley 6482 in the British Library). In the table "The Characters of the Sixteen Figures of Geomancy" (found on page 20 of the manuscript), Rudd assigned to sixteen select Enochian letters both their geomantic figures and their astrological attributes. Mathers spent many hours in the British Museum for research leading to the esoteric teachings of the Golden Dawn, and he used these attributes and combined them with the astrological values for the Hebrew alphabet. By this combination he numbered sixteen select Enochian alphabet letters by substituting the number values for the Hebrew alphabet.

As an example, Dr. Rudd showed that the Enochian letter *Pe* was the geomantic shape *Puer* and also Mars in Aries. Mathers knew that *Aries* in Hebrew was the letter *Heh*, valued at 5. Therefore, he numbered Pe as 5.

Crowley, in studying this system, realized that five additional Enochian letters were without astrological or number value. He intuited that these five remaining letters should be aligned to the five points of the pentagram, and based on their elemental attributes he paired these five additional Enochian letters to the appropriate Hebrew alphabet letters and gave them a number value. These attributes can be seen in Crowley's notes to his own *The Vision and the Voice* when he numerically deciphered the three-letter Enochian calls.

Where Mathers depended on Rudd's previous research in order to establish a number value for the Enochian alphabet, Crowley based his additions on his own magical insight. Neither Mathers nor Crowley utilized Dee's own use of the Enochian alphabet as numbers as it appears in his calls to the 30 Aethyrs. To see a discussion of Dee's own number code for Enochian, refer to the introduction of chapter 11 in the second volume of my *Western Mysteries*.

Table 15 lists the corresponding Hebrew letter and Major Arcana card based on the astrological qualities of the geomantic shapes. Where table 14 linked the sixteen counterchanged elements to the sixteen court cards, table 15 links the sixteen counterchanged elements to sixteen select Major

· · · · · · · ·

Arcana cards and their Hebrew letter equivalents. The number value of the Hebrew letter determines the number value of the corresponding Enochian letter, which link back to the geomantic shape for each of the sixteen counterchanged elements.

Element	Major Arcana	Hebrew	Number Value	Enochian	Name	English
🜂 of 🜂	Temperance	ס	60	ʅ	Gon	I
🜄 of 🜂	Emperor	ה	5	V	Pe	B
🜁 of 🜂	Strength	ט	9	ɓ	Ged	G
🜃 of 🜂	Judgment	ש	300	ҳ	Orth	F
🜂 of 🜄	Moon	ק	100	ε	Don	R
🜄 of 🜄	Chariot	ח	8	Ω	Mals	P
🜁 of 🜄	Death	נ	50	ɜ	Drun	N
🜃 of 🜄	Hanged Man	מ	40	C	Ur	L
🜂 of 🜁	Lovers	ז	7	˥	Graph	E
🜄 of 🜁	Justice	ל	30	L	Med	O
🜁 of 🜁	Star	צ	90	ε	Tal	M
🜃 of 🜁	Fool	א	1	P	Ceph	Z
🜂 of 🜃	Hermit	י	10	˥	Fam	S
🜄 of 🜃	Devil	ע	70	a	Vau	U
🜁 of 🜃	Hierophant	ו	6	Ɣ	Un	A
🜃 of 🜃	World	ת	400	/	Gisa	T

Table 15. Sixteen Sub-elements as Tarot, Hebrew, Number, and Enochian

The Major Arcana cards associated with the sixteen sub-elements and the sixteen court cards are derived from the geomantic astrological attributes. The number value for each Hebrew letter associated with the Major Arcana is the source for the number value of sixteen select Enochian alphabet letters in the Golden Dawn system of magic.

The Golden Dawn magical symbolism for the Enochian alphabet covered only 16 of 21 letters. The remaining five excluded Enochian letters were numbered by Aleister Crowley in his analysis found in *The Vision and the Voice.* Crowley, realizing there were five additional Enochian letters to be given symbolic value, came up with his own system based on the elemental values of the pentagram. He intuited each of these attributes, for there was no corresponding system of attributes for these five missing letters found in the Golden Dawn teachings on Enochian.

In table 16 are the number values for the five excluded Enochian letters that Aleister Crowley was able to decipher by means of the elemental pentagram and the corresponding Hebrew letters for the four elements plus spirit. Crowley gave for spirit the value of the Hebrew letter Daleth (ד) at 4, since the key number to his *Liber Legis* was 31 as AL (אל) for God, which reduces to 4 as 3 + 1. ד = 4 = 1 + 3 = 31 = אל .

Enochian	Name	Letter	Hebrew	Number	Element
⊃	Gal	D	ד	4	✴
(ງ)	Na-Hath	H	א	1	△
⊔	Ger	Q	מ	40	▽
l3	Veh	C	ש	300	△
Γ	Pal	X	ת	400	▽

Table 16. The Five Excluded Enochian Letters

The teachings of the Golden Dawn by means of astral projection explored the inner landscape of each of the sixteen combinations of elements. The doorway to enter these elemental landscapes was the Eastern system of tattvas (derived from Rama Prasad's *Science of Breath*), which combined five elements (in the form of a yellow square, silver crescent, red triangle, blue circle, and blue-violet oval) into twenty-five sub-elements. The primary element was first drawn, and then the secondary element was drawn as a smaller shape within the larger symbol. Sixteen of these combinations correspond directly to the sixteen combinations of elements. Thus, the tattva for air of fire was a blue circle within a red triangle, while the tattva for fire of air was a red triangle within a blue circle.

Sixteen select hexagrams composing the divinatory oracles from the Chinese *I Ching* can also be associated with these sixteen combinations of the four elements, for each hexagram is made of a primary trigram at its base and a secondary trigram above this base. The trigrams themselves are made up of three lines each, and are eight in number. Four of these trigrams were allocated to the four elements by Aleister Crowley in his own working with the *I Ching*. These four trigrams are Chen (☳) as fire, Tui (☱) as water, Sun (☴) as air, and Ken (☶) as earth. Table 17 describes the astral landscape of the sixteen sub-elements.

Element	Tattva	Image	Astral	I Ching	Image	Astral
△ of △	Agni of Agni	Triangle in triangle	Hot climate	51–Chen		Lightning storm
▽ of △	Apas of Agni	Crescent in triangle	Tropical, rainbow	17–Sui		Lightning in center of lake
◔ of △	Vayu of Agni	Circle in triangle	Hot winds	42–I		Lightning below clouds in sky
▽ of △	Prithivi of Agni	Square in triangle	Volcano, earthquake	27–I		Lightning at the foot of a mountain
△ of ▽	Agni of Apas	Triangle in crescent	Hot springs	54–Kuei Mei		Lightning rippling a lake
▽ of ▽	Apas of Apas	Crescent in crescent	Wet climate, ocean	58–Tui		River flowing from lake
◔ of ▽	Vayu of Apas	Circle in crescent	Rain, fog, mist	61–Chung Fu		Wind moving water
▽ of ▽	Prithivi of Apas	Square in crescent	Waterfall, riverbank	41–Sun		Water under-ground
△ of ◔	Agni of Vayu	Triangle in circle	Sunshine	32–Heng		Wind spreading fire
▽ of ◔	Apas of Vayu	Crescent in circle	Snow, ice	28–Ta Kuo		Lake rising over tree tops
◔ of ◔	Vayu of Vayu	Circle in circle	Windy, clouds	57–Sun		Wind dispersing clouds
▽ of ◔	Prithivi of Vayu	Square in circle	Cliff, valley	18–Ku		Wind eroding mountain
△ of ▽	Agni of Prithivi	Triangle in square	Desert	62–Hsiao Kua		Fire at top of mountain
▽ of ▽	Apas of Prithivi	Crescent in square	Beach	31–Hsian		Lake at moun-tain summit
◔ of ▽	Vayu of Prithivi	Circle in square	Mountain	53–Chien		Tree at mountain peak
▽ of ▽	Prithivi of Prithivi	Square in square	Forest, garden	52–Ken		Tower upon a high mountain

Table 17. Sixteen Sub-elements as Astral Landscapes

As the four suits of ten cards each in the Minor Arcana correspond to the ten sephiroth on the Tree of Life, and the 22 Major Arcana cards form the 22 visible paths that join these ten cosmic stations, the sixteen court cards corresponding to the sixteen sub-elements have two special allocations on the Tree of Life, one known and the other secret.

The Golden Dawn places the sixteen court cards on four specific sephiroth on the Tree of Life corresponding to the formula of the Tetragrammaton. This subtle symbolism has been misinterpreted by most commentators on the Tarot, for the Knight and the King are typically confused in this formula. The four letters of the Tetragrammaton as the family unit of father, mother, son, and daughter are placed on the Tree of Life at Chockmah (2), Binah (3), Tiphereth (6),and Malkuth (10). These in turn are the stations for the Knight, Queen, King, and Page.

Since there are four sephirotic Trees in the four worlds, the sixteen court cards correspond to four unique sephiroth in each world. The sixteen unique sephirotic attributes for the sixteen court cards are shown in table 18.

Element	Court Card	Family	Sephirah	World	Color
△ of △	Knight of Wands	Father	Chockmah	Atziloth	Pale sky blue
▽ of △	Queen of Wands	Mother	Binah	Atziloth	Crimson
△ of △	King of Wands	Son	Tiphereth	Atziloth	Pink rose
▽ of △	Page of Wands	Daughter	Malkuth	Atziloth	Yellow
△ of ▽	Knight of Cups	Father	Chockmah	Briah	Gray
▽ of ▽	Queen of Cups	Mother	Binah	Briah	Black
△ of ▽	King of Cups	Son	Tiphereth	Briah	Yellow
▽ of ▽	Page of Cups	Daughter	Malkuth	Briah	Citrine, russet, olive, black
△ of △	Knight of Swords	Father	Chockmah	Yetzirah	Bluish-gray mother of pearl
▽ of △	Queen of Swords	Mother	Binah	Yetzirah	Dark brown
△ of △	King of Swords	Son	Tiphereth	Yetzirah	Rich salmon
▽ of △	Page of Swords	Daughter	Malkuth	Yetzirah	Citrine, russet, olive, black (flecked gold)

Table 18. The Sixteen Court Cards on the Sephiroth of the Tree of Life (continued)

Element	Court Card	Family	Sephirah	World	Color
△ of ▽	Knight of Pentacles	Father	Chockmah	Assiah	White flecked red, yellow, blue
▽ of ▽	Queen of Pentacles	Mother	Binah	Assiah	Gray flecked pink
△ of ▽	King of Pentacles	Son	Tiphereth	Assiah	Gold amber
▽ of ▽	Page of Pentacles	Daughter	Malkuth	Assiah	Black rayed yellow

Table 18. The Sixteen Court Cards on the Sephiroth of the Tree of Life (continued)

There is a second secret allocation for the court cards to the Tree of Life. Paul Foster Case, in his mail-order lessons on the Tree of Life, gave a diagram showing the sixteen invisible paths on the Tree of life. These sixteen paths are the channels not shown on the Tree of Life that connect the various sephiroth. Case did not give any allocations to these sixteen invisible paths. However, I was able to devise a system of allocations for these sixteen invisible paths shown in figure 4. They are based on the elemental nature of each court card based on the suit for each card.

· · · · · · · ·

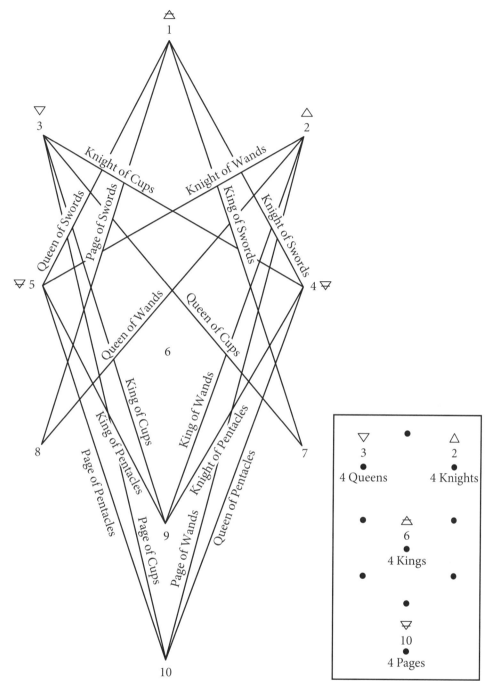

Figure 4. The Court Cards as Sixteen Invisible Paths and Four Select Sephiroth on the Tree of Life

The Origins of the Sixteen Invisible Paths

The diagram of the sixteen Invisible Paths on the Tree of Life (figure 4) does not exist in the esoteric magical teachings of the Hermetic Order of the Golden Dawn. This diagram also does not appear in the copious magical writings of Aleister Crowley nor in the Qabalistic studies of his student Frater Achad. However, this obscure diagram does appear in the correspondence course dealing with the Tree of Life by Paul Foster Case for his own fraternal order of the Builders of the Adytum.

Case provided this diagram without any attributions or commentary. When first encountering this diagram, I discovered a pattern to interpret these sixteen invisible paths based on the symbolism found in the teachings of the Golden Dawn.

Since the forty Minor Arcana cards of Ace through Ten are the ten sephiroth, while the 22 Major Arcana cards are the 22 visible paths on the Tree of Life, the remaining sixteen court cards can be attributed to these sixteen invisible paths.

Twelve invisible paths emanate from the first three sephiroth on the Tree of Life known as the supernal triad of Kether (1), Chockmah (2), and Binah (3). Each of these three sephiroth is the source for one of the three elements flowing down the Tree of Life: Kether is the element of air, Chockmah is the element of fire, and Binah is the element of water.

By this symbolism, twelve of the court cards correspond directly to four paths, each emanating from the three sephiroth making up the supernal triad. The Wands suit of four court cards emanates from Chockmah as the element of fire. The Cups suit of four court cards emanates from Binah as the element of water. The Swords suit of four court cards emanates from Kether as the element of air.

The Pentacles suit of four court cards is the element of earth, and falls to the four remaining paths below the abyss emanating from Chesed and Geburah. Two of these invisible paths end in Malkuth, which is the element of earth on the Tree of Life.

These sixteen invisible paths are governed by sixteen select Enochian alphabet letters, since the sixteen court cards are ruled by sixteen Enochian letters based on the symbolism of both geomancy and astrology. Thus, the visible paths that form the Tree of Life are governed by Hebrew, while the invisible paths are governed by Enochian.

The first three sephiroth on the Tree of Life form a supernal triangle and are the source of the threefold elements of air, fire, and water. The first station, Kether, is air; the second station, Chockmah, is fire; and the third station, Binah, is water. These three supernal elements flow through the rest of the sephiroth on the Tree of Life, ending in Malkuth as a summation of the three elements in the fourth element of earth. Kether flows down the middle pillar to Tiphereth and Yesod, Chockmah zigzags to Geburah and Netzach, and Binah zigzags to Chesed and Hod.

• • • • • • •

All meet in Malkuth to combine the three elements into a fourth element of earth. The flow of the elements on the first ten stations of the Tree of Life is shown in table 19.

Element	Sephiroth	Astrology
△̲	1. Kether→ 6. Tiphereth→ 9. Yesod	First Cause: ☉: ☽
△	2. Chockmah→ 5. Geburah→ 7. Netzach	Zodiac: ♂: ♀
▽	3. Binah→ 4. Chesed→ 8. Hod	♄: ♃: ☿
▽̲	10. Malkuth	△▽△̲▽̲

Table 19. The Flow of Elements across the Sephiroth

If we look at the sixteen invisible paths, we will discover that the sephiroth forming the supernal triad each have four invisible paths, while Chesed and Geburah each have two invisible paths. Using the logic of the elemental flow from the supernal triad, Kether is the source of air (which corresponds to the suit of Swords), Chockmah is the source of fire (which corresponds to the suit of Wands), and Binah is the source of water (which corresponds to the suit of Cups). The remaining four paths emanating from Chesed and Geburah fall below the supernal triad and are the element of earth and the suit of Pentacles. These four lower invisible paths terminate in Yesod and Malkuth, the two lowest points of the Tree of Life.

Table 20 shows the court cards as sixteen invisible paths on the Tree of Life. Note that the 22 visible paths on the Tree of Life correspond to the 22 letters of the Hebrew alphabet, while the sixteen invisible paths correspond to sixteen select Enochian alphabet letters:

Court Card	Path #	Connecting Sephiroth	Enochian	Name	Color (Court)
Knight of Wands	33	2 to 5	⌇	I—Gon	Pale sky blue
Queen of Wands	34	2 to 8	Ѵ	B—Pe	Crimson
King of Wands	35	2 to 9	ϐ	G—Ged	Pink rose
Page of Wands	36	2 to 10	✗	F—Orth	Yellow
Knight of Cups	37	3 to 4	Ɛ	R—Don	Gray
Queen of Cups	38	3 to 7	∩	P—Mals	Black

Table 20. The Sixteen Invisible Paths on the Tree of Life (continued)

• • • • • • • •

Court Card	Path #	Connecting Sephiroth	Enochian	Name	Color (Court)
King of Cups	39	3 to 9	כ	N—Drun	Yellow
Page of Cups	40	3 to 10	C	L—Ur	Citrine, russet, olive, black
Knight of Swords	41	1 to 4	ך	E—Graph	Bluish-gray mother of pearl
Queen of Swords	42	1 to 5	ㄴ	O—Med	Dark brown
King of Swords	43	1 to 7	ε	M—Tal	Rich salmon
Page of Swords	44	1 to 8	ף	Z—Ceph	Citrine, russet, olive, black flecked gold
Knight of Pentacles	45	4 to 9	٦	S—Fam	White flecked red, yellow, blue
Queen of Pentacles	46	4 to 10	ה	U—Vau	Gray flecked pink
King of Pentacles	47	5 to 9	ﭏ	A—Un	Gold amber
Page of Pentacles	48	5 to 10	╯	T—Gisa	Black rayed yellow

Table 20. The Sixteen Invisible Paths on the Tree of Life (continued)

Before we end this lengthy discussion of the symbolism behind the sixteen counterchanges of elements, two more systems used in the Golden Dawn should be delineated: the sixteen possible combinations of color for the sixteen variations on the Tree of Life in the four worlds, and the four quadrants of the four elemental tablets known as the Enochian Watchtowers (table 21).

Element	Sephiroth Color	Path Color	World	Watchtower Tablet	Sub-element	Quadrant on Tablet
△ of △	King	King	Atziloth	△	△	Lower right
▽ of △	King	Queen	Atziloth	△	▽	Upper right
🜁 of △	King	Prince	Atziloth	△	🜁	Upper left
🜃 of △	King	Princess	Atziloth	△	🜃	Lower left

Table 21. The Sixteen Tree of Life Color Variations and the
Four Quadrants of the Four Enochian Watchtowers (continued)

· · · · · · · ·

Element	Sephiroth Color	Path Color	World	Watchtower Tablet	Sub-element	Quadrant on Tablet
🜂 of 🜄	Queen	King	Briah	🜄	🜂	Lower right
🜄 of 🜄	Queen	Queen	Briah	🜄	🜄	Upper right
🜁 of 🜄	Queen	Prince	Briah	🜄	🜁	Upper left
🜃 of 🜄	Queen	Princess	Briah	🜄	🜃	Lower left
🜂 of 🜁	Prince	King	Yetzirah	🜁	🜂	Lower right
🜄 of 🜁	Prince	Queen	Yetzirah	🜁	🜄	Upper right
🜁 of 🜁	Prince	Prince	Yetzirah	🜁	🜁	Upper left
🜃 of 🜁	Prince	Princess	Yetzirah	🜁	🜃	Lower left
🜂 of 🜃	Princess	King	Assiah	🜃	🜂	Lower right
🜄 of 🜃	Princess	Queen	Assiah	🜃	🜄	Upper right
🜁 of 🜃	Princess	Prince	Assiah	🜃	🜁	Upper left
🜃 of 🜃	Princess	Princess	Assiah	🜃	🜃	Lower left

Table 21. *The Sixteen Tree of Life Color Variations and the Four Quadrants of the Four Enochian Watchtowers* (continued)

The Seven Sacred Planets

There were seven sacred planets to the ancient world of magic. These seven planets did not include Earth but did count the luminaries of the Sun and Moon as two of the seven planets. The other five planets were Saturn, Jupiter, Mars, Venus, and Mercury. Our modern planets of Neptune, Uranus, and Pluto did not figure into this count, though recently Pluto was declassified as a planet.

The mystery of the seven planets and their proper allocation to seven select Major Arcana cards is the most difficult set of correspondences for deciphering the allocation of the seven double letters of the Hebrew alphabet. Different versions of the *Sepher Yetzirah* give conflicting attributes to the seven planets. Mathers and Westcott used the imagery of the corresponding Tarot cards to correctly attribute the seven planets to the Tarot.

Westcott and Mathers struggled over the mystery of the planets in the *Sepher Yetzirah*. The Hebrew alphabet has seven double letters, which have two distinct pronunciations. In every printed text of this esoteric manual over the mystery of the alphabet, the three elements and the twelve signs were clearly delineated without any confusion. But when it came to the seven double letters, different versions of the printed text gave the planets in conflicting orders.

· · · · · · · ·

The most common attribute for these seven double letters is the Platonic order of the planets, where the first letter, Beth, equals Saturn and the 7th and last letter, Tav, equals the Moon. Eliphas Levi adopted this order in placing the planets with the double letters, but his scheme led with the Magician card as Aleph, whereas the Golden Dawn adopted the Fool as Aleph.

Westcott and Mathers compared the cards in their revised order with the seven double letters and determined that the Platonic order would not work. They studied intently the actual symbols in the corresponding Major Arcana cards and used the symbolism to guide their allocations. As such, the Magician, which corresponds to Beth, became the planet Mercury rather than Saturn, for they saw in the Magician an image of Hermes-Mercury-Trismegistus. Table 22 shows both Levi's and the Golden Dawn's Tarot allocations for the seven planets.

Hebrew Double Letter	Planet	Levi: א = Magus	Golden Dawn: א = Fool	Secret Order	Symbol in Major Arcana
ב =Beth	♄	High Priestess	Magician	☿	Magician as Hermes
ג =Gimel	♃	Empress	High Priestess	☽	Priestess as Isis lunar goddess
ד =Daleth	♂	Emperor	Empress	♀	Empress as Earth Mother
כ =Kaph	☉	Force	Wheel of Fortune	♃	Jupiter as god of good fortune
פ =Peh	♀	The Star	The Tower	♂	Lightning bolt as Mars
ר =Resh	☿	Judgment	The Sun	☉	Sun in card as the Sun
ת =Tav	☽	The World	The World	♄	Alternate symbol for Saturn as Earth

Table 22. The Seven Planets in the Major Arcana

Paul Foster Case was able to decipher every mystery concerning the Hebrew alphabet and the Tarot except this mystery of the planets. Case admitted in his first published book, *An Introduction to the Study of the Tarot* (gleaned from his magazine articles found in the occult periodical *Azoth*), that he needed to rely on Aleister Crowley's *777* to correctly decipher these planetary attributes. Crowley learned of this secret order through his exposure to the Golden Dawn system of magic. In a footnote in regard to using the *Sepher Yetzirah* to correctly identify the astrological nature of the Tarot, Case states, "The planetary attributes are from *Book 777*, London, 1909."[6]

6. Case, *An Introduction to the Study of the Tarot*, 14n.

The use of these seven planets is fundamental to the practice of alchemy, which works with seven metals corresponding to these seven planets. This doctrine is the same as the chakra system of the Eastern Tantric tradition, which places seven interior stars in the spiritual body that can be contacted through ritual and meditation.

The Tree of Life orders these seven planets as Saturn, Jupiter, Mars, Sun, Venus, Mercury, and the Moon, and places them at station 3 through 9. This order is sometimes referred to as the Platonic order of the planets. However, the days of the week are also ordered by the seven planets in a different order. Starting with Sunday, the seven planets are Sun (Sunday), Moon (Monday), Mars (Tuesday), Mercury (Wednesday), Jupiter (Thursday), Venus (Friday), and Saturn (Saturday).

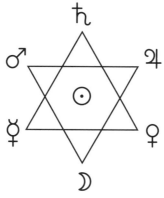

Figure 5. Hexagram of Seven Planets

The classic symbol for the Platonic order of the planets used in the Tree of Life is the hexagram of seven planets (figure 5). The seven planets are laid upon the points and center of the hexagram (which is both the Star of David and the Shield of Solomon) in the Platonic order, starting with Saturn and ending with the Moon. At the center is the Sun, whose geometric shape is the hexagram. This is the position for the seven planets as the sephiroth on the Tree of Life, starting with Binah and ending with Yesod.

The names and signs for the seven planets are derived from Greek mythology and form the seven vowels in the Greek alphabet. The seven planets are seven shades of the rainbow as well as the first seven notes of the octave and the seven directions in space composing the directional cube found in the *Sepher Yetzirah*. The Western symbolism for the seven planets is shown in table 23.

Planet	♄	♃	♂	☉	♀	☿	☽
Sphere	7th	6th	5th	4th	3rd	2nd	1st
Roman Greek	Saturn, Kronos	Jupiter, Zeus	Mars, Ares	Apollo, Helios	Venus, Aphrodite	Mercury, Hermes	Diana, Artemis
Symbol	Scythe	Throne	Spear, shield	Chariot wheels	Mirror	Caduceus	Crown
Shape	Triangle	Square	Penta-gram	Hexa-gram	Hepta-gram	Octa-gram	Ennea-gram
Greek	$\Omega = 800$	$Y = 400$	$O = 70$	$I = 10$	$H = 8$	$E = 5$	$A = 1$
Hebrew	ת	כ	פ	ר	ז	ב	ג
Tree of Life	3 Binah	4 Chesed	5 Geburah	6 Tiphereth	7 Netzach	8 Hod	9 Yesod
Color (Tree of Life)	Black	Blue	Red	Yellow	Green	Orange	Violet
Magic Square	$3 \times 3 = 9$	$4 \times 4 = 16$	$5 \times 5 = 25$	$6 \times 6 = 36$	$7 \times 7 = 49$	$8 \times 8 = 64$	$9 \times 9 = 81$
Tarot	XXI	X	XVI	XIX	III	I	II
Color (Tarot)	Indigo	Violet	Red	Orange	Green	Yellow	Blue
Cube of Space	Center	West	North	South	East	Above	Below
Path (Tree of Life)	32nd	21st	27th	30th	14th	12th	13th
Angel	Zaphkiel	Zadkiel	Camael	Raphael	Haniel	Michael	Gabriel
Stone	Onyx	Sapphire	Ruby	Carbuncle	Emerald	Diamond	Crystal
Face	Right ear	Left ear	Right nostril	Right eye	Left nostril	Mouth	Left eye
Body	Right foot	Head	Right hand	Heart	Genitals	Left hand	Left foot
Octave	B (Ti)	A (La)	G (Sol)	F (Fa)	E (Mi)	D (Re)	C (Do)

Table 23. Platonic Order of the Seven Planets

In table 23, there are two scales of color, one based on the sephiroth of the Tree of Life and the other based on the paths connecting the sephiroth. There are five variations: ♄ = black and indigo (blue-violet), ♃ = blue and violet, ☉ = yellow and orange, ☿ = orange and yellow, and ☽ = violet and blue. Both scales are valid color attributions. You should use the first set when

• • • • • • • •

dealing with the sephiroth of the Tree and the first ten numbers, and use the second set when dealing with the Tarot and the Hebrew alphabet.

The other major set of correspondences for the seven planets is based on the alchemical tradition of associating the seven planets with the seven metals involved in alchemy. These seven metals are the Western equivalent of the seven interior stars of the body referred to as the *chakras* in the Hindu Tantric tradition. *Chakra* in Sanskrit means wheel, and these seven interior stars are seen as spinning wheels of energy and light.

The seven planets are aligned in the human body from the base of the spine to the crown of the head (figure 6). At the base of the spine is Saturn, the metal lead, and the first chakra, Muladhara, while at the crown of the head is Mercury, the metal quicksilver, and the seventh chakra, Sahasrara.

Figure 6. Seven Chakras as Seven Planets

The chakra order of the planets and metals is ♄ (lead), ♂ (iron), ♃ (tin), ☉ (gold), ♀ (copper), ☽ (silver), and ☿ (quicksilver). The alchemical operation of changing lead into gold can be seen as raising the energy from the base chakra (lead) to the heart (gold).

When the Tarot cards representing the seven planets are applied to the seven chakras, an interesting order opens up when counting from the last card to the first: the World (1st/root chakra), the Sun (4th chakra), the Tower (2nd chakra), Wheel of Fortune (3rd chakra), the Empress (5th chakra), the High Priestess (6th chakra), and the Magician (7th/crown chakra). This flow of energy raises the root chakra to the heart center before descending to the lower chakras. It opens the heart to love and compassion before descending to the lower energies of the genitals and the solar plexus. Table 24 illustrates the symbolism for the seven chakras found in the Eastern Tantrik tradition and the Western traditions of both the Golden Dawn and Theosophy.

In the language of alchemy, each of the seven planets corresponds to an alchemical metal. These seven metals refer to the seven interior stars of the body known as the seven chakras in the Eastern Tantric tradition. They are situated along the spine, which in the Theosophical tradition is divided into 33 divisions.

These seven chakras are seen as seven flowers, each with a different number of petals that contain the 50 letters of the Sanskrit alphabet. The first six chakras total to 50, while the 7th chakra is $20 \times 50 = 1,000$ petals. In the Theosophical tradition, the petals of the chakras are replaced by rays of light. The first six chakras total to 360 rays, while the 7th is 360 rays on its own.

In table 24, there are many variations on the color scheme for the seven chakras. The Tantric tradition uses the symbolism of the tattvas. Theosophy and the Major Arcana of the Tarot use the seven shades of the rainbow in various orders. The modern vision for the chakras uses the rainbow in the natural order, starting with red at the base of the spine and ending with violet at the crown of the head. This is similar to the twelve zones of the body divided by the twelve signs of the zodiac, where the head is red and the feet red violet.

This overview has detailed the elements as a division of 3, 4, 5, and 16 and the seven planets. It will end with a discussion on the esoteric nature of the twelve signs of the zodiac in light of the Golden Dawn system of magic.

Planet	♄	♂	♃	☉	♀	☽	☿
Metal	Lead	Iron	Tin	Gold	Copper	Silver	Quick-silver
Tarot	XXI	XVI	X	XIX	III	II	I
Chakra	1st	2nd	3rd	4th	5th	6th	7th

Table 24. Seven Planets as the Seven Chakras (continued)

· · · · · · · ·

Planet	♄	♂	♃	☉	♀	☽	☿
Body	Perineum	Genitals	Solar plexus	Heart	Throat	Third eye	Crown of head
Joints of Spine (33)	1st, 2nd, 3rd	7th	16th	26th	31st	32nd	33rd
Sense	Smell	Taste	Sight	Touch	Hearing	Mind	Higher self
Name	Muladhara	Svadhis-thana	Mani-pura	Anahata	Visud-dha	Ajna	Sahas-rara
Meaning	Root, entrance	Own place	City of jewels	Sound-less sound	Pure-ness	Beyond knowledge	1,000 petals
Sanskrit Syllable	Lam	Vam	Ram	Yam	Ham	Om	Hum
Petals	4	6	10	12	16	2	1,000
Rays	56	62	52	54	72	64	360
Tattva	Prithivi	Apas	Agni	Vayu	Akasha	Mahatattva	Bindu point
Tattva Color	Yellow	White	Red	Blue	Blue violet	Rainbow of five colors	Clear
Color (Tantra)	Yellow	Light blue	Flame red	Smokey green	Smokey purple	White	Rain-bow
Color (Theosophy)	Orange red	Rose	Green	Golden	Light blue	Blue violet	Violet
Color (Tarot)	Blue violet	Scarlet	Violet	Orange	Green	Blue	Yellow
Color (Modern)	Red	Orange	Yellow	Green	Blue	Blue violet	Violet

Table 24. Seven Planets as the Seven Chakras (continued)

The Twelve Signs of the Zodiac

Each of twelve signs of the zodiac is ruled by a planet and corresponds to a specific element. As elements, the signs are also classified as *cardinal* (the first sign of an element), *fixed* (the second and middle sign of an element), or *mutable* (the third and last sign of an element).

· · · · · · · ·

Each sign rules part of the human body. There are two major divisions of the body, one from Greek astrology starting with the head and ending with the feet, and the other from the *Sepher Yetzirah*. Table 25 shows the basic symbolism for the zodiac.

Sign	Symbol	Element	Ruler	Type	Body (Greek)	Body (*Sepher Yetzirah*)
♈	Horns of ram	△	♂	Cardinal	Head	Right hand
♉	Horns of bull	▽̶	♀	Fixed	Throat	Left hand
♊	Twins in an embrace	△̶	☿	Mutable	Shoulders, hands	Right foot
♋	Crab's claws	▽	☽	Cardinal	Chest	Left foot
♌	Lion mane and tail	△	☉	Fixed	Heart	Right kidney (testicle)
♍	Three ears of corn	▽̶	☿	Mutable	Stomach	Left kidney (testicle)
♎	Beam of a balance	△̶	♀	Cardinal	Intestines, kidneys	Liver
♏	Feet, tail & stinger of a scorpion	▽	♂	Fixed	Genitals	Spleen
♐	Arrow notched in a bow	△	♃	Mutable	Thighs	Gall
♑	Head & horns of a goat and a fish tail	▽̶	♄	Cardinal	Knees	Stomach
♒	Twin streams from two vases	△̶	♄	Fixed	Ankles	Bladder, genitals
♓	Twin fishes joined by a chain	▽	♃	Mutable	Feet	Rectum, bowels

Table 25. Basic Astrological Symbolism for the Zodiac

The planetary rulers for the zodiac divide the tweve signs into two groups of six signs each, one group ruled by the Moon and the other group ruled by the Sun. The planets are arranged in an alchemical hierarchy, where Saturn and Jupiter are at the bottom of the ladder and Mercury is at the top, crowned by the Sun and Moon. This pattern has five planets ruling two signs each, and the luminaires ruling one sign each (table 26).

Sign	Planet	Planet	Sign
♋	☽	☉	♌
♊	☿	☿	♍
♉	♀	♀	♎
♈	♂	♂	♏
♓	♃	♃	♐
♒	♄	♄	♑

Table 26. Alchemical Ladder of Planetary Rulers

The twelve signs of the zodiac correspond in the Hebrew alphabet to the twelve simple letters (which have only one pronunciation). Westcott and Mathers detailed the zodiac in the Major Arcana of the Tarot. The zodiac is placed in the Major Arcana as twelve cards starting with the Emperor as Aries and ending with the Moon as Pisces.

The zodiac is divided into twelve shades of the rainbow as well as twelve notes of the octave. The corresponding Hebrew alphabet letter can be chanted in the appropriate tone and visualized in the appropriate color. This can also be coordinated with the twelve zones of the body, shown in table 25, for healing rituals. Any sacred word in Hebrew can be chanted as a mantra and visualized as color using these sound and color attributes.

The *Sepher Yetzirah* describes a model of the cosmos as an expanding cube. The three elements are the three inner coordinates, the seven planets are the six faces and center, and the twelve signs of the zodiac are the twelve edges of the cube. The *Sepher Yetzirah* also gives a permutation of the Tetragrammaton for the twelve signs, as well as twelve distinct human activities.

Table 27 delineates the symbolism for the twelve signs found in the Major Arcana.

Sign	Tarot	Hebrew	Color	Note	Path on Tree of Life	Cube *(Sepher Yetzirah)*	God	Human *(Sepher Yetzirah)*
♈	Emperor	ה	Red	C	15	NE	יהוה	Seeing
♉	Hierophant	ו	Red orange	C#	16	SE	יההו	Hearing
♊	Lovers	ז	Orange	D	17	E Above	יוהה	Smelling
♋	Chariot	ח	Yellow orange	D#	18	E Below	וההי	Speaking

Table 27. The Zodiac in the Major Arcana (continued)

Sign	Tarot	Hebrew	Color	Note	Path on Tree of Life	Cube (*Sepher Yetzirah*)	God	Human (*Sepher Yetzirah*)
♌	Strength	ט	Yellow	E	19	N Above	הויה	Tasting
♍	Hermit	י	Yellow green	F	20	N Below	ההוי	Coition
♎	Justice	ל	Green	F#	22	NW	והיה	Working
♏	Death	נ	Blue green	G	24	SW	והיי	Walking
♐	Temperance	ס	Blue	G#	25	W Above	ויהה	Anger
♑	Devil	ע	Blue violet	A	26	W Below	היהו	Laughter, mirth
♒	Star	צ	Violet	A#	28	S Above	היוה	Contemplation
♓	Moon	ק	Red violet	B	29	S Below	ההיו	Sleep

Table 27. The Zodiac in the Major Arcana (continued)

All versions of the *Sepher Yetzirah* are clear in assigning the zodiac to the alphabet. However, the human functions of coition and working are sometimes swapped for the Hebrew letters of Yod and Lamed.

The order of the twelve Tribes of Israel can be paired to the twelve signs of the zodiac and can be found in the Golden Dawn tradition. The Twelve Apostles are also symbolic of the zodiac. Twelve unique icons are used in Church architecture to symbolize these Twelve Apostles. Agrippa paired to the zodiac both angels and Roman deities. The zodiac is also reflected in the Greek alphabet of twenty-four letters. They are grouped into twelve pairs and placed on the zodiacal zones of the cosmic body of Sophia, the Gnostic goddess of wisdom

Table 28 shows the zodiac symbolized by these cosmic principals.

• • • • • • • •

Sign	Tribe/ Banner	Hebrew	Apostles/ Icon	Angel	Roman Deity	Greek
♈	Gad/ Cavalry	גד	Simon, Peter/ Two crossed keys	Malchidiel	Pallas	Α Ω
♉	Ephraim/ Ox	אפראים	Andrew/ Saltire cross	Asmodel	Venus	Β Ψ
♊	Manasseh/ Vine, wall	מנשה	James the Elder Three scallop shells	Ambrial	Phoebus	Γ Χ
♋	Issachar/ Ass	יששכר	John/ Serpent in chalice	Muriel	Mercury	Δ Φ
♌	Judah/ Lion	יהודה	Thomas/ Carpenter square and spear	Verchiel	Jupiter	E Y
♍	Naphtali/ Bird	נפתלי	James of Alphaeus/ Vertical saw	Hamaliel	Ceres	Z T
♎	Asher/ Cup	אשר	Philip/ Cross and two loaves	Zuriel	Vulcan	Η Σ
♏	Dan/ Eagle	דן	Bartholomew/ Three flaying knives	Barbiel	Mars	Θ Ρ
♐	Benjamin/ Wolf	בנימין	Matthew/ Three money purses	Adnachiel	Diana	Ι Π
♑	Zebulon/ Ship	זבולן	Simon the Zealot/ Fish on open Bible	Hanael	Vesta	Κ Ο
♒	Reuben/ Man	ראובן	Jude of James/ Ship with cross-shaped masts	Gabriel	Juno	Λ Ξ
♓	Simeon/ Sword	שמעון	Judas Iscariot/ Money bag with thirty coins	Barchiel	Neptune	M N

Table 28. The Zodiac in the Cosmos

As the last table gave the cosmic symbolism for the zodiac, the next table will give the natural symbols in nature corresponding to the zodiac (table 29). The attributes for plants and incense as well as drugs (with some modifications) are from Crowley's *777*. The attributes for stones, trees, birds, and beasts are from Agrippa.

• • • • • • • •

Sign	Stone	Plant	Tree	Incense	Drug	Bird	Beast
♈	Hematite	Geranium	Olive	Dragon's blood	Coffee	Owl	She-goat
♉	Emerald	Mallow	Myrtle	Storax	Sugar	Dove	He-goat
♊	Multicolored stones	Orchid	Laurel	Worm-wood	Ergot (LSD)	Cock	Bull
♋	Adularia	Lotus	Hazel	Onycha	Psilocybin	Ibis	Dog
♌	Ruby	Sunflower	Aesculus	Frankin-cense	Cocaine	Eagle	Hart
♍	Beryl	Lily	Apple	Narcissus	Beer	Sparrow	Sow
♎	Agate	Aloe	Box	Galbanum	Tobacco	Goose	Ass
♏	Amethyst	Cactus	Dog	Siamese benzoin	Peyote	Pie	Wolf
♐	Turquoise	Rush	Palm	Ling aloes	DMT	Daw	Hind
♑	Onyx	Indian hemp	Pine	Musk	Cannabis, indica	Heron	Lion
♒	Amber	Olive	Ramthorn	Euphor-bium	Wine	Peacock	Sheep
♓	Coral	Opium	Elm	Amber-gris	Opium	Swan	Horse

Table 29. The Zodiac in the Natural World

The 36 Decans

The zodiac in the Golden Dawn tradition is symbolized in the Minor Arcana in two ways: twelve of the court cards correspond to the twelve signs, while the pip cards numbered 2 through 10 in the Minor Arcana are allocated to the zodiac (of 360 degrees) divided into 36 decans of 10 degrees each. Each sign is made up of three decans, and each decan is approximately ten days.

Each court card is composed of the last decan of a zodiac sign and the first two decans of the next zodiac sign. Thus, the court cards are a hybrid of two zodiacal signs, rather than one sign. The first two decans represent the elemental nature of a specific sign at the peak of its power. The third and last decan represents the decline of the element as it changes into the elemental nature of the next successive sign. This is the reason each court card is composed of the last decan of the preceding sign and the first two decans of the primary sign: to show this shift of elemental energy from one sign to the next.

Table 30 lists the symbolism for the Minor Arcana as the 36 decans.

• • • • • • • •

Court Card	Decan	Ruler	Sign	Pip	Color	Title (Lord of)
Q of W	0°–10°	♂	♈	2W	Sky blue	Dominion
	11°–20°	☉	♈	3W	Crimson	Established strength
K of P	21°–30°	♀	♈	4W	Deep violet	Perfected work
	0°–10°	☿	♉	5P	Red flecked black	Material trouble
	11°–20°	☽	♉	6P	Gold amber	Material success
Kn of S	21°–30°	♄	♉	7P	Olive flecked gold	Success unfulfilled
	0°–10°	♃	♊	8S	Red russet	Shortened force
	11°–20°	♂	♊	9S	Dark purple	Despair and cruelty
Q of C	21°–30°	☉	♊	10S	Citrine, russet, olive, black flecked gold	Ruin
	0°–10°	♀	♋	2C	Gray	Love
	11°–20°	☿	♋	3C	Black	Abundance
K of W	21°–30°	☽	♋	4C	Blue	Blended pleasure
	0°–10°	♄	♌	5W	Orange	Strife
	11°–20°	♃	♌	6W	Pink rose	Victory
Kn of P	21°–30°	♂	♌	7W	Amber	Valor
	0°–10°	☉	♍	8P	Yellow brown flecked white	Prudence
	11°–20°	♀	♍	9P	Citrine flecked azure	Material gain
Q of S	21°–30°	☿	♍	10P	Black rayed yellow	Wealth
	0°–10°	☽	♎	2S	Bluish-gray mother of pearl	Peace restored
	11°–20°	♄	♎	3S	Dark brown	Sorrow
K of C	21°–30°	♃	♎	4S	Deep purple	Rest from strife
	0°–10°	♂	♏	5C	Scarlet red	Loss in pleasure
	11°–20°	☉	♏	6C	Yellow (Gold)	Pleasure
Kn of W	21°–30°	♀	♏	7C	Emerald	Illusionary success
	0°–10°	☿	♐	8W	Violet	Swiftness
	11°–20°	☽	♐	9W	Indigo	Great strength

Table 30. *Golden Dawn Symbolism for the 36 Decans (Continued):*
Kn = Knight, Q = Queen, K = King, W = Wands, C = Cups,
S = Swords, P = Pentacles

• • • • • • • •

Court Card	Decan	Ruler	Sign	Pip	Color	Title (Lord of)
Q of P	21°–30°	♄	♐	10W	Yellow	Oppression
	0°–10°	♃	♑	2P	White flecked red, blue, yellow	Harmonious change
	11°–20°	♂	♑	3P	Gray flecked pink	Material works
K of S	21°–30°	☉	♑	4P	Deep azure flecked yellow	Earthly power
	0°–10°	♀	♒	5S	Bright scarlet	Defeat
	11°–20°	☿	♒	6S	Rich salmon	Earned success
Kn of C	21°–30°	☽	♒	7S	Bright yellow green	Unstable effort
	0°–10°	♄	♓	8C	Orange	Abandoned success
	11°–20°	♃	♓	9C	Violet	Material happiness
Q of W	21°–30°	♂	♓	10C	Citrine, russet, olive, black	Perfected success

Table 30. Golden Dawn Symbolism for the 36 Decans (Continued):
Kn = Knight, Q = Queen, K = King, W = Wands, C = Cups,
S = Swords, P = Pentacles

Note that the twelve signs of the zodiac fall to a different point in the calendar than the twelve court cards that have hybrid zodiacal attributes. Table 31 shows the difference.

Zodiac	Period	Court Card	Hybrid Zodiac	Period
♈	3/21–4/19	QW	♓/♈	3/11–4/9
♉	4/20–5/20	KP	♈/♉	4/10–5/10
♊	5/21–6/20	KnS	♉/♊	5/11–6/10
♋	6/21–7/22	QC	♊/♋	6/11–7/12
♌	7/23–8/22	KW	♋/♌	7/13–8/12
♍	8/23–9/22	KnP	♌/♍	8/13–9/12
♎	9/23–10/22	QS	♍/♎	9/13–10/13
♏	10/23–11/21	KC	♎/♏	10/14–11/12
♐	11/22–12/21	KnW	♏/♐	11/13–12/11
♑	12/22–1/19	QP	♐/♑	12/12–1/10
♒	1/20–2/18	KS	♑/♒	1/11–2/8
♓	2/19–3/20	KnC	♒/♓	2/9–3/10

Table 31. Days of the Year and the Zodiac

• • • • • • • •

430

Symbolism of the Rose Cross

We will end this book with one final use of the rainbow and the zodiac. The supreme symbol for initiates of the Golden Dawn can be seen in the Rose Cross (figure 7). This cross of gold has at its center the Rose of 22 Petals: three petals in the center, seven in the middle, and twelve at the outer edge. Each petal has a Hebrew letter corresponding to one of three elements, seven planets, or twelve signs. The color scale utilized is the King (Atziloth) scale for the 22 paths.

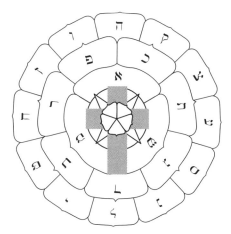

Figure 7. Rose Cross of 22 Petals

The petals themselves are based on the rainbow scale of twelve shades, while the Hebrew letter is drawn in the flashing (or opposite) color. This is a technique for constructing all magical talismans based on elemental, planetary, or zodiacal influences, where the background color is the specific element, planet, or zodiac sign while the symbol itself is in the complementary flashing color. This flashing color is always the opposite sign (180°) of the zodiac (360°).

Table 32 shows the rainbow scale on the Rose Cross. The Hebrew letters are shown as three columns representing the three rings of Hebrew letters on the Rose Cross. The elements are the inner ring, the planets are the middle ring, and the zodiac is the outer ring of rose petals on the cross. Also shown is the corresponding musical note for the rainbow scale of color, which can be used in conjunction with the Hebrew letters listed as a means of chanting all 22 letters of the Hebrew alphabet.

Color	Flashing Color	Note	Hebrew	Zodiac	Hebrew	Planet	Hebrew	Element
Red	Green	C	ה	♈	פ	♂	ש	△
Red orange	Blue green	C#	ו	♉				
Orange	Blue	D	ז	♊	ר	☉		

Table 32. The Rainbow Scale on the Rose Cross (continued)

. . . .

Color	Flashing Color	Note	Hebrew	Zodiac	Hebrew	Planet	Hebrew	Element
Yellow orange	Blue violet	D#	ח	♋				
Yellow	Violet	E	ט	♌	ב	☿	א	△
Yellow green	Red violet	F	י	♍				
Green	Red	F#	ל	♎	ד	♀		
Blue green	Red orange	G	נ	♏				
Blue	Orange	G#	ס	♐	ג	☽	מ	▽
Blue violet	Yellow orange	A	ע	♑	ת	♄		
Violet	Yellow	A#	צ	♒	כ	♃		
Red violet	Yellow green	B	ק	♓				

Table 32. The Rainbow Scale on the Rose Cross (continued)

Bibliography

Agrippa, Henry Cornelius. *Three Books of Occult Philosophy*. St. Paul, MN: Llewellyn Publications, 1993. First published in 1553.

Barrett, Francis. *The Magus*. Secaucus, NJ: Citadel Press, 1967. First published in 1801.

Blavatsky, Helena Petrovna. *Collected Writings, Volume XII: 1889–1890*. Wheaton, IL: The Theosophical Publishing House, 1980. First published in 1890.

Case, Paul Foster. *An Introduction to the Study of the Tarot*. New York: Azoth Publishing Company, 1920.

Crowley, Aleister. *The Book of Thoth*. New York: Samuel Weiser, 1969. First published in 1944.

———. *Liber L. vel Legis*. In *Thelema, Volume III*. Lincolnshire, UK: Hell Fire Club, 2015. First published in 1909.

———. *The Magical Record of the Beast 666: The Diaries of Aleister Crowley, 1914–1920*. Edited with annotations by John Symonds and Kenneth Grant. London: Duckworth, 1972.

———. *777*. San Francisco, CA: Level Press, 1969. First published in 1909.

———. *Shih Yi*. Oceanside, CA: Monthelema, 1971.

———. *The Vision and the Voice*. Dallas, TX: Sangreal Foundation, 1972. First published in 1952.

Foucault, Michel, et al. *IO Magazine, No. 5: Doctrine of Signatures*, Summer 1968. Ann Arbor, MI.

Goodman, Tali, and Marcus Katz. *Abiding in the Sanctuary*. Keswick, UK: Forge Press, 2011.

Hulse, David Allen. *The Key of It All: Book One: The Eastern Mysteries*. St. Paul, MN: Llewellyn Publications, 1993.

———. *The Key of It All: Book Two: The Western Mysteries*. St. Paul, MN: Llewellyn Publications, 1994.

Küntz, Darcy, ed and trans. *The Complete Golden Dawn Cipher Manuscript*. Edmonds, WA: Holmes Publishing Group, 1996.

Levi, Eliphas. *The Magical Ritual of the Sanctum Regnum*. London: George Redway, 1896.

———. *Transcendental Magic*. New York: Weiser, 1974. First published as *Doctrine and Ritual of High Magic* in 1896.

Mathers, S. L. MacGregor. *The Kabbalah Unveiled*. New York: Samuel Weiser, 1974. First published in 1887.

McLean, Adam, ed. *A Treatise on Angel Magic*. Magnum Opus Hermetic Sourceworks series, no. 15. Edinburgh: Magnum Opus Hermetic Sourceworks, 1982.

Papus [Gerard Encausse]. *The Tarot of the Bohemians*. North Hollywood CA: Wilshire Book Company, 1975. First published in 1916.

Prasad, Rama. *The Science of Breath and the Philosophy of the Tattvas*. New York: Theosophical Publishing Society, 1894.

Regardie, Israel. *The Complete Golden Dawn System of Magic*. Phoenix, AZ: Falcon Press, 1984.

———. *The Golden Dawn*. St. Paul, MN: Llewellyn Publications, 1970. First published in four volumes in 1939–1940.

Stenring, Knut, trans. *The Book of Formation (Sepher Yetzirah)*. New York: Ktav Press, 1970. First published as *Sepher Yetzirah* in 1923.

Tatlow, Ruth. *Bach and the Riddle of the Number Alphabet*. New York: Cambridge University Press, 2006. First published in 1991.

Waite, Arthur Edward. *The Pictorial Key to the Tarot*. New York: University Books, 1959. First published in 1910.

Westcott, William Wynn, trans. *Sepher Yetzirah: The Book of Formation and the Thirty-Two Paths of Wisdom*. New York: Samuel Weiser, 1976. First published in 1893.

Wirth, Oswald. *The Tarot of the Magicians*. York Beach, ME: Samuel Weiser, 1985. First published in 1927.

• • • • • • •

About the Author

David Allen Hulse is a published author in the field of Eastern and Western magic and mysticism. He has contributed to various publications including *Tree Magazine, Holy Beggars' Gazette, OTO Newsletter*, and *The Tarot Journal*. He was able to contribute the last chapter to Israel Regardie's *The Complete Golden Dawn System of Magic* regarding a numerical key for the Enochian alphabet. Llewellyn Publications has published *The Eastern Mysteries* and *The Western Mysteries* (formerly *The Key of It All*), which is an extensive study of the sacred alphabets both East and West, as well as *The Truth About Numerology*. Weiser has published *New Dimensions for the Cube of Space*, which deals with the Tarot cards of Paul Foster Case placed upon the spatial cube described in the *Sepher Yetzirah*. Hell Fire Club Books has published *Genesis of the Book of the Law* (previously published by Holmes Publishing Company), which deals with the myth and legend behind Aleister Crowley's *The Book of the Law*. The author currently resides in Sacramento, California.

Art Credits

Figures 1, 3–5, and 7 by the Llewellyn Art Department.

Figure 2 is from Arthur Edward Waite's *The Pictorial Key to the Tarot*.

Figure 6 by Mary Ann Zapalac.

The Future of Ceremonial Magick
by Brandy Williams

Figure 1. Hope in the Prison of Despair *by Evelyn de Morgan*
(Image courtesy of the Art Renewal Center® www.artrenewal.org)

Story: The Future

"I invoke the spirit of the future. Come to me, powerful spirit, and show me what will be!"

A spangled mist appears before me, forming into a human shape with hands outstretched and huge eyes welling with compassion. "What will be cannot be shown," the spirit says in a voice like chiming bells.

"Why can't it be shown?" I ask. My deepest fear is that there is no future. "Is it because it doesn't exist?"

"Yes. No," the spirit says.

That kind of answer generally means I'm not asking the right questions. I try a different tack. "What can you show me?"

"Before you can know me," the figure says, "you must understand the present." Folding both arms against a slender chest, the figure vanishes.

Those eyes! They promised all the joy and sorrow in the universe. Was the figure male or female? What color was that mist? It seemed to be white and blue, dark and light at once. Was it a god, a spirit, an illusion, an angel? What did the spirit have to show me —what knowledge, what warning, what certainty of well-being?

What Is the Future?

We talk about time as if it is a river. The river flows only one way, like an arrow. The present is a little boat floating on the river, always changing, moving away from the past toward the future.

We talk about the future as if it is a place we are all journeying toward together. We hope that it is a utopia, a Star Trek world where everything we need appears when we ask for it, work and creativity are rewarded, hatred fades, and acceptance rules. We fear we will arrive at a dystopia where only a few have whatever they want, everyone else has too little to live, and brutality rules.

Magickians read cards and cast horoscopes and perform divinations to catch a glimpse of the future. This implies that we believe the future is at least partially predetermined and available for us to view. Forewarned is forearmed—if we can predict a future, we can avoid the worst effects and maximize the best ones. We hope that the future is changeable and that the choices we make today will help to determine the life we will experience. We fear that it is too late to change our future, or worse, that we never had the power to change it at all.

The future does not yet exist. How can we know what choices to make to steer ourselves down the river of time toward the destination we choose?

What fixes meaning is story.

Story: The Present

"I invoke the spirit of the present. Come to me, powerful spirit, and show me what is at hand!"

Crash! A young man falls on his knees in front of me. He struggles to his feet, twisting his torso weirdly beneath a slick silver cable that binds his arms together at the wrists and snakes up his chest. He gasps for air through his constricted throat. As I watch in horror, the cable grows up around his mouth and reaches for his eyes.

I cry out and grasp the cable, tearing it away from his mouth. The stuff feels oily; I smear my hand down my thigh. I see despair and gratitude in his eyes. "To save me," he gasps, "you must challenge fate." With a loud clap he disappears. I feel the rush of air on my face as he vanishes.

Shaken, I take a deep breath. It is clear something is terribly wrong. The pain in his eyes haunts me. What happened to him? He seemed so strong. What is the dreadful cable that imprisons him?

To my horror I see a sliver on my hand where I touched the cable. As I watch, the tiny shard grows into a silver thread. It winds around my wrist and slowly grows up my arm, colder than ice, thicker and weightier with every passing second.

I grab at the wire with my free hand to pull it away. Instead it leaps to twine around my other wrist, binding my hands in front of me. The thing wraps my arm and slithers across my chest. I watch fearfully as the silver cable climbs toward my throat. Am I trapped? Is his fate to be my fate?

The Present as Foresight

Futurists make educated guesses about what will happen if current trends continue, using the present as a form of foresight. Just now there is a dominant story that says:

> The future is a place on the linear flow of time. We can never return to an earlier time, the past is fixed and unchangeable, we can only move forward. What the human race does in the present affects what will happen to nature in the future. The power to decide human action lies with large corporations and nation states who set the policies that govern our lives. Since we know the effects these policies are having in the present we can project what will happen going forward. These projections show us the inevitable future arising from the present.[1]

Projecting our present into the future presents a grim prospect:

• The climate crisis has already led to species extinctions, the drowning of islands, and the first climate refugees.

---

1. Gidley, *The Future*, 13.

- The oceans choke with plastics and industrial processes contaminate land and rivers.
- The world economy bestows unimaginable wealth on a very few while leaving millions of people starving.
- Wars and droughts drive millions of refugees from their homes.
- The power to shape the future collects in the hands of increasingly authoritarian governments and corporations who exclude individuals and communities from the decision-making process.

Dystopia seems increasingly more likely. We imagine awful futures in which the rivers and oceans die, animal life is extinguished, massive population crashes reduce the human population, and we all end up as serfs to unapproachable warlords. At its worst we imagine a future that threatens our existence as a species.[2]

If this is our future and it is out of our hands, what hope do we have for a better life for ourselves and our children?

This is an urgent question. People are literally killing themselves for lack of hope. The World Health Organization reports that close to a million people commit suicide each year. The vast majority of suicides occur in low- and middle-income countries. Our most vulnerable populations are at highest risk—people undergoing discrimination and experiencing disaster or personal violence, and migrants and refugees escaping those conditions. Worse, it is the leading cause of death among 15 to 29-year-olds, the people who carry our hopes into the future.[3]

How can we regain control over our fate? How can we liberate our present and rescue our future?

Story: Soteria

The slick silver cable makes the first turn around my throat. Panicking, I fall to my knees and choke out, "O friendly spirits who aid humanity, whoever and wherever you may be, save me!"

A flash of light heats the air around me. I see a golden hand touch the cable at my throat, igniting it like a fuse. Golden sparkles dissolve the cable down my chest, my arms, and my bound wrists. The sparkles fizzle out just at the last wrap around the hand that touched the spirit of the present.

I take a grateful breath and look up into the face of my savior. The spirit is all of gold yellow hair and dark amber skin and shining eyes, draped with glittering cloth. I say, "Thank you for saving me. Who are you?"

He says, "Soter is a good name."

2. Gidley, *The Future*, 1.
3. World Health Organization, "Suicide Data."

• • • • • • • •

438

"Soter?" I say, getting to my feet. "You're a man?" His hair is short and his face is covered with downy hair like a young man's.

While I watch, his face becomes smooth and his hair grows out to his shoulders. "Soteria then," she says, with a voice as sweet as honey. "Tell me, magician, how did you fall into such a dire trap?"

"I was trying to summon the future."

Soteria shakes her head. "Wandering in the ways of time is dangerous without a guide."

I feel a movement at my wrist. The thread is growing again, much more slowly this time, inching its way up my arm. "Will it grow back?" I ask, panicking again. "Can you free me of this?"

"I have hampered it, but I cannot remove it entirely," she says regretfully. "Only you can free yourself, when you understand your destiny."

"The spirit of the present told me to challenge fate," I tell her. I am wary now to do this on my own. Invoking the present didn't seem all that risky, but what would have happened to me if Soteria hadn't responded to my plea? "Will you guide me?" I say.

"Every service comes with a price," she warns.

I open my mouth to agree and stop myself. This is not the first time I have bargained with a spirit. "What is your price and when is it due?" I say cautiously.

Soteria smiles warmly. "Just as I have helped you, so must you provide your help to one who needs it."

Rapidly I try to think through the possible consequences. "What happens if I fail?"

"I will not ask you for a task beyond your power." Soteria holds out a hand. "I will not linger. Do you agree?"

I am anxious to question the future and desperate to rescue the present. I decide to trust this daemon whose very name means Savior. "Yes," I say, putting my free hand in hers. "How can I challenge fate?"

Rescuing the Future

Futurists actively work to democratize the future. The field of futures studies draws on history, economic theory, sociology, psychology, and philosophy to propose multiple futures that benefit humanity.[4]

Futurists propose a new story:

---

4. Gidley, *The Future*, 67.

The future is not a single fixed destination. Instead there are many possible futures. Evolutions in human consciousness and communication have linked us together in newly powerful ways. We create our futures collaboratively through imagining possibilities.

We can think of futures as stacking up in layers: our individual future, the future of our local community, the future of our nation, the future of the world as a whole. Each life plays out in a specific place on the planet and a specific time in history. The closer we are to a level in the futures stack the more influence we have over how that future turns out. Each person has the most control over the individual level and the least influence at the global level.[5]

Magick has layers too. Just as there are multiple futures, there are multiple magicks. Magick today focuses almost entirely on the individual. To be fully effective, our magick needs to address the other layers of the stack. We need community, national, and global magicks. But magick hasn't been a player on the Western stage for about a century, and it hasn't been a dominant worldview for several millennia. We may believe we can make changes in our own lives, but it's very difficult to overcome the skepticism that magick can make a change in the whole world.

Our most urgent task is to meet the challenge of that skepticism, because as it turns out, magick may actually be the Western world's best hope for having a future at all.

Story: Despair

Soteria transports me to a stone room built from enormous bricks. A woman bows before a barred window, one arm pulling her robe to herself protectively, the other cradling her head. Her fear and grief overwhelm me. "Who is she?" I ask Soteria.

"Despair wears her," Soteria says. "She is trapped in it as in a prison."

I long to comfort this hopeless woman. "How can we help her?"

"This is the task I have asked you to undertake," Soteria says. "Will you free her from this prison?"

It is a heavy burden. How can I lift the heart of another? But her plight is riveting. Nothing seems more important than relieving her torment. "I will do everything in my power," I promise. Soteria nods approvingly.

The woman turns her head toward me and I realize she can hear me. "What troubles you?" I ask softly.

The hand holding her robe opens a little and something flutters to the floor. Carefully I pick it up. It's a papyrus filled with rows of Greek letters. I show it to Soteria. "What is this?"

Soteria says, "It's a horoscope."

---

5. Udayakamar, "Futures Studies and Futures Facilitators," in *Rescuing All Our Futures*, 110.

"Can you read it?"

"I am not an expert, but I know one who is. Shall I take you to her?"

This time I do not question the cost. "Yes!"

Facing the Past

How did we get to the place where the future of life on our planet is actually in doubt?

Between the 1400s and the 1900s, Europe colonized the world. *Colonization* is a bloodless word that means brutal exploitation. In those centuries, Britain, France, Spain, Germany, Holland, and Portugal killed much of the population of North America, claimed the lands of South America, kidnapped and enslaved people from Africa, conquered India and the South Pacific, and went to war with China.

European civilization justified this conquest by presenting itself as the pinnacle of human achievement. The Christian religion was the finest development of human morality. Western science explained the world so clearly it is unassailably true. Western philosophy took human reason to its greatest heights.

If European civilization was the most advanced, other civilizations were less so, and available for exploitation. Enlightenment philosophers helped to shape slavery. Isaac Newton, Robert Boyle, and John Locke all participated in the slave trade and even wrote apologetics for it.[6]

Today the European empire has given way to the American empire, which itself already seems to be fading. India is shaking off the effects of British colonization. China allies with the South Pacific in what will almost surely form the next great world power. European civilization is slowly facing the realization that the religion and the science spread to the world as great gifts have turned out to be massively destructive. Rather than elevating the peoples of the world, they benefited a few at the top while exploiting the vast mass of humanity. Ruthless exploitation of resources has so damaged the natural world that there is a real danger we will kill life altogether.

The Western Magical Tradition solidified among European upper-class intellectuals in the Victorian-Edwardian era. The British and European magicians who shaped our tradition into its current form embraced the power of colonization. They saw their magick as accurately describing the workings of the cosmos and saw themselves as superior to everyone else in the world. After all, their work was indisputably successful. Spiritualist circles, magickal lodges, and occult societies attracted famous artists, actors, poets, and politicians. Magick had real influence in the spheres that mattered. At the dawn of the twentieth century, magickians stood triumphantly at the top of the world.

6. Williams, "White Light, Black Magic," 11.

Our experience as magickians has changed. It is difficult to stand triumphantly at the top of the world when that world is suffering. How do we hold ourselves in this new era? Does our magick have anything to offer to the world?

Story: Urania, Muse of Astrology

Soteria says, "Urania, bring us into your realm and show us what we may see."

We are on a hill beneath the sky. A great plain surrounds us, rippling as if covered with water. Urania's dark hair is bound with a circlet of stars. Her bare feet are planted in the mud, but her eyes are fixed on the heavens, a dark bowl filled with points of light. "Look," she says. "This is the cosmos visible to the human eye from Earth. There is the circle of animals," she goes on, pointing to the zodiacal wheel where the lion and scorpion and goat and ram spin around the rim. "You trace your individual lives through them. Here you see what will be."

I hold the papyrus out to her. "What does this say?"

Urania takes it from me, glances at it, and shakes her head. "The stars have written a terrible fortune here," she says. "Health turns to sickness, wealth dissipates, what is loved is lost."

"Can you alter it?" I ask.

Urania turns away. "The stars display what Fate decrees."

Was this what the spirit of the present meant when he said I would need to challenge Fate? I say to Soteria, "Take me to Fate."

Uncertainty

We all experience the future as it unfolds. That means that all of us have the right to be included in shaping that experience. Not only should we be included, but we have a responsibility to shape the future. Science, Christianity and other religions, Western economics—all must coexist with other forms of thinking and imagining.[7]

Just now, capitalism drives the decision making. But what capitalism does the least well is invest in the distant future. The decisions most planners make today do not take into account the entire impact of the decisions they make in time.[8]

An important move to regain democratic control of the future is to challenge the fixed nature of the future. In fact, we can point to numerous predictions that did not come true and numerous events that humanity has not foreseen. What happens next continues to surprise us. Our understanding of the future is fallible. This opens up a window of possibility for a different future than the one predicted by projection of the present.[9]

7. Udayakamar, "Futures Studies and Futures Facilitators," in *Rescuing All Our Futures*, 110–113.

8. Fuller, "Futures Studies and Foresight," in *Rescuing All Our Futures*, 141.

9. Fuller, "Futures Studies and Foresight," in *Rescuing All Our Futures*, 135.

· · · · · · · ·

When we say we are uncomfortable with uncertainty and want to know the future, what we really want is to know that we will be well and happy in the future. When the future seems both fixed and grim, uncertainty is a blessing.

Story: The Fates and Fortune

We are on a hill beneath a tree. Three women are making thread in the shade. One flicks a drop spindle and adds fibers to the lengthening line. She hands it to the second, who unspools the thread and measures it. Then she in turn hands it to the third, who cuts it.

I clear my throat. "Greetings and respect to you, O Fates."

They look at me but don't stop their work. The spinner says, "Greetings, traveler. Do you come to beg for a child? Or to lengthen a life? Or to cut a life short for someone you despise?"

That is a startling set of choices. "To lengthen a life," I say.

The measurer says, "Many a mortal has asked us for a favor. Yet our decrees will not be overturned."

I try another idea. "I ask to lessen the misery of a life."

The cutter says, "That is not in our power. Fortune determines this." She points behind me.

I turn and look into the eyes of a very beautiful young woman dressed in the finest gold cloth. She stands beside a wheel fastened to a board that she can spin. "The wheel of Fortune," I murmur.

"Step up!" Fortune says gaily. "Shall we take your life for a spin?" She pulls down sharply on the wheel. As it spins, I see her age rapidly, her beauty become hideous, and her fine clothes turn to rags. The wheel suddenly stops and she is once again young and beautiful and richly dressed. "Will you try your luck?"

I hold out the horoscope. "Will you change what is decreed here?"

Fortune glances at the papyrus. "She's had her chance." She winks at me. "Come back when you're ready to play."

The Fates and Fortune vanish and we are alone on the hill. "They say their decrees are fixed," I say. "Is there anyone who can tell me how to alter them?"

"There is one teacher," Soteria says.

Challenging Fate

Fatalism is not a new idea in the Western experience. Astrology as we know it solidified in Alexandria as a fusion of Egyptian, Babylonian, and Greek systems. What emerged was the idea that the stars determined an immutable fate decreed by the gods. The astrologer could predict but could not influence what would happen. This grim determinism imagined each human as

· · · · · · · ·

a helpless victim of circumstance.[10] Christians in the same time period also saw fate as decreed by the One God. The Christian response to a fixed fate was to counsel acceptance and even welcome suffering on Earth, with the promise of redemption in the afterlife.

The Platonic teacher Asklepigenia refused to accept the idea that fate was unalterable. She articulated a difference between Christian theology and the Pagan knowledge of the gods. Asklepigenia taught that an understanding of the gods coupled with ritual could influence what happened in the world. Asklepigenia practiced *thaumaturgy*, a word that translates roughly to "making miracles."[11]

Asklepigenia's greatest student was Proklos, who succeeded her as the leader of the Academy in Athens. In the biography of Proklos, we learn that he performed miracles routinely. Proklos himself was healthy and unusually energetic. He was guided by dreams all his life, which helped him avoid political trouble and steer the course of his work. Importantly, his magick did not benefit himself alone. He brought rain to Athens to end a terrible drought. He predicted earthquakes. He healed people with his art and by invoking Asclepius, the god of healing. With his knowledge of ritual and his commitment to the gods, he changed the lives of his friends and his community.[12] He lived out the teachings of Asklepigenia: magick overcomes fate.

Story: Asklepigenia and Proklos

We are on a hill beneath a tree, a summery place redolent with the scent of fennel and cypress. In front of us a young man and an older woman sit side by side on a stone bench. His arms are bare, and her head is covered with her himation. All around them, young men and women sit on the ground, some holding their knees, some crossing their legs, all hunched as if weathering a crushing blow.

One of the young men is speaking to the teachers. "Proklos, Asklepigenia, how can you be so calm! They have moved what should not have been moved." His arm sweeps toward the hill above us where the marble columns of the Parthenon gleam in the sunlight. "They have taken Athena from her home. She no longer lives here."

"They have only taken a statue," Proklos says strongly. "Athena lives here, in the soil," he says, touching the ground, "and here, in our hearts."

One of the women students says, "Isn't the earth Ge?"

"Of course," Asklepigenia says, "as the sky is Zeus, but this ground is sacred to the goddess of our city."

10. Fowden, *The Egyptian Hermes*, 92–93.

11. Waithe, *Ancient Women Philosophers: 600 BC–500 AD*, 9.

12. Marinus of Samaria, *The Life of Proclus, or, Concerning Happiness*, 15–55.

• • • • • • • •

A man bursts out, "How can we contemplate the gods when the Christians are destroying our way of life? Is it inevitable? Has Fate decreed it?"

"No!" Asklepigenia's voice rings out strongly. "Fate is never certain so long as we have magick."

This is what I have come to hear. I step out of the shadow of the tree that has concealed me. "How can we challenge fate?"

The great teacher turns her eyes on me. She whispers to Proklos and rises to move away from the group. He continues to teach them as she draws me aside.

"I do not know you, stranger, but I welcome you," she says, in the ancient Greek tradition of hospitality. "What troubles you?"

I show her the papyrus. "There is a woman in despair because of this. Urania tells me that the stars have decreed a terrible fortune for her. I have met with the Fates and Fortune, but they refuse to change her future."

Reading the papyrus, Asklepigenia becomes grave. "It seems her need is desperate. She will need powerful aids to overcome this." She looks around her on the ground. "Here," she says, picking up a smooth oval rock. "This is a stone from the sacred hill of Athena. It carries with it the virtue of her power." She places it in my palm and closes her hands around mine. "May she grant you success."

As she leaves us, I look down at my arm. The silver cable continues to grow.

The Pagan Worldview

Asklepigenia and Proklos were Pagan. Their ritual practices, called *theurgy*, or "god work," brought them into direct communion with Hellenic deity. Here are the pillars of their religious and philosophical worldview:

- **Earth:** The earth is sacred.
- **Spirit in matter:** As above, so below—spirit is contiguous with matter.
- **Paganism:** The One spirit is a unity in the forms of multiple gods and goddesses. Deity can have a female face.
- **Women:** Priestesses, mothers, and women philosophers are indispensable teachers.
- **Revelation**: We come from the gods, and every individual can directly experience contact with the gods.
- **Reincarnation:** The soul's journey is to improve character through successive incarnations in order to return to the realm of the gods.

These elements came under direct attack in the Christian era. Once the urban temples had been closed, Christian monks fanned out into the countryside throughout the Hellenistic world, overturning altars, destroying statues, and writing "One God!" on the walls of the temples. They preached to the populace that the fact they could destroy the statues meant that the gods they had worshipped were powerless spirits, not truly divine. The shrines were rededicated to Christian use.[13]

By the fifteenth century, educated Europeans believed they were surrounded by supernatural forces directed by Satan and the women who allied themselves with him.[14] Here are the pillars of their worldview:

- **Earth:** The world is corrupt.
- **Spirit and matter:** Spirit is entirely separate from the world.
- **Paganism** is evil, and the only legitimate religion is Christianity.
- **Women** are inferior to men and ally easily with the forces of evil.
- **Revelation:** Any contact with spirits in this world is with evil spirits.
- **Reincarnation:** There is only one life before the soul faces God's judgment.

It seemed that the worst fears of the theurgists had come true and the Pagan worldview had disappeared from the world.

Story: Tycho and Sophie

I have learned a great deal from Proklos and Asklepigenia, but I'm still not sure how to alter what the Fates and Fortune have decreed. I ask Soteria, "Is there anyone else who can help me understand the magick of shaping the future?"

"Tycho Brahe," Soteria says.

We are on a hill beneath a tree. In the landscape below, I can see the famous garden of the Danish island of Hven, laid out according to Tycho's meticulous directions, its precise geometry reflecting the harmony of the spheres. In the distance I can see the famous castle dedicated to the muse of astrology, Uraniborg itself. It stands three stories high, built on a straight north-south orientation to enable the astronomers to make accurate measurements of the stars.

Just now there's no one outside observing the sky. "Let's try the laboratory," Soteria says.

Without transition we stand in an alchemical workshop. A boy shoves a handful of coal into the bottom of a five-foot-high furnace, but there's no one else in the basement room. Soteria says, "Let's try the library."

In a blink we are in a room with windows set high on the wall to let light fall on the tables below. Tycho consults an almanac and makes a mark on a sheet of paper. I can read this horo-

---

13. Trombley, *Hellenic Religion and Christianization*, 220–225.
14. Easlea, *Witch Hunting, Magic, and the New Philosophy*, 1.

· · · · · · · ·

scope. It has the familiar wheel of houses marked with symbols for the zodiacal signs and the planets. "Sophie," he says without looking up. "The light is fading. Bring me a candle."

"In a moment," Sophie calls from across the room.

Tycho looks up from his work and sees me. "I wasn't expecting a guest." He looks me over. Fortunately Soteria has dressed me in the costliest fashion of the day. "Although nobility is always welcome. Have you come to see the celestial observatory or the terrestrial one?"

I decide not to mention that I've seen them both. "I have a friend in trouble," I say. "I hoped you could help me."

Sophie appears with a beeswax candle in her hand. "We can try," she says, carefully placing the candle away from the papers.

Tycho turns to his sister with a smile. "Check my figures," he tells her, pushing the horoscope at her. To me he says, "I forbade her to learn astrology but she taught herself anyway."

"And he's been boasting about me ever since," Sophie says, bending over the desk. "Are you sure about this placement?" When Tycho reaches for a book, she takes it from him. "Here, I'll look it up. You help our visitor."

Tycho settles back into his chair and looks at me expectantly. "What is the trouble?"

"My friend has a horoscope that predicts a terrible life," I say. "She has fallen into despair. How can I convince her that her fate is not fixed?"

"Tell her to pray," he says immediately. "God comforts all."

That wasn't the answer I was hoping for. One of the papers on his desk is inscribed with his famous mottos: *Despiciendo suspicio*, "By looking downward I see upward," and *Suspiciendo despicio*, "By looking upward I see downward." I point to the paper. "I thought I might counter the influence of the heavens with the influence of Earth."

Tycho considers this. "How did you think to do that?"

I hold out the stone. "I have this from the Acropolis."

He touches it reverently. "It has its own virtue," he says. He pushes himself away from the table and rummages among the shelves on the wall. "Earth calls out for sea. Here we are." He pulls out a little clay container with a wooden stopper. "This contains alchemical water. A drink of this can ease the heart."

"What of air?" Sophie says.

"Yes," Tycho says. "Air links the celestial with the terrestrial." He looks at her. "What could carry the virtue of air?"

Sophie picks up the candle and holds it out to me. "Let this light your way."

Taking the gifts from them, I say, "Thank you." I wonder what I can give them in return. "You are a great man and a great woman. Your work will be remembered for many centuries."

"Well," Tycho says, pleased.

· · · · · · · ·

Sophie's eyes light up. *"What a kind wish. Thank you."*

As we fade into the shadows of the room, I see that the silver cable on my arm has nearly reached my chest.

The Pagan Renaissance

After the Roman Christian emperors closed the Alexandrian and Athenian academies, cities farther to the east took in escaping Platonic teachers. The eastern part of the Roman Empire and the Islamic world continued to study Platonic and Hermetic texts. In contrast, the western Roman Christian church depended on Aristotle but rejected Plato.

In the fifteenth century, western European intellectuals rediscovered Hermeticism, starting with Marsilio Ficino's translation of the *Corpus Hermeticum* from Greek into Latin in 1463. The Platonic and Hermetic worldview encouraged learning about the world directly rather than through Aristotelian theory alone. This experiential approach sparked a renaissance in art, science, and spiritual understanding. The people who studied these texts called themselves *natural philosophers* to emphasize their study of nature.

It was impossible to ignore that Pagans had written these important texts. The natural philosophers developed a number of approaches to handle this. Some, like Giordano Bruno, held that the Christian Church had overturned the true Egyptian religion and converted to Paganism altogether. Others, like Pico della Mirandola, expounded on the idea of perennial philosophy: all philosophies share a common root, and the Pagan texts were rough drafts of the perfection of the Christian ones. Pico included the Bible, Platonic texts, and Jewish Qabbalah, along with many other sources, in his work.[15]

Tycho Brahe's work epitomizes the new sciences inspired by Platonic and Hermetic thought. For Tycho, both astrology and alchemy were necessary to explain the world. He developed a cosmology of earth, sea, and sky, with air forming the connection between the celestial and terrestrial realms.[16] Sophie Brahe's work exemplifies the importance of women to alchemy. Women worked in their kitchens and gardens to produce medicines and cosmetics.[17] Alchemists sometimes worked in male-female pairs. Sophie assisted her brother in his astronomical observations and in his laboratory and later married an alchemist. Their marriage centered on their joint work.

The natural philosophers developed a worldview that Proklos would recognize. They taught that humanity is at the center of a cosmos connected end to end by a network of spirit, and

15. Schmitt, "Perennial Philosophy: From Agostino Steuco to Leibniz," *Journal of the History of Ideas*, 505–532.

16. Christianson and Brahe, "Tycho Brahe's Cosmology from the Astrologia of 1591," *Isis*, 312–318.

17. Ray, *Daughters of Alchemy*, 3–4.

· · · · · · · ·

that studying the cosmos leads to an experience of the love of the divine.[18] Our magick today descends directly from natural philosophy.[19]

Story: Hope in a Prison of Despair

I tell Soteria, "Take me to the woman in despair. I want to see if these remedies will help her." I hold up the stone, the alchemical water, and the candle.

I find myself looking again at the woman I have been trying to help, the woman in despair, clutching herself before a barred window. I am not in the brick room with her though. Instead I am looking at a painting of her on an easel. I am in an art studio. Other paintings hang above one another all the way up the walls to an enormously high ceiling. The fireplace in the corner barely warms the drafty space.

An artist perches on a wooden chair in front of the easel. She leans back, dabs at her palette, and touches the brush to the panel, shaping another line of care on the face of the despairing woman.

"Who is she?" I whisper to Soteria.

"Evelyn Pickering de Morgan. She's a spiritualist," she answers softly.

The artist pauses and looks around the room. "Who's there?"

I step into the light and Evelyn spots me. "Welcome, spirit, whoever you may be," she says comfortably.

"I am here to help the woman in your painting," I tell her.

"Despair?" She looks from the panel to me and back again. "Life has trapped her, but she will have relief in the end."

"How can she know that?" I say.

The artist puts down her brush and grabs a sketch pad. "Wait," she says. "Don't move. Hold the candle out just a little more."

Suddenly self-conscious, I pose for her while she roughs out an outline of a slight figure holding up a lamp. "There!" she says. "I've given her Hope." She smiles at me. "You have given me a gift."

"You have given me hope," I tell her.

As she turns back to her painting, I look down at my chest. The silver cable has wrapped around twice and is inching toward my neck.

---

18. Easlea, *Witch Hunting, Magic, and the New Philosophy*, 108–109.
19. Williams, *For the Love of the Gods*, 219–220.

· · · · · · · ·

Magic, Religion, and Science

The Church recognized the threat posed by natural philosophy. The Renaissance magickians were conversing with spirits, exploring Pagan ideas, and challenging Christian doctrine. Many natural philosophers were imprisoned and killed by the Inquisition. Giordano Bruno was burned at the stake.[20]

The natural philosophers wanted to continue to study nature and also wanted to continue to live free and happy lives. Some proposed an alternative to natural philosophy: mechanical philosophy. The Church held that God had created the world and then left, leaving it to run by itself. The mechanical philosophers built that conception into their worldview, rejecting Paganism and the Pagan thought that the world itself was alive. Instead the world and its creatures were all mechanisms without souls which could be explored and exploited.[21]

The category human separated from the category animal. Humans have a soul, intelligence, and emotion; animals do not. This conceptualization led to the immediate and immensely cruel exploitation of animals (including live vivisection—the screams of the animals were explained as the squeaking of a mechanism) and the ongoing loss of the sense of life in the world.

Story: Urania, Muse of Astronomy

"Take me back to Urania," I tell Soteria urgently.

My guide hesitates. "Are you ready?"

"I have to be. I need to act before the chain chokes off my air." I hold up the stone, the flask of alchemical water, and the candle. "I have earth, water, fire, and air. I can challenge her now."

We are on a hill beneath the sky. The cosmos is filled with washes of light, spirals of pink and blue, towering pillars of smoke and diamond. Urania perches on a rock with her arms on her knees, holding a sextant loosely in one hand. I say to her triumphantly, "You told me the stars show what must be, but I know that isn't true."

"Of course it isn't," Urania says carelessly. "Why did you think the stars show the future?" She waves an arm at the sky. "The light we see now travelled millions of years to reach us. When we look at the universe we look at the past. Look there," she says. "That is where stars are born." In one of the clouds the gas blows away and dozens of pinpoints of light blaze into existence. "And there is where stars die." In a section of the sky filled with reddish haze, a circle of light explodes and blasts blue stuff in all directions, and when the haze clears, the point is gone, leaving only the red background behind.

I hesitate. "But where is the meaning?"

---

20. Easlea, *Witch Hunting, Magic, and the New Philosophy*, 104.

21. Easlea, *Witch Hunting, Magic, and the New Philosophy*, 111–112.

"There is no meaning in the stars," she says. "The universe is a mechanism. I can show you its movements and its processes. You must find meaning on your own."

"If we're looking at the past, are we standing on the present?" I ask. "Is that why we're not moving?"

Urania looks at me. "Why do you think we're not moving?"

As she speaks, I feel the ground beneath me tremble like jelly. I am spinning in infinity, with no solid place to stand. I stumble and lose my footing. "Soteria, take me somewhere safe!" I cry out.

The Rational and the Esoteric

The European Enlightenment did not reconcile mechanical and natural philosophy, but instead completed the rejection of the Pagan worldview, a process sometimes called the *disenchantment* of the world. We are indebted to Wouter Hanegraaf's important insight that the Enlightenment actually defined itself against esotericism. Enlightenment scholars divided the field of human endeavor, placing some subjects in the categories "true" and "serious" and others in the categories of "foolish" and "superstitious," a process Hanegraaf terms *eclectic*. Scientific methodologies specifically excluded clairvoyance, intuition, correspondences, and noncausal influences in nature.[22]

Hanegraaf asserts that what academics have meant by "magic" or "esotericism" is Paganism. The Pagan worldview understands the divine as immanent, in the world, while Christian monotheism places an invisible creator entirely outside the visible temporal creation. This failure to recognize Paganism is an academic blindspot.[23]

Put another way, the voluminous academic discussion about the relative definitions of religion, science, and magic can be usefully reframed as a discussion about Christianity, mechanical philosophy, and Paganism.

Story: The Dark Night of the Soul

I grab for Soteria, miss, and fall.

I lose my candle instantly. I fall until all the stars fade and there is only blackness. I fall until I lose all track of time. I fall until all emotion washes out of me and leaves me numb. I fall until I cannot even feel myself.

Gradually I realize I am no longer falling. I have not landed, I have just stopped. I seem to be held up by something, but I can't tell what it is. I am surrounded by darkness and silence.

I try to speak, but no sound passes my parched lips. I realize I am perishingly thirsty. After some time I remember that I carry water with me. Fumbling in the hush of blackness, I find the

---

22. Hanegraaff, *Esotericism and the Academy*, 372–375.
23. Hanegraaff, *Esotericism and the Academy*, 370.

flask. I put the stopper between my teeth and worm it out carefully. A gush of liquid flows down my throat.

I can feel again. Waves of feeling pass over me, sorrow, joy, fear, peace. I breathe deeply and stop shivering. "Soteria," I breathe as a prayer. "Save me."

There is no answer. Did I invent her? Does she really exist? Am I just making up stories to protect myself from the meaningless truth of the universe?

I am alone. I'm not even sure I believe in my own soul.

Overcoming Skepticism

Every marginalized person inhabits two worlds. People of color live in a white-controlled world. Women live in a male-controlled world. Magickians too inhabit two worlds, the world of the Enlightenment and the esoteric world. We look at the night sky and see the brilliant face of the divine, and at the same time see a mechanical universe completely indifferent to life.

When we look at the sun and say "our mother" or "our father," we have on our ears the ringing of a century and a half of laughter at us: what a silly superstition! That was just a way to explain the world before intellect kicked in. This skepticism, the Enlightenment rejection of the esoteric worldview, is the source of our doubt in our own power.

The mechanical universe is hostile and lonely. It also doesn't match our experience. We realize that the physical sun is a ball of gas, but we also know that the sun is the source of our life. It isn't stupid to be grateful for that. We know the world is alive, that other animals do have emotions, and that when they scream they are in pain just as we feel pain. The world is not a mechanism to be taken apart but an organic whole. We long for a way to express our deep conviction that life deserves care.

We challenge the arrogant belief that one type of knowledge can understand the world's tremendously complex living system in its entirety and predict all the effects of changes we make in the system. Our attempt to master nature is killing her. In a visceral physical sense, the sun and Earth are our parents. Using this language to describe them indicates our respect for life. We need to recover that respect and listen to our hearts. We need our mother.

Story: Neith

At the first moment and the last breath there is one name that we call. "Mother."

"I wondered when you would hit bottom," a voice says. There is a shape in the darkness, a deeper velvet.

"Who are you?" I whisper.

"Ama, Ma, mother," she says. "Before I am Athena I am Neith. Before I am Neith I am Nut, the sky. Before I am Nut I am Niw, the dark water from which everything arises."

• • • • • • • •

I do not know if I am worthy of her care. Yet I have been brought into being. The gift of life is given without asking. "Are you my mother?" I ask her.

The darkness lessens and I see more of her shape. "I am the mother of all things," she says warmly.

I see now that I am lying on a rise that keeps me out of an infinite dark sea. "I'm on a hill," I say.

"Creation always starts on a hill," she says. "The mound rises from the fertile water."

The relief and gratitude that fill me are so profound they shake my soul. They make my soul. I'm crying, huge gasping sobs of grief and joy, and laughing, filled with amazement for the wonder of the universe. The only word I have for this is love. Creation is the love given without asking, and love is the only possible thanks for this. "I love you, mother."

Remembering the Mother

All around the world we find indigenous and religious peoples calling the Earth their mother and father, the sun their mother and father, the stars and rivers and weather and cosmos their mother and father. The creatures of the Earth are brother and sister to humanity. The living world is bound by a network of interdependence. From this comes a sense of contentment, that there is a place for us and we belong in it, and a sense of gratitude, that we are found to be worthy of nourishment, that we are given what we need without asking, and that the gifts we receive are sufficient to sustain our life.

We remember our mother. She is Demeter, Aphrodite, Hera. The ancients said that Neith moved to Greece and became Athena. One of the sources of our tradition is Egyptian/Kemetic religious philosophy. The ancients told us this. For centuries the academy rejected this knowledge in the effort to establish European civilization as superior. This is still largely true, although academic voices today argue that we should take the ancients at their word. Esotericism never forgot this—we have long asserted that our tradition roots in Egypt.

Greek and Hellenistic women philosophers studied in the Pythagorean and Platonic schools, and they taught too, even while having families. This was so common that the woman philosopher was a familiar figure, and some famous men were known as mother-taught.[24] The Roman Christian world targeted the academies as strongholds of Pagan thought, taking particular aim at the work of the women philosophers and systematically destroying their work. The closure of the academies also ended for many centuries women's involvement with philosophy, women's involvement in the academy, and the development of philosophical discourse.[25]

24. Glassman, *The Origins of Democracy in Tribes, City-States and Nation-States*, 1204.
25. Glassman, *The Origins of Democracy in Tribes, City-States and Nation-States*, 1205.

• • • • • • • •

We need our mothers back, goddesses and philosophers both. Women magickians are called to be mothers ourselves of the new stories, the new rituals, the new philosophical frameworks of the twenty-first century.

Story: Indra

The sky flares into brilliant life.

The shape of the mother is gone. She surrounds me in the waters and the vault of heaven. I find I am lying beneath a tree blossoming with millions of fragrant flowers in a myriad of colors.

Beneath the tree a beautiful god is drinking from a cup shaped like the moon. Or is it the moon itself? His skin ripples with the colors from the tree, pink and blue, red and gold, green and purple, smoke and light.

I am profoundly grateful that I am no longer alone. A wave of ecstasy washes over me. I reach out a hand and touch his feet, trembling. "Honor to the guru. Honor to Lord Indra. Will you teach me?"

Indra smiles down at me. "You seek meaning," he says. "Look up." He waves his hands at the sky. Every pinpoint of light flashes brightly as a web of threads link each to the others in uncountable combinations. "The meaning is in the net itself. Each of these jewels reflects every other jewel. All are connected. You were never alone; you can never be alone. All of creation is in relationship."

He takes another drink from the moon. "Look down," he says. The water near the mound flows in little streams; as they flow out over the plain, they vanish into each other in a shimmering haze. "All things change, yet what is possible is born from this. Each of these streams creates a possibility." The stars are reflected in the water below; we are in the center of a jeweled bowl, water blending into space, past dissolving into the future.

"You are here," Lord Indra says. "You have always been here."

I pull myself up into a sitting position. I feel the slimy silver cable licking around my neck. "It's winning," I say. "It's going to surround me."

"Let it," Lord Indra says.

All this time I have been fighting this thing, with my mind, with my will, with my desperate seeking. Now I let that all go. I surrender to whatever will be.

As soon as I stop fighting the cable flashes all over my body. It surrounds me from head to toe completely. Once the shell is complete, its weight vanishes, the sense of restriction lifts, and the slimy sensation turns into tingling and then vanishes. I am brilliant. I myself have become a jewel reflecting all the other jewels in Lord Indra's net. For an instant that is an eternity, I see, hear, feel, know, understand, am everything that is.

It is a bliss beyond bliss. It seems as if I am rising and I will go on expanding forever.

· · · · · · · ·

Honoring the Guru

Our tradition has roots not only in Egypt (Kemet) but also in India, Bharata. Pythagoras studied there and brought back the doctrine of reincarnation to Greece. Plato and all subsequent philosophers built on a base of Pythagorean philosophy and practice.[26]

Ceremonial magick, esotericism, and Western culture are all younger siblings to the religions of India. It is time for us to recover our humility, express our gratitude, and honor Bharata as our guru. Westerners have pulled off pieces of Hindu practice that we find useful and studied Tantra to have better sex and yoga for health without acknowledging that these are embedded in a cultural matrix. When we approach Hinduism and Tantra with reverence on their own terms, we can learn from an intact system how to organically regrow the unity of our own partially preserved system.

Story: Athena Sophia

I cannot expand into the infinite universe forever. I must return to my own form. A golden hand offers to help me up. "Soteria!" I say happily. I leap up and hug her.

She is warm and sweet-smelling and laughing. "I see you have found your way."

"Neith, the mother, gave me life. Lord Indra, the guru, gave me meaning," I explain inadequately.

She seems to understand. "We are all the children of our mother and our father. This is true for cultures as well as bodies." She looks me over. "I see you have completed your transformation. Are you ready to complete your task?"

"Do you think I'm ready?" I have learned to ask.

She smiles approvingly. "Do you know how to go home?"

I have lost the candle and I have drunk the water, but I still have one talisman left. I close my fist around the stone and say, "Take me home."

The stars fade to daylight and the tree turns to cypress. I am standing on a summery, fragrant hill looking up at a temple. This one is not so grand as the Parthenon, which was meant to impress and intimidate. This is a small temple whose doors open invitingly.

I recognize that I don't know how to enter with respect for the ways of this place. "Will you guide me?"

Soteria leads me through the columns into the temple itself. On a marble dais sits a golden throne, and on that throne sits the goddess. Her armor lays to one side. She is clad in a simple himation, spinning thread on a drop spindle.

"Athena," I say, dropping to one knee.

---

26. Williams, *For the Love of the Gods*, 202.

· · · · · · ·

"Rise," she says. "Before I am Athena, I am Neith. And I am always a spinner."

Indra showed me that there is a web. I realize that the thread Athena is spinning is salvation. "Can you spin a new future?" I ask her.

"You mean to challenge Fate?" Her voice fills the space with an awful beauty. "For I am Athena Soteria, the savior. I am the daughter who has remembered the mother. I am the child who has inherited the authority of the father. I have returned, although I never left you. I am Athena Sophia and my wisdom brings both reason and inspiration." She lowers her gaze to me. "What future would you have me spin?"

"I would comfort Despair," I say.

If her voice filled me with awe before, now it fills me with terror. "I summon you, Heimarmene! Appear before me and account to me!"

There is a flash of light and a spirit stands before the throne. She is Fortune but not Fortune, brighter, grander; she is not only my personal fortune but also the fate of the cosmos. Heimarmene puts a hand on her waist and tosses her hair. "Account to you, sister? Haven't we grown all high and mighty?"

They both laugh and move to embrace each other. "How goes the spinning?" Heimarmene says.

"How goes the web?" Athena says.

As I look on this happy scene my mouth floods with the bitterness of betrayal. "I thought I was supposed to overcome Fate," I say to Soteria.

The goddesses do not take offense. They turn to me, smiling. "You have not lost," Athena says.

"You have won," Heimarmene says.

They hold out their hands to me. I look to Soteria, who nods and gestures to me. Hesitatingly I step up onto the dais.

"There are always three of us," Athena says. "One of us spins the stuff of the cosmos." She flicks her spindle.

"One of us weaves the pattern of relating." Heimarmene unspools the thread and makes a cat's cradle pattern from it. She holds it out to me.

I realize what I have to do. I take the net into my hands. "And one of us lives the meaning."

Magick in the Twenty-First Century

The lodges of the late nineteenth and early twentieth century shaped esotericism to meet the challenges of the modern age, in particular admitting women into the lodges.[27] After the First World War, magick retreated from being active in the world and reconfigured as a self-help sys-

27. Williams, *The Woman Magician*, 11–12.

tem. As the academic and popular worlds take an interest in us again, we have a great deal of work to do to shape our ceremonies to meet the demands of the next century.

We have already talked about some of the tasks in front of us:

- Understand the world as a living organism embedded in a living cosmos
- Recover the mother and women teachers
- Relinquish imperialism and approach other cultures with respect on their own terms

We also have these tasks:

- Establish the relationship to the academy on our own terms
- Reknit the relationship of theurgic ritual to Pagan philosophy
- Visualize the future together

The Esoteric Relationship to the Academy

As the walls come down between the academy and esotericism, we will need to manage the relationship proactively on our own terms. After a century and a half of being denigrated as foolish, it's flattering to receive some validation. We may seek academic recognition of our work as legitimizing. However it is important to recognize that magick and the academy have different aims. Our ultimate goal is to experience the living world as divine. Magickians can partner with the academy, but we must develop our own standards of scholarship and our own sense of who we are in relationship to the world. In particular we can insist that the people we accept to help us shape who we are and what we do are practitioners, whether or not they are academic.

Non-Western thinkers accuse the West of foraging among intact non-Western cultures for material to prop up the exhausted Enlightenment project.[28] The academic interest in esotericism is partly a move toward inclusion and partly an example of this kind of foraging. What better place to find material than the methodologies that were specifically excluded as defining the Enlightenment? We must resist the attempts to raid esotericism to bandage the failure of mechanical philosophy.

The worldview of the Pagan theurgists is a living whole. The animal nature of the body, alive in the world, with direct access to the experience of spirit—these are the qualities whose exclusion has led to the destruction of the natural world, and human meaning. Theurgy offers a living science, seeking the sources of life and nourishing them within ourselves and the world.

---

28. Goonatilake, "De-Westernizing Futures Studies," in *Rescuing All Our Futures*, 74.

• • • • • • • •

Reknit the Relationship of Ceremonial Ritual to Pagan Theurgy

When the Roman Christian emperors suppressed public Pagan practice, these rituals were split from their philosophical foundations. Both the rituals and the philosophical texts were passed down to us through the centuries through different routes. Theurgic ritual forms the foundation of the ceremonial magick rituals we have practiced in the twentieth century and the beginning of the twenty-first.[29]

For the Platonists, particularly Asklepigenia and Proklos, theurgy was grounded in Hellenic religious observance. Our theurgy must also ground in Pagan practice. That can include but need not be limited to Hellenic Paganism. The important thing is to enter into any religious practice with respect for its cultural rules and study the system on its own terms.

As academics reknit the Platonic philosophies with the rituals practiced by the philosophers, magickians must engage in the same operation. Academic scholars read the Platonic texts, find instructions for practices, and search among the surviving ritual texts for those that correspond with them. They have the texts, we have the rituals. Our operation works the other way around. What Platonic principles underlie the rituals we have been practicing for centuries?

The Renaissance magickians borrowed Jewish Qabbalah to explain the ritual practices, but that system was not original to the rituals. There is a consonance between the Platonic understanding of the soul and the Qabbalistic soul. However, the Renaissance magickians did not approach Jewish Qabbalah with respect. Theurgy offers a way to confront our colonialist past and begin to make reparations.

Should we relinquish Qabbalah altogether? It is deeply embedded in the framework of ceremonial magick today, a historical part of the system. Individuals and communities will have different responses. What we can do immediately is acknowledge that Jewish mysticism is an intact cultural system with its own rules. We can learn something about the people who practice it today and understand their rules of engagement.[30]

We understand the divine through loving the divine. Theurgy teaches both what is divine and how to experience the divine. This is why theurgy is emerging as critical to our future. As we knit together the theory and practice of ceremonial magick we recover a path to our own spirituality. Theurgy brings our stories back. It is our past, and it is also our future.

Visualizing the Future Together

Futurists say that "what we can imagine we can create."[31] Futurists encourage individuals and communities to create visions of the future that we want to live in. This is an exciting conver-

---

29. Williams, *For the Love of the Gods*, 219–220.
30. Tilles, "Kosher Kabbalah for Non-Jews?"
31. Milojevic, "Feminising Futures Studies," in *Rescuing All Our Futures*, 67.

· · · · · · · ·

gence between the field of futures studies and esotericism. Visualization is a key esoteric skill. Magickians learn early on in detail how to build an image and hold it. We pair this skill with the ability to create a statement of intent, a clear declaration of what we want to happen.[32]

We can create statements of intent about the future we want to see for our communities as well as our nations and the world. Today individual magickians create rites to shape the future and release them for general use. Our next step is to come together physically and virtually to co-create them, test them, and refine them. We can partner with futurists in the academy and in the community to learn effective methodologies for working in groups to accomplish this. We can also offer our outputs to other communities for their use and invite them to join with us. These partnerships will lead to new forms of group endeavors that will look very different from the magickal lodges today, less secretive and rigid, more inclusive and fluid, changing dynamically as the need arises.

Magickians have always been the people who make the future. Every jewel in Indra's net reflects every other jewel.[33] All pasts lead to all futures. Through divination, precognition, prophecy, and revelation we chart a path through the myriad continually changing possibilities to the future we choose together.

In our future the West rejects mechanical philosophy with the overdue recognition that the world is alive. We learn from older cultures. The peoples of the world make decisions based on the long-term needs of life. The net of relationships that holds us up regenerates. We acknowledge our debt to the trees, the hills, the animals, the sun, the power of life itself. We recognize the sacredness in the universe and in ourselves.

Story: The Magick of Hope

I am standing in a stone room built from enormous bricks, facing a barred window. I am bent over, pulling my robe to myself with one arm, cradling my head with the other.

Soteria did not say, "She is despair." She said, "Despair wears her."

Despair wears me.

All the futility and hopelessness of a future of torment washes over me. If the future is fixed, if I am powerless, why should I go on?

A light flickers on the wall in front of me. I know that light. It is cast by a lamp. Hope is standing behind me, holding it in her hands. Slowly I straighten, letting my arms fall, bringing myself up to my full height. The light reminds me that I am a jewel in the net of the cosmos, and I am never alone.

In this picture I am also hope. I am a magickian, and I am free to choose my future.

---

32. Williams, *Practical Magic for Beginners*, 25–33.

33. Malhotra, *Indra's Net: Defending Hinduism's Philosophical Unity*, 5.

* * * * * * * *

Bibliography

Christianson, John, and Tycho Brahe. "Tycho Brahe's Cosmology from the Astrologia of 1591." *Isis* 59, no. 3 (Autumn 1968): 312–318.

Easlea, Brian. *Witch Hunting, Magic, and the New Philosophy: An Introduction to Debates of the Scientific Revolution, 1450–1750.* Brighton, UK: Harvester Press, 1980.

Fowden, Garth. *The Egyptian Hermes: A Historical Approach to the Late Pagan Mind.* Princeton, NJ: Princeton University Press, 1993.

Fuller, Ted. "Futures Studies and Foresight." In *Rescuing All Our Futures: The Future of Futures Studies*, edited by Ziauddin Sardar, 134–145. Westport, CT: Praeger Publishers, 1999.

Gidley, Jennifer. *The Future: A Very Short Introduction.* New York: Oxford University Press, 2017.

Glassman, Ronald M. *The Origins of Democracy in Tribes, City-States and Nation-States.* New York: Springer International Publishing, 2017.

Goonatilake, Susantha. "De-Westernizing Futures Studies." In *Rescuing All Our Futures: The Future of Futures Studies*, edited by Ziauddin Sardar, 72–82. Westport, CT: Praeger Publishers, 1999.

Hanegraaff, Wouter J. *Esotericism and the Academy: Rejected Knowledge in Western Culture.* Cambridge, UK: Cambridge University Press, 2012.

MacLennan, Bruce. *The Wisdom of Hypatia: Ancient Spiritual Practices for a More Meaningful Life.* Woodbury, MN: Llewellyn, 2013.

Malhotra, Rajiv. *Indra's Net: Defending Hinduism's Philosophical Unity.* Noida: HarperCollins Publishers India, 2014.

Marinus of Samaria. *The Life of Proclus, or, Concerning Happiness.* Translated by Kenneth Sylvan Guthrie. Yonkers, NY: Platonist Press, 1925. http://www.tertullian.org/fathers/marinus_01 _life_of_proclus.htm.

Mierzwicki, Tony. *Hellenismos: Practicing Greek Polytheism Today.* Woodbury, MN: Llewellyn Publications, 2018.

Milojevic, Ivana. "Feminising Futures Studies." In *Rescuing All Our Futures: The Future of Futures Studies*, edited by Ziauddin Sardar, 61–71. Westport, CT: Praeger Publishers, 1999.

Ray, Meredith K. *Daughters of Alchemy: Women and Scientific Culture in Early Modern Italy.* Cambridge, MA: Harvard University Press, 2015.

Schmitt, Charles B. "Perennial Philosophy: From Agostino Steuco to Leibniz." *Journal of the History of Ideas* 27, no. 4 (October–December 1966): 505–532. University of Pennsylvania Press. https://www.jstor.org/stable/2708338.

Tilles, Yerachmiel. "Kosher Kabbalah for Non-Jews?" *Kabbalah Online*, March 1, 2006. https: //www.chabad.org/kabbalah/article_cdo/aid/380259/jewish/Kosher-Kabbalah-for-Non -Jews.htm.

Trombley, Frank R. *Hellenic Religion and Christianization*. New York: E. J. Brill, 2001.

Udayakamar, S. P. "Futures Studies and Futures Facilitators." In *Rescuing All Our Futures: The Future of Futures Studies*, edited by Ziauddin Sardar, 98–116. Westport, CT: Praeger Publishers, 1999.

Waithe, Mary Ellen, ed. *Ancient Women Philosophers: 600 BC–500 AD*. Boston: Martinus Nijhoff Publishers, 1987.

Williams, Brandy. *For the Love of the Gods: The History and Modern Practice of Theurgy: Our Pagan Inheritance*. Woodbury, MN: Llewellyn, 2016.

———. *Practical Magic for Beginners*. St. Paul, MN: Llewellyn, 2005.

———. "White Light, Black Magic: Racism in Esoteric Thought." Brandy Williams, 2018. http: //brandywilliamsauthor.com/wp-content/uploads/2018/05/WhiteLightBlackMagic.pdf.

———. *The Woman Magician: Revisioning Western Metaphysics from a Woman's Perspective and Experience*. Woodbury, MN: Llewellyn, 2011.

World Health Organization. "Suicide Data." *World Health Organization*, accessed October 9, 2019. https://www.who.int/mental_health/prevention/suicide/suicideprevent/en/.

About the Author

Brandy Williams has spent four decades in the magical communities as a priestess, ritualist, writer, teacher, and thought leader. She is an ordained priestess of Ecclesia Gnostica Catholica and an initiate of Georgian Wicca, the Golden Dawn (as Via Amore Gnostike), the Ordo Templi Orientis, and the Nath Tantrika Sampradahya (as Satya Vana Nath).

Brandy's organizational work includes serving as High Priestess of Anahata Rose Croix Chapter of O.T.O. She is past master of Vortex Oasis of O.T.O. and past president of Covenant of the Goddess. In addition, she is a founding member of Seattle Pagan Scholars and of Sisters of Seshat, a sororal order in the Western Magical Tradition. She frequently presents at conferences, including PantheaCon, Paganicon, TheurgiCon, the Esoteric Book Conference, and Babalon Rising. Brandy's published works include *Ecstatic Ritual: Practical Sex Magic, The Woman Magician: Revisioning Western Metaphysics from a Woman's Perspective and Experience*, and *For the Love of the Gods: The History and Modern Practice of Theurgy*.

Each volume of her work is a step toward transforming Magia Traditionis into Magia Humana, addressing the challenges of the twenty-first century. These include recognizing and protecting the living biosphere, harmonizing the cultures of the world through respectful collaboration, and

· · · · · · ·

framing a new metaphysics accessible to esotericism, the academy, and popular culture. The special focus of her work is the articulation of Magia Femina, traditional magic reshaped around the physical form, emotional center, and spiritual needs of women, an essential precondition to Magia Humana.

Brandy lives in rural Washington state with two partners, three cats, and a dog. She is active in local and national human rights organizations and is an avid gardener and a singer of medieval music.

Art Credits

Hope in the Prison of Despair by Evelyn de Morgan. Image courtesy of the Art Renewal Center® www.artrenewal.org.

About the Editors

American singer-songwriter and recording artist **Lon Milo DuQuette** is also an internationally recognized authority on ceremonial magick, Qabalah, tarot, and the life and teachings of noted English occultist Aleister Crowley (1875–1947). He is senior initiate member of Crowley's magical order, Ordo Templi Orientis, and currently serves as its United States Deputy Grand Master General. He is arguably the most visible member of this secret magical society.

He travels extensively and teaches and lectures on esoteric Freemasonry, tarot, Qabalah, and magick. DuQuette has authored a score of books (translated into twelve languages), several of which are considered modern occult classics.

He resides in Costa Mesa, California, with Constance, his wife of fifty-two years.

Author photo by Paul Muska/muskavision.com.

Dr. David Shoemaker is a clinical psychologist in private practice, specializing in Jungian and cognitive-behavioral psychotherapy. David is the Chancellor and Prolocutor of the Temple of the Silver Star (totss.org), which offers a complete system of training in Thelemic magick and mysticism. He is also a senior initiate of the Ordo Templi Orientis and A∴A∴ (onestarinsight.org) and has many years of experience training initiates in these traditions.

He is a Past Master of 418 Lodge, O.T.O., in Sacramento, having succeeded Soror Meral (Phyllis Seckler), his friend and teacher. He also serves as a Sovereign Grand Inspector General of the order. David was the founding President of the O.T.O. Psychology Guild and is a frequent speaker at national and regional events. His instructional podcast *Living Thelema* has been presented since 2010, and the popular book of the same name appeared in 2013. He is also the author or editor of numerous other publications focusing on Thelema, psychology, and magick.

In addition to his work in magick and psychology, David is a composer and musician. He can be contacted through his website at livingthelema.com.

Author photo by Kevin Fiscus.

Index

· · · · · · ·

• • • • • • •

• • • • • • •

To Write to the Editors

If you wish to contact the authors or would like more information about this book, please write to the authors in care of Llewellyn Worldwide Ltd. and we will forward your request. Both the authors and the publisher appreciate hearing from you and learning of your enjoyment of this book and how it has helped you. Llewellyn Worldwide Ltd. cannot guarantee that every letter written to the authors can be answered, but all will be forwarded. Please write to:

Lon Milo DuQuette and David Shoemaker
℅ Llewellyn Worldwide
2143 Wooddale Drive
Woodbury, MN 55125-2989

Please enclose a self-addressed stamped envelope for reply,
or $1.00 to cover costs. If outside the U.S.A., enclose
an international postal reply coupon.

Many of Llewellyn's authors have websites
with additional information and resources.
For more information, please visit our website at
http://www.llewellyn.com.

GET MORE AT LLEWELLYN.COM

Visit us online to browse hundreds of our books and decks, plus sign up to receive our e-newsletters and exclusive online offers.

- Free tarot readings • Spell-a-Day • Moon phases
- Recipes, spells, and tips • Blogs • Encyclopedia
- Author interviews, articles, and upcoming events

GET SOCIAL WITH LLEWELLYN

Find us on  @LlewellynBooks

www.Facebook.com/LlewellynBooks

GET BOOKS AT LLEWELLYN

LLEWELLYN ORDERING INFORMATION

 Order online: Visit our website at www.llewellyn.com to select your books and place an order on our secure server.

 Order by phone:
- Call toll free within the US at 1-877-NEW-WRLD (1-877-639-9753)
- We accept VISA, MasterCard, American Express, and Discover.

 Order by mail:
Send the full price of your order (MN residents add 6.875% sales tax) in US funds plus postage and handling to: Llewellyn Worldwide, 2143 Wooddale Drive, Woodbury, MN 55125-2989

POSTAGE AND HANDLING

STANDARD (US): (Please allow 12 business days)
$30.00 and under, add $6.00.
$30.01 and over, FREE SHIPPING.

CANADA:
We cannot ship to Canada. Please shop your local bookstore or Amazon Canada.

INTERNATIONAL:
Customers pay the actual shipping cost to the final destination, which includes tracking information.

Visit us online for more shipping options. Prices subject to change.